Mr. Pitt

AND AMERICA'S BIRTHRIGHT

PAINTED BY COOK   ENGRAVED BY H. T. RYALL

William Pitt, Earl of Chatham.

Mr. Pitt

AND AMERICA'S BIRTHRIGHT

A biography of William Pitt
the Earl of Chatham
1708 ~ 1778

by J. C. Long

With many Illustrations, a
Bibliography, and an Index

Frederick A. Stokes Company
New York ~ 1940

Printed in the United States of America

To

DIXON RYAN FOX

MR. PITT

"Power without right is the most odious and detestable object that can be offered to the human imagination."

"Where law ends tyranny begins."

"Unlimited power is apt to corrupt the minds of those who possess it."

"The colonies . . . are equally entitled with yourselves to all of the natural rights of mankind, and peculiar privileges of Englishmen; equally bound by its laws, and equally participating of the Constitution of this free country."

—WILLIAM PITT

CONTENTS

PART ONE

"I Know That I Can Save England"

PART TWO

"An Empire for Freemen"

ix

PART THREE

"I Rejoice That America Has Resisted"

LIST OF ILLUSTRATIONS

MR. PITT

William Pitt, the elder, Earl of Chatham, prime minister of England.

No calendar can mark his days. Born 1708, died 1778,—he lived for seventy years, and for the generations which followed.

It was Pitt who built the foundations of the present Anglo-Saxon empire, Pitt who reclaimed the Magna Carta from the archives, and Pitt who was the protagonist of constitutional democracy against Bourbonism, dictators, and the mob.

He raised a nation from the dust and democracy from the scrap heap. He scorned monarchs and peers, plutocrats and place-holders. He brought honesty to the Army, integrity to the State, and dignity to the common people. He defined the philosophy of democracy, and trained men to defend it.

With it all, he was vain and arrogant, theatrical, ambitious, absurd, incredible, a seething man, and at the end, a seeming failure. But he proclaimed a society in which the lowliest could affirm the rights of an Anglo-Saxon freeman.

Whether he made destiny or whether destiny made him, Pitt's flamboyant energy, his incandescent certainty of purpose, his perception of the inevitable worthiness of individual man, marked him for the ages.

PART ONE

"I Know That I Can Save England"

CHAPTER I

WHO SPEAKS OF SUPERIORS?

In England, in the year 1755, there was one Mr. Pitt. There were, to be sure, a George Pitt, member of Parliament for Dorset, and another member, John Pitt, from Encombe. From Wareham Borough there were two more of the Pitt cousinhood, John Pitt and a William Augustus Pitt. That made four Pitts in the House of Commons, aside from Mr. Pitt.

There were Pitts in trade and at the bar; in shipping and in the Church. There was the head of the Pitt family, the elder brother Thomas, a man who once had enjoyed great wealth and still retained some degree of prominence. But though many bore the name, whenever "Mr. Pitt" was mentioned one particular individual was intended: namely, William Pitt, M.P., member for Aldborough, citizen of Bath, and gadfly of Parliament.

Mr. Pitt's rocket once had shot far into the sky. He had been a pet of great nobles, a minister of the Crown; but now, in December, 1755, the King's Cabinet had marked him for destruction. The powerful Duke of Newcastle, who was First Lord of the Treasury and political boss of the nation, had placed "an indelible negative," as Mr. Pitt expressed it, against Pitt's future. Newcastle had at one time been friendly to the young man and had admired his talents. But Mr. Pitt could not be relied upon to take orders, had ideas of his own; and the Newcastle plan was well hatched.

The plot was simple. Mr. Pitt's chief possession in life was his reputation. He was a man known for his daring and his integrity. The London merchants had found him to be an honest supporter of their interests, and worshiped him because he refused to take a penny of graft or subsidy. The common people regarded him as the champion of their

3

rights, a tribute which his record justified. Newcastle was aware, however, that support of that kind was intangible and should be easy to destroy. Rob Mr. Pitt of his reputation and there would be nothing left. He had already alienated himself from one clique after another on issues of principle.

Newcastle proposed to give Pitt a stomachful of principle, to turn loose the best minds of the Government on the job of showing that Mr. Pitt was a malcontent and a poltroon. Orders were to shout him down, pour denunciation upon him, make him a Catiline, until he would hesitate to open his mouth in the House of Commons. That was the plot.

The word of this proposed butchery had been passed around, and the sessions of Parliament, in December, 1755, had an attendance so full that the benches of St. Stephen's Chapel, which housed the Commons in those days, were jammed to overflowing.

Mr. Pitt arrived early on December 2, well aware of what was in the wind; and seated himself in the front row. He was urbane and faintly smiling, even if a trifle aloof in manner. In contrast to the bright-colored silks and satins of his fellows, he wore a suit of black velvet. This sober habit, his long white hands, and his hawk-like face, pale and lined with illness, gave him the aspect of Hamlet at the court of his lustful stepfather.

Mr. Pitt, however, was more cheerful than Hamlet. His colleagues, in their memoirs, commented on his self-possession. He was at high tension, but good-humored; in fact, even pleased at being the conspicuous central figure at his proposed execution. It was the Government whips who were nervous; and the House as a whole buzzed with murmurs.

Mr. Pitt's choice of a front-row seat was in itself audacious; for by the custom of the House a member might sit anywhere. There were no assigned places, and a member might even stretch his legs by withdrawing occasionally to the narrow gallery. Pitt could have sat in an inconspicuous place, had he chosen to do so.

The small auditorium of St. Stephen's Chapel had been converted to the use of the Commons some three centuries before, and had a makeshift appearance. The pews had been removed from the center of the hall, which was clear; and the members sat on five tiers of benches in the shape of a horseshoe. Where the altar had once stood was a white stone pediment carved with the King's arms. In front of the pediment the speaker sat at a vast table which jutted out into the room. The table was flanked by the clerks and by the four representatives for the City of London, who, at the opening of each session, wore scarlet gowns. Mr. Pitt's position in a lower tier of the horseshoe placed him where all could see the least flicker of emotion on his face or a tremor of his hands. If he should break under the sweating in this bull-pen, his disaster would be public and complete.

The session had opened with the reading of the King's address, namely, the official statement of the Government's policy. The Government speakers droned on for hours explaining and expounding their general program for the year, while the members were impatient for the action against Mr. Pitt to get under way. The chief men whom Newcastle had appointed for that task were a well-assorted team, Fox, Murray and Campbell. Henry Fox was calm, practical, an even-tempered cynic. He was a former schoolmate of Pitt's, knew him like a book. Fox was fearless in his way, too. He was a self-indulgent fellow with pursy lips, thick legs and a well-rounded belly; but he took the exchanges of political blows cheerfully. He had his price, the large price of being Secretary of State, which provided for him handsomely, and he was willing to do the necessary when occasion demanded.

The pale, sour William Murray, in his black robe of the bar, had neither courage nor good temper; but his scholarship was immense. He could outquote and outcite anyone in the Commons. He could feed points to his colleagues. Murray knew Pitt, too, and hated him with the hate of the dyspeptic theorist for the man of action. He feared Pitt and had suffered many a tongue-lashing from him on the floor of the House. But Murray this time had at his elbow the tough-skinned Hume Campbell.

Campbell, dressed like Murray in the black robe of the bar, sat two rows above Pitt. He had been retained by Newcastle as the most abusive counsel he could find for the chastising of Mr. Pitt. Campbell looked the part. He was a large man, ruddy and hard, with the high cheekbones of the Scotchman. Horace Walpole, the letter writer, said of Campbell that he was "arrogant, acute, abusive, corrupt and insatiable." Campbell had enjoyed the hospitality of Pitt's relatives, and knew Pitt even better than did Fox or Murray.

While Newcastle's pack strained at their leashes, Mr. Pitt listened attentively and appraisingly to the exposition of the King's address. The policies which it outlined gave little encouragement to a true patriot. The Court was continuing to play its game of intrigue with European powers, claiming to be enhancing the glory of England, while actually assisting King George II's ambitions in Germany at the expense of British blood and money. Now the Ministry asked the Commons to approve new treaties on the Continent and to vote more subsidies.

Mr. Pitt listened to one speaker after another and at length rose to his feet. A stir went through the house, a gasp of involuntary admiration. Mr. Pitt was clearly not planning to take it lying down. He removed his hat and bowed to the speaker. The light from the large windows back of the pediment illumined his face, emphasized the piercing gray eyes, the hawk-like nose, and the mobile lips.

Mr. Pitt, in his authoritative penetrating voice, declared himself against the treaties. He declaimed against the misrepresentation of the true situation by the Ministry.

"We have suffered ourselves to be deceived by names and sounds," he said, " 'the balance of power,' 'the liberty of Europe,' 'a common cause,' and many more such expressions, without any other meaning than to exhaust our wealth, consume the profits of our trade and load our posterity with intolerable burdens. None but a nation that had lost all signs of virility would submit to be so treated."

Pitt's action was typical. To the ministerial group it proved that Newcastle was right in thinking that Mr. Pitt must be destroyed. He was incorrigible. He had opposed the impressment of seamen. He had demanded a fair trial for Admiral Byng. He had defended the Jews, and had called the Cabinet to account for violations of the Constitution. The man's impertinence was colossal.

Pitt continued speaking against the treaties at some length, and then Henry Fox rose to reply. If Newcastle, or the Commons, expected Fox to strike a hard opening blow, they were disappointed. Fox had no love for Mr. Pitt, but was too shrewd to underestimate him. He did not wish to be the one to draw fire from such an antagonist. He was fully conscious of how long it had taken Newcastle to break with Pitt.

Newcastle, in fact, had not wished to tangle with Pitt. Indeed, he had tried to reward Mr. Pitt handsomely. Newcastle had given to Pitt the post of Paymaster-of-the-Forces which was worth £4,000 a year. In addition, the office customarily provided enough perquisites to make a man enormously wealthy. Mr. Pitt had refused the perquisites, and had finally been dismissed from office. The £4,000 pounds had not been enough to shut his mouth when a question of the Constitution was at stake.

Hence the Fox reply was guarded and courteous, feeling out Pitt. If Pitt made a mistake in strategy, Murray or Campbell could pounce, rather than Fox. Fox expressed interest in Mr. Pitt's views, and wondered that he had not spoken to certain points sooner.

"My calling out was more likely to defeat than promote," Pitt replied, recalling how his every opinion had been viewed with suspicion by Newcastle. "When I remonstrated for more seamen, I was called an enemy to the Government. . . . I am traduced, aspersed, calumniated, from morning to night. . . . These are my sentiments and when a man has truth on his side, he is not to be overborne by quick interrogatories."

Fox did not pick up the gauntlet. In any case, it was

clear that Pitt had not yet been worn down. To exhaust him was part of the plan.

The debates continued day after day, with Mr. Pitt bearing the burden for the Opposition. He had, to be sure, some supporters. His family connections were friendly. These included not only the Pitts, but his in-laws the Grenvilles. The London members also were solidly with him, but the Ministry had a huge majority and the best talent. The hope of the Government was that Mr. Pitt could not keep it up forever. He had been ill for months at a time during recent years. A break might come at any moment, and then the worries of the Government would be over, for there was no one else who could rouse the unorganized yet dangerous public opinion.

Pitt, however, continued to lead the attack. The sessions lasted until midnight, sometimes until two or three in the morning. It had been Mr. Pitt's habit to speak early in the day, but now, with a sardonic smile at the Government benches, he timed his assaults late in the evening, when many of the majority (and of the Opposition, too) were sodden with overeating and liquor, waiting until the Government whips would permit an adjournment. If the game was to catch someone napping, Mr. Pitt was willing to play.

Murray, who could not endure criticism or heckling, who cherished the beauty of his own carefully wrought logic, at last screwed himself up to the task of exposing Mr. Pitt's ignorance. Murray reviewed the European treaties learnedly from every angle, a masterly presentation in its way, calculated to show that the Crown ministers had looked into these matters thoroughly, whatever the views of uninformed rabble-rousers might be. It was an important speech from the Cabinet standpoint.

Mr. Pitt was ready for it. He had spent many hours in the Parliament Library during the session—in spite of the length of the daily meetings—studying the treaties and the conditions affecting them.

His reply to Murray began disarmingly: "It is difficult to know where to pull the first thread from a piece so finely spun. Constructions ought never to condemn a great min-

William Murray, Earl of Mansfield, in one of his happier moods, dressed in his robes of Chief Justice. Usually pallid and dour, he resented the popularity and oratory of Mr. Pitt, whom he regarded as his inferior.

PAINTED BY REYNOLDS   ENGRAVED BY H. ROBINSON

Henry Fox, Lord Holland, the cheerfully corrupt and vastly wealthy
Parliamentary whip.

ister, but," and here Pitt touched off a bombshell, "I think this crime of violating the Act of Settlement is within the letter."

The Act of Settlement! The Georges of the House of Brunswick had succeeded to the Throne under the Act of Settlement. Article III, Section 2 of the Act provided:

> That in case the Crown and Imperial Dignity of this realm shall hereafter come to any person, not being a native of this kingdom of England, this nation be not obliged to engage in any warre for the defence of any dominions or territories which do not belong to the Crown of England, without the consent of Parliament.

Murray's fine structure tottered at this exposure of the crack in its foundation.

"I will not suffer an audacious minister to escape the judgment of Parliament," Mr. Pitt continued. "For if a Cabinet have taken upon them to conclude treaties of subsidy without the consent of Parliament, shall they not answer for their action?"

Mr. Pitt had hit upon the weak place in the Cabinet armor. The Ministry had the votes, and their action would presumably be approved; but it was clear that they had exceeded their authority, a dangerous point to be brought so forcibly to public attention.

Mr. Pitt knew, however, that he had not disposed of the Ministry or they of him. Neither side had broken, though each had scored on the other. Day after day the debates continued, with Mr. Pitt still protecting himself by keeping on the offensive. Newcastle—who, of course, sat in the Lords and must rely on his lieutenants—received daily and sometimes hourly reports of the sessions. Apparently, the Cabinet had tried to beat Mr. Pitt at his own game, and he was glorying in it, but time, with its exhausting toll of strength, should be on their side.

Meanwhile Mr. Pitt sat in the front row, listening, waiting for a break, a false move on the part of some Government speaker which would enable him to shake off this pack who "traduced" and "aspersed" him.

He had taken advantage of every error, every point, but even his Act of Settlement answer had drawn little blood. So he waited, where the House could see his every move. By day the light from the windows behind the pediment was upon him; in the evening he was directly under the gleam from the vast low-hung chandelier over the speaker's desk.

He dominated the stage whether speaking or silent. When others spoke, his face was an obbligato. He had coached the actor Garrick and Garrick had coached him, with each the gainer. The least movement of his hands, pale white against the black velvet suit, could express disdain, amusement, or indignation. This was showmanship, but it was not action. It was not results, and Mr. Pitt's future depended on results.

Then one evening Hume Campbell spoke; on December 10, to be exact. He referred to the "invectives" of Mr. Pitt. So that was the keynote! Pitt's long record of protest against the usurpation of rights was to be labeled with the word "invective." Pitt the fault-finder, Pitt the malcontent.

"Let the House punish these eternal invectives," said Campbell. "Gentlemen are suffered to come to the House every day to arraign the conduct of their superiors."

This was the moment for which the House had been waiting. Campbell poured forth a stream of denunciation such as the famous Pitt had never before been called upon to endure. Here at last was someone big enough to discipline the skilful Mr. Pitt with a bludgeon. There were many a chuckle and nudge on the Government benches.

Pitt rose to a point of order. He objected to having the debates of the House described as "invective."

Horace Walpole, the elder, now in his eighties, observed that Mr. Pitt was the last man to talk about rules of order; and there was a murmur of protest through the Commons. The members wished there to be no interruption.

Pitt observed further that Campbell's expression struck directly at the liberty of debate. He was inclined to move to have the words taken down, but he would wait until Campbell had explained himself.

Campbell continued, unaware that he had made the slip for which Pitt had been waiting, and to which Pitt had not replied: namely, the reference to "superiors."

Superiors! If Pitt had made his response immediately on that word, Campbell might have escaped with an apology. As it was, Pitt waited. Campbell bellowed on, shouting down Mr. Pitt as he had been told to do, while the gentleman in the black velvet sat urbane and contemplative in the light of the low-hung chandelier.

Campbell finished; and as Mr. Pitt did not offer to reply, other members rose to speak on this subject and that. A half-hour elapsed, and then Mr. Pitt requested the floor.

"Superiors," he said, "is a word that I disdain."

Instantly, the House comprehended the insult which Campbell had given them, the worse because it was unconscious. More than half of the members had received pay through Newcastle's influence directly or indirectly. Others were attached to the Ministry because of deals made with their political leaders. But all this had been done with some saving of "face."

The House of Commons, in theory, was the source of government, the authority which voted money and approved foreign relations. Though powerful interests controlled most of the members, appearances had been preserved. The man who has sold his conscience hates himself and the buyer. Above all, the public acceptance of the fact is intolerable; and now Campbell had spoken of the Ministry as "superiors," had denounced a member of the House for criticizing his "superiors." If such doctrine were unchallenged, the last shred of self-respect would be lost to every member of the House.

"I do not say *superiors*," Mr. Pitt affirmed. "I hate that miserable word. But if a Cabinet have taken on them to conclude subsidiary treaties without consent of Parliament, shall they not answer it?"

Mr. Fox, the ablest of Newcastle's lieutenants, was pleased that he had not been caught in this *cul-de-sac*. Horace Walpole, the younger, nephew of the eighty-year-old member, took copious notes. This would be history.

"Superiors?" cried Mr. Pitt, in a voice vibrating with contempt. "Superiors?" His gestures, his accent, were loaded with condemnation.

"I grant that the honorable gentleman may have his superiors," Pitt observed with disarming quietness, "but he knows"—the speaker paused—"he knows that the King himself is not his superior"—Pitt's glance embraced his fellow-representatives—"when the honorable gentleman is sitting, speaking and voting in his legislative capacity."

Pitt's audience waited, the several hundred men who represented the liberties of England, but who had almost lost confidence in the powers which were theirs. So many men had tried the independence which Mr. Pitt was trying, but could it be done? Campbell, after all, had the solid backing of the Ministry.

Mr. Pitt advised the honorable gentleman that the freedom of criticism by Parliament was not unparliamentary, however it might be objected to. This freedom had been acknowledged even in the reign of the Stuarts, though Pitt granted that James I "would have been glad of the assistance of a great lawyer—could he have had one—to threaten a member of Parliament!"

Pitt knew that he had struck home. Campbell might be the roaring bull, but Pitt was the toreador with the lance deep in the animal's neck. He stepped from his place to the floor of St. Stephen's Chapel and turned facing toward Campbell on the third tier of benches.

"But I will not dress up this image under a third person!" Mr. Pitt exclaimed. "I apply it to him."

To him, Campbell. The House faced its traducer.

"His is the servile doctrine," said Pitt. "He is the slave, and the shame of his doctrine will stick to him as long as his gown sticks to his back."

Mr. Pitt paused, as the huge Campbell sat bewildered, red-faced and silent.

"After all," said Pitt with icy disdain, "his trade is words; they were not provoked by me," alluding to Newcastle's plot, "but they have no terrors for me; they provoke only my ridicule and contempt."

Mr. Pitt had won.   He knew it, and the Government knew it.   Fox did his duty.   He tried to explain that Campbell had simply referred to persons who were superior to him personally.   Every man, Fox pointed out, will admit that certain individuals have greater merit.   Campbell defended himself, but Pitt did not bother to comment.   The Government might win its majority votes for this or that measure, but Mr. Pitt had identified his cause with that of every member of the House of Commons.

"Pitt had ridden in the whirlwind and directed the storm," wrote young Walpole, even though he sat on a Government bench.   Pitt, in fact, had proved at last that the principles for which he stood were essential to a free England,—but it had been a long journey.

CHAPTER II
THE MAD PITTS

"There was a great deal of madness in the family," said Lord Shelburne, who knew the Pitts; and nearly all of them, including William, gave good reason for the comment.

To outside appearances there was nothing exceptional in the Pitt family to arouse Lord Shelburne's comment. Robert Pitt, the father, was an inconspicuous country gentleman, and his wife was a gentle, high-minded creature, overwhelmed by her brood of children and taking little part in the social world to which she had access. The family ancestry on the maternal side was noted for genius and instability; and on the paternal side also there was eccentricity, though the Pitt connection in the main were solid people.

William Pitt was born in St. James Parish, London, on November 15, 1708, the son of Robert and Harriot Villiers Pitt, and he was baptized in St. James Church. Two years later the family moved to a small country estate called Mawarden Court, at Stratford-under-the-Castle on the banks of the Avon. Mawarden Court was a comfortable, ample, old stone house, shaded by yew trees, with a broad lawn at the rear sloping down to the river.

This quiet manor was a modest dwelling for one of Mrs. Pitt's heritage. She was a Villiers, a family which counted its ancestry from the Norman Conquest. The first Duke of Buckingham was a Villiers. Barbara Villiers Palmer, a mistress of Charles II, was designated Duchess of Cleveland and was the mother of the first Duke of Grafton. The Villiers were intermarried several times with the Stuart house, and were also connected with the Lytteltons, the Grenvilles, the Shirleys, and the Temples.

The Villiers line and connections were conspicuous for

14

daring and for artistic talent. The Villiers blood flowed in
Lord Chesterfield, author of the noted Letters; in Lord
Bolingbroke, one of the chief authors and libertines of his
day; in Henry Fielding, the novelist; in Samuel Richardson;
and in the poet Edward Fitzgerald. It was a family
destined for eminence in statecraft and the arts even to
modern times, appearing, for example, in the person of Lord
Palmerston, in Pelham Grenville Wodehouse, and in the
motion-picture star, Shirley Temple.

While in Pitt's mother, the tempestuous Villiers blood
was in a temporary calm, it stirred again in several of the
children as they came to maturity.

On the father's side of the house there was more common sense, if less distinction. The Pitts were a large cousinhood of substantial property owners, clergy and members of
the bar. While some of the family had married into the
nobility and there were a few titles on the family tree, the
Pitts were mainly a solid, thriving people, representative of
the commercial and lesser land-owning interests.

Though the tendencies of both practicality and genius in
William Pitt's parentage were destined to affect his place in
England's history, the peaceful, dreaming days of childhood
at Mawarden Court gave little hint of conflicts to come.
The broad lawn, sloping to the river, the yew trees, and the
companionship of his brother and sisters, formed a cool
oasis in William's life, to which his thoughts returned again
and again in later years.

When William was ten he had two older sisters, Harriot
and Catherine, and an older brother, Thomas; and two
younger sisters, Ann who was six, and Betty who was five
years of age. There was an unusual loyalty to each other
among the children, perhaps because the family was large
enough to be self-sufficient. William was the hero of the
two younger sisters. He slept in a tiny bedroom adjacent
to Ann and Betty's dressing-room. The latter served as
headquarters for many childhood conferences and strata-
gems, and became a never-never land in his adult reminiscences.

Between William and his sister Ann was a particular

affinity. She was keen, quick and lively, a smiling, happy child, ready for any enterprise. Betty had a special charm, also. She was easily the handsomest of the family, and had intelligence, but was dominated by passion and a craving for admiration. To William, these two younger sisters were incomparable; and his loyalty to the older children of the family was equally strong.

In time Mr. Pitt became a lonely figure who found that many of his supposed friends would sell him out if the price were good enough. He developed an armor of aloofness, but his love for his family was sustaining and permanent even when circumstances drew heavily on his devotion.

It was William who stood by Harriot when the other Pitts deserted her while she was under the shadow of an enforced marriage. He was loyal to his older brother Thomas when the latter ran through the family fortunes and became a bankrupt. He defended Betty's name when virtually every respectable door in England was closed to her; and he endured Ann's eccentricities which would have alienated a less patient spirit.

Pitt's endurance of his harum-scarum family who did not hesitate to revile him, denounce him to others, and exploit him when they could—according to the evidence of their own letters—has created some wonderment; but he loved them and understood them. They were a brilliant crew, eager, quick-witted, temperamental. If they quarreled quickly, they were equally quick to make up. William himself, beaten upon by waves of emotion, subject to violent changes in mood and ridden by a romantic nature, could understand how Harriot and Betty could go off the deep end.

Except for more self-control and self-direction, Pitt had much in common with his erratic brother and sisters, and he knew them to be of his own kind. He knew them, moreover, from the happy days at Mawarden Court before their lives had been hurt by the strains of adjustment to the outside world. Perhaps he realized also that he was particularly fortunate among the children, since he especially enjoyed the favor and help of the dominating figure of the family, his grandfather, Thomas Pitt.

Grandfather Pitt, merchant prince, former Governor of Madras, owner of the Pitt diamond, president of the East India Company, might well have been a Villiers himself, for he was as mad as a March hare. He had gone to India as a poor boy many years before and had had the audacity to start a trading business in defiance of the East India Company. He soon strengthened his position by marrying Jane Innes, a niece of two of the principal agents of the company. His business grew rapidly and as his position increased the directors of the East India Company, which was supposed to have a monopoly, became increasingly determined to destroy him. They brought legal action against him, forcing him to return to England to defend himself. He was arrested and ruin stared him in the face, but he had the resources of personality and wealth. He managed to win the interest and support of the Duchess of Portsmouth, another mistress of Charles II and the mother of the first Duke of Richmond. Thanks to her influence, the Government action against Grandfather Pitt had been quashed. It was then that the directors realized that the only practical course was to have him with them, since they could not defeat him, and they elected him president of the company.

Grandfather Pitt, however, could not be happy unless he was in the midst of some furious controversy. One of the passions of his life was a huge diamond which he purchased in India for £48,000. For years afterward he quarreled with appraisers and abused his agents because they were unable to make a quick and profitable sale. He finally undertook the task of selling the jewel himself and disposed of it to the French Crown for £133,000, paid for partly in cash, partly in gems, and partly by an I.O.U. for the balance of £20,000. The balance never was paid, a fact which supplied Grandfather Pitt with further material on which to expend his rages.

This dominating and choleric old gentleman, in the latter years of his life, while William Pitt was still a boy, turned his temper upon his unfortunate wife who had done much to further his start in life. She was a descendant of a natural son of James V of Scotland. Conceivably, this fact may have aroused, belatedly, the Governor's frenzied respectability. Or perhaps his long absences from home stirred his suspicions. At any rate, whenever he had occasion to travel, his letters became filled with furious comments about the poor woman.

"Your mother has been guilty of some imprudence at the Bath," he wrote to one of his sons, ". . . let it be what it will, in my esteem she is no longer my wife, nor will I see her more if I can help it."

After one of these tirades, Robert Pitt, William's father, as acting head of the family, went down to the Governor's London house and turned his mother and sisters out of the establishment.

If Robert had expected that he would curry favor with the old gentleman by registering enterprise in this fashion, he found himself much mistaken. Grandfather Pitt flew into one of his best rages and denounced his son for "such an unnatural and opprobrious action." "Have all of you shook hands with shame," the Governor continued, "that you regard not any of the tyes of Christianity, humanity, consanguinity, duty, good morality, or anything that makes you differ from beasts, but must run from one end of the kingdome to the other, aspersing one another and aiming at the ruine and destruction of one another . . . not only your letters, but all I have from friends, are stuffed with the hellish confusion that is in my family."

As a matter of fact, the Governor apparently pursued this subject as the mood struck him. One week he wrote that he had "discarded and renounced your mother forever." A short time afterward a letter from him to Robert said, "I would . . . have you put your mother in mind that she gives her daughters good education, and not stick at any charge for it."

There was at least one principle of the Governor's, however, on which he stood firm with continuous conviction.

He was a Whig. The Whigs were responsible for the Revolution of 1688 which had driven the Stuarts from the Throne. The Whigs were the support of the ruling Protestant House of Brunswick. Generally speaking, they stood for constitutional government and were representatives of the trading and small-property classes. Most of the Pitts were Whigs, though Robert was related by marriage to the brilliant Tory leader, Bolingbroke, and in 1715 he was drawn into a conspiracy to restore the Stuart line. Word of this came to the Governor, and his anger knew no bounds. He wrote to Robert, "It is said you are taken up with factious caballs, and are contriving amongst you to put a French kickshaw upon the Throne again."

It was fortunate for Robert that the Governor had called him off from this adventure, the unsuccessful rebellion of 1715, or the son might have lost his liberty if not his head. From then on he was a tamed and obedient follower of his father's instructions; and as far as politics was concerned, the Governor was a good mentor.

Some of the Whigs were constitutional in theory only and had embraced the cause simply as opportunists. But Governor Pitt, even though he was a buccaneer in business, had a deep respect for honor and decency in government. In his lifetime he had seen more than one cabinet and even a royal family fall because of corruption. The same danger was insinuating itself into the Whig régime, and he wished his family never to suffer from such a taint.

"If ever you intend to be great," he wrote to his son Robert, "you must be first good, and that will bring with it a lasting greatness, and without it, it will be but a bubble blown away with the least blast.

". . . If you are in Parliament, show yourself on all occasions a good Englishman, and a faithful servant to your country. If you aspire to fame in the House, you must make yourself master of its precedents and orders. Avoid faction and never enter the House prepossessed; but attend diligently to the debate, and vote according to your conscience and not for any sinister end whatever. I had rather see any child of mine want than have him get his bread by voting in the House of Commons."

The influence of the Governor at Mawarden Court obviously was overpowering. The place itself was a gift from him. On the corner of the property stood a little stone chapel, erected by him in 1711 and bearing across its tower a sign which read: *Thos. Pitt, Esq., Benefactor.* A few hundred feet distant were the grassy mounds and circles of Old Sarum, the ruins of that once populous borough which the Governor had purchased, providing the family with its seat in Parliament.

Fortunately for William, Grandfather Pitt retired from business while the boy was still living at Mawarden Court, and settled at his country place, Swallowfields, where, in his declining years, he enjoyed playing with his grandchildren. Here he seemed to be a mellowed and more tolerant character, realizing that his days were coming to an end and looking hopefully to his descendants.

Grandfather Pitt was generous to all his grandchildren, setting particular store by an education for the girls as well as for the boys, and his favorite among them all was William. William seems to have been spared his bullying and to have had the advantage of his kindness. "He is a hopeful lad," the Governor wrote to William's father, "and doubt not but he will answer your and all his friends' expectations."

Grandfather already had in mind plans for the boy's future which would cause the inevitable break in the childhood circle which comes in the first going away to school. There were two systems of education in vogue for the children of the middle and upper classes of England. One was the system of private tutoring which was prevalent in the homes of the royal princes and to some extent elsewhere. The other was the system of the great private schools, such as Eton and Westminster, which in England are known as "public schools." Frequently children had private tutors in their earlier years and finished at a public school. The defect of the tutoring idea lay in the difficulty of finding good teachers; and for a boy who was destined for public life the acquaintanceship in school with the sons of prominent families had obvious advantages. It was settled, therefore, that William would leave his beloved and tumultuous family group for the rigorous discipline of a British public school.

CHAPTER III

"COWED FOR LIFE"

Pitt was ten years of age when, in the year 1718, he left the idyllic, dreamy scenes of Mawarden Court for eight years of hell on earth at Eton. Grandfather Pitt's influence was evident in choosing Eton for William and his older brother Thomas, as it was the most fashionable school of the Whig aristocracy.

It lacked the prestige of Westminster and other places patronized by some of the great country families, but Whig money and Whig vigor were in the ascendency in the nation. The Whigs were the dominating party; and the choice of Eton had much wisdom, since William Pitt while here would become acquainted with sons of the most influential forces in the nation.

William, however, was not built by nature for regimentation and had not experienced even the usual discipline of normal family life in the helter-skelter atmosphere at Mawarden Court. Therefore, the abrupt change to the schooled orderliness of Eton required a severe adjustment. In the school system, furthermore, there existed a reign of organized youthful brutality. Under the guise of self-government the older students were allowed to bully and beat the younger, and students who were guilty of insubordination could be certified, and often were, for a birching.

No hint of such rigors was suggested by the placid aspect of Eton. The town was situated on the banks of the Thames. On the opposite shore was the rugged gray stone castle of Windsor with its huge tower. The buildings, arranged in ancient quadrangles of brick and stone, gave promise of scholarship, dignity and peace. Dr. Bland, who became the head of the school shortly after William arrived, was a schoolmaster of high reputation, and the remainder of the faculty were persons of family and learning.

To be an Eton boy was to be stamped with a sterling hall-mark which all the world would recognize; but many of the students paid for this distinction with months, even years, of torture. The younger boys were sent on errands to Windsor and were beaten if they made mistakes. They were thrashed at every conceivable excuse and lived only for the time when they would get into the upper forms and take their revenge on the younger classes. Many of them ran away. Henry Fielding, Pitt's cousin, ran away several times and the penalty was ferocious. Tradition says that Pitt, also, once tried to make his escape and was brought back by the truant officer.

The penalty was a thrashing which was horrible not only for itself, but in the ceremony with which it was carried out. An "altar" was kept in a room off the library for such occasions and brought into a public room at the time of punishment. The device consisted of movable steps. The victim was required to kneel on the lower steps, with hands down, while the head-master applied the number of stripes which had been decreed for the crime. Supposedly he was not to draw blood, but Fielding testified of this ritual, "at thy birchen altar with true Spartan devotion have I sacrificed my blood."

Some of the scholars were able to escape from the eternal smothering presence of the school system by boarding with families in the town. They at least were away from the petty bullying in the dormitory, which gained impetus after school hours. These boarders in town were called Oppidans, and came from the richer families or from those who chose to spend more for their children's schooling. William was not so fortunate, for he was entered, as was his brother, "on the Foundation," as one of the King's Scholars, who were marked apart from their fellows by being required to wear long black robes. Their sleeping quarters were a common dormitory known as the Long Chamber, a room used by more than sixty boys, who every evening at eight o'clock were locked in for the night.

Such a school system may have developed a kind of lead-

ership and stoicism, and it presumably strengthened friendships among those who were brought together under
persecution. Pitt's closest companion at the school was
George Lyttelton, a distant relative on the Villiers side.
Lyttelton was an Oppidan with the privileges thereof, as
were his cousins Richard and George Grenville. This was
the beginning of the Lyttelton-Grenville-Pitt friendships
which were to have a large influence on Pitt's future life.

Pitt and Lyttelton at this period were an odd-looking
team. Pitt was thin and scrawny. His long neck, his huge
beak, and his piercing eyes, with the black robe of the King's
Scholar flapping about him as he walked, gave him the appearance of an animated scarecrow. Lyttelton was even
more ridiculous. He was a big lad with long arms that
flapped at his sides as though they were hung on loose hinges.
His neck seemed not strong enough for his head, which
canted toward one shoulder. He had a shuffling gait and
an absent-minded, preoccupied stare. With it all, this fantastic presence was redeemed by a happy disposition and a
gift for writing witty verse. The gawkiness of the two boys
did not relegate them to a queer set, however. William as a
young man had a social ease and an eagerness which was
hidden in his more austere later years. His friendship with
the Grenvilles, moreover, was a passport to the inner circles
of the school. Richard Grenville was a jolly, hearty youth,
fond of games and good at them, while George was a solid
beefy fellow not disturbed by original ideas and likely to be
on the traditional side of any issue.

Pitt and Lyttelton were distinguished in scholarship, a fact
which won them added respect in a school which was con-
sciously a training ground for public life. William Pitt's
tutor wrote with exceptional praise concerning his work to
the boy's father:

> Your younger Son has made a great Progress since his com-
> ing hither, indeed I never was concern'd with a young Gen-
> tleman of so good Abilities, & at the same time of so good a
> disposition, and there is no question to be made but he will
> answer all your Hopes.

The remarks were all the more convincing since the same tutor had far less favorable comment to make on the older brother, Thomas. Years later, William's nephew, Lord Camelford, who usually put the worst possible interpretation on his uncle's activities, conceded that "the surprising genius" of Pitt "distinguished him as early as at Eton School where he and his friend Lord Lyttelton in different ways were looked up to as prodigies." Lyttelton while still at Eton praised William's gifts, writing that good humor "to Pitt's genius adds a brighter grace."

However oppressive the bullying at Eton might be, the class-rooms gave an opportunity for splendid grounding in the classics. Pitt studied the New Testament in Greek, from which the boys were required to recite a passage every Monday morning. He learned Cæsar, Terence, Seneca, Juvenal and Plutarch. He was grounded in Homer, Thucydides, Xenophon, Plato, and the Greek dramatists.

His studies and a few friendships, however, were the chief bright spots in the school which Pitt hated thoroughly. His days were already darkened from time to time by attacks of the gout which he had inherited from his grandfather. While the gout was frequently the result of eating rich foods and heavy drinking, this was hardly the cause in the modest fare provided for scholars "on the Foundation." The attacks of the disease not only affected William's feet and legs, but also ravaged his intestines and stomach. For hours at a time he would be in grueling pain, then the attack might vanish suddenly. His frail constitution may have kept him from excelling in games and given him more opportunity for scholarship. Though he was a cricketer and an accomplished horseman, his repute at the school was based on his personality and his mental powers.

There were other Eton boys than the Grenville cousinhood who were destined to carry out into the world the knowledge of the young man's unusual talents. There were the two sons of Sir Robert Walpole, the prime Minister, one of whom was Horace Walpole who became a noted commentator. There was one of the sons of Bolingbroke, the Tory leader whom Walpole had driven from office.

There was a talented youth named Charles Pratt, later Lord Camden; and Francis Dashwood, later Lord Despencer who was to become notorious as the president of the Hell-Fire Club. These companions were destined to become close associates of Mr. Pitt in political life, and some of them helped him to form his first Cabinet at a time when he had difficulty in finding good material.

Charles Hanbury Williams was also here, a boy with a fluent pen who in later years used it to write verses both for and against Mr. Pitt, depending upon the tides of Mr. Williams' political opinion. Another student was the red-faced

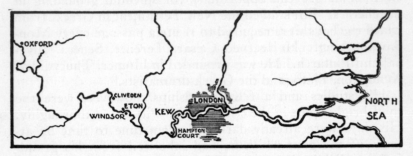

The river Thames as it flowed through the life of Mr. Pitt and his times. At Oxford the Thames is called the Isis.

Hume Campbell, probably even then a vigorous young ruffian, succeeding through sheer determination and lack of sensibilities, who later became one of the three men picked to destroy Pitt's reputation.

The list of young hopefuls during Pitt's time at Eton would be incomplete without mention of the genial and self-possessed Henry Fox, for whom Pitt had a special dislike all of his life, a dislike augmented by Fox's alliance with Hume Campbell. Fox, however, was generally popular. He was never accused of excessive integrity, then or later, but he was not in the least a hypocrite. He could lie deliberately, but bore neither ill-will nor embarrassment when he was caught. His character may not have been so fully developed during the Eton days, but later in life he showed that he could plot with the greatest ingenuity and yet do so without personal malice. He had a happy faculty of running with the popular mood, changing when it changed and giving the soft answer to turn away wrath. Fox was very likely the odious person that Pitt believed him to be, and there are few who have said much in his praise; but he was an ideal type for the week-end atmosphere of the British political scene and was destined to go far. The Fox family had been Tories under Charles II and were now equally prominent as Whigs under George II. That sort of agility required talent, as Mr. Pitt was due to learn.

It would be a mistake, of course, to read back too much of their future characteristics into the boys who were assembled at Eton. Pitt himself was almost pitifully undeveloped at this time in spite of his good record in school work. A letter to his father, the earliest of the Pitt letters which survive, indicates the restraint that was laid upon boys in addressing their elders, a restraint which, added to the hard regimen of school days, left little room for freedom:

Eaton, September ye 29th [1723]

HONORED SIR,—I write this to pay my duty to you, and to lett you know that I am well, I hope you and my mama have found a great benefit from the Bath, and it would be a very great satisfaction to me, to hear how you do, I was in hopes of an answer to my last letter, to have heard how you both did, and I should direct my letters, to you; for not knowing how to direct my letters, has hindered me writing to you. My time has been pretty much taken up for this three weeks, in my trying for to gett into the fiveth form, And I am now removed into it; pray my duty to my mama and service to my uncle and aunt Stuart if now att the Bath. I am with great respect, Honored Sir,

Your most dutiful Son,
W. PITT

The years at school rolled on, eight years in all for William, bringing him some distinction and considerable knowledge, but little relief to his resentments. The cane and switch fell less frequently on the older boys; but the incessant system was there, implacable and durable. Only the merciful visits of Grandfather Pitt brought occasional change of scene.

The Governor from time to time released Tom and William from the confines of the school, coming for them and taking them to Swallowfield Place for the week-end, accompanied by some of their school-fellows. Grandfather Pitt was such an ancient gentleman that he was far above and beyond the rôle of parent, a mixture of Zeus and Santa Claus, who allowed the boys to roam through the woods, took them on long walks and regaled them with yarns of his great days. That free life, the spacious vista, the dream of high accomplishments, was the kind of thing which stirred the young William and released him from the hated routine of the school.

His disapproval of Eton was no passing fleeting fancy to be forgotten when he reached the upper forms, or to be dispelled in the rosy recollections of a graduate. He saw no battles won on the playing fields of Eton. Years later, according to Lord Shelburne, he said that he preferred private tuition to British public-school education, for "he scarce observed a boy who was not cowed for life at Eton." He admitted that "a publick school might suit a boy of a turbulent forward disposition, but would not do where there was any gentleness."

Hence grief must have been mingled with gratitude when William learned in 1726 that Grandfather Pitt was called to Valhalla. In death as in life the Governor brought the breath of freedom to his young grandson, for this turn of fortune returned William to Mawarden Court and started him on new adventures.

CHAPTER IV

GILDED YOUTH

With the death of Grandfather Pitt the dominating influence in the family was removed and the old man's four sons immediately pitched into a furious fight in and out of the law courts, which furnished rich material for the gossips.

Robert, the oldest son, was of course the chief heir. Thomas, the second son, who had become Lord Londonderry, had already benefited by generous payments from the Governor; and the family claimed that he owed the estate £95,000 for loans during the Governor's lifetime. Londonderry vehemently denied this, and alleged that the estate owed him £10,000. Proof of the issue was difficult because his Lordship took the precaution to seize all the Governor's papers before the other sons had had the opportunity to look at them; and he refused to give them up. Lucy, the older daughter, who had married the first Earl Stanhope (a cousin of Lord Chesterfield), and Essex, the younger daughter, were cared for in their dowries.

Col. John Pitt, the remaining son, who was regarded by his brothers as the black sheep of the family, also figured in the suits, for he had been cut off without a penny. The character of this gentleman was defined at a later date by his grandnephew, Lord Camelford, who alleged that he "contrived to sacrifice his fortunes to a flow of libertinism which dashed the fairest prospect, and sank him for many years before his death in contempt and obscurity."

Camelford's words are subject to discount, as his memorandum of the Pitt family from which the words are quoted, gives interesting, malicious, and frequently untrue character studies of most of the clan. Colonel John, in fact, held various positions of trust during his lifetime, and had the friendship of many notables, including the famed Lady Suffolk.

During his younger days, however, Colonel John had been guilty of an act which created prejudice within the family circle. He had been resentful of the modest allowance afforded him by the wealthy Governor; and one day he happened to arrive at home when the rent collectors were bringing in the funds to his father's secretary. No one else of the family was about, and Colonel John seized the opportunity to draw his sword, and with it he swept the money into his hat and departed. Grandfather Pitt naturally had gone into one of the best of his rages and dismissed his son from his good graces forever. Colonel John, nevertheless, now entered into the family squabble and maintained that he was entitled to a pension or some share of the family funds.

Grandfather Pitt's estate was well worth quarreling about. The realty was valued at around £100,000. It included Swallowfield Place, which had been the Governor's favorite estate near Reading, a town house in London, and other properties in Hampshire, Wiltshire, Dorsetshire, Devonshire, and the sizable Mohun estates in Cornwall, among which was the substantial property of Boconnoc; and not the least part of the inheritance was the borough of Old Sarum which provided the family representation in Parliament.

The amount of cash and securities was negligible, for it was now revealed that the Governor had lost substantial sums in the South Sea Bubble. Even so, Robert Pitt estimated that the yield from the estate should come to "full £10,000 a year."

Robert immediately embarked his own family on a tide of considerable splendor. He abandoned Mawarden Court and moved his family to Swallowfields. During the season he opened the town house in London. These circumstances were indeed a change for the young Foundation scholar who had lived so thriftily at Eton. The time had now come for him to attend the university. Cambridge would have been the logical choice, for Oxford was notoriously under the influence of the Tory party. William, however, had remained on good terms with his uncles in spite of the family feuds, and it is probable that he was influenced by Lord Stanhope to matriculate at Trinity College, Oxford, where Stanhope had attended.

Both socially and financially, William Pitt was now in a far better position than he had ever enjoyed before. In addition to the large inheritances, the family had come into public honor through the death of William's maternal grand-mother, Viscountess Grandison. Having married a de-scendant of the first Duke of Buckingham, she was entitled to be buried in the Buckingham vault in Westminster Abbey. The funeral was colossal. Her coffin was covered with crim-son velvet edged with gold lace. The procession included four dukes and eight earls as pall-bearers, sixteen mourning coaches, seventeen noblemen's and gentlemen's coaches with a footman to every coach door, and forty men on horseback. These marks of prestige for the Pitt family had their tan-gible results, and when Robert Pitt came to engage a Mr. Storkwell to prepare William for matriculation, the tutor accepted the position in this letter:

> I had long since determin'd, not to engage any more in a Trust of so much consequence, as the Care of a young Gen-tleman of Fortune is, & have in fact refus'd many offers of that sort; but the great Regard, that every Salsbury-Man must have for your Family, and the Character I hear of Mr. Pitt from All Hands, put it out of my power to decline a Proposal of so much Credit & Advantage to Myself & the College. . . .
>
> I have secur'd a very good Room for Mr. Pitt, which is just now left by a Gentleman of Great Fortune, who is gone to the Temple. Tis thoroughly furnish't & with All necessarys, but perhaps may require some little Additional Expence for Or-nament or Change of Furniture.

William was to be entered as a Gentleman-Commoner, which entitled him to the best privileges of the University. It also involved his father in considerable expense, as Mr. Stock-well had already indicated. There were further costs than the room and board, which the tutor outlined:

> Tis usual for Young Gentlemen of Figure to have a small quantity of Table-Linnen, & sometimes some particular pieces

of plate, for the reception of Any Friend in their Rooms, but
everything of that sort for Common & Publick Uses is provided by the College. . . . Tis much more Customary &
Creditable to a Gentleman of Family to be attended by a Footman—But this I barely mention.

The Other Expences of Mr. Pitt's Admission will be in the
following articles:

	[£	s.	p.]
Caution Mony (to be returned again)	10	o	o
Benefaction to the College...............	10	o	o
For Admission to the Fellow's Common Room	2	o	o
Fee for the Use of the College Plate, &c....	2	o	o
College Servants' Fees...................	1	15	o
University Fees	o	16	o

I have stated Mr. Pitt's Benefaction at Ten Pounds, because that is what we require & receive of every Gentleman-
Commoner, & of very many Commoners; but I know Sir that
you will excuse me for mentioning, that several Young Gentlemen of Mr. Pitt's Gown have besides made the College a
Present of a Peice of Plate of 10, or 12. I am thus particular
only in Obeidience to Your Orders. I believe Sir if You
please to remit a Bill of An Hundred Pounds, it will answer
the whole expence of Mr. Pitt's settlement here and I shall
have the Honour to send you a particular Account of the disposal of it.

At the size of the prospective outlay, Robert Pitt began
to wince. He was always temperamentally inclined to one
moment's extravagance followed by spasms of economy.
William had inherited £100 yearly from his grandfather,
but obviously this was not going to be sufficient for his purposes. A Gentleman-Commoner, to live up to the best
standards of his station, was supposed to have a servant and
Robert Pitt began to think that perhaps William could
share his room with some impoverished student and use him
in the capacity of footman.

Mr. Stockwell, however, suavely waved this aside and
made arrangements to start William out in the proper style,
writing to the father:

Upon receiving the favour of Yours & finding that it was
your intention that Mr. Pitt should keep a Servant, I have

made choice of Another Room much more Convenient for that Purpose, as it supply's a Lodging for His Footman. . . .

I proposed so large a Sum, because I had not mention'd the Articles of Gown, Cap Bands, Tea-Furniture, & some other little Ornaments & Conveniences that young Gentlemen don't care to be without. You will be pleas'd to mention, in what degree of mourning His Gown must be made, [a gown in respect to Governor Pitt]; & I will send you an exact Account of the whole expence.

Pitt was entered at the University in 1727. Though he found it more congenial than the grim days at Eton, the atmosphere was not hospitable to the ideas which he had imbibed from Grandfather Pitt nor to his own temperament. He had little liking for formal education, in the first place, and the air of Oxford was impregnated with principles of which he disapproved. The dominant feeling was Tory and High Church, whereas Pitt's sentiments were strongly on the Whig side; and he was almost a Free Thinker, in his religious views. A leader among the Tory students was William Murray, a youth with a brilliant logical mind who later became a distinguished barrister, a Chief Justice, and was elevated to be Earl of Mansfield. Murray and Pitt competed for the same Latin prize, and Murray took first place. This was the beginning of an acquaintanceship and a subsequent rivalry which lasted through the lives of both men. Murray was the third of the triumvirate chosen by Newcastle in later years to attempt the destruction of Pitt.

The only one of Pitt's close friends from Eton to attend Oxford was George Lyttelton. Lyttelton was entered at Christ Church, where the Wesleys were already beginning their evangelism. To William Pitt this approach to religion was no more satisfying than the High Church movement.

In short, Pitt at Oxford was definitely a fish out of water. Aside from the religious sets, there were the diligent teetotalers; the ale-drinking, tavern-warming boys from the West country; the earnest practical students who were interested in the news and politics of the day; and Pitt's group, the Gentlemen-Commoners. The last were described by a contemporary as "bucks of the first head." They drank port wine and claret and had the privilege of dining at the high table with the Fellows.

In spite of the differences in these groups, they were all for the most part traditionalists, whereas William had been raised by his grandfather not only to respect the new Whig party but also to envision change and expansion in the future of England.

His letters home contained no complaints, but he seemed not to care greatly whether his course continued or not. In sending home his first bills, he was evidently impressed by the high cost of his education, as he wrote to his father:

> I have too much reason to fear you may think some of these articles too extravagant, as they really are, but all I have to say for it is humbly to beg you would not attribute it to my extravagance, but to the custom of this Place; where we pay for most things too at a high rate.

The father shared the son's resentment at the charges. In fact, he was already beginning to worry about the state of his inheritance. In a fit of economy he had reduced the allowance of his older son, Thomas, from £700 annually to £200. He also addressed himself to William in a letter of strong caution as to expenses. To this the boy made a diplomatic reply:

> To pretend to justify, or defend myself in this case would be, I fear, with reason thought impertinent; tis sufficient to convince me of the extravagance of my expences, that they have met with yr disapprobation, but might I have leave to instance an Article or two, perhaps you may not think 'em so wild and boundless, as with all imaginable uneasiness, I see you do at present . . . one considerable article is a servant, an expence which many are not at, and which I shall be glad to spare, if you think it fitt, in hopes to convince you I desire nothing superfluous.

William explained, however, that laundry was the most unreasonable item, costing something over three shillings, six, per week for the washing of a half dozen shirts, a pair of silk stockings, a pair of worsted stockings, and the cleaning of three pairs of shoes.

Father apparently paid the bill and allowed the footman to be retained, as William's next letter is full of gratitude. It also contains a memo of the first quarter's expenses, which gives a further idea of the college costs of the period:

	[£	s.	p.]
Battels [College accounts for provisions from the kitchen and buttery]	15	0	0
Paid Lambert Bd Wages	4	4	0
Three Months learning french and entrance	2	2	0
For a course of experimental Philosophy	2	2	0
For coat & breeches & making	5	18	0
Booksellers bill	5	0	0
Cambrick for ruffles	1	4	0
Shoes, stockings	1	19	0
Candles, coal, fagots	3	10	0
Pockett money, Gloves, Powder, Tea, &c	4	4	0
For Washing	2	2	0
	47	5	0
Remains	9	15	0

This was probably the last bill which William submitted to his father, as Robert Pitt died in Paris on May 20, 1727; and William in the future made his reports to his mother.

The year 1727 was an eventful one in many respects. In May, George I died and George II ascended the throne, destined to reign for thirty-five years. The death of Robert Pitt, of course, brought about new changes in the affairs of the family. Thomas Pitt, the older son, now succeeded to most of the property, and he too, labored under his father's illusion that it ought to yield £10,000 a year. Thomas ran true to the Pitt tradition by adding to the network of lawsuits. He sued his mother for sums said to be due on her dowry, and she in turn sued him for money which she said the estate owed to her. In the confusion, William for a time was left in the dark by everyone as to what effect his father's death might have on his own affairs. Finally, in September, he wrote to his mother:

What part of the world my Brother is in or when he will be in Town, I know not. I hope to hear from him between this and the Coronation.

The chief change in William's life following the death of Robert Pitt was the fact that he was free to leave Oxford, and at the end of the year he took his departure, not to return. It is reasonable to suppose that he did so of his own volition, for Thomas made a handsome allowance to him which would have permitted him to continue at the University. William, however, was impatient to see the world beyond the confines of England, particularly Holland, whose republican ideas attracted him.

CHAPTER V

ARMY WITH BANNERS

From Oxford Pitt went directly to the University of Utrecht. He found the change highly congenial. Here he was bound down by no traditions, by no regimentation of school rules or of what might be expected of an English gentleman.

Furthermore, his financial condition continued to be satisfactory. Thomas Pitt, who held the purse-strings, ultimately became estranged from the rest of his family, disappointed in life, ruined in finance, and hating all about him, but as yet he had not had time to mismanage his inheritance and he was still on friendly and generous terms with William. In fact, in April, 1728, William wrote to his mother concerning Thomas' attitude:

> I receiv'd ye kindest letter in ye world from him: wherein he gives me ye offer of going where I think most for my improvement, and assures me nothing y^t ye estate can afford shall be denied me for my advantage & education.

Thomas at the moment had reason to be in a genial mood. He had just married Christian Lyttelton, eldest sister of William's friend, George Lyttelton. Tradition reports that Thomas saw Christian one night at the Opera, was struck by her beauty, proposed to her the following day, and married her forthwith.

Lyttelton was overjoyed, and wrote to his father expressing the hope that William might marry another Lyttelton sister:

> Would to God Mr. [William] Pitt had a fortune equal to his brother's, that he might make a present of it to my pretty little Molly! But unhappily they have neither of them any portion but an uncommon share of merit, which the world will not think them much the richer for.

37

At Utrecht Pitt had the benefit of pleasant companion-ship. His cousin, Lord Villiers, was there; and also Lord Buchan, with whom he remained on friendly terms for the rest of his life. Apparently the young men had the gayest of times, Lord Villiers a trifle too much so, as Pitt wrote home: "I am depriv'd of my Ld Villiers' Company. he is recall'd perhaps deservedly: if a little Indiscretion arising from too much vivacity be a fault."

This loss, however, could not dampen Pitt's spirits. His mood appeared to be continually high. He wrote home amusingly concerning his sisters, charging Ann with taking up so much time in dancing and in Italian that she would not write to him. He demanded reports on Harriot's conquests, and chided her for being hard-hearted toward his friend Lyttelton, who apparently had a third idea for uniting the Pitt and Lyttelton families. "I am in pain for poor Lyttelton," Pitt wrote to Ann, "I wish there was leagues of sea between him & ye Charms of Miss Harriot. If he dies I shall sue her for ye murder of my Friend."

Even though Pitt was at Utrecht for only a short time, his active mind quickly seized upon the differences in civiliza-tion which the University presented in contrast to the Eng-lish way of life. England and the English point of view were insular, especially in that period under the peaceful premier-ship of Robert Walpole. Holland, on the other hand, had gone through centuries of strife and was entirely cosmo-politan. Pitt's future grasp of international law is credited to his study of Grotius during this period. He absorbed, too, the republican ideas of the country which were con-genial to his temperament.

He considered himself more fortunate than Lyttelton who, imbibing Tory doctrine, was still at Oxford. Pitt re-garded this as a symptom of madness and wrote home in a typically cheerful vein: "Sure there never was so much fine sense & Extravagance of Passion jumbled together in any one Man. Send him over to Holland: perhaps living in a re-publick may inspire him with a love of liberty & make him scorn his Chains."

The happy days at Utrecht came to an end, however, in

less than a year, and Pitt found himself back in England ready to start on a career, but with no occupation, no opportunity clearly indicated, and only such funds as his brother might allot to him. Nominally, he had a legacy of £100 annually from his father in addition to the £100 from his grandfather; but these funds were derived from the confused Pitt estate and may not have been forthcoming regularly.

His condition was not much different from that of many another Gentleman-Commoner. Social tradition barred him from many avenues of trade, and the two major careers which were open to one in his situation were the Army and the Church. There was some talk of his taking Holy Orders, and it was a career in which he might have made a shining mark. He had cultivated the art of speaking in his school days, by industrious practice of the orations of Demosthenes and Thucydides.

His voice was, moreover, singularly melodious, an exceptional instrument which without noticeable effort or forcing could carry to the remotest corner of an auditorium. It had overtones of the whole gamut of emotions which could be called into play at will,—ridicule, kindliness, surprise, horror, righteous indignation, exaltation. With each change of emotion the voice seemed to assume the particular difference of quality appropriate to the occasion. Before Pitt was ever heard in Parliament, before he had even taken a seat there, his powers in the forum were well known. Even though untried in any walk of life his possibilities had made an impression, for Robert Walpole a short time later made the effort to prevent Pitt's entering Parliament, foreseeing shrewdly that the young man would be hard to handle.

Though Pitt's eloquence and platform presence suggested the Church, his own inclinations did not lean that way. The Church would have required more years at the University, more years of regimented study. Though Mr. Pitt's erudition in his later career impressed many of his hearers and gave him the reputation in many quarters of being a man of books, such an appraisal was misleading. He read voraciously in such fields as appealed to him; but his read-

ing was usually for a purpose, to understand government
and the history of peoples, to train himself for accomplishment. He read in order to learn, not for the pleasures of
the library.

From boyhood his interest had been directed toward the
Army. Lord Stanhope, his uncle, had called him "the
young marshal." The boy listened with eager ears to Stanhope's military reminiscences, to Lord Tyrawley, who had
fought with Marlborough at the Battle of Malplaquet. He
was inspired by Sarah, Duchess of Marlborough, the widow
of the great General. The Duchess had been a close
friend of Pitt's lavishly be-funeraled grandmother Grandison, and was herself a noble old warhorse, breathing fire
and brimstone for the glory of England.

The Army was Pitt's natural career, but to enter the
Army in those days required cash. Commissions were purchased, though there was no corruption involved in the
sense of stockjobbing. An officer presumably adopted his
career for life; to resign his commission was frowned upon,
and regarded as well-nigh a disgrace, unless there were unusual, pardonable circumstances; yet to obtain a commission cost money. The Army was then only beginning to
be looked upon as a completely national institution, wholly
supported by the State. It was customary for a private citizen to organize and equip a regiment for the country's
service, often winning high honors thereby. Furthermore,
as the Army was one of the few careers open to young men
of social status, a commission had a special value.

Unfortunately, however, for Pitt's situation, neither the
opening nor the funds was available upon his return from
Utrecht. It appeared as though he were fated to lead a
life similar to that of his father, as a pensioner of the Pitt
property. To the high-spirited William, the situation was
extremely galling. For more than a year following his
return from Utrecht he lived at various of the Pitt estates,
now at Swallowfield Place, now at Boconnoc, at Blandford,
in London, back in Boconnoc again. He was marking time,
waiting for some change in the scene, and highly impatient.
With the future such a vague question mark, no prospect

seemed pleasing. Not even his love of gardening and devotion to nature could console him.

Boconnoc was in many ways an ideal spot. The house was situated in a lawn of nearly a hundred acres. The surrounding gardens were varied and broken, of considerable beauty, wooded and watered by brooks. A park adjoining the lawn was shaded by many beech trees and a few oaks. The house itself was of substantial proportions, having been restored in part by Governor Pitt on the foundations of the original dwelling, which was centuries old. Ancient lead mines were a part of the estate, and the manor had once been the court of Charles I. Here were tradition and romantic beauty in full flower; but not for Mr. Pitt. He wrote to his sister Ann: "I grow more and more out of temper with the remoteness of this cursed hiding place."

Ann among William's sisters was becoming increasingly his favorite, and his interest was reciprocated. She took the time to write to him to ask his views on conduct and in turn to offer her opinions. Like the other Pitts she seemed to suffer considerably from ill health and frequently went down to Bath for the waters. In later years her illness was certainly unfeigned, but from the reports which William received at this time, in 1730, it appeared that the social attractions of the resort may have counted as heavily with Ann as its medical benefits.

"I paint you," he wrote to her, "in the hands of some agreeable Partner, as happy as the new way of wooing can make you. I cannot help suggesting To you here a little grave advice, which is, not to lett your glorious Thirst of Conquest transport You so far, as to lose your health in acquiring Hearts: I know I am a bold man to dissuade One from dansing a great deal that dances very gracefully; but once more I repeat, beware of shining too much; content yourself to be healthy first, even tho you suspend your triumphs a week or ten days."

Ann's thirst of conquest, as a matter of fact, had been gratified by the attentions of Dr. Ayscough, a parson with persistent intentions whom Pitt evidently did not desire as a brother-in-law. Pitt and Lyttelton had both known

Ayscough at Oxford, where he was a tutor. Pitt was too shrewd to oppose the match directly but pursued the fellow with relentless ridicule in his letters to Ann: "You may hear enough of eyes and flames and such gentle flows of tender nonsense from every Fop that can remember," he wrote on one occasion, "but I can assure you Child, a man can think that declares his Passion by saying Tis not a sett of Features I admire, &c. Such a Lover is the Ridiculous Skew, who Instead of whispering his soft Tale to the woods and lonely Rocks, proclaims to all the world he loves Miss Nanny—Fath [sic]—with the same confidence He wou'd pronounce an Heretical Sermon at St. Mary's." Yet Ayscough (apparently pronounced "Askew," as Pitt refers to him frequently as "Skew") may have been maligned.

The relationship between Pitt and his sister Ann was exceptional. Too brilliant to enjoy the stolid roastbeef of English life, and too sane for the more unstable Pitts of lawsuits and frenzies, they understood each other. They had both been through the vicissitudes of wealth, family eminence, family deprivation, the ups and downs which were characteristic of Pitt history. Such experiences shared by sympathetic persons can set up a myriad of vibrations, and William and Ann were on the same wave-length.

William, it will be recalled, had an acute sense of family. He alone of the Pitts seemed to understand and to love them all, perhaps because he was a part of all of them, mad and practical all in one body, and true to himself, a maxim accepted by the Pitts, no matter how grotesque the self might be.

William and Ann in their letters encouraged each other to matrimony; yet winked and leered at any of the prospects in store, while they addressed each other worshipfully. Ann was frankly jealous when her brother seemed to be on the verge of a match. William ostensibly encouraged Ann's marriage prospects, and yet railed at her most ardent suitor. One letter might have dismissed Ayscough, but the succession of criticisms gives basis for reflection on William's jealousy.

Ayscough continued with his attentions month after month, and William continued to throw in a harpoon whenever the opportunity offered. Once when he was at Northampton, he learned that Ayscough was visiting Ann at Boconnoc. He sent her an absurd French ditty suggesting that she warble it "in honour of her gentle loving Shepherd" and he adds: "I can think of nothing so likely to bring her into Temper, as telling Her, her Skew will soon revisit ye groves of Boconnock, where they may pass ye Long Day, and tend a few sheep together."

Pitt's animus on this subject might conceivably have gone to considerable lengths, but suddenly there came a change in his affairs which brought purpose and direction into his life. He obtained a commission in the Army. This event, seemingly impossible of achievement, came about through William's fortunate connections with the Lyttletons. Lyttelton's uncle was Lord Cobham, who was Colonel of the King's Own Regiment of Horse, commonly known as Cobham's Horse. Cobham had served under Marlborough and was a soldier of distinction. Lyttelton was ceaseless in sounding the praises of his schoolmate Pitt, and it may be assumed that the uncle had obtained a favorable impression of the young man from that source.

Furthermore, as Thomas had married Christian Lyttelton, William was now part of the family connection, and therefore a logical candidate for a vacancy in the regiment. The cost of the commission was £1000 and it has been generally assumed that Cobham waived the requirement out of family consideration, though it is equally possible that Thomas may have produced the funds from the Pitt estates.

Pitt entered upon his new life with great eagerness. He was only a cornet, the lowest commissioned rank in the cavalry it is true, but nevertheless an Army officer. The cornet, moreover, had the responsibility of carrying the standards in parade and in battle.

Pitt on horseback leading the regiment, carrying the colors, the banners streaming behind over his shoulder. It was a magnificent prospect. The young man seized every military book he could lay his hands on and read it from cover to cover. In fact he later told Lord Shelburne that he read every military book of the day. He was launched at last; the dreamy days at Mawarden Court, the harsh life at Eton, the Tory towers of Oxford, the gay months at Utrecht, they were all behind him now. Pitt carrying the colors. It was a picture portentous for the future.

CHAPTER VI

A PITT AT COURT

In the same year that William Pitt obtained his commission in the Army his sister Ann also won a conspicuous place in the world of affairs. She was appointed a Maid of Honor to the Queen, an unusual distinction for a girl from such a comparatively modest family.

Even though the Pitts had numerous connections in the nobility and had come into apparent wealth, this was an honor which would have pleased most of the titled young women of the land; and the very fact that Ann could be named to such an appointment was significant of the transient conditions in the social life of England. The Georges had brought with them to the Court a host of Germans from Hanover and had placed them in exalted positions. Other rewards at the King's personal disposal were allotted to friends of the Ministry or favorites of the King's favorites.

Ann had received her appointment through the influence of Lady Suffolk, a favorite of his Majesty. Lady Suffolk had already enjoyed a close relationship to the Pitt family and she crossed the path of William Pitt at many intervals during his life, both in friendship and in politics. She was a woman of exceptional perspicacity who had the devoted friendship of Dean Swift, Bolingbroke, Lord Chesterfield, Pope, and most of the other brilliant minds of her time. Her kindness toward Ann was indicative of the regard which she had for the Pitt family. She was a frequent visitor to Bath, a favorite resort of the Pitt sisters, as it had been of their mother. William Pitt was naturally pleased at this honor which Lady Suffolk had obtained for his sister, but he also viewed it with some degree of apprehension for reasons which will appear.

History has never been certain regarding the degree of intimacy between Lady Suffolk and George II. It was a favorite subject of debate during her lifetime and never proved. She had a host of reputable friends who affirmed that her relationship with royalty was purely Platonic. Even the waspish gossip Horace Walpole said of the lady, "I never knew a woman more respectable for her honour and principles." She was deaf, of high birth, and of very plain appearance; and the quality of well-born ugliness has always been a passport of virtue. Lady Suffolk offered little physical competition to others of her sex, and hence enjoyed their esteem.

Her husband, however, did not seem to look upon the relationship with the same degree of confidence, even though his scheming had been partially responsible for the connection in the first instance. He had recently succeeded to the Earldom of Suffolk, before which, as Henry Howard, he had been possessed of a distinguished name and very limited funds. Early in their married life the Henry Howards had visited Hanover to ingratiate themselves with the future George II, then Prince of Wales. They succeeded better than Mr. Howard had planned (it may be assumed), as Mrs. Howard (the Lady Suffolk to be), became a favorite of the Prince, whereas Mr. Howard received no special honors.

After George II had come to England as crown prince and before he succeeded to the Throne, his connection with Mrs. Howard was conducted so discreetly for a time, that scandal might have been averted. Mr. Howard, however, would not let matters rest. He was Groom of the Bedchamber to George I, the King, who in the Hanoverian fashion cordially hated his son, the heir apparent. George I has been suspected of goading Howard to action. At any rate, the allegedly wronged husband came one night to the quadrangle of St. James Palace and before a considerable throng of witnesses clamored to have his wife delivered to him forthwith. When the guards thrust him out, he produced a letter from the Archbishop of Canterbury endorsing the husband's claim to the person of his spouse.

This arch-episcopal warrant produced no results, and some weeks later Howard made an unsuccessful attempt to kidnap his wife. The Court buzzed with comment on this exciting situation, and it remained an issue of lively possibilities until Howard was pacified by a pension of £1200 annually.

Throughout all this turmoil, the center of it was Bedchamber Woman to the Princess Caroline. In 1731, after Caroline had become Queen and Mrs. Howard had become Lady Suffolk, the latter was appointed to the post of Mistress of the Robes. It was from this high vantage point that she was able to chaperone the social career of Ann Pitt. About this time also Ann thought that she had struck the fancy of the handsome William Pulteney, then forty-seven years of age. Nothing came of this, however, and Ann blamed the slowness of Mr. Pulteney on the opposition of his family.

Brother William had already found that he had his hands full in trying to act as a guide to the lively Miss Ann. He worried about her flirtations, her continued dancing half the night, her frequent visits to Bath, and had even been concerned about her earlier trips to London when she had been staying with her mother. The degree of his anxiety may be measured by the fact that he was becoming tolerant toward Ayscough, and was able to write to Ann on this subject:

> I am glad he is with you: he will prove as good an enlivener of the spirits and invigourate the conversation amongst you, as much as Bath waters do The Blood. . . . I know ye Dog sometimes grows tired of being laugh't at: But no matter: insist upon his being a Man of humour every Day but Sunday . . . there's no Intimacy with one of His Cloath without too much room for Suspicion.

The young Mr. Pitt was not in any position at the moment to throw stones at his sister's goings-on, as he was honest enough to confess to her that the life of the Army post in peace time was painfully dull and the only battles were those which took place in the taverns. He begged Ann to keep him amused with her witty letters lest he "get drunk with bad port to kill time."

He was stationed near Northampton and could occasionally get leave to visit Stowe or other homes of his friends, but frequently his leave was not long enough for such relaxation. On one occasion he wrote to Ann:

> I come from two hours muzzy conversation To a house full of swearing Butchers and Drunken Butter women, and in short all the blessings of a market day: In such a situation what can the wit of man suggest to him? Oh for the restless Tongue of Dear little Jug!

And again he confesses:

> I have neglected you for a course of drunken conversation, which I have some days been in. The service wou'd be the most inactive life in ye world if Charles Feilding was out of it; As long as he is with us, we seldom remain long without pretty smart Action: I am just releiv'd by one night's rest, from an attaque that lasted sixteen hours.

Yet with all his jesting about Army life, with all his tone of banter in writing to Ann, William was seriously worried about the temptations which Ann might find at the Court, and the influences which might be forced upon her. When she wrote to him for advice on how to conduct herself, he had the opportunity to speak out clearly and definitely:

> You can be gay, without holding yourself cheap, while virtue which is never failing is the fixed star which will keep you out of difficulties.

His letter was in French possibly because such forthright advice on an intimate subject might sound more acceptable in French.

He urged her to rely on her good sense and advised her that modesty is the protector of many qualities. He was afraid that she might be dazzled. There was nothing so absurd as the idea that a certain set controlled the Court, hence she need not bow to any one influence.

Envy, deceit, and illegitimacy, he granted, had corrupted the Court beyond recognition. Yet William was practical. He realized that the Suffolk influence was real and considerable. He knew Ann, he knew the instability of the

Pitts. After all, how could he guide her? As for love, what is the nature of love—

"Pour ce qui est de l'amour,"—he admitted it was unpredictable; whatever its guise, it demands its toll,—*"C'est un Personnage à represailles."*

He knew that Ann might or might not take his brotherly advice. He told her that in one circumstance she may find that love is consistent with Christian upbringing. In other circumstances: *"révérez le afin qu'il ne vous fasse point de mal,"*—be careful that it doesn't turn out badly.

CHAPTER VII

A Midsummer Night's Dream

Ann had become a woman of the world, and William was restlessly desirous to establish himself as a sophisticated member of society. He had seen Eton, Oxford, and the University of Utrecht, but he had yet to make the grand tour of the Continent which was regarded as virtually essential to a young man of fashion. Such a project was expensive, but brother Thomas was still generous. William, accordingly, obtained leave from the Army and arrived in Paris in May, 1733, ready to see the world.

The career of debauchery which was often thought to be a proper accompaniment for the grand tour was not included in William's program. Perhaps he recalled the injunction of Governor Pitt: "If you ever intend to be great, you must be first good, and that will bring with it a lasting greatness and without it, it will be but a bubble blown away with the least blast." Perhaps he had accepted that injunction, or perhaps his interest in many things made a libertine's tour of Europe seem too dull a way in which to pass the time.

However that may be, he embarked at once on a strenuous tour of sightseeing. He took lodgings with a M. Banquier in the Rue St. Appoline near the Porte St. Denis, but a few hundred yards from the Memorial Arch with its grotesque carvings of nymphs, shepherds and fleurs-de-lis. From the moment of his arrival, as he wrote to Ann, he did nothing "but run up and down and see; so that believe me it is a sort of Novelty to set down and think."

Paris undoubtedly opened Mr. Pitt's eyes. As a personable young cavalry officer, tall, erect, with flashing eyes, he found no lack of opportunity for companionship. His separation from Ann was now much more easily borne.

"It may sound oddly to say I love you best at a great distance," he wrote, "but surely absence best shows us the Value of a Thing, by making us feel how much we want it."

He could even face the fact of their lives traveling by divergent paths. He wished her happy days at the Court, and concluded: *"Bon voyage ma chère,* and may you find at your journey's end as good an inn as matrimony can afford you." In fact, it may be suspected that he himself was now looking for such an inn.

Unfortunately, or so it seemed, his activities in Paris brought on a return of the gout. He decided, therefore, to visit Besançon in Lorraine, which was famous for its thermal and saline baths.

Besançon was a romantic spot, a city dating from Roman times, conquered by Cæsar in 58 B.C. It nestled in a cup of hills and was situated on a peninsula almost surrounded by the river Daube. Shut in by the hills, shadowed by the great St. Jean Cathedral which had been started in the fourth century and was still being added to, served by a university which dated from 1287, Besançon was sufficient unto itself, with the world well lost.

Pitt wrote to his sister Ann on his arrival: "I can say but little of Besançon yet; The Place is externally pretty enough; how it will prove upon a more intimate knowledge of it, I can't say. My Lord Walgrave was so good as to procure me letters For the Commandant and a Lady of this Place who passes for the finest Woman here. I have had the honour to dine with her at her campagne, where I was very handsomely regaled; what ressource Her acquaintance will be, I shall be better able to judge after another visit or two."

There is no more word of the "finest Woman" and there was a lapse in his letters until he finally left the place. Meanwhile the young cavalryman met the daughter of a riding-master, and the acquaintanceship grew apace.

The thrust to the heart was quick and deep. Lyttelton's hopes for his sister Molly had little basis this summer. The riding-master's daughter—according to Pitt's later testimony, was a marvel of attractions: "a young heart, but not immature in sense, an innocent manner yet touched with nobility, a tall figure of perfect proportions, features which combined to form great beauty, and an expression which bespoke an admirable soul!"

The scene, the girl, and youth, provided an ideal midsummer night's dream. The isolation of Besançon, its noted tree-lined promenades and its romantic atmosphere helped to make the moment more intense, but the Continental requirements for marriage were overwhelmingly practical; and at the end of August Pitt tore himself away. The summer idyll was over, or so he tried to persuade himself.

He arrived at Marseilles, and on the first of September wrote to his sister after the long lapse in their correspondence. His letter touched on many things and finally mentioned Besançon. "I have just left Besançon with infinite regrets; do you want me to confess to you? I was more strongly attached to it than I believed I was going to be, before finding myself on the point of leaving it; so true is it that one never feels so deeply the worth of a thing as when it is necessary to lose it."

The "worth of a thing" must have seemed too cold an expression under the circumstances, and the letter continued: "We had some very pleasant acquaintances there and I find now more than sixty leagues away from it, that I would have spent the winter there gladly. It doesn't fully occupy my heart, but nevertheless I have something of it in me."

Ann was evidently much too skilled in the affairs of the heart to be fooled by these masculine generalities. *Cherchez la femme.* In her reply, she asked to be told all about the girl, a complete description.

Before he wrote again, William had moved on to Lyons, to Geneva, to Strasbourg, and had finally settled at Luneville for the winter. In writing to his sister he did not immediately answer her request and tried to evade it: "You asked the portrait of La Belle of me, do you know in what you are going to involve me? I am Beginning to breathe again and you want to plunge me back into the grief which her loss has caused me by obliging me to renew in my mind the features which had taken possession of it."

Why go into it now that it is all over? "Absence is a great doctor; I find myself so improved by its remedies, that I do not despair of being able to get over it; let it be for a little while and I will make the portrait for you which you have asked me for rather easily."

Then having proved the folly of dwelling on the subject, he agreed to make "only a portrait in pencil in haste"; and the damage was done.

All her beauty was described and lived again. But the affair could not go further. This was a practical world and he was an impecunious officer: "she has no title nor distinguished family; and that's the devil of it."

He railed at his sister for having got it out of him: "Clairvoyant! You have indeed said that I will speak about it gladly. Why do you get a man to talk about his love affairs? You know that when one is there you never know where it is going to end, and you expose yourself to endure everything which comes at the end of the episode. That's talking too much about my business; let's speak a little bit about yours."

Enough was enough. Why didn't she give him some news: "Let's ask questions concerning people known under the title of lovers," alluding evidently to the affair between Lady Suffolk and the King. "Speak frankly and give me some news about them."

After all, he suspects that she, too, may have some confessions to make: "You wouldn't be so happy as you are if you hadn't put some heart under your control; goodbye: let's always love each other and let's try to make each other happy."

Evidently poor William was harder hit than he chose to admit even to himself, yet the thing just couldn't be done. How would it be possible for him to bring back to England a little French girl with no mark of worldly distinction to justify the match? It was against custom, against the practicality of the European marriage system. He had no means of his own to support a family. It was better to forget the thing entirely,—so he kept assuring himself.

But when he wrote to Ann six weeks later he was so sure that he, at last, was cured, that he brought it up all over again: "I have nothing more to say to you about Mlle. It was one of those fleeting flames, a flash that passed so quickly that not the slightest trace of it remains," absolutely not a trace. He was so determined that there was not a trace. "I have forgotten even the portrait of her that I have made for you: don't start accusing me of lightness; that's how it should be when one is on a trip."

Again he tried to divert Ann's attention by asking her to make some confessions on her part: "Remember to keep your word in confiding to me about your first love affairs; don't let the term shock you, I mean it in a proper sense. I don't doubt that you will confide in me soon, at least if you are as frank as I imagine."

This letter, like the preceding one from France, was written in French. But the trip was almost over. It was time to be thinking of home and of English scenes. He would soon be seeing the Lytteltons again, George, Christian, and perhaps, Mary. At the end of his letter to Ann he wrote a postscript in English: "If Miss Molly Lyttelton is in Town, I wish you may see one another often, and make a friendship."

CHAPTER VIII

COBHAM'S CUB

On his return to England Pitt found that the happy conditions he had left were changed in many ways. Molly Lyttelton, his particular friend in that household, next to George, had died suddenly, even before William's letter mentioning her to Ann could have reached England. There was no chance for the two girls to "make a friendship."

Added to this sadness, William also was obliged to face a coolness on the part of his brother. The boys had never been great intimates, but Will had kept the peace with Thomas, and the latter had been generous and fair. Now the mother, urged on by her relatives, had brought suit against her older son and had made William a party to the action. She had written to him while he was on his trip, urging him to agree to endorse a Bill of Complaint, without telling him the contents of it.

William had signed his consent to it under protest:

> I cou'd wish you had pleased to have let me know in general that that bill is, for at present I have no Idea of it. You assure me, Madam the answer you wou'd have me make is a form, and can lead me into no farther consequences, by engaging me in Law, or disobliging My Brother; neither of which I am persuaded you wou'd upon any consideration involve me in: upon these grounds I readily send you my consent to the answer proposed by Mr. Martyn in your letter.

As William suspected, the suit was more than a form. It accused Thomas Pitt of misappropriating his mother's property, and William's participation in the charge widened the barrier between the two men. The suit was only one of the burdens put upon Thomas Pitt by his eccentric relatives. His troubles were multiplied by their ceaseless demands for money. Though his estimate that the estate

should yield £10,000 a year was undoubtedly sadly optimistic, even at par it would have been strained to support
the style of living of the Pitts at this period. They made
use of three separate houses which Grandfather Pitt had
left, as well as a town house in London. In addition, the
sisters had frequent spells of illness and continued to visit
Bath several times a year.

Bath was definitely the most fashionable place for a cure,
and colossally expensive. Groaning at the cost, the Duchess
of Argyle wrote to Lady Suffolk, Ann's patroness and occasional chaperone at Bath: "Oh Gad, I am so sick of
bills . . . I have paid one this morning as long as my arm
and as broad as my bottom."

Aside from financial worries, the Pitts had other troubles.
Harriot had had a secret love affair with a Sir William Corbett, an attractive young blade, a nephew of William Pulteney, who was a friend of the Grenville brothers, and more
or less an admirer of Ann's. The Corbett affair had gone
further than anticipated, and a forced marriage was in prospect. William held the view that the couple were taking the
step that the circumstances required and that there was no
need for making a great to-do about the matter: "Harriot's
complaint is far from giving me any uneasiness, I think
nothing but such a necessity wou'd have made Them do
what they indisputably ought to do. My concern for Her is,
that her situation is so bad as to render this circumstance,
(distresfull as it is) necessary to put her into a better."

His censure was reserved for his brother Thomas, who,
William felt, should have rallied to Harriot's support:
"Poor Girl, what unnatural cruelty and Insolence she has to
suffer from A Person that shou'd be her support and com-
fort in this distress: I have heard him say so many hard
Things upon this affair."

Harriot herself, infinitely more sensitive to public opinion than either Ann or Betty Pitt, was crushed by the event,
and permanently retired from general society in spite of the
efforts of William then and later to restore her self-confidence and self-esteem.

Then to add further to the family distresses, Ann's status

at the Court was jeopardized by the dismissal of Lady Suffolk. George II had been bored with Lady Suffolk for some time past; but the Queen had intervened in her favor, for her Majesty always preferred the competition of old and plain favorites to the newer talent which caught her husband's eye.

Pitt was distressed lest this situation react with permanent harm on Ann's future prospects: "Your Griefs are so much mine that it wou'd be needless to tell you I am sorry for your Loss; I foresee a very disagreeable consequence to you from this change, which is, that your Friendship with Her may be charg'd upon you as a crime, and what was before a support may now be a prejudice to you." Though Ann, in fact, did not lose her post, the end of the Suffolk régime impaired whatever political influence she might otherwise have achieved at the Court.

Even Pitt's personal career had suffered an unexpected blow. His patron, Lord Cobham, had dared to oppose the Excise Bill which was championed by the chief Minister, Sir Robert Walpole. Walpole was furious at this insubordination, for he so regarded any opposition; and he used his influence with the Court to have Cobham deprived of his regiment.

Pitt immediately concluded that this put an end to his own prospects of a rapid rise in the Army. His appraisal of the matter was sound. To rise in the Army required influence. With his patron as colonel of the regiment he could look for rapid advancement, but hardly otherwise.

Opportunely, however, another career opened before him, very congenial to his wishes and his talents. His brother Thomas' inheritance of the Boroughs of Okehampton and Old Sarum provided the control of four seats in Parliament. The control was not an absolute affair, as the electorate went through the motions of voting and had to be kept in line by favors. Thomas expended more than £2000 in election costs and was returned for both constituencies, which gave him the right of nominating their members for Parliament.

Thomas nominated himself and George Lyttelton, his

brother-in-law, for Okehampton, and put in the name of his brother for Old Sarum. But William was still far from taking the coveted seat in the House of Commons.

Sir Robert Walpole had been watching Pitt's career and had already decided that the young man was not a desirable person for the national legislature. Walpole had been in virtually absolute control of the government since 1720, and in fourteen years had strongly consolidated his position. He was a genial boss, a jovial fellow when not crossed, but he ruled with an iron hand.

His firmness had been learned in the school of necessity. He had entered Parliament in the year 1700 and had suffered many vicissitudes. The Whig control and the whole Brunswick dynasty of the Georges who had been called to England under the Act of Settlement were on a precarious footing. In Walpole's early days civil war was at all times an active threat. Walpole had impeached Viscount Bolingbroke; and on another occasion had himself for a time been confined in the Tower. As late as 1715, there had been an uprising aimed at the restoration of the Stuarts, the affair in which Robert Pitt had narrowly escaped a prominent rôle, thanks to Governor Pitt's intervention. Walpole had no intention of letting power slip through his hands again.

In many respects, his rule was kind and wise. He kept England continually at peace, knowing that any military engagement carried with it the hazard of revolution. But as his power became less questioned, so it became less tolerant. Like Peter Stuyvesant, in Maxwell Anderson's portrayal, he could smell opposition. The slightest whiff of it in the air would distend his nostrils.

He could sniff the odor of independence from afar off, and did not fail to investigate the source. Pitt, to him, was already a noisome scent. Pitt in the eyes of the world was still a nobody, but the sagacious Walpole was looking ahead. He was aware of the ownership of Okehampton and Old Sarum. His sons were at Eton with Pitt, where William's record had attracted the notice of the school. He knew, of course, that Pitt had an obligation to Cobham, that he was on friendly terms with some of the Bolingbroke

set, and that his father had been sympathetic with the 1715
uprising. Such a man was dangerous.

Walpole's first move had been to offer Pitt a promotion
in the Army even before the elections had been held, but
this Pitt had wisely refused, knowing that his tenure would
continue only as long as he acknowledged Walpole as master. Then when Thomas made known his nomination of
William, Walpole tried to make a deal. He proposed that
a certain Mr. Harrison buy the seat from William at a
price of £1200. The matter was broached to the Pitt
brothers discreetly, through Harriot (shortly before her
difficulties had become known). Thomas was inclined to
take a rather favorable view of the proposed sale. After
all, a place in Parliament was a luxury for a young man,
unless he were open to constant corruption. William's
funds were exceedingly meager, and £1200 was a tidy sum.

William, however, was scandalized that his brother could
even consider the offer. He ranted and raved, stirred up
the family, made a great issue of it, and finally suggested to
the hesitant Thomas that if pay were involved the only
decent offer would have been to reimburse Thomas for the
£2000 he had spent for the election. That put the affair
in a new light to the older brother, who cut off the negotiations and finally certified William to the House of Commons.

William Pitt took his seat in Parliament on February 18,
1735. It is doubtful if anyone, except possibly Pitt himself,
realized the significance of the day as the beginning of a
career which would shape England's history. There was
little to suggest dignity or glory in the little makeshift
chapel, robbed of its altar and lecterns, fitted with tiers
of horseshoe benches. Its wainscoted walls were dull. Its
narrow gallery supported by thin pillars crowned with Co-
rinthian capitals overshadowed the rear upper benches. The
great speaker's desk added to the cramped feeling. The
building fronted on the Thames, the river which flowed by
Oxford (though there known as the Isis), by Eton, by the
palaces of kings, by the chief city of England, the Thames
which led to England's natural domain, the sea. But within

St. Stephen's Chapel, the river could not be seen and much of its meaning had, for the era, faded.

Under the regulations of that period Pitt was allowed to retain his commission in the Army, where in times of peace the duties were exceedingly light. From then on, however, his field was destined to be political rather than military. Lord Cobham immediately recognized Pitt as a possible candidate for his coterie of Opposition members, who were known as Cobham's Cubs.

Richard, Viscount Cobham was a connoisseur of bright young men, slapped them on the back, placed them in Governmental posts, and taught them how to stick pins into the seats of the mighty.

He invited Pitt to come down to Stowe, the Cobham estate, in July, 1735, where he remained as a guest for several months. It was a training of exceptional advantage for a political neophyte. A great galaxy of talent was foregathered there, social, literary, and political. Pope, the chief poet of the day, was a constant visitor. Martha Blount, a protégée of Pope's and one of his favorites since her fifteenth year, was also a visitor. She had become a noted wit and was now forty-five years of age. Miss Blount was a Roman Catholic, and her family was prominent among those of that faith. Her influence at Stowe, in a period of sharp Protestant feeling, gave Pitt an opportunity to understand the Roman Catholic view, and served to explain his approval, years later, of General Amherst's terms on the surrender of Canada. In these, the French Canadians were allowed to retain their religion even though in England there were strong strictures against Catholics.

Lady Suffolk had joined the group, George Lyttelton was there much of the time, so were Chesterfield, Bolingbroke and Pulteney, who were notable wits as well as persons of great influence. Here too were Richard and George Grenville, nephews of Cobham, and destined for high places in the Government.

The diversions at Stowe were by no means all political. Pitt played at cricket and indulged his passion for horseback-riding. Cobham had a flair for lavish entertainment and the estate was planned on the most elaborate scale. There were vast fields, a lake, and a stalactite grotto. Cobham had amplified nature with Doric arches, groves, fountains and temples dedicated to Venus, to ancient and modern Virtue and to Friendship, the last containing busts of those who had won Cobham's esteem.

All in all, there were four hundred acres to the estate, which was bordered on four sides by a broad gravel walk extending four miles and shaded by lofty elms. And, in addition, there was a two-hundred-acre deer park. Cobham had developed the grounds with infinite care and throughout his life kept adding to and remodeling the estate. Unfortunately his taste was not equal to his devotion. In an age which was inclined to formal and artificial landscape, Stowe outdid them all. Not even the excuse of current practice was able to prevent the comment of Alexander Pope, who, though for years a favorite guest of Cobham, could not help observing:

The suffering eye inverted nature sees;
Trees cut to statues, statues thick as trees.

Plots were hatched and plans were laid at Stowe all through the long summer evenings. The Cobham Cubs were due to form a conspicuous nucleus in the new Parliament. The chief behind-the-scenes leader of the Opposition was the veteran Bolingbroke, who had been restored to citizenship after the Walpole impeachment. Among the younger men in addition to Lyttelton, Richard Grenville, and his brother George, were Thomas Pitt, a cousin John Pitt, and two sons of Lord Marchmont, Polwarth Campbell and, surprisingly, Hume Campbell. Hume Campbell had not yet won fame as a lawyer or infamy as a king's pawn.

The Opposition, as was customary, centered itself around the leadership of the Prince of Wales. Frederick, Prince of Wales, was a singular character. His idiosyncrasies were frequently embarrassing to his followers, but at this stage the nature of his character was less important than the fact that the Prince was in opposition to his father and hence, of course, in opposition to the Ministry. Not only was it advisable for the anti-Government party to be close to the Prince for whatever prestige he might shed on their activities, but also there was the practical thought that at any time the King might die and that those who had supported the Prince would have the best opportunities to come into favor under the new reign.

Pitt did not immediately appear conspicuously for the Cobhamites in Parliament. In fact, he was silent for more than a year. Then, out of the affairs of the Prince, came the opportunity for his maiden speech, in April, 1736.

It had been notorious throughout the kingdom that his Majesty had a violent dislike for his eldest son, that the father on more than one occasion had thwarted the Prince's desire to marry and had finally chosen a bride for him whom the Prince had seen for the first time only a few days before his marriage.

The King, to accent his dislike of his son, had arranged that the marriage should take place with little ceremony, and both the King and Queen had intimated to their followers that any respect shown to the Prince would be looked upon as a lack of respect to themselves.

The Opposition, aware that any mention of the marriage would be distasteful to his Majesty and to Walpole's Ministry, decided to express their hearty congratulations in the Commons. Pulteney moved the address, Lyttelton seconded the motion, and Pitt rose to speak to the question.

His tone was one of elaborate respect for the Crown. He alluded to his Majesty's "high satisfaction" in bestowing marital happiness on the Prince. He referred to "the parental delight of tenderly indulging the most dutiful application, and most humble request of a submissive indulgent son."

The House caught the point, and Walpole took notes.

Pitt expanded on his theme, praising the Prince in the highest terms; and, ostensibly assuming that his words would be gratefully enjoyed by the royal family as a whole, he reminded the Throne of Frederick's popularity—"a generous love of liberty and just reverence for the British Constitution—those are public virtues and cannot escape the applause and benedictions of the public."

In those words Pitt advised George II of two subjects which were not calculated to please,—first, that Frederick was the leader of the younger generation; and, second, that the Georges ruled by sufferance of the Constitution. It was couched in most respectful terms, but the barbs were apparent, as Pitt expressed the hope that this marriage "may afford the comfort of seeing the royal family (numerous as I thank God it is) still growing and rising up in a third generation: a family, Sir, which I most sincerely wish may be as immortal as those liberties and that Constitution it came to maintain."

Walpole was infuriated at this piece of effrontery, and is reported to have growled, while the speech was in progress, "We must muzzle this terrible cornet of horse." The speech was, however, hardly more than the impertinence of an infant member of the House who was undoubtedly put up to it by the Opposition whip. It created no issues as such, joined no principles, and nominally was offered in all respect. Had Walpole ignored it, it might well have been immediately forgotten. But Pitt was a Cobham man. Here was the trouble-making crew coming to the fore again. Walpole lost his head. Before the session closed he dismissed Pitt from the Army, and thereby made him a hero overnight.

CHAPTER IX

THE ONE-HORSE CHAISE

The dismissal of a major opponent by Sir Robert Walpole would have been taken as a matter of course, but for him to stoop to the punishment of a young officer merely aroused public resentment.

To the mass of the public the ruin of a peer, the exiling of a viscount, the sending of a duke to the tower, were familiar historical spectacles, and pleasantly remote from the experience of the average citizen. But the revenge upon a petty officer and a commoner came uncomfortably close. The entire Army was incensed, seeing that, as Pitt observed: "An old officer . . . may be dismissed and reduced, perhaps, to a starving condition, at the arbitrary will and pleasure, perhaps at the whim of a minister; so that by the present establishment of the Army the reward of a soldier seems not to depend upon the services done to his country, but upon the service he does to those who happen to be ministers at the time."

One of the Prince of Wales' household wrote to her brother Lord Carlisle: "The King . . . two days ago turned out Mr. Pitt from a cornetcy for having voted and spoke in Parliament contrary to his approbation. He is a young man of no fortune, a very pretty speaker, one the Prince is particular to, and under the tuition of my Lord Cobham. The Army is all alarmed at this, and 'tis said it will hurt the King more than his removing my Lord Stairs and Lord Cobham, since it is making the whole army dependent, by descending to resent a vote from the lowest commission, which may occasion a representation in Parliament to prevent all officers of the Army from sitting there."

Even Lord Hervey, a stalwart supporter of Walpole,

The House of Commons in the eighteenth century. The auditorium was
originally a chapel, and in Pitt's time it was still frequently referred to as
St. Stephen's Chapel. Note the huge chandelier, which was the chief source
of light in the evening sessions.

St. James Square, probably the most fashionable residential park in London from 1750 to 1800. Mr. Pitt lived at No. 10 during his great Administration. In the background is St. James Church, where he was baptized in 1708.

Stowe, the lavish residence of Viscount Cobham, later the property of Richard Grenville, Lord Temple. Pitt was at first the pupil and ultimately the instructor of the political group which gathered here.

said: "Cornet Pitt was broken for this, which was a measure at least ill-timed if not ill-taken."

Walpole was unmoved by the criticisms. He had driven from power every opponent who had raised his head and every colleague who showed independence. He had exiled Bolingbroke, had dismissed from the Army Lord Stair and Lord Cobham and had driven Pulteney and Carteret, two of his most brilliant colleagues, into Opposition. He saw no reason to be soft with respect to Pitt. In fact, when he was attacked on this score in the House of Commons he replied, "If an officer, of whatever rank or merit, wished to meddle with affairs of state . . . which were outside his sphere, or even show aversion to a minister, that minister would be the most wretched of creatures if he did not cashier him."

This bold position, however, received little support from any direction. The theory that a member of Parliament could not talk freely upon public affairs if he held a commission in the Army could not stand the light of inspection. Bolingbroke's publication, *The Craftsman,* came to Pitt's support, though the Government organ *The Gazetteer* attacked the young member with ridicule, jeering at his tall thin figure and his long neck.

The continued clamor on the affair naturally did Pitt far more good than harm. "I should not be a little vain," he wrote to Lady Suffolk, "to be the object of the hatred of a minister, hated even by those who call themselves his friend." So much stir was made over the affair that knowledge of the circumstances went beyond the Army circles and became a matter of general knowledge. Pitt, seizing the opportunity in this popular interest, drove around the countryside by himself in a one-horse chaise; and was received everywhere with acclamation as the brave young man who had dared to stand up against the King and Ministry.

This appeal to the people was significant of Pitt's future political course. It gave him a strength, the nature of which was little appreciated by either his enemies or his supporters. Other men of the time, such as Chesterfield, Bolingbroke, and Pulteney, were his superiors in learning. There were those who could match him in oratory, except perhaps in his peak periods. In logic and financial acumen he had many peers; yet from his early days he was recognized to have a singular power. That power was fundamentally an adherence to the public weal, a recognition that government derives from the consent of the people.

The one-horse chaise was symbolic of his political sympathies. William had made his Parliamentary début under the auspices of Viscount Cobham. His early friendship and most of his social contacts were with the ruling classes, not only the Temple-Grenville group, but the wide ramifications of his Villiers kinship; yet fundamentally his thinking was that of the English commoner. The stalwart views of Grandfather Pitt were deeply implanted in him, the belief that goodness is essential to greatness, that to sell one's vote is an unpardonable disgrace, and that the welfare of the country demands government by constitution which must limit the king as well as the lowliest citizen.

Nominally the Georges were constitutional kings. The House of Brunswick, as Pitt reminded George II at frequent intervals in Parliament, was ruling according to the Act of Settlement and at the election of the English people. George himself periodically accepted this point of view in theory and repeatedly maintained that his ministers were fully responsible for the Government and must take the responsibility for its mistakes.

The position of the King under the Constitution was like that of the leading actor in a play. The houses of Parliament wrote the script and the head of the Ministry was the director. Actually, of course, the prestige of the monarch gave him very considerable power, just as the wishes of a theatrical star may dominate the production. Though the preferences of the King were influential, there was a higher power; for beyond the Throne, beyond the Ministry, and beyond even the voice of Parliament, was the ultimate dictum of the box office. The taxpayers and the people at large had the final decision.

The very existence of the Georgian succession had been possible because of popular feeling. It was the outcome of a long train of events dating from Charles I. Popular discontent had fostered the revolt of Oliver Cromwell. Dissatisfaction with Cromwell had brought about the Restoration. The Revolution of 1688 had been engineered by the ruling families of the country, and it reflected the strong Protestantism of the country. The Act of Settlement which had called George I from the little Electorate of Hanover to the Throne of England after Queen Anne had died without issue, not only ensured a Protestant monarchy but also defined in detail the place of the Throne under the Constitution.

The accidents of politics, however, had created a situation in which the rights of the citizen had become obscured. The habit of each party in power of taking revenge upon its predecessor had created a tendency toward absolutism in Government which had many evil effects. Walpole was arbitrary because, with good reason, he felt that his very life and liberty depended upon his staying in power. The Opposition to Walpole, in turn, was a coalition of independent Whigs with the few remaining Tories. Their only common principle was the desire to oust the current Ministry.

Pitt's political existence depended upon being allied either with the Governmental party or with one of the minor groups in opposition. There was no direct way in which he could represent the general public merely by canvassing the countryside. His zeal in appealing to the popular will was therefore merely laying the groundwork for his future career. For the present he continued to avail himself of the advantages of the Cobham cousinhood. Having now suffered the same persecution as Viscount Cobham, Pitt's bonds with the family connection were greatly strengthened. The Cobham family influence was considerable, not only because of the wealth of the Viscount but also because of the considerable aggregate of talents which were manifest in his nieces and nephews, even though no single one was outstanding. The extent of this connection is illustrated by the following table listing Richard Temple, Viscount Cobham (who was childless), his sisters and their children:

Mary Temple	Christian Temple	Richard Temple,	Hester Temple
m.	m.	Viscount Cobham	m.
Rev. West,	Sir Thos. Lyttelton		Richard Grenville
Prebendary	‖		‖
of	George		Richard (later
Winchester	Christian		Earl Temple)
‖	(m.		George
Gilbert	Thos Pitt)		James
Temple	Ann		Hester
Mary	Mary		
	William		

The Wests and the Lytteltons were the dramatic and literary members of the cousinhood, while the Grenvilles were on the practical side, solid men of property. Richard was selfish and ambitious. As a young man he was jolly and even light-hearted, but his desire for importance ate into him like a cancer until he became a dandified and ill-tempered mortal. George Grenville was the plodder of the household, meticulous, diligent, and without imagination. These Grenville boys, lacking the fire of Pitt, warmed themselves at the flame of his genius. They realized that in him the family had an excellent property. They loved him as a peasant loves his farm. And, as is the manner of many stolid burghers toward their more brilliant kin, their love had a touch of condescending superiority. Genius is unorthodox, and in the Grenville eyes as patent a genius as William Pitt could never quite equal their own sterling worth.

Though the estate of Stowe had been in the Grenville family for many generations, it was at present the home of Lord and Lady Cobham, and not that of the Grenville brothers. Sir Richard Grenville, husband of Lord Cobham's sister and father of the Grenville boys, was far less prosperous than the Temple connection, and when he died left very little property. The family home at this time, however, was a considerable estate containing about 2800 acres. The estate was called Wotton Underwood, and had been in the possession of the Grenville family since the eleventh century. The manor house was very spacious and the grounds were notable for the fine old oaks, one of which measured twenty-four feet in circumference and was said to have covered an area fifty yards in diameter with its branches, a tall tale which indicates at least that the estate was shadowed by mammoth oaks.

The Lyttelton branch of the cousinhood was less prosperously situated. They lived in an old black and white house at Hagley which had been condemned as unfit to live in about 1690 but was the principal family residence until 1760. George Lyttelton's habit of canting his head to one side may have been due to a glandular affliction of the neck caused by unsanitary conditions. Molly Lyttelton died under conditions which suggested tuberculosis, and five of the twelve Lyttelton children died young, while the others suffered continually from sore throats, agues, and fevers. The family lived there presumably because they had inherited the property and did not have the money either to move elsewhere or to improve it. When George Lyttelton made the grand tour in 1728 he went without a tutor and corresponded with his father frequently in respect to expenses. He even wrote that he would "marry the first advantageous match that his father offered him," though actually he did not marry until 1742.

The childless Lord Cobham, however, embraced the whole cousinhood in his affections and all the connection felt at home in Stowe and basked in its opulence.

The lavish worth of the Cobham-Grenvilles measured in real property was indeed oppressive in size. A one-horse chaise driving up to the portals of Stowe would shrink to a peanut by comparison. The Cobham house was colossal, resembling in general the twentieth-century Metropolitan Museum of Art in New York, only larger. It stretched from east to west a distance of 916 feet. The main salon, built at a cost of £12,000, was oval in shape, 60 feet long, 43 broad, with a ceiling 56½ feet high. From a pavement of Carrara marble rose sixteen Doric columns with white marble capitals and bases. The room was lighted by four bronze and gilt candelabra six feet in height, and above the cornice encircling the room was a frieze of three hundred figures representing a Roman triumph and sacrifice. The other rooms were proportionately vast. The state gallery, for example, was 70 feet long by 25 feet wide, furnished with settee chairs covered in blue silk damask. The state bedchamber was 50 x 35 feet with an 18-foot ceiling and a mammoth bed. The library was the same size as the state gallery. It contained 10,000 volumes and a huge celestial globe on which were inlaid 4,944 stars.

In good solid art-gallery investments the Cobham-Grenvilles had a notable position also. Aside from scores of paintings by Reynolds and other fashionable artists of the day, they could boast the ownership of Rembrandt's portrait of his father; Van Dyke's *Sir Richard Leveson;* Dürer's *St. Catharine and St. Barbara;* the *Head of St. Peter, Head of St. Paul,* and two compositions of the Holy Family by Rubens; *Venus Reclining* by Titian; *The Adoration of the Magi* by Veronese; *The Holy Family* by Corregio, and a multitude of lesser paintings, in addition to scores of sculptural works.

Before the portals of this ostentatious mansion the presence of a one-horse chaise was extraordinarily democratic. This aspect of young Mr. Pitt's activities must have lifted many an eyebrow of the rich Whig aristocracy. Cobham and his wealthy friends must have looked upon Mr. Pitt's democracy with an amused tolerance, thinking of it as something that would pass, not deep rooted; but they would have been wrong; for if country houses are haunted, it may be surmised that the robust spirit of Grandfather Pitt hovered near, while William, amid the marble halls and gilt candelabra of Stowe, contemplated the lot of the common man.

CHAPTER X

The Cliveden Set

While Mr. Pitt was identified with the minority which gathered at Stowe, he was also closely linked with the group of Opposition members who frequented Cliveden, the country seat of Prince Frederick. Stowe and Cliveden were related in politics, and many political and social figures were conspicuously present at both establishments.

The estate of Cliveden had been built by George Villiers, Duke of Buckingham, ancestor of Mr. Pitt, in the reign of Charles II. The house was located on a hill which sloped toward the Thames, affording an exceptionally charming view of meadows and river. Frederick made lavish additions to the main house—which, except for the wings, was destroyed by fire on May 20, 1795. When the Astor family occupied the current structure on this site in the twentieth century, some shrewd historian revived the legend of the Cliveden Set, of political plotting around sumptuous dinner tables. While the modern Cliveden Set is apparently a myth, in the days of Frederick it was real, vigorous, and avowed.

Frederick was a host of the first water. The vast lawns of Cliveden were the scene of picnics and torch-lit garden parties. There were boating on the Thames near at hand and musicales, amateur dramatics, and balls in the great house. Prominent in these affairs were Alexander Pope, "the Wasp of Twickenham," Martha Blount, Lady Hamilton, Mr. Pitt, in fact, most of the Cobham crowd. Amid all of this jollification there was scheming by Prince Frederick and his versatile guests to embarrass the King's ministers, and particularly to overthrow the occupant of 10 Downing Street.

With Walpole's occupancy in 1735, 10 Downing Street

had become, for the first time in history, the official address of the English Government. The house had been built in the mid seventeenth century by George Downing, a member of the first class to be graduated from Harvard University. It had subsequently been purchased by the Earl of Lichfield, who had remained loyal to James II in 1688 when that monarch had abdicated. The new Government had seized all of Lichfield's property, and for many years 10 Downing Street had been used for varied purposes. In 1731, George II offered it as a gift to Sir Robert Walpole. Walpole, however, had been wary and had declined to accept so handsome a bribe as his personal property. At length, in 1735, he had agreed to use the house, but only as his official residence in his capacity as First Lord of the Treasury. For many years it was the headquarters of the First Lord of the Treasury, regardless of who was chief minister in the Cabinet.

Walpole was keeping his own skirts clear and at the same time had his punishing eye on the Cliveden Set, including its Cobham-Grenville affiliations. He had already struck now at Cobham and now at Pitt, in dismissing each from the Army. It was but the first round of a battle which might go to any lengths. Pitt, in the Cobham scheme of things, was a useful pawn in this contest. To a doubter of Pitt's abilities, Cobham had observed, "Sir, you do not know Mr. Pitt's talent for insinuation; in a very short quarter of an hour he can persuade anyone of anything."

The Prince, however, was Walpole's chief target, because in striking at Frederick he would smite all the Opposition party with one blow, for the popularity of the Prince was the chief asset to the Cliveden Set.

To understand the position of Walpole it is necessary to look for a moment at the peculiar personalities of George II, Queen Caroline, and their son, Prince Frederick. The un-English nature of the royal trio created a situation in which all three were subjected to being used by those struggling for power.

George II was a red-faced, coarse-looking little man who in his royal regalia resembled a small-town German brewer dressed up for a masquerade ball. He was German to the core. Like his father, he was bewildered by these peculiar English people who invited him to be a king and yet treated him far differently than royalty were treated by the Electorate of Hanover. In Hanover, everything was done according to a fixed routine year in and year out. Even when the monarch was absent from Hanover, as he was most of the time in occupying the English kingship, the Hanoverian ceremonies remained virtually the same, except that the King's portrait sat upon the throne, to be knelt to in lieu of his Majesty.

The King preferred German mistresses and German companions. He favored his countrymen at every turn. Many of the best plums in the royal household were taken from the English families to fatten Hanover courtiers. His Majesty in the early days of his reign seemed to regard England as a mysterious pudding which had been unexpectedly laid before him and might vanish at any moment. He not only lived in great extravagance, but encouraged his companions to rifle the public till at every opportunity.

Strangely enough, George's city palace of St. James was a relatively mean affair compared to the grandeur of Hampton Court and other dwellings belonging to the Crown. The palace stood on the site of a hospital dedicated to St. James founded by the citizens of London, whence the building and the Court got its name. The building itself was an irregular brick affair having little exterior beauty. The front, next to St. James Street, had a little square courtyard and there were two other small courtyards. The buildings were low, plain, and of mean appearance compared with some of the lavish homes of London's wealthier families. George II always disliked London, lived there as little as possible, and these relatively plain accommodations of his city establishment may have accounted in part for his attitude.

He seemingly made no attempt to understand his subjects. His chief virtue was a willingness at most times to remain a figurehead. Unfortunately for his popularity, the Germanic design of his kingship was not appealing. He even introduced German pronunciations so that the Court adherents were found to be saying "eyether" and "nyether," a version which was hitherto foreign to the English tongue. The King was not popular, but the Administration Whigs had imported him, had "sold" him, more or less, to the people, and were well advised to uphold his hands.

While Queen Caroline lived, and she was living at the beginning of 1737, the ship of state was moving on a steady keel, thanks to the lady's perceptiveness and to her executive gifts. It was Caroline who wore the royal breeches, even though in public she was most submissive to his Majesty. She encouraged his having mistresses, especially old and homely ones. She approved the mammoth Countess of Yarmouth, a favorite brought over from Hanover. While George engaged in various diversions, Caroline was watchful of the interests of the Throne.

Her diligence was ceaseless. She received company while at her toilet, settling affairs of state, hearing social gossip and listening to Divine Service without interrupting the complicated processes of an eighteenth-century boudoir. Occasionally a chaplain would rebel at this cavalier treatment. Once, when the maids of honor closed a door in a clergyman's face as they were on the verge of changing the Queen's undergarments, her Majesty called out to inquire why he did not keep on preaching.

"Because," the clergyman replied, "I will not whistle the word of God through a keyhole."

The Queen ingratiated herself with the English politicians and social leaders, whom the King largely neglected. She kept posted on the activities of Parliament through Sir Robert Walpole, and supplemented her information by the aid of Lord Hervey, her undercover man. Hervey was a bizarre and bilious gentleman who for years lived on a prescribed diet of dried biscuit and ass's milk. His toothless gums, his pallid face, and his high thin voice earned him the nickname of "Lord Fanny." He was feminine and dangerous,—both venomous and personally courageous. He was quick to challenge to a duel and ever ready to devise a plot. Next to Walpole there was probably no more influential figure in the Court.

Against the influence of the King and Queen, who were a unit, stood the rather pitiable figure of the Prince. In 1737 Prince Frederick was thirty years of age. His chief assets were his youth and the expectancy of an early accession to the Throne. The king was fifty-four years of age, in poor health and not expected to live many months.

To support the Prince against his Majesty was, accordingly, an attractive gamble for the Opposition, with the possibility that when Frederick put on the Crown he would scatter rewards to those who had aided him. Walpole realized this possibility so fully that for a time he maintained private negotiations with many of the Cliveden group, expressing an interest in the Prince's well-being, and in turn suggesting that they be moderate in their demands. This was good sense on both sides. The Opposition chiefs did not wish to be too offensive to his Majesty, in case he were to live for a long time. Similarly Walpole desired to show some reasonableness to a prince who might become king at any moment.

Prince Frederick nevertheless was an ace card for the Opposition, and they made much of him. He was a frequent guest at Stowe. He made Bath one of his favored resorts. He was patronized and encouraged by Sarah, the Duchess of Marlborough, widow of the General. In fact, she once had offered him £100,000 to marry her favorite granddaughter. The Prince was willing, but Walpole had learned of the plan and thwarted it. The Duchess was devoted to all who challenged the ruler. In her eyes, since the death of her great husband nothing of real importance had happened. She disdained the gross Hanoverian entourage of the Court, and from the splendor of Marlborough House she looked at the nearby royal residence and referred to his Majesty as "Neighbor George." The Duchess, in brief, fêted the Prince and Pitt and Chesterfield and any others who might stir up some excitement in a world that seemed much too dull.

The Prince was a genial enough fellow with a smattering of good manners, a touch of education, and a flair for lavish entertainments, for the populace as well as for the Cliveden Set. He attended cricket matches, boat races and public gardens, mingled with the crowd and appeared cordially disposed. He was a little over five feet, slender and inclined to be foppish. He lacked the tough fiber of his father and the driving intelligence of his mother, but his informal and friendly manner won him an increasingly popular esteem.

Early in the year of 1737, the Cliveden and Cobham groups conceived the idea of sponsoring the Prince's desire for an allowance from his father of £100,000 per year. This was the amount that George II had enjoyed when he was Prince of Wales and the request seemed equitable. The Prince's current allowance was £50,000 and he was already heavily in debt.

The address on the subject was moved by Pulteney (whose nephew had married Harriot Pitt), followed by a diatribe by Pitt. Pitt's remarks have not been preserved but were said to be violent and abusive. The attack was essentially a gratuitous interference with his Majesty's personal affairs. It was not regarded as the province of Parliament to tell the King what proportion of his Civil List should be allocated to the Prince, and the motion did not carry. The move, however, was popular with the masses and, naturally, popular with the Prince.

Pitt was rewarded with a place in the Prince's official household, and his friend Lyttelton was similarly honored. Pitt's appointment was that of a Groom-of-the-Bedchamber, a post with only nominal duties, which paid £400 per year. It seemed as though the Pitt fortunes had made a good forward move.

Walpole, Lord Hervey, and the Queen, however, were watchful of the rising tide of popularity of the Prince and his associates. They shortly hit upon a scheme which blackened the Prince's reputation and led to the proscription from Court functions of all that came to his support.

The plot centered around the birth of the first child of Prince Frederick and Princess Augusta. The Princess Augusta in the spring of 1737 was strongly under the Queen's suspicion. Their Majesties had been so harsh to their eldest son that they apparently feared reprisals. When the Princess Augusta was pregnant, they feared that the birth of a son would bring the limelight of favorable national attention to the Prince's household. The Queen had the suspicion that if the childbirth were not successful a changeling would be substituted. Such at least was an excuse which she gave for her animosity toward the young mother.

The Prince and Princess several weeks in advance of the expected event had made arrangements for the accouchement at St. James Palace. It was in the heart of fashionable London and had the advantage of the best medical facilities which the time afforded.

Late in July the young couple were visiting their royal parents in Hampton Court. The estate was a summer palace on the Upper Thames about one and a half hours' drive from London. On the evening of July 31, toward midnight, after the King and Queen had retired, Augusta was taken suddenly with labor pains and wished to be rushed back to St. James Palace where all was in readiness.

The Prince hastily summoned a carriage. In a short time he, the Princess, one of her friends and two bedchamber women were in a coach rushing to London.

Within an hour after their arrival the Princess was delivered of a tiny daughter in the presence of a doctor, a midwife, Lord Wilmington, and the Earl of Godolphin (the Lord Privy Seal). The two last, according to custom, were present as officers of state to certify that the child was, in fact, delivered of the Princess, and not an adoption. The Prince had notified other members of the Government but the news had come so suddenly that only these two ministers arrived in time.

Before the child was born a courier rode back to Hampton Court and roused one of the women of the palace who went to the royal bedchamber to give the news that the Princess was in labor.

"My God!" the Queen cried, "my dressing gown! I'll go to her at once."

"Your dressing gown, madam?" said the woman. "Your coaches, too. The Princess is at St. James."

"Are you mad?" the Queen exclaimed.

At this the King popped his head up and shouted in German. "You see how they have done this. It's all your fault. A false child will be put on us. . . . I told you it would be like that."

The Queen hurried into her clothes and within half an hour two coaches were tearing along to St. James bearing her Majesty, ladies-in-waiting, and three peers of the realm, including the ubiquitous Lord Hervey.

On their arrival at St. James the Queen was met by her son, and then hurried in to see the Princess. The baby was brought to her Majesty and after a few affectionate words the Queen retired to an adjacent room to confer with Lord Hervey.

"Well, upon my honor!" she said, "I no more doubt this poor little bit of a thing is the Princess' child . . . though I own I had my doubts upon the road that there would be some juggle; and if there had been a brave jolly boy instead of this poor ugly little she-mouse I should not have been cured of my suspicions."

Hardly had the household settled down for the night when Sir Robert Walpole appeared with witnesses, in great haste and highly perturbed. He roused Prince Frederick from his bed and demanded an account of the course of events.

In the succeeding hours, the King, the Queen, and Walpole became increasingly offended at the surprise party which nature had sprung upon them. The picture of Frederick and Augusta rushing away in the dead of night from their Majesties, without notification, to their own apartments in the city might well reflect upon the hospitality of the King and Queen. It was a mark of disrespect and a sign of independence which they could not tolerate.

Hervey and Walpole saw in the situation an opportunity to fan the King's anger and blacken the Prince in public esteem. They saw the usefulness of a version of the story which would show the Prince to be so heartless as to drive his wife from the summer palace, rushing her to town in a mad hour-and-a-half drive, while she was in the agonies of childbirth. What a monster of refined cruelty he might be painted to be, perhaps even hoping by his actions to cause the death of the Princess! Hervey and Walpole, accordingly, concocted a message to be sent by his Majesty to the Prince. The letter denounced the Prince for cruel treatment to his wife and disrespect to his parents. It ordered him out of St. James Palace, and concluded with the admonition:

> To this I will receive no reply. When you shall, by a consistency in your words and actions, show that you repent of your past conduct and are resolved to return to your duty, parental affection may then and not till then induce me to forgive what parental justice now obliges me to resent.

The message was laid before the Cabinet for discussion, and was received with much skepticism. In fact Walpole's chief associates were stoutly opposed to countenancing such a libel. The Duke of Newcastle, who has appeared in history as one of the least squeamish politicians of the eighteenth century, could not stomach this performance. He went privately to one of the Queen's daughters saying, "For God's sake, stop such a message going to the Prince."

Walpole, however, controlled the Cabinet and he was adamant. Here was a chance to strike at the popularity of the Prince and at the prestige of the Opposition who were gathered about him. Let it be seen that anyone who trafficked with the Prince would have no shadow of approval from the Throne. He was firm that "it would be better for the administration to have a total declared separation."

The letter was sent, and all England buzzed with the story. It registered with the public as Walpole and Hervey had expected. Prince Frederick was never able to stem the tide of the slander with his side of the story. He was driven from St. James Palace and took up his residence at Norfolk House on St. James Square where for a time few visited him except for the more extreme members of the Opposition and their intimates.

The job had succeeded, but Walpole was getting old. He had been in office continuously for more than a quarter century. He had come increasingly to rule by the purchase of votes and by political strategems, and in November, 1737, his political system received a severe blow in the death of Queen Caroline. She had always believed in him and she saw to it that the prestige of the Throne was always in support of his Administration. With the death of the Queen the King's chief mistress, the Countess of Yarmouth, gained the ascendancy over George II, and the Countess had been sedulously cultivated by persons in the Opposition.

Walpole had, according to his plan, killed the Prince's cause as a popular issue in Parliament, but he found that the young and tireless Opposition could find other measures. Pitt and Lyttelton seemed to have a genius for finding holes in his armor. Foreign affairs proved to be a fruitful ground for discussion. Spain, always hostile to England, had been seizing British privateers on the high seas. Englishmen were languishing in Spanish prisons. Mr. Pitt brought that to public attention, and Walpole found that his troubles at 10 Downing Street were far from over.

CHAPTER XI

TROUBLES AT 10 DOWNING STREET

Though Mr. Pitt had flirted with the populace in his time of dismissal from the Army and doubtless found some comfort in reciting his wrongs, his gesture had little importance except as an indication of the trend of his thinking and of his future methods.

Mr. Pitt had an acute sense of his own destiny, vague at first but growing in content and sharpening in design as the years went on. At present the design was blurred in outline and the young man was still in his political novitiate. He can hardly have expected to arouse a strong popular outcry against the treatment which he had received, and if such a protest had arisen there was little chance of its being effective. In theory, the people elected Parliament in 1738, as before and since, and physically they cast ballots; but as a practical matter virtually every district or borough was under the control of some overlord, and such changes as there were usually reflected a fight between overlords rather than a change in mass opinion.

There were, of course, some vestiges of popular representation. The members of the Commons from the City of London were frequently independent of the governmental cliques, and in times of unusual crises the people could affect the opinion of the Commons. Mr. Pitt, many years later, came to discover the evil of "rotten boroughs," to appraise the extent to which the supposedly democratic structure of the Government had been distorted, but at this time Mr. Pitt's tours of the countryside were primarily self-educative and exploratory. As a soldier he had read military books, and as a representative he was now reading the public.

In spite of the warm approval which had been so be-

stowed upon him by the Cobham group, there was in their
benediction a note of condescension. At the age of thirty,
he could no longer afford to be a glorified errand-boy for
the Grenville projects, and he was ready at every opportunity to take the riskier positions in the political battle-
line, to accept responsibilities which the Grenvilles could
disavow if the sorties did not turn out well. Pitt, in short,
entered upon the current phase of his Parliamentary career
with a rashness which is best understood by an appraisal of
the competitive position of his colleagues in the Opposition.

He was allied with many who had greater prestige than
he, many who were so gifted with experience, knowledge and
savoir faire to be in the lead. There was Bolingbroke,
whose learning Pitt admired extravagantly; yet Bolingbroke
had been a Tory favoring the Stuarts and the divine right
of kings. He was almost an old man, debarred through impeachment from sitting in Parliament. There was Pulteney,
handsome, erudite, a fluent speaker, wealthy, influential.
Pulteney was easily top man of the Cobham cousinhood.
Lord Carteret, related to Pulteney and, less closely, to the
cousinhood, was obviously in the quieter battlefields of the
House of Lords; but by his gifts, his sophistication, experience in embassies and the home government, he was one
of the abler men in the kingdom. Among the rest of the
Cobham group were Chesterfield, Lyttelton, Richard Grenville (later Earl Temple), George Grenville, Sir William
Wyndham (who was growing old), and William Murray,
the dour, precise, and exceptionally able scholar.

Pitt was, nevertheless, a considerable citizen, among
them, probably top man of the second flight, a position far
from satisfactory to his ultimate intentions. He was, at this
stage, the most daring, the most imaginative and certainly
the most vituperative of the Opposition. Dr. Johnson at
this period referred to the "yelping of Pitt." He was a
sharp tool in the Cobham kit, though less experienced than
the talented Pulteney and a mere amateur beside the vener-
able Wyndham. Accepting his subordinate status for the
time being, he welcomed opportunities to attack Sir Robert
Walpole and his Ministry.

Walpole, with all the patronage of the Government at his command nevertheless was vulnerable. His urbane and good-humored rule of the country was suffering from the paralysis of inactivity. Moreover, a new generation had grown up since the days of his first climb to power and he had lost whatever he might once have had of "the common touch."

Walpole relied strongly on the fact that there was a solid group of 260 members of the Commons (out of a total of approximately 500) who were on the Government payroll, most of them owing their appointments to him and virtually all of them subject to dismissal if they should incur his displeasure. It was also true, of course, that he himself was subject to dismissal if he incurred the displeasure of the majority of the House of Commons. That was where events worked against him.

In 1738, for example, the Government had attempted to enforce the act against spirituous liquors known as the "Gin Act." Gin drinking had become a widespread vice throughout England, and Walpole's intentions were for the public good. Within a year he brought about twelve thousand arrests for illegal selling of liquor, but the result, instead of approval, was loud public protest!

Walpole in this instance recognized the popular voice as an element in political power. He aimed, ineptly, to influence opinion by heavy secret subsidies to the press, even though the press, as yet, had no wide-spread appeal. Occasionally certain pamphlets on political issues won a large audience, but the daily newspapers were of small circulation. Sarah, Duchess of Marlborough, was at this time considering investing in a proposed paper which would be edited in a way to be of interest to the public at large, and such a notion was considered novel and venturesome.

An awareness of the common man was spreading through many circles of society. George Whitefield, the noted evangelist, on February 17, 1739, gave his first sermon from a field pulpit, addressing the miners near Bristol. This concept of taking the Gospel to the oppressed was revolutionary, in a century in which the Church had become to a large extent an apathetic adjunct of the State. The Countess of Huntingdon "got religion" in the good old evangelical sense. At her soirées she forced the dissolute café society of the times to get down on their knees and pray for the brotherhood of man.

The dapper Prince of Wales, possibly instructed by his friends, intensified his natural inclination to cultivate the people. Assisted by William Pitt, George Lyttelton, and others of his household staff, he went about the countryside with all the antics of a congressman. He kissed the babies of the poor, danced with the populace in public gardens, gave conspicuously to charity, and shouted until he was red in the face with excitement at horse and dog races.

Quite in line with this appeal to the public was the strategy used by the Opposition in continuing their attacks on the proposed agreement with Spain known as the "Spanish Convention." In opposition to an amicable settlement, Alderman Beckford introduced a Robert Jenkins into the House of Commons. Jenkins appeared wearing a huge wig and carrying a strangely shaped package of cotton in his hand. Jenkins was Master of the sloop *Rebecca*. He declared that his ship had been attacked by Spaniards and that they had given him a present to take to King George. The present was wrapped in the cotton which he had brought into the House, and when displayed to the view of the members proved to be a human ear, one of Jenkins' ears. Jenkins said that as the Spaniards had cut off his ear he had "committed his soul to God, and his cause to his country." Some said that the ear had been carefully preserved in a bottle since 1731. Others said later that if someone had snatched at Jenkins' wig, two entirely good ears would have been seen attached to his skull. However that might be, the ear which Jenkins held in his hand was a real ear and it caused a tremendous sensation both in Parliament and outside the walls of St. Stephen's Chapel.

Jenkins' testimony came in the first session of Parliament in February, 1738. Other petitions were heard from numerous merchants and sea captains who had suffered from

Spanish aggression. On March 28, the Opposition wheeled up all its big guns, hoping to blast Walpole out of a majority in his attempt to get support for the Spanish Convention.

The session opened at eight o'clock in the morning with close to five hundred present, one of the largest sittings of the House in many years. The Prince of Wales was seated in the long dim gallery, and he stayed through the session, which lasted until one o'clock the following morning.

Pulteney led the attack for the Opposition, followed by Wyndham. Then, late in the day, Pitt swung into action in his attack on a motion by Horace Walpole, brother of the chief Minister. Pitt's strategy here was typical. Sometimes he prepared himself with the greatest diligence on some subject at issue, but often he spoke extemporaneously, usually waiting until some remark of an opponent lighted the flares of his indignation.

Horace Walpole had evaded bringing a motion in favor of the Spanish Convention and had proposed, in what he thought to be a more tactful approach, to move an address to the King, congratulating him on his "final determination" of the Spanish issue.

Pitt blasted this subterfuge in an attack which carried his name to the far corners of the kingdom:

"We have here the soft name of a humble address to the Throne, and for no other end than to lead to an approbation of the Convention. Is this cursory disposition of matter of such variety and extent all we owe to ourselves and to our country? *When trade is at stake, it is your last entrenchment; you must defend it or perish.* . . . Here we are taking sanctuary in the Royal name, instead of meeting openly and standing fairly the direct judgment and sentence of Parliament upon the several articles of this Convention.

"You are moved to vote a humble address of thanks to his Majesty for a measure which is odious throughout the kingdom. . . . But be what it will, is this any longer a nation? Is this any longer an English Parliament, if, with more ships in your harbors than in all the navies of Europe, with above two millions of people in your American colonies, you will bear to hear of the *expediency of receiving from Spain an insecure, unsatisfactory, dishonorable Convention?* It carries fallacy or downright subjection in almost every line.

"As to the great national objection, Sir, the searching of your ships, it stands merely in the preamble of the Convention, but it stands there as the reproach of the whole, as the strongest evidence of the fatal submission that follows. On the part of Spain, an usurpation, an inhuman tyranny, claimed and exercised over the American seas. On the part of England, that which is an undoubted right by treaties, and from God and nature declared and asserted in Parliament, is referred to plenipotentiaries, to be discussed, limited, and sacrificed.

"The Court of Spain has plainly told you that you shall navigate by a fixed line to and from your plantations and in America; if you draw near to her coast (and this is an unavoidable necessity) you shall be seized and confiscated. If upon these terms only she has consented to refer disputes, what becomes of the security which we are flattered to expect? I will take the words of Sir William Temple:— *It is vain to negotiate and to make treaties if there is not dignity and vigour enough to enforce their observance.*

"Under the misconstruction of these very treaties, this intolerable grievance has arisen. It has been growing upon you, treaty after treaty, through twenty years of negotiation. Spain seems to say, We will treat with you, but we will search and take your ships; we will sign a Convention, but we will keep your subjects prisoners in Old Spain; the West Indies are remote; Europe shall witness in what manner we use you."

Pitt admitted that the assertion by Spain of the right to search British ships suspected of engaging in privateering in Spanish America, might be tenable, but he claimed that the abuses which had grown up under that excuse made the situation unbearable.

"The right claimed by Spain to search our ships is one thing," he continued, "and the excesses admitted to have been committed under this pretended right is another.

Giving an indemnity for excesses is no cession of the claim to search. The payment of the sum stipulated is evidently a fallacious nominal payment only. I will not attempt to enter into the detail of a dark, confused, and scarcely intelligible account. Can any verbal distinctions, any evasions whatever, explain away this public infamy? To whom would we disguise it? To ourselves and to the nation? I wish we could hide it from the eyes of every court in Europe. They see that Spain has talked to you in the language of a master.

"This Convention, Sir, I hold from my soul to be nothing but a stipulation for national ignominy; an illusory expedient, to baffle the resentment of the nation."

The speech gave Pitt a new stature both in the House and with the public. The direct appeal to "your despairing merchants and the voice of England" was a new note in Parliament debates. The suggestion that the "two millions of people in your American colonies" had a right to be heard in determining the policies of the nation was a revolutionary idea to which the Ministry and Parliament might have listened profitably.

Walpole, however, carried his motion by a vote of 260 to 232.

Another blow to the Opposition cause was the death of Sir William Wyndham, in June, 1740. Though Wyndham, in his early career, had been a supporter of the Stuart cause, this had been largely forgiven him in a career marked by ability and straightforwardness. He had been consistently in opposition to Walpole and was above being bribed into submission. Moreover, as the elder statesman of the Opposition, he was a counselor and guide who was badly needed.

The Opposition, to an extent, had won prestige on the Spanish issue even though not defeating the chief Minister, for it had aroused public opinion to the point where Walpole was forced to wage war with Spain if he were to stay in office, and he had consented to a break in relations in the autumn of 1739. War, accordingly, was officially proclaimed at Charing Cross, the Royal Exchange, and at

Temple Bar amid the huzzahs of citizens and the ringing of church bells. For a time the country gloried in the excitement of war preparation and in their dream of a glorious England repeating the history of the Armada.

It required only a short time before the nation realized far more of the pains than of the glories of war. In February, 1740, the Ministry issued orders for a general embargo. Naturally the shippers and merchants yelled to high Heaven. British manufactures were being sold to the far corners of the globe and this restriction pinched many industries and occasioned unemployment.

In July there were riots in London and along the seacoast in protest against the high price of grain. And as the year advanced, Spain, and not England, proved to be the superior on the seas. By the time Parliament met at the close of the year, England had lost 407 ships to the Spanish forces. Walpole was on the defensive again, and on January 26, 1741, Pitt fired an opening shot from which Walpole never wholly recovered. Mr. Pitt demanded an investigation of the conduct of the war.

"Our time cannot be more usefully employed, during a war, than in examining how it has been conducted," he said, "and settling the degrees of confidence that may be reposed in those to whose care are entrusted our reputations, our fortunes, and our lives.

"There is not any inquiry, Sir, of more importance than this; it is not a question about an uncertain privilege, or a law which, if found inconvenient, may hereafter be repealed. We are now to examine whether it is probable that we shall preserve our commerce and our independence, or whether we are sinking into subjection to a foreign power.

"But this inquiry, Sir, will produce no great information, if those whose conduct is examined are allowed to select the evidence; for what accounts will they exhibit but such as have often already been laid before us, and such as they now offer without concern? Accounts, obscure and fallacious, imperfect and confused; from which nothing can be learned, and which can never entitle the Minister to praise, though they may screen him from punishment."

An investigation on the conduct of the war was the thing that Walpole most dreaded. His gifts as a man of peace were considerable, and history has recognized them as such, in spite of his record of political corruption. But war was not his business. He had become involved in it only because he could not avoid it and he was definitely not the man to be at the head of the Government during a time of war.

A graceful retirement, however, seemed improbable. Walpole had been too vindictive to his enemies in the early days to be allowed to withdraw quietly. He needed his power for self-preservation. An investigation of the conduct of the war would fall on him personally. He had been accused of being a "sole" minister, a prime minister, a chief minister. He was this, to be sure, and in general his predecessors had been. But the designation of "Prime" Minister was used first with respect to Walpole, and was employed as an accusation. While for many reigns it had been the custom for one individual to form a ministry, and, in a very general way, to be responsible for the Government, nevertheless it had never been accepted that various members of the Cabinet must be subordinate in their duties to the head man, or must take their ideas from him. Cabinet policies were developed in conference and in many instances were decided by a poll of the members. Cabinet members were colleagues with approximate equality, man for man, in their voting powers. In a strong ministry, of course, the chief of Administration usually dominated the others, though at times a figurehead might be chosen to form the Cabinet while the actual leader stayed in the background.

Again, in certain ministries the Cabinet was hardly more than a loose federation of departments, each of which was largely ignorant of the activities of the other. In any case, for the chief Minister to be portrayed openly as the "sole" Minister was untraditional and invited reprisals. Walpole was shrewd enough to foresee the possibilities, but he preserved his urbanity without a tremor. He was even outwardly unruffled when Sandys of the Opposition came up to him in Parliament on February 11, 1741, stating his intention to move an address to the Throne asking for Walpole's dismissal.

The Minister paused for a moment and thanked Sandys for warning him, answering that he desired "no favour, but fair play."

"Having invested me with a kind of mock dignity," Walpole observed, "and styled me a *Prime Minister,* they impute to me an unpardonable abuse of that chimerical authority which they only created and conferred.

"As I am not conscious of any crime, I do not doubt of being able to make a proper defence. *Nil conscire sibi nulli pallescere culpae. . . ."*

At this Latin quotation Pulteney pricked up his ears and told Walpole that his logic was as bad as his Latin, affirming that Walpole should have used the ablative *nulla culpa* instead of the dative.

Walpole offered to bet Pulteney a guinea that he had given the quotation correctly. Nicholas Hardinge, a clerk of the House, was agreed upon as the judge. Hardinge decided against Walpole, who thereupon tossed a guinea to the winner.

Pulteney caught it in his hand, exclaiming as he held up the coin, "This is the only money I have received from the Treasury for many years, and it shall be the last."

Two days later Sandys brought in his motion for dismissal. Both the Government and the Opposition were eager for a decisive vote and many of the members of the House were in their seats at six o'clock in the morning. Pitt again was in the forefront of the attack, censuring the conduct of the war and affirming that Walpole, who had "lost the countenance of all mankind," should not be permitted to continue at the head of the Government.

But Walpole still had plenty of fight in him. He ridiculed Pitt and his followers who were rejoicing in their popular designation of the "Young Patriots."

"A patriot, Sir!" Walpole exclaimed, with no little truth. "Why, patriots spring up like mushrooms! I could raise fifty of them within the four-and-twenty hours. I have raised many of them in one night. It is but refusing to gratify an unreasonable and insolent demand, and up starts a patriot."

The Sandys motion was lost by a large majority, but the fact that it could have been made at all was ominous, and the continued mismanagement of the war was still working against the prestige of the Government.

In March the Ministry brought in a bill with the innocent title "for the encouragement and increase of seamen, and for the better and speedier manning of his Majesty's fleet." Actually the measure authorized search-warrants to arrest seamen anywhere, even in private houses, and press them into service. This threat to the liberty of the subject aroused Pitt to white heat.

"Will this increase your number of seamen?" he declaimed, "or will it make those you have more willing to serve you? Can you expect that any man will make himself a slave if he can avoid it?

"Can you expect that any man will breed up his child to be a slave? Can you expect that seamen will venture their lives or their limbs for a country that has made them slaves? Or can you expect that any seaman will stay in the country, if he can by any means make his escape?

"If you pass this law, Sir, you must do with your seamen as they do with their galley-slaves in France—you must chain them to their ships, or chain them in couples when they are ashore. . . . For God's sake, Sir, let us not put our seamen into such a condition as must make them worse than the cowardly slaves of France or Spain.

"I say, and I do not exaggerate, we are laying a trap for the lives of all the men of spirit in the nation. Would any of you, gentlemen, allow this law to be executed in its full extent? If, at midnight, a petty constable with a press-gang should come thundering at the gates of your house in the country and should tell you he had a warrant to search your house for seamen, would you, at that time of night, allow your gates to be opened? I protest, I would not.

"Would any of you patiently submit to such an indignity?

Would you not fire upon him, if he attempted to break open your gates?

"I declare I would, let the consequences be never so fatal; and if you happened to be in the bad grace of a Minister, the consequence would be, your being either killed in the fray, or hanged for killing the constable or some of his gang."

At this, Horace Walpole (the elder, and brother to Sir Robert) rose to reprove Pitt for "formidable sounds and furious declamation." He suggested that the young man might have curbed his vehement gestures, his theatrical emotions and his exaggerated expressions, if he had permitted himself to be guided by more experienced speakers who had "more successful methods of communicating their sentiments."

"The atrocious crime of being a young man—which the hon. gentleman has with such spirit and decency charged upon me," Pitt replied sarcastically, "I shall neither attempt to palliate nor deny, but content myself with wishing that I may be one of those whose follies may cease with their youth, and not of that number who are ignorant in spite of experience."

As to the charge of his being theatrical, he replied:

"I am at liberty, like every other man, to use my own language; and though I may, perhaps, have some ambition, yet . . . if any man shall, by charging me with theatrical behavior, imply that I uttered any sentiments but my own, I shall treat him as a calumniator and a villain. . . . I will not sit unconcerned while my liberty is invaded nor look in silence upon public robbery."

When a fellow member arose and sharply called him to order Pitt turned upon his new critic:

"If this be to preserve order, there is no danger of indecency from the most licentious tongue. . . . Order may sometimes be broken by passion or inadvertency, but will hardly be re-established by a monitor like this, who cannot govern his own passion whilst he is restraining the impetuosity of others. . . ."

In spite of all the fireworks, the press bill passed, the

Parliament adjourned, three members who had strongly supported Walpole were rewarded with peerages, the King sailed on May 6 for his beloved Hanover, and Robert Walpole was left to carry on as best he could.

The sarcastic and violent attack on the elderly Horace Walpole, who had merely twitted the young Mr. Pitt, was characteristic of Pitt's sophomore days in the House. In later years he shivered at the recollection of his gaucheries and disavowed them; but with all his crudeness, he had a courage, as well as a brass, which others could not equal. His attacks disturbed the Ministry, and paved the way for the urbane leader Pulteney. Pitt's violence was useful. He was, moreover, making a reputation which placed him on the side of liberty and Constitutional practice.

During the intense political sessions of the past two or three years Pitt's private life had not contributed to his meager supply of serenity. He and his sister Ann had lived together in one of a row of small houses in Pall Mall looking into St. James Square. The turbulent devotion between brother and sister had continued, though not without violent flare-ups of the Pitt temperament. Samuel Rogers, a contemporary of the two, observed that "Ann Pitt . . . was a very superior woman. She hated him, and they lived like cat and dog. He could only get rid of her by leaving his house and setting a bill on it,—'this house to let.'".

The comment by itself is misleading in the light of Pitt's devoted letters to her, both before and after the period of their living together, but it may reflect the high tension of relationships between the Pitt sisters and brothers. They could and did quarrel furiously with each other and yet could be on friendly terms a short time afterwards.

Ann at this stage was becoming a little difficult. She was twenty-nine, an age which in that era marked her for spinsterhood. In the days of her youth she had enjoyed great popularity and had had numerous suitors. She had rejected the pious Ayscough, George Lyttelton after he had sought Harriot's hand, and possibly many others. Now she found herself traveling with a married set who were on the fringe of her brother's friends.

She was reputed to be highly intelligent; but she was becoming progressively odd in her mentality. The Bolingbrokes, Lady Suffolk, and Lord Chesterfield were among the group of notables who were cordial to Ann, but in the main these people were slipping from a dominating place in public affairs. With the death of Queen Caroline, Ann's post at the Court was unnecessary, and she no longer occupied any place in the royal household. The relatively irresponsible and brilliant circle who centered around the Marble Hill estate of Lady Suffolk were seemingly more entertaining to Ann than either the Court coterie or the sturdy diligence of the Grenville cousinhood. She could swear like a trooper and exchange repartee with Chesterfield, but she seemed to lack the art or else the desire to accommodate herself to the more earnest sections of the society in which her brother mingled.

In this respect she was a handicap to him, especially as the hostess of his home. Nevertheless it is only fair to her to say that her popularity with the Duchess of Queensberry and the Duchess of Marlborough may have done much to aid William Pitt with those useful dowagers, and may have helped to strengthen the substantial backing given to him from Marlborough House.

The tart and vigorous widow Marlborough had much in common with Ann Pitt, including a love of profanity. Lord Campbell in his *Lives of the Chief Justices* reports that the Duchess was a very troublesome client and became testy if kept waiting. One evening she called at the home of William Murray, the noted Parliamentarian and intermittent colleague of Pitt, who was also her solicitor. Murray was not at home. She called again later, waiting until after midnight and finally went away without seeing him.

Murray's clerk, in reporting the matter the next morning, said, "I could not make out, Sir, who she was; for she would not tell me her name; but she swore so dreadfully that she must be a lady of quality!"

While eccentricities would be tolerated in the Duchess they were less favored in a single woman. It is significant that in spite of the very close bonds between William and his sister her name virtually had disappeared from the correspondence between William and the Lytteltons. In view of Pitt's fierce loyalty to his kinfolk it may have been a relief to him that in the summer of 1741 Ann decided to go to France for her health. The project had the approval of Lady Suffolk and of Lady Bolingbroke, the Viscount's second wife who was a French woman and well-connected in French court circles.

After Ann had been in Paris for a time under adequate chaperonage, she thought it would be fun to set up an apartment for herself in Paris. In spite of her liberal and independent attitude, however, she had the caution to consult her brother and Lady Suffolk on the subject by letter.

Pitt was extremely disturbed at the idea and wrote to Lady Suffolk that he could not see the scheme in any light that would be fit for Ann. "I thought Paris the most improper place for a single woman to live at," he said, "nor could I like her settling abroad anywhere if her health did not make it necessary." He conceded that Lady Bolingbroke's introductions and sponsorship in France would be most reputable, but he pointed out that "the world here would not know (and perhaps part of it would not choose to know) anything more of her situation than that she was living at Paris, a single woman."

Ann accepted her brother's decision and continued to live for several years at health resorts in France, becoming more and more preoccupied with her symptoms. Meanwhile Pitt diverted himself with visits to many of the country places of his friends. He spent much time at West Wickham, where he was entertained by Gilbert West and his sister Molly, who later married Admiral Hood. He visited Lyttelton at the lugubrious Hagley, the Grenville brothers at Wotton, and of course was a frequent guest at Stowe.

Aside from these social commitments, he attended to nominal duties as a member of the Prince of Wales' household staff. While he had the post of Groom of the Bedchamber his duties were chiefly those of political manager for the Prince. Prince Frederick continued to indulge in a continuous round of petty entertainments, amateur dramatics, dances and levees, and Mr. Pitt occasionally forgot politics enough to lead cotillions at Cliveden, and to stroll along the banks of the Thames with the personable Lady Archibald Hamilton.

Mr. Pitt was a thoroughly eligible bachelor by now, worth only a few hundred pounds per year, but well-connected and a good mate for some rich widow, or gilded spinster. He was tall, erect, and of good proportions. His bones had taken on some flesh but not too much. The neck had lost its scrawny appearance. The fine head, the piercing gray eyes and the strong Roman nose made him a figure to win the attention of feminine eyes. Lady Hamilton was attractive. She had wit, a flair for politics, and a roving eye. People began to talk. It made a pleasant subject for summer evenings. Was the affair Platonic or was it not? There was a nice complication in it, because some affirmed that the lady was a mistress of Prince Frederick, and that brought forth all the possibilities of what jealousy might do to the career of the rising Parliamentarian. Others held that the whole discussion was absurd, that Lady Hamilton was a great friend of the Princess Augusta, that the attentions of Prince Frederick and Mr. Pitt were only the natural courtesy of two gentlemen to a lovely creature of the weaker sex.

The mystery was never solved, as there were so many more provocative riddles which sooner or later entered into the lives of all concerned; but at least it was certain that if Lady Hamilton was a friend of the Princess Augusta, William Pitt was considerably less so.

He was never so foolish as to lose a reasonably cordial relationship with Princess Augusta, but, for a man who did not hesitate to use the friendships of women for the purpose of politics and his career, Mr. Pitt in this instance was peculiarly diffident. Augusta was now the mother of

Promenade at Tunbridge Wells. The three figures in the rear center are, left to right, Beau Nash, Elizabeth Chudleigh, and Mr. Pitt.

Marlborough House, which was frequented by the Rabelaisian Lord Chesterfield and the ambitious Mr. Pitt in the days of Sarah, the turbulent Duchess.

PAINTED BY J. B. VAN LOO

Augusta, wife of Frederick, Prince of Wales, whose unfortunate influence over his son George III did much to warp the life of that unhappy monarch.

a three-year-old boy named George, who would be Prince of Wales and ultimately the King, if Frederick should die. Frederick's health was excellent, and to Mr. Pitt the prospect of George's coming to the Throne probably seemed far, far distant. Pitt's immediate policy was to keep the confidence of Frederick, and perhaps that could not be too easily done in conjunction with paying great attention to Augusta.

Augusta was reputedly at this time a devoted wife, but she was not averse to attention. On the other hand, she was strong-willed, possessive, and a German. Between her and Pitt, whose nationalist feelings were exceptionally strong, there may have been a barrier which he could not have broken down without conspicuous effort, but at least a formal cordiality was preserved between them.

There was much to be done; and Pitt, together with most of the Prince's supporters, spent a considerable part of the summer stirring up the country for a further drive against Walpole. Sentiment was in their favor, as the nation was greatly disappointed in the progress of the war. The Government was adopting more and more stringent measures. On three different days a general fast had been proclaimed to give support to the war. This was supposed to have a moral and patriotic effect. The public had clamored for the war, but had apparently been under the delusion that England could easily defeat her enemies; and this tightening of the belts was a development which had not been foreseen and was highly unpopular.

The Ministry during the summer had founded Woolwich Academy for the training of artillery forces and had embarked upon a stiff enforcement of the Impressment Act. The gazettes reported "a very hot press" on June 2, 1741, and in thirty-six hours a total of 2,370 seamen were enrolled. As Pitt had predicted, this was a dangerous threat to the liberty of the subject, and the commoners everywhere were terrified. No able-bodied man, especially if he had ever shipped before the mast, dared to walk the streets alone or to be found alone in a public tavern. Men traveled in groups for self-protection and the threat of press-gangs created the psychology of a Reign of Terror.

William Pulteney was now definitely the leader of the Opposition group. He was a tall, handsome man with particularly well-formed hands which assisted his gifts as an orator. He had great wealth and ample family connections. He was descended from the first Earl of Bath and was connected by cousinhood and marriage to Lord Carteret, and more distantly to the Grenvilles. In addition to the marriage of his nephew to Harriot Pitt he was also a kinsman of William Pitt through the Villiers line.

Pulteney, at this stage, was brilliant, urbane, and magnetic, while Pitt was still a sophomore in politics,—daring, forceful, but raw. It was Pulteney who had the leading influence at Stowe, at Cliveden, and at the Fountain Tavern where he was accustomed to assemble with Pitt, Lyttelton, and other lights of the insurgent Whigs with their remnants of Tory adherents. Pulteney was the guiding force in the forthcoming elections and in the drive to embarrass Mr. Walpole.

Pulteney, Pitt, and other supporters of the Opposition, aided by the money and social lobby of the Duchess of Marlborough, bent every effort to win in the Parliamentary elections. The Prince was reported to have spent some £12,000 in the Westminster election alone. In most cases Government officials were in control of counting the returns; but at the opening of Parliament, on December 4, numerous election districts were sufficiently close to warrant a series of contested decisions to be passed upon by the Commons.

Still more significant was the fact that the public in many sections of the country had sent in memorials to their representatives to oppose standing armies, to reduce the sales tax, and to repudiate various other policies of the Government.

On the opening of the new session the House was in a ferment. The King's address to the Parliament, which dealt with unimportant topics, was promptly criticized by

various members, who contended that the Ministry was
avoiding public issues. A contest on the Westminster election was immediately brought before the House by the
Prince of Wales' adherents; and the Opposition in triumph
defeated the Ministerial forces by four votes.

Walpole was desperate. He made secret overtures to
the Prince and his advisors, offered to double Frederick's
income, to pay his debts, and to make any other reasonable
adjustment. Frederick, however, declined to compromise
and insisted that Walpole, having lost the support of the
House, must follow the Constitutional practice of retirement.

The chief Minister, nevertheless, was determined to sit
tight, if it should be any way possible. The tide of condemnation was rolling in from all directions. On December 18, there was a meeting of great merchants at the
Crown Tavern behind the Royal Exchange, and resolutions
were passed complaining of losses due to Spanish privateers.
In January, 1742, petitions against the naval losses of the
war were received from London, Liverpool, Lancaster, and
Southampton. On January 21, in a crowded session of
503 members, Pulteney moved that the papers on the conduct of the war be obtained from the Ministry and referred to a secret committee.

While the Opposition lost this measure by a bare majority of three, it was such a show of power that Walpole
was terrified. An investigation by a committee could
readily turn into a man hunt. He himself had hunted with
the hounds and knew what that could mean. Day and night
he pulled political strings and offered favors in the effort
to save himself. On February 2, however, came the contest on the Chippenham election. Even as the roll was
being called it was evident that the tide was overwhelming.
As one former adherent after another voted against the
Ministry, Walpole beckoned to Sir Edward Baynton to
sit beside him, while he recited the favors that he had conferred on scores of members who were leaving him in his
extremity.

When the tellers announced the vote, it was 241 for the Opposition to 225 for the Ministry. Walpole promptly said that he would never sit in the House again. Parliament adjourned to the 18th to get its breath, and Pulteney, chief of the Opposition, was the man of the hour.

CHAPTER XII

AN UNPLEASANT LESSON FOR THE KING

The triumph was Pulteney's rather than Mr. Pitt's. Pitt, indeed, had made a strong impression in the long battles of the Opposition. He had championed the cause of Prince Frederick. He had dared to criticize the Hanoverian bias of the King. He had appealed to the voice of the people in the Commons and in his trips around the countryside. He had endeared himself to the merchants in understanding their side in the Spanish war. He had pointed to England's unused strength in her American colonies. He had championed the cause of the English freeman in his opposition to the Impressment Act. But with all of this he was only one of Pulteney's lieutenants.

There were other conspicuous men in the fight. Sandys had dared to move for the impeachment of Walpole. Lyttelton had spoken repeatedly for the Opposition cause. Murray, the solicitor, had been one of the Opposition orators. Pitt's elder brother Thomas, who was head of the family, had been an election manager for the Prince. The Grenvilles had been loyal supporters of the Opposition, not too brilliant but united and diligent.

Pulteney was clearly the man. Chesterfield and other Opposition peers had done conspicuous work in the Lords; but it had been necessary to accomplish the defeat of Walpole in the Commons and in this Pulteney had had the acknowledged leadership.

Pulteney, it will be recalled, had great wealth, family connections, ability as an orator, and a large personal following. Though a close friend of Mr. Pitt, he was one of the few who stood between Pitt and the post of leadership. In worldly advantages and in talent, in all respects, except the two qualities of audacity and integrity, he was the superior of Pitt at this time.

In the few days which intervened before the reopening of Parliament, Walpole had worked furiously for the preservation of his own hide. On January 11, 1742, he had resigned all employments of the Government and had accepted the title of the Earl of Orford. This was an open confession to the House that they need never again fear his direct management of Parliament. But with his old-time shrewdness, he had worked zealously to divide the ranks of the Opposition as they closed in on him. He had been long enough in politics to realize that a substantial proportion of men are readily susceptible to temptation. He was still in a position to tempt, because George II hated every last man of the Opposition, hated his eldest son, Frederick, hated those who derided his love for Hanover, and was himself devoted to the Walpole whom they had driven from office. Walpole still had a free hand to offer anything that was at the personal disposal of the Crown.

Pulteney was the key man, and to him Walpole went for secret conferences. The old Ministry had been in office so long that some degree of consultation was unavoidable; and it was apparently flattering to Pulteney to be recognized as the particular individual whose word would have the most weight with the new Ministry. He enjoyed being the fellow who could make the decisions and, in his own good time, tell the lesser men what was going to be done. Accordingly, Pulteney and Walpole put their heads together. Pulteney was not willing to promise to forego the proposed inquiry on the conduct of the war, and the ex-Minister for the moment let that pass. Sandys was to be Chancellor of the Exchequer. Murray was to leave the Opposition to become Solicitor General, and from that time on Murray and Pitt were personal and political enemies.

The post of Lord Chancellor was filled by the able jurist Hardwicke, who was not active in the political rivalries. Some of the more obnoxious Walpole ministers were to be removed; but Walpole's chief clerk, Henry Pelham, was to become Paymaster General, and Pelham's brother, New-

castle, was slated to be one of the Secretaries of State. As
to Pulteney, Walpole proposed that he deserved to be elevated to the peerage and it was promised that he should
become the Earl of Bath.

Walpole had read Pulteney's character more shrewdly
than his colleagues, for Walpole had written to the King,
regarding Pulteney: "If I know anything of mankind . . .
he may be won, if it be done with dexterity. For as the poet
Fenton says, 'Flattery is an oil that softens the thought-
less fool.'

"If your Majesty can once bring him to accept of a coronet, all will be over with him; the changing multitude will
cease to have any confidence in him; and when you see that,
your Majesty may turn your back to him, dismiss him from
his post, turn out his meddling partizans, and restore things
to quiet: for then, if he complains, it will be of no avail;
the bee will have lost his sting, and become an idle drone,
whose buzzing nobody heeds."

This arrangement, of course, left in doubt the matter of
Walpole's successor. If Pulteney was no longer in the
House, it would seem better to have the Ministry headed
by a peer, as had been the practice at many times in the past.
Lord Wilmington, a nonentity, was chosen as the nominal
head of the new Ministry in the post of First Lord of the
Treasury. The actual head was to be Lord Carteret, acting
as one of the Secretaries of State. Carteret was sufficient
of a diplomat to be friendly both to Prince and King; and
had been a mild sympathizer with the Opposition. This
left no one in the Commons with a chief place in the Cabinet, though there was an abundance of talent available.
Pitt, Lyttelton, and the Grenville group were to be ignored.

For a brief time those arrangements were not known to
the public or to most of Pulteney's associates. The Parliament reconvened on the 18th and Pulteney within a few
days made the gesture of calling a meeting of three hundred
of the former Opposition at the Fountain Tavern to discuss
the disposal of offices, though the arrangements had already
been made.

In Parliament, Pulteney voted for investigation of Walpole's conduct and made a strong speech on the subject. Pitt, however, made the more memorable impression on this occasion by his retort to young Horace Walpole, later the author of the famous letters. The young man had made a valiant defense of his father; and Pitt, addressing the Commons in a kindly tone, said that young Walpole's speech "must have made an impression on the House. But if it is becoming in him to remember that he is the child of the accused, it also behooves the House to remember that we are the children of our country."

Pitt spoke in the full confidence that he and his associates were now the dominant party in the Government; but within a short time Pulteney's deal became public knowledge and, as Walpole had predicted to the King, the wrath both of the country and of those who were excluded was unbounded. It was said by Pulteney's contemporaries that his vast popularity vanished overnight. He himself was reported to have said that he had been swept off his feet, and it is said that he sought the recall of his patent of nobility; but Walpole held him to his bargain. Whether these were facts or rumor, nothing Pulteney could do was able to win back his former followers. They held a public meeting to disown him; and the new coalition Cabinet hobbled into office leaving a splintered and angry Opposition, bent on retribution.

Carteret was the logical man to head the new Cabinet. After all, the old Opposition had been able to muster only a bare majority; and Carteret, by winning a small section of that group to the established Ministry, would be able to carry on with little disturbance,—or so it seemed.

Carteret personally, of course, did not sit in the Commons. Other chief ministers, if they were peers, usually had their managers or representatives in the House. To Carteret this was of secondary importance. Henry Pelham was nominally the ministerial representative in the Commons, but Carteret disdained to regard him as an equal. "He was only chief clerk to Sir Robert Walpole," Carteret said. "Why should he expect to be more under me? . . . He did his drudgery and he shall do mine."

Carteret, in short, was a minister on the Continental pattern. He chose to deal with principals only, with kings and ambassadors and not with the commonalty of the Parliament. Governmental business was an old matter to him. As far back as 1719 he had been ambassador to Sweden. In 1721 he had been Secretary of State for the Southern department. For six years, 1724-1730, he was Lord Lieutenant for Ireland,—most of his career had been in exalted positions apart from the rough and tumble of legislatures. In his temperamental aloofness from Parliament he had the sympathy of the Throne. On one occasion when George II had been urged to hurry back to England from Hanover, the monarch had remarked testily: "I am nothing there; I am old and want rest, and should only be plagued and teased there about that damned House of Commons."

Carteret's policy upon taking office was to ignore Parliament. He spent much of his time abroad in the various courts of Europe, involving England in the many shifting and obscure feuds of the rival European governments. He even went to the extreme of hiring Hanoverian troops without any sanction from the legislature.

This calm and bold separation of the Ministry, not only from the people but even from deference to the Commons, was, in the long run, a great stroke of fortune for Pitt. Pitt's unquestioned gifts would never have left him wholly submerged; but it was lucky for him that the political suicide of Pulteney was followed by the autocratic aloofness of Lord Carteret. Within a few months the genius of Pulteney had been removed from Mr. Pitt's path and the spirit of Carteret was seen in its true colors. Philip Yorke, a son of the Lord Chancellor, was now able to say that Pitt was "the most popular speaker in the House of Commons and at the head of his party."

The importance of Mr. Pitt as leader of the Opposition may be easily exaggerated, however, for he was merely the head of a remnant in the Parliament which generally was considered too inconsequential to be given recognition. It was a sizable remnant, but the quality was held to be inferior, at least by those in control of the Government. Pitt himself, at this period, was a good bit of a vulgarian and his methods still were crude. He continued to sit at the feet of the ancient Duchess of Marlborough, that proud and vigorous hag who looked like the ruins of a once handsome castle. The Duchess considered herself above caste and the ordinary rules of courtesy. As the wife of the noted General she had been astoundingly beautiful, and she gloried in her rise from comparative obscurity to mistress of the palace of Blenheim. As has been mentioned, she had become a great favorite of Queen Anne. With the favor of the Throne, the strength of her late husband's reputation, and her enormous riches, she had been able to indulge a naturally domineering nature.

She regarded her children as little better than worms and was infuriated if they disregarded her slightest wish. When one of her daughters encouraged a grandchild to make a match of which the Duchess disapproved, the latter took the daughter's portrait, blackened the face of it, and wrote on it "Now her outside is as black as her inside."

The Duchess emphasized her scorn for her own family by gathering favorites about her, especially those prominent in political affairs. She doted on the independent Lord Chesterfield, who refused to be bullied by her, and she was devoted to the brilliant young Murray until he took the post of Solicitor General which removed him from the Opposition camp. The obstreperous Mr. Pitt was to her liking, and she frequently entertained him and George Lyttelton at Marlborough House.

Pitt and Lyttelton at this stage made a more curious appearance to the eye than in their schoolboy days. Pitt, as has been said, had become tall, erect, well-proportioned and distinguished in appearance, whereas with age Lyttelton had become more awkward, if possible. His large head was still canted toward one shoulder, his arms flapped at his sides, and he had the habit of bumping into objects and stepping on his own toes. The team of Pitt and Lyttelton was a case of Hamlet, Prince of Denmark, in partnership with Ichabod Crane.

Lyttelton, however, had a grace of expression and a gift

for writing light verse which made him a welcome addition at the Marlborough levees, while Mr. Pitt lent a more serious, high-spirited note.

The influence of the Duchess may not have been as helpful to Mr. Pitt now as in his more obscure days, for his conduct during the Ministry of Carteret was marked by recklessness which he later regretted. His manner in particular was calculated to create many enmities, for he was merciless in attack, using both denunciation and ridicule frequently in respect to trivial issues. He had a dangerous flair for repartee and extemporaneous address. The Duchess always applauded a good fight, and it is probable that many of Mr. Pitt's thrusts at the stuffed shirts in the Ministry were made with one eye on Marlborough House.

The tragedy of the political situation in respect to the welfare of the country was that essentially nothing had resulted from the supposed Opposition victory and, moreover, there was no target and no issue immediately at hand whereby any change could be brought about. Not even Carteret's personality was a subject for attack. He was not opposed to mass opinion but rather was sincerely uninterested in it. In fact, he lived in a species of dream world peopled by heroic memories of the past. He worshiped the ancients and cultivated Bacchus, whose slave he ultimately became. He was one of the classical scholars of his age and, according to his friend Swift, Carteret carried away from Oxford "more Greek, Latin and philosophy than properly became a person of his rank."

He had, moreover, the strength of the man who is indifferent to consequences. "As I have courage enough to risque in a good cause my natural life," he said, "I am much less solicitous about my political life, which is all my enemies can take from me"; and he stated his intentions without a blush. "What is it to me," he said, "who is a judge or a bishop? It is my business to make kings and emperors, and to maintain the balance of Europe."

This was a noble attitude, but Mr. Pitt saw very early that Carteret was not translating his principles into any tangible program. Intermingled with his persistent oratory

on many subjects, Pitt kept returning to the question of
why England was involved in Continental wars, and in time
the public began to echo the question.

Carteret neither then nor at any other time could explain the befogged policy of his Administration. If he
had a policy, he was of the temper to disdain to send a
reply to the lower House. But it seems likely that there
was no fixed policy. Carteret simply liked to participate
in the game of empire, having a vague notion of preserving
some balance of power through the intervention of England
but actually achieving nothing, for England at that time was
too weak to have much weight in the divided European
councils. Such weight as she might have had was considerably vitiated by the unreliability with which she vacillated,
favoring first one group and then another, and this had led
the country into the War of the Austrian Succession, supposedly on the Spanish issue—which, however, had become
confused with many other issues of ambassadorial intrigue.

The Pitt-Carteret controversy, in fact any of the con-
troversies on the War of the Austrian Succession in which
England participated from 1740 to 1748, are not worth
discussion in detail because fundamentally they had no
meaning. There was no goal, no principle, no program at
stake, and such pretenses as were offered along those lines
were often shifted and changed, to the inevitable confusion
of current popular opinion and posterity. Leslie Stephen,
the historian, has referred to these conflicts as, "That
complicated series of wars which lasted some ten years,
and passes all power of the ordinary human intellect to
understand or remember. For what particular reason Englishmen were fighting at Dettingen, or Fontenoy, or Lauf-
feld is a question which a man can only answer when he has
been specially crammed for examination, and his knowledge
has not begun to ooze out."

Mr. Pitt's persistent queries on what the Ministry was
about were peculiarly embarrassing. And they had the
advantage to Mr. Pitt of making him one of the chief topics
of conversation of the day. His friend George Grenville
said "He spoke like ten thousand angels" in his address on

November 16, 1742. An agent of the French Government reported to his home office that Pitt's remarks were distinguished by eloquence and knowledge in a debate otherwise tumultuous and ill-informed.

Carteret, while disdaining the House of Commons, needed to have some kind of leadership and representation there, as he foolishly looked down upon Henry Pelham; and he gave to William Murray the particular assignment of holding Pitt in leash. This was an error in judgment, for Murray lacked the ability to meet Pitt in the rough and tumble of Parliamentary heckling. Pitt, moreover, took particular pleasure in meeting this adversary, not alone because of their rivalry during Oxford days but also because of Murray's apostasy, as Pitt regarded it, and because every gibe at Murray was now pleasing to the Duchess of Marlborough.

On December 7, 1742, Murray took the first fling at Pitt by attacking the inconsistency of the Opposition. Pitt in his reply apparently registered a triumph. Oswald, a fellow member of the House, said of the affair: "The one (Murray) spoke like a pleader, and could not divest himself of a certain appearance of having been employed by others. The other (Pitt) spoke like a gentleman, like a statesman, who felt what he said, and possessed the strongest desire to convey that feeling to others, for their own interest and that of their country . . . for this talent he possesses beyond any speaker I ever heard—of never failing from the beginning to the end of his speech, either in thought or in expression . . . I think him sincerely the most finished character I ever knew."

There was one man in the House, however, who was equipped to locate the chinks in Mr. Pitt's armor. This was the elder Horace Walpole, brother of Robert and uncle of young Horace. He was aided by a calm philosophy and an even temper which enabled him to appraise his fellows with an annoying coolness. He rose in Parliament to rebuke Mr. Pitt for "inciting the dregs of society to insult their superiors." This was a blow which struck home, for Pitt's activity in catering to the masses was well known.

Ultimately this became a bulwark of strength to him, but as yet neither the society of the times nor the members of the Commons had come to accept in practice the importance of public opinion. Pitt himself had not yet fully developed his philosophy of the people as the ultimate source of the Constitution; and was unable to meet the charge. The incident was important, however, for events of later years illustrated the thoroughness of Mr. Pitt's thinking and the creative imagination of his mind. Again and again, he would return to some subject after it had been first presented in the Commons, and each occasion would witness a new and improved development of the subject. Years later, when the word "superiors" was tossed into Parliamentary debate in the same spirit, Pitt was ready for it and blazed forth in overwhelming reply. Had there been more philosophers than the elder Walpole in the Commons, Mr. Pitt would have trod a thornier path, but as it was he had the good fortune to face little real competition.

Carteret's indifference to the House of Commons forced his Administration into the policy of conducting war largely on the basis of giving subsidies to various foreign powers and hiring troops. Conceivably the country could have been roused to enthusiasm for some particular conflict. The war against Spain, it will be recalled, was a popular movement and there had been dissension only because of British incompetence in conducting the conflict. Carteret, however, could not add to the forces of the Army and Navy without bills in the House approving the expenditures, which in turn would raise the issue of what should be the proper size of the army and navy forces. Accordingly, it seemed simpler to Carteret to commit the nation to financial donations to the Allies, hoping that the Parliament would include these in the general budget.

Pitt naturally enough saw the weakness of that position. "Neither justice nor policy required us to engage in the quarrels of the Continent," he declaimed in the House on December 10, 1742. ". . . The confidence of the people is abused by making unnecessary alliances, they are then pillaged to provide the subsidies . . . now to remedy this deficiency we have taken Hanoverian troops . . . but why should the Elector of Hanover [George II]," he added in words which were to widen the breach between him and the King, "exert his liberality at the expense of Great Britain? It is now too apparent this great, this powerful, this formidable kingdom is considered only as a province to a despicable electorate." There was too much truth in this charge to be palatable to the Throne.

In the following June, George II distinguished himself at the Battle of Dettingen. It was the last occasion on which an English king appeared on the field of battle, but in the conflict he wore not the British colors but those of Hanover. Furthermore, the contest was between the English and the French forces even though at this time England was nominally at peace with France.

The Ministry, however, made the most of the King's personal courage on this occasion; and attempts by Mr. Pitt to diminish the credit of the monarch were looked upon as not very sporting. The young member from Old Sarum, in fact, was in a somewhat precarious position. He was obliged to attack the Ministry in order to give effective leadership to the Opposition, and yet he would need to win over large blocks of votes from the Government side in order to make any real progress. He needed, therefore, to be careful, while opposing the majority position, to deal with subjects which would divide opinion rather than consolidate it. He had unfortunately been robbed of the opportunity which promised the most drama, namely, the investigation of Robert Walpole, by the astuteness of that gentleman. Pitt had been named on an investigating committee, but due to a corps of lawyers which protected the Government and the benefits which Walpole was still able to bestow from the Treasury of the Throne, upon the right persons, no important documents were forthcoming; and the work of the Committee had fallen into nothingness. Mr. Pitt, therefore, was obliged to keep hammering on the foreign situation as the one point concerning which the country and many in the Commons had smoldering doubts.

Carteret's star, never too bright, was beginning to dim.

In July, 1743, Wilmington, the nominal head of the Ministry, died. Carteret urged the King to appoint his old friend Pulteney, now Lord Bath, in the place of Wilmington. In view of Pulteney's unpopularity with the country this suggestion was absurd. Robert Walpole, now Lord Orford, who had remained on friendly terms with the Throne, advised the King that Carteret's suggestion was utterly impossible. He insisted wisely, and successfully, that Henry Pelham, who had been Walpole's chief assistant, would be the logical man. Walpole's judgment on this score was sound and probably patriotic. His own political career was over; with all his faults he had been an efficient administrator, and was now appalled by the present slipshod management of the Government's business.

Pelham had the advantage of being a commoner and his presence in the Ministry brought it considerable strength. He was a realist and desired to bring into the Government the important personalities from all groups. Chesterfield said of Pelham that he was anxious to offer peace and "save himself from Pitt in the House of Commons"; and Pelham soon made an informal agreement with Pitt in which the latter agreed to support an English army in the Low Countries to protect England against France, and Pelham in turn agreed that no foreign subsidies should be paid unless England had a controlling voice in the conduct of operations.

It began to be noised about that Pitt, Lyttelton, and others of their character were to be included in the Cabinet. A cartoon of the period portrays Pitt as very thin and gaunt, saying, "Who knows but I may be puffed into something by and bye. . . . Am not I an Orator? Make me Secretary at War." There was some basis to these rumors. Pelham was quietly forming the so-called Broadbottom Administration, which included an increasing number of men from various groups of influence. He was not ready to further the cause of Mr. Pitt; but his informal agreement with Pitt included a recognition that the latter be free to attack the Government on all points except those on which a truce had been effected. In this move, Pelham showed profound shrewdness, for he realized that Pitt could not be expected to commit political suicide. Either the young man must be given a place of conspicuous honor, or else he must be free to keep himself prominently before the eyes of the Commons and the public as Opposition leader. The chief danger in this arrangement from Pelham's point of view was the fact that with all of its political strength the Carteret-Pelham Ministry was not providing a satisfactory Government.

A disquieting factor in the national scene was the fact that in September France renewed the "Family Compact" with Spain, which had been in effect in 1733, thus uniting the Bourbon powers into the strongest alliance in Europe. England met the action with a Quadruple Alliance which combined her with Holland, Saxony and Austria. This, however, was a relatively feeble affair as the purposes of the participants had little in common except dislike of the Bourbons.

The "Family Compact," moreover, was an aggressive as well as a defensive union. Charles Stuart, the claimant to the British Throne in the Stuart line was still hoping for his restoration; and at any time France might use his cause as an attack against Great Britain. With all of these threatening circumstances it can hardly be said that Carteret was a great figure, even in those circles of diplomacy in which he fancied himself to be a statesman. He was indeed so urbane, so glib, and so learned that many of his contemporaries gave him credit for greatness in one particular or another, yet the facts seemed to be that he was a gracious and self-possessed gentleman who bungled badly any public business which he attempted to handle.

The public at large was more and more aware of this sense of uncertainty and mismanagement in the Ministry. At the opening of Parliament in December, 1743, Pitt exposed the situation in his speech on the address of the King and predicted that events might lead to an attempt by the Pretender to gain the Throne.

"If the present system is continued," he said, "our credit will be ruined, our troops will be obliged to live upon free quarters, the farmer will no longer sow nor reap to have the produce seized by the starving soldiers, the Pretender will land and will be joined by a despairing people as a last hope against an execrable, a sole minister, who has renounced the British nation and seems to have drunk of the potion described in poetic fictions, which makes men forget their country."

Five days later one of the ministerial speakers rebuked a member of the Opposition for criticism of Government policy regarding Hanover and called it "Disaffection to His Majesty's Person." This gave Pitt the opportunity to define the difference between the King as a private individual and the King in his official function. It was a distinction which George II did not always understand; and George III later tried to obliterate it; but it was at the very heart of Pitt's concept of constitutional government.

"I have always looked upon it as a principle of the British Constitution," he said, "that the King can do no more wrong in camp than in the Cabinet; that, whatever is done in either, his advisors are accountable for it. . . . His Majesty is now situated upon the brink of a precipice. At such a time at least it little becomes his faithful Commons to be strewing flowers of flattery and panegyric under his feet. They should rather, with a rough but friendly hand, snatch him from the abyss he is ready to fall into, and with their timely aid place him again upon the secure basis of the affections of his people."

Pitt's notion, at the moment, of the best way to rescue his Majesty was to get rid of Carteret. He kept hammering at the unpopular policy of the Ministry in paying the Hanoverian troops. He abused Carteret as "a Hanover troop minister, a flagitious task-master, whose only party are the 16,000 Hanoverians, the place-men by whose means he has conquered the Cabinet."

Pitt also sounded a popular note in striking at Carteret's neglect of the opinion of the Parliament. "I have a contempt," said Pitt, "for the abilities as well as the honesty of any minister in this country who will not endeavour to gain the confidence of the people. Their sense about any point was never more strongly or universally declared than against taking these troops."

Day after day and week after week Pitt led the attack. When France formally declared war against England in March, 1744, Pitt again assailed Carteret as "the rash author of those measures which have produced this disastrous impracticable war." The evidence of the strength of his oratory is seen in the fear and resentment which it aroused. He was frequently called to order by the Speaker of the House, but was unabashed. On one occasion when he was ordered not to pursue certain criticisms of the Ministry, he said blandly that his train of thought "was disordered by the interruption" and went ahead to develop his subject.

He was steadily gaining ground in national affairs. The French agents, again reporting on him to their Government, referred to him as "the famous Mr. William Pitt, so well known for his patriotic zeal." Edward Montagu wrote of him that he was "a greater man than ever I have sat with, and if he preserves his integrity will be transmitted to posterity in the most illustrious of characters."

Events continued to play into Mr. Pitt's hands. In February, 1744, the British fleet met the combined French and Spanish navies near Toulon in the Mediterranean and came off a bad second. A few days later London was shaken by a rumor that a French fleet was on its way to England, and that the Pretender with an army was ready to land on British soil. The House of Commons met in permanent session. At the seacoast the shore was lined with people waiting for the expected event. On the 17th of February the British fleet did, in fact, sight the French vessels, but on the next morning observed them in full flight under a strong northeasterly gale.

The scare served to dramatize the weakness of the Administration and revealed Pitt's position in time of national danger. He deprecated the spirit of panic and said, "My hope is that good may be drawn out of evil by this event, as it will tend to unite the nation"; and he warned the Ministry against using the situation as an excuse to exercise special powers. "In cases of extreme necessity extraordinary measures might be resorted to," he said, "and the utmost stretch of prerogative is then constitutional; but there is no such extremity here."

The spring sessions continued in an atmosphere of gloom. Both the Army and the Navy were in a deplorable condition. There were reports of ships which capsized due to faulty construction, of incompetence and drunkenness on the part of the officers, and of continued difficulties in getting enlistments in spite of the Press Act. The Army was in charge of superannuated incompetents, and the service of supply was badly disorganized. While the Opposition continued to battle for reforms, the Administration continued to go along solemnly with little change in its ways.

Pelham, it is true, tried to institute some order in the management of public affairs; but he was still secondary in power to Carteret. He made an attempt to encourage trade, by extending the privileges of the Levant Company to all merchants who were willing to pay £20 and observe the company's rules. This measure was in line with the early efforts of Grandfather Pitt, who had broken up the monopoly of the East India Company many years before. William Pitt naturally gave his support to the Levant proposal.

One of Pitt's last acts in this session was to endorse the Government's subsidies to the other members of the Quadruple Alliance. In view of Pitt's general opposition to subsidies, the action brought him not a little criticism; but it was part of the agreement which he had made with Pelham and it strengthened him with the Pelham group—which was gaining more and more influence at Court and in Parliament. It convinced Pelham that Pitt was a man of his word, an individual with whom a plan of action could be undertaken without fear of betrayal; and Pelham, as an experienced politician, realized that this was a valuable asset in either a colleague or an opponent.

In this 1743-44 session of the Commons, Pitt had addressed his attention to major issues to a greater extent than at any previous time in his career. He had definitely become leader of the Opposition, not only in the opinion of his friends, but in being an effective negotiator for the anti-ministerial forces.

The strain, however, made heavy demands on his weak constitution, and at the close of the session he went down to Bath, suffering acutely from a violent attack of gout in the stomach. He was there through most of the summer and fall months and suffered so acutely that in the autumn George Grenville despaired of his recovery.

Pitt had already become a favored citizen of Bath, and had been made a freeman of the town when he had accompanied Prince Frederick there in 1738. It was characteristic of Pitt's sympathies that his activities at Bath were not primarily with the Court set or with others of the gambling social group who participated in the lavish and elaborate entertainments planned by the famous Beau Nash. Pitt's chief friendships there were with the business interests, especially with Ralph Allen, who had been responsible for the physical rebuilding of the place.

Allen was the son of an innkeeper. He had come to Bath about 1715 and obtained a place as a clerk in the Post Office. He then became Postmaster. He discharged dishonest officials and improved the postal system. In conjunction with the Wood family he had furnished the materials for the local hospital and had supported many other town improvements both by donations and organizing energy. He had made a fortune in the Bath quarries. Finally, in 1735, he had built himself a substantial manor known as Prior Park. Allen's talents, moreover, included more than civic consciousness and public gifts. He was elected to Parliament in 1732 and his personality attracted to his home many of the chief figures of the day. Pope had visited him in 1726 while Allen was comparatively a poor man. Gay, the author, and Arbuthnot, the physician, were his friends. Henry Fielding and his sister, Sarah, were also among Allen's intimates, as was Richardson, the novelist; and in later years even the Princess Amelia, daughter of George II, and the Duke of York were guests there.

To Pitt, therefore, Bath was his place of great mental

and spiritual relaxation whenever his illness abated. Here he enjoyed his great love of the stage, chatting with Gay, Quin and Garrick, advising them on the presentation of plays and on topics of stage direction. He spent long hours with his kinsman Fielding, and mingled with Allen's fellow townsmen. While most of the leaders of Government moved in their limited social sets Pitt was hearing the opinions of postal clerks, storekeepers, building contractors and professional people. The time had passed when Stowe could give him useful instruction in the arts of Government. Cobham evidently sensed that his one-time pupil was no longer taking orders or guidance, for at about this time he complained to Chesterfield, "Mr. Pitt is a young man of fine parts, but he is narrow, does not know much of the world, and is a little too dogmatical."

Another circumstance occurred in this summer of 1744 which added greatly to Pitt's ability to maintain his independence. The Duchess of Marlborough died, and left £10,000 to Pitt, "for the noble defense he made for the support of the laws of England, and to prevent the ruin of his country." In addition to the immediate bequest he was to become the ultimate heir of most of her vast estates. These properties were bequeathed first to her favorite grandson, John Spencer, with the condition that Spencer should leave these properties and other inheritances received from his mother to Mr. Pitt, if Spencer's sickly child should not survive. An exception was made in favor of Chesterfield, who was to have the Wimbledon estate under the same contingency.

It is probable that the Duchess had a motive in this bequest of which most of the commentators on the subject seem to have been unaware. Years before, John Churchill, ultimately the first Duke of Marlborough, had been a page to James, Duke of York. At that time, Barbara Villiers, Duchess of Cleveland, had made the page a present of £5000 with which he was able to purchase an annuity of £500. Chesterfield has written that this windfall was the foundation of the Churchill fortune; and in a sense it was, for it enabled Churchill to accept a commission in the Army, which was possible in those days only to men of some independent means. From the Army career, ultimately, came the great Marlborough wealth. Since Chesterfield and Pitt were two notable descendants of the Villiers connection, it is probable that the Duchess was intentionally repaying the Villiers favor of years gone by.

The effect on Pitt's personal fortunes and prestige was electric. It immediately increased his meager income of £400 annually to nearly £800. Shortly after this bequest the Duke of Bedford provided him with an annuity of £300, probably as a settlement in relation to the Marlborough will, for Bedford's wife was a sister of John Spencer and may have had a claim on some of the properties. This has been generally considered to be the basis of the Bedford annuity as there was no political alliance that would have given reason for such a payment, and Pitt would hardly have been so unwise as to accept a gratuity from Bedford.

Spencer died within two years after this. As his child continued to be sickly, Pitt for many years was thought to be prospectively one of the richest men of the kingdom, and unfortunately handled his personal finances in a manner which suggested that he expected that contingency to materialize.

While this immediate inflow of cash, coupled with expectations, relieved Mr. Pitt from worries and brought him financial independence, it was to some degree a liability to his popularity. When he later supported certain ministerial measures of which the Duchess might not have approved, a popular lampoon depicted her ghost returning to Pitt and saying, "Return, base villain, my retaining fee."

Pitt, however, had no intention of being bound to any course by the acceptance of this bequest, and in thanking the executor for notifying him "of the Duchess of Marlborough's great goodness to me," he remained vague as to the particulars of his admiration, saying, "The sort of regard I feel for her memory I leave to your Lordship's heart to suggest to you."

The Marlborough bequest actually enabled Pitt to occupy

the place once held by Pulteney, for it added financial prestige to his mellowing Parliamentary talents. What he had to say was now regarded more as his own personal opinion, as it was clear that he was no longer obliged to be the spokesman of Stowe.

Pitt's ill health, for the time being, prevented him from enjoying the effects of this stroke of fortune, or from participating actively in the negotiations which Pelham and the Duke of Newcastle, Pelham's brother and a protégé of Robert Walpole, were now making with the intent of ousting Carteret. Pitt was on a committee which had been appointed by the Opposition to deal with Pelham, and, though Pitt was too ill to guide the affair, Pelham realized that Pitt would have to be recognized. Pelham approached Cobham as representing Pitt and the Grenville interests. "Do what you will," Cobham had said cheerfully, "provided you take care of my boys."

Pelham and Newcastle, who expected to come into real power by the deal, agreed to name George Grenville and George Lyttelton to subordinate posts in the Ministry and sent word to Pitt through Cobham that he should be Secretary of War as soon as they could obtain the consent of the King to that measure.

This procedure, of course, was handled without the consent of Carteret, who was already complaining that he was tired of being continuously in the minority in the Cabinet. He pursued his own wishes, in any case, but the continual votes against his policies in his own Ministry were beginning to break him down.

Finally, in November, Newcastle presented to the King an elaborate memorial drawn up by Lord Hardwicke, the Lord Chancellor. It recited a long list of grievances against Carteret and his policies. It supported, without naming Pitt, much of the position which he had taken in the Commons. Carteret himself, foreseeing the end, in October had made private though unsuccessful overtures to the Opposition, offering concessions in both places and policies. The King had supported Carteret in this move, but when the same program was proposed with the elimination of his beloved Carteret that was a different story. His Majesty resisted and procrastinated for three weeks, finally calling upon Walpole, now Lord Orford, as he had previously in regard to Pelham's elevation. Orford advised the King that the only possible course under the circumstances was to dismiss Carteret.

This to George II was well-nigh intolerable. He had the concept of himself as a figurehead yet as a monarch with some personal powers, and to be forced to accept ministers whom he did not like, and, above all, to give up his favorite minister, was inconsistent with his notions of kingship.

Therefore, when he at last advised Hardwicke that he would yield he did so with considerable ill feeling. "I have done all you have asked me," he said. "I have put all the power in your hands, and I suppose you will make the most of it."

Hardwicke felt obliged to instruct the monarch subtly that a constitutional king must be in harmony with his ministers.

"The disposition of places," said Hardwicke, "is not enough, if your Majesty takes pains to show the world that you disapprove of your own work."

"My work!" the King roared, "I was forced, I was threatened."

But Hardwicke could not let that stand. The King officially is the emblem of the State, Hardwicke indicated. He is served humbly by those who tell him what is good for him. The King, in short, must take it and like it.

"No means were employed," Hardwicke said, "but what have been used in all times,—the humble advice of your servants supported by such reasons as convinced them that the measure was necessary for your service."

The King, at this, gave up the struggle. Before the month was out Carteret had handed in the Seals of State, and Pitt, though ill at Bath, could have the satisfaction that he had done more than any other man to force the resignation of an unconstitutional minister and to bring about a useful lesson in government to an unwillingly constitutional king.

CHAPTER XIII

THE STUART UPRISING

King George II, worrying about his own prerogatives, little realized that he was sitting on a powder-keg, and perhaps cared less. He went to his Electorate of Hanover every summer always with seeming relief to be free of England, and actually the possibility of his remaining in Britain was insecure. His Ministers realized this to be the fact even if he did not; and in the early spring of 1746 there were already rumors in England that Charles Edward the Pretender might attempt an invasion on British soil.

If Charles Edward landed and made a successful campaign the Stuart sympathizers would again be in power and the Tories would turn the Whigs out of office, doubtless executing a few as a helpful example to the public. This possibility was very real. Dr. Samuel Johnson, Lord Bath, and Henry Fox were among those who estimated that there was a predominant Stuart leaning among the people.

This threat against Whig control now sharply altered the central issues in Parliament. Since the accession of Walpole and throughout Mr. Pitt's political lifetime the struggles in Parliament had been essentially within one party. Those Whigs who had not been admitted to the public trough kept trying to nose their way in. Even Mr. Pitt, who was actuated by principle as well as by the desire to be a figure, carried on his campaign under the Whig banner. In clamoring for changes in the Walpole and Carteret Ministries he had at no time contemplated a return to the Stuart and Tory domination.

Mr. Pitt believed that in Whig principles and party lay the opportunity for greater individual freedom and for an improved lot for the English people. These were aims still pitifully short of accomplishment, yet he believed that they would come about under Whig leadership if at all.

The so-called "great Whig families" had been so adroit in identifying popular causes with themselves that the realities of the situation were beneath the surface. This group in control of the country was, in 1746, far from being the people's party, and was still a long distance from swallowing the medicine which Mr. Pitt, Burke, Charles James Fox and others finally poured down its throat.

The Whigs, it may be recalled, had come into power in 1688 by virtually a *coup d'état* which they had described as "The Glorious Revolution," or again as "The Bloodless Revolution." Their victory, in forcing a change in the Throne and in the Cabinet, was due to the fact that for some time they had been the real financial powers in the kingdom and were increasingly so.

The Whig party, in its beginnings, was the result of the change of English economics from a feudal and rural society to the concentration of wealth in the cities. The leading Tories were the landed aristocrats, frequently land poor. Nevertheless they had prevailed in Government for some time after their real economic power had been superseded. With the growth of the cities had come vast new fortunes created by the rise in urban land values, rents, distilleries, and the financing of transactions in trade. The great Whig families, including such names as Bedford, Halifax, Granville, Devonshire (Cavendish), Wilmington, Lincoln, and Pelham, were dynasties built on urban money. They were the Astors, the Goelets, the Drexels, and Morgans of their day. At the outset the conflict of interest between them and the Tories was comparable to the contest between the industrial North and the plantation South at the time of the American Civil War, or War Between the States—as the South viewed it. The Tories had been in the position which Virginia encountered a hundred years later. Rightly or wrongly they represented a declining mode of life, and when the opportunity offered the stronger power took over.

The Whigs initially had been shrewd enough to identify themselves with two causes dear to the heart of the average Britisher: the Constitution, and Protestantism. The Tories had cherished the romantic idea of a godlike, beneficent king who would shed radiance on his people, without the interference of too much man-made restraint. Viscount Bolingbroke had already jotted down in his notebooks an ecstatic exposition of the Tory theory under the title of "The Idea of a Patriot King." The work was yet to be published, but the ideas were extant in many quarters. This doctrine was incompatible with the conviction of the British citizen that he had his rights, whatever they might be, guaranteed by the Constitution. Furthermore, the Stuart line was Roman Catholic in faith, which was a further handicap to their cause.

The public, however, had become restive under the Whig rule, for it became apparent that the nation had done little more than to trade the old set of overlords for a new set. A few of the Whigs had sincerely determined to provide a constitutional Government, and Hardwicke, Pelham and Pitt had fought for that cause valiantly.

The Whig party, nevertheless, had failed woefully as the expression and support of a potentially growing nation. Bedford, rich from his rentals in the Bloomsbury section of London, had little thought beyond conserving his own wealth, and his colleagues in the ruling party were little better. The term "party," in fact, was almost a misnomer, for it was primarily an oligarchy, a vaguely defined aggregation of economic interests. This wealth-consciousness of the Whig leaders explains why they did not early in his career embrace Mr. Pitt as a natural leader. With all of his attributes and worthy family connections he did not enjoy one of the great city fortunes and hence was essentially an outsider.

Pitt, however, had appraised the weakness of the Whig attitude both from its own standpoint and that of the national welfare. By limiting themselves to their own group they were unwittingly plotting self-destruction. The city merchants, the sea traders like Grandfather Pitt, the general public, and the prosperous colonies beyond the seas were all great sources of power hitherto unorganized. Pitt

realized that here were enormous reserves of strength which
could be brought under the Whig banner and which, moreover, could ultimately demand their place in the Governmental scheme, even as the wealthy urban Whigs had
overthrown the Tory aristocrats. Pitt saw the potential-
ities of all these elements welded together, the vitality of
each protected by the Constitution; in short, he saw empire.

Though belonging to the Opposition, though he was
charged with none of the responsibility of Government, it
was he who voiced the practical application of this broad
policy. While the English peerage, including the Whigs,
looked down upon the Scottish lords, and while the English
public had a violent prejudice against the Scotch, Pitt was
noted for his friendliness to them. "I would walk bare-
footed from one end of the town to the other to gain Mr.
Pitt," said Lord Marchmont, one of the Scottish peers.

Still more prophetic was Mr. Pitt's attitude toward
America. It will be recalled that in the debate on the Spanish Convention he had pointed out that "above two millions
of people in your American colonies" had interests which
should be safeguarded by British foreign policy. At a time
when even the Government Ministers were largely ignorant
of America Pitt was well informed on the subject. In this
respect he was aided by his intimacy with the Temple-Grenvilles, a family which had many relatives on the American
scene. There were Scotch Temples who emigrated and settled
in New York and Pennsylvania. A Sir Thomas Temple
had been Governor of Nova Scotia in the preceding century;
one of whose nephews had married Elizabeth Taylor of
Dorchester, near Boston. Another kinsman of the family,
Robert Temple, had been born in Boston in 1694, and his
son married the daughter of General William Shirley. This
couple had a child, Shirley Temple, in 1761; but the twentieth-century Shirley Temple was descended from the Scotch
Temples who settled in Pennsylvania. American connections were strongly rooted in the New World. In the next
generation and before the American Revolution Temple
children had married into the colonial families of Whipple,

Fitch, Bowdoin, and Winthrop. Pitt was already absorbing information for his future colonial policy.

If the Whigs could see their opportunities and grow with the nation the promise of the future was bright; but in July, 1745, the long dreaded invasion of Charles Edward the Pretender became a reality and the Whig Government was shaken to its foundations.

The *dies irae* which Pitt had predicted had come to pass. "Bonnie Prince Charlie," the Pretender Charles Stuart, had landed in northern Scotland on July 20 and in a short time had raised two thousand Highlanders. For weeks, the Pelham Government was paralyzed, and, incredibly, did nothing; at first glance incredibly, but perhaps wisely. No one knew the real sentiment of the nation. Jacobite clubs were numerous throughout the kingdom; Oxford was Tory; and the very brother of William Murray, the Attorney General in the Cabinet, was on Charles Edward's official staff.

The King's Ministers were in command of the Army and Navy, and in a more meek nation this would have been the moment to declare supreme power. Pelham knew his fellow Englishmen too well to attempt that, even though the trend of the Whig régime had been toward absolutism, toward rule by one personality such as Walpole, but rule by tacit consent. It is significant that the Revolution of 1688 was the "bloodless revolution." A few of the defeated leaders had suffered, but there was no "purge," no commune, no "terror." In fact, rarely in England's history since the Norman Conquest had there been assertion of the right of the sword over civil rights. Walpole, the strongest of the Whigs, had been their unchallenged ruler for many years, but as soon as his absolutism was questioned, as soon as the vote of the Commons was clearly and continuously against him, he had resigned without question.

The Pelham Government ruled theoretically by the consent of the governed, and now in this time of crisis it trembled to force a proof of consent. The Cabinet had already, in periods of domestic peace, endured riots by the weavers, riots against impressment, riots opposing the Gin Act, and had been obliged to accept the disturbances philosophically. By the law of the land, riots were *de facto,* if not *de jure,* protected. Troops were not permitted to fire upon a riotous mob until one hour after a magistrate had read the Riot Act to them ordering them to disperse. Thus the "reading of the riot act" actually had a meaning quite different from what the idiom came to suggest in later times.

Invasion from abroad was different from domestic revolt, but was Prince Charlie's appearance an invasion or a reassertion of the popular will? That query struck terror to the heart of the Cabinet. If the Government tried to be despotic that would alienate the public at once and almost any champion might seize the power of vengeance. An ax which could cleave the neck of Charles I would not quiver at the flesh of a Pelham. If the Cabinet remained passive, on the other hand, "Bonnie Prince Charlie" might gain headway at an overwhelming rate. Word came early in September that the Pretender was beginning to advance and was occupying Perth and Edinburgh without resistance. The Cabinet, driven to action at last, sent Government troops to check his progress. On September 21, 1745, the Stuarts and English army forces met at Prestonpans a short distance from Edinburgh, and the English were driven back.

Each side recoiled in apprehension from the possible effect of this trial at arms. The Government dared not risk another engagement at this juncture. Prince Charlie was content for the moment to rest on the prestige of this victory. The Pretender, in fact, was not a leader, but a weak and confused young man who happened to be the Stuart heir. He was, moreover, an anachronism, picturing himself as a king in exile called home by his people and his nobles. Basking in this belief, he delayed his advance and established his headquarters in the palace of his ancestors at Holyrood.

This pause gave the Ministry at London time to regain its breath and to plan for resistance by Constitutional processes which could not be used against them. Parliament was summoned early, on October 17, 1745, in special session to act on the national crisis.

Revolt was in the air from the Tory benches, which had

long been in hopeless minority. A speaker moved an amendment to the King's address praying for purer elections, shorter Parliaments (viz.: triennial instead of septennial elections) and the prevention of undue influence on members.

At this moment, the stand of Mr. Pitt who also sat on the Opposition side was of chief importance. If he threw his weight with the Tories, the dissatisfied elements among the Whigs would doubtless follow him. He might, indeed, become a new Bolingbroke, and this time a successful one, the chief man in restoring a Stuart king.

But the doctrine of Grandfather Pitt had been too strongly implanted in his grandson for that to happen. Mr. Pitt sought to make the Whigs worthy of their high calling, not to destroy them. Dissension now was a peril to orderly government. He rose to his full six feet in the shadowy light of St. Stephen's Chapel. He paused while the members on both sides of the House bent anxiously forward to learn where he would take his stand.

"At a time when our all is at stake," he said, "whatever opinion we may have of our own Ministers for the time being, surely it is unseasonable to attempt anything that may raise discontents among the public, or lessen their confidence in those who are placed in authority over them. . . . Shall we spend our time in projects for guarding our liberties against corruption when they are in such immediate danger of being trampled underfoot by force of arms?"

The Pelhams were in transports of gratitude at this essential and timely aid. Henry Pelham at once became energetic. He proposed to use hired Hessian and Dutch troops against the Pretender, and to keep the bulk of the English army aiding the British allies in Europe. In this way, France and Spain would be kept too busy to send help to Prince Charlie and if the Pretender had another victory it would be against hirelings and therefore less impressive.

Pitt could not agree to so timid a program. Englishmen must defend English soil. Any other course would be a confession of national failure. He conceded that ten thousand British troops might be left in Holland as a token of good faith to the allies, but held that all other forces must be called home as long as the Civil Government was in danger. Pelham yielded promptly to this demand and wrote to the British Minister at The Hague: "Whatever puts a speedy end to the rebellion is the best measure for our allies as well as ourselves. Till that is done we are not a nation: and whatever good words we might send you, I am sure it would not be in our power to keep them."

Meanwhile, Bedford and a number of other rich Whigs agreed to organize militia troops if the Government would subscribe the major share of the cost. This proposal was agreed to, but shortly brought forth an attack by Hume Campbell, son of Lord Marchmont, charging that troops were not being raised and that those who had proposed to do so were putting the money into their own pockets. Many believed this to be the case (though it was subsequently proved to be false) but it was a dangerously popular accusation, and Pitt again came into the breach with a speech praising Bedford and his associates, who "have signalized themselves by a very laudable and eminent degree of zeal. . . .They have stood like men of fortitude and integrity in the gap in which war and confusion were breaking in upon us, and have by their influence and example raised the same spirit in others."

Pelham at last realized that Mr. Pitt was a man of rare force and judgment whose voice was badly needed in the Cabinet councils, and he persuaded Newcastle to interview Pitt to learn what conditions he would demand to accept the long-promised office of Secretary at War. It was also understood that this post, usually subordinate at that period, would carry Cabinet rank.

Newcastle "apprehended great difficulties in reaching an agreement." Judging by his future conduct he probably did not wish to reach an agreement, and may have fomented the King's dislike of Pitt at this time, as he did later.

Pitt's terms were not difficult. He demanded the removal of the Finches, relatives of Carteret-Granville, who were still employed in the King's household, where they kept feeding the monarch with tales of distrust of Pitt and his friends. There were other minor points, with which the Pelhams were willing to agree; and finally Mr. Pitt advanced his major demand which was "to increase our Navy, and act as principals at sea in the war against France and Spain."

This, of course, was an entire departure from Carteret's system and from the modified support to the Continental wars given by Pelham. The English trading families and the colonials in America knew the value of a navy, but to the insular members of Parliament in either Ministry or the Opposition the idea had no particular appeal.

Pitt gave emphasis to his views on November 21, 1745, by introducing a motion in the Commons to increase the fleet. He made the point that the strength of the Stuart uprising depended to no small extent upon France, and therefore a navy which could cope with France was needed to assure civil tranquillity; but the Commons were not ready as yet for so sharp a departure from the practice of recent years and only thirty-six members voted for the measure.

Pitt nevertheless still desired to pledge Pelham to a strong navy policy and continued to make it a condition of his joining the Ministry; and Newcastle underscored the difference in their views by saying "to bring Mr. Pitt in against his own will is impossible."

In the midst of this impasse the Pretender at last started out from Scotland on his march toward the conquest of England. He advanced with virtually no opposition and reached the town of Derby on December 4.

The English troops which had been sent out to meet him had steadily fallen back. Charles Edward, now within two weeks' march of London, had a clear path to the Capital. As the news spread throughout the city, panic seized upon all classes. Trade virtually ceased. Gangs of laborers were set to placing sandbags along the banks of the Thames. Throngs stormed the Bank of England, which was able to meet the demands of depositors only by paying everyone in sixpences.

As Prince Charlie, for the second time, delayed in pressing his victory, public apprehension gradually abated; but

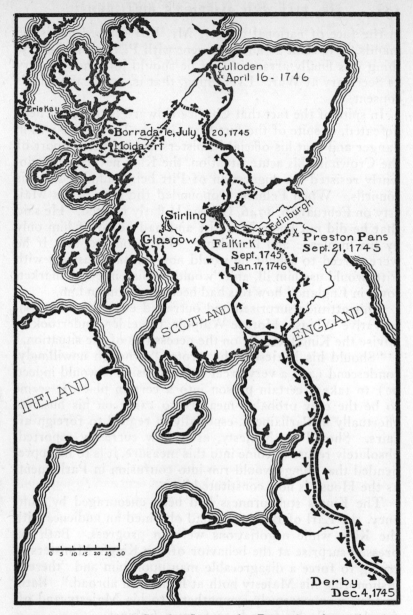

Route of invasion of Charles Stuart, the Pretender, from the time of his landing in Scotland to the Battle of Culloden. Dotted lines show his advance and solid lines his retreat.

in the face of national danger, Mr. Pitt relaxed in his demands. He came to an agreement with Pelham, and everything was finally arranged that he should join the Ministry as Secretary at War. Everything, that is, except the King's consent.

In spite of the fact that Charles Edward had not yet been defeated, in spite of the fact that George II's throne was in danger and that his official Ministers needed the support of the Crown in this acute situation, the King nevertheless violently resisted the suggestion of Pitt being admitted to his councils. When Pelham propounded the idea to his Majesty on February 6, 1746, George II flatly refused. He said that he did not know Mr. Pitt and had heard of him only by his insolence and impudence. He promised that if he were forced to submit he would not transact business with Pitt, would use him ill, and "would publish in every market-town in England" how this had been forced upon him.

This attitude surprised and outraged even the most conservative Whigs. Horace Walpole, the elder, undertook to advise the King tactfully on the necessities of the situation.

"Should his Majesty," he wrote, "although unwillingly, condescend (and a very great condescension it would indeed be) to take a certain person into a certain place, it seems to be the only probable measure to carry on his business effectually in Parliament, especially in regard to foreign affairs. Should his Majesty, as is now currently reported, absolutely refuse to come into this measure, it is to be apprehended that things would run into confusion in Parliament, as the House is now constituted."

The King's stubbornness had been encouraged by Pulteney, the Earl of Bath, who had obtained an audience with the King while negotiations were in progress. Bath expressed surprise at the behavior of the King's Ministers in trying to force a disagreeable man upon him and "thereby dishonoring his Majesty both at home and abroad." Bath, in fact, was extremely sympathetic to his Majesty and offered to rally his friends to form a Cabinet.

Henry Pelham, nevertheless, was determined to stand his ground. The Cabinet position was desperate. Pitt offered to withdraw rather than precipitate a crisis. But the Ministry were now in a high fever of resentment at the monarch and demanded that he show them some mark of royal confidence. Instead of this, on February 10, the King greeted a visit from the Cabinet with violent reproaches; and the Pelham Ministry resigned in a body. This was what the King had hoped for and he expected Bath would be able to form a Government.

William Pulteney, Earl of Bath, accepted the seals on February 10, 1746, and called in Carteret, now Earl of Granville, as his first colleague. A more unsuccessful combination than these two discredited gentlemen could hardly have been concocted by anyone. The whole Parliament laughed at the idea, including Carteret himself. Bath tried for forty-eight hours to name a Ministry but no one of influence would join his forces. In fact only two of the major offices were filled in addition to himself and Granville. By February 12, the Bath Cabinet was virtually ended.

The King at first shut himself up in the palace and refused audience to various persons who desired to decline Cabinet appointments. When he emerged from the royal apartments he found the foyer cluttered with staves, keys, and seals of office which had been returned by the unwilling recipients. At this, George II sent for Bath and told him that evidently the effort was of no avail. Bath then proposed that George try to unite with Prince Frederick and the Tory party, but even George II was able to appraise that suggestion as hopeless. The last two days had demonstrated to the King that the Whig leadership was the only competent group on which he could rely, even though to rely was to submit.

When the Pelhams returned, Pitt urged them not to humiliate the monarch by immediately pressing his cause. Pelham gratefully agreed to defer the issue until the national danger receded, and meanwhile persuaded him to accept the temporary post of Vice-Treasurer of Ireland, which would not, however, require residence there. Pitt, accordingly, entered the Ministry, even though in a minor post, on February 22, 1746.

While the Cabinet crisis was in progress, Prince Charlie, to the dismay of his English supporters and the relief of his enemies, had shown the yellow streak. To advance on London, to challenge the very citadel of English strength, to come within the shadow of the Tower. . . . Ah, no . . . one should have surely greater forces before attempting that, so he had yielded to his Scotch advisers and retreated to the north of Scotland levying tribute on Glasgow on his way. On January 17, 1746, he defeated the English at Falkirk, north of Glasgow, but the English were now panting for blood, free from fear, and angry that this nincompoop should have frightened them. The British lost battles but continued to pursue the Stuart forces.

By flanking movements, the Duke of Cumberland at the head of the British Army drove Charles Edward farther and farther north. Then, at Culloden on April 16, 1746, Prince Charles had another of his hapless ideas. The day was a holiday, and he assumed that the British camp, including its general, would be celebrating and unprepared for attack. Prince Charlie's plan was to steal down upon the enemy and rout them in a surprise move. In order to avoid suspicion, he deployed his army in a thin line two miles long, approaching the British forces by a spear-like movement.

The Stuart forces struck and found Cumberland not celebrating but prepared and waiting for the movement. The British Army immediately charged in formation and slaughtered the unprotected rebel line. Thousands were slain. "Butcher" Cumberland, the people called him afterwards. The carnage was terrible, but in a few hours every vestige of the Stuart revolt had been wiped from British soil. Culloden had saved the country. The Army had belatedly saved the United Kingdom; and Pitt's magnanimity had enabled the Whigs to present a serene front to the nation and to bask in the prestige of the victory. Pitt, indeed, was now in a new light, before the Parliament and the public. At a time of national danger he had proved himself to be a patriot. Above all, when his own career was at stake he had shown the forbearance and good judgment to submerge his claims in the interest of a united country.

CHAPTER XIV

The Famous Legs of John, Lord Bute

Mr. Pitt's legs were frequently swollen with gout. They impaired the picture of the tall, lean Hamlet in black velvet which he liked to affect. Mr. Pitt's legs, in fact, were his tragedy, spoiling his symmetry, keeping him from the scene of battle at times when he was sorely needed. But the legs of John Stuart, Lord Bute, were his fortune.

In a later trousered generation, shapely calves on the male are useless if not ridiculous. But not so in the eighteenth century. In those days the legs of a gentleman of fashion were a matter for note and comment, especially in the idle circles hovering about the Court. The legs of the pallid Lord Hervey were thin and stringy. Henry Fox, the future Lord Holland, the henchman of the Duke of Cumberland, had the sturdy pins of a country squire. The legs of Lord Bute, however, left little to be desired.

If such a discussion seems trivial, the facts were serious enough, for the personal shapeliness of Bute, the Scottish peer, was destined to bewitch a princess, dominate a king, and drive a popular government from office. But that is looking ahead; in 1747, Bute was unknown, an inconsequential son-in-law of the fabulously rich Edward Wortley Montagues, who felt that their daughter had made a misalliance. Had it not been for the Egham races, an obliging apothecary, and a convenient rainstorm, Bute might never have crossed the path of Mr. Pitt, and his famous legs might have been as lost to history as the library at Alexandria.

Bute was precisely the type of idle trifler to fit ideally into the residue of the Cliveden Set centered around Frederick, Prince of Wales. Due to the astuteness of Pelham, most of the more influential persons who had formerly followed

the Prince were now attached to the Government, or at least
were convinced that the Prince was too weak a character to
command their support. The amiable Frederick's reputation was unable to survive the scandal which the King had
put on his name, and he was virtually helpless against intrigue, a born playboy (which was natural to an eighteenth-
century prince), and, in the midst of the avaricious self-seeking political circles of his time, a rather lonely figure. There
was more than one occasion when the Court calendars listed
only his official family in attendance at his levees, but for
Bute, who had no connections, a place in the Prince's
ménage would be a step upward. As yet, however, Bute
had had no introduction to his Royal Highness.

Then came the day of the Egham races. Some accounts
state that the scene was at races elsewhere. Some give the
event as a cricket match, others say it was a hunt, but all
are agreed that Prince Frederick was in attendance at some
athletic event on the fateful day and that Lord Bute was
also present.

Lord Bute was able to be a spectator at the event because
of his acquaintanceship with a neighboring apothecary who
owned a handsome carriage. Class distinctions of the
period were somewhat fluid. The peers were willing at
least to accept favors from those lower in rank; Bute was
not abnormally condescending in accepting a place in the
druggist's handsome carriage. .Bute, moreover, was only a
Scottish peer, and to the true Englishman of the times a
Scotchman of whatever rank was hardly admissible to full
membership in the human race.

While Lord Bute and his plebeian neighbor were watching the athletic contest, whatever it may have been, a rainstorm interrupted the occasion and shortly afterward a
messenger approached the druggist's carriage, stating that
his Royal Highness was also in attendance at the event and
was in the situation of needing a fourth person of eligible
rank for a game of whist. Someone had informed the
Prince that Lord Bute was present and Frederick therefore
had commanded the presence of the delighted gentleman
to join the game.

John Stuart, third Earl of Bute, whose famous legs compromised a princess, dominated a king, and roused the hatred of the populace.

By Permission of R. T. H. Halsey

"The loaded Boot or Scotch preferment in Motion." This complicated cartoon satirizes the affair of Lord Bute and the Princess Augusta.

Frederick and Lord Bute were immediately congenial. It is not surprising. Not since 1745, when the engaging Mr. Pitt had left his staff, had Frederick found so talented a companion. In those days he had had a lively following, the provocative group from Stowe, the Grenvilles, the Lyttelton brothers, and still earlier the brilliant Pulteney. Many of them still retained the shell of a friendship for him, but their loyalty was uncertain and their time much occupied. Never, it may be guessed, had Frederick associated with a peer who was at the same time as deferential and as gifted as John, Lord Bute.

The game went on and on, and when the weather cleared Lord Bute discovered that the apothecary had not been sufficiently obliging to wait indefinitely by himself in his handsome carriage, and had driven home.

This, too, turned out to be an unexpected and happy circumstance, for the Prince invited Bute to go with him to Cliveden. In the evening and in the days which followed the young Scottish peer formed an attachment to the household which was never severed throughout the remainder of his life. He became, as might have been expected, one of the Prince's staff, occupying the same official position as had once been enjoyed by Mr. Pitt.

While Mr. Pitt had concentrated his attention on the Prince, Lord Bute found the Princess at least equally congenial. For the next quarter century the gossips speculated on the extent of the attachment between the Princess Augusta and the Scottish peer. Proof on the issue is lacking, but is essentially unimportant. The significant fact was that this proud, if inconspicuous, Scottish lord soon gained an influence with her Royal Highness which was unshatterable.

The fact was not surprising. The poor Princess Augusta had been brought to England from Germany to live among a strange people. The German courtiers of George II from whom she might have expected some racial loyalty were, instead, a part of the King's entourage and as such participated in the hostility of his Majesty toward the Prince and the Prince's family. The Englishmen who had surrounded her husband hitherto were ambitious for their own careers, saw little assistance in cultivating her, and were far more inclined to aid the Prince in his escapades than to waste time at his domestic fireside.

Bute, on the other hand, became a new and delightful member of the family circle. Deferential, entertaining, and devoted, he organized plays, dances, and picnics. He brought a pleasing note of gaiety for its own sake into the halls and gardens of Cliveden. In doing so he perhaps lost something of his influence with the Prince.

Horace Walpole, the younger, reported that Frederick "used frequently to say that Bute was a fine showy man, who would make an excellent ambassador in a court where there was no business . . . but the sagacity of the Princess Dowager has discovered other accomplishments, of which the Prince her husband may not perhaps have been the most competent judge."

But if the Prince was jealous he also had his own axes to grind. About the time of making his acquaintance with Lord Bute, Frederick was having a rather active affair with Lady Middlesex, and the acquisition of the Scottish peer helped to simplify the situation. A happy foursome was to be seen frequently at Vauxhall, at Henley, and at other pleasure resorts, the Prince with Lady Middlesex and Lord Bute with the Princess.

Lady Bute seems to have accepted the situation without protest and certainly without effective opposition, nor did the attachment alienate her parents. The wealthy Lady Montague had long been convinced that her daughter had married a nobody, and she was now relieved to find that her son-in-law was capable of enterprise. The intrusion of Lady Montague into the scene, even at the sidelines, was due to give the matter added publicity. She was a vigorous, indomitable woman who wrote voluminous letters to numerous of the public persons of her time and had herself achieved fame through her enormous riches and her eccentricities. Her blowsy appearance had caught the attention of the younger Mr. Walpole, but she was perhaps better known because of her avowed preference for Turks as compared to Englishmen. The colorful alliance of the Mon-

tague family with the household of the Prince was pleasing
to those immediately concerned, but for the time being was
a liability to the influence of Cliveden.

Mr. Pitt was fortunate to be free from immediate contact with that situation. He had, in fact, been advanced
materially both in public position and in popular esteem.
On May 6, 1746, he had been appointed Paymaster-of-the-
Forces, and on May 31 was made a member of the Privy
Council. The Paymastership was not a principal office in
the Cabinet, such as he desired and had been promised to
him, but it carried a salary and allowance worth £4,000 per
year. More than that, it had opportunities for legal self-
enrichment which made it the richest plum in the offer of
the Government.

It had been the accepted practice for the Paymaster to
put in his own pocket the interest on all public funds on
deposit in his office. He was supposedly entitled also to
one-fourth of one percent as a handling charge. The huge
possibilities may be indicated by the fact that during one
month of Mr. Pitt's office he handled government payments
totaling £1,139,548, and during most of the time the
monthly funds amounted to several hundred thousand
pounds.

Pitt could have made himself vastly rich as several of
his predecessors had done, as well as those who succeeded
him. In fact, that was probably what the Cabinet had in
mind in giving him the position. It was a bribe of stagger-
ing proportions. He was supposed to be satisfied with it
and henceforth to cease being a nuisance with his unpredictable ideas. Moreover, it was a bribe with honor, generally
considered proper and acceptable. It could hardly seem
comprehensible to the practical politicians that any relatively poor man would neglect this opportunity to become
established for life among the wealthiest families of the
kingdom.

Pitt's initial move on taking office was, accordingly, a
bombshell to the Cabinet. He announced that interest on
the public funds belonged to the public Treasury and he
deposited the monies of his office with the Bank of Eng-

land so that interest therefrom would not even pass through his hands. The public greeted this evidence of integrity with astonished adulation. The more cynical felt that it must be merely a political gesture with some catch in it. The King of Sardinia, for example, who knew that Mr. Pitt would have been entitled to a commission of £5,000 from the Sardinian subsidy, tactfully endeavored to make Mr. Pitt a present of that amount, but the offer was declined.

It was fortunate that Mr. Pitt had been appointed a member of the Privy Council before his unusual ideas of integrity in office became known, as otherwise it is questionable whether he would have been admitted as closely to the councils of the Government. Pelham could understand such honesty, for Pelham himself was moderately honest, but in an age when the powerful Whigs were enriching themselves at Government expense and when the Tories out of office would have liked to do so, Mr. Pitt's conduct was not of the sort to commend him to those who considered themselves practical men.

It was, as a matter of fact, a distinctly dangerous move. Pitt had accepted office under the Government. He was expected to go along with it and not to indulge in novelties of conduct which would bring him to public attention. It separated him in the eyes of the public from the circles of his colleagues. This was an advantage, of course, in the opinion of the populace, but it was not a recommendation to those who had the power over his advancement.

He was getting closer and closer to the position of being politically isolated. In previous years he at least had the opportunity of falling back on the Prince of Wales and rebuilding the organization at Cliveden. Now he had aroused the suspicions of the Cabinet as to his manageability, and at Cliveden the suave and amiable Lord Bute was in the ascendant.

CHAPTER XV

"I Have Sown My Wild Oats"

Mr. Pitt's political isolation in the latter part of 1746 was partially a matter of his own choice. Unless Pelham and his brother, the Duke of Newcastle, were willing to give him a conspicuous, if not a dominating, part in their Ministry, he was better off to be in a subordinate post where he would not have any public responsibility for a ministry in which he had little voice. It was, on the other hand, more advantageous to be in office with Mr. Pelham, who at times thought Pitt worthy of Cabinet rank, than to be identified with any of the minority groups which were too weak to offer any political promise.

As a practical matter, also, the legitimate income from the Paymaster's Office, amounting to £4,000 per annum, was a very tidy sum for a single man, and for anyone except an impractical Pitt it well could have formed the basis of a fortune; and despite Pitt's own vague notions of financial matters he was able to live in considerable style at this time and save something for the future.

Had Mr. Pitt been less ambitious, less convinced of his own destiny, he might well have felt that he had achieved as much success as he might hope for. The very top places in the Cabinet were usually occupied by men of title or at any rate by the sons of families of highest rank. There had, of course, been various exceptions, notably that of Sir Robert Walpole; but Pitt had already risen from a political zero to one of the most profitable places in the Ministry, and as long as he remained loyal to those in authority he could look forward to a lifetime of well-paid service in Government employ.

Pitt, however, had higher notions for himself over the long run. He still expected to be made Secretary at War, with Cabinet standing, and he was not willing to look forward to anything less. For the time being, however,—and the period unexpectedly stretched over several years—he was willing to play an inconspicuous part, for the Pelham-Newcastle Ministry was rapidly becoming more notoriously corrupt than that of Walpole, and Pitt did well to be identified with it as little as possible until such time as the Pelham brothers might call him to their rescue.

Henry Pelham was a statesman of high character, but the weakness of the Ministry was his brother, Thomas Holles, the Duke of Newcastle. Newcastle had the characteristic, usually considered feminine, of being lost unless he were attached to some man of stable character who could calm his twitching nerves and reassure his injured vanity. Unfortunately, like a certain type of woman, he was unable to be loyal to any man for an extended period of time, and as soon as peace began to reign at his political hearthstone he would ogle some distant politician and begin to frame a new alliance.

Why Newcastle, with the influence of his title and a diligence of sorts, should have become an absurd and ridiculous figure, subject to many fears, is unexplained by history. Perhaps the death of his mother while he was a young child, and his adoption by his uncle, may have sown early the seed of a thousand apprehensions. At any rate, in 1746, while he was still only fifty-three years of age, he was coming to be looked upon as an old man. His large head set on a stooped and mincing body gave the impression of an aged courtier. His solemnity of manner, his air of always being busy, yet uncertain, made him peculiarly ridiculous. Lord Wilmington said of him "he loses half an hour every morning and runs after it during the rest of the day without being able to overtake it."

Pitt obviously felt the need to watch his step when marching along the same political pathway as the Duke. He could not, however, afford to ignore his Grace, for Newcastle's power in part came from the fact that he worked at his job twenty-four hours a day, and gave his whole life to it, where other men looked upon Government as only one of their interests. Even the zealous Mr. Pitt was interested in gardening, horsemanship, the affairs of his family, and the arts; but to Newcastle the politics of the Court was ever present and his mind was ever active to trap or betray any strong man on the scene so that he might no longer be a contender.

There were two other political camps which Pitt might have joined. One was headed by the Duke of Cumberland, who had gained some repute in the victory at Culloden, even though he had won the nickname of "Butcher" Cumberland at the same event. Cumberland, however, had demonstrated his military incapacity on other occasions, and Pitt was sufficiently versed in tactics to appraise the man's shortcomings. Cumberland, also, was *persona non grata* in the household of the Prince of Wales, as the Princess was jealous of his influence with the Crown. Though Pitt, while serving in the Ministry, could no longer officially represent the interests of the heir apparent, he had never separated himself wholly from his friendship with the family, and that was an obstacle to enlisting under the Cumberland banner. Most objectionable of all was the fact that Cumberland's chief political manager was Henry Fox. Fox and Pitt were occasionally on the same side of political issues, but Pitt always mistrusted Fox while recognizing his abilities.

The other alliance open to Mr. Pitt was the group of satellites around John Russell, Duke of Bedford. Bedford was often in the political camp of the Whigs and was related to various of the leading Whig families. He usually, however, played an independent rôle, in part because he differed on issues of state and mainly to get his share of offices for himself or his followers. Bedford had a large Parliamentary interest, and a man like Pitt would have been a great asset to him, but Bedford was stubborn and self-willed, and he was far better satisfied in having the notorious Lord Sandwich as his chief henchman.

Bedford's lack of squeamishness and his satisfaction with a reputation for being a tough and intractable citizen, had roots in the circumstances of his childhood and adolescence.

There had been two boys in the family, Wriothesley, the
elder, and John (the present Duke) who was two years
younger. Their father had died when they were young children, and their mother had raised them in the sheltered innocence of hothouse plants.

The effect on Wriothesley, then Duke of Bedford, was
recited in a letter by Lady Mary Wortley Montague to her
sister, in 1725, the year of Wriothesley's marriage. This
was the rowdy Lady Montague, mother-in-law of Bute, she
who preferred Turks to Englishmen:

> I am in hopes your King of France behaves better than our
> Duke of Bedford; who, by the care of a pious mother, certainly
> preserved his virginity to his marriage-bed, where he was so
> much disappointed in his fair bride, who (though his own in-
> clinations) could not bestow on him those expressless raptures
> he had figured to himself, that he already pukes at the very
> name of her, and determines to let his estate go to his brother,
> rather than go through the filthy drudgery of getting an heir
> to it.
> N.B. This is true history, and I think the most extraordinary
> that has happened in this last age. This comes of living till
> sixteen without a competent knowledge either of practical or
> speculative anatomy, and literally thinking fine ladies composed
> of lilies and roses. *A propos* of the best red and white to be
> had for money, Lady Hervey is more delightful than ever. . . .

Apparently "true history" it was. Wriothesley died
childless on October 23, 1732, and the estate and title
passed to his brother. Wriothesley's widow, despite her
first husband's reported opinion, was married again within
exactly eight months of his demise to the 3rd Earl of Jersey
(a cousin of Mr. Pitt), by whom she had two children.
Meanwhile John Russell, who became Duke of Bedford, had
reacted in reverse pattern to his brother. No delicate
flower he. By 1745 he had married twice and begot-
ten two children. In reality, Bedford's letters and state
papers show him to be a man of perception, and no more
grasping than most of his fellows; but he chose the purple
cloak of wickedness. His followers were known as "the
Bloomsbury gang." He was reputed to be loud, avaricious,

and lustful. He loved it; but in a country devoted to fine appearances it made him a dubious political ally.

At this period nevertheless the Cumberland and Bedford forces were in mild alliance, like two drunks going home in a London fog. Newcastle, however, broke this up when Chesterfield resigned as Secretary of State in February, 1748. Newcastle asked Pitt's advice on a successor to Chesterfield, and Pitt nominated Fox; whereupon Newcastle invited the Duke of Bedford to take the office and Bedford promptly accepted, thus ending the Bedford-Cumberland loyalties. Pitt was aware that there was no spirit of cohesion in these two circles with which to form an Opposition.

All in all, Pitt decided to continue with Pelham, even though it seemed probable that the Ministry did not plan to redeem its promise to include him in the Cabinet. Pitt, on his part, left the Ministers to run the Government as best they could without his active co-operation, and devoted himself mainly to private life, indulging his favorite hobby of landscape gardening.

In 1747 he purchased the lease of South Lodge, an estate of sixty-five acres, in Enfield Chace. He began remodeling it with the typical Pitt extravagance and within a few months had paid £1358 for carpenters' bills.

The greatest attention, however, was paid to the garden. Gilbert West, the minor poet, exclaimed over "every sequestered nook, dingle, and bosky bower . . . in that little paradise." Molly West, Gilbert's sister and a great admirer of Pitt, is said to have walked many times over the grounds by herself in defiance of wind or rain. The lodge and grounds were well stocked with woodcock and snipe; and crowds came down from London for the hunting and for the long evenings at which, as Legge put it, "we will discuss politics, poetry, or that greatest of all the Nepenthes, nonsense." The Legge referred to was Henry Bilson Legge who had long been an acquaintance of Pitt's. He had been a private secretary to Robert Walpole, sat in Parliament for East Looe, Cornwall, and was currently an envoy to Prussia. He was an uncle of the 2nd Earl of Dartmouth, for whom Dartmouth College was named.

The grounds at South Lodge brought Mr. Pitt considerable fame as an amateur landscape designer. Sanderson
Miller, the poet and sculptor, Lyttelton, and Lord Chancellor Hardwicke called upon Mr. Pitt for guidance; and
Miller subsequently wrote in gratitude:

> *A Laurel walk and Strawberry Bank*
> *For which the Paymaster I thank,*
> *The Paymaster well-skilled in Planting,*
> *Pleased to assist when cash was wanting.*
> *He bid my Laurels grow, they grew*
> *Fast as his Laurels always do.*

As the months rolled on, the laurels did not grow as well
in Britain's official garden. The Government weathered an
election in the summer of 1747, thanks to the weakness of
the Opposition. The Prince of Wales now had only the
feeblest lieutenants, headed by William Pitt's erratic
brother, Thomas, aided by the inept Dr. Ayscough. As
Thomas Pitt remained loyal to the influence of the Prince
and since he was the owner of Old Sarum, William was
obliged to find some other constituency since he was running as a Government candidate.

It was a most unpleasant situation, for the only opportunity available appeared to be the Borough of Seaford,
which was under the Duke of Newcastle's control, and not
a very secure control at that. Newcastle was by no means
sure that the voters would accept his candidate without
some urging and he addressed a polite but firm letter to the
constituents:

> Mr. Pitt's zeal for H.M.'s service and for the Interest of
> His country and his known ability and inclination to promote
> them are such qualifications as I doubt not but will make him
> as agreeable to you, as the choice of him will be serviceable to
> the Publick. Mr. Pitt intends to be with me at Bishopstone the
> end of the week where he will have an opportunity of being
> personally known to you, and as no man is better able to serve
> you I am sure nobody will be more willing. Your favor to
> Mr. Pitt and Mr. Hay upon this occasion will ever be grate-
> fully acknowledged by . . . Holles Newcastle.

This communication was augmented by instructions to an agent addressed as "Sam." Sam was to go around the town and inform the voters "how considerable a man Mr. Pitt is and how able he will be to serve them." This sentiment was to be emphasized by treating the freemen to a bowl of punch. Even so, Newcastle encountered some opposition, and on the election day he took Mr. Pitt down to Seaford and sat all day by the returning officer to overawe the voters.

The technique was successful, but it was a blot on Mr. Pitt's reputation, for on the opening of Parliament in November a petition was brought into the Commons to review the circumstances of the Seaford election. Pitt was in a tight place and he called upon all of his powers of ridicule to turn the subject off as a jest by saying, "Was the dignity of the House of Commons on so sure foundations that they might venture themselves to shake it by jokes on electoral bribery?" Thanks to the heavy majority of the Government and thanks to the fact that few men cared to compete with Mr. Pitt in debate, the subject was dropped, but it was one more example of Pitt's embarrassment in being tied to a ministry in which he was subordinate. Newcastle could have nominated Pitt to a sure borough in which these circumstances need not have arisen, but undoubtedly preferred the situation as it was.

For this and other reasons Pitt, in the fall of 1747, was profoundly gloomy. In Navy affairs England had been successful during the year. Anson had been victorious off Finisterre in May, and in October Hawke had captured six men-of-war off Belle Isle; but the Finisterre victory had been dampened for Mr. Pitt as Thomas Grenville, one of the brotherhood, had been killed in action. Furthermore, the naval victories had little significance, as England's part in the war against the Bourbon allies was being carried on without any coherent plan. On the Continent the English troops, fighting sporadically against the French, had established a poor record and in the summer had been decisively defeated at Lauffeldt. Pitt was convinced that the English allies in Europe could not cope with the French combination, unless Prussia could be induced to join the Northern Alliance. He had attacked Carteret in the past for meddling in European affairs, for Carteret had not had a consistent policy. Neither, in fact, did Newcastle have a policy, except that he was opposed to being involved in Europe any more than necessary and yet seemed unable to disengage the country from European embroilments, especially as the King expected his Electorate of Hanover to be protected.

Pitt, however, was eager to win Newcastle to a definite policy. On December 17, 1747, commenting on the "melancholy scene of public affairs" he wrote to the Duke:

> I will not teaze your Grace with the repetition of things which don't meet with your approbation, nor agree with your view of publick affairs. I will sum up my whole political creed in two propositions: this country and Europe are undone without a secure, lasting peace; the alliance as it now stands has not the force ever to obtain it without the interposition of Prussia. The umbrage of that Prince, justly taken at the language of the Court of Vienna ever since the cession of Silesia, once effectually removed, it is his interest and therefore his inclination to see Europe pacified and France contained within some bounds. I am not sanguine enough to imagine he would on any account engage in the war, but I must believe, if the proper steps were taken and taken in earnest, he might be brought to care for such a peace as we ought to think ourselves happy to obtain.

Newcastle was not persuaded, and Pitt took no further conspicuous stand in this session of Parliament except to defend the Grenvilles when Sir William Stanhope charged them with being greedy upstarts who were hogging governmental favors.

Pitt immediately sprang to arms with the not too eloquent retort than the "violent torrent of abuse on a whole family is founded on no reason in the world, but because that family is distinguished by the just rewards of their services to their King and country."

The Grenvilles were probably neither more nor less grasping than most of the dominant families. There was a considerable fashion in accusing one's neighbors of peculation, while grabbing for oneself as avidly as possible. A notable instance was the Walpoles' continuous criticism of the Bedfords, though Sir Robert Walpole started in the government service as a poor man and had emerged rich. The Temple-Grenville money had been made through smart management of their properties and in some cases by useful marriages, though most of the property was on the Temple side, in the hands of Viscount Cobham; and the current generation of Grenville brothers had little in their own right.

The Grenville cousinhood at this stage was, in fact, in a relatively low state, as none of the boys inherited the strong personality of their uncle Cobham. Richard, who had once been a jolly, amiable person, was beginning to turn into a self-important young man, rather pleasing to look at though almost effeminate in appearance. The stocky, stolid George Grenville was a dull, industrious fellow, rather ill-tempered, and made faintly ridiculous by a thin querulous voice. Jemmy Grenville, the youngest of the boys, had the charm of the family. He was a gay and loving personality who was content throughout his life to bask in the light of others, especially in that of Mr. Pitt. In the Lyttleton branch of the cousinhood, the gawky, absent-minded George had the most scholarly brains, but not much political sense, and his brother, William, showed no particular signs of distinction. Of the West cousinhood, Gilbert was the most talented, and, like George Lyttelton, had won some success as a minor poet.

This was a creditable enough record but not a distinguished one, especially for a family which laid claim to Villiers blood. Certainly the cousinhood could not in this generation match the abilities of the Keppels, the Howes, the Stanhopes, and the Townshends. It was fortunate for them that they had virtually adopted Mr. Pitt and that he continued to be their guiding star.

Though Pitt was devoted to them and visited frequently at their several homes, his taste for friendship in his leisure hours ran to the literati or other persons of keen intelligence. Except in his official contacts he spent little time with the nobility, even those active in Government, yet he could have sought that society both because of his family connections and because of his own abilities. Among many of the leading families, however, public exercise of the brain was not considered well-bred. There were a few exceptions such as Carteret, now Lord Granville, with "more learning than became his rank" but in the main those close to the Court were interested in gambling, drinking, and other light pursuits. Pitt was willing to devote untold energy to his ambitions in respect to Government work, but he chose to spend his leisure hours more entertainingly.

When he visited Tunbridge Wells in the summer of 1748, his companions were the actor Garrick, Dr. Samuel Johnson, George Lyttelton, Molly West, Mrs. Elizabeth Montagu and, not least, the famous Elizabeth Chudleigh.

Miss Chudleigh, who was to crop up later in his life, was a beautiful creature, now twenty-eight, who in her young girlhood had been a protégé of William Pulteney, who was thirty-six years her senior. Pulteney had taken the position that he was very much interested in her mind and over a considerable period had guided her studies. He apparently had been a successful tutor, for though Miss Chudleigh had an extraordinary range of admirers, she seems to have been interested in and accepted by the most brilliant minds of her time.

In 1743 she had been appointed Maid of Honor to Augusta, Princess of Wales, some said through the influence of Pulteney, though he had deserted the Prince the year before. At any rate, this had been the beginning of a lurid career which was not yet in full glow. Actually, and secretly, Miss Chudleigh was the wife of Augustus John Hervey, subsequently Earl of Bristol and nephew of the painted Lord Hervey commonly known as "Lord Fanny." She had eloped with Hervey in 1744, and some said that she left him after the first night, whereupon he went to the West Indies. In any event, they both kept the marriage a secret lest she lose her place as Maid of Honor. On his return from the West Indies Hervey had repeatedly sought a reconciliation, and in the summer of 1747 Miss Chudleigh had a child secretly at Chelsea, who died shortly afterward.

Rumors of this leaked out, but she chose to treat them only as rumors.

"Do you know, my Lord," she said to Lord Chesterfield, "that the world says I have had twins?"

"Does it?" said his Lordship. "For my part, I make a point of believing only half of what it says."

Miss Chudleigh had not, however, been sobered by her experiences. Her beautiful figure and her vivacity won her the attention of the most eligible gentlemen in the nation including the King, and she was not backward in displaying her advantages.

In the spring following this summer at Tunbridge Wells, on May 8, 1749, to be exact, Mrs. Elizabeth Montagu, Pitt's particular friend, wrote to her sister regarding Miss Chudleigh's costume at a masked ball at Somerset House:

> Miss Chudleigh's dress, or rather undress, was remarkable; she was Iphigenia for the sacrifice, but so naked the high priest might easily inspect the entrails of the victim. The maids of honour (not of maids the strictest) were so offended they would not speak to her.

The Princess of Wales was likewise shocked at seeing the curves of her Maid of Honor so publicly displayed, and threw a veil over her person.

This rebuke from the Princess whose scandal with Lord Bute was notorious, was too much for Miss Chudleigh, who could not resist the pun, and commented: *"Votre Altesse Royale sait que chacune a son but."*

Miss Chudleigh perhaps dared to risk offending the Princess because of the influence which La Chudleigh had with the King. In the following year his Majesty appointed her mother housekeeper at Windsor, and at a royal levee said that he hoped Miss Chudleigh would not think a kiss too great a reward. "Against all precedent," wrote Horace Walpole, "he kissed her in the circle; he has had a hankering these two years."

This stimulating group at Tunbridge Wells was joined by Colley Cibber, the actor and dramatist, Richardson, the novelist, and Whiston, the translator of *Josephus*. There is no record of any Iphigenia balls enlivening the scene, but it was apparently enlivening for Mr. Pitt, who improved under the treatment.

The climate of Parliament, however, in the autumn session of 1748 was neither stimulating nor refreshing. The chief event of the session was the news that England had signed the treaty of Aix-la-Chapelle, which lined up Britain, Holland and Austria on one side against France and Spain on the other. The treaty also guaranteed Prussia in the possession of Silesia, which was a step toward the friendship which Pitt believed should be cultivated. On the other hand, the treaty damaged the position of England in her American colonies, for it returned to France the important fortress of Louisbourg which had been captured through Colonial efforts, and it failed to deal with the protection from search of British vessels navigating the American seas, which had been a primary reason for England entering the war.

Pitt, however, was powerless to offer any protest, even if it had been politically feasible for him to do so, for England was not in a position to conduct a successful war under the present inept Ministry.

Pitt, in fact, continued to have very little to say, breaking forth only occasionally with some sharp commentary which kept his personality alive before the public. In April, 1749, he had the courage to support a bill to indemnify Glasgow to the extent of £10,000 for the fine which had been levied on it by the Pretender. English opinion was strongly against all Scotch, loyal or not; but Pitt, as usual, recognized that sane statesmanship should encourage unity of feeling throughout the kingdom. "There are not many cities in the United Kingdom," Pitt said, "that have so often and so remarkably distinguished themselves in the cause of liberty . . . it is the whole tenour of this city's conduct from the time of the Reformation that drew the resentment of the rebels upon it."

In the same session he made one of his more noted speeches against lawyers. "The Gentlemen of the Black Robe," as he often described them, were, with a few ex-

Elizabeth Chudleigh, afterwards Duchess of Kingston, a friend of Mr. Pitt and Dr. Johnson, and twice kissed by George II. She eloped at an early age, concealed her marriage, had countless admirers, and finally was tried for bigamy by the House of Lords.

Horace Walpole, the younger, the premier letter-writer and gossip of eighteenth-century England.

ceptions, his particular enemies. Whenever any ministry was hostile to Pitt it was customary to set the dogs of Westminster Hall upon him, for no lay speaker of the time (except Fox) could cope with him. Pitt naturally resented the procedure and, confident of his own learning, was irritated by the assumed superiority of the legal profession. He frequently retorted by jeering at those who "spoke from a brief," and in this session of Parliament he said: "The Constitution may be shaken to its center, and the lawyer will sit calm in his cabinet. But let a cobweb be disturbed in Westminster Hall, and out the bloated spider will crawl in its defense."

Such fireworks, however, were merely exercise for Mr. Pitt, who still could see no way out of the political cul-de-sac in which he was now placed. Personal matters were more important on his horizon. Thomas Pitt, his brother, was now reaching the end of a badly misguided career. The failure of the Prince in the recent elections had dramatized Thomas' incapacity and had finished him financially. Virtually all of the estimated £100,000 left to Thomas Pitt from his father's and grandfather's estates had been dissipated, chiefly through mismanagement, and Thomas was now hawking Old Sarum on the market, though there were no offers at a satisfactory price. Thomas, moreover, had made a complete wreck of his marital affairs in spite of his romantic courtship of Christian Lyttelton twenty years before. He treated the poor woman with utmost contempt, encouraged, it is feared, by both Ann and Betty, who lived with him part of the time at Boconnoc. It was his custom in the winter to bring Ann and Betty to town, leaving his wife and children in the country. This conduct had led to a separation and it was only through the intervention of the Lytteltons and Mr. Pitt that some provision was made for Mrs. Thomas Pitt, who went to live with her brothers at Hagley. Thomas' conduct had obviously reflected on the Pitt name and gave emphasis to their reputation as an erratic tribe.

In the Grenville cousinhood likewise there were changing events which had influence on the future. In the year 1749

George Grenville married Elizabeth Wyndham, a close friend of his sister, Hester. Miss Wyndham was the daughter of Sir William Wyndham the great Tory leader who, years before, had instructed Mr. Pitt in Parliamentary tactics. She was the sister of the Earl of Egremont and a loyal friend of Pitt. Through the new Mrs. Grenville's friendship, Pitt's relationship with the cousinhood was further strengthened, and as a result of the marriage, on the other hand, George Grenville's self-importance was increased, as his alliance with Egremont made him feel less dependent on either his older brother or Mr. Pitt.

The most radical change of all, in this year, was the death of Richard Temple, Viscount Cobham, on September 13, 1749. With him went the last glimmer of the early days when Opposition had been so brilliant. His sister, Hester Temple Grenville, mother of the Grenville brothers, now inherited his huge properties, with the condition that they were to go to her oldest son, Richard Grenville; and in October of the same year she was created Countess Temple.

The new wealth and the honors which came to his immediate family, and which he would inherit ultimately, instilled in Richard Grenville a pride which progressively possessed him like a disease. He was now avid to inherit the title of Lord Cobham and pressed for the honor when his uncle had been dead only fifteen days. Even the hardened Newcastle was shocked by this hasty demand and suggested a postponement of the action on the ground of common decency. Richard, however, was importunate, and through the aid of Pitt soon obtained his wish.

Shortly after these changes in the affairs of the Grenville cousinhood, there was an unforeseen crisis in the Pelham Ministry, thanks to the restlessness of the Duke of Newcastle. Newcastle had always been discontented under the leadership of his younger brother, but had not found any plausible reason for dissension. In 1750, however, he had become violently dissatisfied with his own Cabinet appointee, the Duke of Bedford, because Bedford refused to be a rubber stamp. Newcastle was for dismissing Bedford at once, but Pelham, who was by nature a conciliator, disagreed. Upon this, Newcastle began to cast about to form a new ministry. He made overtures to Mr. Pitt and was ready to accept any combination which would place the Newcastle influence in supreme and undivided control. If Pitt had been interested solely in the eminence of office, this would have been a golden opportunity, but he realized that a schism between the Pelham brothers would be ruinous to the Whig party and would offer no real leadership to himself. Accordingly, he chose the path of peacemaker.

On July 13, 1750, he wrote to Newcastle: "I don't hazard much in venturing to prophesy that two brothers who love one another, and two ministers essentially necessary to each other, will never suffer themselves to be divided further than the nearest friends by difference of opinion or even little ruffles of temper may occasionally be. Give me leave," he continued, "to suggest a doubt. May not frequent reproaches upon one subject gall and irritate a mind not conscious, intentionally at least, of giving cause?"

These mollifying words had the desired effect upon his Grace, especially as they informed him by inference that Mr. Pitt would not be available as a support in a quarrel against Pelham. Newcastle realized that he must make peace, and accordingly the Pelham-Newcastle Ministry again presented a united front. The fact that Mr. Pitt through the force of his own personality had been able to patch up the quarrel which threatened the stability of the Government added greatly to his prestige both in the House of Commons and among the Cabinet officers. It was, in fact, a major political achievement. Hitherto he had shown himself to be an incomparable speaker in St. Stephen's Chapel, a devastating critic, and a man of high integrity, but this was the first time that he had appeared as a principal negotiator among the chief figures of the kingdom.

Pelham wrote to his brother: "I have had a long discourse with Pitt. He seems mighty happy with an opinion, that his interposition, and his truly friendly offices, have had a good effect in bringing you and me nearer to each other. I most sincerely desire you to go on in your correspondence with him, with all the frankness and cordiality you can: I do so, in all my conversations with him. I think him, besides, the most able and useful man we have amongst us: truly honourable, and strictly honest. He is as firm a friend to us, as we can wish for; and a more useful one there does not exist."

Newcastle seemed grateful to Pitt for extricating him from a bad situation and addressed a circular letter to his supporters giving testimony to Pitt's friendliness and assistance.

Pitt, in turn, was wise enough to disclaim credit for bringing the two men together and wrote to Newcastle on August 24: "You are both infinitely too good to mention, as you are pleased to do, my poor little part between you. My good wishes were sincere, and wishing well was all I could possibly have to do. I should be foolishly vain with a witness, if I ascribed the least part of the perfect union between you to any thing but your own good hearts and understandings. I need say nothing of the interior of administration. Your Grace and Mr. Pelham, united as you are, must certainly be masters to give it such a shape as may best suit your situations and views; of which you alone must be judges. Whatever determination you come to, I heartily wish it may more and more secure and strengthen power and authority in your hands."

The high favor which Pitt now enjoyed from the Administration gave him reason to believe that the Pelhams would take steps to include him officially in their Ministry as they had promised to do for so long a time. He addressed a note to Newcastle in October, 1750, which, in tortuous and cryptic language, gave a hint of his thoughts on that subject: "The alteration thought of at home I have always seen so full of difficulties in itself and in the consequential arrangements, that I felicitate your Grace upon seeing your way through it. Whatever it be the King proposes in this matter, *himself,* and *from himself* (as your Grace terms it), I can only say with great truth for now, that I wish it may meet with perfect acquiescence from all quarters. I find Mr. Pelham (whatever inconveniences he may apprehend) in all the general dispositions to acquiesce and accommodate, that your Grace could wish. I understand from him, that the arrangement for the Duke of Bedford will probably lie between Master of the Horse and President: * and fortunate I shall think it, if he is quieted and disarmed by either; which it is, I imagine not very material.

"I cannot conclude without assuring your Grace of my warmest gratitude for the kind use you were so good as to make of some expressions in my letter: nothing can touch me so sensibly as any good office in that place, where I deservedly stand in need of it so much, and where I have it so much at heart to efface the past by every action of my life."

Though expressing these hints that his services should be recognized, Mr. Pitt was now old enough to get something of a perspective on the political course which his life had taken up to that time. He evidently realized that his incessant criticism of the conservative elements in the Government was not likely to commend him to a high place. He had frequently seen examples where an agitator, often himself, plowed the way for a change, and then more conservative temperaments such as Henry Pelham were brought in to take the helm of administration. Furthermore, his associations had not been of the sort to give him the most stable reputation. His connection with the Prince, his friendship with Bolingbroke, his legacy from the Duchess of Marlborough, and his acquaintanceship with Miss Chudleigh and her group were all marks of a man in Opposition rather than one likely to be called on to guide the destiny of the nation.

He felt called upon to declare a change of heart in a speech in Parliament on January 17, 1751, which contained this somewhat naïve paragraph: "Those who endeavour to quote from my former speeches, the outpourings of my hot and fractious youth, are hereby warned off. I have sown my wild oats; henceforward I am to be regarded as a prudent and sagacious statesman."

---

* President of the Council, a sinecure office in the Cabinet. Bedford would be transferred from Secretary of State, if room were made for Mr. Pitt in that office.

He knew well enough that this outburst might bring forth many jeers from those who could quote chapter and verse against him; and he met the issue by recantation of the errors of his youth before his enemies had an opportunity to present them. He was now convinced that to demand guarantees of "no search" from Spain was impracticable, though he recognized that once he had criticized the Government on that very stand. "I confess I did, Sir," he said, "because I then thought it right, but I was then very young and sanguine. I am now ten years older, and have had time to consider things more coolly."

In fact, Horace Walpole, the younger, wrote of the reborn Pitt: "Where he chiefly shone was in exposing his own conduct; having waded through the most notorious apostasy in politics, he treated it with an impudent confidence that made all reflections upon him poor and spiritless when worded by any other men."

In general, however, the change in Mr. Pitt was more a matter of attitude than an alteration of principles. He supported the Pelham position whenever he could, but he did not hesitate to go into opposition when some of his strongest beliefs were attacked. He refused to endorse Pelham's proposal to reduce the naval establishment, and in January, 1751, he made a spirited address on the subject. It is true that his first recorded act in the House of Commons years before had been to vote a reduction in Walpole's proposal of thirty thousand men for the Navy, but since then he had been consistently and repeatedly a big Navy advocate. Pelham was able to defeat Pitt in this instance by a majority of 180, and yet the First Lord of the Treasury had apparently been convinced by his colleague, for in succeeding years he complied with Pitt's demands in respect to Navy establishment.

Mr. Pitt's loyalty to the Pelhams and his proclamation of himself as a substantial citizen still failed to bring him the desired recognition; and even the hopeful possibility of Prince Frederick succeeding to the Throne was ended in March, 1751, by the death of the Prince. Pitt loyally if inadvisedly addressed himself in Parliament to the memory of Frederick, referring to him as "the most patriot prince that ever lived, to whom I had such infinite obligations and such early attachments, which I am proud to transfer to his family." Then recalling the undying hatred which his Majesty had felt for his son, Mr. Pitt could not resist adding sarcastically: "I wonder at his Majesty exerting a fortitude at this calamity which Edward III was not master of when he lost the Black Prince."

Mr. Pelham lost no time in letting Pitt see what could happen to those who had supported Cliveden, and he promptly deputized Pitt to inform his brother Thomas that he would be no longer employed as Warden of the Stanneries, a post which was worth £1500 per year, though the blow was softened by an annual pension of £1,000.

Pelham, in general, however, was more interested in statecraft than in political punishment or rewards, and Pitt was often actively as well as passively on his side. Throughout the spring of 1751 Pelham was badly in need of help in supporting a bill which he introduced for offering naturalization to foreign Protestants, especially the Huguenots from Holland and France. The Huguenot refugees in England had already proved to be industrious and capable workers and Pelham believed that his measure would bring new forms of industry to the United Kingdom and improve England's economic position.

Popular prejudice against the foreigner was, however, strongly against the bill, and found expression in the voice of Henry Fox. Pitt entered into the issue with enthusiasm, supporting the Pelham cause, and in the numerous debates on the bill clashed again and again with Henry Fox. Fox was dogged and unafraid. In his dispassionate way he realized that Mr. Pitt made a better presentation, but Fox adhered persistently to his position and commented at the end of the struggle, "Pitt is a better speaker than I am; but thank God I have more judgment." Though the subject was closed for the time being, it was due to recur again and to cause Mr. Pitt no small embarrassment.

Another issue of this Parliament, affecting Mr. Pitt's career, was the debate on the Regency Bill. Frederick's oldest son, Prince George, who was later to become George III, was now only thirteen years of age, and if his grandfather should die before the Prince was of age, a Regency would be required. The political importance of the Regency was paramount. In May, 1751, a bill was brought into Parliament naming the Princess Dowager as Regent, aided by a Council presided over by the Duke of Cumberland. The issue hinged on the powers of the Regency Council. Fox, as Cumberland's aide, was continuously pressing to increase the power of the Council, while Mr. Pitt declaimed eloquently in favor of the rights of the Princess, urging that she should have no restrictions which might prove irksome to her.

Probably as a result of Pitt's ardent support of Augusta, his sister Ann, in June, 1751, was appointed Keeper of the Privy Purse of the Dowager Princess of Wales and superintendent of the education of the younger Princess Augusta. This arrangement was dangerous to many interests: to Fox, to Cumberland, to the Pelhams, and, not least, to Lord Bute. Ann Pitt in the heart of the Wales household and Mr. Pitt in the heart of the Commons!—a strong combination, especially in view of the well-known devotion between brother and sister. Someone, probably Bute judging by later events, promptly began to work upon Ann to set her against her brother. She was led to disagree with him, to challenge his views, and finally to break with him on the basis of a conversation in which the two had quarreled.

No one could ever work upon William to be disloyal to his relatives. In fact, he was astoundingly loyal to them throughout their most outrageous conduct, but they were all sensitive, high-strung, quick to quarrel, and it had been an apparently easy matter to stir up Ann's feelings. When Pitt realized that his sister had definitely turned against him he wrote to her on June 19, 1751, in bewildered astonishment and pain, making every effort to effect a reconciliation:

DEAR SISTER:—As you had been so good to tell me in your note of Monday that you would write to me again soon *in a manner capable, you hoped, of effacing every impression of any thing painfull that may have passed from me to you.* I did not expect such a letter as I found late last night. I have well weighed your letter, and deeply examined your picture of me, for some years past; and indeed, Sister, I still find something within, that firmly assures me I am not that thing which your interpretations of my life (if I can ever be brought to think them all your own) would represent me to be.

I have infirmities of temper, blemishes, and faults, if you please, of nature, without end; but the Eye that can't be deceived must judge between us, whether that friendship, which was my very existence for so many years, could ever have received the least flaw, but from umbrages and causes which the quickest sensibility and tenderest jealousy of friendship alone, at first, suggested.

It is needless to mark the unhappy epoque, so fatal to a harmony between sister and brother unexampled almost all that time, the loss of which has embitter'd much of my life and will always be an affliction to me. . . . 'Absolute deference and blind submission to my will,' you tell me I have often declared to you, in the strongest and most mortifying terms, cou'd alone satisfy me.

I must here beseech you cooly to reconsider these precise terms, with their epithets; and I will venture to make the appeal to the sacred testimony of your breast, whether there be not exaggeration in them.

I have often, too often reproached you, and from warmth of temper, in strong and plain terms, that I found no longer the same consent of minds and agreement of sentiments; and I have certainly declared to you that I cou'd not be satisfy'd with you, and I could no longer find in you any degree of deference towards me. I was never so drunk with presumption as to expect absolute deference and blind submission to my will.

A degree of deference to me and to my situation, I frankly own, I did not think too much for me to expect from you, with all the high opinion I really have of your parts. What I expected was too much (as perhaps might be). In our former days friendship had led me into the error. That error is at an end, and you may rest assured, that I can never be so unreasonable as to expect of you, now, anything like deference to me or my opinions.

I come next to the small pecuniary assistance which you accepted from me, and which was exactly as you state it, two hun-

dred pounds a year. I declare, upon my honour, I never gave
the least foundation for those exaggerations which you say have
been spread concerning it. I also declare as solemnly, before
God and man, that no consideration could ever have extorted
from my lips the least mention of the trifling assistance you
accepted from me, but the cruel reports, industriously propa-
gated, and circulating from various quarters round to me, of
the state you were left to live in.

As to the repayment of this wretched money, allow me, dear
Sister, to entreat you to think no more of it. The bare thought
of it may surely suffice for your own dignity and for my humiliation, without taxing your present income, merely to mortify
me; the demonstration of a blow is, in honour, a blow, and let
me conjure you to rest it here. When I want and you abound,
I promise you to afford you a better and abler triumph over
me, by asking the assistance of your purse. I will now trouble
you no farther than to repeat my sincere wishes for your welfare and to rejoice that you have so ample matter for the best
of happiness, *springing from a heart and mind* (to use your own
words) entirely devoted to gratitude and duty.

There were more letters exchanged on the same theme.
For the time being, nothing that William could say changed
Ann's attitude; and his attention soon was even more painfully occupied with the lurid affairs of his sister Betty. The
beautiful and impulsive Betty had become involved in a
scandal with Lord Talbot. She had been living near the
Talbots at Grately Lodge, a home which William had provided for her, and there had become interested in Talbot,
whose attentions extended to various ladies. Gossip drove
her from the neighborhood and then she lived openly with
his Lordship.

Pitt had tried to remedy this situation by sending his
sister to Europe and providing her with a charming young
companion by the name of Miss Taylor. For a time this
apparently worked well, and on October 10, 1751, Betty
wrote to Mr. Pitt from Tours, calling him the best of
brothers and of men. Also, about this time, she was attracted to a Frenchman named Dutens who was on his way
to England, and she gave Dutens a warm letter of introduction to her brother.

Betty's heart, however, seldom stayed very long in one place, and on June 1, of the following year, she wrote to her brother from Tours referring to Lord Talbot and saying that he had promised to marry her as soon as he could be divorced from Lady Talbot.

Betty had, in fact, become incensed at Dutens for falling in love with her companion, Miss Taylor, a fact which she had not discerned in its early stages; but on June 11 she wrote to Mr. Pitt alleging that Dutens had treated her shabbily and had scandalized her name, and she begged William "to order one of your footmen to give him the treatment he merits."

Pitt had treated Dutens with marked courtesy on the strength of his sister's earlier introduction, and now broke with him. He was apparently, however, not entirely convinced of Betty's judgment, for he took the peculiar step of appointing as her guardian the Rev. Dr. Ayscough. In view of Pitt's opinion of the somber "ridiculous Skew," it may be suspected that he did this not without some sardonic reflections on the effect on both parties. Ayscough, at any rate, found it a most trying assignment, as he later referred to Betty as "the worst, the wickedest and the most wrong-headed woman in the world."

It was an exhausting period for Mr. Pitt. To cap it all, the Countess Temple died on October 6, 1752, and Richard Grenville succeeded as Earl Temple. Lyttelton wrote to Sanderson Miller: "Lord Cobham will now be the richest man in England, so you may expect to see new beauties at Stowe, for I daresay her thousand a year will all go that way. I beg his pardon: I should have called him Earl Temple." Temple was now head of the cousinhood, and was still loyal to Mr. Pitt; but the rise of his fortunes, while in many ways helpful to the Pitt-Grenville influence, also meant that Temple was included in all the Pitt calculations, which more than once proved to be a handicap. In fact, Pitt extended to the cousinhood the same uncritical devotion which he felt for his own family, except in the periods when the Grenvilles openly and conspicuously broke with him.

The year 1753 fortunately opened more happily for Mr. Pitt's affairs. He was less concerned in politics and more interested in regaining his health. On January 14 he wrote a letter to his friend, Sanderson Miller, asking him to purchase a horse:

I am always very obliged to you for every mark of your friendly remembrance; this concerning the horse you mention is most welcome as my stable is in want of a recruit and my health stands much in need of the help of riding. I have an entire confidence in your skill in horse flesh, and believe no man a better judge in either of those Capital articles of life, which is, in a word, to be well mounted.

I would ask but one question: is the horse gentle and steady? If you find he is, I shall be much obliged if you will buy him for me and send him to me by my groom, who will deliver this letter to you. I think there is nothing unreasonable in the price if he comes six years old. I send you enclosed a draught on my Banker for six and twenty pound five shillings, payable to you on order, and desire you will be so good as to lay down the money for the horse.

I am happy to hear Mrs. Miller already enjoys the laurels; I make no doubt the myrtle still blooms at Radway and that all the laurels there are not sufficient to bind your victorious brow. I saw your widow at Bath * looking very thin and with the charming air of a lady who had tasted largely of the myrtle. Poor little Molly Cobby † is delightful . . . I applaud your noble zeal for the Arts; go on and prosper, making Angels in bas relief and alto relief as fast as you can.—I am in great truth, my dear Miller,

Your faithful and affectionate Humble Servant.

Happily, also, Pitt had at last prevailed upon Ann to be reconciled, and wrote to her on February 8, 1753:

DEAR SISTER:—I am unable to express the load you have taken off my heart by your affectionate and generous answer to my last letter; I will recur no more to a subject, which your goodness and forgiveness forbid me to mention. The concern I feel for your state of health is most sensible; wou'd to God, you may be shortly in a situation to give me the infinite comfort

* Possibly their mutual friend, Mrs. Elizabeth Montagu.
† Probably Molly West.

of hearing of an amendment in it! I hope Spring is forwarder, where you reside, than with us, and that the difference of climate begins to be felt. I will not give you the trouble to read any more; but must repeat in the fulness of my heart, the warmest and tenderest acknowledgements of your goodness to,
My Dear Sister, Your most affec. Brother

W. PITT

Another cheerful event from Mr. Pitt's point of view was the trial of William Murray before the Privy Council, Murray of Oxford who had left the Opposition at the time of Pulteney's ill-fated deal. Charges had been made by the Opposition that Murray some years before, with certain other persons named, had drunk the health of the Pretender. Murray's position was damaged by the fact that his brother had been on the Pretender's staff. Murray defended himself ably, pointing to his long record as a Whig and in the service of the current dynasty. No one took the charges very seriously, as it was plainly a political move based on an alleged event of years before, but it gratified Mr. Pitt to see the man who had so often attacked him (and Pitt felt had betrayed him) in so uncomfortable a spot. Moreover, the affair had a permanent effect on the sensitive Murray who ever afterwards was suffocated whenever anyone alluded to him as a Stuart sympathizer.

The winter passed along with Mr. Pitt suffering less than usual from the gout, and on April 5 he wrote to Ann expressing the hope of receiving benefits from the horse which Miller had purchased for him:

MY DEAR SISTER:—Nothing can be felt more sensibly than I do the goodness of your letter, in which you talk to me circumstantially of your own health, and desire to hear circumstantially of mine. . . . I am infinitely glad that the concurrent opinions of Physicians of both Countries are the foundations of expecting the Spa will relieve you. . . .

I have been ill all the winter with disorders in my bowels, which have left me very low, and reduced me to a weak state of health. I am now, in many respects, better, and seem getting ground, by riding and taking better nourishment. Warmer weather, I am to hope, will be of much service to me. I pro-

pose using some mineral waters; Tunbridge or Sunning Hill or
Bath, at their proper seasons. As the main cause of my complaint is much abated and almost removed, I hope my Horse,
warm weather and proper nourishment will give me health
again. The kind concern you take in it is infinitely felt by,
   Dear Sister,
   Your most affectionate Brother
                                            W. PITT

There was only one event now to stand between Pitt and
vacation time. This was the proposal by Pelham to introduce into the Commons a bill permitting the naturalization
of the Jews. Certain Jews, such as Sampson Gideon, had
assisted Pelham in the floating of public loans, and many
Jews, though not citizens, had volunteered for the British
Army at the time of the Stuart uprising. The Government
Treasury was in need of financial aid because of the war,
the extravagance of the royal house, and Newcastle's costly
system of vote-buying. Pelham believed that the measure
would bring the aid of Jewish finance to England and would
naturalize a useful group of citizens. Pitt heartily supported the bill, as it coincided with his principles of toleration. The bill was similar in principle to that in favor of
the Huguenots, which had aroused so much opposition; but
in this instance the Commons appeared to be apathetic, and
the measure passed by a small majority in a lightly attended
house.

Pitt was now ready to indulge in one of the pleasantest
summers of his career. He decided to sell his place at South
Lodge, disposing of all of the furnishings with the exception of a portrait of the Duchess of Marlborough, and he
returned to Tunbridge Wells where he had spent such an
enjoyable season in the summer of 1748. Elizabeth Chudleigh apparently was not there this summer, but Mrs. Montagu was. In fact she and two young ladies had a home
near Mount Ephraim which Pitt was occupying with Gilbert
and Mrs. West and Miss Molly West. Both households
were together frequently. They visited all the parks in the
neighborhood, and Pitt was lavish in taking the crowd to
dinner at noted resorts and in planning picnics. On one

occasion, Mrs. Montagu reported, "in the most beautiful rural scene that can be imagined . . . he ordered a tent to be pitched, tea to be prepared, and his French horn to breathe music like the unseen genius of the wood."

George Lyttelton and wife came to visit him in July, and on July 7, 1753, Lyttelton wrote enthusiastically to Sanderson Miller:

Mr. Pitt wants nothing of being quite well but to think himself so, and to sleep soundly all night. He has recovered his flesh, rides fifteen miles a day, eats like a horse, and has as much wit as ever he had in his life. I hope another month's use of the Tunbridge waters will quite remove all his complaints real or imaginary. Miss West and her brother and his wife are still with him, and I suppose will stay as long as he does, which may be till the end of September.

He talks of a visit to Hagley * after that time. Miss West is much out of order, but her brother is better than he has been for some years. Dr. Ayscough is also at Tunbridge, but proposes to leave it before the end of this month.

Billy † is here, and will return to Mr. Pitt as soon as a very troublesome boil upon his posteriors (saving your reverence) will give him leave.

My wife is well and joins with me in compliments and congratulations, and so does Billy. We intend being at Stowe on Tuesday next, this day sennight, and with you on Saturday the 4th of next month in the evening. I can't get any birds or other animals upon painted glass for love or money to putt in her dairy windows, which is very vexatious. Adieu.

At the conclusion of the Tunbridge Wells season Pitt went on a series of visits to the homes of the cousinhood, ending up at Bath in November. From there, on October 24, he wrote to his youngest sister, Mary, in terms which showed that his confidence in Ann was now thoroughly restored:

I am very glad to hear in the Conclusion of my Dear Mary's letter that she will be under no difficulty in getting to London; my Brother is very obliging, as I dare say he intends to be in all things towards you, to make your journey easy and agreeable

---

* The dilapidated home of the Lytteltons.
† Sir William Lyttelton (later Governor of South Carolina).

to you. I propose being in Town by the meeting of the Parliament; if I am able; when I shall have infinite joy in meeting my Dear Sister after so very long an Absence and seeing Her in a Place where she seems to think herself not unhappy. If I shou'd be prevented being in Town so soon, the House will always be ready to receive you.

I think you judge very right not to produce yourself much till we have met; Mrs. Stuart, and my Sister Nedham,* if in Town, will be the properest, as well as the most agreeable Places for you to frequent.

My Dear Child, I need not intimate to your good understanding and right Intentions, what a high degree of Prudence and exact attention to your Conduct and whole behaviour is render'd necessary by the sad errors of others.† It is an infinite misfortune to you that my Sister Ann is not in England; her Countenance and her Advice and Instructions, superior to any you can otherwise receive, wou'd be the highest advantage to you. Supply it as well as you can, by thinking of Her, imitating her worth, and thereby endeavouring to deserve her esteem, as you wish to obtain that of the best Part of the World.

I can not express how anxious I am for your right behaviour in all respects, upon which alone your happiness must depend. Whatever assistance my advice can be to You, you will ever have with the truest affection of a Brother.

Yrs

W. PITT

As Pitt said in his letter, he was planning to go up to Town at the opening of Parliament, and for once his conditional phrase, "if I am able," had little significance. He was as strong as Sanderson Miller's horse, and he was resolute to obtain the recognition which had long been due him, either in the Ministry or out of it. He had been the chief negotiator in holding the Pelhams together, and he had supported the Ministry in its major crises. If they did not choose to recognize him they would have the opportunity to face a new Opposition.

Pitt had discussed the idea of an Opposition with the

---

* His plain and respectable sister, Catherine, who had married a Robert Needham (also spelled Nedham).
† viz.: Betty.

Grenvilles and the Lytteltons. The plan was in tentative form, perhaps to be used merely as a political threat, a bit of pressure to start action.

Pitt was concerned that everything should be done according to careful program, and secrecy was of greatest importance in the early stages. In October he had a visit with George Lyttelton and instructed him carefully in all of the details.

The absent-minded Lyttelton had the practice of confiding everything to his father, and accordingly wrote down the whole scheme in a paper which he planned to send by messenger to Hagley, in order to avoid risk of its contents being discovered in the postoffice.

At the same time Lyttelton addressed a note of no consequence to someone else. In his absent-mindedness he gave this note to the messenger for his father. The secret plan he mailed in the postoffice, with the further neglect of not addressing it to anyone.

The postal authorities naturally perused the unaddressed message to determine the name of the sender, but when they had read its contents they forwarded it to Mr. Pelham. Pelham was exceptionally decent about the matter and returned the document to Lyttelton by the hand of one of his trusted colleagues, instructing his emissary to be as tactful as possible.

The blow to Pitt's project was, of course, irreparable. Pelham indulged in no reprisals, but something of the fine warm friendship, for whatever it was worth, had been impaired. Pitt's confidence in Lyttelton was also badly shaken, and the brief bright moment in which Pitt had been the prime negotiator among the chief ministers of England had faded, leaving him in new clouds of obscurity.

CHAPTER XVI

"No Jews, No Wooden Shoes"

Mr. Pitt was certainly running into a season of ill luck. George Lyttelton's carelessness had placed Pitt in a position where he could no longer afford to stand idly by waiting for some favorable opportunity to enhance his position with Pelham, or, on the other hand, to delay action until some popular issue might bring him independently to the forefront. Pitt had been pursuing a waiting policy for nearly seven years, but since Pelham now knew that Pitt was contemplating some form of political strategy, it was necessary for the latter to be actively on the scene lest reprisals be effectively carried out against him.

Pitt accordingly attended Parliament in the fall session beginning November, 1753, prepared to take an active part; and here his ill luck continued, for the chief issue of the session was the Jew bill, which had caused a tremendous furore throughout the country.

When Pelham had sponsored his bills offering naturalization to the Huguenots and again to the Jews, neither he nor the Ministry had anticipated that the measures would continue to be public issues after they had been enacted. Severe laws against the Jews existed on the statute books. They were forbidden to hold various offices; they had no right to acquire real property; and they were not legally permitted to have synagogues. Most of the laws, however,— notably the one forbidding synagogues—were dead letters, and therefore the passing of the Naturalization Bill had been in accord with an apparent public trend toward toleration. The introduction of the Jewish measure had not aroused any special interest in the Commons; and Pitt, in favoring toleration, had not found it necessary to exert himself in respect to the Bill, to the extent he had devoted to the Huguenot cause.

Throughout the summer, however, the opposition to the measure had spread like a forest fire, fanned by the merchant class, by the shippers, and, to a large degree, by the clergy of the rural churches. The Huguenots had proved to be such skilful and diligent workers that in a short time they were serious rivals of the native English; and the threat of Jewish immigration offering further competition aroused the deepest resentment.

"No Jews, no wooden shoes!" was the watchword wherever merchants and craftsmen foregathered. No other issue had shaken the country so violently since the turbulent days of the Stuart uprising. Periodicals of the day were filled with the subject, and *The Gentleman's Magazine* had made it a feature of its pages throughout the summer. In the August issue it summarized public opinion on the subject by listing objections to the Bill, and the answers to the objections, as follows:

OBJECTION 1. By this Bill we do not, like Esau, sell our birthright for any consideration however inadequate, but we do worse, we give it away.

ANS. *The privileges here called our birthright are not lost by communication.*

OBJ. 2. Jews will obtain a share in the gov. and will be qualified to vote for members of Parliament.

ANS. *False.* (*A voter could be required to take oaths inconsistent with the Jewish religion.*)

OBJ. 3. The Jews who intend to be naturalized are very wealthy and cannot procure a settlement elsewhere, and will therefore become the highest bidders for every landed estate in this kingdom. Great numbers of poor Jews will then settle in the same vicinity, as they must use their own bakers, butchers, etc.

ANS. *Would have happened already if this were true, as a Jew, without being naturalized, could purchase in the name of some denizen, allowing him possession in the meantime. Also, if it increases the number of purchasers of land, it will therefore increase the value of the land.*

OBJ. 4. Jews who live in Popish countries may come back here to be naturalized, return and profess Judaism, believing

they are secure (being Englishmen), and therefore involve
England in disputes with foreign countries.

ANS. *The fact that he is an English Jew would make no difference. What would the motive be for such conduct? Why
would the same dangers not continue and deter him as now?*

OBJ. 5. Jews are not like other foreigners, for they will always remain a distinct nation, and are not absorbed by the
country or community in which they dwell. Example of Jews
going into Egypt one family, and coming out a distinct people
(600,000) 430 years later.

ANS. *The religion of the Jews united them. At that time it
(the religion) was true; it is now false and grows weaker
before Christianity. The Bill appears to be a means of ful-
filling the prophecy concerning the conversion of the Jews.*

OBJ. 6. By this Bill we are giving the lie to the prophecies,
and invalidating the strongest proof of the Christian religion.
The prophecies on which Christianity is founded say, they
shall be dispersed; we are gathering them together.

ANS. *If the Chr. religion can be thus overturned, it ought not
to stand, for whatever prophecy can be invalidated by facts
is false. If it is true, the most popular argument against the
Bill means nothing, for then the Jews cannot be united as
a distinct people or found the restoration of their nation upon
the ruin of ours.*

OBJ. 7. It is inconsistent with our character to admit the
Jews as denizens without receiving the sacrament.

ANS. *The sacrament would mean nothing to them except an
idle ceremony, and they would feel they were risking nothing
by receiving it; therefore it would be sacrilegious—and it is
up to the Christians to prevent such profanation.*

OBJ. 8. The Jew goes in for merchandizing rather than man-
ufacturing.

ANS. *The Jews have been unable to be manufacturers because
it is not a traveling occupation, but implies a settlement.*

OBJ. 9. If the Jew becomes a shopkeeper instead of a hawker
or pedlar, there will be less Christian shopkeepers, as the number cannot increase. The shopkeepers sell as low as they can
afford, so it would be merely a substitution of Jew for Christian—with no reduction in the price of the commodity.

ANS. *False; the shopkeepers do not sell as cheaply as possible.
Jew shopkeepers would then be hurtful only to those who*

were making a great deal of profit—and therefore the Jews would be beneficial to the public.

OBJ. 10. If the Jews become merchants and shopkeepers they will throw the trade into each other's hands and eventually force the Christians out of business so they will have to do the labor of manufacture.

ANS. *The Christians do the same thing; anyway the act will not give them more power to do this than they had before.*

OBJ. 11. The Jews are enemies of Christian states, for their nineteenth prayer calls the Christians "apostates and heretics."

ANS. *The Sadducees are meant by this. Also, the Jews always pray for prosperity of the gov. under which they live.*

In spite of the logical answers which could be made to the objections, the Ministry realized that popular feeling continued to be strongly against the Bill, and in the opening days of Parliament Pelham brought in a motion for repeal.

This action placed Mr. Pitt in possibly the most embarrassing position of his entire career. He had consistently favored toleration and yet he was equally consistent in consulting the views of the merchant class and the general public, who were the main source of his strength. He could swing into the situation with great gusto, winning popularity and taking credit of the repeal away from Pelham, or he could stand against the new position of the Ministry and against public opinion by supporting toleration. The choice was not clear-cut, even from the standpoint of conscience, for while Pitt believed ardently in the freedom of the individual, he also believed that the Commons should reflect the popular will.

Thoroughly uncomfortable in this dilemma, he waited until there had been expressions of opinion in both Houses of Parliament. In the House of Lords, the Duke of Bedford was the most violent for repeal, expressing the anti-Jewish feeling in extreme form: "The next boon they would probably obtain, would be a general naturalization of all their brethren; and then I may venture to prophesy, that the Jews would be the highest bidders for every landed estate brought to market in this island, by which means they might at last get possession of all the lay fees in the kingdom.

"As dominion always will follow property, could we in this case expect they would submit to continue under the disability now proposed to be laid upon them with regard to the estates relating to the church? No, my lords, they would not only repeal this law, but every law for establishing Christianity, and establish Judaism in its stead.

"They might then call this island their own land, and whatever respect some of the superstitious among them might retain for their prophecies, every sensible man would think, they had made a happy exchange; for this island flows as much with milk and honey as the land of Canaan ever did, and it is more secure by being less liable to be invaded by powerful neighbours."

Bedford was well aware that the issue of toleration would be raised, but he was ready for that, too. "The fashion in this country" he said, "at present seems to be, to profess our being free-thinkers; and I do not know but that in the next age the fashion may be, to profess our being Jews; for nothing is more liable to change, nothing can be less governed by reason, than what we call fashion, and it generally starts from one extreme to the other; consequently, might start from Libertinism to Judaism, which I look upon as the two opposite extremes, because of all enthusiasts the Jews have shewn themselves the most obstinate."

Carteret-Granville was inclined to pooh-pooh Bedford's excitement, saying that he felt that the original Naturalization Bill had not been well phrased and that the purpose could have been achieved if the matter had been handled more tactfully. He saw the value of permitting naturalization, within limits, but suggested that the Bill should be repealed in view of public sentiment and that Jewish immigration could then be handled on a quota basis.

In the Commons there was a very evident reflection of the popular clamor. Some members resented the impertinence of the public in criticizing Parliament for passing the Naturalization Bill, and felt that the members should hold their ground as a matter of principle. In general, however, the members took the anti-Jewish position, and the Administration bloc was committed to repeal by Pelham's orders.

In this situation, where little had been said about toleration, Mr. Pitt attempted the difficult feat of taking several positions at once.

He began by deploring the interjection of the religious issue; "I am fully convinced: I believe most gentlemen that hear me are fully convinced, that religion has really nothing to do in the dispute; but the people without doors have been made to believe it has; and upon this the old High Church persecuting spirit has begun to take hold of them."

On the other hand, he thought that it would be wise to repeal a bill which had proved to be so contentious: "We are too wise to dispute this matter with them; as we may upon this occasion evade it without doing any notable injury to the public. But at the same time we ought to let them know, that we think they have been misled; and that the spirit they are at present possessed with, is not a true Christian spirit."

As he crawled out on this limb, he realized that it was shaky, and he tried to explain what the attitude of Parliament should be in explaining itself to the public: "In the present case we ought to treat the people as a prudent father would treat his child: if a peevish perverse boy should insist upon something that was not quite right, but of such a nature as, when granted, could not be attended with any very bad consequence, an indulgent father would comply with the humour of his child, but at the same time he would let him know, that he did so merely out of complaisance, and not because he approved of what the child insisted on. If he did otherwise, his behaviour would be like that of a sycophant servant, and not like that of a prudent and indulgent parent."

As he warmed to his subject, Mr. Pitt evidently thought that he had discovered a plausible line of reasoning and he continued with a presentation in which he at least seemed to be trying to convince himself. "Thus, Sir, though we repeal this law out of complaisance to the people, yet we ought to let them know, that we do not altogether approve of what they ask; and I would desire nothing more for convincing me, that we ought not to approve of it, than what has been admitted by those that have spoken in favour of this amendment."

He began to lay the groundwork for the education of the public on this subject: "They have admitted, that as good Christians we ought not only to wish, but to use our best endeavours for the conversion of all Jews, Turks, and Pagans. Can we use any endeavours for this purpose, unless we converse with them? Can we converse with them, unless we permit them to live and follow their honest employments amongst us? But by our laws, as they stand at present, were they to be strictly put in execution, no alien Jew could easily follow any employment in this country: he cannot export or import any goods without paying the aliens' duty, except only those goods that are exempted by particular acts of Parliament: he cannot so much as take a lease of a house or shop, nor can anyone let him such a lease: and indeed, as Jews are not included in the Toleration Act, no Jew could so much as live in this kingdom, if our laws relating to religion were to be strictly carried into execution."

By this time, he had apparently forgotten his opening statement that the religious issue was not involved, and he continued: "It is true, Sir, neither our ridiculous laws against aliens, nor our persecuting unchristian laws relating to religion, have of late years been carried into execution; but no one can tell when they may; and we cannot expect that any rich Jew will think of settling his family and fortune in this country, when he does not know but that the very next year he may be driven from hence, by the Government resolving to carry all these laws strictly into execution; for from what has now happened it is plain, that in such a resolution the Government would be warmly supported by the people."

All in all, however, Mr. Pitt was not yet ready to reject the demands of the merchants and the public, as much as he disagreed with them; and he concluded: "Therefore I must still think, that the law passed last session in favour of the Jews was in itself right; and I shall now agree to the repeal of it, merely out of complaisance to that enthusiastic spirit that has taken hold of the people; but then I am for letting them know why I do so, and this, as I have said, cannot, I think, be done in a more proper method than by the preamble now under our consideration; for which reason I am against any amendment or alteration."

This ingenious policy of yielding to popular clamor, while attempting to instruct the public gently in the error of its ways, was not successful. The anti-Jewish forces realized that they had Mr. Pitt and the Ministry on the run. Whatever sophistries might have been indulged in, the fact was that the Administration had yielded to the demands for repeal and the anti-Semitic groups decided to press the advantage. An Act passed in 1740 had permitted Jewish settlers in the plantations to become naturalized. This law now became the object of attack, and in the second session of the new Parliament, a motion was introduced to repeal this act also. This was too much for Mr. Pitt. He had yielded reluctantly, once, under pressure, and not without a great deal of mental squirming; but this time the movement found itself breaking against a stone wall.

"Is this to be the first return to Parliament for its condescension in repealing the last Act?" Pitt declaimed in Parliament. "Here the stand must be made or *venit summa dies!* . . . the late clamour, I believe, was only a little election art, which had been given way to genteelly . . . it is the Jew today, it will be the Presbyterians tomorrow; and we shall be sure to have a septennial Church clamour."

Stiffened by Mr. Pitt's moral courage, and resentful of the position which had been previously forced upon it, the Commons defeated the new repeal measure by a large majority; and this decisive stand disposed of the Jewish issue so thoroughly that it ceased to be a political question. For Pitt, the affair had been ultimately a moral victory, but it was a liability to his career. His stand had weakened him, temporarily at least, with the merchants and the masses, and he had gained nothing in his influence with Pelham and Newcastle, who saw that his "nuisance value" had been decreased by his unpopular stand.

CHAPTER XVII

"To Awaken Men"

The year 1754 opened darkly for Mr. Pitt, thanks to Lyttelton's bungling and other causes, though before it closed it became a turning point in his life. Eventful as these months proved to be, at the beginning of the year Pitt was a prisoner of the gout. He had faith in the waters of Bath, and in the advice of his physicians, but neither at the time was able to save him from acute suffering. In January and February he was in such agony that for hours at a time he was incapable of any activity.

His absence from public affairs, moreover, filled him with anxiety. He was unable to press effectively for the greater influence in the Cabinet which he felt was rightfully his. He had not relaxed in his desire for the post of Secretary at War, or an equivalent post. While he had declined to be forced upon the King during the invasion of the Pretender, that very fact entitled him to consideration when the crisis was over. Pitt's assumption, however, that his patriotic gesture of renunciation would commend him to the Throne or to the Cabinet was naïve. There were a host of hungry claimants for office. He already had the sizable post of Paymaster-of-the-Forces, and no one was disposed to advance him further. Indeed, his illness was used as the highly plausible excuse for not burdening him with new duties, and not jeopardizing public business by awarding a chief secretaryship to a man who could barely hobble.

Pitt thought he should be the best judge of his physical capacities, and in that he had good reason. His illness was partly psychological. Indeed, his enemies claimed that he used it conveniently when he chose to be absent from embarrassing scenes, and that he wore the trappings of illness in Parliament to arouse sympathy when he was as well as the next man. These charges were exaggerations based on a modicum of truth. Success often worked upon him as a healing medicine. He was frequently able to conquer or forget ill health in moments when great things were at stake; and again disappointment plunged him into physical as well as mental pain. Had the Government called him to a high post at the beginning of 1754, it is conceivable that Mr. Pitt would have rallied his strength for the occasion, but he was unequal to the task of carrying on vexatious Parliamentary chores while he remained sick at heart as well as in body.

His restless mind, however, could never be entirely idle. While at Bath he steeped himself in hours of reading. He subscribed to Bull's library, and devoured Hume, Locke, Shakespeare, Abernethy's *Sermons,* Thucydides, and Spenser's *Faerie Queene.* When he was too ill to read, he had the library attendant read aloud to him, notably from Josephus' *History of the Jews.* His own library was stocked with works on history, not only of England but of the colonies, including *The State of North America,* Colden's *Indian Nations of Canada,* Labat's *Voyage en Amérique,* Voltaire's *Historie d'Allemagne,* and Grotius' works on international law.

The titles given are typical examples. Some may have been acquired after 1754, and the Grotius was probably a survival from Pitt's studies at the University of Utrecht; but it is known that at this time as well as others he fortified himself with a knowledge of history and the classics. Something of his appraisal of his reading, something of his philosophy of life, in fact, may be gleaned from his letters to his nephew Thomas written during this year. The letters, to be sure, reflect the stuffy customs of the day. It was usual for a man of parts to write letters to a son, or to some other lad, in terms of what was thought good for the boy. Pitt's letters to young Thomas at Cambridge have, at times, the odor of sanctity; yet there are some passages which have individuality, which give an insight into the mind and character of the writer. Notable among these are the paragraphs on politeness in the letter of January 24, 1754:

> Now as to politeness: many have attempted definitions of it. I believe it is best to be known by description; definition not being able to comprise it. I would, however, venture to call it *benevolence in trifles,* or the preference of others to ourselves in little daily, hourly, occurrences in the commerce of life. A better place, a more commodious seat, priority in being helped at table, &c., what is it, but sacrificing ourselves in such trifles to the convenience and pleasure of others?
>
> And this constitutes true politeness. It is a perpetual attention (by habit it grows easy and natural to us) to the little wants of those we are with, by which we either prevent or remove them.
>
> Bowing, ceremonious, formal compliments, stiff civilities, will never be politeness; that must be easy, natural, unstudied, manly, noble. And what will give this, but a mind benevolent, and perpetually attentive to exert that amiable disposition in trifles towards all you converse and live with.
>
> Benevolence in greater matters takes a higher name, and is the queen of virtues. Nothing is so incompatible with politeness as any trick of absence of mind.

In his letter of January 14, Mr. Pitt had dealt with a particular problem of politeness, namely what to do when it seems necessary to contradict someone:

> There is likewise a particular attention required to contradict with good manners; such as, begging pardon, begging leave to doubt, and such like phrases. Pythagoras enjoined his scholars an absolute silence for a long noviciate.
>
> I am far from approving such a taciturnity; but I highly recommend the end and intent of Pythagoras's injunction, which is, to dedicate the first parts of life more to hear and learn, in order to collect materials, out of which to form opinions founded on proper lights and well-examined sound principles, than to be presuming, prompt, and flippant in hazarding one's own slight crude notions of things, and thereby exposing the nakedness and emptiness of the mind—like a house opened to company, before it is fitted either with necessaries, or any ornament for their reception and entertainment.

Another passage in the same letter gave Mr. Pitt's views on religion. It is significant that the advice contained noth-

ing on formal doctrine. Pitt was baptized in the Church
of England, raised in it, and as a member of Parliament
was obliged to be a communicant. The state church, however, had fallen into a condition of spiritual paralysis.
Clergymen owed their posts to political influence. The
grotesque Dr. Ayscough, for example, who had sought the
hand of Ann Pitt, was an election manager for Thomas
Pitt and the Prince of Wales, without any apparent sense
of incongruity. Parallels may be found in all ages, to be
sure, and there were presumably many vicars who were
devout believers; yet it was the general state of apathy
which gave rise to the Wesleys and Whitefields in this period;
and contemporary comment is full of reference to the low
estate of the Church. In any case, Mr. Pitt referred his
nephew to the essence rather than the ritual of the subject,
in almost evangelical terms:

I come now to the part of the advice I have to offer to you,
which most nearly concerns your welfare, and upon which every
good and honourable purpose of your life will assuredly turn; I
mean the keeping up in your heart the true sentiments of religion.
If you are not right towards God, you can never be so towards
man: the noblest sentiment of the human breast is here brought
to the test. Is gratitude in the number of a man's virtues? If it
be, the highest benefactor demands the warmest returns of gratitude, love, and praise. "Ingratum qui dixerit, omnia dixit." *

If a man wants this virtue where there are infinite obligations to excite and quicken it, he will be likely to want all others
towards his fellow-creatures, whose utmost gifts are poor compared to those he daily receives at the hands of his never-failing
Almighty Friend. "Remember thy Creator in the days of thy
youth," is big with the deepest wisdom: "The fear of the Lord
is the beginning of wisdom; and, an upright heart, that is understanding."

This is eternally true, whether the wits and rakes of Cambridge allow it or not: nay, I must add of this religious wisdom,
"Her ways are ways of pleasantness, and all her paths are peace,"
whatever your young gentlemen of pleasure think of a whore and
a bottle, a tainted health and battered constitution.

Hold fast, therefore, by this sheet-anchor of happiness, reli-

* "To be called ingrate is complete condemnation."

gion: you will often want it in the times of most danger; the storms and tempests of life. Cherish true religion as preciously as you will fly with abhorrence and contempt superstition and enthusiasm.* The first is the perfection and glory of the human nature; the two last the deprivation and disgrace of it. Remember, the essence of religion is, a heart void of offense, towards God and man; not subtle speculative opinions, but an active vital principle of faith.

In addition to recommendations on conduct and belief, Mr. Pitt had definite notions on education. He was clearly not a pure classicist, and his syllabus was somewhat similar to the arts curriculum in colleges a hundred years later. How ardently Pitt felt on this question is open to conjecture. He loved neither Eton nor Oxford where he had attended. His own education was largely self-directed. He may have felt the lack of a formal basis in his own studies. Though he was no special student of teaching, he desired Thomas to persuade his tutor to agree to a given course of study, that certain books be read, "and such only." The books were listed unequivocally in the letter of January 12, 1754:

They are as follows: Euclid; a course of Logic: a course of experimental Philosophy; Locke's *Conduct of the Understanding;* his treatise also on the *Understanding;* his *Treatises on Government,* and *Letters on Toleration.* I desire, for the present, no books of poetry but Horace and Virgil: of Horace the *Odes,* but above all, the *Epistles* and *Ars Poetica.* These parts, *"nocturna versate manu, versate diurna."* ** Tully † *De Officiis, De Amicitia, De Senectute;* his Catilinarian *Orations* and *Philippics.* Sallust. At leisure hours, an abridgment of the *History of England* to be run through, in order to settle in the mind a general chronological order and series of principal events, and succession of kings.

Proper books of English history, on the true principles of our happy Constitution, shall be pointed out afterwards. Burnet's *History of the Reformation,* abridged by himself, to be read with great care. Father Paul on beneficiary Matters, in English.

---

* According to Murray's *New Oxford Dictionary,* "enthusiasm" in the eighteenth century meant ill-regulated or misdirected religious emotion.
** Study night and day.
† Quintus Tullius Cicero.

A French master, and only Molière's plays to be read with him, or by yourself, till you have gone through them all.
Spectators, especially Mr. Addison's papers, to be read very frequently at broken times in your room. I make it my request, that you will forbear drawing totally while you are at Cambridge, and not meddle with Greek, otherwise than to know a little the etymology of words in Latin, or English, or French; nor to meddle with Italian.

It should be said for Mr. Pitt, however, that the proposed curriculum was merely the basis for advanced study, for he added:

I hope this little course will soon be run through. I intend it as a general foundation for many things, of infinite utility, to come as soon as this is finished.

Young Thomas replied to all these admonitions with the respectful acquiescence which was required from the young to their elders in the eighteenth century. Of the uncle's devotion there can be little doubt. When Thomas Pitt, the father, was unable to continue to support his son at the University a year later, Uncle William assumed the obligation. Young Thomas, however, may not have returned the affection. If he did at the time, it soured later, for as Lord Camelford he wrote a memoir which vilified his uncle in many particulars, though Camelford treated his aunts and parents with similar vitriol and may have been merely exercising the family habit of mutual denunciation. To be just to Camelford, it should also be said that in later years he paid his father's debts, provided portions for his sisters and had a creditable record in politics. Apparently, he profited by his uncle's advice, even if critical of the donor.

Fortunately, in this dark time of Mr. Pitt's ill health and poor political prospects, his sisters were in a state of apparent quiescence. Ann was in France for her health, and Betty had gone to Florence, Italy.

Mary, the youngest sister, who had been born after the days of Mawarden Court, was now active in London circles and gratifyingly showed her individuality by being a credit to the family. Pitt's friend Mrs. Montagu said of her at this time: "Miss Mary·Pitt, youngest sister of Mr. Pitt, is come to stay a few days with me; she is a very sensible, modest, pretty sort of a young woman, and as Mr. Pitt seems to take every civility shown her as a favour, I thought this mark of respect to her one manner of returning my obligations to him."

The year had begun gloomily, and then occurred an unexpected and untoward event which called Mr. Pitt to action. On March 9, 1754, he wrote to Ann:

> DEAR SISTER,—I write to you under the greatest affliction, on all Considerations Private and Publick. Mr. Pelham died Wednesday morning, of a Feaver and St. Anthony's fire.* This Loss is, in my notion of things, irreparable to the Publick. I am still suffering much Pain with Gout in both feet, and utterly unable To be carry'd to London. I may hope to be the better for it hereafter, but I am at present rather worn down than reliev'd by it: I am extremely concern'd at the last accounts of your health. I hope you have Spring begun at Nevers, which I pray God may relieve you.
>
> I am Dear Sister, Your most affectionate Brother,
>
> W. PITT.

Pelham's death was, indeed, catastrophic, for there was no one of equal character available to take his place. Pelham was not brilliant, he had no high conception of England's destiny, but he was diligent, tolerant, and a man of his word. He was a firm Constitutionalist, ready to forego office and daring to discipline the King if principle were at stake, and yet he was cordially willing to consider the advice of friend or enemy. He had been able to conciliate many factions, because all could rely on his integrity. His death caused a bankruptcy in Cabinet morale, and Pitt felt that the moment had come for himself and others of the Grenville-Temple connection to direct the affairs of state.

Mr. Pitt's self-esteem in the circumstances was fully justified. Without the guiding hand of Henry Pelham, the Duke of Newcastle, now the chief figure in the Ministry,

* Erysipelas.

was a deplorable bungler. He loved personal power, resisted parting with a shred of it, and yet had no notion of how to use it. His chief confidant was Lord Hardwicke who had been Lord Chancellor since 1741. Hardwicke was a wise and mellow friend who had the respect of his fellows and had survived many changes of administration. His pen was active in placating foes. He lent his influence to conferences, soothed wounded feelings, had real gifts as a negotiator, and yet remained in the background, evidently preferring the security of his post to the responsibilities of leadership. Hardwicke was no barrier to Mr. Pitt's ambitions and was cordially disposed to his advancement.

While Newcastle commanded the largest following, the Pitt-Grenville contingent had the talent for government which was now acutely needed. Carteret and Bath were wholly discredited. Bedford and Henry Fox represented factions which were too small to dominate unless they could win allies. Fox was popular, a good mixer, and a thorough journeyman politician. He might lead as a compromise candidate, even though he would never be one to arouse the country, to restore England's prestige, or to hold George II in proper check.

Though the logic of events called for Mr. Pitt and the Grenville group to head the Government, the situation was delicate. Pitt was sitting in Parliament from Aldborough, one of Newcastle's districts. This was doubly a favor, for it was a more secure berth than that of Seaford, where Pitt had had election troubles seven years before. Under the circumstances, any outright defiance of Newcastle would be bad ethics and would be charged to ingratitude. Moreover, Pitt and his associates were hoping for control of the Ministry while they were already a part of it in minor capacities. If through bad judgment they should be forced to resign, they might lose the opportunity of the great moment. Pitt was well aware that his group could win only by sagacity, luck, and a sufficient recognition by King and Cabinet that Pitt was the man needed to organize them.

Pelham had died on March 6, and two succeeding incidents had given hope to Mr. Pitt. Within a few hours, Henry Fox had called at his London home. Though Pitt was at Bath and could not know what this might signify, it at least indicated that Fox regarded Pitt as a key man in the crisis. Similarly, when the Princess of Wales made inquiry as to his health, the fact suggested that the Regency were thinking of Mr. Pitt's importance in Government.

Pitt was greatly perturbed that he could not summon strength to go to London to conduct negotiations personally; but between March 6 and April 8, 1754, he did manage to write twenty-two letters to his lieutenants, to Newcastle, and to others concerned in the revision of the Cabinet.

The letters were masterpieces of political maneuvering, of feeling one's way, feinting, releasing trial balloons. They illustrate the quagmires which may be in the path of the most alert public figures. Oratory, statesmanship, and magnetism may command public applause, but Pitt found that generalship was equally important. If he could not himself take to the field, because of ill health, the next best thing was to guide someone to act for him.

Pitt's chief reliance was on Sir George Lyttelton, in spite of the incident of the mixed letters. He trusted Lyttelton's loyalty, even if he feared his judgment. Pitt's brother had married Lyttelton's sister. Lyttelton had been Pitt's lifelong friend and champion. Pitt might have asked Temple to serve as his ambassador, but this was a matter in which the choice of a leader from the Commons was to be considered, and Earl Temple's seat in the Lords would not be very helpful. George Grenville might have been an emissary, but he was a stolid plodding fellow who had no gift for finesse, and Pitt looked to Lyttelton as his most devoted follower who would have the most zeal for his cause. Accordingly on March 7, Mr. Pitt addressed "Sir George Lyttelton and the Grenville brothers" on a program of action.

"MY DEAREST FRIENDS,—I will offer to the consideration of my friends but two things: the object to be wished for, the public; and the means; which the object itself seems to suggest; for the pursuit of it, my own object for the public, is, to support the King in quiet as long as he may have to live; and to strengthen the hands of the Princess of Wales, as much as may be, in order to maintain her power in the Government, in case of the misfortune of the King's demise. The means, as I said, suggest themselves: an union of all those in action who are really already united in their wishes as to the object: this might easily be effected, but it is my opinion, it will certainly not be done.

"As to the nomination of a Chancellor of the Exchequer. Mr. Fox in point of party, seniority in the Corps, and I think ability for Treasury and House of Commons business stands, upon the whole, first of any.

"Dr. Lee* if his health permits is Papabilis, and in some views very desirable. *Te Quinte Catule,* my dear George Grenville, would be my nomination.

"A fourth idea [about the Chancellorship of the Exchequer] I will mention, which, if practicable and worth the person's while, might have great strength and efficiency for Government in it, and be perfectly adapted to the main future contingent object, could it be tempered so as to reconcile the Whigs to it: I mean to secularise, if I may use the expression, the Solicitor General,† and make him Chancellor of the Exchequer. I call this an idea only; but I think it not visionary, were it accompanied by proper temperaments. I write these thoughts for Lord Temple, his brothers' and Sir George Lyttelton's consideration only, or rather as a communication of my first thoughts, upon an emergency that has too much importance and delicacy, as well as danger in it, to whoever delivers their opinion freely, to be imparted any farther.

"I am utterly unable to travel, nor can guess when I shall be able: this situation is most unfortunate. I am overpowered with gout, rather than relieved, but expect to be better for it. My dear friends overrate infinitely the im-

* Sir William Lee, then Lord Chief Justice of the King's Bench. Pitt may have been alluding to the bench in using the term Papabilis.
† William Murray.

portance of my health, were it established: something I might weigh in such a scale as the present, but you, who have health to act, cannot fail to weigh much, if united in views.

"I will join you the first moment I am able, for letters cannot exchange one's thoughts upon matters so complicated, extensive and delicate.

"I don't a little wonder I have had no express from another quarter.

"I repeat again, that what I have said are the breakings of first thoughts, to be confined to you four; and the looseness, and want of form in them, to be, I trust, excused in consideration of the state of mind and body of

Your ever most affectionate,
W. PITT"

Mr. Pitt was obviously speaking in riddles, vaguely, fearing that his letter might fall into the wrong hands, or that Lyttelton rashly might quote him. But it was equally dangerous if Lyttelton did not understand him. What was the real strength of Fox? How sincere were the compliments which had been paid to the Pitt group, and how could they command public confidence unless they had adequate public recognition? The ground must be felt out along these lines; and Pitt, therefore, added a postscript:

"As nothing is so delicate and dangerous, as every word uttered upon the present *unexplained* state of things,—I mean *unexplained,* as to the King's inclinations towards Mr. Fox, and his real desire to have his own act of Regency, as it is called, maintained in the hands of the Princess; too much caution, reserve, and silence cannot be observed towards any who come to fish or sound your dispositions, without authority to make direct propositions.

"If eyes are really turned towards any connection of men, as a resource against dangers apprehended, that set of men cannot, though willing, answer the expectation without countenance, and additional consideration and weight added to them, by marks of Royal favour, one of the connection put into the Cabinet, and called to a real participation of councils and business. How our little connection has stood at all, under all depression and discountenance, or has an existence in the eyes of the public, I don't understand: that it should continue to do so, without an attribution of some new strength and consideration, arising from a real share in Government, I have difficulty to believe.

"I am, however, resolved to listen to no suggestions of certain feelings, however founded, but to go as straight as my poor judgment will direct me, to the sole object of public good.

"I don't think quitting of offices at all advisable, for public or private accounts: but as to answering any further purposes in the House of Commons, that must depend on the King's will and pleasure to enable us so to do."

As Pitt thought further on the matter he was increasingly concerned lest the gawky, none too skilful Lyttelton upset the negotiations somehow, and he was moved to write a note of caution to Temple on the subject:

"MY DEAR LORD,—I return my answer to Jemmy's † and Sir George's dispatch directed to you, and accompany it with this line to give you my apprehensions of Sir George's want of discretion and address, in such soundings as will be, and have been, made upon him, with regard to the disposition of his friends.

"I beg your Lordship will be so good to convene your brothers and Sir George, and communicate my letter to them which is addressed to you jointly. It is a most untoward circumstance that I cannot set out immediately to join you. I am extremely crippled and worn down with pain, which still continues. I make what efforts I can, and am carried out to breathe a little air. I write this hardly legible scrawl in my chaise.

"Let me recommend to my dear Lord to preach prudence and reserve to our friend Sir George, and if he can, to inspire him with his own.

† James Grenville, one of Temple's brothers.

"I heard some time since that the Princess inquired after my health; an honour which I received with much pleasure, as not void, perhaps of some meaning.

"I have writ more today than my weak state, under such a shock, as the news of today will well permit.

Believe me, my dearest Lord,
Ever most affectionately yours,
W. PITT."

"Fox will be Chancellor of the Exchequer, notwithstanding any reluctancy to yield to it in the Ministers; George Grenville may be offered Secretary at War; I am sure he ought to be so.   I advise his acceptance.   The Chancellor * is the only resource; his wisdom, temper, and authority, joined to the Duke of Newcastle's ability as Secretary of State, are the dependance for Government.   The Duke of Newcastle alone is feeble, this not to Sir George."

Pitt in referring to Newcastle's "ability as Secretary of State," with the addition that "Newcastle alone is feeble," put his finger on the nub of the matter.   Alone Newcastle was helpless; Hardwicke was his moral prop.   Yet with a prop, Newcastle's patronage-dispensing abilities were the controlling influence.   Pitt could not resist making that point to Temple, but he dared not disclose it to Lyttelton.

Lyttelton started off well enough in his efforts, but was confronted with queries from Hardwicke, as to what the position of the Pitt group would be, and that brought forth further elaboration from Pitt in the form of two letters, the first a private schedule of instructions for Lyttelton's eyes only, the second the letter to be shown to Hardwicke.

The private letter:

Bath, Mar. 10, 1754

"DEAR LYTTELTON,—I am much obliged to you for your dispatch, and am highly satisfied with the necessary reserve you have kept with respect to the dispositions of yourself and friends.   Indeed, the conjuncture itself, and more es-

* Hardwicke, the Lord Chancellor.

pecially our peculiar situation, require much caution and measure in all our answers, in order to act like honest men, who determine to adhere to the public great object; as well as men who would not be treated like children. I am far from meaning to recommend a sullen, dark, much less a double conduct.

"All I mean is to lay down a plan to ourselves; which is, to support the King's Government in present, and maintain the Princess's authority and power in a future, contingency. As a necessary consequence of this system, I wish to see as little power in Fox's hands as possible, because he is incompatible with the main part, and indeed of the whole, of this plan; but I mean not to open myself to whoever pleases to sound my dispositions, with regard to persons especially, and by premature declarations deprive ourselves of the only chance we have of deriving any consideration to ourselves from the mutual fears and animosities of different factions in court: and expose ourselves to the resentment and malice in the *closet* * of the one without stipulations or security for the good offices and weight of the other there in our favour. . . .

"I would be open and explicit (but only on proper occasions) 'that, I was most willing to support his Majesty's Government upon such a proper plan as I doubted not his Majesty, by the advice of his Ministers, would frame; in order to supply, the best that may be, the irreparable loss the King has sustained in Mr. Pelham's death: in order to secure the King ease for his life and future security to his family and to the kingdom. . . .'

"This and the like, which may be vary'd for ever, is answer enough to any *sounder*. As to any things said by Principals in personal conference, as that of the Chancellor [Hardwicke] with you, another manner of talking will be proper, though still conformable to the same private plan which you shall resolve to pursue.

"Professions of personal regard cannot be made too strongly; but as to matter, generals are to be answered with generals; particulars, if you are led into them, need not at

* Closet: viz.:—in private audiences with the King.

all be shunn'd; and if treated with common prudence and presence of mind, can not be greatly used to a man's prejudice; if he says nothing that implies specific engagements, without knowing specifically what he is to trust to reciprocally. Within these limitations, it seems to me, that a man whose intentions are clear and right, may talk without putting himself at another's mercy or offending him by a dark and mysterious reserve.

"I think it best to throw my answer to the Chancellor into a separate piece of paper, that you may send it to his Lordship. I am sorry to be forced to answer in writing, because, not seeing the party, it is not possible to throw in necessary qualifications and additions or retractions, according to the impression things make.

"As far as, my dear Lyttelton, you are so good to relate your several conversations upon the present situation, I highly applaud your prudence. I hope you neither have nor will drop a word of menace, and that you will always bear in mind that my personal connection with the Duke of Newcastle has a peculiar circumstance, which yours and that of your friends has not. One cannot be too explicit in conversing at this unhappy distance on matters of this delicate and critical nature.

"I will, therefore, commit tautology, and repeat what I said in my former dispatch, viz., that it enters not the least into my plans to intimate quitting the King's service; giving trouble, if not satisfied, to Government. The essence of it exists in this: attachment to the King's service, and zeal for the ease and quiet of his life, and stability and strength to future government under the Princess; this declared openly and explicitly *to the ministers*.

"The reserve I would use should be with regard to listing in particular subdivisions, and thereby not freeing persons from those fears which will alone quicken them to give us some consideration for their own sakes: but this is to be done *negatively* only, by eluding explicit declarations with regard to persons especially; but by *intimations of a possibility of our following our resentments;* for, indeed, dear

Sir George, I am determined not to go into faction.* Upon the whole, the mutual fears in Court open to our connexion some room for importance and weight, in the course of affairs: in order to profit by this situation, we must not be out of office: and the strongest argument of all to enforce that is, that Fox is too odious to last for ever, and G. Grenville must be next nominated under any Government.
I am too lame to move.
Your ever affectionate,
W. PITT."

The letter to be shown to Hardwicke by Sir George Lyttelton, as stating Pitt's position:

"MY DEAR SIR GEORGE,—I beg you will be so good to assure my Lord Chancellor, in my name, of my most humble services and many very grateful acknowledgements for his Lordship's obliging wishes for my health. . . . I can never sufficiently express the high sense I have of the great honours of my Lord Chancellor's much too favourable opinion of his humble servant; but I am so truly and deeply conscious of so many of my wants in Parliament and out of it, to supply in the smallest degree this irreparable loss [the death of Pelham] that I can say with much truth were my health restored and his Majesty brought from the dearth of subjects to hear of my name for so great a charge, I should wish to decline the honour, even though accompany'd with the attribution of all the weight and strength which the good opinion and confidence of the master cannot fail to add to a servant; but under impressions in the Royal mind towards me, the reverse of these, what must be the vanity which would attempt it? These prejudices, however so successfully suggested and hitherto so unsuccessfully attempted to be removed, shall not abate my zeal for his Majesty's service, though they have so effectually disarmed me of all means of being useful to it.

"I need not suggest to his Lordship that consideration and weight in the House of Commons arises generally but

* [viz.: not to leave the Ministry and join the Opposition.]

from one of two causes—the protection and countenance of the Crown, visibly manifested by marks of Royal favour at Court, or from weight in the country, sometimes arising from opposition to the public measures. This latter sort of consideration it is a great satisfaction to me to reflect I parted with, as soon as I became convinced there might be danger to the family from pursuing opposition any further; * and I need not say I have not had the honour to receive any of the former since I became the King's servant. . . . Perhaps some of my friends may not labour under all the prejudices that I do. I have reason to believe that they do not: in that case should Mr. Fox be Chancellor of the Exchequer, the Secretary at War is to be filled up. . . ."

Speaking even this plainly was perhaps dangerous, for Pitt did not wish to ask flatly for the Secretaryship at War and then be refused; yet Hardwicke was the safest man to know his true sentiments. Hardwicke was a realist and would have no urge to embarrass Mr. Pitt. Nevertheless Pitt was worried, and again consulted Temple, taking the opportunity to make further suggestions on their program:

"MY DEAREST LORD,—I hope you will not disapprove my answer to Lord Chancellor. I include in you your brothers, for your Lordship's name is Legion. You will see the answer contains my whole poor plan; the essence of which is to talk modestly, to declare attachment to the *King's* Government, and the future plan *under the Princess,* neither to intend nor intimate the quitting the service, to give no terrors by talking big, to make no declarations of thinking ourselves free by Mr. Pelham's death, to look out and fish in troubled waters, and perhaps to help trouble them in order to fish the better: but to profess and to resolve *bona fide* to act like public men in a dangerous conjuncture for our country, and support Government when they will please to settle it: to let them see we shall do this

* Refers to Pitt's support of George II against the Stuart uprising.

from *principles of public good,* not as the *bubbles* of a few fair words, without effects (all this civilly), and to be collected by them, not expressed by us; to leave them under the impression of their own fears and resentments, the only friends we shall ever have at Court, but to say not a syllable which can scatter terrors or imply menaces.

"Their fears will increase by what we *avoid saying concerning persons* (though what I think of Fox, etc., is much fixed), and by *saying very explicitly,* as I have (but civilly), that we have our eyes open to our situation at Court, and the foul play we have had offered us in the Closet: to wait the working of all these things in offices, the best we can have, but in offices.

"My judgment tells me, my dear Lord, that this simple plan steadily pursued will once again, before it be long, give some weight to a connexion, long depressed, and yet still not annihilated. Mr. Fox's having called at my door early the morning Mr. Pelham died is, I suppose, no secret, and a lucky incident, in my opinion. I have a post letter from the Duke of Newcastle, a very obliging one. I heartily pity him, he suffers a great deal for his loss.

"Give me leave to recommend to your Lordship a little gathering of friends about you at dinners, without ostentation. Stanley,* who will be in Parliament: some attention to Sir Richard Lyttelton I should think proper; a dinner to the Yorkes ** very seasonable; and, before things are settled, any of the Princess of Wales' Court. John Pitt *** not to be forgot: I know the Duke of B——**** nibbles at him: in short *liez commerce* with as many members of Parliament, who may be open to our purposes, as your Lordship can.

"Pardon, my dear Lord, all this freedom, but the conjuncture is made to awaken men, and there is room for action. I have no doubt George Grenville's turn must come.

* Hans Stanley, who was sitting for the Tory interest in Southampton. This is an indication that Pitt was thinking of adding the Tory minority to his group. Though Stanley later was allied with Pitt he always retained his Tory connection.
** The sons of Lord Hardwicke.
*** Mr. Pitt's cousin, M.P. from Encombe.
**** Bedford.

Fox is odious, and will have difficulty to stand in a future time. I mend a little. I cannot express my impatience to be with you.

W. PITT."

"To awaken men," there was the keynote of Pitt's doctrine, the basic strength of his position. While others were working chiefly for the purpose of holding office, Pitt was conscious that England's welfare was threatened within and without. There was no definition of foreign policy, no sense of national duty at home. The King, whose European interests were centered around the protection of Hanover, was bored by domestic issues, and with the death of Pelham the Cabinet had no one who could offer leadership. "To awaken men" was a vital concern, if England were to be more than a little bungling province, an adjunct of European chancellories, virtually a forgotten land. Somnolence and inertia had been her guides over a steady decline for many years past. Without doubt there was "room for action," and Mr. Pitt was the man to bring it to pass.

In this critical moment, Lyttelton conducted negotiations while Pitt waited impatiently for news of events; and Lyttelton, as Pitt had feared, fumbled the ball. The crafty Newcastle, afraid only of Pitt, was willing to placate the Grenville connection at a reasonable price. He explained to Lyttelton, first of all, that Mr. Pitt was unacceptable to his Majesty. This excuse was of long standing. Newcastle stuck to his story, and he had had much practice in the telling of it. He had no objection to others of the Grenville group, and Lyttelton was slated for Cofferer of the Household, while George Grenville was named for Treasurer of the Navy.

Lyttelton accepted the deal, and it was a cheap price, for neither post was a major Cabinet office. Worst of all, of course, it left Pitt, the Grenvilles' source of strength, on the sidelines. After it was all concluded, Lyttelton himself apparently had misgivings. He delayed writing to Pitt until the 18th of March, and even then asked Grenville if he should do so.

Lyttelton's misjudgment was underscored by still another circumstance. Fox had been appointed Secretary of State as everyone had expected, but Newcastle had refused to delegate any power to Fox or even apprise him of which Parliament members were under obligations to the Cabinet. This was intolerable even to as callous and indifferent a politician as Fox, and he promptly resigned the office. Had Lyttelton followed instructions, remained coy, asked leave to consult his friends, the situation would have been exactly what the Grenvilles needed. If the Grenvilles had not been comprised, Newcastle could not have ignored Pitt, now that Fox was disgruntled. As it was, Newcastle continued to neglect Mr. Pitt and appointed Sir Thomas Robinson in Fox's place. Robinson was an amiable protégé of the Duke who had spent most of his life abroad, knew almost nothing of procedure in the House of Commons, and, accordingly, suited Newcastle perfectly.

Mr. Pitt at Bath, torn with pains and anxiety, received Lyttelton's report in horrified astonishment. He had expected that Lyttelton might be indiscreet, but he had not looked for betrayal; and to Pitt it seemed to be just that. Poor Lyttelton had believed that something was better than nothing. He worshiped Pitt, wanted to help him, and simply had been outsmarted; but Pitt was stung to the heart and could regard Lyttelton only as his enemy. Yet in the midst of this heartburn, stunned by the rebuff which had been administered to him personally while his colleagues were honored, Pitt had the sense to write Newcastle in terms which moved the timorous Duke to wails of apprehension. He congratulated Newcastle on succeeding to Pelham's post as First Lord of the Treasury. He admitted no disloyalty in the Grenville ranks, deplored his own situation, and allowed himself for the first time in silken words to express a note of "menace":

"MY LORD DUKE,—I have heard with the highest satisfaction by a message from Sr. George Lyttelton the effectual proofs of his Majesty's great kindness and firm confidence in your Grace for the conduct of his Govern-

ment. You have certainly taken most wisely the Province
of the Treasury to yourself, where the powers of Government reside, and which at this particular crisis of a General
Election may lay the foundations of the future political
system so fast as not to be shaken hereafter. But this will
depend upon many concomitant circumstances. For the
present the nation may say with consolation, *uno avulso non
deficit alter aureus.*

"The power of the Purse in the hands of the same family
may, I trust, be so used as to fix all other power there along
with it. Amidst all the real satisfaction I feel on this great
measure so happily taken, it is with infinite reluctance that
I am forced to return to the mortifying situation of your
Grace's humblest servant and to add some few considerations to those which, I have the satisfaction to learn from
Sr. George Lyttelton, had the honour to be receiv'd by your
Grace and my Lord Chancellor without disapprobation.

"The difficulties grow so fast upon me by the repetition
and multiplication of most painful and too visible humilia-
tions that my small store of prudence suggests no longer
to me any means of colouring them to the world; nor of
repairing them to my own mind consistently with my unshaken purpose to do nothing on any provocation to disturb
the quiet of the King and the ease and stability of present
and future Government.

"Permit, my Lord, a man, whose affectionate attachment
to your Grace, I believe, you don't doubt, to expose simply
to your view of his situation, and then let me entreat your
Grace (if you can divest your mind of the great disparity between us) to transport yourself for a moment into my place.

"From the time I had the honour to come into the King's
service, I have never been wanting in my most zealous endeavours in Parliament on the points that laboured the
most, those of military discipline and foreign affairs; nor
have I differ'd on any whatever, but the too small number
of seamen one year, which was admitted to be so the next;
and on a crying complaint against General Anstruther: for
these crimes how am I punish'd?

"Be the want of subjects ever so great and the force of

the conjuncture ever so cogent, be my best friends and pro-
tectors ever so much at the head of Government, an indelible
negative is fixed against my name. Since I had the honour
to return that answer to the Chancellor which your Grace
and his Lordship were pleas'd not to disapprove, how have
mortifications been multiply'd upon me. One Chancellor of
the Exchequer over me was at that time destin'd, Mr. Fox:
since that time a second, Mr. Legge, is fixt: a Secretary of
State is next to be look'd for in the House of Commons;
Mr. Fox is again put over me and destin'd to that office:
he refuses the seals: Sir Thomas Robinson is immediately
put over me and is now in possession of that great office.

"I sincerely think both these high employments much
better fill'd than I could supply either of them in many
respects. Mr. Legge I truly and cordially esteem and love.
Sir Thos. Robinson, with whom I have not the honour to
live in the same intimacy, I sincerely believe to be a gentleman of much worth and ability. Nevertheless I will venture to appeal to your Grace's candour and justice whether
upon such feeble pretensions as twenty years' use of Parliament may have given me, I have not some cause to feel (as
I do most deeply) so many repeated and visible humilia-
tions.

"I have troubled your Grace so long on this painful subject that I may have nothing disagreeable to say, when I
have the honour to wait on you; as well as that I think it
fit your Grace shou'd know the whole heart of a faithful
servant, who is conscious of nothing towards your Grace
which he wishes to conceal from you.

"In my degraded situation in Parliament, an active part
there I am sure your Grace is too equitable to desire me to
take; for otherwise than as an associate and in equal rank
with those charg'd with Government there, I never can
take such a part.

"I will confess I had flatter'd myself that the interests
of your Grace's own power were so concern'd to bring
forward an instrument of your own raising in the House of
Commons that you cou'd not let pass this decisive occasion
without surmounting in the Royal mind the unfavourable

impressions I have the unhappiness to be under; and that the seals (at least when refus'd by Mr. Fox) might have been destin'd as soon as an opening cou'd be made in the King's mind in my favour instead of being immediately put into other hands.

"Things standing as they do, whether I can continue in office without losing myself in the opinion of the world is become a matter of very painful doubt to me. If anything can colour with any air of decency such an acquiescence, it can only be the consideration given to my friends and some degree of softening obtain'd in his Majesty's mind towards me.

"Mr. Pelham destin'd Sir George Lyttelton to be cofferer, whenever that office shou'd open, and there can be no shadow of difficulty in Mr. Grenville being made Treasurer of the Navy.

"Weighed in the fair scale of usefulness to the King's business in Parliament, they can have no competitors that deserve to stand in their way. I have submitted these things to your Grace with a frankness you had hitherto been so good to tolerate in me, however inferior.

"I wou'd not have done it so fully for my own regard alone, were I not certain that your Grace's interests are more concern'd in it than mine: because I am most sure that my mind carries me more strongly towards retreat than towards courts and business. Indeed, My Lord, the inside of the House must be consider'd in other respects besides merely numbers, or the reins of Government will soon slip or be wrested out of any minister's hands.

"If I have spoken too freely, I humbly beg your Grace's pardon: and entreat you to impute my freedom to the most sincere and unalterable attachment of a man who never will conceal his heart, and who can complain without alienation of mind and remonstrate without resentment.

I have the honour to be, etc., etc.,

W. PITT.

"I cannot hope to leave Bath in less than a week. My health seems much mended by my gout."

One sentence in the letter was particularly ominous, because inescapably true: "the inside of the House must be consider'd in other respects besides merely numbers, or the reins of Government will soon slip or be wrested out of any minister's hands." Newcastle could not fail to understand the meaning of that. Walpole had had numbers, so had Carteret. The mere majority of votes would not, over the long haul, be enough, if Newcastle were unwilling to recognize men with a capacity for leadership. Moreover, it was Mr. Pitt who had "wrested the reins" from ministers in the past.

Newcastle was neither as hard-boiled as Walpole nor as urbane as Carteret, and the dark prophecies of Mr. Pitt threw him into a bad state of nerves. He called upon Hardwicke to placate the terrible invalid of Bath. He himself endeavored to assure Pitt of his devotion with what Pitt called a "beautiful foliage of fine words."

Very well, Mr. Pitt was not irreconcilable, and addressed the Duke again on the 4th of April:

"MY LORD DUKE,—I was honour'd with your Grace's letter of the 2nd inst. yesterday evening. How shall I find words to express my sense of the great condescension and kindness of expression with which it is writ? It would be making but an ill return to so much goodness, were I to go back into the disagreeable subject that has occasion'd your Grace so much trouble, and wou'd be tearing and wounding your good nature to little purpose.

"Whatever my sensations are, it is sufficient that I have once freely laid them before you, and that your Grace has had the indulgence to pardon that freedom, which I thought I used both to your Grace and myself.

"As for the rest, my attachment shall be ever found as unalterable to Government as my inability to be of any material use to it is become manifest to all the world. I will enter again, but for a word or two, into a subject your Grace shall be troubled no more with. It is most obliging to suggest as consolations to me that I might have been much more mortify'd under another management than un-

der the present: but I will freely own I shou'd have felt
myself far less personally humiliated, had Mr. Fox been
placed by the King's favour at the head of the House of
Commons, than I am at present: in that case the necessity wou'd have been apparent: the ability of the subject
wou'd in some degree have warranted the thing.

"I shou'd indeed have been much mortify'd for your
Grace and for my Lord Chancellor: very little for my own
particular. Cou'd Mr. Murray's situation have allow'd
him to be placed at the head of the House of Commons, I
shou'd have served under him with the greatest pleasure:
I acknowledge as much as the rest of the world do his superiority in every respect.

"My mortification arises not from silly pride, but from
being evidently excluded by a negative personal to me (now
and for ever) flowing from a displeasure utterly irremovable. As to the office of Chancellor of the Exchequer, I
hope your Grace cannot think me fill'd with so impertinent
a vanity as to imagine it a disparagement to me to serve
under the Duke of Newcastle at the head of the Treasury;
but, my Lord, had I been proposed for that honour and
the King been, once reconciled to the thought of me, my
honour wou'd have been saved and I shou'd with pleasure
have declin'd, the charge in favour of Mr. Legge from a
just regard to his Majesty's service.

"I know my health, at best, is too precarious a thing to
expose his Majesty's affairs in Parliament to suffer delay,
perhaps in the middle of a session by being in such improper
hands. As to the other great office, [Secretary at War]
many circumstances of it render an uninterrupted health not
so absolutely necessary to the discharge of it. Were I to
fail in it from want of health, or, what is still more likely,
from want of ability and a sufficient knowledge of foreign
affairs, a fitter person might at any time be substituted without material inconvenience to publick business.

"To conclude, my Lord, and to release your Grace from
a troublesome correspondent, give me leave to recur to your
Grace's equity and candour: when the suffrage of the party
in one instance, and a higher nomination, the Royal designa-

tion in another, operate to the eternal precluding of a man's name being so much as brought in question, what reasonable wish can remain for a man so circumstanced (under a first resolution, on no account to disturb Government) but that of a decent retreat, a retreat of respect, not resentment: of despair of being ever accepted to equal terms with others, be his poor endeavours ever so zealous.

"Very few have been the advantages and honours of my life: but among the first of them I shall ever esteem the honour of your Grace's good opinion: to that good opinion and protection I recommend myself: and hope from it that some retreat, neither disagreeable nor dishonourable, may (when practicable) be open'd to me.

"I see with great joy Sr. George Lyttelton and Mr. Grenville in this arrangement, where they ought to be. I am persuaded they will be of the greatest advantage to your Grace's system. They are both connected in friendship with Mr. Legge and with Mr. Murray, who in effect is the greatest strength of it in Parliament. May every kind of satisfaction and honour attend your Grace's labours for his Majesty's service. I have the honour, etc. etc.

W. PITT

"I wrote your Grace by the Post ye 2nd inst., which I hope came to your hands."

Mr. Pitt had left the door open for Newcastle to offer belated recognition; but he did not rely on such hopes. The time had come "to awaken men" and the Government might as well know it. In this situation Pitt chose finally to express his thoughts in a letter to Lyttelton,—if they should indiscreetly be passed along to others so much the better:

"I am really compelled, by every reason fit for a man to listen to, to resist (as to the point of activity in Parliament) farther than I like to do. I have intimated retreat and pointed out such a one in general as I shall really like. Resolved not to disturb Government; I desire to be released from the oar of Parliamentary drudgery. I am (un)willing to sit there and be ready to be called out into action when the Duke of Newcastle's personal friends might require, or Government should deign to employ me as an instrument. I am not fond of making speeches (though some may think I am). I never cultivated the talent, but as an instrument of action in a country like ours."

These were bold words from a man who still held a Government post, and daring sentiments from one whose closest friends had, in effect, deserted his standard. But Mr. Pitt had tried the way of patience, of co-operation, of cajolery, of practical politics. None of them had served, and he was now ready to appeal to the country with unqualified abandon, let the result be what it might be.

CHAPTER XVIII

THE MYSTERY OF HANNAH LIGHTFOOT

Mr. Pitt's elaborate political program by which he expected to bring himself into power was outlined in March and April, 1754. His letter to Newcastle, giving warnings to the Duke in considerable detail, was dated April 4, 1754. Two days following the writing of this letter Parliament was prorogued (a circumstance certainly not displeasing to Newcastle), and on April 8 dissolved. On May 31, the newly elected Parliament met briefly and adjourned until the following November. The plan "to awaken men," therefore, had to be held in abeyance during the recess, as a revolt in Parliament was the only way in which the hand of Newcastle might be forced.

Meanwhile, in the summer of 1754, Prince George, the heir-apparent, became involved in an affair with a young Quaker girl named Hannah Lightfoot; and the names of Mr. Pitt, Miss Chudleigh, and other friends of Leicester House (the residence of the Princess of Wales) were ultimately dragged into the story. The tale has been reiterated so frequently, even to the twentieth century, that any account of Mr. Pitt should delve into this mysterious event, and appraise which part of it may be true and which fancy.

Prince George, in this summer of 1754, was sixteen years of age, but less experienced in most respects than other boys of his age because of his over-sheltered upbringing. It is well to understand something of the pitiable Prince George. Soon after he became King George III, and throughout most of his reign, he was looked upon as a stubborn, dull and ill-tempered monarch. He became pious and thrifty, narrow and mean, yet these characteristics were at variance with all accounts of him as a young man. The training of his boyhood days was such as to smother any youngster, and George was ultimately suffocated; but only after more than one struggle.

The first serious blow in his life was the death of his father. Frederick, in contrast to his own parents and grandparents, was a genial and loving father to whom his children were devoted. When the death of Frederick was announced to Prince George he broke into bitter crying.

"I feel," he said, placing his hand over his heart, "something here, just as I did when I saw the two workmen fall from the scaffold at Kew."

After Frederick's death, the boy was at the mercy of various persons who sought to mold his career. His chief tutor was Dr. Francis Ayscough, "the ridiculous Skew," Ann Pitt's one-time suitor; his governor was the amiable Lord North. Most influential, however, were his mother's favorite, Lord Bute, and the Princess of Wales herself.

In the Princess, the maternal instinct and the desire for domination led to a policy under which George's individuality was bound and gagged. "The Princess Dowager and Lord Bute," Lord Chesterfield wrote, "agree to keep the Prince entirely to themselves." The mother justified herself by the belief that she was keeping her son immune from the world's temptations. Gloucester, George's youngest brother, affirmed in later years that this policy was carried to extremes. "No boys," he said, "were ever brought up in a greater ignorance of evil than the King and myself. At fourteen years old we retained all our native innocence."

Even a royal prince, however, has eyes in his head and human emotions. Even a prince may walk abroad and observe the populace. Young George occasionally visited his grandfather, the King, in the plain brick palace of St. James. On a street near the palace was the shop of a linen-draper by the name of Wheeler. Wheeler is said to have had a niece by the name of Hannah Lightfoot, a young Quakeress who had come to London from Yorkshire to live with her uncle's family and assist in his shop. She was said to be a girl of great beauty, firm virtue, and several years older than the Prince.

Some stated that Miss Chudleigh, maid of honor to the

Princess, and kissing acquaintance of George II, had assisted the young Prince in being introduced to the Quaker girl. Others have hinted that Mr. Pitt, the friend of commoners, acted as the go-between. It is possible, of course, that the Prince in strolling near the palace grounds may have made his own introductions. It is not unusual for boys of sixteen to fall desperately in love with girls several years their senior. Such girls usually have poise, and, sometimes, kindness. To the young timid male heart, such an one may be as luminous and angelic as the guardian who kept Adam from the gates of Eden. So it was with Prince George. It was easy for the two to meet. The lovely Hannah's home at her uncle's was on the southeast corner of Carlton Street and St. Alban's Place, near the royal palaces, about half-way between the Prince's and the King's. Acquaintanceship leaped to adoration and passionate devotion. Frequent meetings fed the flame, and, rumor said, led to a marriage.

Whatever the facts might be with respect to the reported marriage, the interest of the young Prince in Hannah Lightfoot was of more than a transient nature. Letters supposedly from her relatives, printed in the *Monthly Magazine,* Volumes 40 and 41, concede the Prince of Wales' devotion to the young Quakeress, though affirming that this was nothing more than a kindly protective affection. It is further significant that a portrait, said to be that of Hannah or her daughter, was painted by the noted artist, Joshua Reynolds, and ultimately was hung in the gallery at Knole Park, the birthplace of Lord George Sackville. The magazine, *Notes and Queries,* Volume 8, has stated that a sizable home was provided for Hannah on the Hackney Road near London, where she lived in virtual seclusion until the end of her life.

Curiously enough, almost nothing seems to have been known about the affair at the time. The incident is not related by the arch-gossip, Horace Walpole, in his *Memoirs of George the Third,* nor is it to be found in the *Letters* of Mrs. Elizabeth Montagu, or those of Lady Mary Wortley Montague.* All three were avid retailers of scandal, not

* The husbands of the two ladies were cousins who disagreed on spelling.

neglecting the royal family in their comments, and well-acquainted in the circles of the Court. Kindness to the unhappy boy or fear of reprisals from the Throne may have sealed their lips, though this seems unlikely. Possibly the affair at the time was known only to Mr. Pitt, Miss Chudleigh, and a few intimates at Leicester House. Even Reynolds may not have known of it, as his portrait was made after Hannah Lightfoot took the name of Mrs. Axford. Public discussion of the matter took place many years later, when all of the principals were dead, and the story of the marriage which has been accepted, sometimes as speculation and sometimes as fact, by a long series of writers, seems to have originated in a magazine article which was based on very flimsy grounds.

The basic article appeared in the *New Monthly Magazine,* Volume 72, page 216, and purported to be the report of a conversation with William Beckford, Jr. This Beckford was the son of William Beckford, Mr. Pitt's lifelong friend. He was, in fact, the godson of Mr. Pitt and on intimate terms with the Pitt family. This report recited that the marriage between the Prince and Hannah Lightfoot was performed at Kew in the presence of Mr. Pitt and a Miss Ann Taylor. The clergyman was stated to be Rev. James Wilmot, D.D., who was known to be a close friend of the Pitts. Dr. Wilmot, Beckford was quoted as saying, "had opportunities of being fully acquainted with everything"; but the weakness of the article, "Conversations with the late Mr. Beckford," lay in the fact that Mr. Beckford, being deceased, was unable to confirm or deny the conversations.

This article was the foundation of a suppressed work published in the year 1832, entitled *A Secret History of the Court of England.* Another edition of the material, published in the same year under the title *Authentic Records of the Court of England,* gave a different account of the marriage, stating that it took place in the Curzon Street Chapel, in the presence of Miss Chudleigh and the Duke of York. Furthermore, the date of the marriage has been stated variously to be from 1753 to several years later, but usually in the summer of 1754.

The story of a marriage was perpetuated in *Memoirs of the Life and Reign of King George the Third* by J. Heneage Jesse, published in 1867. Again, William Makepeace Thackeray alludes to the subject in *The Four Georges* in an edition of 1877, saying of George III, "I pass over the stories of his juvenile loves—of Hannah Lightfoot, the Quaker, to whom they say he was actually married (though I don't know who has ever seen the register)." Paul Kester, twentieth-century dramatist, wrote a play on the subject which assumed that the marriage took place, and Compton Mackenzie, as late as the 1930s, wrote a book in which the legend and the evidence were again examined.

Jesse made considerable of the point that the Royal Marriages Act was not in existence at that time, and that the children of the Prince and the pretty commoner would therefore have been legal heirs to the Throne, and, consequently, that suppression of news of the affair was of great importance to the Hanoverian dynasty. Jesse also points to the letters of Miss Lightfoot's relatives, which state that she eloped in 1754 and was married to an Isaac Axford with whom she apparently did not live. It is hinted by Jesse that this marriage was to protect the future George III against future claims, and some reports say that the wedding of Hannah to Axford was arranged by the Cabinet.

These various accounts, coming years later, might suggest that the marriage of Prince George and Hannah had been an established fact, handed down by word of mouth and coming into print when time had made publication no longer dangerous. The reports, however, ignore one circumstance of overwhelming importance which virtually explodes the entire marriage theory: The Regency Bill, designed to provide for all matters relating to Prince George insofar as they affected his succession to the Crown, had been passed in 1751. The debates on the subject had been extensive and thorough, and had been participated in by Mr. Pitt and other major leaders of the time. The provisions of the Act were widely known, and a clause in the

Act stated "If the minor [Prince George] marries without consent of the Regent and Council, such marriage shall be void, and all persons concerned guilty of high treason."

It may be concluded without doubt that no clergyman would risk his life by the performance of such a ceremony. It is equally clear that Mr. Pitt, even if he had no other reason for refraining, would not place himself in the position of being charged with high treason for conniving at such a match. The rumored marriage was undoubtedly a myth, and perhaps the affair itself was simply the love of a lonely neglected boy for a sweet sympathetic girl. This, if undramatic, seems the most probable explanation.

The intimates of Leicester House were doubtless familiar with the infatuation of the Prince. Mr. Pitt years later, in his old age, may have told young Beckford about the romance between George and the Quaker girl; and from that point on the writers began to embroider the tale. Whether Mr. Pitt had any close and influential relationship to this love affair can be only a matter of conjecture. It is known that in this particular summer he spent little, if any, time in London, and was, in fact, much more active than usual in the social whirl, visiting numerous watering places and going for week-ends to the homes of friends and relatives, especially those of the Grenville cousinhood.

Among the places which he visited was Ealing, the home of Mr. and Mrs. George Grenville. It will be recalled that Mrs. Grenville was the former Elizabeth Wyndham. She had become increasingly devoted to her sister-in-law, Hester Grenville, who was much younger than her brothers and, of course, younger than the group in which Mr. Pitt usually traveled. She was thirty-three, while Mr. Pitt was forty-six, and most of the Temple-Grenvilles in her generation were in their forties.

Elizabeth, however, for the past several years, had had her eyes on the fate of Mr. Pitt, and in her correspondence had kept Hester informed of his activities, his health, his witty remarks, and anything else which might reflect in his favor. Pitt's visits to Ealing had been timed by his hostess to coincide with the visits of Hester. The strategy at least had some results. Between William and Hester there was an affinity of mind and interest, but also there was the strong cellophane-like barrier of an acquaintanceship long and uneventful. What point of newness could there be between the Grenvilles' young sister and their old friend Mr. Pitt; yet somehow a basis had been established, reflected in a steady correspondence.

So now there were notes and visits, visits and notes, and the only obstacle to Pitt's seeing Hester more frequently was the fact that he had filled up his social calendar solidly until the opening of Parliament. Had correspondence led him to that decision? Was the eagle-like Mr. Pitt in full flight? Whatever the reason, he had accepted a series of invitations which would leave him no time for Ealing.

CHAPTER XIX

THE COURTING OF HESTER GRENVILLE

In spite of the parties and the visits, accompanied by feasts of philosophy and experiments in amateur landscaping, Mr. Pitt was finding his life profoundly unsatisfactory. While he had achieved a considerable success in his public career, personal happiness had passed him by. At the age of forty-six, he was still single, one of the most eligible bachelors in England, and yet unlikely, as far as he could see, to find a way to change the situation.

There were several circumstances which stood in his way, the chief of which, naturally enough, was himself. Though he had consummate self-confidence with respect to his political abilities, he was modest and humble in his estimate of his personal attractions. The memoirs of his contemporaries, both men and women, speak with enthusiasm of his charm in conversation, his erect carriage, his kindliness; there was a sense of elation and excitement when they wrote of him; but Pitt himself seemed almost overwhelmed by his frequent illnesses, his advancing years and his inner loneliness. His letters to his sister Ann in which he tried to clear up their misunderstandings had been amazing in their abjectness. He seemed to lack the confidence to believe that anyone did, or would, actually care for him. Perhaps it was this sense of inferiority which he had in mind when he later spoke to Shelburne of boys being "cowed for life" at Eton.

He had been late, of course, in getting started on his career, due to the slightness of his family fortunes and the act of Walpole in dismissing him from the Army. His first love affair with the daughter of the French riding master had come to nothing; and it will be recalled that Molly Lyttelton had died just at the period when she might have consoled him for the affair in France.

Molly West, sister of Gilbert West, the poet and cousin of the Lytteltons and Grenvilles, adored Mr. Pitt; but seemingly won only a friendly affection in return. She ultimately married Admiral Hood, even though her devotion to Mr. Pitt continued undimmed. Sarah Robinson, Mrs. Montagu's sister, who wished to dance "only with Mr. Pitt," had apparently made little impression on him.

Aside from the girls of the Grenville cousinhood, Mr. Pitt's women acquaintances were for the most part married or had reputations so scandalous that they would not occur to Mr. Pitt in terms of marriage. Curiously enough, although Pitt was straight-laced and strongly disapproved of the immoralities prevalent in his times, his political and literary life had involved him with some of the more lurid characters of a highly dissolute age.

The circle of Prince Frederick, for example, had been notorious. Here Pitt had known Lady Archibald Hamilton, Miss Chudleigh, Miss Vane, and other attractive mistresses of the era. The women at Marlborough House and at the home of the Duchess of Queensberry were more conservative, but these homes were salons of wit and philosophy rather than romance.

For some years Pitt had been compensated for his lack of a normal home life by his devotion to his sister Ann. She had been everything to him but a wife—a confidante, companion and the hostess of his home. His love for Ann was a conspicuous and consuming affair. It is a safe guess that both Ann and Betty had done their part to keep their brilliant brother to themselves and to break up any prospective match, just as they had absorbed the attention of their brother Thomas and broken up his home.

In this combination of circumstances, Hester Grenville, with the able managership of her sister-in-law, led the field. In 1754 Mr. Pitt's interest in Hester had developed rapidly. It was evident that, up until his flight from Ealing, they were meeting about as often as he could arrange it. If Pitt was blind to where this path was leading him, it must at least have been clear to others. Hester had an apartment in the Argyle Buildings in London which, during her absence in the country, she offered to Mr. Pitt to use for political and social engagements, and he gladly availed himself of the courtesy.

It was increasingly clear that Hester had been waiting with one thought in mind. Her brothers for some time had been worried about her single state. In fact, when she was only twenty-two Jemmy Grenville had written to her with a brotherly lack of tact expressing pleasure "that there is a prospect of getting you off with Simon Truelove. He really deserves to have you, and it is impossible to hope for a more advantageous prospect. My dear Meg you grow old, and it is time to think of a decent retirement." She had refused Mr. Truelove, however, and had also rejected her cousin, Mr. Berenger. In fact, in view of her reputed wealth, she had doubtless declined many offers.

Hester, however, knew whom she wanted. Better than her brothers, she knew who was the real man of the whole Cobham connection. While women may guess wrong in their appraisal of minor men and may be deceived by the pretensions of a cad, yet they have a sensitivity to real greatness, even as Mary Todd knew early the greatness of Abraham Lincoln. So Hester Grenville knew that the raw youthful Pitt was a man for the ages, kind and incomparable; and she had waited for him.

Just what circumstances opened Mr. Pitt's eyes to the situation is not recorded. Perhaps there was no one circumstance, or very possibly the use of Hester's apartment, the presence of her things there, her gesture in offering it, made him realize the state of her feelings. At any rate, in September, 1754, after he had rejected Ealing, he suddenly gave himself up and rushed down to visit Hester in her own home at Wotton. Soon after his arrival, as he and Hester were walking by the edge of the pond under the great oak trees, he proposed to her and was immediately accepted.

In the days which followed, Pitt for the first time knew unalloyed happiness. There were long walks, and hours of horseback riding. There were discussions of future plans and the decision that the marriage would take place promptly. They were both past their youth and there was no reason for delay. The date was agreed upon for November 6.

The effect on the middle-aged lover was electric, not only in his personal happiness, but in everything.. He was once again agog with ambition, out to conquer against all odds. The next session of Parliament would be opening in November, and he needed to go down to Bath to get himself in physical condition for the rigors of political activities. Hence it was necessary for him to tear himself away from Wotton, but the lovers poured out their devotion in a constant stream of letters, daily and several times a day. "Nothing I could ask of Heaven and you, but soon to return to your feet," Pitt wrote. And again: "I . . . feed my soul upon this infinitely endearing mark of confidence and sweetest pledge of all I wish to live for?"

The thought of Stowe brought him some troubled reflections. In spite of his long deep intimacy with the Grenville family, would they welcome him as a brother? He knew, better than anyone, Temple's insatiable ambition. Even though he had been the one who had helped Richard to obtain his first patent of nobility and had later aided him in obtaining an earldom, Temple might well have in mind a more advantageous match for his sister. The Grenville nose was pointed toward a dukedom, a fact which was no secret, and perhaps the family would desire Hester to marry a coronet.

In these doubts, Pitt was suffering from his customary personal self-depreciation. He had actually done more for the Grenvilles than they could have done for themselves, and their ponderous wagon was still hitched to his star. He was, moreover, at this time a person of very considerable wealth. He had the income of £4000 from his Government post, the annuity of £300 from Bedford, and something may still have remained from the grandfather's bequest, unless that had vanished along with Thomas Pitt's mismanagement of the estate. In addition to his handsome income, Pitt still had the expectancy of receiving the Marlborough properties if the one remaining heir did not survive. This heir, John Spencer, had reached the age of twenty, but was in ill health and not expected to live. Pitt, nevertheless, was apprehensive of what the Grenville views would be.

Pitt's anxieties, however, were needless. Temple and the other Grenvilles were delighted with the match, as they well should have been. In fairness to them it should be said that with all of their unabashed self-seeking they apparently had a deep love for this tall, brilliant, dynamic man, so different from themselves and yet so devoted to them. Hester was able to write to William happily:

"All visitants receive a notification from my brother Temple which speaks his vanity on the subject."

Pitt, of course, was beside himself with joy at this family welcome. He replied to Hester on October 14 in an extravagance of enthusiasm:

> If I was reconciled to our Post for going Saturday, how infinite are my obligations to it for coming yesterday? how rich a Packet fraught with two such letters? I seem to live only for and by your adored self, and yours my days, my happy days . . . and I can mark and reckon time by nothing but fresh and accumulated proofs of the most generous goodness and kindest partiality to me from that dear House, to whom alone it belongs to have such a Sister and such Brothers. . . .

William was equally proud to have his own family participate in the felicitations. Catherine had sent her congratulations, and Pitt urged Lady Hester "to read the letter, such as it is, of an unshining, but a most good and affectionate and honourable woman. . . . Kitty's letter has all the marks of herself, and for a principal one, consequently, the most cordial, sincere and warm affection. I love her for it: my dearest Lady Hester, too, will love her for it, I am sure, and be diverted with it, as well as affected with esteem and goodwill to the honest writer of it."

Now that everything was settled he was free to write to his beloved Ann and tell her of his good fortune, though he delayed writing for a week. The delay was caused by a sudden cloud over the bright sunlight of the romance. Hester's triumph had been too long deferred to permit her a sense of immediate security, and when the slowness of the

post left her without word from Mr. Pitt for a day or
two, she was in a frenzy. Even when a devoted letter arrived, she could not refrain from letting him know what she
had suffered:

> Tuesday night, October 15
>
> I did not write to you by the Post of this morning, tho' it was
> the most natural Time for my indulging myself in my favourite
> employment, but a gloom had seized my mind and filled it with
> Ideas not pleasing to me. . . .
>
> A thousand ways your Silence hurt and alarmed me, but I
> chuse you shou'd judge at present of what my feelings were by
> contraries and by my expression of the excessive pleasure which
> I have received in reading yr. Letter to 'night which is a full
> compensation for the Past.

She followed up this letter with a stronger protest on
Thursday evening, Oct. 17:

> How could yesterday bring me half a dozen letters without
> one from you . . . shou'd I repress my impatience and with a
> Philosophical Indifference quietly wait to the latest day to be
> inform'd of what I can never hear soon enough for my pleasure,
> or often enough? It would be in vain to propose it. Too rare a
> proportion of my happiness is staked upon the information I am
> to receive.
>
> I am angry . . . I am not unreasonable, am I?
>
> If I am, forgive me for the Cause, which is being devoted to
> you by an unalterable affection.

Pitt, in fact, had written to Hester from Bath on the
14th and 16th, but the letters had been delayed in transit.
When he received her first pained letter of the 15th in
which she had expressed herself as hurt at not hearing from
him, he wrote to her on the 19th in tender and mollifying
terms. Pitt could not resist this plea for pardon and he
was so relieved that the cause of her anxiety had really been
due to agitation at not hearing from him, that he was only
too happy to meet her more than halfway:

> The thought that my ever amiable and most ador'd Lady
> Hester Grenville was seized with gloom of mind, hurt and
> alarmed for worthless me, is almost too much for me.

Her second letter alarmed him, however, especially her statement that she was angry, which seemed out of proportion to a mere delay in the mails. Perhaps, after all, she was regretting her decision. He answered her on the 20th in a tumult of distress:

> The word you use is a large one, may it not imply more than the non-arrival of a Letter you were so good to expect with an impatience delightful to me, but which it is now known was out of my power to send? Can I have been wrong to you?
> I implore of you to tell me in what? that I may correct and atone the crime, if it has been in my manner or behaviour, or (what I more dread) if in my nature; tell me where it lies, that I may despise and hate myself, as much as I venerate and love you. . . .

> I said once to you that you cou'd end my being when you pleased. 'Twas not a lover's exaggeration; be you unhappy and I soon shou'd cease to be, not only my happiness, my existence depends upon the most amiable of women: she is too, the best, and to my unspeakable felicity the most generous and compassionate. Will she forgive me? I know she will, if I entreat Her upon my knees not to distrust the Passion she has rooted in my soul. . . .

The comedy of errors continued, for before Pitt had had the occasion to write his letters of the 19th and 20th, Hester had already received his previous affectionate letters of the 14th and 16th, and she was overcome with self-reproach. "I am in disgrace with myself," she hastened to write him on October 18. She conceded that her temper was not pardonable, but attributed her rebuke to the "infinite depression" she had felt in not hearing from him:

> Perhaps you cannot Comprehend my having given way to such a weakness . . . How is it possible you shou'd, since you never can have known the flattery of receiving applause from anyone superior to yourself, who have the Superiority over all.

The storm at last was over. On the 21st, in a letter from Bath, he closed the incident in the following graceful and irresistible words:

How ill does the word Superiority, apply'd to me or to any ten times me fit the lips of Lady Hester Grenville! The tender warmth of your feeling, loving Heart has almost sweetly robbed me of the only superiority I gave myself: that of loving you more than you cou'd love.

Pitt was now ready to write to Ann:

Bath. Oct. 21, 1754

. . . Lady Hester Grenville has consented to give herself to me, and by giving me every thing my Heart can wish, she gives you a Sister, I am sure you will find so, not less every other way than in name.

. . . she has generosity and goodness enough to join part of her best days to a very shattered part of mine; neither has my fortune any thing more tempting. I know no Motif she can have but wishing to replace to me many things that I have not.

I propose staying here about ten days, if my patience can hold out so long. You will wonder to see a letter on such a subject dated from Bath; but to a goodness like Lady Hester Grenville's, perhaps, my infirmities and my Poverty are my best titles.

Your ever affectionate Brother,

W. PITT

Poor Ann! This notification was the beginning of the end of the long devotion which had existed between herself and her brother. Hester did in fact write to her a dutiful, sisterly note which was no more than that. William, wishing for the best, saw in the letter only the intent of good will, but there was no love lost between the two women. Though head of William's household for many years, Ann evidently had not cultivated a friendship for the Grenville contingent, and Hester may have suspected that Ann had been responsible for the engagement not taking place long before. In any case, Hester's formal letter to Ann foreboded that the wife would thoroughly displace the sister as the dominating person in the affections, friendships and affairs of William Pitt.

Though the Pitt-Grenville match was infinitely satisfactory to those directly concerned, the world naturally buzzed with speculation and comment. Since Temple's fortune was one of the greatest in England, the gossips assumed that

Hester was an heiress of great possessions and that Mr. Pitt had feathered his nest handsomely. Lord Shelburne later commented that there was certainly no romance in Mr. Pitt's marriage, while Lord Camelford, Pitt's nephew, still later gave an elaboration of the same view:

> His marriage was unexpected. He was no longer young, and his infirmities made him older than his years, when, upon a visit to Mr. Grenville * at Wotton, Lady Hester made an impression upon him that was the more extraordinary as she was by no means new to him. The first hints he gave of his intentions were eagerly seized by her, saying she would be unworthy the honor he proposed to her if she could hesitate a moment in accepting it.
>
> With a very common understanding and totally devoid of tenderness, or of any feeling but pride and ambition, she contrived to make herself a good wife to him by a devotion and attachment that knew no bounds. She lived only in his glory, and that vanity absorbed every other idea of her mind.
>
> She was his nurse, his flatterer, his housekeeper and steward, and, though her talent was by no means economy, yet she could submit to any privation that would gratify his wants or his caprices. If he loved anyone it must be her who had no love but for him, or rather for his reputation. Yet I saw no sacrifices on his part for her ease and quiet or to the essential comforts of her life.†

Hester Grenville did not fare any better from the tongues of the ladies. She was not distinguished for her beauty. Her face was kindly and intelligent, and in figure she was a Grenville, rather heavy of hip and thigh, a solidly built person. She had rich auburn hair, a longish upper lip and a nose slightly uptilted. If she was personable in a Percheron fashion, she at least had not conquered through physical charms. Mrs. Montagu appraised the matter in a comment which may have had a feline overtone. "I believe Lady Hester Grenville is very good-humored, which is the

* Camelford was confused on his dates. Mr. Grenville, Sr., was dead. George Grenville was at Ealing. James Grenville may have been at Wotton, but Pitt had gone there especially to see Hester.

† Camelford had been named as Mr. Pitt's heir, prior to his engagement to Hester Grenville, and his tongue may have been sharpened by disappointment.

principal article in the happiness of the Married State. Beauty soon grows familiar to the lover."

Guided by Camelford and Shelburne, and naturally influenced by Pitt's own self-abasing comments in his letters to Ann, to Hester and others, history has accepted the view of Hester as a great financial prize whatever other attractions she may, or may not, have had for Mr. Pitt. Actually, the Grenville estate was "land poor," and Hester was a pensioner on the bounty of her brothers. The detail of the family finances was described in her father's will, in a letter by her mother, and in the marriage settlement with Mr. Pitt. These documents were preserved in the collection of family papers at Stowe; and, 185 years later, were acquired by the Huntington Library at San Marino, California.

The will of Richard Grenville, Sr., disclosed that Wotton and his other properties were entailed, mortgaged and otherwise involved so that he was able to leave nothing to the children. At the time the will was drawn, Hester was not mentioned, as she had not been born, but there was nothing available for her, anyhow.

When Grenville died, his widow was protected by an inheritance from her brother, Viscount Cobham, though this was limited by the fact that Richard Grenville, Jr., (Earl Temple) was the ultimate legatee. Mindful of this circumstance, the widow Grenville (Countess Temple and mother of the Earl) had written a letter to Richard in 1750, asking him to care for his sister, Hester:

June 25, 1750

. . . be kind to yr poor sister who has ever bin most affectionate and dutyful to me: and worthy and loving to you and all her brothers . . . you will be far from thinking her undeserving of your giving her a thousand pounds addition to her fortune which to be sure I much wish to procure her: but if my interest will not go so far: at least let me prevail with you to furnish handsomely two rooms for her at whatever friend's house she chooses to reside: and bestow on her the little quantity of plate I took from Wotton: I must also desire that you would pay whatever debts I shall be unable to discharge. . . .

Hester's two rooms in the Argyle Buildings, London, were apparently Temple's response to this admonition from his mother, and her "fortune" was whatever marriage portion Temple and his brothers should elect to give her.

In the marriage agreement, the Grenville brothers drove a good bargain with the prospective bridegroom. Hester's dowry, as in the case of many of the important marriages of the times, was not a sum at the free disposal of the husband, but property in trust for the bride, the children, and the prospective establishment, under terms precisely defined.

While the bride's family might contribute the larger share, the prospective husband was also expected to provide a part. As both of Hester's parents were dead at the time of her marriage this complicated the question of her appropriate portion. If she had been Temple's daughter rather than his sister the proper sum would have been £20,000. Lord Hardwicke's wife, for example, had prevailed on him to delay accepting an earldom until their two daughters were married, on the grounds that a daughter of a baron customarily had a £10,000 dowry, whereas an earl's daughter should have double the amount.

The Grenvilles compromised between the two figures, and provided their sister with £12,000 in Bank of England three-percent annuities. Pitt, for his part, deposited £5000 in cash, and rights in the Marlborough inheritance valued at £65,000. The Grenvilles were trustees for the quick assets, and the Lytteltons for the Marlborough contingency. The terms of the Pitt-Grenville agreement ran to more than ten thousand words.

The Grenvilles urged Pitt to include in the agreement everything that he expected from the Marlborough bequest, but he desired to make certain exceptions. It began to appear that the wedding must be postponed until the matter could be settled, but Pitt wrote to Thomas Nuthall, the solicitor, "May I most respectfully implore that the small niceties of the Law may be waved." Hester, however, named the settlement and "a hundred combining circumstances," of which she detailed several, as reasons for delay. Finally, it was agreed that Pitt might retain a portion of the

Marlborough inheritance, if received, for the purchase of a town house, a country estate, and other concurrent expenditures.

The financial note should not be over-emphasized. Pitt himself continued to be in the most romantic and adoring mood, while many of his friends were more charitable than Camelford. George Lyttelton wrote to his cousin Hester: "As your friend I congratulate you, and as his I love you for the choice that you have made." Pitt's colleague in politics, H. B. Legge, wrote in lighter vein, rejoicing at "the acquisition to the corps of us married men . . . I think the breed will be a good one, and can't fail to speak as soon as they are born." Gilbert West was not only generous with congratulations, but offered the use of his house in West Wickham for the honeymoon, a courtesy which was accepted.

As the time drew near, Pitt grew increasingly impatient. Hester (before the discussion on the marriage settlement) had postponed the date from November 6 to November 14, an idea which Mr. Pitt had accepted protestingly if good humoredly; and now many details still crowded their days. The most pressing questions were where and when the wedding should be held. Pitt desired the utmost of simplicity. "The less preparation, the less spectacle," he wrote to Hester, "the less of everything but of your lovely tender self, is surely best."

It was not so easily settled. Lady Temple at the very outset had offered to Hester the auspices of Stowe. Its magnificent marble halls, its untrammeled splendor, would make a grandiose setting, and if Earl Temple should run the affair it was sure to be colossal. Mrs. George Grenville, neé Elizabeth Wyndham, also had a claim to ask that the wedding be held at the Ealing estate; and Temple favored Ealing as a second choice; but Mr. Pitt remained firm.

Poor Hester was under fire from all sides and wrote to William for help:

> I submit it to you, and provided I am not exposed to the embarrasment of having the honours done to me by either of the parties I am satisfied.

I cannot with justice to my brothers omit to say that they
have both declared themselves depending on your orders. . . .
If it was not too much trouble, I wish you would by a few lines
to each of them let them know that I have done truely by
them. . . .

I will say that I feel I shall expect it with an impatience that
will affect every thought. . . . Oh! may your journey be prosperous free from every thing that is disagreeable and secure from
any disasterous accident! You see that I grow acquainted with
fears by what I pray to be averted from you. . . . Without indulging weak terrors, is not traveling by night an alarming
circumstance?

Then there was the question of a clergyman for the wedding. Any bishop or archbishop would have jumped at the
chance; but it was decided that none other than Dr. Ayscough should officiate. Poor stupid old "Skew," the tutor
from school days, the rejected suitor of Ann Pitt, the butt
of the Cobham cousinhood,—good old Skew would at last
have one job which he could do creditably and well, to
marry Hester Grenville and William Pitt in the simplicity
of her apartments in the Argyle Buildings, London.

The day, now definitely November 16, was drawing near;
and the decorations of the future home of the bridal couple
were not yet completed. At least, so Hester decided, and
William had his first hint of his future position as a husband:

"Has it ever occurred to you," she wrote to him three
weeks before the wedding, "to recommend having the paper
match'd to the blue of the half-damask that is to compose
the Chairs, Cushions and the rest of the furniture of your
room above stairs, for I think it possible you may not have
considered that different shades is not to be chosen if it
can with the same care be avoided."

On this he had the sense to be appreciative: "How good
of you to think of it! . . . Mr. Hall has had orders to match
the paper and the other furniture in colour, and all is
promised to be ready the last day of this month."

As the final day drew near, Pitt himself was pressed for
time to clear up many tasks of office. Parliament was about

PAINTED BY THOMAS HUDSON   *In the Possessions of George Pretyman, Esq.*

Lady Hester Pitt, wife of Mr. Pitt.

Letter from William Pitt to Sir George Pocock, Jan. 26, 1763, welcoming him back to England. Pocock was one of the numerous geniuses inspired by Pitt's call to action.

to open and there were many details of government with which he was concerned. William Lyttelton, for example, brother to George, was anxious to go to America as Governor of South Carolina, and Pitt was asked to use his influence in the appointment, which he did successfully. More burdensome was the work which Pitt was doing on a bill for the relief of Chelsea Pensioners, and there were various election disputes to be heard in the Commons.

Nevertheless, after both he and Hester had come up to London several days before the wedding, he found time to write her brief notes every few hours telling of his program and making appointments to see her.

His health was reasonably good, as he was strong enough to ride horseback nearly every day, though the intense work had affected his digestive system. "I am as well as rhubarb will let me be, and hope to be better tomorrow for it."

In another note he said: "I am still not quite well. The worst of my little disorder is that I cannot banquet (for such a delicious chicken is) in Argyle Street. Dr. Wilmot thinks the attack bilious; apprehends little from it. Has ordered me an emetick."

He was still hopeful that his family and hers would get along happily, as he wrote: "Will my kindest Lady Hester visit my sister [his youngest sister, Mary] this evening and early? 'Twill be charity as well as love."

November 16 at last arrived.

The Grenvilles poured forth from their town house in Cavendish Square to Hester's modest apartments in the Argyle Buildings. A few other intimate friends attended. The Rev. Dr. Ayscough read the service, and shortly the couple were on their way for a ten-day wedding trip in West Wickham.

It was the beginning of a match which would make history for England.

CHAPTER XX

"HE WILL COME AS A CONQUEROR"

The marriage of William Pitt did far more for him than any advantage of finance or social connection. There was little change in his life from a material point of view, but emotionally and through the whole gamut of his character there was a perceptible change. His life now had unity and purpose. He did not need the assurance of political victories to justify his existence. His exceptional feeling for family ties could now look to the future, rather than being dependent upon devotion to his erratic brother and sisters. Instead of wandering restlessly around the countryside during vacations from Parliament, visiting one country house after another, he devoted his spare time to the building of his new country home at Hayes Place and to the companionship at his own hearthstone.

If the devoted Hester wove a net about him, discouraged new acquaintances and insisted on being the chief ambassador between Mr. Pitt and the outer world, it was a prison which he entered willingly. To be free from vexations, exploitation, from making decisions about his social calendar, was a relief to the high-strung Pitt whose life had known very little of restfulness.

This sense of inner peace and of augmented strength was reflected in his political powers. He had not relaxed from his intention "to awaken men"; but there was more patience in his attitude, more sureness and less nervous anxiety. This was apparent to the apprehensive Duke of Newcastle. It would be tiresome and pointless to relate in detail the endless conferences which Newcastle indulged in to sound out Pitt at this period. The pattern was virtually the same each time. Newcastle would have an attack of jitters, he would send an emissary to Mr. Pitt asking on what terms he would accept a Cabinet post, and then before an agreement could be reached, Newcastle would shrink away from sharing any of his power and would disavow his messenger.

Such procedure, which was by no means secret, naturally put the Ministry in a ridiculous light. Newcastle soon had difficulty in getting anyone to act as his spokesman and on one occasion he himself interviewed Mr. Pitt, asking him to give all his personal views on Government policy in absolute confidence in order that they might work out a *modus operandi*. Pitt had barely left, when Newcastle blabbed the entire story to the King, using Pitt's views to place him in as bad a light as possible with his Majesty. Pitt learned later that his confidence had been betrayed, and Newcastle in defense claimed that he had reported the views "to do you good."

Such assurances left Mr. Pitt entirely cold, and when Newcastle approached him the next time Pitt said icily, "Fewer words, my Lord, if you please, for your words have long lost all weight with me."

The cool retort was sickening to Newcastle, whose stomach was literally responsive to his political digestion. It is said that this rebuff by Pitt doubled up the Duke with an attack of internal twinges, as though he had eaten green apples; yet, despite his sufferings, Newcastle continued to pack his Ministry with sycophants.

His greatest weakness was in the Commons, where poor Sir Thomas Robinson, the spokesman of the Cabinet and a newcomer to the House, was subjected to constant bullying by Mr. Pitt and Mr. Fox.

William Murray, who was now Attorney General and a leading figure in the Cabinet, was also subjected to frequent grilling. Pitt delighted in throwing out innuendoes which stuck pins into Murray and yet gave no opportunity for logical answer. On November 27, 1754, for example, the Stuart cause was mentioned in the Commons, and Mr. Pitt became quietly discursive on the subject of Oxford University and its Tory principles. He described a recent visit he had made to Oxford in which he had seen a picture of the Pretender inscribed with a Latin motto praying for his

return. No, Jacobitism was not dead yet, Pitt indicated.
He wished it were. It was even suspected in high places.
Here Mr. Pitt looked at Murray, whose brother had been
on the Pretender's staff. Oxford was paved with Jacobites,
he continued, and there was no trusting any man who had
been bred there in Tory principles. He looked at Murray
again. In fact, as the younger Horace Walpole described
it, "Every word was Murray, yet so managed that no public
notice could be taken of it." Fox declared that Murray,
who was sitting next to him, suffered for an hour.

Such treatment of the King's ministers, who had all the
prestige of office and authority, would have been impossible
if the incumbents had been worthy of their posts. It was
patent to the most casual observer that Mr. Pitt and Mr.
Fox were outstandingly superior to anyone on the Government side, and the King accordingly asked Lord Waldegrave
to try to negotiate changes to strengthen the Ministry.

Waldegrave at first contemplated including Fox, but
neglecting Pitt. This amused Lord Bath, who said that it
reminded him of a story of the Gunpowder Plot: the Lord
Chamberlain was sent to examine the vaults under the Parliament House, and, returning with his report, said he had
found five-and-twenty barrels of gunpowder, that he had
removed ten of them, and hoped the other fifteen would
do no harm.

Fox felt that Pitt's support was essential, but he was in a
difficult position, as such an alliance might ruin his own
chances, leaving Pitt on the inside with Mr. Fox excluded.
He finally laid the situation before Pitt in a letter, dated
April 26, 1755:

> The King, about four this afternoon, sent me word by Lord
> Waldegrave, *that he graciously condescended to admit me into
> his cabinet council.* I want to tell you more than I can pretend
> to write. My house has proved as bad for our meeting at as
> yours. Pray think of some other place, and let me know a sure
> one. Whether the determination is likely to be wise or foolish
> with regard to you, I have taken so much pains in vain to learn,
> that I conclude there is no determination yet. I find nothing is
> so terrible as what, if they knew us, they ought to wish, our

being in conjunction with them and in their service. This makes
it important that we should not be known to meet—and yet we
should. Adieu!

H. Fox

The bearer, Calcraft,* will wait for your answer, at what hour
you please tomorrow or next day, unless you approve of our not
meeting; and then I can contrive to lay the whole before George
Grenville. I hate this mystery; 'tis their fault.

Even though Mr. Fox's proposal seemed reasonable
enough from his standpoint, Pitt was infuriated that all this
had taken place behind his back, as he regarded it. Why
hadn't the Ministry treated jointly with him and with Fox.
How could he take office as Fox's beneficiary. He had assumed that the discussions he had had with Fox had contemplated a joint effort.

On May 9, Pitt attended a party at Lord Hillsborough's
home, and standing conspicuously on the staircase declared
loudly to his host that all connection between him and Mr.
Fox was over, that the ground was altered, that Fox was
of the Cabinet and on the Regency Council and that he,
Pitt, would consent to be second to nobody.

Fox, who was also at the party, joined them. Pitt repeated what he had said and added more. He declared
he would not accept the seals from Mr. Fox's hands, for
that would be owning an obligation and superiority which
he would never acknowledge, that he would owe nothing
but to himself.

Fox asked what would put them on the same ground.

"A winter in the Cabinet and a summer's Regency," Pitt
replied.

Fox asked if he were suspected of trying to place himself
before Mr. Pitt.

"No," said Pitt, "but we act on different lines, sometimes
together, sometimes apart, for I am independent and can
act on my own responsibility; you will sometimes act with
me, sometimes you are tied down in implicit obedience to
the Duke of Cumberland, whose soldier I am not, and whose

* John Calcraft, solicitor, then a clerk under Fox in the Pay Office, but
later an M. P. and a major supporter of Pitt.

commands might at the end of a campaign counteract all that had been jointly done."

Lord Hillsborough tried to calm the excited gentlemen and succeeded sufficiently so that Pitt and Fox did confer again in the next few days, but the fundamentals of the situation made agreement impossible. Pitt was black with discouragement. The Fox betrayal, as Pitt viewed it, was just one more instance of what he had endured from former colleagues, notably Pulteney, Murray, and George Lyttelton. And Pitt did not know to whom to turn for a new alliance.

He seriously considered complete retirement, and he appended to his file of letters from Fox a "to be or not to be" soliloquy:

> If Mr. Fox should be treated with by the Duke of Newcastle, what must be our situation? He must either close with the offers made him, to our prejudice, or demand that satisfaction should be made to us; that is, in effect, treat for us. If he takes the first part, that of dropping us; possessed as he is of the Duke, pushed and supported by Lord Granville, reconciled with and assisted by Stone, favoured by Lady Yarmouth [mistress of the King], and liked and trusted by the King, we shall be left without a remedy. If he takes the other honourable part, that of treating for us; we are thereby reduced to a very inferior situation in point of figure, and entangled inextricably by such an obligation (no matter for the motives of his seeming generosity) not only for the present, but embarked in his bottom, in all appearance, for times to come.
>
> Is not some remedy to be thought of against so disadvantageous, mortifying, and dangerous a situation? May not that remedy be to resolve to talk for ourselves, and endeavour to bring things to some explanation, before the above-mentioned conjuncture is actually come upon us? Is not the sort of overture, made through Mr. Walpole,* a sufficient and natural foundation for some conversation, in which I might avail myself of the dispositions intimated in my favour?—take them for sincere and real, and ground on them a desire that, at least, my state with the King might be brought to an explicit point?—that I could no

---

* Horace Walpole, the elder, brother of Sir Robert, who had been one of the many emissaries from Newcastle to Pitt.

longer remain in the dark, concerning a thing upon which all my conduct ought in reason to turn?—that, if I am so unhappy as to lie under his Majesty's irremovable displeasure, and an unalterable determination, in consequence of it, that I am at no time and in no exigency, to be suffered to have the honour to be admitted to the closet; that, at least, I might humbly hope to hear the grounds of his Majesty's so deep rooted aversion?— whether it grows out of an opinion *that my services would be useless there,* in which his Majesty would but do me right; or from impressions on the Royal mind, infinitely more mortifying to me, namely, that I am *not worthy to be trusted* there, in which I am willing to flatter myself his Majesty would have been misled to do me some wrong. Whichever the fatal cause of my depression may be, is it not reasonable, just, and necessary, that I should know it, in order that I may no longer look towards impossible things, perhaps continue to do injustice in my thoughts to endeavours in my favour that may have been sincere though fruitless, and waste my life under a delusion that must prove fatal to the little credit I may still be fortunate enough to have to manage with the world?

If I have flattered myself in vain with the hopes the Royal mind must relent,— when the hard, irrevocable decree, together with the grounds of it is known to me, I may take my final part as reason with warrant, according to the necessity imposed on me. I shall then be enabled, upon certainty and knowledge, to determine either for acquiescence as I am, or resistance of what I hope I don't deserve, or for a retreat from both.

The chief reason why Pitt had been excluded from office in ministry after ministry was the fact that he had put his finger on abuses and special privileges which those in power, including the Throne, wished to retain, at no matter what cost to the country. The difference between the faults of Newcastle and those of his predecessors was that the Duke was incompetent and vacillating even in the business of trying to maintain party harmony. This state of affairs naturally did not help the general unrest of the country, in the face of the continued military and naval defeats which had been going on over a period of a dozen years with very few victories to counterbalance them. In midsummer the country had word of the defeat of General Braddock at Fort

Duquesne, a major frontier post in the American colonies, in which the General was killed and many of his troops were massacred. This new disaster, dramatic in the extreme, brought great condemnation on the Cabinet. Newcastle's only remedy for the situation seemed to be an increasing number of subsidies to various allies, including the pay of the eight thousand Hessians in Europe who had been supported by the British treasury in one guise or another for many years past.

Mr. Pitt as Paymaster-of-the-Forces was in a strategic position to know about the subsidy situation and to delay payments. When the warrant for the levy monies came to his office he discussed the subject with the Duke of Devonshire and with certain others who had weight with Newcastle. As Mr. Pitt pointed out, there was no end to the drain of expense which Hanover could cause England. It was an open country which could not be defended without thousands of men, and it would be far cheaper, if Hanover were attacked, to bargain for its return at the conclusion of peace than to attempt to fortify it. He said that he would support a naval war to the utmost, but that a Continental war spelled bankruptcy.

Newcastle was much alarmed to have such talk going about, and asked Hardwicke to get in touch with Mr. Pitt and to hint that his long desire for Cabinet rank might be satisfied. Pitt replied that he did not remember making any application for office, certainly not to Newcastle, and that until both the King and his ministers desired such a move he would have none of it. Hardwicke then asked if Pitt would be willing to talk to Newcastle, and Pitt agreed only if his Grace sent for him. Newcastle did so, and Pitt was more blunt than he had been with the Lord Chancellor, saying that he sought neither flatteries nor exalted office, what he was concerned with was the Duke's system of carrying on the business of the House, which would not do.

"There must be men of efficiency and authority, in the House," he said, according to the account given by Lord Shelburne in later years, "a secretary and a Chancellor of the Exchequer, at least, who should have access to the

Crown; habitual, frequent, familiar access, that they might tell their own story, to do themselves and their friends justice, and not be the victims of a whisper."

Pitt went on to say that he esteemed both of the Secretaries of State, but he supposed something was wanting, or why was he sent for. For his part, if the Ministry asked nothing of him he asked nothing of them.

Mr. Pitt observed further that the King could not have chosen a worse policy than to journey to Hanover at this unfortunate time, a move "which all people should have prevented, even with their *bodies*. A King abroad, at this time, without one man about him that has one English sentiment, and to bring home a whole set of subsidies!" Newcastle spoke plaintively of the King's dignity and the King's honor. Pitt replied in the terms of greatest respect for his Majesty's person and the dignity of the Throne. He said that he was speaking to prevent the King from taking steps which were so dangerous to his own quiet and to the safety of his family. He felt that the issues were of such national moment that he must oppose these subsidies in the Parliament.

Newcastle, however, was content to let things drift, and while Parliament was in recess there was little recourse against him by either the Ministry's friends or its opponents. Pitt used the vacation period to recover his health and to spend time with Hester. These were happy days for him in his private life and he could readily afford to treat Newcastle in a cavalier fashion. There was a new member expected in the Pitt family and Hester was remaining in their London apartment, presumably because of the better medical facilities in the city. Pitt, when not in London, was supervising improvements to his home at No. 7 The Circus, Bath, an additional establishment to his new country home at Hayes Place. The feature of the house at Bath was to be a blue dressing-room for Hester, similar to the one which she had in town. All of these activities kept him busy, with little opportunity to brood. He wrote to his nephew that he was living in post-chaises, dashing about the countryside; and the tone of his letters was high-spirited. Early in the fall the newcomer arrived, a girl, whom they named Hester. The experience of paternity seemed to give Pitt a new confidence in the continuity of life, and by November this terror of the Ministry was in the best form that he had ever been.

He began, as he had warned Newcastle, with a general onslaught on the ministerial policy. Under ordinary circumstances, propriety would have required his resignation from the Paymaster's office before taking a stand so sharply in opposition, but Pitt was determined that the Government should either dismiss him or accept his recommendations. On November 20, 1755, Newcastle obliged Mr. Pitt with dismissal, and also removed George Grenville, James Grenville, and their colleague, Henry Bilson Legge. As a nice touch of insult Pitt's former intimate, Sir George Lyttelton, was promoted to the office of Chancellor of the Exchequer.

Poor Lyttelton. He had cut a fair figure when supported by the coaching of Mr. Pitt; but after leaving that alliance, as will be seen later, he sank progressively deeper into obscurity. Lyttelton's absent-mindedness had increased with the years, and Lord Chesterfield described him as "wrapped up like a Laputan in intense thought, or possibly in no thought at all." Chesterfield expressed the fear that if his son, who was equally absent-minded, should meet Sir George at dinner the pair would "run their heads against each other, cut each other's fingers instead of the meat, or die by the precipitate infusion of scalding soup."

Lyttelton, it may be gathered, was of little constructive help to the Administration. Newcastle, by this time, however, was firm and clear about one thing, and that was the destruction of Mr. Pitt. His Grace, therefore, embarked on a campaign of vilification against Pitt, using Fox, Murray, and Hume Campbell, as already narrated in the opening chapter. The complete failure of Newcastle's best troops to get their man left his Grace in an even weaker position than before.

Pitt, of course, no longer received his £4000 a year income from the Paymaster's office, and Temple, his brother-in-law, immediately offered him £1000 annually until better times, an assistance which Pitt cheerfully accepted. If Pitt was in need of ready cash, he doubtless still considered himself as one of the future rich men of the kingdom, because of the Marlborough bequest. At any rate, he went cheerfully ahead with his housebuilding program at Bath, in the bland indifference to finance which was characteristic of the Pitt family.

Pitt lost no time in organizing an effective Opposition centered around his own ideas. His first move was to strengthen his relationships at Leicester House. Bute, who hitherto had enjoyed little prominence, except for his unwelcome fame as a favorite of the Princess, heartily welcomed the overtures, and Pitt became the spokesman for Prince George at the Court. The old Duke was representing the old King; the relatively young Pitt was representing the young Prince. The sardonic overtone to the situation would not be lost on the Duke of Newcastle.

Pitt kept making himself vigorously felt in Parliament and spoke twenty-six times during the session. Indeed, after his shattering of Hume Campbell no one on the ministerial side dared to face him or call him to account; and events outside the kingdom continued to clamor for the attention of the Ministry. Through elaborate machinations, England had brought about and had signed the Westminster Convention. This was supposed to keep Prussia and Austria at peace, to protect Hanover, and to hold France in line, with Prussia and Austria as threats at her back door; but on March 23, 1756, the King informed Parliament that the French were contemplating an invasion of England.

Meanwhile Mr. Pitt in the House was attacking the Russian, Hessian, and Prussian treaties—which did not accomplish the benefits which the Ministry had expected from them. British policy had failed in North America, was uncertain in the Mediterranean, and no one seemed to be concerned about the status of British affairs in India. Pitt's chief objection to England's part in power politics at this stage, however, was the ineptitude, in fact the chaos, of the Administration, and the unwillingness of anyone to accept responsibility.

"They shift and shuffle the charge from one to another," he declared. "Says one, 'I am not the general.' The Treasury says, 'I am not Admiral.' The Admiralty says, 'I am not Minister.' From such an unaccording assemblage of separate and distinct powers with no system, a nullity results. One, two, three, four, five lords meet—if they cannot agree, 'Oh! we will meet again on Saturday.' 'Oh! but,' says one of them, 'I am to go out of town!' "

The chief retort which the Government was making to the French threats was to send a squadron under Admiral Byng to relieve the island of Minorca, a major British naval base in the Mediterranean. The French were laying siege to it, and British prestige and public morale demanded a successful defense.

Pitt was apprehensive about the relief expedition. Byng had never proved himself in an important naval engagement. He was sent out with a small squadron which was short of its full complement of men. He was led to expect that he would get reinforcements at Gibraltar, but after he had sailed Anson, the First Lord of the Admiralty, felt that additional men could not be spared.

"I pray to God," exclaimed Pitt in the Commons, "that the King may not have Minorca like Calais written on his heart."

Pitt was equally alarmed over the whole military problem, and urged that the Ministry should adopt a strong naval policy and should assist home defense by the establishment of a militia.

The Pitt Militia Bill was similar in its pattern to the structure of the National Guard currently in practice in the United States, but for those times the idea was revolutionary. Kings and Cabinets were accustomed to have their paid standing armies, and the notion of citizens at large having access to arms was not a pleasant thought for rulers. Newcastle protested to Devonshire in the greatest apprehension, fearing the risks of guns in the hands of the people and deploring the expense. The measure, however, was highly popular in a country fearing immediate invasion, and in spite of the normal large majority of the Ministry Pitt was able to carry the bill in the House of Commons. It was, however, defeated in the Lords.

Pitt was not alone in realizing that England needed to reform her military situation from top to bottom. Cumberland, Fox, and Bedford were the center of a war party, which had considerably more political influence in upper circles than did Mr. Pitt; but he could not ally himself with Cumberland, not only because of Fox, but equally because of Cumberland's incompetence. A war in the hands of Cumberland might be almost as bad as the pretense of peace under the direction of Newcastle.

Pitt, accordingly, relied largely on his new acceptability at Leicester House, the headquarters of Prince George, where Fox said that he was "quite master . . . acting and being treated as the minister there as much as Sir R. Walpole in Queen Caroline's drawing-room." The Princess and Lord Bute in turn looked to Mr. Pitt to further the cause of young George with the Throne. The Prince, on reaching eighteen years of age, was seeking the substantial allowance from the Crown to which he was entitled, and he also desired to name Lord Bute as Groom of the Bedchamber in his household; but the King wished to make conditions which were unwelcome to the Prince.

A lively correspondence regarding Prince George's affairs now ensued between Bute and Pitt. Bute was grateful for the progress which Mr. Pitt seemed to be making with the Crown through Newcastle; and Newcastle gave assurances which looked promising. Meanwhile, however, the old Duke was running true to form, influencing the King to delay action, and telling Bute that the bungling of Pitt was spoiling everything. Bute was naïve enough to take Newcastle at his word, and Pitt began to lose ground at Leicester House.

There were, however, matters on the national scene far more important than Court intrigue. No word had been received from Minorca. At the end of May, it had become known that Byng was lingering at Gibraltar, and it was also realized that time was desperately pressing on the small British garrison which was holding Minorca under a state of siege. Then on June 2, 1756, came the astounding report that after a brief skirmish with the French fleet Byng had sailed away without even attempting to land troops on the island.

The news was a profound shock to the entire country. A severe naval defeat would have been bad enough, but to leave the scene of action and abandon the army post to the French forces smacked of a cowardice that was almost unbelievable.

The public rage knew no bounds, though the cooler heads awaited Byng's report. George Grenville wrote to Mr. Pitt on June 7: "Though in the venality of this hour, it may be deemed sufficient to throw the whole blame upon Byng, yet I will venture to say, the other is a question that, in the judgment of every impartial man, now and hereafter, will require a better answer than, I am afraid, can be given to it. Whatever faults Byng may have, I believe he was not reckoned backward in point of personal courage; which makes this affair the more extraordinary, and induces me to wait for his own account of it, before I form an opinion of it."

Newcastle, who was terrified at the incapacity which might be charged to his Government, determined to make Admiral Byng the scapegoat, and promised that he would be brought to trial immediately. Some, indeed, reported that Newcastle had promised that Byng would be hanged immediately. When Byng's report was received by the Ministry, it detailed all the handicaps and delays to which he had been subjected by the Cabinet. These criticisms were carefully deleted, and the report was published in a form which made it a self-condemnation.

The word of this disaster was still fresh in the public mind when more bad news arrived. Calcutta, it was learned, had been attacked by Indian forces, the Governor had deserted his post, and 146 English subjects of both sexes were crammed into a dungeon, called "the black hole," where 123 perished from suffocation.

The black hole of Calcutta, added to Minorca, made a

scandal which shook the Ministry. The rats began to leave the sinking ship of Newcastle's Cabinet. William Murray, who had served the Duke faithfully, now demanded to be given a peerage and to be elevated to the post of Chief Justice, where he would be removed from the political scene. Newcastle was in a frenzy of apprehension, and begged Murray to reconsider, but Murray said flatly that he would resign if his wishes were not granted, and Newcastle was obliged to yield,—though of course it was some weeks before he kept the promise.

Pitt's friends began to see that the time was ripe for organizing a group which might be called to take over the Ministry. Legge wrote to Mr. Pitt on June 16, 1756, making several nominations as the nucleus for an Opposition group, saying "we shall out-lawyer them upon the whole, notwithstanding the enemy are possessed of the grand magazine of legal preferments." Meanwhile, the Government's position grew steadily worse. On August 11, Montcalm defeated the English at Fort Ontario near Oswego, New York. The victory protected the French pathway from the St. Lawrence westward and was part of their plan to unite their settlements on the Great Lakes and the Mississippi, threatening the ultimate encirclement of the English colonies on the Atlantic seaboard.

Newcastle could no longer conceal from the public the true state of affairs, no matter how he might try to shed blame upon others and make excuses. *The Gentleman's Magazine* in August of 1756 said: "Thus has our money been squandered, our strength by land and sea either not exerted or misapplied, the lives of veterans sacrificed, and a most valuable fortress lost while the French, against whom we still boast our superiority, have executed every project which they have formed, and have not only eluded, but despised, the impotent and ill-directed attempts that have been made to disappoint them."

Voices on all sides within and without the Government were now crying for Mr. Pitt. Pitt had said to the Duke of Devonshire, "I know that I can save England and that

no one else can." While others were running from responsibility in fear and dismay, Mr. Pitt was confident that he
could save the State; and virtually everyone believed that
he, if anyone, could. The Duke of Cumberland, who did
not know Pitt personally, said to Mr. Fox that if all he
heard was true, "Pitt is—what is scarce—a man."

Newcastle snatched eagerly at this hope and now delegated Hardwicke to entreat Pitt to join the Newcastle
Cabinet on his own terms. That was not what Pitt had in
mind. Hardwicke obtained an appointment with Pitt at the
home of Lord Royston, where he argued with Pitt for
three and a half hours, but the latter's first condition was
the dismissal of Newcastle and his following. He refused
to be affiliated in any Government with the Duke, under
any circumstances.

Mr. Pitt had now a mandate from the people which, in
the circumstances of the times, the King, the Cabinet, and
the Commons could not long ignore. The gentry, clergy,
and freeholders of the county of York—to cite but one instance—instructed their representatives in Parliament: "We
hope that you will endeavour to introduce a change not only
of men, but of morals and measures."

Memorials to this effect poured in from all over the
country. William Beckford, one of the members for the
city of London and one of the most influential men of
the city, summarized the situation in a letter which he
addressed to Mr. Pitt on November 6, 1756:

> Let my esteem and regard plead an excuse for the imperti-
> nence of this letter. The dismal accounts received, and the mel-
> ancholy prospect of public affairs, make a change of men
> necessary; but as a change of measures only can save the nation,
> I hope and trust, as you can, so you will be the instrument of
> our deliverance. . . .
>
> A new system is now absolutely necessary; which cannot be
> established without an almost total removal of those men who
> have brought these miseries upon us. I have, during my whole
> life, acted as a private man. In the militia of Jamaica I was
> no more than a common soldier: in our present political warfare,

I intend to act as one of your private soldiers without commission; and be assured I will never desert the cause of liberty and my country, as long as the heart beats in the breast of,

Dear Sir,
Your most obedient
and faithful servant,
WILLIAM BECKFORD

Faced with the inescapable realities, his Majesty now accepted Mr. Pitt's suggestion that the Duke of Devonshire be urged to form a ministry to whom he, Pitt, would lend his full support.

The nomination of Devonshire as the titular head of the Cabinet was a shrewd and broadminded move on the part of Mr. Pitt. William Cavendish, Duke of Devonshire, had a prestige with the old Whig families which would add materially to the strength of a new ministry. He was closely related to Hardwicke and, in fact, to Newcastle. He was a nephew of the Duke of Bedford. He was also a man of great wealth and amiability who would be an influence for union rather than friction. Moreover, Pitt had conferred with him frequently during the past year and knew that Devonshire was familiar with his policies and would not oppose them.

The King and Newcastle, as might have been expected, immediately began to hedge on their commitments and insisted that the new Administration must contain many leading persons of the Old Guard, as well as Mr. Fox.

His Majesty went to the point of calling a conference of the Cabinet ministers and prominent members of both Houses, at which a slate was agreed upon. It was decided, for example, to refuse Mr. Pitt's proposal of Legge as Chancellor of the Exchequer, and to name Fox for that office. Devonshire for the moment agreed; but at this juncture the wise old Horace Walpole, who frequently had enjoyed stirring up Mr. Pitt in the House of Commons, pointed out to Devonshire that Pitt, in view of everything, could not possibly submit to any such dictation, and that the Government was obliged to meet his wishes. Henry

Fox, while disappointed, agreed that this was good sense, and withdrew from the situation.

The path was now clear. Virtually everyone now earnestly desired to see Mr. Pitt in office, and even his bitterest enemies did not oppose the elevation of Mr. Pitt, on December 4, 1756, as Secretary of State and actual head of the Ministry.

Even Newcastle gave his hearty assent.

This was too much for Hardwicke, who had endured so many of Newcastle's confidences.

"Are you really for it in your heart?" he asked.

"I am hand and heart for Pitt, at present," answered the old Duke, with his usual caution. Then he added ruefully, "He will come as a conqueror. I always dreaded it."

PART TWO

"An Empire for Freemen"

CHAPTER XXI

CAPTIVATING THE PEOPLE

William Cavendish, Duke of Devonshire, was only thirty-six years of age when he accepted the office of First Lord of the Treasury as the nominal head of Mr. Pitt's Administration. The Cabinet was composed chiefly of young and daring spirits not afraid of risk and new ideas. They had come into office by the singular circumstance that the Majority leaders lacked the courage to steer through the disasters which they themselves had caused.

Newcastle had controlled a majority of one hundred and fifty in the Commons at the time of his resignation, but he could not find a dozen men willing to accept responsibility in the Government under his leadership or in the face of current circumstances. Mr. Pitt, therefore, enjoyed the dubious position of a victor by default. The elder statesmen were content for him to guide England out of her low estate if he could. If he could not,—only a noncommittal shrug could be found for that contingency. Pitt had embraced his destiny for better or for worse.

The Pitt Administration necessarily was made up largely of Pitt's personal friends and relatives, and Horace Walpole the younger jeered that Pitt did not have enough cousins to fill the available places. Temple became First Lord of the Admiralty, George Grenville was Treasurer of the Navy, Henry Bilson Legge, one of Pitt's first lieutenants, became Chancellor of the Exchequer. Sir Robert Henley, a schoolmate from the Eton days, was named Attorney General in the place of William Murray. There was no one of the stature of Hardwicke to take the office of the Lord Chancellor, and the Great Seal accordingly was placed in a Commission of three men.

Other positions were filled by some of the older incumbents. Carteret-Granville remained as President of the Council, forgiving Mr. Pitt for earlier attacks upon him and indulging a vocal and sardonic glee at the troubles which he saw ahead. The Earl of Holdernesse was Pitt's colleague as one of the principal Secretaries of State. He was ostensibly a Pitt man, but actually was an industrious spy for Newcastle, keeping the latter informed of the moves and private counsels of the new Government.

Mr. Pitt was undaunted by the inexpert and divided character of his Cabinet. Its very weakness served his immediate purposes, for he planned to revolutionize policy and to rebuild the Government in every particular; and stronger colleagues might have proved to be obstacles.

The first task of the Ministry was the composition of the King's address at the opening of Parliament, which was customarily drafted by the chief Minister.

Pitt, and not Devonshire, prepared the address, and Pitt's actual leadership of the Government was therefore officially established, if there had been any question of it in any quarter.

Pitt wrote the address at Hayes, his country place, and aimed to put in it the essentials of the policy on which his Administration would stand or fall. It was an epoch-making document. America received his first attention. In America, Mr. Pitt foresaw the great chance for expansion of the British Empire under conditions of constitutional liberty. This was a revolutionary and farseeing idea in a Government which had been neglectful of the colonies, largely ignorant of them, and essentially conscious of the provincials as inferior to the inhabitants of England.

Mr. Pitt next advanced his plan for a militia, the proposal which had been recently defeated in the Lords. He also desired to place in the royal mouth a promise that the Electoral troops, namely the Hanoverians, would be returned from England to Germany; and he called for more vigorous efforts in prosecuting the war. England thus far had been drained of subsidies and men to further the schemes of European monarchs. Mr. Pitt contemplated that she now would conduct the war in the interest of her own nationals.

Finally, Mr. Pitt was mindful of the hardships of the poor, and wrote a paragraph calling for a reduction in the price of grain and for other measures to relieve poverty.

It was a document calculated to invigorate the nation, by giving a vision of empire, by training the populace in self-defense, by sending home the unpopular German troops, and by having sympathy for the sufferings of the common people. Mr. Pitt forwarded the draft to Devonshire, with the enthusiastic comment:

> I have drawn it captivating to the people, but with all regard to the King's dignity, and have avoided any word offensive or hostile to those who no longer serve his Majesty. I extremely recommend the mention of the electoral troops in the Speech. As it stands, it will go over the whole kingdom and spread a satisfaction which a subsequent message cannot do; the length is very moderate, and the King need not trouble himself to read a third part of it in the House of Lords. I hope Mr. Legge will approve this plan of opening the Session. If it should meet with your approbation and that of a few friends, I should be sorry that way were to be given to the criticism of quarters that may not think a thing the better for coming from my hand.

"Captivating to the people"—presumably not even the astute Mr. Pitt was aware of the full significance of his phrase. No other minister in his time, and probably none in prior time (except perhaps Cromwell) had made such a frank and unhesitating appeal to the public. The very casualness of the allusion, without any attempt to argue to the principle, revealed that Pitt regarded himself as a minister of the people, a concept incomprehensible to many who belonged to the ruling classes of the day. It was this basic attitude of Pitt, even more than his particular program, which made him an exponent of modern democratic government. He regarded himself not as a king's minister enlightening the people, but as one of the people's ministers enlightening the King. The next step was, in fact, to present the address to George II for his consideration. That was Devonshire's task.

Devonshire was pleased with the paper and promptly took it to the King who was at Kensington Palace. His Majesty received the Duke politely but coolly, and listened sullenly while Devonshire read the declaration of faith which the King would be called upon to lay before the Parliament. Here in the royal palace were expounded the hopes for America, the plans for a greater empire, the call for relief of the poorer classes. Devonshire paused, waiting for the royal opinion.

"Stuff and nonsense!" said his Majesty.

The King was indifferent to most of the address, but he was annoyed at the suggestion that his German troops were unwelcome in England. He insisted that if he gave this speech (though he actually had little choice in the matter), the House of Lords in reply should thank his Majesty for bringing over the Hanoverian troops. Devonshire transmitted this message to a meeting of the Cabinet at Mr. Pitt's home two days before the opening of Parliament. Opinion was divided. Temple was greatly incensed at the proposal, saying, "This is a very unfortunate step at the outset."

Others felt that his Majesty was being asked to swallow a bitter pill and that granting the one request might have a mollifying effect without destroying the essentials of policy.

Pitt naturally was not pleased at the King's suggestion, but he hesitated to force the issue and perhaps needlessly alienate some of the Cabinet who might feel that he was sticking at a fine point. Accordingly, Pitt reluctantly acquiesced in this concession to George II's pride.

On Dec. 2, 1756, came the great day, the opening of the session of Parliament in which the policy of the Pitt Administration would be proclaimed to the world through the King's address. The event took place, as customary, in the House of Peers. This room was a trifle smaller than St. Stephen's Chapel, being eighty feet long by forty feet wide, but gave the appearance of greater space because it was less cluttered and simpler in arrangement. Its seating plan consisted of two rows of benches along either wall and about a dozen center benches occupying the main section of the floor. Crimson was the dominating color. The benches were upholstered in crimson baize. At the front of the room was a huge crimson curtain and canopy reaching two-thirds of the way to the ceiling, serving as a setting for the throne. The throne itself was a sizable armchair placed upon a dais which was about twenty feet wide and six feet deep.

The room achieved a touch of grandeur by its vaulted ceiling, which was some thirty feet high at its apex. The ceiling was composed of hexagonal panels, except for two large skylights at either side which supplied most of the light of the room. The walls were paneled with tapestries framed in wood, depicting scenes of the defeat of the Spanish Armada.

On the day of the King's address, George II, small and redfaced, looked more squat than ever in his ample robes with his face dwarfed by the huge crown. Standing behind the throne were a score of young peers who were not yet eligible to vote. At either side of the King sat members of the royal family. At his right, on the side benches, were the Archbishops of Canterbury and York. Next to the Archbishops there was a large fireplace in the right-hand wall, and on the remaining benches on this side sat the other bishops.

Sitting opposite the spiritual lords, on the wall benches to the left of the King were the temporal peers, robed in crimson and ermine. Nearest the King (on these benches) sat the dukes of the blood royal, then the other dukes, the marquesses, the earls and the viscounts. On the center benches, were the barons, also in crimson robes, who constituted the lowest order of the peerage. Directly in front of the throne, below the dais, was a broad seat having a cushion stuffed with wool, called the woolsack, with two similar seats at either side. For fifteen years Lord Chancellor Hardwicke had occupied the woolsack. Now that he had retired, the three seats were occupied by the three Commissioners of the Great Seal, clad in black robes. The total of this august assemblage was slightly over two hundred, not including the young ineligible peers and the members of the royal family.

The Lords had remained standing as his Majesty entered, and were seated after his Majesty was seated, but remained uncovered, holding their coronets in their laps.

The Gentleman Usher of the Black Rod was then sent by the King to command the attendance of the Commons. In a few moments the members arrived from the nearby precincts of St. Stephen's Chapel and stood behind the wooden railing at the rear of the room, the railing known as the Bar of the House of Lords. The physical arrangement gave little evidence of the true state of affairs. Seated close to the King was his son, the huge and beefy Duke of Cumberland. Far up toward the front of the room were the Dukes of Newcastle, Bedford, and Devonshire,—but back of the Bar, among the Commoners, stood the tall commanding figure of Mr. Pitt, writer of the script and director of production of this epoch-making scene.

His Majesty then spoke the brief but significant words which Mr. Pitt had prepared:

"MY LORDS, AND GENTLEMEN:

"I have called you together in a conjuncture which highly requires the deliberation, advice and assistance of Parliament; and I trust that (under the guidance of Divine Providence) union and firmness in my affectionate people will carry me with honour through all difficulties; and finally vindicate the dignity of my Crown, and its indubitable rights, against the ancient enemy of these kingdoms.

"The succour and preservation of America cannot but constitute a main object of my attention and solicitude; and the growing dangers to which our colonies may stand exposed, from our late losses in those parts, demand resolutions of vigour and dispatch.

"An adequate and firm defence at home must have the chief place in my thoughts; and, in this great view, I have nothing so much at heart, as that no ground of dissatisfaction may remain in my people.

"To this end a national militia, planned and regulated

with equal regard to the just rights of my Crown and people, may, in time, become one good resource, in case of general danger; and I recommend the framing of such a militia to the care and diligence of my Parliament.

"The unnatural union of councils abroad, the calamities which, in consequence of this unhappy conjunction, may, by irruptions of foreign armies into the Empire, shake its constitutions, overturn its system, and threaten oppression to the Protestant interest there, are events which must sensibly affect the minds of this nation, and have fixed the eyes of Europe on this new and dangerous crisis.

"The body of my Electoral troops, which I ordered hither at the desire of my Parliament, I have directed to return to my dominions in Germany; relying with pleasure on the spirit and zeal of my people, in defence of my person and realm.

"GENTLEMEN OF THE HOUSE OF COMMONS:

"I will order the proper estimates to be laid in due time before you: and I rely on your wisdom, that you will prefer more vigorous efforts (though attended with large expense) to a less effectual, and therefore less frugal, plan of war.

"I have placed before you the dangers and necessities of the public; it will be your care to lay in such a manner the burdens you may judge unavoidable, as will least distress and exhaust my people.

"MY LORDS AND GENTLEMEN:

"I cannot here be unmindful of the sufferings of the poorer sort, from the present high price of corn, and the disturbances which have arisen therefrom; and I recommend to you to consider of proper provisions for preventing the like mischiefs hereafter.

"Unprosperous events of war in the Mediterranean have drawn from my subjects signal proofs how dearly they tender my honour and that of my Crown; and they cannot, on my part, fail to meet with just returns of unwearied care, and unceasing endeavours for the glory, prosperity, and happiness of my people."

It was a high moment of triumph for Mr. Pitt and his policies, to stand at the Bar of the Lords and hear his own words coming from the mouth of the King, framed in all the panoply of State. Scores of other chief Ministers had had an outwardly similar experience, but rarely with words which had foreboded a new epoch or so boldly faced a national crisis.

Results, however, and not words would be the test. Pitt promptly pressed for action on all the points of the King's address. General Loudoun was in charge in North America, that ill-fated area. Braddock, Shirley, Webb, and others had done badly on the American scene. Loudoun, like his predecessors, had no inspiring record of achievement; but Pitt was determined to give him every possible support. Loudoun proposed to attack the fortress of Louisbourg on Cape Breton Island near the mouth of the St. Lawrence, advance up the river, and take Quebec, Montreal, and the rest of eastern Canada. There were to be other subordinate campaigns, under Loudoun's general direction. It was a top-heavy, over-ambitious program, but Pitt, new to office, was ready to accept Loudoun's advice. When an attempt was made to refuse additional supplies for the American campaign Pitt wrote to Devonshire:

> I am confident I may speak freely to your Grace, because I know you love your country, and are as much convinced as I am that efforts in America alone can save us. I must therefore use the plainness of a man who means right, and declare that I cannot acquiesce in a negative upon sending another battalion and a bigger battering train, &c.; let the negative arise where it may, the ruin of the kingdom shall not be at my door.

On December 16, 1756, he called a meeting of the Cabinet to send "an expedition of weight," not less than eight thousand men, as well as a fleet, to America. While his colleagues were digesting this, he made the startling proposal to recruit regiments from the Highland clans who had taken part in the late Rebellion. The Highlanders had shown themselves to be gallant fighters, and loyal clans had been used in the Army before, notably the Black

Watch, which saw action in 1739. Mr. Pitt was convinced of the valor and patriotism of the Highlanders, and believed that they would respond to this evidence of confidence in them. In the face of considerable wagging of heads the plan was adopted.

The Navy, of course, was a vital part of Pitt's program. He demanded from the Admiralty a list of ships "requisite for the total stagnation and extirpation of the French trade upon the seas and the general protection of that of Great Britain upon the seas." He found that sixty-six of the two hundred warships were out of commission and that the forces were in general below the authorized strength. Pitt thereupon launched upon a program of shipbuilding which within four years brought the Navy to a total of four hundred ships of all classes. He provided for a new design of frigate and in his first year of office the Commons were asked to vote the unprecedented number of 55,000 sailors.

Throughout January and February he personally followed the detail both of troop raising and Navy preparation. On Feb. 7, 1757, he ordered the Admiralty to send twelve ships of the line with frigates to await the transports at Cork and to escort them to America.

Meanwhile, on December 4, Pitt had arranged for the reintroduction of the Militia Bill. It was passed in the Commons and though strongly opposed in the Lords, became law in June, 1757. It was the beginning of a National Guard which served the country in many emergencies. The Bill in the Commons had called for a total of 60,000 men, but the Lords had cut it down to 32,000. Even so, this was a respectable addition to the defense of the realm when compared, for example, to the total forces in America under Loudoun, which did not exceed 17,000 men.

On the European scene, Pitt had less scope for originality. He was confronted with that morass of entanglements which had entrapped the English for several generations past. As an Opposition minister he had clamored for a stay-at-home policy, but now he found himself in the position of having inherited an aggressive treaty with Frederick of Prussia. Fortunately for Pitt's face-saving, Frederick was a philosopher as well as a field campaigner. He avowed to Pitt that Prussia was essential to England's self-fulfillment; that France would like to drive England out of America and India; France was a threat to the Channel countries, indeed to the coast of England itself. Assist Prussia, and he, Frederick, would keep France occupied so that England could go her own way. Specifically, Frederick asked for an auxiliary army to protect his flank against France, while he attacked Austria.

The King of Prussia's shrewd appraisal of how his advancement could help England convinced Pitt, and ultimately became a fundamental of Pitt's European policy. On February 18, 1757, in the Commons, Pitt requested £200,000 to provide 24,000 Hessians and other mercenaries for Frederick's operations. George II in turn had agreed that the Electorate of Hanover would contribute 36,000 Hanoverians. Pitt made an eloquent speech expounding his policy, and met opposition only from Mr. Fox, who, with mild sarcasm, reminded Mr. Pitt of the many times when he had spoken against European alliances. The House in general was for Pitt, not only the Newcastle contingent but also the Tories and the city members. Frederick of Prussia appeared to be a winning horse, and England had seen so much defeat that the nation was prepared to bet some money on the hope of placing in a successful race.

The readiness of the Commons to vote funds was, however, more a tribute to Pitt's personal leadership than an expression of inner conviction. It may be repeated that Pitt's Ministry came to power by default. He had promptly expounded new and vigorous policies. He had committed the country to military action on many fronts. The real test of confidence would be the public attitude toward the national budget.

Legge, as Chancellor of the Exchequer, brought in a budget of over £7,500,000, of which more than £4,000,000 was to be raised in taxes. The remainder was to be obtained by selling £2,500,000 in life annuities and £500,000 in a lottery.

The financial program was a conspicuous failure. The

annuities were only one-eighth subscribed and only half the necessary tickets for the lottery were purchased by the public.

This practical demonstration of the basic lack of confidence by the nation in the ability of the Government to meet its obligations was a searching criticism of the Pitt Administration. It demonstrated that regardless of the personal popularity of Mr. Pitt, the absence of the big Whig fortunes in Government affairs was a serious weakness. The people might be captivated, but as yet at least the investing public was not convinced that the new leader could provide a successful and stable Government. Moreover, before Pitt had been in office three months he felt obliged to take a moral stand which was to badly impair his hold on those masses who were usually his supporters even in adversity.

CHAPTER XXII

REVOLT IN THE CABINET

Admiral Byng had returned to England and had been committed to the Tower pending court-martial proceedings. Public feeling had continued to run high against him. Minorca was the Gibraltar of its day, England's chief post in the Mediterranean, and Byng's alleged cowardice was held responsible for a national calamity which had been fully dramatized. America and India might be vague remote countries in the British mind, but the loss of Minorca was a disgrace hardly to be endured.

Newcastle, it will be recalled, had promised that Byng would be brought to justice without delay. Since the Duke was now out of office the responsibility rested upon the new Administration. There was still, however, the risk of a Parliamentary investigation hanging over the heads of Newcastle and his former Cabinet. The sooner that Byng could be done away with the better for them. The blood of the Admiral would serve to appease the public wrath.

On February 14, 1757, the court-martial on the Admiral found that though not guilty of cowardice or disaffection he had not "done his utmost to take or destroy every ship, which it shall be his duty to engage," and sentenced him to death according to the 12th Article of War. The sentence, however, recommended the Admiral to the mercy of the King.

The court-martial proceedings, it developed, had not been entirely regular. The senior officer who should have been named to preside at the trial was passed over, and Admiral Smith, an illegitimate brother of George Lyttelton, was in the Chair. Lyttelton, who had served in Newcastle's Administration, had endeavored to influence his half-brother in the following letter:

256

The House of Lords in the eighteenth century. The King and peers are seated. On the walls are tapestries depicting the destruction of the Armada by the British fleet. In the foreground are members of the House of Commons, standing below the bar.

Thomas Pelham, Duke of Newcastle, painted in a state of calm and poise which he rarely exhibited. A genius in political-machine management, he was a master of intrigue, afraid of sleeping alone, and pathologically incapable of adhering to a decision.

I will only observe that his not having shown any symptoms of fear when he was in scarce any danger will not be sufficient to acquit him of cowardice in the sense of the law. His not going into danger when he ought to have done so is that criminal negligence which the law has made capital. You seem to think that the law is too severe; but it was the intention of the Legislature to make it severe; and till they repeal it, the judges of a court-martial must act in a strict conformity to it: and you know the whole nation has called on the King to let the law take its course.

Byng may have been criminally negligent, but affirmations made then and later indicated that he did not have a fair trial. Temple West, a nephew of Gilbert West, who served under Byng and was severely wounded in the brief skirmish at Minorca, was firm in his praise of his commanding officer, but the Court limited his testimony to the answers to certain questions. Capt. John Amherst, who was also serving under Byng on this occasion, wrote to his brother, Col. Jeffery Amherst, that he had not been allowed to testify to matters which would have served to exonerate the Admiral.

While Pitt did not know of all the circumstances, he felt that there was reasonable doubt and that the recommendation to mercy should be supported. When the sentence was discussed in the Commons on February 17 and 23, he attacked the severity of the 12th Article of War and pleaded that the Admiral should receive the King's pardon.

This attitude on the part of Mr. Pitt drove Newcastle and his former colleagues into a state of frenzied apprehension. It will be recalled that Newcastle had made the rash move of editing Byng's dispatches before they were made public, striking out all references to the failure of the Cabinet to provide the necessary supplies. This now left Newcastle in a hideous situation. Byng apparently was unaware of the tampering with his reports, and unless he were executed promptly this would come to light. Newcastle, accordingly, was fighting not only to gain popularity by persecuting Byng, but to save himself from ruin.

The evidence on this subject did not become known fully until many years later, but the actions of Lyttelton and

Hardwicke indicated that they at least had strong personal fears in the situation, whether or not they knew the full depths of Newcastle's plotting.

Hardwicke, at any rate, now became guilty of apparently the only black deed in an otherwise fine and noble career. It was Hardwicke who hit upon the idea of publishing an anonymous pamphlet, further to stir up public indignation. He arranged to have David Mallet write a history of the Byng case under the title *A Plain Man on the Loss of Minorca*. Mallet had previously done some ghost-writing for the Treasury, but he was an author of some reputation who could not be counted upon to write according to order, regardless of the truth.

Hence this piece of strategy was extraordinarily dangerous; and Mallet had been approached indirectly by an under-Secretary named Cleveland. When the manuscript was submitted to Cleveland and turned over to the principals it did not satisfy them, but the task of making the desired changes was a delicate one, as that might come back to the door of the Newcastle contingent. Hardwicke wrote his misgivings concerning the manuscript to Admiral Anson, his son-in-law and a party to the anti-Byng cabal:

> I cannot find much fault, but own I am not much enamoured with it. This *entre nous,* for authors of this kind must not be discouraged by too much criticism. However, I have ventured to put down some remarks and queries, which I desire you will take the trouble to peruse, and to consider whether you think any of them improper, especially in what relates to maritime affairs.
>
> Whatever you disapprove strike out, and then deliver to Cleveland to copy it over fair for Mr. Mallet, keeping the original. I am not fond of giving a handle to be named as a joint author with this gentleman; but I have written him a very civil letter, informing him that he will very soon receive such a paper from the Secretary; and I have suggested to him to add something further, by way of observation and argument, upon the points of conduct objected to; for in this part I suspect this performance to be chiefly deficient.

The pamphlet in its final form had the desired effect, and the fury of the public turned against Pitt for daring to suggest mercy. He was informed in the House of Commons that the Byng case would be the means of turning him out of office, even as it had the late ministers. He was flooded with anonymous letters denouncing him for his stand; but he refused to be moved.

A few men supported him, including Bedford, Temple, Sir Francis Dashwood, and the younger Horace Walpole.

Pitt called a special meeting of the Cabinet, and induced them to draft a message from the King, granting a reprieve on the basis of certain statements which had been made in the House of Commons. It was unconstitutional for the King to allude to proceedings in the House, but Pitt was willing to take that chance. The Cabinet, with some doubts, yielded to his pleas, and his Majesty consented that the message be sent.

Mr. Pitt then rushed to St. Stephen's Chapel, went up to the Speaker's table, and presented the message to the Speaker.

Fox immediately raised the point of a breach of privilege, and the Speaker ruled that the proposal was unconstitutional.

Pitt answered that time had been too pressing to consult precedents, and he had no thought that the life of a man was to be trifled with while clerks were searching records.

"May I fall when I refuse pity to such a suit . . ." he said, "justifying a man who lies in captivity and in the shadow of death. I thank God I feel something more than popularity: I feel justice." But the ruling stood.

The only hope that remained was an absolute pardon by the King. Strong pressure was brought upon him from both sides. An unsigned memorandum, submitted to his Majesty, probably by the Newcastle advisors, said:

> Be steady, Sir, for God's sake, and nothing will go wrong; your Majesty never was more popular than at present; and the Minister [Pitt] has lost by this factious job all that he had acquired with the City. If he presumes again, sir, discard him; your people will stand by you; but if this miscreant escapes we shall be a laughing-stock to our enemies.

Temple, on the other hand, pleaded for Byng's life, but Temple's unpopularity with the monarch did not help the cause. The King exclaimed that he could not forgive conduct which manifestly implied cowardice. To this Temple replied, "What will you say if he dies game?"

Unfortunately the Admiral was destined to be put to this test. The King refused pardon; and on March 14, 1757, Byng was shot on the quarter-deck of the *Monarch*. He died game.

In Pitt's stand on this issue was revealed an essential quality of his character. There was room here for a less conscientious man to have had doubts. A lesser man could have yielded to the popular clamor. A lesser man might have loved the acclaim of the public for sending a supposed coward to his death, without facing the fact that, unless the case were fully proved, the accuser might be robbing an innocent man of his life and his honor.

In the Byng case, Pitt's moral courage, the main buttress of his greatness, was evidenced for all time. Pitt was avid for power, often arrogant, occasionally Machiavellian, inconsistent on many issues, but never failed at any cost in a choice between integrity and advantage; he was never untrue to the spacious concept. The populace, which was the mainstay of Pitt's political strength, shouted for Byng's execution, but Pitt had fought every inch of the way for a fair trial, and for mercy.

Mr. Pitt was soon called upon to pay a high price for his courage. Immediately after the execution the Newcastle faction began to peer out from their rat-holes. Holdernesse and other Newcastle sympathizers in the Cabinet kept obstructing Pitt's aims and policies. Pitt's supporters in the House, on the other hand, brought in a motion to inquire how far the loss of Minorca had been due to the want of naval and military preparations for its defense. They apparently had the forlorn hope that there would be some value in keeping the affair alive, some justice in seeking retribution.

It was expected that Pitt, who was ill with the gout, would not be able to come out in the wintry weather. But on the day when the motion was presented he appeared, wrapped up in garments so extraordinary as to attract the attention of the younger Horace Walpole. His legs were encased in long woolen riding-stockings, he wore a beaver jacket and a waistcoat embroidered in gold, and over all this he had on a red frock coat, while his right arm, swollen with the disease, was carried in a crêpe sling. The astonished House wondered what line Pitt would take, and he did not leave them long in doubt.

Since he had failed to save the life of Admiral Byng, he said to the House, that matter was now essentially a closed issue. He observed that any investigation of the past should not descend upon a few ministers, but should involve all of Newcastle's Cabinet. This may have been a horrifying hint to Hardwicke and some of the others, letting them know that Pitt at least had his suspicions of how far they may have been involved. He also observed that a number of the late Cabinet were now his present colleagues, and that, accordingly, any blame for negligence might involve the present Administration as well. He was shrewd enough to be, in fact, highly skeptical of any investigation in Parliament while it was under the control of Newcastle's minions, and he expected that any procedure would turn out to be a clearance for the Duke and his fellows.

The House was much relieved that Mr. Pitt had taken this line of reasoning and even went so far as to pass a series of resolutions which virtually concluded the whole matter, outlining the steps which the Newcastle Government had taken for the defense of Minorca, and reaching the conclusion that the necessary had been done.

It will be recalled that Pitt had come into the Government through the default of Newcastle and all the other leaders who were afraid to take responsibility in such dangerous times. Now that the public clamor had been satisfied by the execution of Byng, Newcastle and the powerful Whig families began to regret their tremors and to resent the presence of Mr. Pitt at the head of the Government. Pitt's Cabinet was weak. Holdernesse and certain other members were Newcastle men. Legge, who was supposedly Pitt's second in command and presumably a loyal friend, was, in fact, flirting with the Holdernesse group and preparing to desert his chief if he could make a satisfactory deal. Temple, then and later, was distinctly a liability. He was not yet avidly jealous of his brother-in-law's fame, but he at no time considered himself second in merit to Mr. Pitt. Unfortunately, Temple aped Pitt's most arrogant moods without having his redeeming qualities. Where Pitt was disdainful Temple tried to be more so. Pitt was unyielding in policy in conferences with his Majesty, while Temple was so rude and arrogant that the King could hardly bear to see him. Such conduct naturally brought unpopularity to the Pitt group in Court circles.

The chief Minister, accordingly, was treading on very shaky ground. The Newcastle party needed only to find a successful Cabinet coalition, after which they could defeat Mr. Pitt on any measure in Parliament and require his resignation. His one sure source of support, aside from the vague value of such popularity as he had left with the general public, was the support of Leicester House. The Earl of Bute, who was now the chief advisor there, looked upon Pitt with greatest favor, addressed him as "my dearest friend," applauded his efforts, and wrote on March 2, 1757, "Go on, my dear Pitt, make every bad subject your declared enemy, every honest man your real friend. I, for my part, most desire ever to share with you in both."

The Leicester House support proved, however, to be inadequate. Frederick of Prussia, who felt that he was not getting enough help from Mr. Pitt, asked the Duke of Cumberland to accept the command of the Army of Observation allied with Frederick's forces. Cumberland accepted on the condition that Pitt must be dismissed, for he would not take orders from a Secretary of State who was so closely allied with Leicester House. This was a grievous error of judgment on the part of Cumberland, as he discovered before the year was out; but it was fatal to Pitt's continuation in office. As Pitt had no Parliamentary majority, and as he apparently had lost his hold on the public because of his part in the Byng affair, he was at the mercy of the King's wishes. On April 4, George II dismissed Temple, thinking that Pitt would take the hint; but Pitt chose to leave the responsibility to the Throne. Accordingly, on April 6, his Majesty demanded Pitt's resignation and ordered the Newcastle contingent to form a Government.

There followed immediately one of the most curious interludes in British history. When it came to the crisis, few of Newcastle's friends actually had the courage to undertake the job. In the first place, to everyone's surprise, there was a tremendous popular uproar at Pitt's dismissal. The public hero had been denounced by the people for defending Byng, but to see him thrown out of office by the Crown and the old crowd called back to power was an entirely different matter. London, Exeter, York, Dublin, and scores of other cities and towns, voted him the freedom of the city and sent him their certificates in the form of elaborate presents. Exeter offered hers in boxes made of hearts of oak, and Lady Hervey observed of this deluge of honors that "it rained gold boxes."

The next three months were a repetition of the Carteret-Bath fiasco. The main business of the country was carried on informally by Holdernesse and William Murray, now Lord Mansfield. The King commissioned Lord Winchelsea to take the post of First Lord of the Admiralty, which he did with reluctance. Fox refused to serve in any capacity. Though Newcastle was aided by Hardwicke, and though the Duke was itching to return to the high command, on every hand, his friends gave him the unpalatable advice that no ministry could be formed unless Mr. Pitt had the principal part. The Primate of Ireland, one of the Duke's chief advisors, told him that an administration with Pitt "is what the whole nation calls for."

Accordingly, on June 3, Newcastle proposed to the King a ministry which included both Pitt and Temple. The red-faced little monarch was furious.

"I know," he replied, "that by inclination Pitt will distress my affairs abroad which are so enough already."

The King called in a dozen leaders of the Whig families,

including Bedford and Carteret-Granville, and with this support prevailed upon Fox to accept a prominent place. For a moment everything looked happy for the King's wishes, but at this point Mansfield had a private audience with the King in which he affirmed simply that the arrangement would not work. Pitt had no more bitter enemy than Mansfield but the latter had a practical regard for his own hide, and had sense enough to realize that public affairs were in a critical state. At last, in profound disgust, his Majesty told Hardwicke to bring in the best ministry that he could.

This could mean only one thing. Mr. Pitt was immediately approached with the request to return to office and again assume the direction of the Government. Hardwicke was to serve without portfolio. Newcastle was to be included, but on terms which were extremely painful to his Grace.

The Duke's face was saved by placing him in the office of First Lord of the Treasury which had been occupied by Devonshire. He was, however, to have even less voice in policy than Devonshire had enjoyed.

Newcastle obviously had something to offer or he could not have returned to office so persistently. He had an unquestionable flair for political management. He knew what the boys in the back room wanted and he managed to give it to them, even at the expense of his private purse. Newcastle's job, in the revived Administration, was to bring to Pitt the Parliamentary majority which had hitherto been uncertain or lacking.

The proposal to include Newcastle in the new Administration naturally raised considerable adverse comment among Pitt's independent supporters. Pitt saw no alternative. Without Parliamentary support he was in constant jeopardy. If he took the time to be a Parliamentary manager his chief work would be neglected; and there was no assurance that he would be successful in a field for which he had no taste and no proved ability. He described his dilemma in a letter to Glover, one of his supporters at that time:

But what is to be done? Do not imagine that I can be induced to unite with him unless sure of power—I mean power over public measures. The disposition of offices, (except the few efficient ones of administration), the creating of deans, bishops, and every place man besides, is quite out of my plan, and I would willingly relinquish them to the Duke of Newcastle.

Thus it was arranged. On June 29, 1757, Pitt's interrupted Ministry, much fortified, received the approval of his Majesty. Hardwicke declared that it was looked upon as the strongest administration that had been formed for years. Even the King seemed reconciled.

"Then this thing is done," he said to Hardwicke, "and may I thank you heartily."

With his own men in the strategic offices, and with the backing of the powerful Whig machine, Pitt now had such facilities as the country could offer for raising the nation from the deplorable and almost hopeless state into which it had fallen.

CHAPTER XXIII

"This Almost Degenerate England"

The task which Mr. Pitt had set for himself and his country was seemingly an impossibility. England had a population of only 7,000,000 persons, compared with 10,000,000 in Spain, 5,000,000 in Prussia, 29,000,000 in Austria, and 27,000,000 in France. For a time, under Elizabeth, England's great energy on the sea had given her a sense of confidence which exceeded her position in terms of actual relative force. Her success in the colonization of America and the relative peacefulness of her internal affairs had created the illusion of her being a first-rate power.

Other nations, however, particularly France, had increased their naval strength and on land had notable superiority. For the past forty years England had endured a process of being whittled away. Her generals and her European policy had been as stupid as that of the competitor nations, and without marked superiority in intelligence she was inevitably overshadowed by superior force. The repeated series of British defeats in her sporadic and ill-conceived attempts to participate in European affairs had convinced foreign powers, and at last England herself, of her relative weakness.

Pitt, however, was determined to develop England into a vast empire for free people. He was a typical British subject in his conviction of the superiority of the British system; and, what was less common, he was dedicated to the purpose of maintaining as a fact the freedom which existed in theory in the British Constitution.

His problem in rejuvenating the kingdom was internal as well as external. For years he had tried to impress upon Parliament and the Crown that the liberty of the subject was the cornerstone of the nation. He had repeatedly pointed to two to three million subjects in America as an essential part of the Empire, part of the family in trade, peace, and war. The American population increased the strength of the mother country by a third,—a stalwart, independent, combative third. If England and her American colonies could act on a unified basis the English system thereby would be bolstered by a formidable force. Pitt's initial goal, therefore, was the cultivation of the American colonies, and an extension of British colonial rule throughout all North America, including Canada. Such a conquest, he felt, would restore the self-confidence of the nation at home, would spread the liberties of mankind, and would check the growing prestige of the totalitarian Bourbon powers.

In this purpose Mr. Pitt demonstrated the truth of his claim that he was fundamentally a man of action, that his exceptional eloquence was cultivated not for the sake of virtuosity but to achieve results. At the closing session of Parliament following his return to the Government, Mr. Pitt had these words included in the King's address:

> The succour and preservation of my dominions in America have been my constant care. And, next to the security of my kingdom, they shall continue to be my great and principal object: and I have taken such measures, as I trust, by the blessing of God, may effectually disappoint the designs of my enemies in those parts.
>
> I have had no other view, but to vindicate the just rights of my Crown and subjects from the most injurious encroachments; to preserve tranquillity, as far as the circumstances of things might admit; and to prevent our true friends, and the liberties of Europe, from being oppressed or endangered by any unprovoked and unnatural conjunction.

It will be noted that the King's address alluded to "the liberties of Europe" as well as to the colonial situation. This was pertinent in more ways than one. France was now the greatest obstacle to Britain's colonial expansion. Furthermore, Pitt was planning to embark on the European scene more actively than before, if necessary. Frederick of Prussia, on June 18, 1757, had been defeated at Kolin, and it now seemed evident that Frederick could not be counted upon as a secure protector for England's back door. As Chesterfield wrote to a Mr. Dayrolles:

> The King of Prussia, the only ally we had in the world, is now, I fear, *hors de combat*. The French are masters to do what they please in America. *We are no longer a nation. I never yet saw so dreadful a prospect.*

Pitt, undeterred by the gloomy outlook, was applying himself with the utmost diligence to get his campaign under way on all fronts, often working far into the night, and upsetting the tempers of his colleagues who were not accustomed to such industry. Holdernesse in particular, his co-secretary, complained greatly at being obliged to sit up until three in the morning while Mr. Pitt was composing a dispatch to the King of Prussia, "weighing words more than matter."

"Tout ceci est bel et bon pour un temps!" Holdernesse wailed to a friend, "but I would not pass such another evening for the King's revenue, or for what is still more valuable, Mr. Pitt's abilities . . . for I neither can nor will be detained for hours upon the introduction of a monosillable."

Such a whirlwind of effort bewildered the Ministry as a whole, including the Duke of Newcastle, and left him, correctly, with the impression that he was far behindhand in knowing what was going on. Pitt called frequent Cabinet meetings and made a point of informing Newcastle and Hardwicke of his general procedure; but this was quite a different situation from the days when Newcastle was top dog. On July 11, 1757, the Duke wrote to Mr. Pitt, almost pathetically:

> I beg you would order Mr. Rivers to send me your letters and instructions to the Earl of Loudoun and Admiral Holbourne, that I may have the pleasure of seeing them. I am sure I shall most entirely approve of them.

Times, indeed, had changed, and Pitt, with his gift for the theatrical, conducted himself so that it was clear, even to the general public, that he was accepted by both King and Parliament as the chief Minister. Though he did not hold the Treasury office, and hence was not entitled to live at 10 Downing Street, the seat of Government was wherever Mr. Pitt might choose to reside. He rented a house at 10 St. James Square, London's most fashionable section, and there set up a ménage suitable to his position. Where once he had traversed the countryside in a one-horse chaise, or clattered along country roads in a two-seater, he now set forth in a coach, attended by footmen in livery of blue and silver. On the outside of the carriage was carried a huge boot to accommodate Mr. Pitt's gouty leg. If the commoners failed to recognize the ownership of the carriage, the boot gave the identifying mark.

The boot was doubtless necessary, even so it was a touch worthy of Pitt in his most Garrick mood. Whenever he had audience with the King, the huge leather piece of footwear stood outside the door, an advertisement that the people's tribune was holding conference with his Majesty. Again, the boot stood for hours before doors at the Admiralty, at the Treasury, and outside the Parliamentary Library. Mr. Pitt was diligent and ubiquitous; and, thanks to the boot, all the world knew it.

The indefatigable Secretary of State was not deluded, however, by any impression that his zeal could overcome a bad situation promptly. He was struggling to restore a Government which had been conducted on a disorganized and whimsical basis. Favoritism, rank, and seniority competed for Army and Navy leadership, regardless of ability. During the ten weeks when there had been no Ministry in England whatever, important military and naval expeditions had been under way. As they had lacked Government support their success would depend upon the enterprise of the commanders in the field, and Mr. Pitt was not optimistic. Lord Loudoun, in North America, had an army of regulars, presumably adequate for the reduction of Louisbourg, but whether the General could accomplish the elaborate series of victories he had projected was a matter of some doubt.

On the Continent, the Duke of Cumberland was in charge of the Army of Observation allied with Frederick of

Prussia. Unfortunately Cumberland, on July 25, 1757, was surrounded by the French at Hastenbeck, in Germany. Thanks to the activity of his aide-de-camp, Col. Jeffery Amherst, in organizing a rear-guard action, the Duke made his personal escape, though he was soon afterward compelled to sign a humiliating treaty at Closter Seven, which delivered Hanover to the French and agreed to disband the Hanoverian and Hessian troops, about which there had been so much controversy in Parliament for many years.

The catastrophe was a severe blow to British prestige. England had proved unable to protect the Electorate of Hanover, which was her monarch's most treasured possession, and Cumberland, the King's own son, had proved himself to be scandalously incompetent. The Earl of Bute, now chief mentor of the Prince of Wales, expressed the general sentiments in his letter to Pitt of August 5, 1757:

> I do not know that in my life I ever felt myself so affected with any foreign transaction. Oh, my dear friend, what dreadful auspices do we begin with! And yet, thank God, I see you in office. If even the wreck of this Crown can be preserved to our amiable young Prince, 'tis to your efforts, your abilities, my dear Pitt, that he must owe it. Let what will happen, one thing comforts me. I know you have a soul fit for these rough times, that, instead of sinking under adversity, will rise and grow stronger against it. Farewell, my dearest friend. No event shall ever make me cease to be one minute,
> Most affectionately, etc.

In the long run Cumberland's disaster was not without its compensations for Mr. Pitt personally. It was Cumberland who had demanded and obtained the dismissal of Pitt before starting out on this expedition. It was Cumberland who at last had lost the Electorate of Hanover for his father. The King's objection to Pitt as the man who would not protect the King's German possessions was now obscured by the deep pain of actually losing them through the bungling of his own son.

The defeat at Hastenbeck encouraged Spain to take a more active interest in the Bourbon alliance, as the defeat of England would provide rich plums of conquest in the

New World. On August 23, 1757, Pitt wrote a long dispatch to Sir Benjamin Keene, British Ambassador at Madrid. Essentially, it proposed an English and Spanish alliance, promised to satisfy certain complaints which Spain had made against England for some time past, and spoke seductively of the importance to Spain of preserving her independence from French domination. This missive also proposed that the Spaniards capture Minorca and trade it to England for Gibraltar.

While Pitt was waiting to hear the outcome of this negotiation, more trouble arose at home. The new Militia Act, which had been put through the Parliament with so much difficulty, was looked upon by the public with very considerable suspicion. The administration of the Act was in the hands of lord-lieutenants of the various counties, and in some sections the measure had been introduced with an arbitrary procedure which intensified public suspicion. Many feared that the Act was only an excuse for impressment, that once men were enrolled for the Militia they would be at the mercy of the military.

The Militia Act, in fact, was enforced in strict compliance with its promises; but it was nevertheless enforced. Pitt could not afford a demonstration of weakness at home, added to all the disturbances abroad, and the regular Army was used to support the lord-lieutenants of the counties wherever necessary. Within a short time the public saw that the Act was being carried out in good faith, and the resentment died down; but it had been a nerve-shaking issue.

Then on August 30, Pitt received dispatches from Loudoun bearing the incredible news that the General had abandoned even the beginnings of his plan. He was retiring from Louisbourg, as the French, he was advised, had a force strong enough to defend it. He added that it would be too late to do anything further in America that season.

Pitt's untried Government was in the depths of despondency. The chief Minister virtually alone saw that the remedy was to keep at it until some particular effort would hearten the public and start his program on a forward course. His immediate plan was for the Navy to make an attack on Rochefort. Rochefort was an important point on the coast of France near the Basque Roads. It contained wharves and arsenals, and a successful blow would have a strong effect in dampening French morale. Pitt's colleagues were extremely doubtful as to the wisdom of this enterprise, but he forced it through, saying to Newcastle that he would defend it with his head and "whoever stopped it should answer for it."

Pitt was eager to have a young vigorous man in charge of the expedition. He was satisfied with the appointment of Admiral Hawke in charge of the naval command, but he needed enterprising officers for the army half of the expedition. Rochefort was to be in the nature of a test case, and Pitt saw in it a chance to try out the qualities of the younger men. He requested that Col. Henry Seymour Conway be put in charge, but the King insisted that Sir John Mordaunt, an older man, should be the superior officer. Besides Conway there were two other notable young officers on the staff. One was Col. James Wolfe, serving as Quartermaster, and another was William Petty Fitzmaurice who, years later as Lord Shelburne, became one of Pitt's chief supporters.

The expedition set out on September 9, 1757, and did not reach the Basque Roads until eleven days later. At this point dissension broke out among the officers. Wolfe made a landing and reported favorably on the possibility of taking Rochefort. Hawke supported him; but Mordaunt, Conway, and others could not agree. The result was that the squadron returned to London early in October having accomplished nothing, and causing by its failure a further depletion in public confidence.

There was gloom on all fronts, even among Mr. Pitt's closest friends. William Beckford, the London and Jamaica merchant, outlined the public view in a letter of October 22, 1757.

DEAR SIR,

It gave me great pleasure to find, by your favour of the 18th instant, that there was no seeming want of bodily health, which is what, I confess, has given me the greatest uneasiness; for as to health, vigour, and fortitude of mind, no man enjoys it in a greater degree than yourself. This is a blessing few have the comfort of; it gives cheerfulness, affords resources in misfortunes, and prevents despair. I wish I could say as much of some of your associates, who are constantly croaking to the world the weakness of Great Britain and the strength of France.

We are truly sick at heart; but the constitution is good. I think of the public, as I do of a robust patient,—get it but out of the hands of quacks, and it will recover of itself. To attack and destroy one of the principal naval arsenals and docks of France was a noble project; success in the undertaking would have made amends for all our losses and disappointments. I do from my soul believe, that if courage or conduct had not been wanting, we must have succeeded. Heaven and earth seemed to favor us.

It is to be wished, rather than hoped, that something might be undertaken, decisive in its consequences; for if we go on in our military operations as we have begun, we shall be ruined, by being beat and baffled in detail. Cape Breton, Louisbourg, the only port the French have in all the Atlantic, seems to be the object: the greater naval force they have there, the greater influence will such a conquest have. Let them make what efforts they will, Great Britain is able to send a greater; and such a one as may ensure success, provided a commander can be found that has courage and capacity equal to the undertaking.

> Your most obedient
> and faithful humble servant,
> W. BECKFORD

Louisbourg,—Beckford was right enough about that. It was in fact, the chief French post in the New World, commanding the entrance to the St. Lawrence River, which led to all the French possessions to the westward. Loudoun, who had been so absurdly over-confident, had recognized its value,—Loudoun who was going to take Louisbourg and eastern Canada in one campaign, and then had turned back from the initial attempt. Pitt was formulating a general plan, but individual successes had to come first. Louisbourg, indeed, was essential, and Pitt agreed with Beckford that it could be taken "provided a commander can be found that has courage and capacity equal to the undertaking."

To find such a man became Pitt's determined purpose. He turned for advice on the subject to Sir John Ligonier, who, on October 29, succeeded the Duke of Cumberland as Commander of all the British forces. Three names for the command against Louisbourg received serious consideration. They were Col. Jeffery Amherst, Col. Henry Seymour Conway, and Col. James Wolfe. All three had served with distinction. Conway probably would have been first choice, except for his excessive caution at Rochefort. Wolfe was impetuous, daring, and ready to court any danger for a desired goal. He was thirty years of age, ten years younger than Amherst, less balanced, and less schooled in strategy. Ligonier recommended Colonel Amherst.

Amherst, though virtually unknown to the general public, had many scores to his credit. He had served as an aide-de-camp to Ligonier in several campaigns and had obviously won the hearty approval of that gentleman. He had organized the rear-guard action which saved the Duke of Cumberland at Hastenbeck, and Cumberland, for whatever little influence he still had left, supported Amherst's cause. Two other strong influences favored the young officer. In his early days he had been a tent-mate of Sir Joseph Yorke, now Ambassador at The Hague, a son of Hardwicke, and Amherst had Hardwicke's endorsement. Again, during the Hastenbeck campaign, Amherst had taken pains to pay his respects repeatedly to the Princess of Hesse Cassel who was a sister of the King and an ardent Whig supporter. She, too, was a believer in the competence of the young Colonel.

In spite of all these recommendations which Mr. Pitt was able to lay before the King, his Majesty was strongly opposed to the radical procedure of elevating a Colonel to such a command. The King had not yet become convinced that his new firebrand Minister was a trustworthy manager for the kingdom, and, indeed, Pitt had not as yet produced any results to win such a confidence. Pitt, however, had no intention of being balked this time. He could have forced the issue on the Throne; but he employed the more tactful method of outlining the difficulties to the King's mistress, the Countess of Yarmouth, and she, in turn, convinced his Majesty.

While these negotiations were in progress, Pitt received a lengthy reply from Benjamin Keene which made clear that no help could be obtained from Spain. Keene reported that Wall had been personally friendly, but had said that the failure of the English to pay attention to Spanish complaints against English privateering and the seizure of Spanish ships had created an invincible barrier to co-operation. In fact, Wall's friendships in England had proved very embarrassing to him with his own Government, and he saw no possibility of supporting any British proposal under the circumstances.

In respect to the plea that Spain should support England in the interests of liberty, Wall had coldly reminded Keene again of England's failure to keep her promises, saying—

> Are these times and circumstances to talk on such points as the liberties of Europe and a closer union with Spain, when you have given *us* so much room to be dissatisfied with you? And not only *us* but your enemies the French and the Austrians, who are continually blowing up the coals against you, for your be-behavior towards *us*? What worse can happen to *us,* when the liberties of Europe are gone, than what you do to us? If we are to be despised, let it be by the strong, and by our own blood and relations; and what are we to expect from you in your successes, if such is your treatment in the present state of your affairs?

The one bright spot on the scene was the revival of strength on the part of Frederick of Prussia. On December 5, 1757, he defeated Count Daun at Lissa, and on the 25th he recaptured Breslau. Pitt determined to push the alliance with Frederick for all it was worth. To win the Throne to this view, he agreed to support the King in the latter's desire to recapture Hanover. The mercenaries who had been disbanded under the convention of Closter Seven were re-enlisted. On January 17, 1758, Pitt sent a royal message to Parliament, asking for supplies to aid Prussia. It was a desperate procedure, but the one alliance which promised immediate continued victories. It was, likewise, a very costly enterprise, more so than Pitt had imagined.

Newcastle's staff at the Treasury estimated that the expenses of an army of 50,000 to aid Frederick would be £1,800,000 for one season. Pitt was flabbergasted, and wrote to Newcastle, "The demand of forage for Hessians last year is preposterous, and would revolt all the world. I wish to God I could see my way through this mountain of expense. I confess I cannot, unless your Grace can reduce things to a reasonable bulk." The Treasury had included, however, the cost of graft in buying supplies from the King's friends in Hanover, and the accountants maintained that the estimates were over-conservative. Regardless of the expense, it was deemed necessary to go ahead with the plans.

Fortunately for Pitt's American schemes, his success in the appointment of Amherst had placed control of the war more closely in his own hands. Amherst had been delayed for several weeks in returning from the European front, because of the winter weather, and finally arrived at London on Sunday morning, the 26th of January. On March 3, 1758, Mr. Pitt delivered to him a message:

> Mr. Secretary Pitt presents his compliments to Major General Amherst and sends him herewith his Majesty's commission to be Commander-in-chief at the siege of Louisbourg, which has been prepared without notification from the War Office, and is not proposed to be at present entered there, or at the other offices where commissions are usually entered, in order not to make the object of this commission too public.

Amherst naturally accepted this dazzling promotion, though he, like the other army officers, preferred a European command; and for family reasons of no small urgency, he obtained Mr. Pitt's promise that he might return to England at the time of the campaign. Amherst made an auspicious beginning, for he set sail within thirteen days after his appointment, to attempt the conquest of the formidable Louisbourg.

Meanwhile Pitt, who had been in office more than a year, still hoped impatiently for some note of military victory to justify his Ministry. He had recalled Loudoun and had appointed General Abercromby as the Commander in the New World, except for the Louisbourg expedition. Abercromby was charged with the task of taking Ticonderoga. He was a dull senior officer addicted to lengthy reports on what could not be done, but Pitt gave him an excellent staff and 15,000 trained troops to facilitate his task.

At home, the Parliament seemed less concerned with Mr. Pitt's anxieties than with their own squabbles. In the House of Commons a bill had been introduced to extend the provisions of the Habeas Corpus Act which, over a period of years, had been increasingly restricted. The bill passed the Commons with little debate, but met with great opposition in the House of Lords. When Mr. Pitt was emphasizing to the world the liberty of the Anglo-Saxon system, when he particularly needed this moral force, both at home and abroad, the opposition in the Lords to a more liberal Habeas Corpus was dangerous and disheartening. As Bute, who was still a supporter of Mr. Pitt, wrote him on June 4, 1758:

> What a terrible proof was Friday in the House of Lords of the total loss of public spirit, and the most supreme indifference to those valuable rights, for the obtaining which our ancestors freely risked both life and fortune! These are dreadful clouds that hang over the future accession, and damp the hopes I should otherwise entertain of that important day—I say *damp,* for while you keep your health, I never will despair of better times.
>
> I am ever most affectionately yours,
>
> BUTE

The calendar moved around toward midsummer, and there was still no news from America or the Continent. Pitt had removed to his country place at Hayes, and Lady Hester was visiting the Temples at Stowe. Pitt's home life in these dark days was the one comfort which renewed his strength. There were now three children in the family. In addition to Hester who was two-and-a-half, there was a son John who was a year-and-a-half old, and a second daughter Harriot under three months. The youngest was with her mother at Stowe, but the two older remained to keep father company. He wrote to Hester on the 1st of July:

Hayes is as sweet with these showers, as it can be without the presence of her who gives to every sweet its best sweetness. The loved babes are delightfully well, and remembered dear mamma over their strawberries. They both looked for her in the prints, and told me, "Mamma gone up there—Stowe garden." As the showers seem local, I may suppose my sweet enjoying them with a fine evening sun.

But not all the pleasantness of the scene could blot out his anxiety for the fate of the nation; and he continued the letter, speaking in despondent terms about the public scene:

The messenger is just arrived, and no news. Expectation grows every hour into more anxiety.

I trust, my life, in the same favouring Providence that all will be well, and that this almost degenerate England may learn from the disgrace and ruin it shall have escaped, and the consideration and security it may enjoy, to be more deserving of the blessing.

CHAPTER XXIV

The Critical Year

Pitt was in a position where he must have victories. For years, in season and out, he had preached the doctrine of the Constitution, of the liberty of the subject, and of the empire of freemen. He had been then in the position of a critic, and now, as head of the Government, it was his job to prove whether or not democracy could stand up as a world power.

Pitt had committed himself to a program which involved sending expeditions around the globe; he did not hesitate, believing that the democratic procedures of England could match the Bourbon strength, and believing, too, that the United Kingdom had to be well armed and effective if it were to command worldwide respect. Since Pitt's accession to the Ministry, England's part in the war had become avowedly for "the liberties of Europe" and for a free empire, as he conceived it, in the New World.

Thus far, events had been disappointing, though Pitt's exclamation of an "almost degenerate England" had been penned in a mood of excessive despondency. His dynamic leadership had already begun to have an effect on the personnel of the Army and Navy, even on some of the old personnel. Anson had occupied the office of the First Lord of the Admiralty from 1751 to 1756, at which time he had been hamstrung by Cabinet policy. Now, reappointed to his post under Pitt, he was given chief responsibility for all Channel operations, without political interference; and he had become a new man. In fact, Anson had written to his father-in-law, Hardwicke, soon after being given this command:

> I do assure your lordship when I began to exercise my fleet
> I never saw such awkwardness in going through the common

manœuvres necessary to make an attack upon an enemy's fleet at all. What we now do in an hour, in the beginning took eight. . . . Most of the captains declared they had never seen a line of battle at all, and none of them more than once.

The situation in the Army was more problematic; for it was only necessary to think of Braddock, Loudoun, Mordaunt, and Cumberland to visualize the Army's appalling capacity for being defeated. Whatever excuses might be found for each of these generals, they were clearly not of the stuff which makes for victory; and Pitt needed victories.

His political as well as his strategic edifice rested largely on the showing which he might be able to make in this critical year of 1758. His Ministry was spending money for the war at a rate which terrified Newcastle and the other Cabinet officers, and if the results should not justify Pitt's judgment, his fall would be certain and lasting.

In the initial stages of his war policy, Pitt had sent out expeditions as quickly as he could win approval for them, while his general plan of strategy was being formulated. Now, however, the whole titanic plan had taken shape, and if a successful beginning could be made on some one front, the Administration might hope for adequate support to carry the program through to its conclusion.

The pattern of Pitt's strategy was unknown to Newcastle, who lived in a state of continued apprehension at Pitt's unexpected moves. The plan was not laid in its entirety before either Newcastle or the Cabinet, as the details were subject to alteration in Pitt's own mind, and furthermore he could not rely on the loyalty of his colleagues either to preserve secrecy or to stand by him. His manifold orders to the various commanders of the Army and Navy, however, now stemmed from the principles of a well-ordered and brilliantly conceived system of operations.

The Pitt strategy was based upon England's position in the society of nations and on his conception of what was necessary to her future. England, inferior in population to her chief enemies, and limited in area, could have a future only in colonization which would be in partnership with the mother country. England could have no importance as a nation if self-contained within the British Isles. Trade was necessary to her for wealth, for the existence of her diversified industries, and to maintain the balanced standard of living to which her people had become accustomed. Without trade she must revert to a primitive agricultural society, and without strength in home waters and beyond the seas she would have difficulty in preserving her trade.

The Pitt system, accordingly, had a co-ordinated purpose, divided into five major parts:

1. To extend the British nation in North America.
2. To protect the West Indies trade.
3. To maintain a mobile Atlantic fleet.
4. To hold an adequate position in the Mediterranean.
5. To have a policy and voice in European affairs.

(The objects named above were supplemented by subordinate and related expeditions in Asia and Africa.)

Each of the five points of strategy was important to the other, for an outstanding failure in any one sector might compel such concessions on the other points as to lose every object of the war. In the Treaty of Aix-la-Chapelle, for example, England had not only failed to win protection for her West Indies trade against the practice of search,—the object for which she had engaged in war at that time,—but she had also been obliged, because of failures on the European scene, to return the fortress of Louisbourg which had been captured by the American provincials. The return of that fortress to France, as has already been noted, was a moral as well as a military loss, for it disgraced the mother country of the English colonies before the Bourbon powers in the New World.

In the year 1758 the American scene was of particular concern in Pitt's strategy, for on this front, above all others, England had sustained so many humiliating defeats. America, too, was the major area in which the conflict between the democratic idea and the Bourbon idea was clearly dramatized. As long as the English colonies were threatened by Bourbon invasion from the North and by Bourbon encirclement through the Great Lakes down the Mississippi valley, English freedom was imperiled.

In Pitt's North American program for 1758, there were three enterprises of especial importance, namely:

    a. Louisbourg
    b. Ticonderoga
    c. Bradstreet's expedition.

Louisbourg was a crucial expedition in itself, and was a test of Pitt's assertion that he was the one individual who "could save England." Loudoun had said that Louisbourg could not be taken; the army forces were in command of the untried General Amherst, appointed at Mr. Pitt's personal solicitation; the naval part of the Louisbourg enterprise was headed by Admiral Boscawen, a man intimately known to Pitt and having the Minister's full confidence; and even a portion of the enlisted men in the expedition were a Pitt experiment, namely the Highland regiments that he had organized despite the skepticism of his Cabinet. If Amherst, Boscawen, and the Highlanders should fail, Mr. Pitt's personal judgment would be publicly discredited.

Ticonderoga was almost as important as Louisbourg from a military standpoint. It was the great French fortress between Lake George and Lake Champlain, protecting the major interior route leading from Montreal to Albany. As long as Ticonderoga was in French hands, northern New York was in constant fear of invasion from the French forces and their Indian allies. The Ticonderoga expedition, it will be recalled, was in charge of General James Abercromby, commander-in-chief in the New World, who had been provided with a picked army of 15,000 men. Abercromby was a doddering old fellow, so pettifogging that the colonial troops dubbed him "Mr. Nabbycromby." Pitt had opposed this appointment, but the King had insisted on it. Pitt, however, was able to name the youthful and enterprising Lord Howe as second in command. Howe was counted upon to infuse spirit into the campaign, and, with the generous supply of troops at his command, Abercromby was expected to take the fortress easily, to capture

Crown Point and advance toward Montreal, the capitol
of New France. This would divide the French forces and
diminish any aid which the French might send to Louisbourg. If both Louisbourg and Ticonderoga should be
taken, it was possible that the Abercromby and Amherst

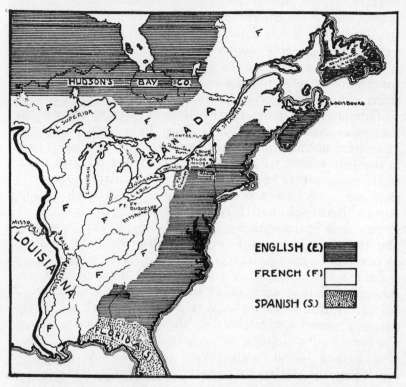

Colonies of England, France and Spain in the New World; the
shaded portion is English, the white French, and the dotted Spanish.
West of the Mississippi the sovereignty was largely undetermined.

forces could effect a juncture and force the surrender of
eastern Canada in the current season.

The third phase of the North American program, namely
the Bradstreet expedition, was the result of a Pitt innova-
tion contained in orders which he had authorized in December, 1757, which gave provincial troops equal status

with those of the regular British army.   This revolutionary step had immediately fired the enthusiasm of the colonials, and Col. John Bradstreet of Maine had volunteered to raise a force to attempt an attack on Forts Oswego and Frontenac.   The capture of these forts, which were on Lake Ontario, would impair the French communication to the West and prevent the enemy from attacking from the West on Abercromby's left flank.   The colonial troops, however, were held in greatest contempt by most of the British officers, to say nothing of the armchair critics in the London coffee-houses, and nothing was expected from the Bradstreet enterprise by others than the first Minister.

Though Pitt's most cherished hope was to extend the Empire in North America, the West Indies was a scene of immediate political importance and, therefore, a main item in the Pitt system.   Many of the rich Whig families made their money either in owning West Indies plantations or in shipping to and from the West Indies.   Pitt's strong supporter, Beckford, had large interests in Jamaica.   Both France and Spain owned rich islands in this area,—vulnerable islands.   The capture of one such prize might be both an easy and a showy victory.

In the Pitt system, as stated above, the principle was fundamental that each point had a bearing on the other points.   Pitt, for example, was determined to regain Minorca, England's stronghold in the Mediterranean (Point 4), but he now decided to accomplish this by the capture of a French island in the West Indies (Point 2) which could be later traded to France for Minorca.   He was a genius at this policy of oblique pressure instead of direct attack, which always kept the enemy guessing.   Martinique was the island he had selected for the present purpose.   The fleet which protected the trading ships to and from England and her West Indian possessions could be used, and Martinique, if unprepared for attack, could not be adequately defended by the few ships on the local station.

While waiting for news from the American and West Indies fronts, Pitt was developing his third point,—a mobile Atlantic fleet,—for years he had been a "big navy" man, and the furious and brilliant strategy which he now employed became the basis of England's future tactics of protecting her worldwide empire by means of a strong navy.

The general patrol duty of the Atlantic fleet extended from the Channel, southward off the west coast of France, around the coast of Spain and Portugal, through the straits of Gibraltar and into the Mediterranean. Sometimes different sections of the fleet were under independent commands and at times the Mediterranean squadron was almost wholly divorced from the operations of the main fleet; but, though the various units of the Navy might have their temporary diverse objectives, Pitt fundamentally used the entire Atlantic fleet as a dynamic center flinging out expeditions with centrifugal force for the protection of British interests everywhere.

Pitt's demand for ships and more ships to augment his Atlantic fleet was insatiable. Day after day and week after week the many-sailed ships of the line and the smart swift frigates could be seen making their way down the Thames. The spectacle of squadron after squadron setting out for some glorious unknown destiny excited the public and lent glamour to the strange eagle-like commoner at the head of the Government.

This factor of unknown destination, this Pitt policy of sending captains to sea with sealed orders, had the flare of romance, yet was adopted for practical reasons. Pitt was unable to trust either the discretion or the loyalty of his colleagues and particularly could not trust the gossipy and hysterical Newcastle and, therefore, felt that the less the Duke knew about operations the better. Newcastle in this summer of 1758 was torn between admiration and terror. He was dazed by Pitt's whirlwind energy and observed that "there had never been such diligence in government." On the other hand, Newcastle and the rest of the Cabinet were alarmed at the continuous flow of expeditions, and were infuriated at not knowing their purpose. Finally, stung by neglect, Newcastle beat up the winds of criticism against Pitt, claiming that the Minister was planning a huge naval engagement with France, alleging that such a battle might cripple the entire British navy, and howling that it was impossible for the British fleet successfully to engage the French and their allies on an extended line.

Pitt, actually, had no such intention.   He had a concept of the use of the Navy which had been adopted by Drake, was later used to enormous effect by the American free-lance, John Paul Jones, and again was used by German sub-marines and planes against England in 1939.   Pitt's naval game was not to attempt to capture French towns, nor

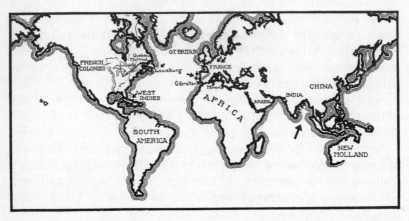

Pitt's world strategy.   Note the arrows pointing to North America, the West Indies, the coasts of France and Spain, the Mediterranean, the northeast border of France, and India.

even to engage any part of the French fleet, if avoidable, but to dart hither and yon on the French coast, pouncing sud-denly, burning docks, destroying shipping, moving rapidly away, and then pouncing again at some distant point.   In this way the French were to be kept in a perpetual state of alarm.   The seacoast regions would clamor for protection from their home Government, and the French Cabinet would be terrified, not knowing at what point the British might be planning an invasion.

This conception was not original with Mr. Pitt.   It had been suggested by Frederick of Prussia, by Beckford, by Anson, and by other advisors, but Mr. Pitt was the one who had to take the responsibility and make the policy effective. An element in the success of the scheme, on which Mr. Pitt counted, was the temperament of the French Court and Cabinet, who reacted as he expected. Louis XV and his advisers were Continental-minded. As Pitt had foreseen, these mosquito bites on the French flank were interpreted as threats of invasion. The Bourbons thought in terms of armies on European soil, and they expected Mr. Pitt to think in the same terms. Each sortie upon the French coast had the effect of shifting the armies of France from one point to another, and bewildered the high command. In fact, during the summer of 1758 approximately 10,000 mobile British marines were able to divert the movements of some 90,000 of the French forces,—all of which was extraordinarily helpful to Frederick of Prussia, to his ally, Ferdinand of Brunswick, who was in charge of the Hanoverian forces and to the British troops attached to Ferdinand's command.

While concentrating his energies on Navy policy, Pitt did not neglect Point 5 of his system, which was to take part in the war on the Continent. In this he had the ardent support of Newcastle and the King, who believed that he had at last come over to their way of thinking. The old Army crowd were equally pleased, as they had been brought up to think in terms of the battlefields of Europe. What was a victory in some remote place such as Albany or Martinique compared to a well publicized and understandable conquest on the Rhine? Even the eager and ambitious wolf had his eyes set on a European appointment as his ultimate goal.

Pitt had already changed from his position of his earlier days by approving the hiring of Hessian troops for Ferdinand's army in Hanover. He now took a further step in proposing to add to the few British troops under Ferdinand's general command. His real purpose was quite different from the days in which England had confined her chief activities to meddling in the affairs of Europe. Pitt did not have the slightest interest in who might sit on the throne of Austria or who might be elected as emperor of the confederacy of German states known as The Empire.

His purpose was to keep France and her allies so occupied at home that they could not interfere with his building of an Anglo-Saxon system.

Legend: A. N.—Austrian Netherlands. H.—Hanover. M.—Mecklenburg. Detail of Pitt's strategy in the home territory. Note the elaborate system of naval attacks on the Atlantic Coast and in the Mediterranean.

The Pitt scheme of reinforcements for Europe was ingenious. He advised sending twelve squadrons of cavalry to the aid of Ferdinand. This move was helpful to the European forces, where cavalry were needed, and yet did not deplete Pitt's resources for other expeditions. Extensive use of cavalry was impractical in North America or the Orient because of the problem of transporting the horses. The cavalry were not needed for home defenses and were, as Beckford pointed out in a letter to Pitt, "a great burden to the poor inn-holders, etc." In fact Beckford favored sending all the cavalry to Europe.

As soon as the proposal for sending the twelve units of cavalry had been approved there was a great squabble among the leading influences of the kingdom to obtain the posts of commander and assistant commander. Here was a chance for glory near at home, without the long absences and the inconveniences of colonial warfare. Since, in Pitt's mind, this was a minor expedition from the military standpoint, he used it to the utmost to strengthen political support for his Ministry. He first named Gen. Bligh, an old Army man to the command. This pleased the Throne and the old Army group, but Bligh was unable to win the backing of the chief Whig families. Pitt accordingly transferred Bligh and appointed the young Duke of Marlborough, a choice which was highly popular among the old-school political nabobs. As second in command Pitt appointed Lord George Sackville, who was a favorite of Prince George, heir apparent. Sackville was a snob of the first water. As a soldier, according to the younger Horace Walpole, he was "not among the first to court danger." He was, however, a son of the Duke of Dorset and represented the Dorset interests in Parliament. He had considerable influence furthermore in the upper social ranks, some of whom were inclined to look with misgivings on having a commoner at the head of the Ministry. All in all, the appointment of Marlborough and Sackville substantially strengthened Pitt's political fences even though more skillful soldiers could have been named from the point of view of Prince Ferdinand, under whom they were to serve.

While the politicians at home were exciting themselves over the war in the European area, Pitt had occasion to have fresh worries regarding the Louisbourg expedition. The great peril there was that some of the French fleet might get into the harbor of the city, interfere with Boscawen's transports, and prevent them from supplying Amherst's army. The support of the Army, both in food and munitions, was necessarily from the sea, as the land adjacent to Louisbourg was barren and the few settlers were hostile. Rumors came to England on July 3 that the French had, in fact, been able to run the loose blockade of the seas which Britain attempted to maintain, and that some French ships had reached the stronghold. Temple on hearing this wrote to his brother-in-law Pitt:

> What alarms me most, is the account Lady Hester brought of some men-of-war, a few, very few, being got into Louisburgh; because, upon the issue of that attempt, I think the whole salvation of this country and Europe does essentialy depend, and any French force at all in that harbour, bringing comfort and reinforcement, may blast all our hopes: but . . . I will still depend upon success there, and wish it everywhere else.

Before July was ended the British forces representing the entire range of Pitt's strategy, were engaged or preparing to engage in North America, against the French coast, the Mediterranean, in the West Indies, and on the continent of Europe. A few weeks would tell whether he had planned and chosen wisely, whether his Administration would go down as one of the greatest fiascos in history or whether it would give promise of the rise of a new England. The suspense was hard to bear. News from the various fronts was anywhere from a week to three months late. On July 28 Pitt wrote to Admiral Boscawen at Louisbourg: "I have received your letters of May 10th and 27th, and his Majesty waits with great impatience for some news from you."

Time dragged along without encouragement from the various fronts until August 11, when news came to England that the elderly Bligh, transferred to a division of the fleet commanded by Admiral Howe, brother of Lord Howe at Ticonderoga, had landed at Cherbourg, and, thanks to Howe's direction, had captured the forts, burnt the docks and numerous ships in the harbor. The Cherbourg raid was the first notable success of the season, one of the few successes of British arms in many years. Pitt naturally was elated, and he made the most of it. He promptly reinforced Bligh with new infantry forces to convert the raid into a more lasting attack. If Bligh could make a real bite at Cherbourg, that would create fresh alarm in France whenever other raids might be made, as the enemy would never know the extent of the British objective.

Ridden as Pitt was by the cares of office, he found time to write to his sister Mary. She, the youngest, who was now in her early thirties, had become a thin frail girl suffering from the afflictions of gout. Whatever the needs of the Empire, Pitt continued to feel the tug of family loyalty and love. Indeed, again and again, in public disaster or triumph, his first impulse was to write to wife, sister, or nephew. So, on August 10, 1758, he wrote to Mary concerning her health, her philosophy, and Cherbourg:

St. James's Square, Aug. 10, 1758

DEAR SISTER,—I wait with much impatience to hear you are arrived well at Bath, and that you are lodged to your mind. I will not entertain any doubts, after having had the satisfaction of seeing you, that your progression to a perfect recovery will be sensible every Day, and as soon as you can bear a stronger nourishment, that Spirits, the concomitants of Strength, will return. as a part of the necessary regimen, solid nourishment for that busy craving Thing call'd Mind must have its place, and I know of no mental Alteratives [?] of power to renovate and brace up a sickly Constitution of Thought, but that mild and generous Philosophy which teaches us the true value of the World, and a rational firm religion, that anchors us safe in the confidence of another. but I will end my sermon and come to the affairs of the world I am so deeply immersed in. this day had brought us an account that our Troops effected their landing, with little Loss, ye 7th and 8th two Leagues from Cherbourgh, in the face of a pretty considerable Number, who gave some loose fires and run. I am infinitely anxious till we hear again, as I expect something serious will ensue. I must not close my letter without telling you that the most particular enquiries after your health have been made by the Lady you sent a Card to, and I, very obligingly reprimanded for keeping your arrival a secret from Them. Lady Hester shares my Impatience to hear news of you, and all my sentiments for your health and happiness. our Love follows dear Mary, whose merits you must, to your great satisfaction, more and more feel every day.

I am ever my Sister's most affectionate Brother

W. PITT

Newcastle had a new attack of nerves at the moving of additional troops to Cherbourg, fearing both the added drain on the Treasury and suspecting, rightfully, that Pitt in approving this coastal attack was neglecting the German battlefront as the main theater of war. This was a blow to the Duke, who had flattered himself that, at last, Pitt had been converted to the Continental system. Pitt, however, was too occupied to be swayed by the wailings of his colleague; and Newcastle, as usual, poured out his fears and resentment to Hardwicke, writing that Pitt "had a sword at his throat" and that he, Newcastle, did not dare to protest because of the public temper.

The cautious Duke had a certain amount of sense on his side. He was terrified at the thought of any more defeats, except on the Continent. There, the blame for a reverse would at least be shared by Britain's allies, but an attack on the seacoast of France was a constant courting of potential defeat by the English forces alone, and that would recoil on the Ministry of which he was a part. The poor Duke felt himself to be linked to a madman. "Pitt," as Anson had observed in a letter to Hardwicke of June 29, 1758, "said everything possible to his generals to make them risk action." No wonder that the situation brought terrors to Newcastle. The ghost of Byng stood at his shoulder to remind him of what might happen to one who failed. In the Cherbourg instance, as it turned out, Newcastle's fears were needless, for Bligh and Howe completed the destruction of Cherbourg and sailed away without further action.

As late as August, there was still no word of the campaign in North America, and Mr. Pitt decided to go down to the country for a few days of rest. He came back to London on August 17. As his coach clattered up to his house in St. James Square, about ten in the morning, he was informed

that Captain William Amherst, brother and aide-de-camp
to the General, had arrived from Louisbourg with Amherst's dispatches, and had been waiting since seven in the
morning. At last, news from Louisbourg!

Pitt received the young emissary and embraced him
warmly, declaring him to be "the most welcome messenger
that had arrived in this kingdom for years." Pitt hastily
pressed for news of the siege. The report was all he had
wished for, a notable co-ordination of the Army and the
fleet. Boscawen had defeated a French naval force and had
blockaded the harbor. His flotilla and transports had anchored along the seacoast, giving support to the troops.
Amherst had landed three divisions simultaneously along the
coast toward the rear of the city, had built an arc of encircling batteries, and, with combined artillery and infantry
encircling the city, had choked the French into submission.

Captain Amherst continued with further details.

"This is the greatest news!" Mr. Pitt interrupted. He
could not wait to advise his colleagues of the momentous
triumph. He and Captain Amherst must proceed at once
to inform Ligonier.

The veteran campaigner heard the report with great enthusiasm and joined the two as they set out to inform his
Majesty of the happy outcome. At the palace at Kensington, where the King was stopping, they were also accompanied by Captain Edgecumbe, the emissary from Admiral
Boscawen.

The King took the occasion to indicate again his disapproval of the Amherst appointment by addressing his inquiries to Edgecumbe,—even his questions regarding the
army maneuvers. Mr. Pitt and Ligonier observed that Captain Amherst had brought the account from the Army, but
the King did not repeat his questions.

Perhaps it was this incident which reminded Mr. Pitt that
Lady Yarmouth deserved particular credit for the appoint-
ment of his young Major General, and the entourage then
visited the Yarmouth apartments where they were joined by
Lord Holdernesse, Pitt's fellow Secretary of State. The
Yarmouth comments were enthusiastic regarding Amherst.

"His friends in Germany will rejoice; he is much beloved there."

At last it occurred to the party to pay their respects to the Duke of Newcastle. His Grace received them at Newcastle House and was well-nigh delirious with joy. He kept repeating that he had sent "orders for two corporations (stomach-fulls) to be made drunk."

The victory went far to cement smoldering dissension between various political factions. It will be recalled that Cumberland had recommended the appointment of Jeffery Amherst and Captain Amherst went down to Windsor in the evening where he reviewed the entire siege with the Duke and was urged to spend the night. In view of Cumberland's long opposition to Pitt, and in view of the Duke's present disgrace, the visit was a gracious gesture which was cordially received.

On the following day Captain Amherst learned that Prince George, the heir apparent, was in London, and sought leave to wait upon him. The Prince was most gracious, said that he had expected great things of Amherst, but that this news exceeded the expectations.

After the many failures on the part of generals and admirals, after the odor of defeat which had hovered about so many of the leaders of the English forces, this clean-cut victory on top of the Cherbourg success was a refreshing breeze. Pitt's family were naturally beside themselves with joy. Temple addressed Pitt as his "dear brother Louisbourg." The chief Minister had dispatched a rider to take the news to Hester at Hayes and she wrote him that she was "so happy and glorious for my loved England, happy and glorious for my most loved and admired Husband. I feel all your joy, my Life, the joy of the dear brothers, the joy of my friend Mrs. Boscawen, and the joy of the people of England." Ann, who was down at Bath, obtained the Mayor's permission to build a huge bonfire in front of her brother's house, hired a company of musicians, held a community sing, and dispensed ten hogsheads of strong beer.

Officially and through the nation Pitt capitalized the victory to the fullest extent. He had a Louisbourg medal struck, depicting the co-operation of fleet and Army. The French standards taken at Louisbourg, which Captaim Amherst had brought with him, were paraded before the King at St. James Palace and deposited in St. Paul's Cathedral. The guns of the Tower fired salutes of victory, bonfires were lit near the royal palace, and the Archbishop of Canterbury issued a special form of prayer and thanksgiving to be used in churches and chapels.

In the dispatches which Captain Amherst had brought from his brother to Mr. Pitt the General had said, "If I can go to *Quebeck,* I will.'

"General Amherst will make nothing of Quebec after this," Mr. Pitt had observed on first hearing the news, encouraged to believe that the campaign in America would be completed in the present season. He had full reason to think so, for Abercromby at the gates of Ticonderoga had the pick of the Army in the New World, 6,000 regulars and 9,000 Provincials to be used against a garrison of only 4,000 men under the French general, Montcalm. The overwhelming of Montcalm, followed by a siege and probable capture of Montreal would strike at the heart of New France, leaving Quebec an easy task for Amherst's elated troops.

Nothing could be more propitious. The situation seemed almost incredibly good. In fact, it was too good. Within two days after Captain Amherst's arrival in London the news arrived that Abercromby's army had been slaughtered at Ticonderoga and that the old General had abandoned all action for the season.

CHAPTER XXV

"THE WONDERFUL YEAR"

The circumstances of the defeat at Ticonderoga could hardly have been worse. The brilliant young Howe, who was counted upon to supply the energy which Abercromby lacked, had been killed from ambush in a skirmish prior to the main attack. Abercromby had forthwith exceeded even the most pessimistic view of his idiocy and cowardice. He had ordered a frontal assault by his best battalions against the ramparts of the French fort, while he himself, with the remainder of the army and a number of the guns, remained at his base camp some twelve miles away. His conspicuous incapacity as Commander-in-Chief had proved as damaging to British repute as the fact of the repulse and the ghastly slaughter of men.

Obviously it was necessary for the Government to replace Abercromby at once. The Commander-in-Chief in the New World should be the pivot man of Pitt's strategy in North America and the West Indies. It was vital not only to win victories in that sector, but also to secure the support and respect of the colonies. Loudoun had antagonized the provincials by his tactlessness, and now Abercromby had made the British staff an object of contempt. Someone was needed who would re-establish the prestige of the mother country, and carry the flag to victory.

The proper selection for the job clearly was General Amherst. He was already in the New World, had the conquest of Louisbourg to his credit, and was known to be a good administrator as well as an effective general.

Accordingly, within less than two weeks after the General's brother had arrived in London with the news of Louisbourg, Mr. Pitt summoned Captain Amherst and gave him the official dispatches to be taken to the colonies, including the commission of Major General Amherst as Commander-in-Chief in North America. Pitt was not forgetful that these new honors interfered with his promises that General Amherst could return home after the Louisbourg campaign. Amherst's wife had been frantic at his appointment to the American front after several years' service on the Continent. Pitt urged Captain Amherst to express the Government's regret for the trouble which might be caused, but to explain that "the King's dependence is entirely upon him to repair the losses we have sustained."

On the other side of the Atlantic the disaster at Ticonderoga hampered General Amherst's contemplated advance up the St. Lawrence to Quebec. Abercromby was already calling on Amherst to detach some troops to his aid, which would weaken any forces available for Quebec. Boscawen, moreover, said that the ships could not be put in condition to transport the forces up the St. Lawrence. A further complication in Amherst's situation was the attitude of James Wolfe, his impetuous Brigadier General, who wished to push ahead to Quebec at all costs. Amherst was unwilling, under the circumstances, and Wolfe begged leave to resign his command. Amherst was eager to have no dissension in the ranks, and wrote Wolfe a mollifying letter:

DEAR WOLFE,

I have your letter this morning, to which I can say no more to you than what I have already done; that my first intentions and hopes were, after the surrender of Louisburgh, to go with the whole army (except what is absolutely necessary for Louisburgh) to Quebec, as I am convinced 'tis the best thing we could do, if practicable. The next were to pursue my orders as to future operations, and this affair unluckily happening at Ticonderoga, I quitted the thoughts of the future operations in part, as ordered, to assist Major General Abercromby.

My wishes are to hasten everything for the good of the service, and I have not the least doubt but Mr. Boscawen will do the same. Whatever schemes you may have, or information that you can give, to quicken our motions, your communicating of them would be very acceptable, and will be of much more service than your thoughts of quitting the Army; which I can by no means agree to, as all my thoughts and wishes are confined at present to pursuing our operations for the good of his Majesty's service; and I know nothing that can tend more to it than your assisting in it.

The assault on Quebec, accordingly, had to be postponed, and Ticonderoga remained on the list of unfinished business. Fortunately, the third phase of the American campaign, namely, the expedition under Bradstreet, had been wholly successful. Bradstreet had taken both Fort Oswego and Fort Frontenac, in spite of desertion and illness among his troops. For a time the enterprise had appeared to be hopeless, but Bradstreet's zeal had won out, and in the period of greatest discouragement he had said, "Should the numbers be reduced so low, as that we cannot make out above 1,000 men fit to proceed to Lake Ontario, with them I will do my best."

Bradstreet's accomplishment served to strengthen Mr. Pitt in his conviction that the future of the Empire depended on the development of the English colonies in the New World, and his admiration for the character and abilities of the colonial subjects was increasingly a governing influence in his general policy.

A further if less important phase of the year's campaign was the victory of British forces in India and Africa. The extension of British sovereignty in the Orient was only a supplementary part of Pitt's plan, used by him primarily to bring pressure on France. In this, Pitt was endorsing the theory of Frederick of Prussia, who believed that France would make many concessions in return for her Indian stations if they should come into the possession of the British.

Robert Clive, who was already distinguishing himself in India, had sought aid from Pitt. Pitt greatly admired Clive and had referred to him in Parliament as "that man not born for a desk; that Heaven-born general! He . . . had never learned the arts of war or that skill in doing nothing, which only forty years of service can bring!" India, however, was the battle-ground of the East India Company and Clive's operations were essentially a private warfare, now aided by the very modest support of ships and men which Pitt felt he could allocate for the purpose.

Pitt, with his usual flair for the essentials of strategy, knew that Senegal and Goree in Africa were the French bases in the East from which they outfitted for expeditions against India. The least expensive way to aid Clive, accordingly, would be an attack on these French-African posts which would not anticipate any hostilities. The idea had worked. A small British squadron had arrived at the Senegal River on April 23, 1758, and within a week had forced the surrender of Fort Louis and all possessions of the French Company. When Pitt had learned of this in the middle of June, he had authorized another expedition against Goree under Admiral Keppel, which had set sail in the middle of August.

The year 1758 drew to a close, however, with the Pitt program uncompleted in many particulars. The most irritating delays had blocked the contemplated attack on Martinique, and the expedition did not sail until November 12. Anson had opposed it, on the grounds that he could not spare a ship, though he was willing to defer to Pitt's decision. Newcastle had been less pliant, and protested that the nation could not bear the expense of both the American and the European war. Pitt replied that if that were so, he would recall all of the troops from the Continent and use them for America. His Majesty, curiously enough, came to Pitt's aid in this controversy. George II had been swept up into the spirit of victory, and for the first time had become a violent champion of Pitt, even to the point of brushing Newcastle aside. Addressing himself to Newcastle, the King went even further than Pitt, saying, "We must keep Cape Breton, take Canada, drive the French out of America, and have two armies in Germany, consisting together of 80,000 men."

Then he turned to Pitt and said, "We must conquer Martinique as a set-off to Minorca."

Eighty thousand men on the Continent! If these were to be British soldiers, it was a fantastic notion, but it demonstrated to Newcastle the hold which Mr. Pitt now had

upon the monarch, as well as on the rest of the country.
The King's remark regarding Martinique as an offset
to Minorca was also significant. It may have been his
Majesty's idea before Pitt first proposed it. Virtually all
of Pitt's ideas in military and naval strategy were suggested at one time or another by someone else. One of the
great sources of his strength was an open ear to all such
suggestions from laymen and professionals alike. He was
interested in the fighting possibilities not only as tactics in
the field, but also in the weighing of their moral impact.
The receptiveness of Pitt in listening to and adapting the
views of others cannot be overemphasized as one of the
foundation stones of his genius. No one mind, however
spacious and informed, could compass all the details of
world strategy unless open to information and counsel.
The tradition-bound ministers of former years had centered English strategy on the Continent, and had disastrously used Continental habits of warfare in America.
Pitt had had the sense to see that English traditional
methods had been wrong and he was incessantly seeking to
remedy them as new ideas and possibilities presented themselves. He asked no praise for originality on his own part.
What he sought, demanded and pleaded for, was victory.

The work in North America was well begun with the
taking of Louisbourg, but the campaign for the ensuing
year had to be determined, and in November, 1758, this operation was Mr. Pitt's chief concern. The main question
was the strategy to be employed. Pitt did not lack for advice
upon this subject. Beckford, in particular, was certain that
Canada could be taken only by the St. Lawrence route, and
he deplored any proposed attempts on Ticonderoga. On
December 17, 1758, he wrote to Pitt:

> DEAR SIR:—Let no persuasion or plausible reason determine
> you to leave the plan of operations by the river St. Lawrence.
> To go by the lakes, through wild and almost inaccessible for-
> ests, has already proved dangerous, tedious, and expensive, will
> prolong the war, and at the same time enrich your commanders
> and contractors. What is more, we have seen that our regulars

do not fight well in woods; the Indian yell is horrid to their ears, and soon throws them into confusioʃ

Beckford, whose views usually carried weight, was overruled this time. The opinion of seasoned campaigners in America was strongly against him. Amherst had the view that the French could never be subdued through the capture of individual forts and cities alone. They could always retreat before a drive up the St. Lawrence, falling into the back country, and they had already demonstrated versatility in developing settlements in remote quarters such as Detroit and Dubuque. Governor Pownall of Massachusetts held the same opinion.

The Pownall plan, in brief, was to attack French Canada simultaneously from three different directions. One attack was to be up the St. Lawrence, directed at Quebec. A second army should move upward from Albany, take Ticonderoga and Crown Point and advance northward on Lake Champlain to Montreal. A third force should come in from the West, from Lake Ontario down the St. Lawrence, cutting off any retreat of the French inland.

Pitt was favorably inclined toward this strategy, and now moved to determine the choice of men for the different parts. Amherst as Commander-in-Chief, would need to be at New York or Albany during most of the season. On him depended the co-ordination of the services of supply, the raising of money, and the maintaining of good relationships between the British regulars and the colonial forces. It seemed probable that he would be the best person to undertake the attack on Ticonderoga, as this expedition would keep him on the mainland and in direct touch with colonial affairs.

The nomination of an officer for the Quebec task was less certain. Alderman Beckford proposed a certain Captain Winslow, but Mr. Pitt evidently did not take this recommendation seriously. Wolfe's fine record and his justified reputation for dash and bravery made him a favorite candidate for the expedition, though it was known that he was anxious to be transferred to the Continent. Wolfe, how-

302 MR. PITT AND AMERICA'S BIRTHRIGHT

ever, on hearing that he was being considered for Quebec, promptly wrote of his willingness to serve:

SIR:

Since my arrival in town, I have been told that your intentions were to have continued me upon the service in America.

I take the freedom to acquaint you, that I have no objection to serving in America and particularly in the river St. Lawrence, if any operations are to be carried on there. The favour I ask is only to be allowed a sufficient time to repair the injury done to my constitution by the long confinement at sea, that I may be the better able to go through the business of the next summer.

I have the honour to be, with the utmost respect,

Sir, your most obedient,

and most humble servant,

JAM. WOLFE

Mr. Pitt was delighted at this solution. Wolfe, in fact, was the perfect choice for the task. He was not an administrator, not a co-ordinator, not tactful in his relationships with others, but he was a genius with a quick and daring thrust. He had a super degree of zeal; he had been the first to make a landing at Rochefort, and again was the first ashore at Louisbourg. His fault would always be a reckless disregard of consequences, a failure to count the costs, but his impetuosity was just the quality which was needed for the attempt on Quebec, and a quality which was painfully rare in British military circles.

Mr. Pitt promptly promoted Wolfe to the rank of Major General, and invited the young man to dinner at St. James Square to discuss the details of the task before him. The dinner was a considerable occasion. Temple was present, and, in fact, Wolfe was taken right into the heart of the Administration's eagerness to win the great objective of Quebec. Wolfe caught fire with the excitement of the idea. His bulging blue eyes blazed with interest as he predicted what he would accomplish. Though he had refrained from drinking during the dinner, he was intoxicated by the opportunity before him. After the meal was over he strolled up and down the reception room, running his hands through his shock of red hair and brandishing his sword, boasting of what he would do to the Bourbons. Temple, who was offended by his naïve conduct, said afterwards that Mr. Pitt began to have misgivings as to whether he had not appointed the wrong man to such a responsible task; but since Temple's testimony is the only evidence on the point, it seems likely that he was speaking for his own views, and it is more than likely that the dramatic Mr. Pitt was delighted with the fire-breathing antics of his new commander.

At any rate, within the month he sent elaborate instructions to General Amherst, telling him of Wolfe's appointment, and directing him to organize troops and supplies to be in complete readiness for Wolfe at Halifax, Nova Scotia, on approximately the 20th of the following April. Amherst was also informed that Wolfe's new title applied to the Quebec expedition only. It would not create an equality of command in respect to the New World as a whole. In fact, the setup was similar to the appointment of Amherst in the case of the Louisbourg expedition. After expressing the hope that the proposed invasion of Canada "will be attended with a happier & more honorable Event than heretofore," Pitt proposed alternative methods:

. . . by Way of Crown Point or La Galette [the western route], or both, according as you shall judge practicable, and proceed, if practicable, and attack Montreal or Quebec, or both of the said places successively . . . in one Body, or at one and the same time, by a Division of the Forces into separate & distinct Operations, according as you shall . . . judge all or any of the said attempts to be practicable.

The amount of leeway which Pitt permitted in these instructions was contrary to his general practice, and indicated the amount of confidence he had come to have in Amherst's capabilities. It will be observed that he had not specifically adopted the Pownall plan, but merely hinted at it, in saying "that you do attempt an invasion of Canada by way of Crown Point or La Galette, or both, according as you shall judge practicable." The approach by way of Crown Point was the Ticonderoga route which Abercromby had attempted the year before. La Galette was on the

upper St. Lawrence. This was the western route referred
to by Pownall. The practical difficulty with respect to the
western route was the fact that the upper St. Lawrence was
filled with cascades and eddies shortly above Montreal
which were thought to make the river virtually unnavigable.

As it developed, Amherst prepared to adopt the Pownall
system as far as was in his power. He first organized the
forces for Wolfe, according to instructions. Next he decided to use the main part of the remaining forces for a
march on Ticonderoga and Crown Point, with Montreal as
the ultimate goal. Thirdly, he sent a detachment westward
under General Gage with the purpose of attacking La
Galette and approaching Montreal from the west, making
at least a feint from that direction which would add to the
confusion of the French forces.

In the midst of Pitt's tremendous military exertions, he
was again troubled by the vagaries of his sister Ann. Her
typical Pitt eccentricity was apparently developing into
flights of madness. Over a long period of years her letters
to Lady Suffolk had exhibited hypochondriac tendencies,
and in the year 1758 she had reached the point of being
forty-six years of age, restless and thoroughly unhappy.
She proposed a remedy for that condition in a letter addressed to Lady Suffolk, containing a most astonishing proposal:

DEAR LADY SUFFOLK,
. . . I hear my Lord Bath is here very lively, but I have not
seen him, which I am very sorry for, because I want to offer
myself to him. I am quite in earnest, and have set my heart
upon it; so I beg seriously you will carry it in your mind, and
think if you could find any way to help me. Do not you think
Lady Betty [Germaine] and Lord and Lady Vere would be
ready to help me if they knew how willing I am? But I leave
all this to your discretion, and repeat seriously that I am quite in
earnest. He can want nothing but a companion that would like
his company; and in my situation I should not desire to make
the bargain without that circumstance. And though all I have
been saying puts me in mind of some advertisements I have seen
in the newspaper from gentlewomen in distress, I will not take

that method; but I want to recollect whether you did not once tell me, as I think you did many years ago, that he once spoke so well of me that he got anger for it at home, where I never was a favourite.

It was, perhaps, not too surprising that the unabashed and original Miss Pitt should offer herself in marriage to a man who was now seventy-four years of age, an earl, very rich, and not expected to live long. As she hinted, the fact that he seemed to have liked her in the days of her youth gave her encouragement.

But granting all this, the proposal of a marriage between Ann Pitt and the Earl of Bath was an idea so preposterous as to be almost fantastic. Lord Bath, some years before, had abandoned his famous education of the beautiful Miss Chudleigh, who had gone on to postgraduate studies of her own selection. Bath had married, had a son and had become a widower. He was now a sad and notable wreck of the once handsome Pulteney, and politically, of course, he was notorious. He had never recovered from his secret betrayal of the Whigs and he had become a diligent, if feeble, devotee of the Throne, consistently and sarcastically opposed to Mr. Pitt's policies. If Bath had sought the hand of Ann Pitt, that would have been another matter, but the thought of the sister of the first Minister trying to arrange a marriage with the ancient earl was humiliating.

Either Pitt or Lady Suffolk was apparently able to discourage Ann from persisting in this notion, and Pitt himself urged his sister not to live in London. Obviously, Ann could not understand that attitude, nor could she comprehend why there was no longer the opportunity for the intimacy which had lasted for so many years between her and her brother. She could not realize that she had failed him, that Hester inevitably had dislodged her. Or perhaps she did comprehend that time and fate had defeated her, and her pitiful thought of Pulteney, Lord Bath, was a desperate, sick attempt of a once brilliant and beautiful girl to conclude her days in some vestige of dignity.

It is reasonable to surmise that Ann believed that as the Countess of Bath she might aid William's career. If now and in later months she was an embarrassment to Pitt, he had only himself to blame. He had broken up her affair with the pedantic Ayscough, who had ultimately married Anne Lyttelton, sister of George. Ayscough was clearly no ball of fire, but Ann Pitt in her younger days had been willing to give him much of her time. She probably would have married Ayscough, but for her brother's ridicule, and it would not have been the first time, nor the ten thousandth time, that a brilliant woman decided that a "Mrs." was, after all, to be desired, even if the prospective spouse had, in his infancy, been dropped by his nurse on a stone pavement.

Pitt, however, could not afford to assume his sister's burdens at this stage of his career. When Parliament reconvened on November 23, 1758, the stage was all set for the following year. The King's address, prepared of course under Mr. Pitt's direction and approval, gave in broad terms the basis of Pitt's military strategy, sounded the keynote of the war as a struggle "for liberty and independency," and had the British tone of combined idealism and unctuousness which has always riled Britain's enemies. The address said in part:

MY LORDS, AND GENTLEMEN:
It has pleased the Divine Providence to bless his Majesty's measures and arms with success in several parts; and to make our enemies feel that the strength of Great Britain is not to be provoked with impunity.
The conquest of the strong fortress of Louisbourg, the taking of Frontenac, of the highest importance to our operations in North America, and the reduction of Senegal, cannot fail to bring great distress upon the French commerce and colonies; and in proportion to procure great advantages to our own. That nation has also been made sensible, that, whilst their forces are sent forth to invade and ravage the dominions of their neighbours, their own coasts are not inaccessible to his Majesty's fleets and armies.
In Germany, his Majesty's good brother, the King of Prussia, and Prince Ferdinand of Brunswick, have found full employment for the armies of France and her confederates; from which

our operations, both by sea and in America, have derived the most evident advantage.

His Majesty has further commanded us to observe to you, that the common cause of liberty and independency is still making noble and vigorous efforts against the unnatural union formed to oppress it; that the commerce of his subjects, the source of our riches, has, by the vigilant protection received from his Majesty's fleet, flourished in a manner not to be paralleled during such troubles.

The address was the occasion for a personal triumph for Mr. Pitt in both Houses of Parliament. Speakers vied with one another in outbursts of patriotism. One said that he would lend all he was worth to support the war. Another said that he would give all he was worth. Lord Bath sneered that Mr. Pitt had promised to take all that both the gentlemen had.

Pitt in the Commons, in fact, had warned that the war was costing millions of pounds and would cost millions more, but the House was ready to vote all that he might ask. As he stood before the House, under the huge chandelier of St. Stephen's Chapel, and faced his fellow members it was a far cry from the time only three years previously when he had fought single-handed to maintain his reputation and political life against the onslaughts of Murray (now Lord Mansfield), Hume Campbell, and Henry Fox. He was now accountable to nothing but the Constitution and his own judgment on the conduct of public affairs.

Already France was learning the lesson that she was facing a new and very different England under the leadership of Mr. Pitt. The Bourbon King, Louis the XV, was being shaken out of his complacency by the failure of French arms, and his incompetent advisers were seeking retirement from public life before a storm of criticism should overtake them. In September the leading French minister, Abbé de Bernis, had taken sanctuary in a Cardinal's hat and had been succeeded by the Duc de Choiseul.

Choiseul was prepared to fight without quarter to regain the losses which France had endured.

"In our hearts and in all our actions we are the enemies of England," he said, "enemies now more than ever, and we neither see nor wish to see the end of this enmity."

Choiseul's initial policy was to check Pitt's series of raids on the French coast by an aggressive program which contemplated the invasion of England. If France could be bewildered and terrified by the frequent assaults which the British Navy had made upon her harbors, the same doctrine could be reversed and magnified. Choiseul opened the 1759 campaign with a plan to unite the French fleets from the Mediterranean and the Channel, using them to convoy a French army of 50,000 men for the invasion of England.

The project was hampered by one error, which Pitt had avoided in his naval tactics, namely its magnitude. For complete success it required that the French Mediterranean fleet be able to run the British blockade at Gibraltar, avoid the British Atlantic squadrons, and actually join forces with the Channel fleet. Hence it was much more unwieldy than the Pitt system of minor raids, whereby a few swift-striking vessels could create terror out of all proportion to their size and importance.

Pitt at first refused to believe in rumors of the proposed French attack and pooh-poohed Newcastle's fears on this score. Ultimately he learned, however, that the Duke, who had an efficient spy system, had obtained copies of communications between the French Court and Sweden and, while keeping Pitt in the dark, had shown the information to the King. Pitt was so outraged at Newcastle's conduct that he resisted all effort to recall troops for home defense, organized more expeditions for foreign service, and convinced the chastened Duke that he must never again keep secrets from the chief Minister.

It was generally known around the Court that Newcastle resented the ascendancy of Pitt and hoped to curb his power, possibly by alliance with Bedford. The Duke, however, was in general ill-favor, as may be gathered from an incident at a ball given by the Duchess of Bedford, as described in a letter from Horace Walpole to George Montagu, April 26, 1759:

The delightful part of the night was the appearance of the Duke of Newcastle, who is veering round again, as it is time to betray Mr. Pitt. The Duchess of Bedford was at the very upper end of the gallery, and though some of the Pelham court were there too, yet they showed so little cordiality to this revival of connexion, that Newcastle had nobody to attend him but Sir Edward Montagu, who kept pushing him all up the gallery. From thence he went into the hazard-room, and wriggled, and shuffled, and lisped, and winked, and spied, till he got behind the Duke of Cumberland, the Duke of Bedford, and Rigby; the first of whom did not deign to notice him; but he must come to it.

You would have died to see Newcastle's pitiful and distressed figure. Nobody went near him; he tried to flatter people; they were too busy to mind him; in short, he was quite disconcerted; his treachery used to be so sheathed in folly that he was never out of countenance but it is plain he grows old.

To finish his confusion and anxiety, George Selwyn, Brand, and I, went and stood near him, and in half-whispers, that he might hear, said, "Lord, how he is broke! how old he looks!"

Then I said, "This room feels very cold; I believe there never is a fire in it."

Presently afterwards, I said, "Well, I'll not stay here; this room has been washed today." In short, I believe, we made him take a double dose of Gascoign's powder when he went home.

While Pitt in dealing with Newcastle assumed an attitude of reckless indifference to the power of France, he was actually giving sober and intense thought to meeting the French threat. His strategy was a defensive version of his raiding system, whereby he maintained a British encampment at the Isle of Wight, together with a fleet of transports ready to move troops on short notice to any point which might be subjected to attack. Further, he called out the militia of twenty-four counties, assigned them to home-defense duty, and with this addition of man power was able to leave the regular army forces virtually undisturbed. Thus the Choiseul threat of invasion had only limited success. It did not divert any considerable number of British troops nor did it bend the determination of Mr. Pitt.

England's European position, however, was weakened
not only by the enterprise of Choiseul, but also by a disgraceful failure on the part of Lord George Sackville.
Prince Ferdinand of Brunswick, under whom Sackville was
serving at the head of the British forces on August 1, 1759,
began an attack on the French forces near Minden in Hanover. At a crucial moment in the battle Ferdinand ordered
Sackville to attack with the British cavalry. Sackville pretended not to understand. Five times he was ordered to
advance and consistently refused to move. In spite of this
failure, Ferdinand won a decisive victory which drove the
French out of Hanover, but he might have turned it into
a complete rout of the French forces, and regained all of
the territory belonging to the Electorate, if Sackville had
obeyed orders.

The popular explanation of Sackville's conduct was that
of sheer cowardice. Some said that he was drunk. Others
held that his conduct was due to his steady resentment at
taking orders from anyone, especially from a foreigner.

His Majesty, who cared more for his German possessions than his English Crown, left no doubt in Sackville's
mind as to the opinion of the Throne. He ordered Sackville's dismissal from all military posts and with his own
hand struck Lord George's name from the list of Privy
Councillors. Sackville, however, was a man of incomparable brass and aplomb. He contested the justice of his
punishment, seeking the support of the Prince of Wales,
Lord Bute, and Mr. Pitt. In the first two instances he was
successful, and in the third he was able to create for Pitt
a most embarrassing situation.

Pitt at all times in his long political career had endeavored to keep the peace with the household of the heir apparent. Even when he had become a member of the
Cabinet, and therefore one of the King's servants, he had
been careful to avoid a break with the circle at Leicester
House. Now, unfortunately, Prince George violently es-
poused the cause of Sackville, ably abetted by Lord Bute.
On learning that Pitt had taken no immediate steps to

come to the rescue of Sackville, Bute addressed him a letter
on August 7, 1759, which was far different from the affectionate tone of those only a few months before:

DEAR SIR:

I am extremely concerned to observe by your letter, that all
endeavours have proved hereto unsuccessful, in regard to a business the Prince has so much at heart. I need not tell you that
he complains bitterly of the extreme neglect he ever meets with
in any matter (be it what it will) that immediately concerns
himself. The most gentle, patient dispositions may be at last
so soured, that all the prudential reasons and arguments in the
world will not prevent very bad effects—very pernicious consequences. Nothing shall be wanting on my part to preserve peace
and good-humour, but at the same time, I will not be answerable
for the consequences of this treatment. I ever am, dear sir,

Your most affectionate humble servant,

BUTE

Pitt replied on August 15 in a conciliatory tone, and he
proceeded to examine the facts of Sackville's case with
every sympathy; but even from the man's own account Pitt
was unable to find justification for Sackville's action. Accordingly Pitt on September 9 wrote to Sackville expressing
"infinite concern" at not being able to offer his support,
knowing regretfully that he was making Sackville his enemy
for life.

It was getting late in the 1759 fighting season and, as
in the preceding years, Pitt was waiting impatiently for
news from across the seas. Good news was again urgent,
for the stability of the Ministry. The political backing of
Sackville was now withdrawn, the Duke of Marlborough
had died, Bute and Leicester House were cool. The first
report which had come in from the New World in the
early summer had been reassuring. The expedition to
Martinique had been diverted from its course because of a
superior French naval force at the Island, but thanks to
the enterprise of General Barrington (brother of Viscount
Barrington at the War Office), the squadron had sailed for
Guadeloupe, another valuable island in the West Indies,

had promptly subdued it, and had captured a vast quantity of rich stores.

Then, on September 8, 1759, came news of more triumphs in the New World, which stiffened Mr. Pitt's backbone and reduced the Sackville incident to unimportance for the time being. Amherst, the dispatches reported, had captured Ticonderoga with the loss of only a few men. He had then advanced upon Crown Point, a few miles north, to find that the French had evacuated the fort. He was

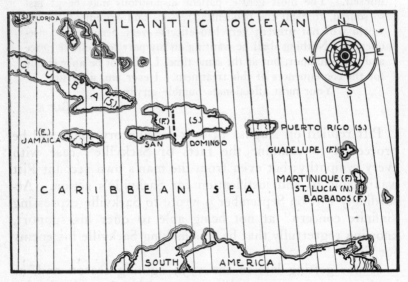

Detail of West Indies Islands.

now encamped near the fort on the shores of Lake Champlain, waiting to hear from Wolfe in order that the advance of each might be timed to inflict the greatest damage on the enemy.

In addition to the success at Ticonderoga, came word that Sir William Johnson had captured Fort Niagara. Again, it was learned, belatedly, that in Pennsylvania Col. John Forbes had taken Fort Duquesne, once the scene of Braddock's defeat. From this event came the naming of Pittsburgh, as Forbes' prophetic message to Pitt indicated:

Pittsbourgh, 27th Nov., 1758

SIR:—I do myself the Honour of acquainting you that it has
pleased God to crown his Majesty's arms with success over all
his enemies upon the Ohio . . . I have used the freedom of giving your name to Fort Du Quesne, as I hope it was in some
measure the being actuated by your spirits that now makes us
Masters of the place. . . . I hope the name Fathers will take
[it] under their Protection, In which case these dreary deserts
will soon be the richest and most fertile of any possest by the
British in North America.

In both Africa and Asia, also, new triumphs had been
achieved. Goree had surrendered to the British forces,
and Clive, with 2200 sepoys and 800 Europeans had defeated an army of 50,000 at Plassey. In the Baltic, a
squadron of the British fleet had established a naval base
for the Prussian forces by the capture of Emden from the
French. In the roll-call of glory, only Wolfe remained to
be heard from.

The news from that sector of operations was ominous.
Amherst reported that he had heard nothing from Wolfe,
and that General Gage had failed to advance from La
Galette. Then, on October 14, Pitt received a dispatch
from Wolfe which was profoundly discouraging:

Upwards of twenty sail of French ships got in before our
squadron, and brought succours of all sorts; which were exceedingly wanted in the colony. . . . These ships serve a double purpose: they are magazines for their provisions, and at the same
time cut off all communication between General Amherst's army
and the corps under my command; so that we are not able to
make any detachment to attack Montreal, or . . . open the
General's way into Canada; all which might have been easily
done if there had been no ships in the river. . . . I am so far
recovered as to do business; but my constitution is entirely
ruined, without the consolation of having done any considerable
service to the State; or without any prospect of it.

Pitt, who never concealed either losses or victories from
the public, published the ill news in the official gazette,
and admitted that he saw little hope for the outcome. The
dramatic seizure of Quebec which he had visualized as the

thing which would arouse the people to renewed efforts and sacrifice now seemed to be a lost cause.

Then, only three days later, came the news of Wolfe's heroic and seemingly impossible accomplishment. He had stormed the Heights of Abraham and while fatally

Detail of 1759 campaign in the New World, with inset showing General Wolfe's locations at Quebec. Note also Amherst's march north of Albany, and the location of Gage at La Galette.

wounded had defeated the surprised Montcalm in a sudden battle. Quebec had surrendered to the British flag.

Nothing could have been more electric. The long suspense, the almost certain defeat, and then the blaze of victory, even the tragic loss of Wolfe in the moment of triumph, added to the popular acclaim. England at last was producing heroes, commanders who would give to the utmost for the British cause.

The excitement throughout the nation was at fever pitch, and the whole world wondered at the accomplishment of the British arms. Frederick of Prussia said, "England has been a long time in travail and though she suffered greatly in producing Mr. Pitt she at last brought forth a man."

This final triumph led Walpole to describe the last twelve months as the *annus mirabilis*, "the wonderful year," enabling the Pitt Ministry to record a series of victories such as England had never witnessed before:

> In Africa, Senegal and Goree.
> In India, Plassey.
> In Europe, Cherbourg, and the rewinning of Hanover.
> In the West Indies, Guadeloupe.
> In North America, Louisbourg, Fort Duquesne, Fort Frontenac, Oswego, Fort Niagara, Ticonderoga, Crown Point, and Quebec.

Mr. Pitt's system had been justified to the utmost, and he was well on his way to building his Anglo-Saxon empire.

CHAPTER XXVI

"LIBERTY AND INDEPENDENCY"

The victories of "the wonderful year" might have satisfied any minister whose sole interest was that of power politics and the kudos of a successful career. Measured, however, by the yardstick of establishing an empire of "liberty and independency," Mr. Pitt was far short of his goal.

England had won many points in the game, in North America, in Europe, and elsewhere, but the results to date were inconclusive. Canada had not been conquered, the Mediterranean was not secure, and France had only been badgered. To make peace at this time would not establish a foundation for the Anglo-Saxon system. It would not destroy the prestige of the totalitarian Bourbons, or prove the inherent strength and validity of the constitutional state.

Too little had been either won or settled; and yet by the standards of the time, judging the matter solely as the rivalry between two powerful alliances, England was in a better position than she had enjoyed for many generations. Most of Pitt's colleagues were eager for him to make some settlement of the war while the settling was good, but Pitt realized that the time had not yet come; and he expressed the difficulty in a note to Hardwicke:

> Peace will be as hard to make as war. The materials in his Majesty's hands are certainly very many and great, and it is to be hoped that in working them up in the great edifice of a solid and general Pacification of Europe there may be no confusion of language, both that the workmen may understand one another.

This was language which Hardwicke could understand, and Pitt did not express his problem more specifically partly because the Cabinet was unsympathetic to him and partly because the concept was still emerging and taking form in his own mind. Pitt's influence was apparent a few years later in the doctrines of Edmund Burke, Charles James Fox, Benjamin Franklin, George Washington, and Thomas Paine; but in 1759 he himself had not yet formulated his views with the clarity and force which he gave to them in later years. He was certain, however, that he had a mission to build an empire for "liberty and independency," and that the job was not yet done.

Fortunately for Pitt's position, the news came to England on the night of October 17, 1759, that a part of the French fleet had broken through the Channel blockade. That ended for some time any pressure by the Cabinet for a premature peace. In fact, the presence of additional French warships on the high seas, with the threat that more might break the blockade, emphasized the instability of most of the victories which Britain had won. In most sections of the globe, except in the case of well-developed colonies, control of territory was by forts strategically located, and depending for munitions and supplies on the fleet of the home country. A sudden superiority of sail at any point could turn the tide. This was notably true of Louisbourg and Quebec, which were outposts ever open to reprisals by hostile French Canada.

Choiseul, as England soon learned, had ordered Admiral Conflans to press the advantage, turn the flank of the blockade, and drive the British fleet from the French coast, all the way from Brest to the Spanish border. The idea was neither grandiose nor impossible, for France had the resources and the autocratic control which were supposed to make for efficiency. This time not only Newcastle but also Anson, Ligonier and Bedford shivered in their boots, expecting naval disaster and subsequent invasion. As they saw it, Pitt for a year and a half had achieved the incredible through sheer audacity and enterprise, and now the nation was about to pay for his foolhardiness.

If Pitt had qualms or hesitation, he did not display them in his manner or in his conduct of the war. On the other hand, Conflans had been suffering from the actual inefficiency of the Bourbon state, for France with all her show of grandeur had been exploited to the limit by the Bourbons and their Court coterie. The fleet was defective in ships, supplies, and man-power. On November 14, however, the Admiral put to sea from Brest with twenty-one ships of the line (40 to 90 guns each) and five cruisers. His goal was Quiberon Bay about midway down the French coast.

A contemporary cartoon

ADMIRAL KEPPEL

One of the numerous sea commanders stirred to action by Pitt's leadership.

There he expected to drive off a blockading British squadron, release additional French ships and transports which were anchored in the bay, and break the grip of British sea-power.

Conflans, however, had not allowed for the changed spirit which had come over the British Navy under the inspiration of Mr. Pitt. Hawke, who was stationed in nearby waters, on hearing of Conflans' destination, set out after the superior French force under full sail. Conflans, on hearing word of this pursuit, made his first mistake. He vacillated on his course, not believing that Hawke could be so rash, and fearing that French reports must have misjudged the location of the British fleet.

By the time Conflans continued on his original plan he ran into unfavorable winds. This gave time for the arrival of Admiral Saunders, who was returning from his participation with Wolfe in the siege of Quebec. Saunders learned from a passing vessel that Hawke was in pursuit of Conflans, and without waiting for Admiralty orders he sent word to Mr. Pitt: "I have therefore only time to acquaint you that I am making the best of my way in quest of Sir Edward Hawke, which I hope his Majesty will approve of."

A third small force, three ships of the line under Admiral

Geary, put out from England to join in the chase. Conflans became panicky at this sudden, unforeseen, and apparently fearless augmentation of the British forces. He changed his plan of stopping to engage the blockading squadron and made at top speed for the shelter of Quiberon Bay. On the 20th of November, 1759, he sailed into the bay with

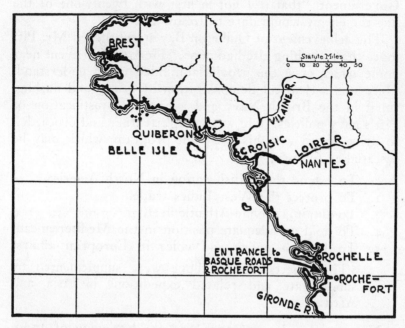

Quiberon Bay with the fortress of Belle Isle commanding the entrance.

Hawke, Geary and Saunders close on his heels, followed by Keppel who had come up under full sail from the south, augmented by Duff, who commanded the blockading squadron.

The British fleet immediately opened battle, again taking the French Admiral by surprise. Many of the French vessels were driven aground, six of their ships were destroyed and about 2500 men were killed, whereas the British lost three to four hundred men and only two ships; in short, the main French fleet was badly crippled and the morale shattered.

The British victory was a vast alteration from the days of Byng when red tape and hesitating councils had prevailed. Conflans himself unconsciously paid tribute to the change. "I had no ground for thinking," he wrote to his Government, "that if I got in first with twenty-one of the line the enemy would dare to follow me."

The achievement of Quiberon Bay strengthened Mr. Pitt more than anything else had done. Here was an event near home which even the provincial-minded could understand. Here was a clear-cut demonstration of a new and dashing spirit in the British Navy and a complete justification of Pitt's navy policies. He was in high feather and proceeded to drive ahead with his five-point program, which may be restated as follows:

1. To extend the British nation in North America.
2. To protect the West Indies trade.
3. To obtain a mobile Atlantic fleet.
4. To hold an adequate position in the Mediterranean.
5. To have a policy and voice in European affairs.

(The objects named above were supplemented by subordinate and related expeditions in Asia and Africa.)

Now, at the close of 1759 and the beginning of 1760, the program which had been originally little more than a daring hope had become a well co-ordinated course of action. Pitt no longer deferred and cajoled, he had less patience than ever with his reluctant fellow Ministers. His house at St. James Place buzzed with secretaries, diplomats, admirals, generals, and members of the Ministry, receiving and carrying out orders. Pitt continued to drive himself unsparingly, and when stricken with his renewed attacks of gout he received callers and transacted business as he lay in bed. On one of these occasions Newcastle came to call and was ushered into Mr. Pitt's bedroom,

FROM THE PAINTING BY BLACKBURN   PHOTO BY JULEY

General Jeffery Amherst, a soldier of the King. Pitt staked his reputation on the unknown commander.

General James Wolfe. His reckless sword offended Lord Temple, but won undying fame.

where the windows were wide open. Newcastle, after fidgeting about for several minutes, fearing to catch cold, spied another bed in the room and clambered into it fully dressed, boots and all, pulling the covers up over him, whereupon the First Lord of the Treasury and the animated Mr. Pitt discussed the affairs of state as their heads bobbed up and down on the pillows.

The year was closing with the third and most perilous part of Mr. Pitt's program now well established, namely, the mobile Atlantic fleet, and for the time being he returned to his policy of periodic raids on the French coast.

The supplementary phase of his program, Asia and Africa, was also brought into the foreground, by Robert Clive, who again solicited Pitt's attention to India. Clive had the vision to see that the East India Company's operations would ultimately be of important concern to the British Government, even though the Company at that time was virtually independent in its operations. In the previous year Clive had written to Mr. Pitt, indicating his sympathy with Pitt's purposes by saying: "I have the liberty of an Englishman so strongly implanted in my nature, that I would have the civil all in all, at all times and in all places (cases of immediate danger excepted)."

Clive was now eager to pursue the subject further; and on November 26, 1759, his agent, John Walsh, called on the chief Minister, bringing specific proposals in the form of a letter.

Clive pointed to the great advantage which had been won for the Company "by the success of the English arms."

"But so large a sovereignty may possibly be an object too extensive for a mercantile company," he added. ". . . I leave you to judge, whether an income yearly of upwards of two million sterling . . . be an object deserving the public attention."

He then suggested that if the Government would take over control, "under the management of so able and disinterested a minister" the East Indian trade would prove "a source of immense wealth to the kingdom" which might be very helpful in diminishing the public debt.

Pitt, having listened appraisingly as Walsh read the letter, then invited him to expound it. As he was doing so Pitt interrupted suddenly with the exclamation "Mauritius!"

Mauritius was an island off the coast of Madagascar, several hundred miles southwest of India. As Senegal and Goree had been, Mauritius was still a French supply depot and now particularly important to France since the two former posts had fallen to the English. In January, 1759, Pitt had already sent a few troops directly to Clive. He now promised Walsh that he would send more when the situation at home permitted, and meanwhile he made a mental note of Mauritius.

Walsh felt that he detected a note of evasiveness, and said that he feared that Mr. Pitt thought the suggestion that the Government take over the East Indian revenues was chimerical.

"Not at all," Pitt replied, saying that Clive was right in thinking it not proper for the Company to retain vast revenues won substantially by British arms, but there were delicate points involved. The revenues might, he said, "endanger our liberties." The voting of funds by the House of Commons was the chief control over the power of the Throne; it was a bulwark of the Constitution. If the East Indian profits should come directly to the Crown or to Government departments without the restrictions by Parliament, —Pitt discussed the matter at length, saw many legal difficulties. On learning from Walsh that Clive planned to revisit England in the coming year Pitt suggested tabling the subject until that time.

In resisting the Clive proposals to appropriate the East India revenues, Pitt exhibited prudence and statesmanship. Now, in the height of his popularity, he might have forced the measure through, but he could realize that basic principles and great dangers were involved so that the problem should be weighed in all its phases. It was, without doubt, a tempting idea, for the financial burden of the war became more pressing each year. The Cabinet had abandoned their clamor for peace, after the naval victory, but they urged upon Pitt to await the result of expeditions already under way and to delay any further programs for 1760. They felt that good luck was now on the English side and it was wise to see what Fate had in store; but Pitt would have none of that.

"There is no such thing as chance," he declared. "Chance is the unaccountable name of nothing. To pursue the war in all its parts is the only way to secure an honourable peace, and the least omission in any part might be fatal to the whole and bring the stone which we have almost brought to the summit rolling down the hill again."

The goal was nevertheless a costly one. The money voted for supplies had been as follows:

1757	£ 8,509,000
1758	£10,486,000
1759	£12,761,000

The program contemplated by Mr. Pitt for 1760 was due to bring the year's budget to a new high, namely to £15,-503,000. An increasing proportion of these revenues was being raised by loans, three million pounds in 1757, five million in 1758, six million six hundred thousand in 1759; and now an eight million pounds loan would be needed for 1760.

The financial question had been persistently the most difficult part of Pitt's Administration. At times he loftily disavowed any connection with the Treasury department, especially if it was under attack, but at other times he stuck his nose into Newcastle's affairs and criticized Legge at the Exchequer. Indeed, if it had not been for the enterprise of some of Pitt's commanders his whole strategy would have been wrecked on the rocks of finance. The burden of financing the Amherst and Wolfe campaigns in the current year had been placed squarely on the shoulders of General Amherst, who was instructed to raise the money in the colonies. Whenever Newcastle complained of the war budget Pitt flew into a torrent of rage and threatened to appoint a committee of inquiry into graft and extravagance. For many months that unpleasant prospect held Mr. Pitt's colleagues in line.

Trouble had arisen on a new front. Charles III had

succeeded to the throne of Spain in August, 1759, upon the death of King Ferdinand. Where Ferdinand had been indifferent, provincial, and pacific, Charles was astute, vigorous, and ambitious. Charles was actively sympathetic with the French cause and had no love for the English. He forthwith sent an ambassador to England, the Conde de Fuentes, to lay the proposal before Mr. Pitt that Spain should act as the mediator for a separate peace between France and England. It was a smart move, aiming to detach England from her alliance with Frederick of Prussia, and aiming to place Pitt, if he should decline, in the unpleasant position of being a war lord. Fuentes concluded with the thrust that Spain could not sit idly by and see the balance of power in America upset.

Pitt stalled for time, gave the appearance of being much interested, and promised an answer in the near future. Meantime, he learned that Newcastle had been meddling with some peace proposals received by Joseph Yorke, English ambassador at The Hague. Yorke had been corresponding on the subject with the Princess Anhalt-Zerbst, mother of Catherine of Russia. Yorke later claimed that he did not regard the correspondence seriously, but he did send the letters to his father, Lord Hardwicke, who in turn showed them to Newcastle and Holdernesse confidentially, and Newcastle had read them to the King. Pitt learned of it only through an inadvertent remark of Holdernesse, and he proceeded to berate Newcastle for daring to discuss peace proposals behind his back. Newcastle protested that the whole thing was "purely for amusement," and added, "I am as innocent . . . as any man alive," affirming that he would not enter into such negotiations "upon any account in the world."

"I believe it," Pitt replied, "for if you did you would not be able to walk the streets without a guard."

The overture from Spain, of course, had to be answered, and the brief period of delay strengthened Mr. Pitt's position materially, for by the time his proposal was in effect he again had his Ministry in hand and the good news of the naval victory had been verified. His answer to Spain was couched in terms of Mr. Pitt at his diplomatic best. He expressed a profound desire for peace, was highly appreciative of the good offices of Spain, and he was prepared to go even further than Charles III had indicated. The British Government, he announced, had decided to propose a Congress of the Powers to meet at The Hague with the purpose of effecting a general peace of Europe.

Mr. Pitt had observed similar congresses before this. He knew their delays in formation, their infinite discussion, and their usual futility. The aim and the scope of such an idea were, however, inescapably noble, and Charles III could not, with good face, reject the proposal. Meanwhile, while the Congress of Powers was getting under way, Mr. Pitt was free to develop and execute the remainder of his worldwide plan. He had no intention of permitting the existence of the Congress to interfere, and on December 11, 1759, he wrote to General Amherst: "It would be unnecessary to caution you, not to suffer this first general step towards peace . . . to slacken . . . any preparations for the Campaign next year or to delay, for a moment, taking every opportunity to annoy and distress the Enemy." He also urged Amherst to be "extremely attentive" to any effect which the Conference might produce in North America and to prevent any such rumors from lessening the efforts of the provincials. Pitt, in fact, had reached a point where he did not need to overlook or tolerate half-hearted performance. In the letter to Amherst he referred to the failure of Thomas Gage on the western route in the last campaign, in terms which showed Pitt's grasp of the situation, and left no doubt of his displeasure. He remarked that Gage had abandoned his advance "a full month before you yourself judged it not too late to attempt, with your whole army, a more difficult and dangerous navigation on the lake Champlain."

This was to be no season for doubting Thomases, or for personal obligations either. On January 7, 1760, Mr. Pitt wrote Amherst again, enlisting him for the coming season, and without apology for ignoring the promise that he could return to England. The task for the coming summer was clear and urgent: "The King continues to place the firmest confidence, in your experience, zeal and abilities; and . . . you will exert your utmost efforts, for compleating the glory of his arms in North America, by the entire reduction of the Enemy." The letter gave Amherst a completely free hand to pursue any method of campaign he might choose, but the demand for the result, to take all of Canada, was imperative.

Having placed this major responsibility on the shoulders of a general in whom he had trust, Pitt for the first time in some months, permitted himself moments of relaxation. He even added a postscript to the Amherst letter, asking that protection be given to a certain Convent in Quebec, at the special request of the wife of a French general. (An interesting commentary on Pitt's humanity in the midst of warfare!) He acted as godfather to the son of his friend, William Beckford, and he accepted, in the same month, the dedication of a new book by a Rev. Laurence Sterne. The book was entitled *The Life and Opinions of Tristram Shandy,* the spirit of which was expressed in Sterne's dedication to Mr. Pitt, saying, "I live in a constant endeavour to fence against the infirmities of ill health and other evils of life, by mirth; being firmly persuaded that every time a man smiles,—but much more so, when he laughs,—that it adds something to this fragment of life."

Conceivably, Mr. Pitt may have been influenced by Sterne's philosophy, or perhaps he was merely exhausted with opposing the Duke of Newcastle. At any rate, in the spring of 1760 he played a conscious or subconscious joke on the Duke. Newcastle, in spite of his clamors against the expense of war, had proposed to send further reinforcements to Ferdinand of Brunswick to protect Hanover. Pitt, instead of his usual air of authority, assumed indifference. He said that he would not sponsor it, but that he would not oppose it if others wished it. This left the Duke in his old-time agony of indecision, a form of self-torture of which he had been almost wholly deprived since Pitt had taken command. After interminable vacillation and intrigue on Newcastle's part he finally maneuvered Pitt into position where the latter had to make a decision, and further reinforcements were finally sent to Ferdinand, largely on Pitt's responsibility.

The step proved to be justified, as both Ferdinand and his ally, Frederick of Prussia, were notably successful throughout the summer. The dilly-dallying at the sessions of the Congress of Powers, as Pitt had foreseen, prevented the embarrassment of premature peace talk. The Spanish Ambassador, Fuentes, was kept occupied and happy by the blandishments of the social lobby, in a series of entertainments, featured by a huge ball on the 4th of June given by Miss Chudleigh, who may be recalled as the literary pupil of Lord Bath and the friend of Mr. Pitt in the Cliveden days. There was minor trouble in Ireland because Bedford, now Lord Lieutenant there, had supported a taxation bill without consent of the House of Commons; but Pitt had ended that difficulty by endorsing the contention of the Irish Parliament that they had sole jurisdiction in the rights of taxation. Pitt held this view to be inherent in the Constitution and he avowed it again later both with respect to Ireland and America, but it brought him the dogged enmity of Bedford. The only serious threat in this relatively easy, if tense, summer—while news was awaited from the Seven Seas—was the fact that the French had laid siege to Quebec and were expected momentarily to recapture it. Fortunately, the news had reached Amherst in time to send a relief squadron from Halifax and the city had been saved. That was in June.

On October 5, 1760, a Major Isaac Barré arrived in London with Amherst's dispatches, bringing the crucial news of the year.

Amherst had adopted Pownall's plan of the three-way thrust at Canada. He had undertaken the westward passage at which Gage had failed in 1759. While Amherst advanced from the west, another army, starting from Ticonderoga and Crown Point had proceeded northward by the central route, and a third army had advanced on Montreal from Quebec. Through wilderness and rapids and a strange country, covering more than a thousand miles of march, Amherst had assembled three armies, scheduled to arrive at a given time, and all arrived within forty-eight hours, a feat unique in military history. Corbett, the historian, a century and a half later called it "one of the most perfect and astonishing bits of work which the annals of British warfare can show"; and Fortescue, historian to

General Jeffery Amherst's campaign of 1760 featuring the three-way thrust on Montreal.

George V, was moved to call Mr. Pitt's chief North American General "the greatest military administrator produced by England since the death of Marlborough; and he remained the greatest until the rise of Wellington."

Montreal and the French forces had been completely surrounded and the French immediately asked for terms.

"I have come to take Canada," Amherst replied, "and I will take nothing less."

The French had surrendered unconditionally. The victory, too, had been without sting or disgrace, for Amherst was able to report that his forces were more than conquerors, exercising kindness and mercy:

> I have as much pleasure in telling you Canada belongs to the King, as I had in receiving the capitulation of it this day, from the satisfaction I know it will give you. The French troops all lay down their arms and are not to serve during the war. Their behavior in carrying on a cruel and barbarous war in this country I thought deserved this disgrace. I have suffered by the Rapids, not by the enemy. I entered the inhabited country with all the savages & I have not hurt the head of a peasant, his wife or his childe, not a house burnt or a disorder committed. The country people, amazed, won't believe what they see; the notions they had of our crueltys from the exercise of their own savages, drove them into the woods; I have fetched them out, & put them quiet in their habitations and they are vastly happy.

At this point Mr. Pitt's doctrine of "liberty and independency" had been put to the crucial test. Was he willing to extend civil rights to a conquered people? The terms which the Commander granted for the province answered the question. The Articles of Capitulation, which were published where all might know of them, were printed, among other places, in the New York *Mercury* for December 15, 1760.

The terms gave to the Canadians the liberties of British subjects, in fact even greater than those enjoyed in England, for the French Catholics were permitted the free exercise of their religion without discrimination, which was in contrast to the anti-Catholic laws in effect in England at the time.

The following Articles were particularly significant:

> ART. II—The troops and the militia, who are in garrison in the town of Montreal shall go out . . . with all the honours of war.

> ART. VIII—The sick and wounded shall be treated the same as our own people.

ART. X—His Britannick Majesty's General shall be answerable for all disorders on the part of his troops, and shall oblige them to pay the damages.

ART. XXVII—The free exercise of the Catholick, Apostolick and Roman religion shall subsist entire in such a manner that . . . the people . . . shall continue to assemble in the churches . . . and to frequent the sacraments as heretofore without being molested in any manner directly or indirectly. (This article also proposed that the British rule agree to collect tithes for the Roman Catholic church. Amherst ruled that that was a taxation question and referred it to the home government).

ART. XXXVII—The Canadians as well in the towns as in the country, shall preserve their entire property and peaceable possession of their goods.

ART. XL—The savages or Indian allies shall not be molested on any pretense whatsoever for having carried arms and served his most Christian Majesty [viz.: the King of France].

ART. XLVI—The inhabitants and merchants shall enjoy all the privileges of trade under the same favours and conditions, granted to the subjects of his Britannick Majesty as used in the countries above.

Amherst judged correctly that he was expressing Mr. Pitt's views and wrote to him on October 14, 1760: "I have fixed the form of Government that I judged would be easiest and best 'till the King's Pleasure is known, and if it meets with his Majesty's approbation, I shall be very happy."

Only fear of a recuperated and vengeful France now seemed to stand in the way of Mr. Pitt's consolidation of his long-awaited Anglo-Saxon empire. The Bourbons must be held definitely, irrevocably in check, particularly the French fleet must never again be feared as a weapon of invasion against England.

Pitt's strategy on the latter score was simple. He proposed to seize and fortify the island of Belle Isle at the mouth of Quiberon Bay. This would give the English a naval base which could observe the movements of the

French fleet, and give adequate warning of any proposed attack. Pitt was most enthusiastic for the plan and won the King's hearty support for it. The older men in the Army and Navy, however, were timid, and probably were jealous of Pitt's victories.

Encouraged by members of the Cabinet, Anson, Ligonier, even Keppel and Hawke made representations to the King that this was a foolhardy enterprise. Accordingly when Pitt obtained an audience with his Majesty on October 24, 1760, he found that the monarch had weakened and was proposing that some other method be undertaken.

The chief Minister retired from the conference in a fury, and announced to by-standers that he refused to consider any naval plan for guarding Quiberon Bay, whether Belle Isle or otherwise. He presumably thought that this attitude would bring the Cabinet and the King to terms, as it had in the past. But on the following morning, before any further discussion had been undertaken, George II, the red-faced, contumacious monarch, was found dead on the floor of his bedroom.

CHAPTER XXVII

THE PETTICOAT KING

George II had died of heart failure in his bedroom, by himself, shortly after taking his morning cup of chocolate. He had been crossing the room from his bed to the doorway when the fatal attack struck him. The date was October 25, 1760.

Mr. Pitt received the news of the King's death from the household early in the forenoon, and at once prepared to notify the Prince that he was now George III. The Minister ordered his coach and six, and soon the blue and silver liveries of the Right Honorable William Pitt were seen by the populace as the procession clattered along the road from London to Kew where the heir apparent was residing.

Before Pitt's entourage had reached its destination, it encountered, coming toward London, the carriage of the new King. Young George III had learned of his grandfather's death through a messenger dispatched by his aunt, the Princess Amelia, and was on his way to London to take charge of his affairs. The King's coach proceeded to London, and that of the chief Minister turned about, following behind the carriage of the monarch.

The incident was both significant and ominous. The young King could hardly be criticized for rushing to pay respects to the remains of his grandfather, but it was customary for the new incumbent to wait to be notified officially by the chief officer of state. The impetuous action of George III was a waving-aside of ministerial form and, in essence, an affront to the dignity of the King's Cabinet.

Mr. Pitt, however, was not in a good technical position to resent the King's cavalier treatment of a formal notification. He was *de facto* the first Minister, so regarded by everyone and so deferred to by his colleagues in the Cabinet. On the other hand, Newcastle, as the First Lord of the Treasury, was nominally the first ranking officer in the Cabinet. As a further slap to Pitt, George III, within three or four hours of arriving at London, granted his initial private audience to the Duke of Newcastle as first Minister of the Crown. Newcastle, as is not surprising, had sought the interview.

The attitude of the new King, swift-moving, decisive, and disrupting, came as a thunderclap to Pitt and his colleagues. They had every reason to expect that the twenty-two-year-old youth, who had been held under wraps all his life, would be a pliant monarch, serving quietly as the figurehead of State, which was his proper rôle. They had reckoned without the peculiar and evil influences which had surrounded his Majesty from his boyhood up. The Duke of Newcastle in his brief interview had learned the extent and power of those influences. To his surprise, he found that the Earl of Bute was present with the King and remained throughout the session. At the conclusion the King paid some formal compliments to Newcastle and then said, "My Lord Bute is your good friend; he will tell you my thoughts."

The unconstitutionality of that procedure was obvious, but a new king could be forgiven almost any error on his first day in office; and the Ministers did not wholly appreciate the implication of the King's words.

Neither the Ministers nor the country realized how deeply George III had been grounded in an absolutist idea of kingship, nor did they realize that the Earl of Bute was George's sweetheart.

The unfortunate George, who was destined to a gloomy and unwise reign, punctuated by periods of insanity, was the victim of his upbringing. His good and natural impulses were balked and twisted to serve the purposes of a jealous and ambitious mother and a pompous and scheming favorite. He was tall, strongly sexed, had bulging eyes, a thick nose, loose, full lips, and a nature inclined to activity and adventure. Everything was done to stamp out this natural character. George had pleaded with the old King to be allowed to go to war, but that had been refused. He had been thwarted in the affair of Hannah Lightfoot, which had frightened the Princess Dowager Augusta into excessive vigilance.

Augusta had not forgiven the harsh treatment shown her by the old King and Queen in the early days of her marriage with Frederick. She had hated a succession of ministries and resented the fact that through the long life of George II she had been deprived of her expectation of becoming Queen. She clung to the young George, surrounded him, smothered him, and, with the aid of Bute, formed his mind.

Bute entered into the scheme with rare skill. The nature of his peculiar relationship to that household has never been proved or disproved. Whether or not he was a favorite of Augusta's bedchamber, he was the chief figure in her life, virtually the only figure of importance outside of their young victim, the new King.

The famous legs of John, Lord Bute, had carried him right up the steps of the Prince's palace, but it was his wits which kept him there. He was known as a dancing man, an amateur actor, a patron of the arts, an amiable nobody. Frederick had underestimated him, and so did most of his contemporaries.

The vigorous mental activity of the young man had needed some outlet, and the keynote set by Augusta and Bute was piety,—piety and economy. Perhaps their own sins made them regard piety as a beautiful and remote jewel, to be worn by the young George, or perhaps they felt that it was a good contrast to the libertine behavior of the old King. Piety would keep Hannah Lightfoots and ribald companions away from the young man. George embraced the virtue with unction and became violently upright.

A companion idea to the particular brand of piety taught by Augusta and Bute was their conception of kingship. George must prepare himself to be a good king, better than his wicked ministers, dispensing through the radiance of his presence and his intentions an atmosphere of goodness to all his people, unhampered by any powerful officers who might wish to interfere, such as the Whigs.

Bute, as tutor to the royal Prince, had found a useful textbook for his purpose. The book was Bolingbroke's *The Idea of a Patriot King.* Only a few copies are extant today and it had little general influence or acceptance in its own time. Bolingbroke had written the tract as a romantic fancy after he had regarded the Tory cause as utterly lost. He had declined to permit publication of the manuscript for many years, doubtless recognizing the danger that it might bring to him in a nation under the control of the Whigs. Bolingbroke, it will be recalled, even though a Tory, had been a political advisor to the young Whigs at Stowe. His charm and the keenness of his mind had capitivated the young Pitt. Something of this amiability pervades the text of *The Idea of a Patriot King.* It was essentially, on Bolingbroke's part, an *apologia pro sua vita.* It was an idealization of the Tory idea, a conception of the perfection of the absolute monarch as he might be in Utopia.

The doctrine was precisely suited for the classroom of teacher Bute and pupil George, as may be seen by sampling a few of its paragraphs:

> The office of kings is then of right divine, and their persons are to be reputed sacred.
>
> When monarchy is the essential form (of government), it may be more easily and more usefully tempered with aristocracy or democracy, or both, than either of them, when they are the essential forms, can be tempered with monarchy.
>
> God is a monarch, yet not an arbitrary but a limited monarch, limited by the rule which infinite wisdom prescribes to infinite power. If governing without any rule and by arbitrary will, be not essential to our idea of the monarchy of the Supreme Being, it is plainly ridiculous to suppose them necessarily included in the idea of a human monarchy.
>
> The constitution will be considered by him as one law, consisting of two tables, containing the rule of his government, and the measure of his subjects' obedience, or as one system, composed of different parts and powers, but all duly proportioned to

one another, and conspiring by their harmony to the perfection
of the whole.

He knows that his (hereditary) right is founded on the laws
of God and man, that none can shake it but himself, and that
his own virtue is sufficient to maintain it against all opposition.

He must fix at once the general principles and ends of all his
actions, and determine that his whole conduct shall be regulated
by them.

Best and most important of all, from Bute's point of
view, Bolingbroke had enunciated two further thoughts for
a King:

He must begin to govern as soon as he begins to reign.

His first care will be, no doubt, to purge his Court, and to
call into the administration such men, as he can assure himself
will serve on the same principles on which he intends to govern.

He will "purge his Court"! The pupil at a later time
did not forget that lesson.

Such was the stuff which filled the mind of the young
and thwarted King. The ideas of piety and absolutism
gave scope for his mental energies, but did not satisfy his
capacity for affection. Cut off from almost all society, the
young George lavished all his devotion upon his tutor. The
King addressed the Earl of Bute as "My Darling," everything was Bute. Bute was the custodian of his heart and
mind. George was King and he meant to be King splen-
didly, without interference from his Ministers. Bute
would be able to tell him how, and he clung to Bute, as a
large and outraged orchid to its tree.

Each day the Ministry realized more clearly that George
III had notions of conduct and kingship which they had
not foreseen. The first shock had been the interview with
Newcastle, when the King had indicated Bute as the royal
mouthpiece. Now came a bolder incident. The young
monarch had established his Court temporarily at Carlton
House, his mother's city residence; and thither he summoned a meeting of the Privy Council. He also instructed
Newcastle, Pitt and Holdernesse to arrive ahead of time
for a conference. On their arrival, the King informed

these Ministers that he proposed to give his views on government to the Privy Council, that he had drawn them up in a paper, and he handed the paper to Newcastle to read aloud. When Newcastle had finished, his Majesty inquired, "Is there anything wrong in point of *form?*"

Form, not policy! the King had his breeches on inside out, for it was his privilege to express preferences for form, and his Cabinet's to affirm the substance.

The three Ministers, unprepared for this surprise, and flabbergasted by it, bowed and retired. Mr. Pitt was in a state of great agitation, for the King had enunciated policies clearly drawn up by Lord Bute, which were aimed directly at the present Administration. The victories of England were referred to as "a bloody and expensive war," and the King expressed his intention of "obtaining an honourable and lasting peace."

The import of the message was clear enough. As long as the war lasted there was no man in England who could replace the work of Mr. Pitt or approach his abilities. The war, then, must be terminated promptly and not treated as a glorious accomplishment. The clamor for peace, coming directly from the Throne, would weaken the hands of Pitt and aid the cause of his enemies abroad and at home.

This expression of opinion by the King was given without alteration at the Privy Council meeting, but Pitt went that evening to Montague House and wrestled for three hours with Lord Bute to have the text altered for the record. Bute unwillingly yielded, for he did not dare to stand out against the combined voice of the Cabinet, which supported Pitt in this issue. Even Lord Mansfield, who was unrelenting in his hatred of Mr. Pitt, could not countenance this effort of the King to seize control of policies without consulting his Ministers. The first phrase in the address, accordingly, was changed to read, "an expensive but just and necessary war," and the peace phrase was altered to read "honourable peace in concert with our allies," which supported Mr. Pitt's strategy of a Congress of the Powers.

The King himself had the bit in his teeth and was ill pleased when his darling Bute told him that these changes would be necessary, and it was not until two of the following afternoon that he finally yielded to the correction of his royal will.

Each day brought fresh evidence of the changed world under the new monarch. On October 26, 1760, the accession of the new King was officially proclaimed at Leicester Square, Charing Cross, at Temple Bar, in Cheapside, and at the Royal Exchange. For a brief period his popularity was high. He aimed to merit the amiable qualities of Bolingbroke's "Patriot King," as well as attempting the seizure of power. At his levees, in contrast to the manner of his grumpy old grandfather, he was gracious and smiling, circulated among his guests, and had a pleasant word for all. The ladies in particular were captivated, so also were courtiers who had been for some time out of favor. Sackville was so frequently received by his Majesty that Pitt put a stop to the practice, lest it be regarded as a repudiation of Sackville's dismissal from the Army after Minden, and thus undermine Army discipline.

Among the newcomers at Court was the awkward Lord Lyttelton, who had never regained the confidence of Mr. Pitt, his friend of school days. He kissed the King's hand as early as October 30, and was loud in his praises of the new monarch. Another gentleman who enjoyed high favor was Lord Talbot, who had promised to marry Betty Pitt if his wife would divorce him. His Lordship had apparently made similar promises in various directions, and his wife finally entered suit for divorce, naming a duchess as co-respondent.

Talbot had seemingly forgotten the warm beauty of Miss Betty, and had entered upon a life of conspicuous reform. He was soon to be appointed Steward of the King's Household, where he endeared himself to the Crown by drastically cutting salaries and supervising the amount of food allotted for each servant. The Duke of Cumberland also benefited from the new accession, as the King treated his uncle with marked kindness.

The Ministry necessarily was quiescent until the opening of the new Parliament on November 18, when it would have the opportunity through the medium of the King's address to state its policies for the coming year.

The new faces seen at Court, the parsimony in the royal household, and the obvious slights accorded to Mr. Pitt and his friends very shortly began to wear down the new King's popularity, and the public who had hailed his youthfulness became disturbed with suspicions. Why had he held his first official gathering at Carlton House which was his mother's winter palace? He might just as well have gone to Saville House in Leicester Square which was his own residence. Why was he seen incessantly with Lord Bute, the Scotch peer? The obvious friendship of the King for his Scotch tutor was conspicuous and disquieting. It aroused the strong anti-Scotch feeling prevalent throughout the south of England, and it was intensified by the fact that Bute's presence reflected on Pitt, the great popular leader who, in public opinion, should influence the King.

Never, in fact, had Mr. Pitt's hold on the people been greater, and as the opening of Parliament approached the public sensed the impending struggle, and was clearly on the side of the Administration.

The Ministry now began to prepare with greatest care the text of the King's address to Parliament. Hardwicke drew up the initial draft. Hardwicke still occupied the curious position of being one of the strongest men in the Government, though having no official portfolio. While actually an opponent of Pitt on many issues, though lacking any considerable personal following or any great family connection, his integrity and intelligence were so marked that all ministers respected his advice. Pitt, who was not gifted as a writer, had again and again welcomed the aid of Hardwicke in the preparation of state papers.

In this case, the former Lord Chancellor was at his best. With respect to the progress of the war he wrote:

> I reflect with pleasure on the successes with which the British arms have been prospered this summer. The total reduction of the vast province of Canada, with the city of Montreal, is of the most interesting consequence, and must be as heavy a blow to our enemies, as it is a conquest glorious to us; the more glorious

because effected almost without effusion of blood, and with that humanity which makes an amiable part of the character of this nation.

Our advantages gained in the East Indies have been signal; and must greatly diminish the strength and trade of France in those parts, as well as procure the most solid benefits to the commerce and wealth of my subjects. . . .

I rely upon your zeal and hearty concurrence to support the King of Prussia and the rest of my allies.

If the King swallowed these statements, and he would be obliged to swallow them, he would learn something of the difficulty of adhering to Bolingbroke's principle that "he must begin to govern as soon as he begins to reign." Lord Bute had evidently learned his lesson, at least in part, for he made no attempt to change these affirmations of policy. The King, however, did take the unprecedented step of writing a paragraph of his own into the address which, added to Hardwicke's paragraphs, he read to the assembled Parliament on November 18:

Born and educated in this country, I glory in the name of *Briton;* and the peculiar happiness of my life will ever consist in promoting the welfare of the people, whose loyalty and warm affection to me I consider the greatest and most permanent security of my Throne.

The Ministry had been given the faint courtesy of the permission to see these words before they were publicly spoken, but were informed that the addition was "by command."

Newcastle was a servile courtier when he could use a King to his purpose, but at heart he was a Whig and this was too much for him. "I make no observation," he wrote to Hardwicke, "but that this method of proceeding cannot last, though we must *now,* I suppose, submit."

Taken from its context, the paragraph introduced by the King might seem like a noble sentiment. He was ruler of the United Kingdom, Scotland as well as England; and the use of the word "Briton" was appropriate. The words about the loyalty and affection of his people as "the greatest and most permanent security of my Throne" had a noble ring, but they ignored Parliament and the Ministry as the Constitutional security of the Throne.

The significance of the royal sentiments, however, as reflecting the voice of Bute, was thoroughly understood by the public and a popular clamor broke out against the influence of Augusta and the Earl of Bute. This was no Constitutional procedure, this was not the English way of doing things. Placards were posted on the walls of Westminster Hall and the Royal Exchange bearing the words "No petticoat government! no Scottish favorite!" The appearance of Augusta at the theater brought such outcries of insults from the gallery that she retired to a temporary seclusion, and one day when the King was being carried in his sedan chair from the royal offices to his mother's apartments, a voice from the mob cried out and asked him if he were going to suck.

CHAPTER XXVIII

THE KING AND SARAH LENNOX

All through the winter, the spring and the early summer of 1761 Mr. Pitt and other personalities around the Throne jockeyed for advantage, yet each advanced tentatively, keeping his position flexible and avoiding decisions and enmities. Mr. Pitt no longer took a high tone toward his Cabinet, but advanced like a horse on an insecure bridge, testing each plank with the hoof before relying on it. Lord Bute, with all the backing that the Throne could give him, was similarly hesitant about making enemies or taking irrevocable positions. Most notably, he took especial pains to conciliate Mr. Pitt and frequently sided with him in Cabinet dissensions. No one wished to make a move, for the air was pregnant with transition, as behind the scenes of Cabinet and Throne a romantic drama was in process. In short, the King was in love.

The object of the King's affections was Lady Sarah Lennox, a girl of extraordinary loveliness. She had a pretty mouth, remarkably fine teeth, a well-turned figure, and an abundance of dark silky hair. She was noted for her fine complexion, a fair white skin with rosy cheeks. Above all she had a vivacity and personality which marked her apart from the ordinary run.

Sarah was eligible both by personality and rank to be a queen. She was the daughter of the second Duke of Richmond and sister of the brilliant Charles Lennox, the third Duke, who had distinguished himself in the Army and in politics. The whole Lennox family had extraordinary vivacity and talent. Her sister Caroline had eloped with Henry Fox and was the mother of the notable Charles James Fox. Another sister was the mother of Edward Fitzgerald, translator of the Rubaiyat. They were related to the Keppels, the Bedfords, the Kerr-Lothians and other noted families of the day. The Villiers blood flowed strong in their veins and by this they were distantly connected with Mr. Pitt for whom the Lennox family had always shown a strong admiration. The first Duke of Richmond, it will be recalled, was the son of Charles II by his French mistress, Mlle. Louise Renée de Perrencourt de Querouaille, but the fact of the bar sinister had not cast a shadow on the family, while its notable gifts had made it one of the chief houses in the kingdom.

The romance between Sarah and the King, which became intense in the spring of 1761, had been brewing for a year and a half. In her early teens Sarah had lived in Ireland, but in November, 1759, at the age of fifteen, she had attended Court and there had met and danced with young George, then Prince of Wales. To the sheltered Prince it had been a memorable experience. Royalty was not awesome to Sarah, for as a little girl she had been a pet of George II; and she treated the young George as though he were any other boy of her acquaintance. There was a new dance step of the day called the Betty Blue, and Sarah instructed the Prince in how to do it.

Sarah was not frequently at Court, and Prince George was too closely guarded to have easy opportunities to see her. When he ascended the throne in October, 1760, however, the memory lingered on, and, significantly, the new King delayed the Coronation ceremonies, in the thought that he would wait until a Queen might be crowned at the same time. This notion did not please Princess Augusta or Lord Bute, but as long as it remained an intangible idea there was little to be feared.

On November 6, 1760, the King had changed his residence to St. James Palace, which removed him from the immediate surveillance of his mother. At about the same time he developed the habit of taking horseback rides along the Kensington Road.

Now it happened that Holland House, the home of Henry Fox, was on the Kensington Road. It also happened that Sarah Lennox was spending much time with her sister, Lady Caroline Fox. There was a meadow between the house and the Kensington Road and Lady Sarah formed the habit of putting on a dress of the peasant style and joining with the workers in hay-making. It was a democratic gesture current in the eighteenth century, and it enabled Sarah to be near the road when King George passed by. It soon developed that he did not pass by but remained to converse, and, to make hay himself while the sun shone.

At first only a few persons were aware of the King's mounting interest in Sarah Lennox. The best informed was Lady Susan Strangways, a niece of Henry Fox and Sarah's intimate friend and confidante. One day, early in March, Susan and Sarah attended Court. They were planning to go down to the country for a considerable period and this was to be their last, or next to last, appearance for some time. The King had learned of this, and at the levee was in a state of considerable agitation. He waited until Susan was on the other side of the room from Lady Sarah and then took Lady Susan aside.

"You are going into Somersetshire," said the young King. "When do you return?"

"Not before winter, Sir," Lady Susan answered, "And I don't know how soon in winter."

"Is there nothing will bring you back to town before winter?" the King asked eagerly.

"I don't know of anything."

"Would you not like to see a Coronation?"

"Yes, Sir," Lady Susan smiled. "I hope I should come to see that."

"I hear it's very popular my having put it off," the King said significantly.

At this Lady Susan was silent and confused, thinking, in fact, that the King was declaring his intentions with herself in mind.

His Majesty continued with his comments on the Coronation.

"Won't it be a much finer sight when there is a Queen?" he said.

"To be sure, Sir," Susan answered.

"I have had a great many applications from abroad but I don't like them," George III observed.

Susan made no comment.

"I have had none at home," he continued, "I should like that better."

Lady Susan again was silent.

The King paused, hesitatingly.

"What do you think of your friend?" he said finally, "You know whom I mean; don't you think her fittest?"

"Think, Sir?"

"I think none so fit," he said decisively.

Before Lady Susan could find any reply to this astounding declaration, the King crossed the room to Lady Sarah and told her to ask her friend what he had been saying, to make her tell her, and to tell her all. It was evident to everyone at the levee that the King had fallen deeply in love with Sarah. It was written all over him, in his eyes, his manner, his eager attention to her. And the prospect, the possibility of Lady Sarah Lennox becoming Queen of England, became the underlying factor in every move of the Government.

It was an unexpected and catalytic factor in an already complicated situation. In the Constitutional view the King was the symbol of the State and acted according to the guidance of his Ministers, but George III had other ideas. The struggle between the royal point of view and that of the Constitutional Whigs was still unresolved.

Ordinarily the marriage of the King might have little bearing on political circumstances, but Sarah's family connections, coupled with her marked personality and influence over his Majesty, gave special emphasis to the situation. She was, in effect, a princess of the Constitutional Whigs. While the Whigs quarreled violently among themselves, they were nearly always united on the issue of Constitutionality. Moreover, Sarah as Queen would in herself serve to unify the Whig party, through her relationship to dissenting elements. She was a favorite of her brother-in-law, Henry Fox, and at the same time devoted to her brother

Charles, the third Duke of Richmond, who disliked Fox. She was a protégé of her relative, Lady Albemarle (Albemarle was the title of the Keppel family), even though the Duke of Richmond and Lord Albemarle were not on good terms. With Sarah as Queen, Mr. Pitt's Administration would have solid strength, the ascendancy of Lord Bute would be at an end, and the Princess Dowager would be relegated to the background. With such a favorable prospect Mr. Pitt could afford to mark time.

Bute thoroughly realized the danger. It was vital to his interest to retain the support and friendship of Mr. Pitt if the marriage should take place. His only salvation in that event would be to have the favor of the Whigs, and it would be necessary to modify quickly and drastically the lessons which he had taught the young King. Contrariwise, if the romance soured, his Majesty would naturally harbor resentment against the Whig families and would be steeled in his purpose to be a dominating ruler. Bute did well to pause and ponder.

Secretly, Bute and the Princess Dowager set about to break up the love affair. Lady Sarah herself proved to be their best weapon. While Sarah had been flattered by the attentions of the King, her favorite at this time was a good-looking, dashing young scapegrace named Lord Newbottle, the future Marquis of Lothian, a more engaging companion than the adenoidal young King. Newbottle, according to Henry Fox, "made love to all the girls"; and had fallen in love with Lady Caroline Russell, a daughter of the Duke of Bedford. This had been a challenge to Sarah Lennox, who proceeded to take him away from the Bedford girl, and in the process had fallen in love with him.

The young man's parents and the Richmonds both were violently opposed to the match,—which only served to strengthen the attachment. This affair was at its height at the time that the King had made his intentions clear to Lady Susan and Lady Sarah at the levee. Unchanged by the King's avowal, Sarah arranged for a meeting with Lord Newbottle in St. James Park under the chaperonage of her brother Lord George Lennox and his lady, who was Lord

Newbottle's sister. Also present at this conference, though unheard and unseen, were the Earl of Bute and his Majesty, George III. Bute had learned of the meeting through one of his many spies, and had prevailed upon the King to hide in the bushes and learn the facts about his true love. While in that unroyal stance, George listened to the declarations of love between Sarah and Newbottle and heard it settled that Newbottle would beg his father's consent to the match.

Even so, his Majesty was not altered in his feelings, while Sarah remained loyal to Newbottle. The Foxes, however, were determined that Sarah should encourage the King, and against her strong protests finally forced her to go to Court, on an occasion shortly after the King's momentous conversation with Lady Susan. She had been crying all morning and was in the worst possible humor. The moment the King saw her, he approached her.

"Have you seen your friend lately?" he said eagerly, referring to Susan.

"Yes," Sarah answered without encouragement.

"Has she told you what I said to her?"

"Yes."

"All?"

"Yes," Sarah answered.

"Do you approve?" the King asked.

To this the beautiful Sarah made no reply whatever, but looked as cross and ill-pleased as she knew how. Affronted and bewildered, the King walked away, and then in confusion left the room.

While the Court society speculated on what this incident might mean, Sarah went down to the country to visit her brother, Richmond. While there she was re-united with Newbottle, became bored with him, and carried on other flirtations. One day she fell from a horse, and broke a leg. Newbottle indicated that she needn't expect any sympathy from him, saying that the leg was ugly enough to start with; and in the period of convalescence Sarah began to think more favorably of the King.

By this time Lord Bute had rallied opposition to the match from a new quarter. Rather surprisingly, the King's relatives, including the Duke of Cumberland, were stoutly opposed to his Majesty marrying an English peeress. All of the old Hanoverian pride came to the fore. The Electorate of Hanover had always seemed to them more important than England. For the King to marry outside of royalty they regarded as outrageous. There were scores of German princesses who, in their opinion, would be far more appropriate, and they made their wishes apparent to the King.

George, however, was not to be deflected from his intentions. Sarah came back to town on May 22, and on May 29 went to the theater. The King learned of her plans and went to the play also, where he greeted her with conspicuous pleasure. On the following Sunday she attended Court, which was more than he had hoped for. When he saw her he blushed, rushed up to her and spent most of the time conversing with her. On Thursday, at the Birthday Ball, he had no eyes but for her, and hardly talked to anyone else. He persuaded her to come forward and stand by the throne where he was receiving, so the entire room could not fail to be aware of his interest. Lady Bute, who had been instructed to keep an eye on Sarah and break up these attentions, sat near at hand and glared at the couple throughout the proceedings, but they were oblivious. The Princess Dowager on meeting Sarah laughed in her face, but the King continued unmoved by opposition. He was ecstatically, gloriously, in love.

He asked his sister to dance the Betty Blue.

"A dance," he said to Lady Sarah, "that you are acquainted with. I am very fond of it because it was taught me by a lady," he continued, looking at her significantly.

Sarah said that she really did not know whom he meant.

"A very pretty lady," the King added, "that came from Ireland November was a twelvemonth."

Sarah still pretended to be innocent.

"I am talking to her now," said the King. "She taught it me at the ball on Twelfth Night."

"Indeed, Sir," Sarah replied, "I did not remember it."

"That may be," said the King. "But I have a very good

memory for whatever relates to that lady. I had got a
pretty new country dance of my own for the late King's
birthday if he had lived to it, and I named it, 'The twenty-
fifth of February.' "

The twenty-fifth of February was Lady Sarah's birthday,
and at this mark of the King's interest and attention Lady
Sarah blushed, which made her look prettier than ever, and
so they continued in eager attention to each other throughout the ball. As the King's time came to leave he started to
withdraw, came back and talked to Sarah again and repeated his action several times before he was able to tear
himself away.

The conspicuous attentions of the King naturally aroused
the royal family and Lord Bute to more furious and determined opposition, and for a time had the effect of discouraging him, and raising doubts. When Lady Sarah appeared
again at Court on Sunday, June 7, 1761, he looked at her
languishingly and talked to her for a long while but made
no new declarations of affection. In fact, he appeared out
of sorts and melancholy; but on Thursday, June 18, the
King had recovered his courage. As soon as he saw Lady
Sarah he said in a loud voice that others could hear: "I was
told you were to go out of town. If you had gone I should
have been miserable. For God's sake think of what I hinted
to Lady Susan Strangways before you went to the country."

And again, as if to leave no doubt in the minds of everyone, he almost shouted: "For God's sake remember what
I said to Lady Susan before you went to the country, and
believe that I have the strongest attachment."

After that, the result seemed to be only a matter of time.
Lady Sarah attended the next two levees, where the King
spoke and looked with great fondness; and on Sunday,
June 28, 1761, he attended church where she was seated
within easy view of him, and he fixed his eyes on her almost
continuously throughout the service. By this time, nearly
all London knew the story; and the country was waiting
for some announcement, when a notice was sent from the
Throne to the Privy Council on July 1 for a meeting on the
8th to consider "urgent and important business."

CHAPTER XXIX

MINISTER BEHIND THE CURTAIN

While the King's love affair proceeded during the anxious early months of the new reign, Lord Bute took many measures to protect himself, to augment his influence at the Throne, and to plot against Mr. Pitt.

It was necessary, of course, for Bute to move with the utmost care. It was risky to trust anyone, for each man in the Cabinet seemed to carry a stiletto ready to jab into the back of his nearest colleague. Bute, though generally regarded as a dilettante and a fop, soon proved to be a professional in politics. His actions, from November, 1760, through July, 1761, revealed a shrewd, resourceful schemer equipped with an organizing talent and self-control.

The King was ready to support Bute in any program and would gladly have consented to the immediate dismissal of Mr. Pitt. A lesser, duller man than Bute might have been tempted to seize the power at once, not realizing the extent of the forces against him. Bute knew that he must move astutely toward the goal of establishing himself and Tory principles as the governing influences of the kingdom. He could not afford to challenge Mr. Pitt's position openly and, in fact, he desired rather to win Pitt as an ally, clip his wings, compromise him, and make use of his hold on the people.

Lord Bute, in his long acquaintance with William Pitt, was well aware of the Minister's devotion to his sister Ann. Bute also knew Ann particularly well, through her services on the household staff of the Princess Dowager during the years 1751-53. In fact, Ann was still on the rolls of the household though ill health had prevented her continuing in active service as Privy Purse. The use of Ann as a means of embarrassing her brother had rather provocative possibilities. Ann was readily excitable, at times half insane, and now both hurt and embittered through having been supplanted in her brother's life by Lady Hester Pitt. Lord Bute regarded that family situation contemplatively, and events began to work in his favor. Ann had decided to come up from Bath to London to see her brother, and Hester had written her a note, making not too plausible excuses as to why William would not be able to receive his sister:

> It is, my Dear Madam, extremely unfortunate that from different circumstances which have interposed themselves, I have not had it in my power to have the pleasure of seeing you since your arrival in the neighborhood of London.
>
> There is to be a meeting of the Cabinet here this Evening, which Always engrosses my Apartment and banishes me to other quarters.
>
> We are but just arrived from the Country, which I think has done your Brother good. He desires I wou'd assure you of his affectionate Compliments, and let you know that his present Pressure of business is so great that it does not leave him the Command of a quarter of an hour of his time, so as to be able to assure himself beforehand of the pleasure of seeing any friend, therefore under that uncertainty, and fearing he may miss of the Satisfaction of meeting You, he desires thro' me to wish you a safe return to Bath, so much the best place, He is perfectly convinced, for Your Health.
>
> I must not end my Note without expressing how much I was flattered by your remembrance of Little Hetty.

This letter was written in October, 1760, just after the accession of the new King; and Bute's new relationship to Mr. Pitt and the Ministry, should be traced from the beginning of the reign. Ann had probably been moved to come up to town by the onrush of Tories and Leicester House favorites who were rapidly surrounding the Throne. It is altogether possible, as may be surmised from subsequent events, that Bute had suggested the trip. In justice to Hester, it should be said that this was the worst possible time for injection of family complications into Mr. Pitt's affairs. Ann's arrival in the city was apparently but a short time before the opening of the new Parliament, and the Cabinet meeting to which Hester referred in her letter probably was the one which dealt with the draft of the King's address. Hester held Ann at a distance on various occasions, but this time, at least, it seemed thoroughly wise. Ann, however, did not accept this rebuff, and arranged to stay elsewhere in the city, whereupon Hester wrote her a second letter:

DEAR MADAM,—Having informed Mr. Pitt, who is this moment come home, that you intend going to the Lodgings in Lisle Street, He wou'd not set down to dinner without desiring me to let you know from Him that this intention of Yours gives him the greatest surprise and not Less concern for *Your sake,* being unalterably persuaded that Retreat is the only right Thing for your Health, Welfare, and Happiness, and that Bath in Your present state seems to be the fittest Place.

St. James Square, Wednesday, past four o'clock.

At this, Ann was grieved and infuriated. Apparently she talked freely to her friends, many of whom were also friends of Mr. Pitt, regarding the treatment she was receiving, for she soon had a letter from her brother outlining his reasons for not wishing her to stay in London:

DEAR SISTER,—I desire to assure you that all Idea of *Quarrel* or *unkindness,* (words I am griev'd to find you cou'd employ) was never farther from my mind than during your stay in this neighborhood. On the Contrary, my Dear Sister, nothing but kindness and regard to your Good, on the whole, has made me judge it necessary that we should not meet during the Continuance you think fit to give to an excursion so unexpected, and so hurtful to you. I beg my Dear Sister not to mistake my wishes to see Her set down, for a time, quiet and collected within her own resources of patience and fortitude, (merely as being best and the only fit thing for Herself) so very widely as to suppose, that my Situation as a Publick Person is any way concern'd in her residing in one Place or another. All I mean is, that, *for your own sake,* you shou'd abstain from all desultory jaunts, such as the present. The hearing of you all at once, at Sion; next at Kensington, then every day going, and now not yet gone, certainly carries an appearance disadvantageous to you in this view; I have refused myself the pleasure of seeing You; as considering your journey and hovering about London, as too imprudent and restless, or as too mysterious, for me not to dis-

PAINTED BY REYNOLDS   ENGRAVED BY DICKINSON AND WATT

George III at the time of his accession. "The Betty Blue" was still his favorite dance.

PAINTED BY REYNOLDS   ENGRAVED BY T. COOK

Lady Sarah Lennox, who jilted Lord Newbottle (later Lord Lothian), flirted with the King, and stymied the politics of the nation.

courage such a conduct, by remaining unmixt with it. This is
the only cause of my not seeing you, nor can I give you a more
real proof of my affectionate regard for your welfare than by
thus refusing myself a great pleasure, and, I fear, giving you a
Pain. I offer you no Advice, as to the choice of your residence.
I am persuaded you want none; you have a right and are well
able to judge for yourself on this point. But if you will not fix
somewhere You are undone. I am sorry to be forc'd to say this
much; but saying less I should cease to be with truest affection
Dear Sister

Ever Yrs.
W. PITT

Pitt obviously was somewhat less than candid in claiming
that his disapproval of Ann's presence had nothing to do
with his situation "as a Publick Person." He knew, however, that his letter was likely to be shown to others, and it
was important to preserve the benevolent tone. His approach, moreover, was successful with Ann, for she replied
with a willingness to do as he advised, and she also revealed
that the chief purpose of her trip to London had been to
see him about getting her a pension:

DEAR BROTHER,—I am going to set out to return to Bath,
but as the letter I received from you yesterday leaves me in
great anxiety and perplexity of mind, I cannot set out without
assuring you, as I do with the most exact truth, that there was
no mistery in my journey here, nor no purpose but the relief I
proposed to my mind. If I had known before I left the Bath
that you disapproved of my leaving that place at this time, or
of my coming to Town, I wou'd not have done as I have done,
and wou'd not even have come near it, tho' the advice given
me at Oxford with regard to my health, made me desire to
make use of the interval in which I was order'd not to try the
waters again, to have the pleasure and satisfaction of seeing You
and some of my friends and as I hoped that satisfaction from
You in the first place, I will not dissemble that I am very much
disappointed and mortified in not having seen you, but as the
hurry of important business you are in, and the relief necessary
to make you go through it, made it possible for me not to inter-
pret your not seeing me as a mark of unkindness, I never used
the word [sic] but to guard against other people using it, upon

a circumstance which I thought they had nothing to do with.
When I writ you word from the Bath that I had thoughts
of coming to Town for Christmas, I desir'd nothing so much
as to do what was most proper according to my situation, and
consequently to have your advice, which I told you very sincerely I wished to be guided by preferably to every other consideration, You best know how I am to attain the end I have
steadily desired for Years, as you know I writ you word from
France (before my spirits were so much disorder'd as they have
been since) that I desired nothing as much as a safe and honourable retreat, that wou'd leave me the enjoyment of my
Friends, without which help and suport I find by a painful experience that it is impossible for me to support myself. I beg
leave to trouble you with my compliments to Lady Hester, and
my wishes for the happiness of you both, and of all the little
family that belong to you.

The request for a pension, of "a safe and honourable
retreat," as Ann euphemistically called it, could not have
been made at a more difficult period, from William's
view, and yet from Ann's standpoint it was just the time.
As she had been one of the King's family circle since his
boyhood days, it seemed entirely proper that his Majesty
might now recognize her worthiness, especially as many
other newcomers to the Court were being rewarded on far
less justification. Pitt, however, could not sponsor the request. He could not afford to be under obligations to the
new King, or to anyone. The very strength of his position
depended upon his having no ties of obligation, and he
wrote to Ann on November 4, 1760, to explain his position:

DEAR SISTER,—I hoped long before now to have been able
to call on you, and in that hope have delayed answering a letter
on a subject so very nice and particular, that I cou'd, with
difficulty and but imperfectly, enter into it even in conversation.
I am sure I need not say to one of your knowledge of the world,
that explaining of Situations is not a small Affair, at any time,
and in the present moment I dare say You are too reasonable
to wish me to do it. In this state I have only to assure you of
my sincerest wishes for your advantage and happiness, and that
I shall consider any good that arrives to you as done to myself,
which I shall be ready to acknowledge as such; but having never

been a Solicitor of favours, upon any occasion, how can I become so now without contradicting the whole tenour of my Life? I think there is no foundation for your apprehensions of anything distressful being intended, and I hope you will not attribute what I have said to any motive that may give you uneasiness, being very truely

Dear Sister Your affectionate Brother

W. PITT

Lord Bute had been watching this situation with a saturnine interest, and had become mingled in it. While applying to her brother for assistance, Ann had also been in conference with Bute. On receiving her brother's refusal to act, she went again to Bute, and within three weeks she was placed on the pension roll. The exceptional promptitude of the act indicated that the matter had been long under consideration, and Bute may well have persuaded Ann to come up from Bath, on the suggestion that her brother ought to get her this reward and that, if the brother did not, he would.

Ann, naturally delighted, wrote a gloating letter to her brother, who replied on December 30, 1760:

DEAR SISTER,—Accept sincere felicitations from Lady Hester and me on the Event you have just communicated, on your account, I rejoice at an addition of income so agreeable to your turn of life, whatever repugnancy I find, at the same time, to see my Name placed on the Pensions of Ireland, unmixt as I am in this whole transaction, I will no doubt that you will take care to have it thoroughly understood. Long may you live in health to enjoy the comforts and happiness which you tell me you owe to the King, singly through the intercession of Lord Bute, and to feel the pleasing sentiments of such an obligation.

I am Dear Sister Your most affectionate Brother

W. PITT

Bute had partially failed in his attempt to compromise Mr. Pitt, to the extent that the latter had been too wise to apply for a pension for his sister, but the move was not without advantage, for at least it could be claimed that a member of the Pitt family was under obligation to his Lordship.

There were so many nuances to the situation in the latter weeks of 1760 that Bute found it necessary to think rapidly and astutely. Mr. Pitt, of course, was plunging right ahead with all his schemes of conquest for the following year. Now that Spain had actively interjected herself into the scene, Pitt was keeping Amherst for yet another year on the American station as a warning to Spain.

On the home-front Pitt was equally vigorous, and on November 13 again laid his Belle Isle proposal before the Cabinet. The public was still strongly in favor of Mr. Pitt, and Lord Bute needed to weigh his own position carefully. Most of the Ministers continued to be critical of the Belle Isle project, but Bute, to everyone's surprise, said, "It would be a blot upon the King's reign to open by laying aside such an expedition." The Cabinet, however, was not persuaded; and Mr. Pitt did not choose to force a decision on the issue at that time.

Bute was attending the Cabinet meetings at the King's request, but had not been invited by his colleagues to take a specific portfolio. To arrange for this would have required someone's resignation or else the elevation of some minor post to Cabinet standing. There was precedent for either step, but no one made either proposal. Bute, accordingly, consulted Mr. Pitt, in a politic fashion, saying that there were those who felt that he ought to have a high Cabinet position in view of his status with the King, but that he himself doubted the wisdom of such a move. It was Pitt's cue, of course, to brush away Lord Bute's modest qualms and urge him to take a prominent post. Bute had reason to expect to be coaxed, in view of his support on Belle Isle; but instead Pitt strongly agreed that the Scottish favorite would be impolitic to take office, and applauded his reluctance to participate in public affairs.

Though defeated in this little strategy, Lord Bute's power was far from being extinguished. The King repeatedly made it clear that the word of his former tutor had the greatest weight with him. Again and again members of the Ministry, seeking advice or authorization from the Throne, were referred to Lord Bute for a decision. To

Pitt, this interjection of a private person into ministerial authority was intolerable.

"I will make way for my Lord Bute's greatness, and assist it," Pitt said to Newcastle, "only I cannot make part of it." And again he said, "I and my Lord Holdernesse dangle at Court with a bag in our hands, but we are not Ministers. . . . People seeing me with that bag come and ask me questions which I am no more able to answer than any man in the outer room." In fact, he accused Bute of intending to be "the Minister behind the curtain."

Bute looked upon Pitt as obnoxious now that Pitt had shown no disposition to share ministerial power. Apparently the thing to do, after all, was to stir up a wave of peace talk which would, of course, be embarrassing to Pitt and perhaps cause his downfall. Bute accordingly organized a group of coffee-house runners to cry down Mr. Pitt, and he co-operated with certain members of the Cabinet in a campaign of printed propaganda.

The clamor for an immediate peace was fomented with especial success by a pamphlet entitled *Considerations on the Present German War*. This booklet was written by Israel Mauduit, and, like the Byng pamphlet, was inspired by Lord Hardwicke. It spoke of the growing expenses of the war, the poor results of the last campaign when the French had invaded Hesse and Hanover, and it demanded that England withdraw from such an expensive and profitless performance. The arguments were persuasive and, in part, were similar to those which Pitt had used in driving Carteret from office. In the present case, there was the difference that the English participation in Germany was part of Pitt's five-point system whereby he aimed to keep France occupied in Europe while pursuing his major plans elsewhere. Many of the people did not see the distinction, however, and the poet Gray wrote, "Ministry are much out of joint, Mr. Pitt much out of humor, his popularity tottering, chiefly occasioned by a pamphlet against the German war, written by that squeaking acquaintance of ours, Mr. Mauduit."

When the subject of the annual subsidy to Frederick of

Prussia was debated in the House on December 22, 1760, the drive for peace came to a head. There were many speeches against the Pitt policy, and very little vocal support for the Ministry.

Pitt was not unaware of the sources of the opposition, and in his reply he said, sardonically, "A certain little book, that was found somewhere or other, has made a great many orators in this House."

The shot reached its mark. Many of the members suspected that the Mauduit pamphlet had been inspired, and at least a few knew that the coffee-house claque had been hired by Lord Bute. When the issue came to a vote, therefore, the Parliament was not yet ready to reject Mr. Pitt, and he carried the motion.

Bute, for some time after this, was careful to disassociate himself from any peace talk, and even had the effrontery to rebuke Bedford for being a pacifist.

Bute was increasingly restless at being without Cabinet portfolio, and there was much to be said for his attitude. He was sensible of his growing abilities, and he was taking a public part at the insistence of the King. Though he could scheme and stoop to the most devious methods when he regarded them to be necessary, he did not, like Newcastle, love intrigue for its own sake. He could follow a straightforward path, and exhibit moral courage on occasion, and he preferred to have the open responsibility of Cabinet office.

As the reign advanced into the early part of 1761, Bute realized that some leading minister must beg him to take a Cabinet post, and he must find a method to bring that about. Since Pitt had refused to take the hint, the question now was, what Minister.

The Duke of Newcastle was obviously the best choice, though he was nominally allied to Pitt and could not be approached directly. There was, however, a strange individual in London who was a specialist in intrigue, and Bute engaged his services. This curious fellow was Count Viry, the Sardinian Minister. Viry, strangely enough, seemed to have gained the confidence of leading persons of the day, including Pitt. The memoirs of the period disclose that Viry was a constant talebearer, continually betraying confidences, never caught at it, or, if caught, able to carry it off without losing status.

In January, 1761, Viry approached Newcastle, Devonshire, and Hardwicke, separately, with the suggestion that Holdernesse retire from his post of Secretary of State for the Northern Department, with the compensation of a handsome pension, and that Lord Bute be requested to take his place. All three Ministers were receptive to the idea in principle, but Newcastle, who was slated to be the chief actor in the little drama, was apprehensive. He avowed that he was committed to Mr. Pitt and that he would hesitate to incur his displeasure if Mr. Pitt did not approve. Viry did not press the point immediately and left the proposal to be mulled over by Newcastle's intriguing mind.

The idea undoubtedly had much charm for the aging Duke. His control of patronage had been rudely curtailed by the accession of the new King, and Lord Bute would be a fresh ally who had recently been strengthened by some changes in his personal affairs. Bute was the nephew of the Duke of Argyle (no relation to the free-spoken Duchess of Argyll). The Duke had died and left to his nephew the political managership of Scotland. In addition to this benison, Bute's wife and his second son had been named as heirs to the riches of Lady Bute's father, Edward Wortley Montague. Bute became administrator of one of the largest fortunes of the kingdom, a fortune which included Montague House which later formed part of the British Museum. The political managership of Scotland, a vast fortune, the favor of the King,—what a combination! The Duke itched to bring the Earl of Bute under the Newcastle influence; yet he trembled at the thought of Mr. Pitt.

Viry approached the Duke again, and at first could not move him. Then the adroit Sardinian suggested that other friends of Mr. Pitt might make the same proposal and Newcastle would lose the credit for doing so. Alarmed by this prospect, the Duke consulted Hardwicke and Devonshire, and learned that they were favorable to the idea.

Newcastle then consented to meet with Lord Bute on March 10 to discuss the matter. The great difficulty, Newcastle feared, would be the question of who should propound the idea to Mr. Pitt; but Bute relieved his fears on that score by saying that he would broach the matter himself. Newcastle was overcome with gratitude and promised his undying loyalty. Bute, in turn, assured him that Pitt's popularity was declining and that even if Pitt resigned it would make little difference because he did not plan to go into opposition. Newcastle departed cheerfully and, as usual, wrote an account of the affair to Hardwicke.

When Mr. Pitt learned, as he soon did, the part which Newcastle had played in this affair, his confidence in his aging colleague was gone forever. Toward Bute and this new move, however, he showed no resentment, and evidently recognized that he must make terms with Bute's now obvious abilities and power. Pitt's demands were simple: complete control over appointments in his own department, free accessibility to the King, and assurance from the Throne of support for the war until a satisfactory peace could be obtained. Bute agreed, and on March 25, 1761, received his appointment in the place of Holdernesse.

The transaction as a whole turned out to be at the expense of Newcastle, for Mr. Pitt had sacrificed only his interest in domestic politics, which in fact had been managed by the Duke. When Bute took office, Lord Barrington replaced H. B. Legge, who had been Newcastle's as well as Pitt's man, as Chancellor of the Exchequer. Charles Townshend, Newcastle's nephew, was made Secretary at War, but wholly subject to Pitt's direction in war policy. The final guarantee of the bargain was the fact that on the day of Bute's appointment to the new post, Pitt obtained the King's signature to secret orders, approving the expedition against Belle Isle.

CHAPTER XXX

PARIS-MADRID AXIS

A new bombshell in international politics burst upon the European scene in the spring of 1761, and in Mr. Pitt's view shattered the current domestic structure. His union with Bute was well-nigh impregnable, and, without interference from King or Cabinet, he might well have expected to finish the building of his Anglo-Saxon system in short order, and to make peace on terms which would solidify it. Spain, however, was the new element which upset all former calculations. The attempts to pacify Charles III had been unavailing. He was champing with impatience over the dilatoriness of the Congress of Powers, and shrewdly enough he was planning to move in on the war actively, now that France and England were near financial exhaustion.

For the first time in many years, "the Family Compact" of the Bourbons was becoming an active and aggressive threat. The greatest peril of it, in Pitt's situation, was that his colleagues refused to take it seriously. Pitt was seeing dangers to the State, at least six months ahead of his fellows, and the fact that he was often ultimately justified made little difference. Spain had been a sleeping giant from the days of the Armada, and the Cabinet thought that Pitt was merely raising another issue to prolong the war and keep himself in office.

Mr. Pitt actually had before him copies of letters obtained by the British Secret Service, establishing the fact of a Paris-Madrid axis. They indicated that Choiseul was to draw England into peace talk and thereby slow up her wartime activities to give Spain time to organize her forces for a major offensive. Pitt laid the documents before the Cabinet, but they aroused little interest. The Ministers were insular in outlook, and besides they were tiring of the strain of Mr. Pitt's intense Administration. Even though Choiseul, as the intercepted letters indicated, offered his proposals for peace on March 26, 1761, the Cabinet treated the offers at their face value and used them, as Choiseul had hoped, to bring pressure on Pitt.

Here, again, the affair of Lady Sarah Lennox cut across the scene, as Henry Fox now became a clamorous opponent of the Pitt policies. As Fox might be the brother-in-law of the future Queen, his words carried weight. Fox, who once had been a genial man-about-town with many friends, whose chief shortcoming had been a cheerful lack of principles rather than evil intent, had undergone a marked deterioration. In his office of Paymaster-of-the-Forces he had, unlike Mr. Pitt, accepted all of the perquisites which the office afforded, and as a result of the war had become colossally rich. He had become an incessant gambler, drinker and glutton. His once stocky frame had become bulbous and his stomach had swollen to an enormous size, even for that corpulent era. Now, his chief ambition in life was to have a title and while Mr. Pitt was in power such an honor for Fox seemed unlikely.

The cord of mutual political interest which at times had tied Fox and Mr. Pitt together had long been frayed by personal incompatability. In a memoir written at the time, Fox said of Pitt, "It seems as if he singly would prevail to our and his own destruction."

Pitt did not expound his views on Fox, though many years later Lord Shelburne offered an explanation:

> It was a long time before I could learn from Mr. Pitt his opinion of Mr. Fox's private character. He then told me that he thought him the *blackest* man that ever lived; that he was a great dealer in anonymous letters to set people at variance with each other, and suggest to each such opinions as he thought convenient; that he carried it so far, that to his latter end, whenever he went about purchasing an estate, he had recourse to methods of undervaluing it, and deterring others from bidding for it; that he dealt much also in newspaper abuse, though he was continually complaining and crying about it; that he educated his children without the least regard to morality, and with such

extravagant vulgar indulgence, that the great change which has taken place among our youth has been dated from the time of his son's going to Eton.

Pitt did not need to worry particularly regarding Henry Fox's influence on Sarah Lennox for, as has been pointed out previously, other branches of Sarah's family were loyal to him, but the Fox adroitness and gusto were to be feared, and served to stiffen the opposition of Bedford, Devonshire and Hardwicke. Pitt did not, moreover, allow the Choiseul proposals to stop his plans. The Belle Isle expedition was on its way, as authorized, and Pitt sent specific instructions to Amherst to outfit further expeditions against French possessions in the West Indies, including Martinique, which had been too well protected in the previous attempt against that island.

Some answer had to be made to Choiseul's proposals, and the French minister in the following months was successful at least in occupying much of Pitt's valuable time in diplomatic correspondence and in causing growing dissension in the British Cabinet.

Choiseul had proposed that peace should be settled on the basis of conquests in hand, as of certain dates, for all regions except North America; and that the latter would be a matter of special negotiation. Pitt answered that England accepted the proposal in principle, which meant, and was supposed to mean, just exactly nothing. After dispatching this message, Mr. Pitt informed the King that he proposed to accomplish "the total destruction of the French in the East Indies." He also expected to retain Canada, Cape Breton (Louisbourg), and all the fishing rights in Newfoundland and the other banks off North America. He also expressed his full confidence in capturing Belle Isle and Martinique. He added further that this was his unalterable schedule and "if he was even capable of signing a treaty without it, he should be sorry he had ever again got the use of his right hand, which use he had but just recovered."

Newcastle, on hearing of this firm tone, called it "strange stuff."

On April 19, 1761, Choiseul made a counter-suggestion that each nation appoint a representative, one at Paris and the other at London, to carry on negotiations simultaneously. This was a shrewd move, as it would create an active platform for peace talk, and it was seemingly impossible to decline the offer. Pitt, accordingly, called a Cabinet meeting on April 23 to discuss the proposition and to recommend Hans Stanley as England's representative for the negotiations in Paris. Stanley was the Tory M.P. who had been noticed by Pitt in 1754 as one of those whom Temple should enlist in the coalition proposed at that time. Stanley had become one of the Lords of the Admiralty, and was said to have won Newcastle's favor. He had apparently kept clear of factional politics, and the Cabinet promptly confirmed the nomination.

On May 13, 1761, Pitt summoned his colleagues again to discuss Stanley's instructions. Pitt proposed that the representative be empowered with "unlimited instructions"; but the Cabinet would not grant that request, which, in effect, would mean that Stanley would carry out whatever instructions Mr. Pitt might dictate, without further need for Cabinet confirmation. Mr. Pitt next attempted to have Stanley instructed to assure Choiseul that England would continue to support Frederick of Prussia. Here again he encountered strong opposition, but compromised by adding the phrase "as an auxiliary."

Pitt was obliged to fight every inch of the way. There was no alternative system suggested, but the Ministry were tired of the war and tired of him.

Finally Pitt dropped his fighting attitude and told his colleagues that he would go along with them on either of two plans:

(1) *Would they agree to continue fighting until France was compelled to give up her German conquests?*

(2) *Would they be willing to trade some of the present*

conquests for the ground which France had conquered in Germany?

He pointed out that either course would permit England to discharge her pledges to her allies. It must not be said later that an alliance with Great Britain had resulted disastrously for her supporters. He was obligated to protect England's allies, and was willing to rest on that minimum as the united policy of the Cabinet.

The two questions were a brilliant and simple statement of the situation. France had conquered and was holding most of the German territory belonging to the English King. Therefore, the Cabinet felt compelled to say that they would continue the war to redeem those possessions.

Pitt, however, with the second question, forced the alternative upon them. They need not continue the German war, if in exchange for George III's lands they were willing to trade back to France the advantages gained in the New World and elsewhere, if they were willing to go before the public on the platform that all the conquests, all the effort and expense, all the heroism of the past three years, were to result in a peace which would leave England just about where she had started in 1757. Such were the realities of the situation, and Pitt knew that the Cabinet dared not make peace on such terms.

The Ministers concluded the session with a virtual endorsement of Mr. Pitt, supported by a vague resolution which stated: "the losses of our Allies in Germany should be considered at the peace and at the final settlement of our conquests."

Stanley arrived in France on May 31, 1761, and the French appointee, F. de Bussy, reached England on the same date. Much has been written about Bussy and his conversations with Mr. Pitt, but aside from being a propaganda agent he was nothing more than a straw-man. He did not belong to Choiseul's political party, and, for a period of five years—in the days of Walpole's Administration—had been in the pay of the British Government and was known as "101" in the Foreign Correspondence.

Choiseul probably knew this, and was prepared to use Bussy as the scapegoat if the negotiations became unpopular at home. While Pitt treated Bussy with notable diplomatic and personal courtesy, he conducted most of his dealings through Stanley at Paris.

Pitt succeeded in prolonging the discussions all through the spring, and on June 5, 1761, the fortress of Belle Isle surrendered to the British forces. This conquest restored Mr. Pitt's prestige and power to a point which he had not enjoyed since the accession of George III. This was the expedition which had been opposed and laughed at, which the chief officials of the Army and Navy had said was impossible. It gave Britain a naval base off the coast of France whereby she could keep informed of the operation of the French fleet from Bordeaux to the Pyrenees. It aroused the public to a new pitch of enthusiasm. By the same token, it threatened the stability of the Choiseul Government and compelled the transfer of French troops from the German lines to the coast defenses.

Meantime, Lady Sarah Lennox had returned to Court, and on June 18, as previously noted, the King had made his public declaration of his attachment to her. It seemed that the influence of Lord Bute was on the wane and that the Whig Government would have a new lease of power with Mr. Pitt as pre-eminently the person to continue in control, with the probable inescapable addition of the Fox and other Bedford Whigs.

Choiseul, quick to sense the change in affairs, promptly sent a new proposal, which was no longer a gesture to create embarrassing peace talk, but an earnest desire to settle. France offered to give up all her German conquests at once in return for Belle Isle, to cede Canada as far westward as Niagara, to make further concessions elsewhere, but to reclaim Cape Breton (without re-fortifying Louisbourg) as a fishing station.

These were sensational concessions compared with Choiseul's original vague memo of March 26, and when the English Cabinet met on June 24, 1761, to consider the offer, sentiment was strongly favorable. The proposals, of course, completely did away with Pitt's earlier formula which had kept the Cabinet in line, by offering to return the King's German possessions and also giving England considerable additional territory.

Such terms, however, would not be responsive to Pitt's original goal, and he pointed out that they were not so attractive as they might appear at first glance: Cape Breton commanded the St. Lawrence and should never be yielded, whatever promises might be made with respect to non-fortification. The use of the North American fishing grounds was a source of strength to France as a training ground for seamen and a bulwark to her Navy. The pretense of yielding all Canada was a fiction, because it was proposed that the southern and western limits should be marked by Niagara. This would leave France in control of the Great Lakes, the Mississippi and Louisiana. It would block the westward expansion of the English colonies, and it would destroy Pitt's great conception of North America as an unfettered territory for the expansion of the Anglo-Saxon system.

Bourbon France was known to be actively negotiating with Bourbon Spain. The terms which Choiseul proposed would enable France to reorganize her forces both in the Old World and the New, and it would be only the matter of a few years when England would face a new and stronger alliance.

Bedford observed that Pitt's conditions would mean the destruction of Bourbon France as a first-class power. Mr. Pitt agreed that defeat of Bourbonism was one of the chief points of the war. This was the time to make the demands which England had earned and could, in his opinion, enforce. His colleagues admitted that they were persuaded in respect to Cape Breton and Canada, but felt that France would never consent to sacrificing her rights in the Newfoundland fisheries.

Granville, Halifax, Newcastle and Bedford were all against Pitt on the fisheries issue. Bedford said that Choiseul had proposed "the most reasonable peace ever offered to this country for some years past." Bute tried to introduce himself as a negotiator by suggesting that England should attempt to carry the point about the fisheries, but should not insist if it proved impossible.

"Puerile and illusory," said Mr. Pitt to this suggestion. Bute muttered something about Pitt's insolence, but no one came to his support, and he subsided. The Newcastle group remained adamant, and Pitt decided not to force the issue. Details were discussed for many hours, six hours on June 24 and six hours at a second meeting on June 26. Immediately following the second meeting Mr. Pitt wrote his dispatch to Stanley to be given to Choiseul: all Canada must be ceded; also Cape Breton without conditions; Belle Isle, Guadeloupe, and Marie Galante (also in the West Indies) to be returned by England in exchange for the German conquests, Minorca, and Bencollen (a settlement of the East India Company in Sumatra which had been captured by the French); both Senegal and Goree would be retained by England; England would retain certain of the West Indies islands; the East India question could be the subject of further negotiation.

Mr. Pitt heaved a sigh of relief. It seemed that little remained now to be done except for diplomatic negotiations on the details. His long conduct of the war appeared to be ending in an atmosphere of triumph, with his own position in Government more secure than ever. On July 2 he was able to write to Lady Hester in the happiest of moods:

MY DEAREST LIFE,
    I have gone through the labours of the *corps diplomatique* from ten this morning till past two, and am not at all the worse for the sweat of my brow. I have just received an epistle from Pam [the nurse], with a continuation of good accounts from the nursery. All are in perfect health. I propose to see them tomorrow evening, and to devote Saturday to children and to hay-making; and I hope Sunday will prove a day of rest from business—a day of impatience, but of a sweeter kind, it is sure to prove, big with the dear expectation of receiving again my delight and comfort on Monday. The enclosed note to Lord

Temple you will be so good as to deliver to him. My compliments to all.

Your ever loving husband,

W. PITT

That was July 2. On July 1 he had received notification of a meeting of his Majesty's Privy Council, called for July 8, the famous notification already referred to which promised "urgent and important business." Apparently the subject of this meeting, whatever it might prove to be, gave Mr. Pitt little or no concern. He was accustomed to urgent and important business; yet hardly accustomed to the news which he and the country were due to receive on July 8.

CHAPTER XXXI

HEDGEHOG AND HORSE

His Majesty's Privy Council, in the late eighteenth century, was a curious institution for which there was no precise parallel to be found in other governments. In earlier times the Privy Council had acted as a Cabinet, but in 1761 it consisted of approximately sixty leading persons of the realm whose duties were chiefly to serve as window-dressing for the King. They had recognized status in public ceremonies, were used as the sounding board for personal announcements by his Majesty, and had general duties similar to those of the house committee of a club. Occasionally they might function like President Roosevelt's Brain Trust in giving the King advice, but they were not, as Privy Councilors, commissioned to take any part in legislation.

The office was honorary, but transient, continuing only at the King's pleasure. The Duke of Richmond, for example, in the spring of 1761, had incensed the King by some truculent language and George had personally, with his own hand, struck the Duke's name off the list of Privy Councilors. This, however, did not deprive Richmond of any of his rights or privileges relating to his dukedom, his place in the Army, or otherwise.

The Council, as might be expected, consisted mostly of members of the peerage. In 1761 only ten of its members were commoners, and these all held high positions in the Government.

On the notable 8th of July, when the Council had been summoned for the "most urgent and important business," they assembled, as usual, in the Painted Chamber, a high-ceilinged room which connected the House of Commons with the House of Peers. An attendance of sixty members included Mr. Secretary Pitt, Bute, Cornwallis, who was later to have an unpleasant time at Yorktown, Hardwicke, Ligonier, Lyttelton, Anson, Newcastle, of course (and all others who had Cabinet rank), George and James Grenville, and Henry Fox, Esq. On his throne, at one end of the room, sat a nervous and uncomfortable young man, George III. He was about to make an announcement which would astonish most of his audience and give profound chagrin to some of them. He began in his adenoidal voice, which sounded as though he had a bad head cold:

> Having nothing so much at heart, as to procure the welfare and happiness of my people, and to render the same stable, and permanent to posterity, I have, ever since my accession to the throne, turned my thoughts towards the choice of a princess for my consort.

The choice of a consort. The state of Henry Fox can be imagined. In recent weeks the King's attention to Lady Sarah had become public property, pamphleteers had dwelt upon the pros and cons of an English subject being chosen as Queen, and a plate of her picture had been made by a bookseller, ready for printing when an announcement might be made. But the King had said "a princess for my consort." Fox had already heard rumors of bad news, and this confirmed it. The King continued with his announcement:

> And I now, with great satisfaction, acquaint you, that, after the fullest information, and mature deliberation, I am come to a resolution to demand in marriage the Princess Charlotte of Mecklenburg-Strelitz.

This was news for which most of the Council were wholly unprepared. Though they were the King's personal advisors they had had no intimation of it. Not only Princess Charlotte, but the tiny principality of Mecklenburg in Germany from which she came, was unknown to virtually all of them. It later became known that this proposed alliance was the artful work of the Princess Dowager and the Earl of Bute. Its significance for the fortunes of Bute was evident to everyone. The royal family would be thoroughly isolated. German in origin, and not allied to any

British subject, its only intimacy with a Britisher was that of
the King's mother with Lord Bute. Bute's special knowledge
of the affair was evident, for it was said that he had given
the facts to Newcastle, Hardwicke, Bedford, and Mr. Pitt
several days before the Privy Council meeting. It is certain that he advised Bedford of the matter in a letter of
July 3:

> The very great regard I have for your Grace has made me
> quite uneasy till I obtained his Majesty's permission to com-
> municate to you the business of the Council to which your Grace
> is summoned on Wednesday next. I do it, my Lord, under the
> seal of the strictest secrecy. The King intends that day to de-
> clare his resolution of taking a consort to his bed. The lady
> pitched upon to be our future Queen is the Princess Charlotte of
> Mecklenburg-Strelitz.

Bedford, logically and properly, looked upon this mark
of confidence as a sign that he was to become a featured
player in the Government. In the succession of events between the meeting of the Privy Council, and the wedding
and Coronation on September 8 and 22 respectively, Bedford's voice became increasingly strong in challenging Mr.
Pitt.

In short, the underlying forces of the political scene had
now been determined. Before the King's announcement,
Mr. Pitt was the strongest man among the Whigs, and to
risk his displeasure was to risk political suicide. Now Bute
became the secure source of Court patronage and royal
favor while Mr. Pitt's strength rested wholly on his personal force of character, his hold on the public, and the
course of events. The calendar brought continuous crises:

JULY 9—Bedford wrote to Bute an open challenge of
the Pitt system:

> The endeavoring to drive France out of any naval power is
> fighting against nature, and can tend to do no good to this
> country; but, on the contrary, must excite all the naval powers
> of Europe against us, as adopting a system, viz.: that of a mo-
> nopoly of all naval power, which would be at least as dangerous
> to the liberties of Europe as that of Louis XIV was, which drew
> all Europe upon his back.

JULY 13—Choiseul offered new terms, but not what England had demanded.

July 20—News arrived that England had captured Pondicherry in India, and Dominica in the West Indies.

JULY 21—Bute rebuked hint by Bedford that Bute succeed as chief Minister. Cabinet rejected new Choiseul proposals. The meeting a Pitt victory.

JULY 22—Pitt urged Amherst to accelerate action against Martinique.

JULY 23—Bussy approached Pitt with the proposal that Spain be invited to guarantee a peace treaty between France and England.

JULY 24—Cabinet authorized Pitt to inform Bussy that the King:

> will not suffer the disputes with Spain to be blended, in any manner whatever, in the negotiation of peace between the two crowns. . . . Moreover, it is expected that France *will not* at any time *presume* a right of intermeddling in such disputes between Great Britain and Spain.

Mr. Pitt still had hope that Spain might only be playing with the idea of a French alliance and he gave every opportunity for a disavowal. He asked the Spanish Ambassador if the Bussy message had been presented with the approval of Spain, and was assured that it had. He then wrote to Lord Bristol, brother-in-law of Miss Chudleigh and now the British Ambassador at Madrid, instructing him to protest at this interference; but, if there was an inclination to disavow it, to "open to the Court of Madrid as handsome a retreat as may be."

JULY 29—Stanley delivered "final" British terms to Choiseul, known as "the ultimatum of July 29," and offering partial concessions on the fisheries. Choiseul renewed negotiations on the Paris-Madrid axis, and a letter of his on the subject was intercepted by the English.

AUGUST 5—Choiseul returned a counter-ultimatum, less conciliatory than his earlier proposals, and said to Stanley that he found Mr. Pitt's words offensive. Mr. Pitt was pained at this accusation and observed to Bussy:

I admit [he said] that I have written in strong language. But the Duc de Choiseul also threatened England, though in the cleverest and politest way imaginable, that he would continue the war if our court did not satisfy Madrid. Only Frenchmen have the art of wounding with perfect courtesy: I should have tried to do so also had I been writing to you in English, but my French is not good enough to allow me to venture on elegant turns of expression.

AUGUST 13—Discussion of French proposals at Cabinet meeting.
AUGUST 14—The same.
AUGUST 19—The same.
AUGUST 20—The same.
AUGUST 24—The same.

The discussions were deadlocked on a trial of strength between Mr. Pitt and his fellow Ministers. At the meeting on the 24th, Pitt pressed for action. Some of his colleagues were sincerely opposed to his policy, and thought England should make further concessions. Most of them appeared to think that the Paris-Madrid axis was a bogey man that Pitt was using to continue the war and to keep himself in power. Nearly all of the men around the council table were opposed to Mr. Pitt for ancient grudges, clashes of temperament, or rebukes of their own conscience.

There was the nervous and timid Duke of Newcastle who had betrayed him repeatedly. There was the burly Duke of Bedford, impatient at receiving directions from this arrogant commoner.

The palsied and rum-soaked Granville, who had once been the suave Lord Carteret, cherished the memory of his own days as a foreign minister, and resented being overruled in foreign policy. There was the sagacious Hardwicke who was exhausted by the strain of Pitt's dynamic leadership.

Devonshire had once served as Mr. Pitt's "front man," and had been lukewarm ever since he had been displaced.

Lord Halifax had never been a zealous Pitt supporter. General Lord Ligonier had been raised to power by Mr.

Pitt; but, secure in his office, took little part in public issues.

Temple was a stanch ally who unfortunately copied Mr. Pitt's moods of arrogance without having his moments of conciliation or his flashes of genius.

The gray-faced, dour Earl of Mansfield, the former William Murray, hated Mr. Pitt steadily and industriously. A noted jurist, an extraordinary scholar, proud of his intelligence, he never for a moment forgave Mr. Pitt for outshining him.

The pertinacious Bute was like Henry Fox in his young days, strong because of his dispassionateness, ready to lose, destroy or reclaim a friend according to the needs of the situation.

All of them, moreover, felt themselves to be right in opposing Pitt's stand, and they were justified in terms of their upbringing and their old-school point of view.

Mr. Pitt spoke on the French proposals, urging that England should stand her ground. He reluctantly yielded to the wish of the Cabinet that an island off Newfoundland should be ceded to France as a station for her fishing boats, though he felt that France would regard this concession as a sign of weakness.

As to accelerating war with Spain, he said that he would prefer to fight France and Spain openly rather than France when she was covertly aided by Spanish money and supposedly neutral services. He then read a draft of his reply to Choiseul. Some of them observed that it expressed Mr. Pitt's views and not their own, that it was couched in too stern a tone.

Mr. Pitt spoke of the haughtiness of France, dwelling on the subject at some length.

Hardwicke then said sarcastically that, while he approved of not submitting to their haughtiness, he congratulated his country on not being behindhand in that respect.

The Earl of Granville reached out his shaking hands for the draft, read it over, and said that it had excellent literary merit but that he did not care for "fine letters on business."

This badgering infuriated Mr. Pitt, who told his colleagues that they were not to alter one iota.

Granville, seemingly delighted that he had touched the chief Minister on a tender spot, repeated that he did not care for Pitt's exalted diction, or for his exalted views either. He then started to say that he had understood from Bussy—

"From Bussy!", Pitt interrupted, "Nor you, nor any of you, shall treat with Bussy: nobody shall but myself."

Bedford then opened his attack, saying that he did not know why he was called to the meeting if he was not at liberty to debate. He said that since he had been informed that the Cabinet would not be permitted to alter one iota of the communication referred to their judgment he would come no more; and forthwith left the room.

Lord Bute, however, realized the dangers of this insurrection. He still had no desire to be responsible for Government in such a crisis, and he spoke up to say that the King's honor was involved in standing by the terms which His Majesty's Government had already announced to France. This warning gave the Ministers their cue, and they all yielded, with the exception of Devonshire. He had said nothing up to this time and finally observed that if they were not permitted to alter the draft he would give no opinion.

Mr. Pitt asked what he should report to the King as to Devonshire's views, but the Duke repeated that he would give no opinion, and the meeting broke up.

AUGUST 27—Pitt instructed Stanley to stand on the terms of July 29, except for the further concessions on the fisheries.

While the Cabinet awaited a further reply from France, the Court prepared for the marriage of the King on September 8. The Princess Charlotte arrived at St. James Palace at three-thirty in the afternoon, and the wedding was held that evening.

The King might have fared considerably worse in his bride, considering the way in which she was chosen. Mitchell, the ambassador at Berlin, had reported "She is no regular beauty; but she is of a very pretty size, has a charming complexion, very pretty eyes, and is finely made. In short, she is a very fine girl." Horace Walpole was less charitable. "She is not tall nor a beauty," he wrote, "pale and thin; but looks sensible and is genteel." He also observed that she had a low forehead, "nostrils spreading too wide," and a wide mouth. He conceded that her teeth were good and hair "darkish and fine."

The young prospective Queen appeared to have a mind of her own. While she was preparing for dinner before the wedding one of her ladies told her that the King preferred some particular type of dress.

"Let him dress himself," she replied, "I shall dress as I please."

Again, when she was told that the King liked to keep early hours she replied that she did not wish to go to bed with the chickens.

Considering the speed with which the nuptials were arranged, they were arranged with considerable pomp and grandeur. Lady Sarah was entitled to be one of the Queen's bridesmaids. This honor was due her as one of the ten unmarried daughters of dukes and earls. The Lord Chamberlain accordingly sent her an invitation and, to the surprise of many, she accepted, though Horace Walpole commented: "Her stooping to bear the Queen's train as bridesmaid did her more prejudice than all that was invented against her."

Henry Fox, however, assumed that she would serve, saying, "Well, Sal, you are the first virgin in England, and you shall take your place in spite of them all as chief bridesmaid, and the King shall behold your pretty face and repent."

The wedding party started for the royal chapel in St. James Palace between eight and nine in the evening. The bride was dressed in white and silver, and her train was a long mantle of violet-colored velvet lined with ermine and fastened at the shoulders by bunches of huge pearls. She wore a tiara of diamonds and a jeweled stomacher. The procession was highly impressive, though there was one incident embarrassing to the Queen. Lady Sarah and Lady Caroline Russell (from whom Sarah had stolen Lord Newbottle) led the bridesmaids holding the Queen's train. As the bride advanced, the great weight of the train, it was said, pulled her dress down from her shoulders in back and neither the Lennox nor Russell bridesmaid remedied the matter, so that according to Walpole's view of the Queen, "the spectators knew as much of her upper half as the King himself."

As the couple approached the altar the eyes of the courtiers were fixed on the King to see whether, in the presence of Sarah Lennox, he could go through the ceremony with composure. The Archbishop of Canterbury began the familiar words:

Dearly beloved, we are gathered together here in the sight of God, and in the face of this congregation—

As the service proceeded the King gave no outward sign of emotion until the Archbishop came to the prayer in the authorized version of that day:

Look, O Lord, mercifully upon them from Heaven, and bless them. And as thou didst send thy blessing upon Abraham and Sarah—

Sarah.

At the mention of the name the King was visibly affected and could not conceal his confusion. This, then, was the ending to the romance which he had contemplated with his Sarah, for whom he had composed the dance entitled "The Twenty-fifth of February," and to whom he had made so many avowals.

And as thou didst send thy blessing upon Abraham and Sarah, to their great comfort; so vouchsafe to send thy blessing upon these thy servants.

The ceremony proceeded to the end and the King once and for all had cast his lot, which he found to be a dull one, with the poor little princess of Mecklenburg.

Lady Sarah conducted herself throughout with flags flying high. Shortly afterwards she had her attention distracted by the death of a pet squirrel. Her grief was then assuaged by the care of a hedgehog that she had saved from destruction in a field. It soon occupied her affections and replaced his Majesty as her reigning favorite.

On September 13, 1761, Bussy called upon Mr. Pitt to present the new memorandum from Choiseul which justified the Great Commoner's contention that any concession to France would be taken as a sign of weakness. Choiseul now demanded an island off the Gulf of the St. Lawrence. Mr. Pitt summoned the Cabinet for approval to recall Stanley, and the Cabinet promptly agreed.

Five days later, on September 18, Pitt called another Cabinet meeting at Devonshire House. He placed before them an unexpected and audacious plan. He presented a number of documents which proved to his satisfaction that France had entered into firm agreement with Spain, whereby the latter agreed to declare war on England in the following year. He also had a memorandum that Spain was going to assert a claim in the Newfoundland fisheries.

Spain's intended delay until 1762 was due to the fact that the Spanish treasure ships were now returning from the West Indies and fifteen Spanish warships had gone out to convoy them. Obviously, Spain would prefer to have the treasure safe in port before embarking on a war.

Pitt, therefore, proposed that England should declare war on Spain at once, particularly as the British fleet now off Martinique could thereupon engage the Spaniards. The Ministers were staggered at the thought of this new burst of activity. They argued that the documents in Pitt's hands were not adequate justification for war.

Pitt contended that Spain clearly was going to proceed against England and that a swift blow at the outset would cripple her strength, dampen her enthusiasm for an alliance with France, and bring about a speedier peace.

No one, however, except Temple would support Pitt in this. Lord Anson was asked for his technical advice on the probability of the British fleet capturing the Spanish treasure ships, but he refused to commit himself. Pitt then demanded a formal vote by the Cabinet that there be written minutes of the Cabinet opinion. The majority decision was to instruct Bristol to inquire at Madrid whether Spain was "under any engagement to take part with France in the present war." This week-kneed policy meant nothing, as it would be at least a month before a reply could be received and by that time the Spanish treasure ships would be safely at home.

Mr. Pitt then determined that he and Temple would draw up an "advice in writing" to his Majesty, setting forth their views and the reasons therefor. It was a shrewdly drawn paper which asked for Bristol's recall and for permission to "take forthwith such necessary measures . . . for the defense of the honor of the Crown and of the just and essential interests of his Majesty's people." The far-seeing Lord Bute was able to appraise this document at its full political value. If the King should refuse Mr. Pitt, that would presumably lead to his resignation or dismissal; and the Cabinet would be committed to a policy which, after all, might prove to be unwise. If England then suffered reverses in the war there would be a Parliamentary inquiry, and Mr. Pitt's written advice might prove highly embarrassing.

In these proceedings Pitt felt, with some justice, that the Cabinet was interfering with his rights as a war minister. War with Spain was not a policy which he had fomented, it was not a policy at the discretion of the Cabinet, but a prospective fact agreed to under the Family Compact. Spain had promised France to make war, and the question before the English Government, therefore, was primarily one of strategy in war maneuvers—which were Mr. Pitt's particular responsibility in the Cabinet.

On September 21, 1761, therefore, he sought an audience with the King, who received him with Lord Bute in attendance. His Majesty, doubtless coached by Bute, now made an adroit move by refusing to accept the paper of the Pitt-Temple advice. Bute made the comment that it was only fair that Pitt's opponents should also give their views.

The King added that he would not decide anything until

Stanley arrived home from Paris since "he might give some necessary light with regard to Spain."

Pitt was blocked by this strategy until Stanley's return, and meanwhile, on September 22, 1761, Lord Bute had the satisfaction of witnessing the Coronation of the King whom he had tutored and the Queen whom he had chosen.

London had not seen such a show in thirty-four years, since the Coronation of George II in 1727. The affair was carried off with great splendor, marred by only a few absurd mishaps.

Westminster Hall, where the procession formed and where the banquet was held following the Coronation, was equipped with a new boarded floor covered with matting. Three wooden galleries were constructed in the Hall, also covered with matting, and large cabinets were constructed under the first gallery to accommodate the side-boards for plates, dishes, and other supplies necessary for the banquet. The route of the procession from the Hall to the Abbey of Westminster was paved with a raised wooden roadway covered with blue cloth, with rails on each side. The procession began at eleven o'clock in the morning and included several thousand persons. It was led by the King's herb woman followed by six maids strewing the way with sweet herbs. Then came the Dean's Beadle of Westminster with his staff, and the High Constable of Westminster in a scarlet cloak. Fife, drums and trumpeters followed. Shortly after them came the thirteen Aldermen of London in scarlet gowns. Then a host of minor officials followed by the Choir of Westminster in surplices, carrying their music books.

The Choir was followed by the organ blower and the Groom of the Vestry.

Numerous other Orders were next in line, followed by the ten Privy Councillors who were not peers, which was the station of Mr. Pitt and Henry Fox. Mr. Pitt, however, did not attend, pleading gout in the foot as his inability to march in the procession. (Hester was in the audience in a Coronation robe for which the materials alone cost £50:14s:6d.) Then came various ranks of the peer-age and their wives.

These were followed by dukes and duchesses, the Lord Chamberlain of the Household (Devonshire), heralds, certain members of the Cabinet, the Archbishop of Canter-bury and the Queen's Vice-Chamberlain (Lord Cantelupe).

Next were the Queen's household and the Queen. This time her Majesty's train was supported by the Princess Augusta and the six unmarried daughters of earls, not in-cluding the daughters of dukes, which excluded Lady Sarah. More notables followed, the Queen leading the way for the King's official entourage. In the vanguard of his Majesty were the Duke of Bedford, carrying what was sup-posed to be the King's sword, the Duke of Richmond bear-ing the sceptre with the dove, the Lord High Steward, Talbot, bearing St. Edward's Crown, the Bishop of Carlyle, carrying the Bible, and the Bishop of Chester bearing the Chalice.

Finally, came the King, advancing under a canopy of cloth of gold, borne by sixteen barons with his train sup-ported by six sons of peers. Behind the canopy came minor officials, and the rear of the procession was brought up by the Yeomen of the Guard.

To the thousands of onlookers the magnificent pageant proceeded without mishap, as only a few persons were aware that the King's Sword of State had been inadvert-ently left behind at St. James Palace and Bedford had been obliged hurriedly to borrow a substitute sword from the Lord Mayor. When the procession reached the altar, the proper sword had been rushed thither so that the cere-monies could conclude without further substitution.

After the strain of the four-hour Coronation service, it was perhaps not surprising that the concluding banquet in Westminster Hall proceded not quite so smoothly. There were certain historic incidents which usually do not appear in accounts of pomp and circumstance. When the Queen went to her retiring room before the banquet, she found that the Duke of Newcastle had unwisely preceded her there, presumably not expecting her arrival so promptly.

The lighting effects in Westminster Hall did not operate precisely according to plan. The intention was to light all of the candles at once by means of fuses of prepared flax which reached from one candle to another. When the Queen entered, the fuses were lighted and created a blaze of splendor, but for a short time the flax fell in large burning flakes, terrifying the Queen and in fact the whole audience, though there was no serious damage.

When the King complained to the Deputy Earl Marshal, Lord Effingham, because the Sword of State had been forgotten and that the Chairs of State for the King and Queen had not been provided for in the banquet hall, so that their Majesties had been kept standing for some minutes, his Lordship did not choose the happiest words of apology.

"It is true, sir," he replied, "that there has been some neglect, but I have taken care that the *next Coronation* shall be regulated in the exactest manner possible."

The King had the unexpected wit to be amused at the ineptness of the reply. More serious was the fact that somewhere during the ceremonies a jewel fell from his crown. This was regarded as an evil omen by many of the superstitious, and it was called to mind in the newspapers in 1782 when the British Crown lost the American colonies.

The most unnecessary unpleasantnesses of the occasion were due to the economies of Lord Talbot, the same who had once been a friend of Betty Pitt. He had decided to save money by not providing places for the Knights of the Bath, the Aldermen of London, and the Barons of the Cinque Ports. As Englishmen are jealous of their rights, Talbot found that he had a lively scrap on his hands.

"To us," said Sir William Stanhope, representing the Order of the Bath, "it is an affront, for *some* of us are gentlemen."

Beckford was the spokesman for the Aldermen.

"We have invited the King," he said, "to a banquet which will cost us ten thousand pounds, and yet when we come to Court, we are to be given nothing to eat."

Talbot was forced to yield to the Knights of the Bath and to the Aldermen, but to the Barons of the Cinque Ports, who were only courtesy barons from a small constituency, he replied, "As Lord Steward, I tell you it is impossible."

Despite the minor incidents, it was a day of triumph for Bute, their Majesties, and the Tory ideals, even though a struggle with Mr. Pitt was still impending. There was one further incident which might also have seemed to be an omen. Lord Talbot was the unfortunate protagonist of this affair. As Lord High Steward it was part of his duty to ride on horseback, during the banquet, up to the royal dais, make his obeisance to the Sovereign, and back his horse out of the Hall. The animal had been so overtrained for these maneuvers that he persisted, when the moment came, in entering the Hall backwards, and was only, with great difficulty, prevented from advancing with his hind-quarters turned toward their Majesties. Lord Talbot might have Tory tendencies, but it is said that his horse was a Whig.

CHAPTER XXXII
VALEDICTORY

His Majesty, with his crown now firmly upon his head, was eager to resume his rôle of being a King who would demand subservience from his Ministers. He was ready, according to Newcastle, to "put an end, at all events, to the uncertainty about Mr. Pitt,"—in other words, to get rid of him. Each member of the Cabinet, except Temple and Pitt, now sought audience with the King to expound his opposition to the Pitt measures. They were not to be caught in the unwisdom of making a written reply which might be held against them later, but they were anxious to make sure that his Majesty would understand that a change would be welcome to them.

Bute and Newcastle were already conferring on the composition of a new Cabinet. Bute recommended Henry Fox, perhaps thinking that this would pacify him for the affront which had been offered to his family. Newcastle said that Fox was too unpopular with the people and would be an unhappy contrast to Mr. Pitt. Instead, he made the artful suggestion that George Grenville might be named. Pitt would be in a difficult position to attack his own brother-in-law. Grenville had indicated a willingness to serve under Bute's leadership and had been on intimate terms with the favorite's secretary, Charles Jenkinson, who later became Lord Liverpool. Bute took the thought under advisement.

Stanley returned from France on September 30, 1761, and brought with him no new information which would lead to a change in Pitt's opinion. Pitt called a Cabinet Council on October 2, determined to make a final drive to win support for his position. Ten members of the Cabinet were present.

Mr. Pitt came immediately to the point, saying that they

were meeting to pass upon instructions to Lord Bristol, Ambassador to Spain. He added that his own view on the subject remained as he had given it in his "advice in writing."

Newcastle at once spoke of the expense of further war, said that he saw no adequate reason for beginning new hostilities, and to fight with Spain would only involve considering the interests of an additional nation in working out some plan of peace.

Hardwicke also discounted Pitt's evidence. He affirmed that France was trying to lead Spain into war with England, but that he thought it was very doubtful that Spain would attempt any overt act, and therefore England would simply be falling in with the enemy's plan to take the aggressive.

Lord Granville tried to adopt a conciliatory tone. He regretted that Stanley had brought no new information of consequence which might have given a new light to everyone on the subject, and might provide a formula for compromise. Without new information he felt that he could not vote for hostilities against Spain. If England embarked on a new war, he felt that some portion of the existing war must be abandoned, as the nation could not increase its present efforts.

Lord Anson said that the British ships "were not in condition to enter immediately into any material operations against Spain."

Ligonier stated that Spain had 15,000 cavalry and 60,000 infantry as well as 20,000 Neapolitan troops. Mansfield said that he was apprehensive of the impression which would be made on neutral powers by the continued vast war projects of England.

Temple made the tension worse by roundly abusing all of Mr. Pitt's opponents and then leaving the room. Pitt himself finally rose to make a last earnest plea for his position. His words were summarized by Edmund Burke in the 1761 issue of the *Annual Register,* as follows:

> This was the time for humbling the whole house of Bourbon;
> that if this opportunity were let slip, it might never be recovered;
> and if he could not prevail in this instance, he was resolved that

this was the last time he should sit in that council. He thanked the Ministers of the late king for their support; said he was himself called to the Ministry by the voice of the people, to whom he considered himself as accountable for his conduct; and that he would no longer remain in a situation which made him responsible for measures he was no longer allowed to guide.

These were the words for which his colleagues had been waiting for many weeks. Lord Granville, perhaps recalling his own fall from power, made reply in words quivering with malicious satisfaction:

I find the gentleman is determined to leave us, nor can I say I am sorry for it, since he would otherwise have certainly compelled us to leave him; but, if he be resolved to assume the right of advising his Majesty, and directing the operations of the war, to what purpose are we called to this council? When, therefore, the gentleman talks of being responsible to the people, he talks the language of the House of Commons, and forgets that at this Board he is only responsible to the King. However, though he may possibly have convinced himself of his infallibility, still it remains that we should be equally convinced before we can resign our understandings to his direction, or join with him in the measure he proposes.

So it was. At the apogee of victory, deserted by timid and resentful colleagues, hated by King and courtiers, Mr. Pitt resigned his great Administration.

It was an occasion marked with a double significance. In the first place, Pitt had raised England to new heights of glory. In the words of the *Annual Register:*

In the conduct of the war he never suffered the enemy to breathe, but overwhelmed them with reiterated blows, and kept up the alarm in every quarter. If one of his expeditions was not so well calculated or so successfully executed, amends was made by another, and by a third. The spirit of the nation, once roused, was not suffered for a moment to subside; and the French, dazzled, as it were, by the multitude and celerity of his enterprizes, seemed to have lost all power of resistance. In short, he revived the military genius of our people; he supported our allies; he extended our trade; he raised our reputation; he augmented our dominions.

Secondly, and more important, the core of his strength had been a zeal for Constitutional freedom. This concern for the liberty of the subject had little interest for most of his colleagues, and few understood that it was the source of his strength. It is significant, however, that in spite of his tremendous prestige with the Army and Navy, in spite of his vast hold upon the public, in spite of the fact that he was often described as a dictator, it apparently never even occurred to him to seize the power illegally. When he reached a Constitutional impasse in his inability to carry the Cabinet with him, he quietly and, as a matter of course, resigned.

"Liberty and independency" had been his watchwords, the basic and indispensable concepts of his empire of free-men. The King and Lord Bute did not approve. They were now in control and ready to develop their experiment of an unconstitutional Crown. They would have done well to study their history, and recollect the fateful day in 1755 when a prior King and his ministers had attempted the extinction of Mr. Pitt.

PART THREE

"I rejoice that America has resisted"

CHAPTER XXXIII

LIBERTY OF THE SUBJECT

From the fall of Pitt to the time of his death, events moved on a worldwide front in a battle to preserve democracy at home and for future generations in both hemispheres.

Pitt had risen to power in a nation which had lost confidence in itself and had begun to imitate the totalitarian powers by tolerating a series of chief ministers who had ignored democratic principles. Such a trend, however, was contrary to English tradition as expressed in the Magna Carta. Therefore, Walpole, Carteret and other ministers who had tried to conduct domestic and foreign affairs without reference to the public had found their paths uneasy and had met with ultimate failure; and not until Pitt called upon the genius of the people as a whole had England risen to a towering resurgence above the Bourbon States.

Mr. Pitt, drilled in English principles by his choleric grandfather and absorbing them from the stolid and sturdy democracy of the Pitt squirearchy, had appeared in Parliament at first as a naïve and emotional champion of the rights of man. With Parliamentary training, wide reading, consultation with men of all types and stations, and the practical tasks of administration, his political judgment had ripened and deepened. The magnificent statements of democratic faith and philosophy which he was to proclaim in the closing chapters of his life were the outgrowth of his long experience in statecraft and human nature.

It was no accident, no temporary outburst of emotion, which had led Pitt at his last Cabinet meeting to refer to his mandate from the people.

Carteret-Granville, in turn, had stood for his old Tory attitude when he welcomed Mr. Pitt's resignation by saying,

"When, therefore, the gentleman talks of being responsible to the people he talks the language of the House of Commons and forgets that at this Board he is only responsible to the King."

Granville, it was clear, had learned nothing in his suave and alcoholic life. He seemingly had forgotten that when the House of Commons would no longer support him the King had been obliged to dismiss the Carteret Ministry. Even the conservative Hardwicke, many years before, had instructed George II that his Majesty's servants were, in fact, the persons who were responsible for outlining his Majesty's policies.

Mr. Pitt had realized that Hardwicke's doctrine of the Constitution was a solid basis on which to build. The liberty of the subject was protected by the basic law of the Constitution. He then proceeded to the question of the ultimate source of all law, to wit, the consent of the governed. Pitt was, of course, aware that the King appointed his ministry and that the ministry, his Majesty's servants, were the administrators of government. The formalities of the procedure did not, however, change the fact that in the long run the King was obliged to accept whatever ministry commanded the confidence of Parliament and the public.

Mr. Pitt, therefore, had affirmed the ultimate source of his strength, while Granville had rested his case on a theory of a personal royal government which was contrary to the Constitution. The Granville view, unfortunately, was a theory now cherished by the Court, who wished to see these principles become the policies of the kingdom.

The struggle which lay ahead of Mr. Pitt was more subtle and more difficult than anything which he had faced before. When he had attacked the Ministers of a ruined England, he had drawn a lance against a group who were already undermined by failure and conscious of their own shortcomings. Now, however, at the end of his Ministry he had resigned the power to a group who would take possession of the country when it was in a state of strength and glory which it had not enjoyed since the Elizabethan era.

Pitt had proved that a democratic people, living under a realm of law, where the military was at all times subject to ultimate civil control, could be rallied to defend itself against all enemies and to take a leading place among the nations of the world. Now he was confronted with the insidious danger that the victories won would be sabotaged and that the empire, presumably to be an empire of free people, would in fact be seized by the young King, the Princess Dowager, Lord Bute and their satellites and become in effect nothing more than another state on the totalitarian plan. For the next eighteen years, in a series of brief crises when he was able to rise from his sickbed, Mr. Pitt encountered the techniques of dictatorship and met them with techniques of democracy, dramatizing the issue and setting it sharply before the English people so that the choice was clear, clear for them and for the democracies of all time.

In October, 1761, when Mr. Pitt had resigned from office he had only a moderate inkling of the strong and determined attempt which would be made to destroy the theory of English government. The King's marriage to a German princess had been ominous. The influence of Bute was unfortunate, but even Mr. Pitt had no way of foretelling that the young King would have absorbed so thoroughly the Tory doctrines of *The Idea of a Patriot King,* or that he would ultimately develop into such a tough-minded and stubborn monarch. In fact, when Mr. Pitt had his audience with George III on October 5, three days after the last Cabinet, he returned the Seals of Office not without some feeling of relief. The monarch received him with a disarming and deceptive courtesy and made various pleasant remarks about Mr. Pitt's Ministry,—though expressing no regrets at his departure.

The King had been so relieved to learn that Mr. Pitt did not plan to go into Opposition that he spoke of giving a reward for past services. Mr. Pitt had replied gracefully that he hoped any reward would be for future services which he might render to his Majesty. The main thing at the moment was to bring the war to a successful conclusion.

Pitt, who had expected that the meeting might be filled with recrimination, was moved to tears by this kindness and retired with the most elaborate and respectful bows, his great Roman nose bobbing between his knees.

He was glad to be free of office. When his colleagues had begun to turn against him he had not, as he had done in the past, made any effort to rally popular support, to stimulate memorials from various cities or in any way to force his retention. He was an ill man; he was exhausted by terrific labors. He wished to finish the war, but as his colleagues thought they could do it better and insisted on doing it according to their own plans, he preferred to resign rather than to make new issues.

Indeed, he took steps to retire to private life as fully as possible. He offered for sale his town house at 10 St. James Place and sold the horses and elaborate equipages from his town stables. As a minister of the Crown he had chosen to dress the part, but now he wished to become "the village philosopher," as he expressed it, and at last to enjoy the company of his family at Hayes.

In spite of the quiet manner of the Pitt resignation and of the relatively unruffled surface of events, the succeeding months brought many sweeping changes. In every avenue of society there were alterations in the habit of thought, public opinion and alliances. It was one of those periods which come occasionally in history when the old ways seem suddenly to break up and for a time the whole nation seems to be without its moorings.

Within a year and a half, for example, the various alliances in which Lady Sarah Lennox had been a storm center were completely altered. Lord Newbottle, the future Marquis of Lothian, married a daughter of the Fortescue family, thereby becoming related, ridiculously enough, to Dr. Ayscough. Lady Caroline Russell, daughter of the Duke of Bedford, from whom Sarah had stolen Lord Newbottle, married the fourth Duke of Marlborough. Since Mr. Pitt expected to inherit properties that normally would have been left to Marlborough, this alliance may not have improved his relationships with the Bedford connection, who had already settled with him for other parts of the Marlborough bequest in which the Duchess of Bedford was concerned. Lady Sarah herself married a Sir Charles Bunbury, a nephew of Henry Fox.

One result of this shift in alliances, as will appear from time to time, was the anger of Charles Lennox, Duke of Richmond, against all the King's friends and an intensification of his feelings for Mr. Pitt. From the worldly standpoint the future of Sarah Lennox proved to be unfortunate. Bunbury was evidently deeply in love with her but preferred to spend most of his time with race-horses. Sarah, thus neglected, ran away with Lord William Gordon, from whom she was rescued by her scandalized family. When this romance was over Bunbury begged her to return. Sarah refused his generosity, however, and ultimately married General Napier, by whom she had numerous children. In spite of modest means she managed to put several sons through the university; and many of her Napier descendants occupied distinguished places in British affairs. She outlived virtually all her contemporaries and closed her days still writing delightful and witty letters to her girlhood cousin and confidante, Lady Susan Strangways. However colorful Sarah's career may have been it was not comforting to the Richmond family; and Charles's resentment at the treatment accorded to his sister by the King remained unappeased.

Another alteration in family relationships was brought about in the new appointments to the Cabinet. With his usual wiliness, Bute induced the King to appoint Lord Egremont in the place of Pitt to be one of the Secretaries of State, and, in line with Newcastle's earlier suggestions, George Grenville was made manager of the House of Commons. Egremont was the son of the Tory leader, William Wyndham, who had been one of Pitt's early sponsors. Egremont's sister Elizabeth, it will be recalled, had married George Grenville and had fostered the marriage between Pitt and Hester Grenville. The appointments of Grenville and Egremont were made to give the public an impression that Mr. Pitt's blessing was on the new

Administration; and were expected to embarrass him in any criticism of the Ministry. Actually, it did not turn out that way. Pitt was embittered at the thought that men supposedly loyal to him would enlist under Bute's banner. He became increasingly estranged from Grenville, who not only accepted the office but was willing to be an instrument in serving the Tory ideas of the King. Egremont was less of an active peril to the State, for he was wholly a Charlie McCarthy for Lord Bute, bringing no ideas or force of his own to the situation.

Though Mr. Pitt had promised to support the Government in prosecution of the war and had expressed a desire to return to country life, Lord Bute was not disposed to put too much faith in these pledges. Bute felt that as long as Mr. Pitt had a popular following the designs of himself and the monarch would not be immune from possible attack. The problem before his Machiavellian mind, accordingly, was to place Mr. Pitt in a situation which would remove him by one means or another from the political scene.

Therefore on October 6, 1761, the day after Mr. Pitt had returned the Seals of Office, Lord Bute wrote to the retired Minister offering him the governor-generalship of Canada or the post of Chancellor of the Duchy of Lancaster with a salary of £5,000 per year. The latter office was a sinecure at the disposal of the Crown.

Mr. Pitt did not accept the proposition of banishment to Canada, nor did he wish any public office, however nominal, under the Bute régime. On the other hand, he did not suspect any trickery in Bute's offer and was touched by the apparent kindness of his Majesty. He hinted that he would welcome a peerage for his wife and would accept a pension, provided it were not loaded on the Irish revenues as so many English pensions had been.

Though Bute had made these offers in the name of his Majesty, the thrifty King, who had greatly resented Mr. Pitt's independence, had consented most reluctantly. Bute had a plot afoot, however, and was determined the Crown should give some distinguished reward to the retired Minister. Accordingly, he made another proposal responsive

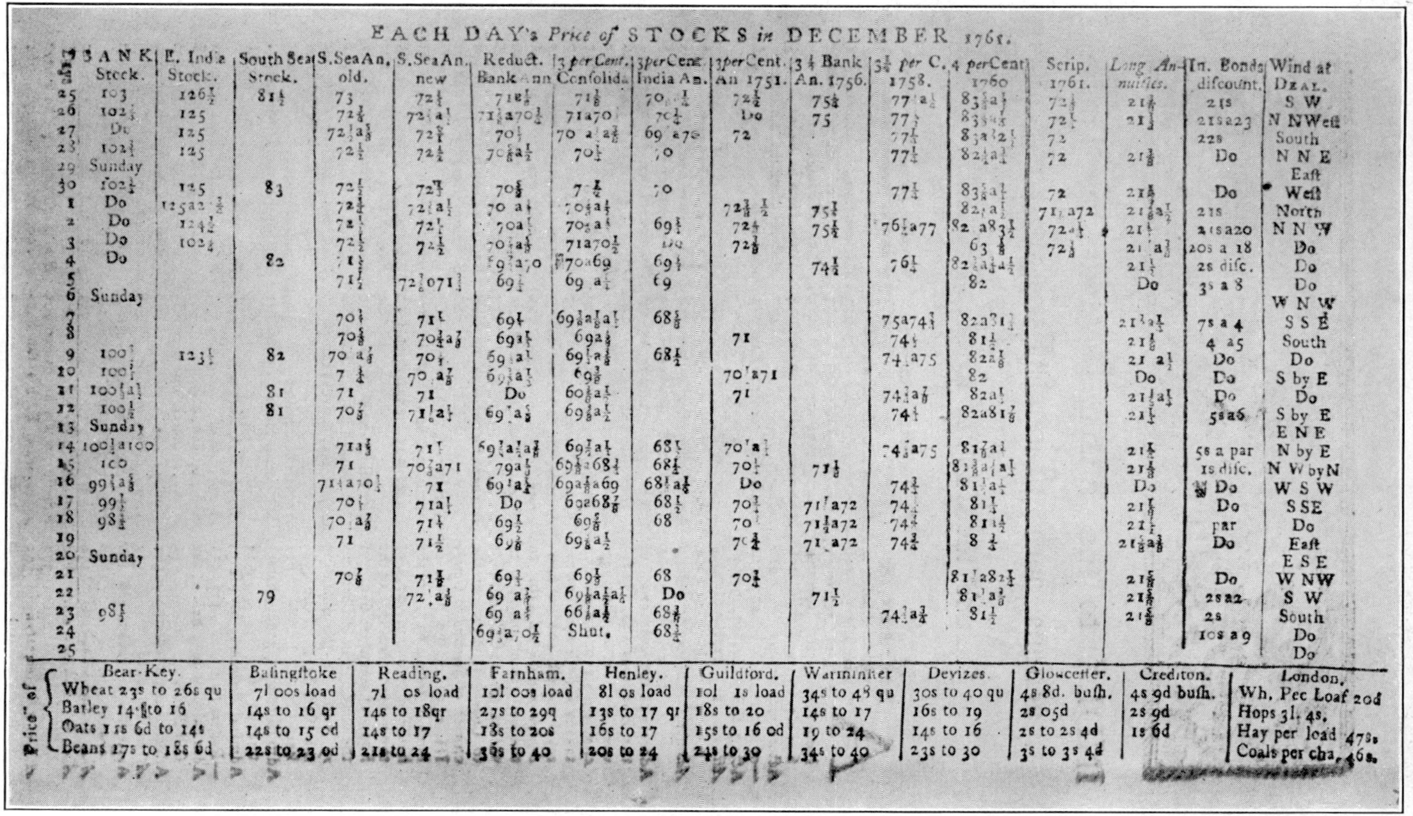

EACH DAY's *Price of* STOCKS *in* DECEMBER 1761.

1761	BANK Stock.	E. India Stock.	South Sea Stock.	S. Sea An. old.	S. Sea An. new	Reduct. Bank Ann	3 *per Cent.* Consolid.	3 per Cent India An.	3 per Cent. An 1751.	3 ½ Bank An. 1756.	3½ *per* C. 1758.	4 *per* Cent 1760	Scrip. 1761.	*Long Annuities.*	In. Bonds discount.	Wind at Deal.
25	103	126½	81½	73	72¼	71⅛	71⅛	70½	72½	75¾	77 a½	83¾a½	72¼	21¼	21s	S W
26	102¼	125		72⅞	72¼a½	71⅛a70½	71a70	70¼	Do	75	77½	83¾a½	72½	21¼	21sa23	N N West
27	Do	125		72½a⅜	72⅜	70½	70 a½a⅝	69¾a70	72		77¼	83a82½	72		22s	South
28	102¼	125		72½	72¼	70⅝a½	70½	70			77¼	82¼a½	72	21⅛	Do	N N E
29	Sunday															East
30	102½	125	83	72½	72⅞	70⅝	70¾	70			77¼	83⅝a½	72	21⅛	Do	West
1	Do	125a124½		72¼	72¼a½	70 a¼	70⅜a¼		72⅜ ½	75¼		82¼a½	71½a72	21⅛a½	21s	North
2	Do	124½		72¼	72¼	70a½	70⅜a¼	69½	72¼	75½	76½a77	82 a83½	72¼	21¼	21sa20	N N W
3	Do	102¼		72½	72½	70¼a⅛	71a70½	Do	72⅜			63 ⅛	72½	21 a¼	20s a 18	Do
4	Do		82	71¾		69⅞a70	70a69	69½		74½	76¼	82¼a¾a½		21½	2s disc.	Do
5				71½	72⅛a71¾	69¼	69 a¼	69				82		Do	3s a 8	Do
6	Sunday															W N W
7				70¼	71¼	69¼	69⅛a⅜a¼	68⅝			75a74¾	82a81¾		21¾a½	7s a 4	S S E
8				70⅝	70½a⅞	69a½	69a⅛		71		74½	81½		21⅛	4 a5	South
9	100¼	123½	82	70 a⅞	70¼	69 a¼	69¼a⅛	68½			74½a75	82a⅛		21 a½	Do	Do
10	100¼			7 ¼	70 a⅞	69¼a½	69⅜		70¼a71			82		Do	Do	S by E
11	100¼a½		81	71	71	Do	69⅛a¼		71		74¼a⅞	82a½		21½a¼	Do	Do
12	100½		81	70⅞	71⅛a¼	69 a⅝	69⅝a½				74½	82a81⅞		21½	5s a6	S by E
13	Sunday															E N E
14	100¼a100			71a⅞	71¼	69¼a½a⅞	69½a¼	68¾	70¼a¼		74¾a75	81⅞a½		21½	5s a par	N by E
15	100			71	70⅞a71	79a½	69⅛a68¾	68½	70½	71⅛		81⅜a¼a½		21⅛	1s disc.	N W by N
16	99¼a⅜			71¼a70¾	71	69½a¼	69a⅛a69	68¼a⅛	Do		74¾	81¼a¼		Do	Do	W S W
17	99½			70¼	71a¼	Do	69a68⅞	68½	70¾	71¼a72	74¼	81¼		21⅛	Do	S S E
18	98¾			70 a⅞	71¼	69½	69⅝	68	70¾	71¾a72	74¾	81½		21½	par	Do
19				71	71½	69⅝	69⅛a½		70¾	71 a72	74¾	81¼		21⅛a⅜	Do	East
20	Sunday															E S E
21				70⅞	71⅛	69¼	69⅛	68	70¾			81¼a82¼		21⅝	Do	W N W
22			79		72¼a⅛	69 a¼	69⅛a½a¼	Do		71½		81¼a⅜		21⅝	2s a2	S W
23	98½					69 a¼	66⅛a¾	68¾			74¼a¾	81½		21⅝	2s	South
24						69¼a70½	Shut.	68½							10s a 9	Do
25																Do

Price of	Bear-Key.	Basingstoke	Reading.	Farnham.	Henley.	Guildford.	Warminster	Devizes.	Gloucester.	Crediton.	London.
Wheat	23s to 26s qu	7l 00s load	7l 0s load	10l 00s load	8l 0s load	10l 1s load	34s to 48 qu	30s to 40 qu	4s 8d. bush.	4s 9d bush.	Wh. Pec Loaf 20d
Barley	14s to 16	14s to 16 qr	14s to 18qr	27s to 29q	13s to 17 qr	18s to 20	14s to 17	16s to 19	2s 05d	2s 9d	Hops 3l. 4s.
Oats	11s 6d to 14s	14s to 15 0d	14s to 17	13s to 20s	16s to 17	15s to 16 0d	19 to 24	14s to 16	2s to 2s 4d	1s 6d	Hay per load 47s.
Beans	17s to 18s 6d	22s to 23 0d	21s to 24	35s to 40	20s to 24	24s to 30	34s to 40	23s to 30	3s to 3s 4d		Coals per cha. 46s.

Stock quotations from *The Gentleman's Magazine,* December, 1761. Stocks had declined from the September schedules after the fall of Mr. Pitt.

iovereigns
Joy in an
prefent to
al Tender
ccafion of

ortance of
We like-
on of that
s Wifdom
efs to ho-
Such a
a poffeffed
vhich can
Royalty,
a happy.

g.
rations _
may Heaven
participate in the �G.
the Felicity of the Royal .
of all your Princely Offspring,
Given under our Common Seal, this twe_ .
    Day of September, in the Year of our La_
    One thoufand feven hundred and fixty one.

Madrid, September 4. A Report having been
lately fpread here, upon the Arrival of the
laft Letters from France, as if there was Rea-
fon to apprehend an immediate Rupture between
our Court and that of Great-Britain ; we underftand,
that the Spanifh Minifters, in a Converfation which
they had lately with the Earl of Briftol, Ambaffador

Extraordinary from his Britannick Majefty, expreffed
their Concern thereat, and declared very explicitly to
his Excellency, that, on the Part of their Court, there
was not the leaft Ground for any fuch Apprehenfions,
as the Catholic King had, at no Time, been more
intent upon cultivating a good Correfpondence
with England, than in the prefent Conjuncture ; and,
at the fame Time, informed the Earl of Briftol, that
Orders had been fent to Monfieur Manfo, Governor
of San Roque, to reprimand fuch of the Inhabitants
under his Jurifdiction, as had encouraged the illegal
Protection given to the French Privateer Row-Boats,
under the Cannon of a Spanifh Fort.

and, in all
Part of H'
called Eng
of Berwic.

The Ki
Barrington
Dignity of
in the Uni
by the De,
the Canor

St. James's, October 9.
The Right Honorable William Pitt having
refigned the Seals into the King's Hands, His
Majefty was this Day pleafed to appoint the Earl of
Egremont, to be one of His Majefty's Principal
Secretaries of State. And, in Confideration of the
great and important Services of the faid Mr. Pitt,
His Majefty has been gracioufly pleafed to direct,
That a Warrant be prepared for granting to the Lady
Hefter Pitt, his Wife, a Barony of Great Britain, by
the Name, Stile, and Title, of Baronefs of Chatham,
to herfelf, and of Baron of Chatham to her Heirs
Male ; And alfo to confer upon the faid William
Pitt, Efq; an Annuity of Three Thoufand Pounds
Sterling, during his own Life, and that of Lady
Hefter Pitt, and their Son John Pitt, Efq;.

ings, as
minated.
the Ente
concluder
Demonft

Public,
to come,
from Eng,
tioned at
Paffport,
of State.
All P,
Packet-B
from His
Majefty's

The paragraphs above, from *The Gazette,* the official Government organ, which appeared on adjacent pages, were designed to embarrass Pitt by indicating that he resigned to obtain a pension, not because of any crisis in Spain.

to the hints of Mr. Pitt and offered to elevate Mrs. Pitt to the rank of countess and award a pension of £3,000 a year to Mr. Pitt. These rewards were gratefully accepted by the Great Commoner.

Meanwhile, no announcement had been made to the public regarding Mr. Pitt's resignation, either of his verbal retirement on October 2 or his official resignation on October 5. Rumors began to circulate around London both with regard to the resignation and the pension; but until Saturday, October 10, nothing was definitely confirmed. Then in the *Gazette* which appeared at ten o'clock Saturday evening, Bute sprung his trap in the paragraphs which he had prepared for the official circular.

A contemporary cartoon
THE DISTRESSED STATESMAN

One of the many cartoons of Pitt, circulated by his enemies, referring to the public uproar over his pension.

The announcement told of Mr. Pitt's retirement and recited the rewards given to his family. Moreover, the notice in the *Gazette* was artfully preceded by foreign notes which reported that there was no need for apprehension in respect to Spain. The statement regarding Spain was designed to refute any statement that Pitt had resigned as a matter of principle, leaving the impression that the King had bought Mr. Pitt's resignation with favors.

The effect was what Bute intended. The public assumed that Pitt had been bought off by the Court party, and there was a torrent of abuse from his opponents, with an embarrassed silence on the part of his friends. Bute fanned the flames by hiring a claque to circulate in the coffee-houses and curse Mr. Pitt for betraying the people. He also subsidized pamphleteers; and there were many who, in all honesty, were staggered at what they believed to be the venality of their hero.

Pitt was crushed by this deluge of criticism, while the King and George Grenville gloated. The Court party as a whole figured that they had secured a real triumph and the King's brother referred happily to the pension as "a damper to Mr. Pitt." Pitt's close friends approached him and urged him to give some public explanation; and, as usual, Alderman Beckford was his friend and spokesman with the public. To Beckford he addressed a letter, October 15, 1761, explaining his position.

> DEAR SIR:
>
> Finding, to my great surprise, that the cause and manner of my resigning the seals, are grossly misrepresented in the city, as well as that the most gracious and spontaneous marks of his Majesty's approbation of my services, which marks followed my resignation, have been infamously traduced, as a bargain for my forsaking the public, I am under a necessity of declaring the truth of both these facts, in a manner which I am sure no gentleman will contradict. A difference of opinion, with regard to measures to be taken against Spain, of the highest importance to the honour of the Crown, and to the most essential national interests, and this founded on what Spain had already done, not on what that court may farther intend to do, was the cause of my resigning the seals. Lord Temple and I submitted in writing, and signed by us, our most humble sentiments to his Majesty; which being overruled by the united opinion of all the rest of the King's servants, I resigned the seals on Monday, the 5th of this month, in order not to remain responsible for measures which I was no longer allowed to guide. Most gracious public marks of his Majesty's approbation of my services followed my resignation. They are unmerited, and unsolicited; and I shall ever be proud to have received them from the best of sovereigns.
>
> I will now only add, my dear Sir, that I have explained these matters only for the honour of truth, not in any view to court return of confidence from any man who with a credulity, as weak as it is injurious, has thought fit hastily to withdraw his good opinion from one who has served his country with fidelity

and success, and who justly reveres the upright and candid judgment of it, little solicitous about the censures of the capricious
and the ungenerous. Accept my sincerest acknowledgments for
all your kind friendship, and believe me ever, with truth and
esteem, my dear Sir,   .

W. PITT

The letter, which was published in the *Gentleman's Magazine,* and the gradual spread of knowledge on the facts of
the case soon restored Mr. Pitt in public opinion. The real
reasons for his resignation became known and the fact that
he had actually been forced out of office because the King
would not endorse his policies, rather than bought out,
erased the public indignation. Letters and memorials of
commendation began to come in from all parts of the kingdom, and Cork ordered a statue to be erected in his honor.

The climax of enthusiasm came on November 9, when
the Lord Mayor and the city gave a banquet for the King
and Queen, the famous dinner which Beckford had said
would cost £10,000.

The procession of notables to the Mansion House where
the banquet was held was a triumphal march for Mr. Pitt
and almost a disaster for Lord Bute. Huzzahs, shouts of
approval, greeted the carriage of Mr. Pitt as it moved
toward the banquet hall. Robert Clive wrote afterwards,
"It seemed as if King William instead of King George had
been invited to that great entertainment."

The royal carriage was treated with respect and greeted
with some applause, but with noticeably less acclaim than
that accorded to Mr. Pitt.

Bute expected no popular welcome. He knew that his
reputation as Augusta's lover, as a Scotchman, and as an
enemy of Pitt might rouse the mob against him. He therefore took the precaution to set out in a carriage which was
trailed by a hundred bruisers who were to quash any hostilities. He further took the precaution to instruct his men
to tell the crowd that this was Mr. Pitt's carriage.

For a few minutes the ruse was successful, but it was a
futile attempt, for the Roman nose and the eagle-like face

of Mr. Pitt were well-known to the public. Soon some curious onlooker peered into the Bute carriage and cried: "By God, this is not Pitt. This is Bute, and be damned to him!"

A great uproar followed this announcement, accompanied by groans, hisses and yells.

"No Scotch rogues!" the crowd shouted, "No Butes!— no Newcastle salmon!—Pitt for ever!"

Someone picked up a clod and hurled it into the carriage, spattering Bute's immaculate laces. A flying wedge charged forward trying to break the shafts and overturn the carriage. Bute's fighters flew into action and there was a free-for-all fight for several minutes before the new chief Minister of the Crown was able to proceed to London's dinner to their Majesties.

This rough handling was an eloquent lesson to the King's favorite that his plan of establishing the King's party had its dangers and that his function should be behind the scenes rather than out in front where vulgar fists were flying. Above all, he saw it was unwise to be known as an anti-Pitt man, and from then on he did not let himself be caught in overt plotting against the Great Commoner.

Mr. Pitt himself was regretful at the incident in several particulars. All his life he had been a champion of orderly procedure. He had hesitated about attending this banquet, foreseeing that he might receive an ovation and knowing that under the circumstances it would be distasteful to the King. Pitt, having taken the step of resigning office, deplored anything that might savor of rancor or cause difficulty to his successors in prosecuting the war. Beckford and Temple, however, had urged him to attend, and now the result had been far more drastic than he had feared. His Majesty naturally was enraged that a subject should pointedly receive so much greater respect than the Crown, and the attack on Bute, whatever his personal characteristics, was a dangerous threat to all orderly government. Pitt was a champion of the liberty of the subject whether of high or low degree, guaranteed by law, and a brawl was a species of mob tyranny, which Pitt hated as much as the King's tyranny.

At the opening session of Parliament Pitt took particular pains to speak calmly and quietly, neglecting his famous gusts of oratory and invective. He supported the address from the Throne, congratulated the Ministry for carrying on the war until it might reach a successful conclusion, and spoke in the general interest of harmony.

Various members who now sought to rise to power by denouncing the fallen Minister exercised their oratory at the expense of Mr. Pitt, but he refused to be ruffled. His chief allusion to his own past was his statement on the policy of continuing support to maintain English troops in Germany in order that France might be prevented from reconquering her former possessions in America and elsewhere:

> America has been conquered in Germany, where Prince Ferdinand's victories have shattered the whole military power of that great military monarchy, France. Recall the troops from Germany, and I should be robbed of my honour, while England, by deserting her allies, would be deserted by God and man. And, honour apart, nothing but that spectre of an invasion which the Ministry of 1755 had not constancy enough to look at, frightened us out of Minorca. So would it be again, if the troops of France found themselves at liberty to quit Germany.

He concluded with Scipio's words: *"Utere sine me consilio me, patria,"*—*Without me, make use of my counsel, oh my country.*

Pitt, in spite of his public urbanity, was bored and disgusted with the turn of affairs. He resented the fact that no voice came to his support when he and his measures were attacked in the House, but he refused to take any notice of younger members who tried to curry favor with the King by attacks on the Pitt Ministry. He had moved into the position of an elder statesman whose record would speak for itself and he needed no defense.

For a second time, on December 9, 1761, he was moved to discuss his past policies, as Lord North attacked his record, and another member, Delaval, reminded Pitt that he had at one time said that Prussia would "hang like a millstone on the neck of any ministry."

"As Germany was formerly managed, it was a millstone around our necks," he replied. "As managed now, it is a millstone around the neck of France. When I came in, I found the subsidy to Prussia dictated by Hanover, not by Great Britain. I insisted that national defense and America must stand first, nor would I agree to the German war until every other service had been provided for."

He then turned to the burly Henry Fox, who, as Pitt knew, was organizing the claque for the King's friends.

"If any gentleman in this country should venture to take the lead on any other plan but the present," he said, glowering at Fox, "I would make his heart ache:—and now I think I have answered the millstone."

The indoor sport of baiting Mr. Pitt nevertheless continued. One of the most active in this game, a man in the pay of Fox, was a certain Col. Isaac Barré. Barré was a huge, dark, truculent Irishman, having a savage glare in one eye which was caused by a bullet wound. He had been with Wolfe at the fall of Quebec and had later been an aide to General Amherst, to whom he still owed money. He was an able officer, though not distinguished, and, lacking family connection, had reached the limit of advancement. Now he was trying to move forward along the political route. His chief method was by attacking the policies of the late minister, but Pitt paid no attention to him until on December 11th Barré accused him of lack of confidence in the King. At the mention of the King's name, which was forbidden in the Commons, Pitt demanded a ruling on a point of order. Barré was embarrassed and wished to withdraw, but Fox urged him on. Barré accordingly continued to speak against Pitt, calling him a chameleon who turned to the color of the ground he stood on, accused him of creating all the trouble with Spain and then promoting domestic confusion by resignation. In itself, the speech had no importance, except that it was a stencil of the ministerial gossip against Mr. Pitt.

The policy of the Ministry, however, was occasioning

great disgruntlement with the general public and with wealthy families who did not happen to be benefiting directly from the King's favor. As long as Mr. Pitt was in office, talk of peace had caused a rise in the stock market. This had influenced Fox, Bedford, and others in their policy toward the war. General confidence, however, proved to be a bigger factor in security values than any other consideration. With the fall of Pitt, peace on some basis seemed to be imminent, the expenses due to war would be greatly curtailed, and the market, supposedly, would be firmer, especially in Government securities, yet the reverse had taken place. With the dismissal of Pitt, public confidence in the Administration was undermined. At the end of September, 1761, shortly before his resignation, the three-percent consols had sold for 74⅜. At the end of December, 1761, they were down to 66⅛. This was typical of the entire list, and it was an eloquent index of public feeling.

The events which Pitt had predicted had come to pass. The Spanish galleons had gotten safely home, bringing in a vast treasure which would aid the French and Spanish armies. The Bourbon Powers, accordingly, became increasingly truculent, with the result that on January 4, 1762, George III declared war against the King of Spain.

Mr. Pitt did not gloat. On the contrary, on January 19, he spoke in Parliament for national unity. "Now it must be the King," he said. "It must be the Administration, the Parliament, nation, Army and Navy, who are to carry on the war; and I pray God it may all be enough. . . . Arm the whole. Be one people! This war, though it has cut deep into our pecuniary, has augmented our military, faculties. Set that against the debt, that spirit which has made us what we are."

Fortunately for the Crown, expeditions set in motion the preceding year were proving successful. Martinique succumbed to the British forces on February 12, 1762, followed by a number of other islands in the West Indies, until France was left with nothing in that area but half of the

island of San Domingo. Within the year Spain lost Havana
and Manila.

In spite of this stronger position, Egremont, Bedford,
and Bute bungled the British diplomacy. Bute began to flirt
with Russia and Austria, neglecting Frederick of Prussia,
who, of course, learned of this plotting and cooled to the
British cause. Bute was afraid of the belligerence of Frederick the Great and his chief aim was to obtain a peace on
any plausible terms as soon as possible. He had the good
sense to realize that neither he nor his colleagues were competent as war ministers. It was impossible, of course, to
admit this officially or to the public, and therefore he and
Egremont adopted the bizarre course of conducting peace
preliminaries through Viry, the Sardinian Ambassador,
whom he had used before in negotiations with Newcastle.

The Ministry outlined terms to Viry; Viry sent them to
the Sardinian Minister in Paris; who, in turn, discussed
them with Choiseul. After months of this performance, in
spite of the victories of the year, Bedford signed preliminary articles of peace at Paris on November 8, 1763, on
terms which were inferior to those which Choiseul had been
willing to give at various times in the past. England was
to retain Canada and certain islands in the West Indies,
and Minorca was exchanged for Belle Isle. In Africa,
Great Britain was allowed to keep Senegal, but the French
retained Goree—which destroyed the whole objective of
that operation. In India, France returned to her status of
January 1, 1749.

Spain gave Florida to Great Britain in exchange for
Havana, and France in turn compensated Spain with Louisiana. Since France had failed in her effort to reserve the
mid-continent section of America, Louisiana no longer had
value in her imperial scheme. England was still well ahead,
compared with her position before the war, but France retained Guadeloupe, Martinique, Marie Galante, and St.
Lucia, which left her in a strong position in the West Indies,
and she was accorded favorable terms of fishing rights in
the Newfoundland and St. Lawrence banks.

These terms were a disappointment to the public and to

the merchant and shipping classes, who had expected to enjoy a monopoly of West Indian trade. The agreement was unsatisfactory to Mr. Pitt for it ignored his hopes of a northern European alliance to hold the Bourbon states in check, and, through the fisheries, it gave France a training ground for seamen and the chance to recoup her naval strength. Pitt, it will be recalled, had addressed himself again and again to these points. The great thing which was salvaged in these negotiations was the inclusion of Canada, permanently, under the British flag, continuing the charter of liberties to her subjects which had been accorded by General Amherst in the terms of capitulation.

Pitt, of course, did not endure silently his disappointment at the meager terms which England had obtained. He was confined, virtually bed-ridden, at Hayes, but was able to see a continual stream of callers. When he learned that the ancient Lord Bath approved the peace terms he observed that his Lordship was damning his country with his last breath. He complained eloquently to Cumberland, Charles Townshend, and others, and regretted that he did not have the strength to appear at the Commons and offer opposition.

Bute, on learning of Pitt's strong feelings on the subject, became alarmed. He had relied, perhaps too much, on the Great Commoner's policy of harmony, and now it appeared that the whole program might be upset by a vote of Parliament. The logical cure for the situation was to enlist Mr. Pitt again in the Government's service. Bute sent an emissary to Hayes to propose that Mr. Pitt might have his choice of virtually any office if he would return to the Bute Ministry. It was a naïve and silly offer, considering the fact that Bute had known Mr. Pitt so well. Though Pitt enjoyed the panoply of office it did not tempt him to abandon his conscience. To expect that he would return and support a ministry which was responsible for the current terms of peace was preposterous, and Pitt promptly made this clear.

Bute then embarked on a campaign of bribery and intimidation. The Court could not afford to lose on an issue of this magnitude. If it did so, the scheme of establishing the kingly prerogative might as well be abandoned. He engaged the rotund Henry Fox as chief-of-staff for this program of reward and punishment. Fox, himself, if he did his job successfully, was to be rewarded with the peerage, which had so long been the object of his heart's desire.

Fox proved to be the ideal man for the task,—genial, corrupt, efficient, and callous. The Walpole memoirs harp on the great unpopularity of Fox and have imprinted this impression on history; but this view was obviously an exaggeration. Fox held office in many ministries and always was regarded as one of the leading figures in Parliament. The very fact that he was chosen for the present negotiations was an indication of confidence, at least in his diplomacy. His letter to Horace Walpole the younger, offering a bribe to Walpole's nephew, the current Lord Orford, is written in the tone of cheerfully unabashed corruption which was typical of Mr. Fox:

Nov. 21, 1762

DEAR SIR,—As soon as I heard that the Parks, which Lord Ashburnham had quitted, were worth £2200 a year (as they certainly are), I thought such an income might, if not prevent, at least procrastinate, your nephew's ruin. I find nobody knows his Lordship's thoughts on the present state of politics.

Perhaps he has none. Now, are you willing, and are you the proper person, to tell Lord Orford that I will do my best to procure this employment for him, if I can soon learn that he desires it? If he does choose it, I doubt not of his and his friend Boone's hearty assistance, and believe I shall see you, too, much oftener in the House of Commons. This is offering you a bribe, but 'tis such a one as one honest good-natured man may without offence offer to another.

If you undertake this, do it immediately, and have attention to my part in it, which is delicate. If you do not undertake it, let me know your thoughts of the proposal, whether I had better drop it entirely, or put it into other hands, and whose.

You'll believe me when I tell you that goodness of heart has as much share in this to the full as policy.

Yours ever,

H. Fox

Walpole claims that while his nephew accepted the offer, the family did not do the bidding of the Ministry. However that may be, there were a vast number of gentlemen who were grateful to Mr. Fox for his attention, and he soon had a solid majority in Parliament. Those who were opposed promptly learned the folly of their attitude.

Devonshire, for example, who had been the façade of the first Pitt Ministry, had developed an exaggerated sense of his own importance. It will be recalled that he had disapproved Pitt's later policies and had taken an active part against him. Since he had been awarded the post of Lord Chamberlain to the King, he fancied himself as one of the chief advisers to the Throne. This proved to be a delusion. Devonshire openly disapproved of the peace, whereupon the King flatly refused to give him further audience. Devonshire then returned his staff of Lord Chamberlain, in reply to which the King struck him off the list of Privy Councillors. At this, Rockingham and other Whig lords resigned their various places at Court, but they were only beating Mr. Fox to the gun. Those who did not resign promptly enough were kicked out with great speed.

The vote on the approval or disapproval of the preliminaries of peace was scheduled in Parliament for December 9, 1762. The Ministry was secure in a safe majority; and Mr. Pitt was ill in bed. In the dim auditorium of St. Stephen's Chapel everything was proceeding according to routine when the noise of people shouting was heard from without. The doors were flung open and at the head of a vast shouting crowd of persons was seen Mr. Pitt, carried on the arms of his servants who brought him in and set him down within the bar of the House. From there he crawled, with the help of a crutch and with the assistance of some few friends, to his seat, while Mr. Fox and some of his friends sneered at this theatrical entrance.

Pitt was authentically ill, but did not neglect the opportunity to dramatize his infirmities. Though he wore his usual black velvet suit, his legs and thighs were wrapped in flannel, his feet were covered with buskins of black cloth and he wore thick gloves. He spoke with difficulty in a low voice and with only occasional bursts of eloquence. He was able to proceed only by taking frequent cordials and by the indulgence of the House which permitted him to address them while seated. He was unusually verbose, perhaps because of the ease of speaking while seated, and his address lasted for three hours and a half, a fact which won the applause of the multitudes when he emerged from the House, but a fact which naturally enough bored the members of the Commons.

It had been an heroic effort, but an ineffectual one. Though he usually was able to stage a *tour de force,* this was not one of his happier occasions; and the lampooners made the most of it, one of them writing:

> At length he tries to rise, a hum
> Of approbation fills the room.
> He bows and tries again; but, no,
> He finds that standing will not do
> And therefore to complete the farce
> The House cries, "Hear him on his ar-e!"

The vote on the preliminaries was 364 for the Ministry and only 65 in opposition, the latter including the votes of Beckford and Clive. When the Princess Dowager heard the result she exclaimed, "Now my son is King of England!"

The Princess was a trifle premature in thinking that George had now gathered the power into his own hands. He had made progress in that direction, but not without difficulty and personal unhappiness. Ever since his marriage, which was supposed to free him from the Whigs and to cheer his private life, he had been morose and ill-tempered. The eager, sociable young monarch who had courted Sarah Lennox and had mingled sociably with his subjects at the royal levees, had turned into a sullen recluse. It was a matter of general comment that the King appeared in public as little as possible, and also kept his family generally confined within the palace walls. Day after day he followed a strict, dull schedule, concluding with early retirement in the evening, so that the Queen in spite of previous protests "went to bed with the chickens." His audiences with his Ministers were commonly occasions of irritation to them and to himself. The more control he gained over the State the less satisfaction he seemed able to command from life.

There were now new faces in almost every place around the Throne. On May 25, 1762, Newcastle had resigned, inevitably, as the King had denied his request for a certain subsidy for the war in Germany, had cut in half the amount which Newcastle said was necessary. The broken old fellow now had his moment of distinction. He refused any reward from the Crown upon retirement, even though he was said to have spent a great deal of his personal fortune in addition to government money in the activities of his office. During recent months he had again sought the favor of Mr. Pitt and had become zealous for Whig principles; and, for this, Henry Fox made him the object of particular persecution.

In speaking of Fox's appointment, the King had said, "We must call in bad men to rule bad men." Fox proceeded to justify the royal comment. All clerks, pilots, stewards, watchmen, anyone who held any place on the government payroll due to the prior favor of Newcastle, was driven from office. A special effort was made to see that

A contemporary cartoon

THE FOX
ELEVATED

Referring to Henry Fox in charge of driving out the Whigs from all places in the Government.

none of Newcastle's friends in his own county of Sussex remained in jobs. Anyone who was known to be a Whig or to be critical of the Government was promptly dismissed. On the other hand, many new jobs were created to be occupied by Tories. It was a complete and ruthless use of the public funds to build and perpetuate the King's party.

As the King's party was strengthened, his Majesty seemed to rely less and less on Lord Bute and to take a growing interest in chicane. Bute had taught the various members of the Cabinet to approach his Majesty for the purpose of backbiting Mr. Pitt, and the habit of plotting with the Throne had increased.

Grenville now appeared to have the chief post of honor next to the Crown, in order, as has been mentioned, to block Mr. Pitt, and it was Grenville's task to organize the defense of Government policies in the Commons. The presence of Grenville in the Court party and backing such measures, as has also been noted, was peculiarly odious to Mr. Pitt. Pitt knew the man's limitations and his incapacity and he felt that Grenville's desertion of Whig principles was unforgivable. The two men, of course, were widely different in temperament. Though Mr. Pitt was deeply devoted to the cousinhood, he could hardly have found Grenville very congenial under the best circumstances. The man's plodding mind, the dullness of his oratory, and his thin querulous voice, were foreign to Mr. Pitt's nature and tastes. Now, whenever possible in Parliament, Pitt made his brother-in-law feel the sting of his contempt, nor did the Government fail to provide Mr. Pitt with proper occasions.

After the successful vote on the peace preliminaries, the confidence of the Throne knew no bounds. On March 4, the Ministry introduced a proposal to levy an excise tax on all cider brewed for home consumption. This was unpopular enough in itself, but the measure carried two riders which were its worst features. They proposed that excise officers could invade private homes and that all offenses were to be tried by commissioners instead of by a jury.

This measure stirred Mr. Pitt to action. He found that a number of the Whig leaders were willing to be roused on this subject, particularly the Duke of Devonshire, whose political principles had been rekindled by his dismissal from office. Devonshire gave a huge dinner at his home, where Mr. Pitt was master of ceremonies, attempting to stimulate his colleagues to a more active part in Parliament. In the debate in the Commons on the cider tax measure Pitt took a leading part, and on March 27, 1763, he was particularly severe in criticism of Grenville for advocating an excise tax and for championing means of enforcement which invaded the rights of the individual.

Grenville replied with an attack on the way in which Pitt had handled finances when in office, and pointed out that it was now necessary to have new revenues. If the Opposition did not like this tax he invited them to say where they would have a new tax laid.

"I say, Sir, let them tell me *where!*" he said in his high-pitched voice. "I repeat it, Sir, I am entitled to say to them, tell me where."

Mr. Pitt sat listening to the speech, regarding Mr. Grenville with cool disdain and suddenly he began humming, so that the House could hear it, the tune of a popular song, *Gentle Shepherd, Tell Me Where.*

The idea of the stolid Grenville with his voice like a shepherd's pipe in the rôle of a Gentle Shepherd struck the House as a piece of apt absurdity. The nickname "Gentle Shepherd" clung to Grenville for a long time afterwards, and was used against him in political pamphlets.

Pitt then rose to pour fresh insults on his brother-in-law and predicted that those who were now following Grenville so closely would ultimately get enough of it, and then he turned, walking toward the door.

Grenville started up, shaking with rage.

"If gentlemen are to be treated with contempt . . ." he began.

Mr. Pitt turned around, made a deep sneering bow to Mr. Grenville, and departed.

The incident was a personal triumph for Mr. Pitt and mildly encouraging to the Whigs, but the Ministry was too well entrenched to be shaken by barrages of oratory. While the Government measure was unpopular, Bute and Fox had moved so adroitly that only a major catastrophe could dislodge the present party. Bute still realized that he, personally, was a liability to the Ministry because of his Scotch blood and the scandal connecting him with the Princess Dowager. Ever since the mob had tried to kill him and had spattered him with mud, public office had lost its charm. He had remained in office long enough to engineer the vote on the peace and to turn out the Whig party. Accordingly, on April 8, 1763, he begged leave to retire, leaving vacant the first place in the Ministry.

This was, in a sense, another victory for the King, for while Bute bowed to Majesty he had also been the tutor, virtually the creator of, Majesty in this instance. The Kingship, as George III knew it, was a synthesis from the brain of Bute, and now he was relieved of too frequent a reminder of that fact. The question immediately arose as to who should succeed as First Lord of the Treasury and chief Minister. The choice was fairly obvious and, as expected, the King appointed to this post none other than Gentle Shepherd George Grenville.

CHAPTER XXXIV

FREE PRESS AND DRUNKEN PORTERS

"I know what liberty is," said Mr. Pitt, "and that the liberty of the press is essentially concerned in this question."

He was discussing with Newcastle the stand which all true Whigs must take on the Wilkes case.

This notorious case, started by the Government on April 29, 1763, was the next move on the part of George III and his courtiers in trying to build the structure of dictatorship.

The first step on the part of the King to obtain supreme power had been to get rid of his enemies and, if possible, to destroy their reputation. The plot to ruin Mr. Pitt in the public eye had, to be sure, failed, but, in general, all the King's critics had been effectually proscribed from participation in Government. The second step, familiar in all such movements, was to fill all the places in the Government with friends of the King and dismiss from any Government employment anyone who dared to raise his voice. George III, it must be admitted, could find ample precedent for his conduct, in Whig tradition as well as Tory. At any rate, as Bolingbroke advised, he had "purged his Court."

To banish, to smear, and to bribe, such were the tactics of the Administration, but their efforts were hampered by the existence of the press. The journals of the day were feeble beginnings compared with the newspapers of later times. They contained only fragments of news and were primarily given over to opinion. Non-partisan publishing was practically unknown, and virtually every paper served some political clique avowedly or secretly. Pamphleteering was a favored form of publishing, and such papers were usually violently partisan expressions of opinion on some particular issue. The press commanded small respect compared with the position it achieved in later generations.

Reporters were not permitted in either House of Parliament and were obliged to obtain their material from members or by other devious ways. In spite of the small standing of journalism, the fact remained that truth, and even half-truth, was mighty; and as long as printing presses were free to be used against the Government, the drive to suppress all power but the Crown would be impeded.

Therefore, in the spring of 1763, swollen with confidence over the successful proscription of the Whigs from every corner of public life, the Administration began its campaign to jail and impoverish any publisher who failed to bow the knee. George Grenville, the apostate from the Whig cause, now exceeded Bute in his stubborn and humorless advocacy of the royal power. He chose the test case with shrewdness in the selection of John Wilkes as the object of persecution. The character of Wilkes made any support of him embarrassing. He was an adventurer and a rogue who had gone into the demagogue business with the frank and cynical intention of making a fortune in rabble-rousing. He was the son of a wealthy distiller, and a Lieutenant Colonel in the Militia who had inherited moderate means and had added to his purse by marrying a wealthy woman ten years his senior, a match which he said had been planned by his parents. He soon made clear to the lady that his interest in her was wholly financial and his substantial house in Great George Street became virtually a brothel for the young bloods of the town and their lady friends.

Wilkes was a tall, hideous man who had the gift of a lively personality, affable ways, and wit. He sopped up scandal like a sponge and exuded it like a garden spray, both verbally and with a scurrilous pen. Like the late Frank Harris, he could and did boast acquaintanceship with most of the leaders of the day in the literary, political, and social world. He had shoved his way at one time or another into the homes of Smollett, Johnson, Gibbon, Hogarth, and Pitt, to name but a few. He was an intimate of the leading rakes of the day. Gibbon said of him, "I scarcely ever met with a better companion; he has inexhaustible spirits, infinite wit and humor, and a great deal of knowledge; but a thorough profligate in principle as in practice, his life stained with every vice, and his conversation full of blasphemy and indecency."

It had been the Wilkes practice to write fawning letters to everyone high in Government office—he had written to Mr. Pitt as early as 1757—promising his infinite loyalty and hinting that he would like to have a worthwhile job. He had succeeded in being elected to Parliament, but otherwise his self-abasement had yielded little profit. This fact had embittered him and he had turned to pamphleteering as a means of making money, gaining political support and paying off some old scores. At first he wrote for journals published by others, but on June 5, 1762, he had founded *The North Briton*. This periodical soon involved him in considerable trouble with various public persons. In the twelfth issue, for example, appearing in August, 1762, he had rashly commented on Lord Talbot's famous, rear-action horse:

> A politeness equal to that of Lord Talbot's horse ought not to pass unnoticed. At the Coronation he paid a new, and, for a horse, singular respect to his sovereign. . . . Some of the regulations of the courtiers themselves for that day had long been settled by former Lord Stewards. It was reserved for Lord Talbot to settle an etiquette for their horses.

Talbot had failed to see the humor in this allusion to an unfortunate occurrence and had challenged Wilkes to a duel, from which both gentlemen emerged unscathed. Wilkes became involved in other encounters and made an increasing number of enemies. Lord Bute had refused the pleas of Wilkes for political recognition and had even attacked Wilkes in subsidized pamphlets. Wilkes, in turn, devoted various issues of *The North Briton* to satires on the King's favorite and to stirring up prejudice against the Scotch, a practice which Mr. Pitt particularly deplored; and *The North Briton* now paid special attention to George Grenville.

Wilkes, in short, commanded little respect; had few friends and many bitter enemies. A proceeding against him on the part of the Crown was considered safe. On April

23, 1763, Wilkes published the famous No. 45 edition of *The North Briton,* containing what was held to be an attack on the King personally. Such an inference could hardly with fairness be drawn from the document. Wilkes had carefully refrained from attacks on the Sovereign, but in this issue he had denounced the Address from the Throne. He had, however, elaborately pointed out that the address was always understood both by the Parliament and the public to be the work of the Ministry. He then wrote:

> Every friend of his country must lament that a prince of so many great and amiable qualities, whom England truly reveres, can be brought to give the sanction of his sacred name to the most odious measures, and to the most unjustifiable public declarations, from a Throne ever renowned for truth, honor, and unsullied virtue.

The merits of the charge against Wilkes were, however, of little concern to the Administration. They desired to set a precedent, and this was the opportunity. On April 26,— at the instigation of Grenville—George Montagu Dunk, Earl of Halifax and a principal Secretary of State, issued a general warrant for the seizure of the authors, printers, and publishers of *The North Briton No. 45,* and of their papers.

On the 29th, the warrant was placed in the hands of the King's messengers who spread a drag-net for any printers whom they suspected of being involved. They arrested a David Leach after midnight, having broken into his house. They seized him, his servants, apprentices, and papers, and threw the victims into jail, where they were detained for several days even though all were wholly innocent of any connection with the publication.

They then apprehended the real printer, Kearsley, treated him in the same way, and proceeded at midnight on a later day to deal in a similar fashion with Wilkes.

Wilkes showed fight; and the messengers called a constable who took him to be interviewed by Lord Halifax and Lord Egremont. By this time, the Ministry were somewhat alarmed at their own boldness, but the step had been

THE NORTH BRITON.

NUMB. XLV.* SATURDAY, APRIL 23, 1763.

The following advertisement appeared in all the papers on the 13th of April.

THE NORTH BRITON makes his appeal to the good sense, and to the candour of the ENGLISH nation. In the present unsettled and fluctuating state of the *administration*, he is really fearful of falling into involuntary errors, and he does not wish to mislead. All his reasonings have been built on the strong foundation of *facts*; and he is not yet informed of the whole interior state of government with such *minute precision*, as now to venture the submitting his crude ideas of the present political crisis to the discerning and impartial public. The SCOTTISH minister has indeed *retired*. Is HIS influence at an end? Or does HE still govern by the *three* wretched tools of his power †, who, to their indeliable infamy, have supported the most odious of his measures, the late ignominious *Peace*, and the wicked extension of the arbitrary mode of *Excise*? The NORTH BRITON has been steady in his opposition to a *single*, insolent, incapable, despotic minister; and is equally ready, in the service of his country, to combat the *triple-headed, Cerberean* administration, if the SCOT is to assume that motley form. By HIM every arrangement *to this hour* has been made, and the notification has been as regularly sent by letter under HIS HAND. It therefore seems clear to a demonstration, that HE intends only to retire into that situation, which HE held before HE first took the seals; I mean the dictating to every part of the king's administration. The NORTH BRITON desires to be understood, as having pledged himself a firm and intrepid assertor of the rights of his fellow-subjects, and of the liberties of WHIGS and ENGLISHMEN.

Genus ORATIONIS *atrox, & vehemens,* cui opponitur *lenitatis & mansuetudinis.*

CICERO.

" THE *King's Speech* has always been considered by the legislature, and by the
" public at large, as the *Speech of the Minister* §. It has regularly, at the be-
" ginning of every session of parliament, been referred by both houses to the consi-
" deration of a committee, and has been generally canvassed with the utmost freedom,
" when

The most famous single page in the struggle for the freedom of the press. These paragraphs from issue "No. 45" of *The North Briton* provoked the famous Wilkes case, in which Pitt was the chief defending voice.

By Permission of the Huntington Library, San Marino, California (Item AM 21228 Chatham)

One of Chatham's last letters, predicting "the end of my political career." It bears only the salutation "Dear Sir," but was probably addressed to Barré, his chief support in the Commons.

taken and Halifax ordered Wilkes committed to the Tower. Meanwhile the messengers returned to Wilkes' home, seized all his papers, broke open every closet, bureau, and drawer, threw the contents promiscuously on the floor, collected all the written material into a sack, including Wilkes' will, which was in his private pocketbook, and carried the material to Lord Halifax.

It was a bold stroke, and coupled with the terrorizing of innocent printers, as a by-product, it must have filled Grenville with some hopes of success. Indeed, if it did succeed, his program of royal dictatorship was well on its way.

Though Wilkes had few personal friends and many enemies the Ministry had far over-estimated their legal power. Wilkes immediately made application for *habeas corpus* and was brought before Pitt's friend, Charles Pratt (later Lord Camden) who was then Chief Justice of the Common Pleas. Pratt held that Parliamentary privilege protected members from arrest, except in cases of treason, felony, or breach of the peace. He ruled that Wilkes was not guilty on any of these counts and ordered his release.

Wilkes had been made a hero, and on his release the mob greeted him with the cry "Wilkes and liberty." The printers who had been arrested brought action against the King's messengers and were awarded heavy damages; but the Ministry foolishly adopted a stubborn attitude, deciding to carry the case further, and, thereby challenged the constitutionality of the freedom of the press.

If Grenville or the King thought or did not care whether Mr. Pitt would be blind to such a challenge, they were singularly obtuse. In fact, this blindness to Pitt's character, though Grenville had known him intimately for so many years, was striking evidence of Grenville's dullness and political incapacity. True enough, on November 13, 1761, Pitt had referred to the press, which was then abusing him, as "that chartered libertine of the air"; but the current issue was too vital to be swayed by his personal resentment against pamphleteers. In the ensuing weeks he urged upon the Whigs that they should unite in challenging the Government on this position as soon as Parliament opened. In his advice to Newcastle on this subject he had also said:

> I disapprove of all these sort of papers, *The North Briton,*
> etc.; but that is not the question.   When the privileges of the
> Houses of Parliament are denied in order to deter people from
> giving their opinions, the liberty of the press is taken away.
> Whigs who would give up these points to humor the Court and
> extend the power of the Crown, to the diminution of the Liberty
> of the subject, I should never call Whigs; . . . and I should never
> agree to act with anybody upon that foot.

On seeing that the Wilkes matter had been badly fumbled
and was still likely to create trouble, the King became impatient with Grenville and longed for some situation which
would permit the return to office of his beloved Bute.

The death of Egremont on August 21, 1763, gave an
excuse for reshuffling the ministerial places.   It was not
feasible to oust Grenville, without the risk of allying him
again with the Whigs, and the easiest system would be to
include him in any new deal, but to surround him with abler
men.

The most satisfactory arrangement of all would be to
devise a ministry which would include Mr. Pitt, and thereby
get the danger of that independent voice nearer to the
Crown, where the King thought it might be controlled.   Bute
was the father of this notion and the emissary between the
King and the Great Commoner.   Pitt conferred with Lord
Bute in London on August 25, and on August 27 was summoned to the royal presence.   He had clarified to Bute
what his program would be, namely, a general control of
basic policies and the restoration of the Whigs to some of
the offices of state.   This attitude, of course, was not what
had been hoped for by his Majesty.   The value of the Pitt
name would be worth almost any personal reward, if the
man would be content to serve as a figurehead.   The King,
nevertheless, gave audience to Mr. Pitt and heard his conditions without demurring.   His Majesty even seemed willing to displace Mansfield as legal adviser to the Cabinet
and accept Mr. Pitt's nomination of Charles Pratt in that
post.

"There is pen, ink, and paper," he said at last to Mr. Pitt. "Make out a list of your Administration at once."

Pitt was unprepared for such sudden acceptance of his program and demurred that he could not make out a list until he had consulted his colleagues. Possibly he feared a trap, and it may be that the King actually only was sounding out Pitt's present point of view. At any rate, the monarch did not press the point and it was agreed that Mr. Pitt would return on Monday, presumably to conclude final details.

While this conversation had been going on in the Queen's house, where the King had arranged the audience, Grenville happened by and recognized Pitt's servant and sedan chair with its huge leg-rest protruding from the front.

He was immediately profoundly upset, and during the weekend he, as well as other courtiers, began to shiver at the prospect of a return of the eagle-like Pitt. The very terms he had laid down were a forecast of his attitude. Pratt as legal adviser! It was Pratt who had ruled that the general warrants were illegal and had freed the scoundrel Wilkes. And now Pratt was proposed as a member of the Ministry. Pitt's audacity and his disregard for royal prerogative were intolerable. The Court party emphasized this view to Bute so insistently that he consented to lay the dangers of the situation before the King. Accordingly, when Mr. Pitt appeared for his audience on Monday the King found fault with various points of the Pitt program, and finally said, "Well, Mr. Pitt, I see this won't do. My honour is concerned and I must support it."

"Sir," Pitt replied, "the House of Commons will not force me upon your Majesty, and I will never come into your service against your consent."

To Pitt the incident caused grief and disillusionment, the dampening of the last flicker of hope. For a time it had seemed that both the monarch and Bute had realized the error of their unconstitutional ways, and were taking a graceful method of returning to a government on Anglo-Saxon principles. Pitt had not asked for patronage or for the dismissal of any of the King's friends except Mansfield, whose voice had been a bulwark of Tory policy. Now it was clear that Grenville and a host of other small-minded men were, after all, the dominating influence with the Crown.

Thoroughly discouraged and in poor health, he tried, nevertheless, to rally the remnants of the Whig party and met with the leaders from time to time during the weeks preceding the fall session of Parliament. The more he consulted with Pratt, the more convinced he became that any general warrant, no matter what the cause, invaded the liberty of the subject. On two occasions Pitt had issued general warrants in time of war against persons suspected of being enemy aliens, but he conceded that the practice was always dangerous and the present instance was particularly iniquitous as it was directed not against spies in time of war but against the freedom of the press, when not the slightest danger of public safety was involved. He tried to impress this view on Newcastle, on Hardwicke's son, Charles Yorke, and on Devonshire; but his former colleagues were luke-warm. Rigby, who was Bedford's secretary, had said of Pitt that he was interested in measures rather than men. On the other hand, both the Whigs and the Tories were chiefly interested in what men were to be in office, and Pitt's insistence on principle at times grew tiresome.

When Parliament opened in November, 1763, Wilkes complained of his arrest as a breach of the privileges of the House, and Pitt was the only prominent Whig who supported that view. The Ministry, at the same time, determined to press the issue. George Grenville moved "that *The North Briton No. 45* was a false, scandalous and seditious libel, tending to excite the people to traitorous insurrections against the Government."

Pitt rose to say that a law court and not the House was the place to try a libel. He also observed that the use of the word *traitorous* was unjustified. An attempt was being made here to create the fiction of a treason trial as a screen for invading the privileges of the House.

He emphasized that he held no brief for Wilkes personally or for his periodical. He regarded *The North*

Briton as a detestable publication and its author as a blasphemer, but that did not justify Parliament in surrendering its privileges. To justify the course of the Ministry would place every member who did not vote with the Administration under a perpetual terror of imprisonment.

The House, however, was largely composed of the King's party and voted for the Grenville motion by an enormous majority. In January, 1764, when Pitt was at home ill, they carried the matter further by expelling Wilkes from the House without a hearing.

In spite of the huge majorities of the Government in the condemning of Wilkes and *The North Briton,* Pitt's words had not been wholly unavailing and a small group in the minority had agreed among themselves to place the issue of warrants as a general principle before Parliament as soon as Mr. Pitt's health would permit him to be present. His eloquence and generalship were necessary for a battle, which was certain to bring out the strongest repressive measures which the Crown could command. Accordingly, on February 13, with Mr. Pitt present, the House came to the discussion of the resolution "that a general warrant, for apprehending and seizing the authors, printers, and publishers of a seditious and treasonable libel, together with their papers is not warranted by law." The proceedings began with an examination of witnesses. Those who had seized Wilkes in his house were asked to explain their conduct. One of them, Philip Carteret Webbe, said that he had acted as a servant of the Secretary of State; further, that he had not intended that Colonel Wilkes should be held a close prisoner in the Tower; and he had taken care that he was made comfortable while there.

This defense was so apologetic that Grenville observed that the hour was getting late and perhaps they should adjourn.

"I think we should not adjourn until we know whether we have a Constitution or not," observed Mr. Pitt.

Lord Frederick Campbell, however, moved the adjournment, which, under the rules of the House, was debatable.

Pitt had no intention of being shut off, and said that it was derogatory to the honor of the House to adjourn.

"My own first wish was to crush foreign enemies," he said truculently. "Now I have come to crush domestic enemies." He then added, with a touch of his old theatricality, that after this had been accomplished he would die willingly. The question of Pitt's prospective death was not gone into; he defeated the motion to adjourn by a vote of 379 to 31; and the House was in a rebellious mood for the first time since the accession of the new King. Attendance at many sessions had been less than 150, but during the general warrants debates there were more than 450, almost a capacity House, present.

The rest of that evening and much of the following day were occupied with matters of routine. Mr. Pitt was in virtually continuous attendance, either in St. Stephen's Chapel or in an adjoining room to which he retired frequently to recover his strength.

The strategy of the Ministry was to introduce as many irrelevancies as possible to cloud the issue, and especially to wear down Mr. Pitt, who was conspicuously in ill health. The battling Whigs, however, stuck to their guns and disposed of interruptions as rapidly as possible. The Administration was eager for adjournment, for its margin was now so slender that any vote on the main issue was hazardous. An attempt to adjourn at four-thirty in the morning was defeated by 208 to 184 and the House did not finally rise until after half-past seven on the morning of the 15th, after a sitting of seventeen hours, the longest in the record of the House, but the business still was not settled.

On the 17th, Pitt made his first speech on the motion. He said that the Crown and the Ministry had accomplished what they desired in the conviction and expulsion of Mr. Wilkes. It was now the duty of the House "to do justice to the nation, to the Constitution, and to the law. The Ministers," he observed, "who affected so much regard for liberty and the Constitution, are ardently desirous of retaining for themselves and for their successors, a power to do an illegal act."

He replied to the charge that he had issued general warrants during his ministry by pointing out that he had issued two in time of war for the seizure of suspected enemies. He conceded that he had done so illegally and was prepared to take the consequences. It was a matter of the public safety and he had been willing to risk his head because of "the real exigency of the time."

He continued: "In the present case there is no necessity for a general warrant. The ministers knew all the parties [hence a specific warrant could have been drawn]; the plea of necessity could not be urged; there was no pretense for it; the nation was in perfect tranquillity; the safety of the State was in no danger; the charge was, the writing and publishing of a libel.

"Parliament has voted away its own privilege," he cried, "and laid the personal freedom of every representative of the nation at the mercy of his Majesty's Attorney General.

"The extraordinary and wanton exercise of an illegal power, in this case, admits of no justification, nor even palliation.

"It was an indulgence of a personal resentment against a particular person. If the House negatives the motion they will be the disgrace of the present age and the reproach of posterity; who, after sacrificing their own privileges have abandoned the liberty of the subject upon a pretense that was wilfully founded in error and manifestly urged for the purpose of delusion."

The Government benches listened to this panegyric with fear and hatred. Sir Fletcher Norton, recently appointed Attorney General, was stung by the allusion to himself. Sneering at his audience, at both the Opposition and at the King's men who had weakened on this issue, Norton observed that he should regard a Resolution of the House of Commons no more than the oaths of so many drunken porters. This gratuitous insult instantly won friends for the motion, and the Ministry realized that a mistake had been made. Dr. Hay, a Government member, hastily moved that the motion be amended to include the word "treasonable," so that it would read: "a general warrant for seizing the authors, printers etc. of a seditious and treasonable libel is not legal."

Mr. Pitt saw that the insertion of "treasonable" was a slap at his having issued warrants on the grounds of public safety, even though the subject then had not been related to printing or publishing.

He said he was willing to have the question extended to cover his own case, that no general warrant to search universally without specifying name or place was allowable, even in case of treason.

"General warrants are always wrong," he affirmed, but he suggested that Dr. Hay stop quibbling and return to the consideration of this one case. All the best speakers on both sides stepped into the fray, including again Norton, who exhibited considerable legal knowledge. After Norton had concluded, Charles Townshend sarcastically complimented him on his great talent for being able to hold the attention of a group of drunken porters.

After several more addresses Pitt paid his respects to Webbe.

"Hear the language of Ministers and their agents," he said sardonically. "Carteret Webbe said that he had settled Wilkes *comfortably* in the Tower with his shaving things! Then, they say you need not pronounce this illegal."

Grenville finally realized that he was facing an opponent of far greater powers than himself, that Pitt at his best retained his ability to arouse the conscience of men, even though the Ministry was supported by all the wealth and prestige of the Crown. The motion clearly could not be defeated and the chief hope for the Administration now lay in the possibility of amendment. Hence the Government forces concentrated on a whittling process. The addition of the word *treasonable* was adopted. The Government also succeeded in adding the qualifying clauses that such warrants had been issued according to the usage of office, that it had been frequently resorted to, that so far as appeared to this House, the validity had never been debated in the Court of King's Bench and that "the parties thereupon have been frequently bailed by the said Court."

Nevertheless, though weighted down by these amendments the House at last adopted the resolution:

> That a general warrant for apprehending and seizing the authors, printers and publishers of a seditious and treasonable libel, together with their papers, is not warranted by law.

Mr. Pitt, taxing his strength to the utmost, with one of the most notable evidences of the force of his personality, had rallied a supine House of Commons and had induced the "drunken porters" to build a lasting foundation for the freedom of the press.

CHAPTER XXXV

AMERICANS ARE SONS, NOT BASTARDS

Though Mr. Pitt had won a victory on the subject of general warrants, the effort had been at the cost of his health and spirits. He alone had carried the burden of organizing this crusade, and he was disgusted at the lukewarmness of his colleagues on the subject. The weakness of the Whigs resided in the fact that most of them could be so easily bought. Charles Yorke, one of the younger sons of Lord Hardwicke, was frank enough to say that he had his own career to consider, and if Whiggism could not advance him he would need to see what offers might be made by the King's party. Whenever Pitt retired to his country place, as he did now for a number of months, the Whigs contented themselves with occasional protest meetings at the Albemarle Street and other liberal clubs, but no one chose to lead with his chin in Parliament.

Pitt, nevertheless, felt that Newcastle, Devonshire, and some of the older men might keep the party on a solid footing, so that it would be prepared and well organized whenever emergencies might arise. This view indicated an unusual spirit of optimism on Mr. Pitt's part, for there was little in the history of his colleagues to suggest that they had such steadiness. Newcastle always needed Pitt or Hardwicke to be his backbone, and when they were absent he was reduced to a jelly. Hardwicke had died in March, 1764; and with Pitt ill, Newcastle now was nothing more than a mass of tearful petulance.

There was a younger group of men who were ready to support Constitutional opposition to the King, but they were an erratic, unreliable crew, divided among themselves. There was the handsome Lord Shelburne, glib, active and deceitful, who was never fully trusted by anyone, in spite of his good record in the Army and a creditable later career. There was the suave and stately Marquis of Rockingham, proud of his birth, insistent on his own eminence, thin, dark and handsome, but a poor speaker, and lacking in political *savoir faire*. James Grenville was a devoted follower of Pitt. A genial, charming fellow without great force.

Most vigorous of the younger men was Col. Isaac Barré. He had left the Fox payroll and desired to be a real statesman, but he lacked both the finesse and the following necessary for Parliamentary leadership. Mr. Pitt saw little to choose from in this assortment of cats and dogs, and now preferred to hold himself aloof from commitment to any clique. He continued to remain at Hayes in the rôle of "village philosopher," a term which he enjoyed applying to himself.

The situation naturally played into the hands of Grenville and Bedford who, having routed opposition, began to bully the unhappy King. George III was beginning to learn that a king is dependent upon one group of ministers or another and that any cabinet which obtains excessive power can use it against the Throne as well as against the people. Grenville, who had been brought into power by Bute, was now jealous of his benefactor and of the Princess Dowager. In the spring of 1765 the King fell ill for a few weeks, in the first of his recurrent periods of insanity. It was necessary to introduce a Regency Bill in Parliament, and Grenville used his influence to exclude the name of the Princess Dowager, fearing a return of Lord Bute if the Princess should become a dominant factor in the affairs of the Throne.

When the King recovered in May, 1765, he was so amazed at this insult to his mother that he determined to teach Grenville a lesson, and decided again to approach Mr. Pitt to form a ministry. Pitt was now receptive, because Grenville, in February, 1765, while Pitt was ill, had obtained the passage of an act in Parliament imposing stamp taxes on the American colonies; and in March, 1765, he had added a Mutiny Bill for guarding against colonial resistance. Pitt had rejected a stamp-tax bill when it was proposed to him in 1757, as he looked upon it as unjust, and as certain to alienate the colonies at the very time when it was important to be building the foundations of an Anglo-Saxon system.

When the King's messenger, Lord Albemarle, came down to Hayes on May 16, Mr. Pitt was willing to meet him with proposals, but Albemarle was not empowered to accept conditions. George III had made the mistake, which Bute had made earlier, in thinking that the Great Commoner would be glad to have office as such. The Albemarle mission accomplished nothing, and then the King dispatched his uncle, the great fat Duke of Cumberland, who arrived at Hayes in elaborate style accompanied by many retainers.

It was a signal compliment for a member of the royal family to visit the home of a commoner with such marks of dignity. It betokened that the Throne would treat Mr. Pitt with the greatest kindness and respect; but Pitt was not flattered. He required assurance that he would be permitted to carry out the policies which he felt were necessary to re-establish Constitutional government. Cumberland, like Albemarle, was not in a position to make such promises, nor was the King ready to give up the powers which he had arrogated to himself.

Reluctantly his Majesty decided to leave himself in Grenville's hands, and then the obtuse Grenville, thinking himself indispensable, decided to sweep out the last of the Bute adherents and force the King to break a promise which he had made to Bute's brother, having assured him of a lifetime job in the Scottish Government. This was too much for the morose and sulky monarch, who decided at last that he would permit Mr. Pitt to write his own terms, and on July 19 he gave audience to the former minister and accepted his conditions. These included the repeal of the Stamp Act, the repeal of the Cider Tax, the inclusion of Pratt, a northern alliance against the House of Bourbon, and a clearer resolution against the use of general warrants; in fact, all the cardinal points of Pitt's policy.

The new Cabinet was to be made up mostly of younger men, and not including the chief Whigs who had proved so unstable in the past. The names of Newcastle and Devonshire were omitted. The only one of the older politicians to be slated for office was Temple, who was nominated for the First Lord of the Treasury, and was to have the responsibility of leadership in the House of Lords.

To the surprise of everyone, and Pitt especially, Temple flatly refused. For a long time his conceit had been growing. As long as he had been in the Ministry he had been able to delude himself that he was on a parity with Mr. Pitt as a fellow member of the Government, but ever since their retirement it had been clear even to him that Mr. Pitt was regarded as the mainspring of that Administration. He, Temple, was the head of the Grenville-Pitt connection by rank and by wealth, and he had found it excessively galling to have his Majesty turn to Mr. Pitt as the chief figure.

He now said that he would come into Government only on a basis equal to Pitt or as his superior. Two years before he had complained to Newcastle that he was unwilling to be "dragged at Mr. Pitt's tail."

Pitt was dumfounded at this turn of affairs, for he had placed solid reliance on Temple's loyalty. Even though Temple was tactless and difficult, his experience would have made him a useful leader in the House of Lords if he were willing, as in the past, to speak for the Pitt program. Now, however, the situation was impossible. The King, of course, had no intention of submitting to a Ministry headed by Temple, even if Temple had been able to enlist a group under his banner. He urged Mr. Pitt to try to form a cabinet without his brother-in-law, but the Great Commoner felt unequal to the task. He realized his own ineffectiveness as a party manager. He dared not trust himself again to the unreliable Newcastle, and he lacked the strength to weld the Cabinet together by the sheer force of his own domination, as he had done in the years 1757-1762.

In bitterness and discouragement, he returned to Hayes while the King was obliged to accept a nondescript Government headed by Rockingham and Newcastle, with General

Henry Seymour Conway (a kinsman of Horace Walpole) as Secretary of State and leader in the Commons. Grenville and Bedford were out of office, and the King's power took on a new lease of life, for the Rockingham Ministry was shilly-shallying and indecisive, refusing to face the Constitutional issues which were before the country.

Mr. Pitt had many things that he desired to do, aside from attending Parliament. He now had five children. William, the second son, who was to approach the fame of· the father, had been born on May 28, 1759. The youngest, James Charles, had been born at St. James Square, April 24, 1761. Pitt wished to devote himself to family life, to which he had been a virtual stranger in his long period of bachelorhood and in the active days as Secretary of State. He now spent most of his hours playing with his children, and helping to educate them. These pursuits were interrupted by periodical attacks of the gout, but his illness was less severe when he had the opportunity to relax at home, to go horseback riding for hours at a time and to enjoy peaceful scenes. The disease was partly nervous, and was always intensified during the strains of parliamentary battles.

The Pitt children, three boys and two girls, were taught by a tutor. Mr. Pitt remained firm in his conviction of the evil of the British public-school system and none of the children were sent away to school until old enough for university training. The value of the Pitt method, in this case, was supported by the intelligence and interest of the parents and the fact that the five children were close together in age. The family conducted amateur shows and often read and conversed in Latin. Mr. Pitt also taught the children to recite passages from the Greek orators and held readings from Shakespeare in which different members of the family took the parts of various characters. The girls, contrary to the general practice of the time, were included in this general educational scheme, and the whole atmosphere of the home was that of the pursuit of knowledge.

Outdoor pursuits were included as well as the classics. The popular vogue of hay-making was part of the program.

Mr. Pitt and the five children would customarily get into work clothes and spend hours in the fields. At other times they chased butterflies, went fishing, and swam on the beach at Lyme Regis.

The results of this system, apparently happy for all concerned, were reasonably successful. William, the second son, was the only child to achieve real distinction, but his record of becoming Prime Minister while in his early twenties was phenomenal. None of the children, moreover, were conspicuous failures, and in view of the number of scapegraces in Mr. Pitt's family this avoidance was no small achievement.

By 1765, financial worries were again beginning to trouble the Pitt household. Mr. Pitt was a curious mixture of extravagance and simplicity. He cared nothing for the pomp of social life, state dinners, jewels, mistresses, objects of art, and the other forms of display of the eighteenth century. The popular vices of drunkenness and gambling were abhorrent to him. On the other hand, he had certain tastes which were extremely costly, the chief of which were landscaping and horseflesh. He had acquired a mania for privacy and wherever possible bought up land around Hayes to protect it. He thought nothing of building a lake here and installing a grove of trees there. On one occasion when he got the notion that he wanted a particular kind of tree, he combed all England to get a sufficient supply, and, in his impatience, hired a crew of men to work day and night for the planting.

Devoted to horses and horsemanship, he kept a large stable and many carriages. On his trips to London he would, at times, lead a procession, driving by himself in a surrey, and followed by a train of carriages carrying his family, retainers and sometimes as many as seventeen servants.

Like his father and his elder brother he was thoroughly incompetent in the management of his private finances. His income was unequal to his mode of living. The pension of three thousand pounds from the Government had been settled by Newcastle in such a way that it was subject to fees and deductions so that there was an actual net of little more than two thousand pounds. Most of his revenues from the Marlborough estates were in trust under the terms of the marriage settlement, and it now seemed clear that the great portion of that inheritance would never come to him, since the grandchild of the Duchess,—an ancestor of Winston Churchill,—had grown up in good health; and it was only through the expected demise of this child that Mr. Pitt was to come into the major properties.

Pitt, nevertheless, had been living for some years in expectation of ample fortune, and lucky windfalls had kept him going. In 1764, Ralph Allen of Bath had left him one thousand pounds. Lord Grandison, his uncle, had made him his residuary legatee in 1761; and early in 1765 Sir William Pynsent, an eccentric old man who had never even seen Mr. Pitt, left him all his estates. These consisted of property worth between £3,000 and £4,000 a year, including a large house and park overlooking the sea at Burton Pynsent near Langport in Somersetshire.

This bequest, while ultimately profitable, involved Pitt in a series of disputes and changes in his living conditions which were an added strain on his frail constitution and his frailer finances. He promptly sold his beloved Hayes Place, on which he had expended thousands of pounds, to Thomas Walpole, brother of Horace the letter-writer. He then began a series of improvements to Burton Pynsent regardless of expense. Meanwhile the kin of Sir William Pynsent brought suit to upset the will, and it was not until 1771 that the title was finally confirmed in Mr. Pitt's favor.

There were political considerations, also, which entered into this bequest. Lord North, who was a relative of Newcastle, ambitious both in politics and finance, had expected to inherit this property. He was distantly connected with Pynsent, had assiduously courted the old man and had at one time been named in his will. Pynsent, however, while inactive in politics, was a passionate believer in Constitutional rights and had greatly admired Mr. Pitt's stand on general warrants. He had become equally disgusted with

Lord North's support of the terms of the Peace of Paris, and on that issue had struck North out of his will. This situation, as will be seen, made North more than ever dependent upon the royal favor and ultimately willing to accept the job of being the King's tool.

While Mr. Pitt was busily engaged on his personal affairs, the Rockingham Ministry suddenly found itself in an embarrassing situation which Grenville had left on their hands. Though Grenville had proposed and achieved the passage of the Stamp Act, he had permitted it to lie inactive on the statute books, and had gone no further toward enforcing it than to appoint Stamp officers; but when it became clear that his Ministry would be forced to retire, he had set the enforcement machine in motion; and now violent repercussions had come from America. There had been riots in many sections. Public business in South Carolina was at a standstill, because the citizens refused to buy stamps to affix to public documents. Officers of the Crown had been mobbed. The provincials had established a boycott on British goods and were refusing to pay the bills for goods previously purchased.

A contemporary cartoon

THE MARQUIS OF
ROCKINGHAM

Handsome, well-intentioned, ineffectual.

In the opinion of King and courtiers this was an insurrection which could not be tolerated. In the judgment of many others, the colonies were making an uproar which seemed out of all proportion to the injustice, if there were an injustice. Legal opinion was divided on the rights of Parliament to lay such a tax, and some of the best minds held that, if Parliament had the right to regulate colonial affairs in many particulars to which the colonies acceded, the addition of a Stamp Tax was only a detail.

The legalistic argument, however, ignored the general state of affairs existing between the colonists and the Mother Country. The home Government thought that the colonials should be willing to pay a considerable part of the expense of the late war, which had driven France from the New World and thereby strengthened the position of the English colonists. This view overlooked the fact that the American War had largely been financed in America. The colonies had raised a substantial portion of the troops. More than that, they had made huge loans to the British Government and had not been repaid. Amherst had financed his two chief campaigns on loans from New York State augmented by aid from Massachusetts. The Crown was deeply in debt to Pennsylvania, and most of the colonial currencies were inflated, due in large part to these loans and the failure of the home Government to redeem its promises. The imposition of a Stamp Tax to bleed the colonies further, after all that they had already contributed, was the last straw. The tax, too, like the Cider Bill, was framed with the obnoxious provision that violations would be tried by officers, without right of trial by jury.

Rockingham in the Lords, and Conway in the House of Commons, were faced with the necessity of urging the coercing of the colonies or the repeal of the Stamp Act. Either course was difficult. The first might mean war, and the second would be asking Parliament to rescind an action which it had taken less than a year previously. Grenville, naturally, was strongly in favor of his pet measure, and used his influence outside of the Ministry to block any consideration of repeal.

Rockingham and Conway, however, decided that they must introduce a bill for repeal, and so notified His Majesty. The King, on Rockingham's representation that the choice lay between coercion or repeal, indicated that he would advise the latter. To the stubborn, morose George III, however, sulking under the rebuffs he had endured on his attempts to extend the royal power, the action of the colonies was outrageous. He was obliged to stomach Rockingham for the time being, since no other ministry seemed to be politically possible, but he hated the Whigs and their Constitutional views. Secretly he took the astonishing step of letting it be known that he would not be offended at members of Parliament who opposed the Ministry. In fact, he informed certain servants of the Crown that they were at liberty to vote against the ministerial repeal bill and retain their places on the royal payroll.

When Parliament met on January 4, 1766, to consider repeal, the Ministers were shaky, even alarmed at what the result might be. They did not know that the King had betrayed them, but could feel that the Court party, at least, was lukewarm. Grenville and his followers, of course, would be for enforcement. Bute and his party took the same position, and Mr. Pitt was an unknown quantity.

After the motion on the King's address, which evaded the issues of the day, several speakers in succession attacked the Ministers for their lack of spirit and for permitting the authority of Parliament to be called in question by the colonies.

"The tax was not a twentieth part of what they could afford to pay," said Hans Stanley, who had re-embraced his Tory views after acting as Pitt's Minister to Paris. "But that is not the point. I would rather have a peppercorn to acknowledge our sovereignty than millions paid into the treasury without it."

The peppercorn metaphor was an unfortunate choice for Stanley, as Pitt referred to it repeatedly in the next dozen years to cast ridicule on the Tory view.

As Stanley was speaking, Mr. Pitt appeared in the House. His manner was austere, quiet, contemplative. His eagle-like glance regarded the Ministerial benches and the Opposition, as though he had come with a message of great moment which would guide Government policy. No one could be sure what side he was going to take now that the colonies had resisted; but it was clear that his action might establish or destroy the Ministry. He took his seat, next but one to the pale and worried Grenville, and rose to speak in an atmosphere of tense silence.

"I came to town but today," he said in a calm and quiet voice. "I was a stranger to the tenor of his Majesty's speech and the proposed address, until I heard them read in this House. Unconnected and unconcerted, I have not the means of information; I am fearful of offending through mistake, and therefore beg to be indulged with a second reading of the proposed address."

The address, namely that of the Commons in reply to the King, was read. It included the passage:

We acknowledge that care for the welfare of his people . . . which his Majesty shews in the early communication, which his Majesty has been pleased to order, of the necessary informations relative to the disturbances in America.

"I commend the King's speech," Mr. Pitt observed, "and of the address in answer, as it decides nothing. Every gentleman is left at perfect liberty to take such a part concerning America, as he might afterwards see fit. One word only I could not approve of,—'An *early*' is a word that does not belong to the notice the Ministry have given to Parliament of the troubles in America. In a matter of such importance, the communication ought to have been immediate. I speak not with respect to parties; I stand up in this place single and unconnected.

"As to the late Ministry," he turned to Grenville, "every capital measure they have taken has been entirely wrong.

"As to the present gentlemen, to those at least whom I have in my eye," looking at the bench where General Conway sat with the Lords of the Treasury, "I have no objection; I have never been made a sacrifice by any of them. Their characters are fair: and I am always glad when men of fair character engage in his Majesty's service. Some of them have done me the honour to ask my opinion before they would engage. These will do me the justice to own, I advised them to engage; but notwithstanding—I love to be explicit—I cannot give them my confidence: pardon me, gentlemen," bowing to the Ministry, "confidence is a plant of slow growth in an aged bosom; youth is the season of credulity; by comparing events with each other, reasoning from effects to causes, methinks I plainly discover the traces of an over-ruling influence.

"There is a clause in the Act of Settlement, to oblige every Minister to sign his name to the advice which he gives to his Sovereign. Would it were observed! I have had the honour to serve the Crown, and if I could have submitted to influence, I might have still continued to serve; but I would not be responsible for others.

"I have no local attachments: it is indifferent to me whether a man was rocked in his cradle on this side or that side of the Tweed," he continued, alluding to the prejudice against Bute and against the Scotch in general. "I sought for merit wherever it was to be found. It is my boast, that I was the first Minister who looked for it; and I found it, in the mountains of the north.

"I called it forth, and drew into your service, an hardy an intrepid race of men," referring to his policy of enlisting Highland regiments for Louisbourg and elsewhere, "men, who, when left by your jealousy, became a prey to the artifices of your enemies, and had gone nigh to have overturned the State, in the war before the last. These men, in the last war, were brought to combat on your side: they served with fidelity, as they fought with valour, and conquered for you in every part of the world: detested be the national reflections against them! they are unjust, groundless, illiberal, unmanly. When I ceased to serve his Majesty as a minister, it was not the country of the man by which I was moved, but the *man* of that country wanted wisdom, and held principles incompatible with freedom."

The reference to Bute made clear that Pitt was not going to rejoin that faction, and Conway's party breathed more easily.

"It is a long time, Mr. Speaker, since I have attended in Parliament," he went on. "When the resolution was taken in this House to tax America, I was ill in bed. If I could have endured to have been carried in my bed, so great was the agitation of my mind for the consequences, I would have solicited some kind hand to have laid me down on this floor, to have borne my testimony against it.

"It is now an act that has passed. I would speak with decency of every act of this House; but I must beg the indulgence of the House to speak of it with freedom.

"I hope a day may be soon appointed to consider the state of the nation, with respect to America. I hope gentlemen will come to this debate with all the temper and impartiality that his Majesty recommends, and the importance of the subject requires,—a subject of greater importance than ever engaged the attention of this House; that subject only excepted, when, nearly a century ago, it was the question, whether you yourselves were to be bound or free."

It was clear now that Mr. Pitt had come to offer what the Ministry and the country needed, which he alone could give, a philosophy of action. Rockingham and Conway had the feeling that repeal was necessary, but were at sea in the midst of conflicting arguments. Yet here was a matter of major state policy destined to affect the future of the realm, and Pitt was ready to define it. His reference to "nearly a century ago" meant the Revolution of 1688, when the Whigs had rebelled against royal prerogative and called a new monarch to serve under Constitutional principles. He was now summoning the House to stand by those principles.

"In the meantime, as I cannot depend upon my health for any future day, such is the nature of my infirmities, I will beg to say a few words at present, leaving the justice, the equity, the policy, the expediency of the Act to another time. I will only speak to one point, a point which seems not to have been generally understood; I mean to the right.

"Some gentlemen seem to have considered it as a point of honour [to enforce the Act]. If gentlemen consider it in that light, they leave all measures of right and wrong, to follow a delusion that may lead to destruction.

"It is my opinion, that this kingdom has no right to lay a tax upon the colonies.

"At the same time, I assert the authority of this kingdom over the colonies to be sovereign and supreme, in every circumstance of government and legislation whatsoever. They are the subjects of this kingdom, equally entitled with yourselves to all the natural rights of mankind, and the peculiar privileges of Englishmen: equally bound by its laws, and equally participating of the Constitution of this free country.

"The Americans are the sons, not the bastards of England.

"Taxation is no part of the governing or legislative power. The taxes are a voluntary gift and grant of the Commons alone. In legislation, the three estates of the realm are alike concerned; but the concurrence of the Peers and the Crown to a tax, is only necessary to close with the form of a law. The gift and grant is of the Commons alone.

"In ancient days, the Crown, the Barons, and the Clergy, possessed the lands. In those days, the Barons and the Clergy gave and granted to the Crown. They gave and granted what was their own. At present, since the discovery of America, and other circumstances permitting, the Commons are become the proprietors of the land; the Crown has divested itself of its great estates. The Church (God bless it!) has but a pittance. The property of the Lords, compared with that of the Commons, is as a drop of water in the ocean; and this House represents those Commons, the proprietors of the lands; and those proprietors virtually represent the rest of the inhabitants. When, therefore, in this House we give and grant, we give and grant what is our own. But in an American tax, what do we do? We, your Majesty's Commons of Great Britain, give and grant to your Majesty, what? Our own property? No!—We give and grant to your Majesty the property of your Majesty's Commons of America. It is an absurdity in terms.

"The distinction between legislation and taxation is essentially necessary to liberty. The Crown, the Peers, are equally legislative powers with the Commons. If taxation be a part of simple legislation, the Crown, the Peers,

have rights in taxation as well as yourselves: rights which
they will claim, which they will exercise, whenever the principle can be supported by power.

"There is an idea in some, that the colonies are virtually
represented in this House. I would fain know by whom
an American is represented here? Is he represented by any
knight of the shire, in any county in this kingdom? Would
to God that respectable representation was augmented to
a greater number! Or will you tell him that he is represented by any representative of a borough—a borough
which, perhaps, its own representatives never saw? This is
what is called 'the rotten part of the constitution.' It cannot continue a century: if it does not drop, it must be ampu-
tated. The idea of a virtual representation of America in
this House is the most contemptible idea that ever entered
into the head of man: it does not deserve a serious refu-
tation.

"The Commons of America, represented in their several
assemblies, have ever been in possession of the exercise of
this, their Constitutional right, of giving and granting their
own money. They would have been slaves if they had not
enjoyed it. At the same time, this kingdom, as the supreme
governing and legislative power, has always bound the
colonies by her laws, by her regulations and restrictions in
trade, in navigation, in manufactures—in every thing except that of taking their money out of their pockets without
their consent. Here I would draw the line."

Pitt was seated, and a long silence ensued. The Ministry
could add little to this plea, and no one in favor of the Stamp
Act chose to take on such an adversary. Finally, General
Conway, deeply grateful for this support, said that he
agreed with virtually everything Mr. Pitt had said, and
would gladly serve under his leadership if he would take the
office. As for himself, he had been unwilling and accident-
ally called to the Ministry,—a statement in which there was
considerable truth, as he had left his army career at the
persuasions of Rockingham and the other Whigs. As to the
delay in notifying Parliament of American troubles, he
would take the responsibility for that, since the first reports

of resistance were vague and uncertain. Only lately had they become specific.

"The excuse is a valid one, if justifiable," said Mr. Pitt. "That much appears from the papers now before the House."

Grenville, who had been stewing with indignation at the attack on his pet bill, rose to defend it at great length, citing precedents, denouncing the Americans as open rebels, affirming that Pitt preached insurrection, stating that many other classes such as stockholders did not have representation, bemoaning the unfair attacks on his recent Ministry, and audaciously affirming that the Magna Carta gave the right to tax the colonies.

Pitt jumped to his feet at that last affirmation, but Grenville was not to be overborne. The tall hawklike Pitt and the pale squat Grenville stood trying to outshout each other, while other members joined in the clamor until the speaker called for order.

"I do not speak twice," said Pitt. "I only finish, what I designedly left imperfect; but if the House is of a different opinion, far be it from me to indulge a wish to transgress against order. I am content, if it be your pleasure, to be silent."

Here he paused; but the House resounded with cries of "Go on! Go on!"

"Gentlemen," he proceeded, "Sir [to the Speaker], I have been charged with giving birth to sedition in America. They have spoken their sentiments with freedom against this unhappy Act, and that freedom has become their crime. Sorry I am to hear the liberty of speech in this House imputed as a crime. But the imputation shall not discourage me. It is a liberty I mean to exercise. No gentleman ought to be afraid to exercise it. It is a liberty by which the gentleman who calumniates it might have profited. He ought to have desisted from his project. The gentleman tells us, America is obstinate; America is almost in open rebellion.

"I rejoice that America has resisted.

"Three millions of people so dead to all the feelings of

liberty, as voluntarily to submit to be slaves, would have been fit instruments to make slaves of the rest.

"I come not here armed at all points, with law cases and acts of parliament, with the statute-book doubled down in dog's ears, to defend the cause of liberty; if I had, I myself would have cited the two cases of Chester and Durham. I would have cited them, to have shown that, even under former arbitrary reigns, parliaments were ashamed of taxing a people without their consent, and allowed them representatives. Why did the gentleman confine himself to Chester and Durham? He might have taken a higher example in Wales; Wales, that never was taxed by Parliament till it was incorporated. I would not debate a particular point of law with the gentleman. I know his abilities. I have been obliged to his diligent researches: but, for the defence of liberty, upon a general principle, upon a Constitutional principle, it is a ground on which I stand firm; on which I dare meet any man.

"The gentleman tells us of many who are taxed, and are not represented. The India Company, merchants, stockholders, manufacturers. Surely many of these are represented in other capacities, as owners of land, or as freemen of boroughs. It is a misfortune that more are not equally represented: but they are all inhabitants, and as such, are they not virtually represented? Many have it in their option to be actually represented: they have connections with those that elect, and they have influence over them.

"The gentleman mentioned the stockholders: I hope he does not reckon the debts of the nation as a part of the national estate. Since the accession of King William, many ministers, some of great, others of more moderate abilities, have taken the lead of government.

"None of these thought, or even dreamed, of robbing the colonies of their Constitutional rights. That was reserved to mark the era of the late Administration: not that there were wanting some, when I had the honour to serve his Majesty, to propose to me to burn my fingers with an American Stamp Act. With the enemy at their back, with our bayonets at their breasts, in the day of their distress, perhaps the Americans would have submitted to the imposition; but it would have been taking an ungenerous and unjust advantage.

"The gentleman boasts of his bounties to America. Are not those bounties intended finally for the benefit of this kingdom? If they are not, he has misapplied the national treasures.

"I am no courtier of America; I stand up for this kingdom. I maintain, that the Parliament has a right to bind, to restrain America. Our legislative power over the colonies is sovereign and supreme. When it ceases to be sovereign and supreme, I would advise every gentleman to sell his lands, if he can, and embark for that country.

"When two countries are connected together, like England and her colonies, without being incorporated, the one must necessarily govern; the greater must rule the less; but so rule it, as not to contradict the fundamental principles that are common to both. If the gentleman does not understand the difference between external and internal taxes, I cannot help it; but there is a plain distinction between taxes levied for the purpose of raising a revenue, and duties imposed for the regulation of trade, for the accommodation of the subject; although, in the consequences, some revenue might incidentally arise from the latter.

"The gentleman asks, when were the colonies emancipated? But I desire to know, when they were made slaves. But I dwell not upon words. When I had the honour of serving his Majesty, I availed myself of the means of information which I derived from my office: I speak, therefore, from knowledge. My materials were good; I was at pains to collect, to digest, to consider them; and I will be bold to affirm, that the profits to Great Britain from the trade of the colonies, through all its branches, is two millions a year. And," he referred to the words of Hans Stanley, "shall a miserable financier come with a boast, that he can bring a pepper-corn into the exchequer, to the loss of millions to the nation? I dare not say how much higher these profits may be augmented.

"Omitting the immense increase of people by natural

population, in the northern colonies, and the emigration from every part of Europe, I am convinced the whole commercial system of America may be altered to advantage.

"You have prohibited where you ought to have encouraged, and encouraged where you ought to have prohibited.

"Does the gentleman complain that he has been misrepresented in the public prints? It is a common misfortune. In the Spanish affair of the last war, I was abused in all the newspapers, for having advised his Majesty to violate the laws of nations with regard to Spain. The abuse was industriously circulated even in handbills. If Administration did not propagate the abuse, Administration never contradicted it. I will not say what advice I did give to the King. My advice is in writing, signed by myself, in the possession of the Crown. But I will say what advice I did not give to the King: I did not advise him to violate any of the laws of nations.

"The gentleman must not wonder he was not contradicted, when, as the Minister, he asserted the right of Parliament to tax America. I know not how it is, but there is a modesty in this House, which does not choose to contradict a minister. I wish gentlemen would get the better of this modesty. . . .

"A great deal has been said without doors of the power, of the strength, of America. It is a topic that ought to be cautiously meddled with. In a good cause, on a sound bottom, the force of this country can crush America to atoms. I know the valour of your troops. I know the skill of your officers. There is not a company of foot that has served in America, out of which you may not pick a man of sufficient knowledge and experience to make a governor of a colony there. But on this ground, on the Stamp Act, when so many here will think it a crying injustice, I am one who will lift up my hands against it.

"In such a cause, your success would be hazardous. America, if she fell, would fall like the strong man. She would embrace the pillars of the State, and pull down the Constitution along with her. Is this your boasted peace? Not to sheath the sword in its scabbard, but to sheath it in the bowels of your countrymen? Will you quarrel with yourselves, now the whole House of Bourbon is united against you? While France disturbs your fisheries in Newfoundland, embarrasses your slave-trade to Africa, and withholds from your subjects in Canada their property stipulated by treaty; while the ransom for the Manillas is denied by Spain.

"The Americans have not acted in all things with prudence and temper. The Americans have been wronged. They have been driven to madness by injustice. Will you punish them for the madness you have occasioned? Rather let prudence and temper come first from this side. I will undertake for America that she will follow the example. There are two lines in a ballad of Prior's, of a man's behaviour to his wife, so applicable to you and your colonies, that I cannot help repeating them:—

> Be to her virtues very kind,
> Be to her faults a little blind.

"Upon the whole, I will beg leave to tell the House what is really my opinion. It is, that the Stamp Act should be repealed absolutely, totally, and immediately; that the reason for the repeal should be assigned, because it was founded on an erroneous principle. At the same time, let the sovereign authority of this country over the colonies be asserted in as strong terms as can be devised, and be made to extend to every point of legislation whatsoever: that we may bind their trade, confine their manufactures, and exercise every power whatsoever," he repeated, returning to his previous forceful statement, "except that of taking their money out of their pockets without their consent."

CHAPTER XXXVI

Mr. Grenville Takes the Hiss

Mr. Pitt's speech on the Stamp Act gave the American issue an importance which it had not had previously. The Rockingham-Conway Ministers welcomed his support, and yet found themselves committed by it far beyond their original position. They might have succeeded in repealing the Act on the grounds of expediency, but Pitt had declared the Act wrong in principle and had proclaimed the colonists to be equal in their rights with all British subjects.

Such a stand was a challenge to a wide sector of British thought, of which the stolid Grenville was the chief exponent. Except for a few wealthy sea-captains, planters, and other entrepreneurs, the colonials were a miscellany of younger sons of nobility, debtors, adventurers, criminals, dissenters, Dutch, Germans, refugees, and Irish. Pitt's concept of them as British subjects on a parity with either the peer or pauper of London was distasteful to many in the home country.

The issue had been posed for both sides of the Atlantic, however, and each batch of news from across the seas gave testimony that the provincials felt they had a common cause against the Stamp Act on the grounds of their rights as freemen. On January 27, 1764, a Mr. Cooke of Middlesex presented to the Commons a petition from a Congress of the North American Provinces protesting the Stamp Act. There were several objectors to receiving this "Petition of Right," as it was called. The Bute faction was among them, and one member of Parliament called the Congress "a dangerous and federal union."

"Dangerous and federal!" Pitt replied. "Why it is the evil genius of this country that has riveted amongst them this union, no more 'dangerous and federal' than a meeting at the Albemarle Street Club or on Newmarket Heath. The Americans originally fled from the Star Chamber and the High Commission Court, and in comparison of this country the desert smiled upon them. Now if, as I assert, Parliament cannot tax America without her consent, the original compact with the colonies is actually broken and they have the right to resist."

Sir Fletcher Norton, who in the last session had referred to the M. P.s as "drunken porters," now thought to batter down Mr. Pitt by roaring at him and misquoting his words.

Pitt then started to explain.

"The gentleman now says I mistook his words," Norton interrupted. "I do not now understand them."

"I did say the colony-compact would be broken," Pitt replied in his most imperious manner, "and what then?"

"The gentleman speaks out now, and I understand him," Norton countered, "and if the House go along with me, *the gentleman will go to another place.*"

At this hint of sending him to the Tower, Mr. Pitt looked at Norton in greatest contempt, raised his chin and cried— "Oh! Oh!—Oh! Oh!," as if to say that Norton had revealed himself in his true colors.

"I will bear that from no man," said Norton. . . . "I say the gentleman sounds the trumpet to rebellion. . . . He has chilled my blood at the idea."

"The gentleman says I have chilled his blood," Pitt replied. "I shall be glad to meet him in any place with the same opinions when his blood is warmer."

This brusque exchange of words served chiefly to advise the ruffians of the Court party that Pitt could not be bulldozed, and had only contempt for their threats. The petition from America was left unheard, however, in the series of wrangles which ensued on the subject; and another week passed before the Ministry met the issue again.

On February 3, 1766, Conway brought in a set of resolutions which he thought would placate all sides. He was weakening somewhat on the repeal question, for his Administration had come near to defeat in certain votes on other matters. His strategy now was to offer a series of dicta which would rebuke the colonies. Having thus satisfied the pride of the anti-repeal forces, he might then carry Parliament with him for repeal. In any case, he was against trying to enforce the Act. Conway, unfortunately, like many a soldier in politics, was honorable but maladroit, a straightforward fellow with neither the arts of persuasion nor domination. His resolutions, as he put them boldly, were as follows:

FIRST: that Great Britain had, hath, and ought to have full right and power to bind the Americans in all cases whatsoever.
SECOND: That tumults have been carried on.
THIRD: That the votes of the assemblies are illegal.
FOURTH: Humbly to address his Majesty to bring the authors of riots to condign punishment.
FIFTH: To address, that the sufferers by riots be compensated.

Immediately, fire came from both sides. William Blackstone, author of the *Commentaries,* held that Parliament had no legal right to impose the taxes, and others also spoke on the colonial side.

The first resolution, affirming Great Britain's right to bind the Americans "in all cases whatsoever," was a form of compromise which appealed to the members of Parliament, as it seemed to save face and would make it less galling to repeal the Stamp Act, if they should come to that conclusion. Mr. Pitt could see the practical politics of the proposal in the House of Commons; but he hoped that Parliament would rather come clean with an unequivocal reversal of what he regarded as a cardinal mistake. If America were to be, as he conceived it, an extension of the British system, as much a part of the kingdom as Middlesex, then any attempt to isolate the colonies by denunciation and punishment would injure the possibility of unity.

The debate on the subject continued all day. Conway, naturally, supported his own resolution, and the Grenville forces seized upon it as at least some concession to their ends. One speaker, thinking it well to relieve the tension,

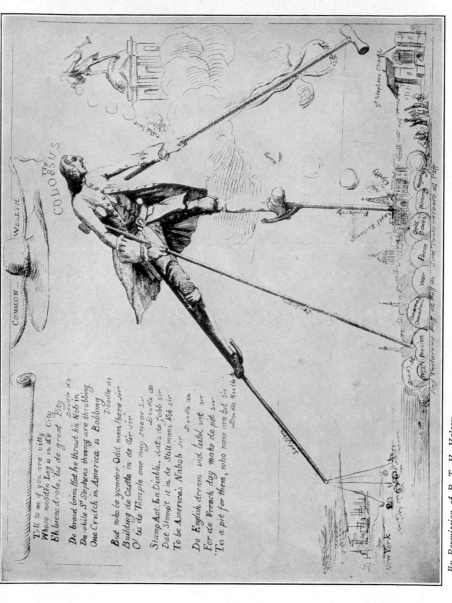

"The Colossus." A cartoon representing Pitt as stirring up sedition in America and striding over England on the props of Pension and Popularity.

By Permission of R. T. H. Halsey

'Gulliver's Flight: or the Man Mountain.' A cartoon satirizing the public adulation of Pitt.

suggested blandly that it was just as well not to enter too closely into fundamentals, such as the right of taxation.

"Not look into foundations!" Mr. Pitt exclaimed. "What else produced the Reformation? What revived liberty in this country? . . . If liberty be not countenanced in America, it will sicken, fade, and die in this country. . . . The colonies are too great an object to be grasped but in the arms of affection. . . . I wish this to be an empire of freemen."

An empire of freemen! Here was the Pitt purpose proclaimed again, the central theme of his statesmanship, little understood by many of his own followers, and stiffly resented by the Throne. Norton had said that Pitt sounded a "trumpet of rebellion," but Pitt conceived of himself rather as a trumpeter of freedom. Whenever liberty had been trampled on, in religious intolerance, in the throttling of the press, and the principle of general warrants, he had sounded the alarm with the trumpets of reveille, the violins of ridicule, the woodwinds of sympathy, and the open diapason of a spacious patriotism.

Norton did well to say that Mr. Pitt sounded a trumpet, but for the moment his blasts were inadequate. The discussion went on until four in the morning; and Conway's first resolution, asserting the unlimited rights of Great Britain over the colonies, was carried with hardly a dissenting vote.

Mr. Pitt, however, was planning to stay in town until the Stamp Act issue was fully settled. He had rented an apartment in Bond Street from the Duke of Grafton, and made that his headquarters for strengthening the morale of the leaders of the Rockingham-Conway Ministry in their campaign for the repeal. On the day following the long session discussing Conway's first resolution, Pitt slept until noon and then addressed a note to Lady Hester:

> I am just out of bed, my dearest life, and considering the great fatigue, not getting to bed till past four, I am tolerably well . . . my hand not worse, my country not better. . . . We debated strenuously the rights of America. The resolution passed, for England's right to do what the treasury pleases with three millions of free men. . . .

It is probable the main question of repeal will not come on till Friday or Monday. Send the coach, my love, tomorrow morning, and I shall then have it in my power to do as events allow. At present, adieu. Kiss our dear babes for me.

Your ever loving husband,

W. PITT

The debate continued on February 5, 1766. Pitt saw no objection to the second resolution, which stated a fact: "that tumults have been carried on." When a member decided to amend the resolution by adding that the tumults had defeated the execution of an Act of Parliament, Pitt was again on his feet to oppose such provocative language. He regretted that his support had proved of so little help to American liberty.

"I stand almost naked in this House," he said, "like a primeval parent; naked because innocent; naked because not ashamed."

In this instance Mr. Pitt prevailed, and the amendment was withdrawn.

Everyone acceded to the third resolution, which held "that the votes of the assemblies are illegal," as clearly they had no legal validity.

The fourth resolution, for punishing the riotors in America, was dropped, as the members realized that this would cause more tumult than anything that had gone before.

The fifth proposition, to compensate the Crown officers who had suffered through the resistance of the Americans, was approved by the House in a modified way, in which Pitt agreed to an amended wording suggested by Grenville.

If the gesture of deferring to Grenville on this point was intended by Pitt to conciliate his brother-in-law, it failed of its purpose, for in the ensuing days both the Ministry and the Opposition showed their colors on the implications of the Stamp Act, which had now divided men according to their basic concepts of Government.

This was a case in which division of opinion surpassed the usual Parliamentary struggles wherein one group or the other was seeking merely jobs and prestige. This was a contest between the idea of a ruling class headed by the Court, as opposed to the concept of a nation of freemen delegating the powers of government to a legislature and cabinet, headed by a king who upheld the Constitution. The idea, the Tory idea, had made great progress under George III, and the protest by the colonies was a blow at that entire theory. Mr. Pitt was regarded on both sides as the moving factor in this issue.

On February 17, 1766, the Ministry announced in Parliament that they had decided to change their intention of printing the official papers on the Stamp Act resistance in America. To print the documents regarding the disputes would disclose the names of many persons and concerns involved, and conceivably make them subject to reprisals. This announcement angered the King's friends, who saw clearly that Mr. Pitt's conciliatory inventiveness had been at work again.

"The oracle has appeared, the oracle has spoken," sneered Mr. Wedderburn, a member of the Court party, gesturing toward the Ministerial benches. "There is the Government they have prostrated themselves before; but I hesitate to think what will become of them for their inconsistencies. How will they expiate their crime? How atone for it? I would advise them to make pilgrimages to Hayes, perhaps he may require human sacrifices."

Mr. Pitt was absent on this day, and others took the opportunity of baiting Conway, now that his chief support was lacking.

"I have heard of a *médécin malgré lui,* never of a *minister malgré lui,*" said Rigby, the Duke of Bedford's party manager, alluding to Conway's remark several days before that he had been brought into office unwillingly. "Nor am I apt to think that people who do not like their situations, exert all their abilities—they do not do their best: I dare say the honourable gentleman does not do his best. I look upon timidity in a minister to be as bad as cowardice in a general."

"May we ever have such a minister *malgré lui,*" added Lord George Sackville, sarcastically, "who is ready to serve his country and rescue the dignity of the Sovereign from being injured!"

Conway kept his temper admirably, realizing that these remarks were meant to stampede him. He observed that Rigby could not have meant to apply the term of cowardice to him.

"I know him too well; he would scarcely have taken an improper occasion to call me coward," Conway said in reply to Rigby. "I have a better opinion of his courage than that comes to. The other gentleman who talked of the oracle had better have said that on the last debate [when Pitt was present]—but why did he say it at all? Is it not known that those gentlemen had courted and idolized the idol, and have been rejected?"

On February 21, 1766, came the major test in Parliament on the repeal of the Stamp Act. Mr. Pitt wrote to Lady Hester before starting to the Parliamentary chambers:

Thank God, I am able to send a good account of myself, legs excepted; more properly, one leg only excepted. I must get up to the House, if I can; when in my place, I feel I am tolerably able to remain through the debate and cry Aye! to the repeal, with no sickly voice.

By this time most of the proceedings of the House had leaked out to the general public. The merchants, the manufacturers, and the urban public were on the side of the Americans and Mr. Pitt, because Mr. Pitt stood for a growing and modern England, for expanding boundaries and opportunities for all who had the will and abilities to grasp them. He stood, moreover, for the rights of the smallest man against imposition from above.

Grenville, in turn, had proved to be the exponent of the older, privileged classes, to him a welcome change from following Pitt's uncomfortable views. Grenville's chilly nature, always needing the fire of an alien genius, was now warmed by the intensity of the King and his Tory ideas, while the glamour of the Throne cast its glow over the tenacious Grenville mediocrity.

Crowds of American merchants, British importers, and other general public hung about St. Stephen's Chapel while the closing debates were in progress. Conway, who had come to the conclusion that repeal of the Stamp Act, was, after all, inevitable, made his final and strongest appeal on the basis of British trade. He pointed out that eight merchants had received cancellations of American orders amounting to £400,000. He said that the city of Nottingham had dismissed 4,000 workers and unemployment was growing elsewhere in proportion. In Manchester, three out of every ten laborers were discharged. He granted that legal opinion might be found to support Parliament in taxing the colonies, but against this he placed the fact that trade was prostrated. He said that he had in his pocket a piece of cloth which had been made in Philadelphia as cheaply as it could be produced in England.

Grenville, in reply, went straight to the matter of principle as opposed to expediency. He called taxation "the brightest jewel of the Crown." How would the Parliament justify the action to his Majesty? How to future administrations?

Mr. Pitt supported his own previous arguments simply by saying that he regarded the repeal as due to the liberty of unrepresented subjects and in gratitude to their having supported England through three wars.

Finally, Conway moved for leave to bring in a bill to repeal the Stamp Act; and, to the surprise of the Ministry itself, the proposal carried by the large majority of 275 to 167.

As the word was passed to the crowds waiting without, at 1:30 in the morning, there were shouts of applause. General Conway was among the first to leave the House and the crowd gave him three cheers, pressed forward to compliment him, and then made a lane for his passage.

As Mr. Pitt appeared in the lobby there was a great roar of welcome. The whole crowd took off their hats, huzzahed, and many followed him on the way to Bond Street with shouts and blessings.

When the stolid Grenville emerged the tone of the public changed. He was jostled, and several pressed close to him with hisses. Grenville, however, was no coward.

Swelling with rage and mortification, he seized the man nearest to him by the collar. The fellow was quick-witted.

"Well, if I may not hiss, at least I may laugh," he said, and laughed in Grenville's face, and Grenville moved on, seething with resentment.

Mr. Pitt, vastly elated over the move to repeal, promptly dispatched a message to Lady Hester at Hayes; and the following day he received an ecstatic reply:

> Joy to you, my dear love. The joy of thousands is yours, under Heaven, who has crowned your endeavours with such happy success. May the Almighty give to mine and to the general prayers, that you may wake without any increased gout, or any cold that may threaten it, bye and bye! I will hope that . . . the gratitude of a rescued people have cured you. . . .
>
> All my feelings tell me that I hate oppression, and that I love zealously the honour of my dear husband. I must not be sorry that I do not see you today: It would be too great a hurry, and it is fit that you should rejoice with those who have triumphed under you.

Wives, however, apparently have much in common from century to century, and from ocean to ocean. Lady Hester was unable to leave this letter of congratulations without adding the postscript:

> I do not understand the House dividing at half-past twelve, and your not being at home till half-past two.

When Mr. Pitt, one of England's greatest prime ministers, replied to his wife's letter, he had wisdom enough to know what was the most important point in her letter, for he said at the outset:

> Happy indeed was the scene of this glorious *morning* (for at past one we divided), when the sun of liberty shone once more benignly upon a country, too long benighted.

Then he continued:

> My dearest love, not all the applauding joy which the hearts of animated gratitude, saved from despair and bankruptcy, uttered in the lobby, could touch me in any degree, like the ten-

der and loving delight, which breathes in your warm and affectionate note. . . .

Thank you for the sight of Smith [the coachman who had come to take Mr. Pitt home]. His honest joy and affection charm me. Loves to the sweet babes, patriotic or not; though I hope impetuous William is not behind in feelings of that kind. Send the saddle horses if you please, so as to be in town early tomorrow morning. I propose, and hope, to execute my journey to Hayes by eleven.

Mr. Pitt went to Hayes as he planned; and meanwhile the friends of Grenville tried to prevail upon him to relax his hold on a clearly unpopular position. Grenville, however, was not to be moved. He was fighting in a cause in which he believed, and he knew that the King and many of the Court party were only waiting the turn of the tide to reassert the rights of royal prerogative, even though his Majesty was obligated to approve the acts of his current Ministry.

Rockingham, too, felt that the large majority for repeal was due to Mr. Pitt's inventiveness, and that there could readily be a reaction unless Mr. Pitt could be persuaded to take an active part in the Cabinet. On February 26, while Rockingham was seated in his coach outside the House of Lords, he saw Mr. Nuthall, Mr. Pitt's solicitor, and called him over for a conversation. Nuthall reported to Pitt that Rockingham said that "he wished to God, Mr. Pitt would fix upon some plan for carrying on administration, putting himself at the head of it." He asked Mr. Nuthall to convey this idea to Mr. Pitt, proposing that Pitt, Rockingham, Conway, and the Duke of Grafton meet in the near future on this subject.

Pitt, however, had been through that situation again and again. It was the custom of public men to ask his aid in forming a ministry. Then, when the time arrived for the King's approval, some hitch would occur. He had no desire to resume the duties of office. Events had proved that he could be very useful to the State in offering his views on major issues, without the necessity of carrying on the details of daily business. He advised Nuthall that he did not wish to give the Rockingham scheme any thought unless the Throne were concurring in it. He had, moreover, been misrepresented so frequently that he cautioned Nuthall that "ambassadorship is a troublesome trade"; and Nuthall replied, "I beg leave to add, dangerous too, and that I envy not the most honourable and expert professors in it . . . and as yesterday gave birth, I conclude this day has put a period, to my glory and achievements in this new occupation."

There remained in this historic struggle with respect to British policy on the Stamp Act only a few concluding matters. The Bill was taken through its final readings, and Mr. Pitt had the faint hope that he might be able in this last stage to obtain the withdrawal of the amendments which Conway had attached to the Bill, particularly the first resolution declaring the right of Parliament to govern all matters concerning the colonies. It was true that this compromise by Conway, later known as the Declaratory Act, had been helpful in obtaining the large majority for the repeal; but Mr. Pitt realized that the amendment would cause great irritation across the seas, would minimize the conciliatory value of the repeal.

On March 4, 1766, he was again in town to address the commons on the subject; and he made a final and unsuccessful appeal to the House, to omit this amendment.

"I doubt," he said, "if there would have been a minister to be found who would have dared to dip the royal ermines in the blood of the Americans for such an act. This country, like a fine horse, to quote an expression of Job, 'whose neck is clothed in thunder'—if you soothe and stroke it you may do anything; but if an unskilful rider takes it in hand, he will find that, though not vicious, yet it has tricks. I repeat it, I never had greater satisfaction than in the repeal of this Act."

George Grenville, pale, angry, entirely disapproving of the policy of his brother-in-law and kinsman, and embittered at Pitt's eminence, could not bear to be silent upon this allusion to the repeal. He rose to state a policy, which forecast the view that he and the Crown would stand for in the next dozen years, come what might.

"No, Sir, not dip the royal ermines in blood," Grenville retorted in his high querulous voice, "but I am one who declares, if the tax was to be laid again, I would do it; and I would do it now if I had to choose; since he [Pitt] has exerted all his eloquence so dangerously against it, it becomes doubly necessary. It is necessary from the increase of the debt in the late war; he knows I was against the enormous expense of the German war. Are all those boasted triumphs shrunk to the meanness of supporting such a measure as this!"

The issue burst upon his mind like a glowering firework taking the image of Pitt, hero of the crowds, incendiary, anathema to Grenville, torturous.

"I envy not the popularity," Grenville cried bitterly. "Let him have the bonfire; I rejoice in the hiss."

Then he added, doggedly and not without moral courage: "Was it to do again, I would do it."

CHAPTER XXXVII

A MINISTRY OF MADNESS

(July 28, 1766–October 14, 1768)

The triumphal march of the Whig Ministry in repealing the Stamp Act was followed by the equally popular repeal of the Cider Bill, but there the momentum stopped. Mr. Pitt had been both the inspiration and the organizer of the Whigs and when he retired to the country the Ministers fell back into their normal state of ineptitude.

The younger generation of Whigs lacked the tough-mindedness of their fathers, were indifferent to policies, and were mentally lazy. Rockingham, C o n w a y, Shelburne, and Grafton, though the principal officers of government, were all serving with varying degrees of reluctance, which was reflected in a general instability of Administration. Rockingham was a notoriously poor speaker who was totally unable to cope with Mansfield, Bute, or Bedford in the House of Peers. He was, further, conscious that the present Whig Ministry represented only a fraction of those who had composed the party in its greatest days, as the Bedford, Grenville, Hardwicke, and Fox factions were now detached from the party and playing their own political games. At every opportu-

A contemporary cartoon

LORD SHELBURNE

Pitt failed' to give him a glass of water.

458

nity he consulted the advice of Mr. Pitt, and when this was lacking he had an acute sense of insecurity.

Lord Shelburne was the most peculiar member of the group, combining an earnest diligence with a certain shiftiness of manner. In spite of his political ties with Mr. Pitt, the relationship there seemed to be on a basis of formality.

"I was in the most intimate political habits with him for ten years," Shelburne wrote of Pitt in his *Memoirs*, "the time that he was Secretary of State included . . . and necessarily was with him at all hours in town and country, without drinking a glass of water in his house or company." A striking comment on Shelburne, in view of the general hospitality which prevailed in the Pitt household. Shelburne, in short, was an efficient colleague, a man of vision and intelligence, and yet somehow deficient in stature.

The Duke of Grafton was the strangest figure of all to find in public life. He was steeped in a variety of vices and was infatuated with a mistress whom he took everywhere, notably to the opera when his wife, as well as the King and Queen, were present. Grafton had long associated with the Richmonds, the Pitts, and others of the Whig connection. While indifferent to public life for its own sake, he had the characteristic of some evil men who seek to redeem their own lives in the service of those whom they know to be their betters. Grafton, thus influenced, had attached himself to Mr. Pitt. He worshiped Pitt both for his mind and his character.

"Under him," Grafton said openly in the House of Lords, "I should be willing to serve in any capacity, not only as a general officer, but as a pioneer; and for him I would take up the spade and mattock."

By far the most capable man in the Ministry was General Conway. He, however, had chosen the Army as his career and preferred it. He conducted his office in a cold, honest, orderly fashion which was inadequate to the crises of the day. When Conway was taken ill in the spring of 1766, there were, accordingly, few friends to lament his absence, yet there remained no one in active life competent to take his place.

The Whigs at once began a desperate drive to get Mr. Pitt to take the leadership of the party and return to office as first Minister. When he declined, the Duke of Grafton retired from his office as Secretary of State, and Richmond took his place. In this very weak Ministry the King hoped to find subservience to his ideas, but Richmond had not forgotten the slight put upon the Lennox family and treated his Majesty with temper and effrontery. Poor George was in a dreadful position. Ever since his beloved Bute had resigned, he had suffered a succession of hard-headed truculent Ministers who seemed painfully unaware of the "Idea of a Patriot King." Even George Grenville, who shared the royal views in many respects had been dull, self-seeking, and lacking in deference. The King finally made up his mind to take the advice which came to him from all quarters to issue a call to Mr. Pitt and to accept whatever terms he might demand.

Pitt had repeatedly refused to take office, sometimes because of ill health and sometimes because he was asked merely to be a figurehead for the policies of others. Following his exertions on the Stamp Act he had been living at Hayes in a state of great pain and distress due to overwork. He had little desire to resume the burdens of office, but the invitation of the King, giving him a complete free hand, was too tempting to refuse, and on July 11, 1766, he rushed up to London to discuss the preliminary arrangements with his Majesty. Pitt was all aglow with an idea, which was acceptable to the Throne, an idea which proved to be the greatest mistake of Mr. Pitt's career.

For a long time Pitt had had the notion of forming a coalition cabinet which would include the best minds of the kingdom regardless of party. Such a system, in his opinion, would relieve the chief Minister of the burdens of party management, making unnecessary the bickerings, the jobbing of places, all of the backstairs work usually required to keep an organization together. A worthy first Minister interested in "measures not men," supported by the best minds from all factions, was an attractive conception; but it demonstrated Mr. Pitt's lack of understanding of the machinery of government. The King, who had smarted under the rule of various parties, naturally applauded the idea. Under a strong ministry, the Pitt plan would make the policies of the country and control the Throne, but under a weak ministry, there would be no effective party organization to oppose the King. The King would then actually, as well as nominally, appoint "his Ministers" and the program of "the Patriot King" would then be fully established. Mr. Pitt was personally obnoxious to his Majesty, but he was well along in years and in conspicuous ill health.

Pitt set to work to arrange his Ministry, as his own health would permit. He felt unable to undertake the strenuous work of leader of the House of Commons where he would nominate someone to carry out his policies; and he looked to Temple, who had also been summoned by the King, to be the leader in the Lords. Pitt, himself, planned to take some sinecure in the Cabinet and act as the general director of policy and administration.

Temple, however, was still jealous of Mr. Pitt's pre-eminence and had, in fact, fatuously imagined that the King had summoned him in order to offer him the leading part. He declined firmly to take any place in the Cabinet, and wrote to Hester regarding "the indignation with which I received the proposition of being stuck into a Ministry as a great cypher at the head of the Treasury, surrounded with other cyphers, all named by Mr. Pitt."

Following Temple's refusal, Pitt decided to take the leadership in the Lords himself, making it necessary for him to be elevated to the peerage. The sinecure which he had determined upon was that of Lord Privy Seal. Though these arrangements were known to the King, the details of the formation of the Ministry were kept a secret by Pitt. The Duke of Grafton expected that Mr. Pitt would take the office of First Lord of the Treasury, and Grafton himself accepted that portfolio only after he had strongly urged Mr. Pitt to take it. When the various new Ministers assembled on July 28 to take office, they were uncertain of what part Mr. Pitt would play, though most of them assumed that he would be one of the Secretaries of State, and that he would be active in the Commons. When the Ministry was finally put together it included the following:

Lord Chancellor—Charles Pratt, Lord Camden.
First Lord of the Treasury—Duke of Grafton.
Chancellor of. the Exchequer—Charles Townshend (nephew of Newcastle).
Secretaries of State—H. S. Conway and Lord Shelburne.
Lord President of the Council—Charles Henley, Earl of Northington.
President of the Board of Trade—Lord Hillsborough.
Paymasters General—Lord North and George Cooke, Esq.
Secretary at War—Viscount Barrington.
First Lord of the Admiralty—Lord Egmont.*
Master General of Ordnance—Marquis of Granby.
Vice Treasurers of Ireland—James Grenville and Isaac Barré.
Treasurer of the Navy—Viscount Howe.
Lord Lieutenant of Ireland—Earl of Bristol.**
Lord Privy Seal—William Pitt, the Earl of Chatham.

This conglomeration of individuals fell considerably short of being "the best minds," as is often the case in a coalition cabinet. The major posts were filled by Whigs who reflected Mr. Pitt's policies, while the Rockingham Whigs were given almost no consideration except for the retention of Conway. Newcastle, who had returned briefly to Cabinet rank as Lord Privy Seal was finally eliminated from public office, never to return. Hillsborough represented the Bedford group. Lord North, though a relation of Newcastle's, was essentially a King's man. Minor offices were given to some of the Bute connection. The public was dazed at seeing this strange assortment of incompatibles. Edmund Burke described the Cabinet as:

Such a diversified piece of mosaic; such a tesselated pavement without cement; here a bit of black stone, and there a bit of white; patriots and courtiers, king's friends and republicans;

* Not to be confused with the late Lord Egremont.
** Former Ambassador to Spain, and brother-in-law of Elizabeth Chudleigh, whose husband later succeeded to the title.

Whigs and Tories; treacherous friends and open enemies;—that it was, indeed, a very curious show;—the colleagues . . . stared at each other, and were obliged to ask, "Sir, your name?—Sir, you have the advantage of me.—Mr. Such-a-one—I beg a thousand pardons—"

The sensation of the day, however, to both the Cabinet and the public at large was Mr. Pitt's acceptancy of an earldom. To many of his followers this was a betrayal of trust, as they considered that the Great Commoner had sold his principles for a title. This attitude was a misconception of Pitt's view of liberty. He was that rare type of democrat who believes in justice for the rich as well as for the poor. To him both a Duke and a Commoner had the rights of an English freeman. He had said only a few weeks before in the House of Commons, "I am no overheated enthusiastic leveller." It is unlikely that he craved the privileges of an Earl which entitled him to call t h e King "cousin" and conveyed the doubtful blessing of being permitted to kiss his Majesty's

A contemporary cartoon
COLONEL BARRÉ
He helped Pitt in the Commons and Cabinet.

cheek. The one satisfaction which inhered particularly in the situation was the fact that it placed Pitt on an equal status with Temple, so that he was no longer dependent upon family connection for a dominating place in the House of Peers.

Mr. Pitt's real motives, of course, can only be a matter of conjecture. Maybe the title did dazzle him. Certainly he could not be blind to the advantage which it might mean for his children. His choice of the name Chatham was from one of the hereditary Villiers properties which had been at one time in his family. The Dukedom of Buckingham was directly in the Villiers line, and it was rumored that the King intended in time to elevate Mr. Pitt to be Duke of Kent. Pitt might bully Newcastle, Devonshire and Grafton, and yet to become a duke himself might have had its fascinations. In any event, he doubtless felt it his right as an English freeman to accept whatever title might be offered to him as a mark of honor.

Financially, Mr. Pitt had made a very poor deal for himself, as the office of Lord Privy Seal yielded only £3,000 per annum, less taxes; and the fees which he had to pay for receiving his office and for his title of nobility amounted to £915. The fact remained that in taking a peerage the Great Commoner incurred almost as much criticism as had greeted his acceptance of a pension. Again, this feeling was fomented by pamphleteers, and Temple was particularly active in commissioning and circulating pamphlets which ridiculed the pretensions and principles of his brother-in-law. Whatever Pitt's reasons might be, the common people generally did not like it. An old soldier wrote to him from a town in Ireland: "My Lord, I will be plain and honest with you and tell you that many people here are displeased with your acceptance of a peerage, as you could not be more honourable than you were. But in all company I am in, I always insist on it you are still the Pitt in your affection to your country, the good and welfare of the people, trade, etc. etc."

The King was thoroughly pleased with the turn of affairs and wrote Mr. Pitt a letter on July 29 which hinted strongly that his Majesty expected to be paid properly for value received:

Richmond Lodge, July 29, 1766
25 m. past five, P.M.

MR. PITT,

I have signed this day the warrant for creating you an Earl, and shall with pleasure receive you in that capacity to-morrow, as well as entrust you with my privy seal; as I know the Earl of Chatham will zealously give his aid towards destroying all party distinctions, and restoring that subordination to Government, which can alone preserve that inestimable blessing, Liberty, from degenerating into Licentiousness.

GEORGE R.

"Subordination to Government." Mr. Pitt may well have felt a sense of foreboding at that ominous phrase, for to George III, "Government" meant the Throne. Pitt had, however, managed the King before this, and at present the new Lord Privy Seal had more immediate problems in the attempt to organize and direct his Ministry.

The duties of Lord Privy Seal required Pitt to attend the office only once a week to witness the affixing of the Royal Seal to charters and other state documents. It was not the lightness of these duties which disturbed Chatham's Ministerial colleagues, but the fact that he had retired from the Commons which had been the theater of his greatest influence. Leadership there was now shared between Conway and Charles Townshend, a combination which was foredoomed to be unsatisfactory. Townshend was a brilliant speaker, a wit and a cynic, whose immediate purpose was to shelve Conway. From the beginning, therefore, there were divided councils in the Commons.

Despite all of these handicaps the Chatham Ministry began in a whirlwind of energy and promise. On August 4, 1766, Chatham renewed his efforts to form an alliance with Prussia and other Northern powers as a counter-balance against the Bourbon Family Compact. He simultaneously made demands upon France and Spain for unsettled payments due under the terms of the Peace of Paris.

On American affairs his new Ministry began with far greater prestige in the New World than it enjoyed at home. The repeal of the Stamp Act had been received with enthusiasm throughout the colonies, and Mr. Pitt was the hero of the occasion. His picture was displayed in thousands of homes throughout the colonies, statuettes of him decorated many an American parlor, and South Carolina

voted a statue to him, to be set up in the city of Charleston,
bearing the inscription:

IN GRATEFUL MEMORY
OF HIS SERVICES TO HIS COUNTRY IN GENERAL
AND TO AMERICA IN PARTICULAR
THE COMMONS HOUSE OF ASSEMBLY
OF SOUTH CAROLINA
UNANIMOUSLY VOTED
THIS STATUE
OF
THE RIGHT HONORABLE WILLIAM PITT
WHO
GLORIOUSLY EXERTED HIMSELF
IN DEFENDING THE FREEDOM OF AMERICANS
THE TRUE SONS OF ENGLAND
BY PROMOTING A REPEAL
OF THE STAMP ACT
IN THE YEAR 1766
TIME
SHALL SOONER DESTROY
THIS MARK OF THEIR ESTEEM
THAN
ERASE FROM THEIR MINDS
THEIR JUST SENSE
OF HIS PATRIOTIC VIRTUES

There was, however, legislation on the books which was
due to jeopardize these happy relationships. The Declaratory Act, that resolution of Conway's which Pitt had opposed, had not yet become a point of issue; but there was
new resistance to the Mutiny Bill, which the Grenville Ministry had passed almost unnoticed in March, 1765. This required the provinces to provide barracks and certain specified
supplies for the regular troops, and also permitted the
billeting of troops in private families. Though the provinces had usually furnished the supplies voluntarily, they
resented the requirement being made a matter of law, and
the clause on billeting they regarded as an invasion of the
Englishman's home. These were principles which would

have been a war cry to Mr. Pitt previously and which won his support at a later time.

Now, however, when the province of New York refused to vote funds for the supplies, Chatham took the astounding step of instructing Shelburne to inform the Governor of New York that the materials must be supplied and the quartering of troops properly conducted. Shelburne carried out his mission with as much tact as possible, knowing that Chatham at any moment might flare up again as an American advocate. To Shelburne and others of the Cabinet the whilom Mr. Pitt as Earl of Chatham had become on most matters unpredictable and incomprehensible.

The fact was, as soon became apparent, that Pitt's mind and physique were cracking under the strain of office, or perhaps of conscience. He was aloof, dazed, obscure, and possessed by delusions of grandeur. At the King's levee, on August 7, 1766, he retired to a corner of the room and wrote out instructions on little pieces of paper, giving them to members of the Cabinet as though they were errands of the day for delivery boys.

Toward the end of the month, however, he started a new issue, destined to become one of the great reforms in English history. This was the investigation of the East India Company, which had developed into one of the scandals of the age. The Company's profits were enormous, it had enjoyed enormous growth during the late war, thanks to Government support, but its revenues went chiefly into the pockets of the directors and the stockholders. It will be recalled that Clive and Mr. Pitt had corresponded on this subject previously, without reaching a conclusion. Now Chatham demanded that the affairs of the Company be investigated by Parliament. In this he had the support of Alderman Beckford and Clive, but here again he was vague, and failed to take the Cabinet into his confidence.

The new Chatham ministry, in fact, was conducted in a vastly different atmosphere from the glorious Administration of Mr. Pitt. There was no house on St. James Square, no appearance of the familiar livery, no sedan chair with the huge boot for the gouty leg, and no frequent view of the

great man on public occasions. Chatham had become virtually a hermit. He had rented quarters at North End
House on Hampstead Heath, and lived an existence of almost complete seclusion, punctuated by sudden violent
declarations on one policy or another. By the end of August
he had become seriously ill and his Ministers, lacking in
direction, representing no party, and afraid to displease the
erratic Chatham, continued business as best they could in a
state of confusion.

It was an era of public discontent. Trade had not yet
recovered from the differences with America and there was
the threat of famine due to the failure of the grain crop.
On this issue Chatham chose to break his silence, and on
September 24, 1766, he sent the following note to Townshend:

> Lord Chatham desires to add here, that his mortification is
> extreme at not being able to go to council to-day, having nothing
> so much at heart as to give his opinion *publicly* for the embargo
> upon corn, which he has strenuously advised in *private;* and that
> he should think himself guilty of neglecting the public safety, if
> any thing could shake his resolution about this measure.

Parliament was not in session and the only way to accomplish the purpose was, as Chatham knew, to declare an
embargo on the authority of the King's prerogative, and so
it was done. Yet Mr. Pitt had been a stanch opponent of
the use of prerogative except under the most crucial circumstances. If Parliament had been in session the difficulty
could have been avoided, and a delay of two months until
the Commons re-convened would have avoided the sacrifice
of the principle. Even Chatham's most devoted friends
were nonplussed.

"I much doubt whether it will reduce the price or quiet
the badness of the times," his beloved and loving Jemmy
Grenville wrote to Hester. "There seems to be something
in the present temper I do not comprehend."

His Majesty also was unable to understand the vagaries
of his chief Minister. Although the King himself was
subject to spells of illness and insanity, he placed no credence

William Pitt receiving the gratitude of America, as symbolized by an Indian child. This Chelsea statuette was a favorite ornament in American homes before and during the Revolution.

Courtesy of R. T. H. Halsey

FROM A MEZZOTINT OF THE PAINTING BY PEALE

"Worthy of Liberty, Mr. Pitt Scorns to Invade the Liberties of Other People." Like the Chelsea statuette, this illustration of Pitt was a great favorite in Colonial American homes.

in Chatham's claims of sickness and believed that his ailments were turned off and on for purposes of political convenience. The partnership of King and Minister was already beginning to wear a little thin, and his Majesty was extremely annoyed at Chatham's failure to attend personally on the Throne, and at receiving evasive replies to the royal messages in the handwriting of Lady Chatham.

The fact was that the coalition idea had failed. Chatham knew it and was in despair. The King's letter of July 29 had been the first betrayal, and every subsequent letter had indicated that George III assumed that Chatham would be his tool, not knowing or not caring that Pitt and the principle of Whig Constitutionality were inseparable. In October, when Chatham took a trip to Bath, he encountered Horace Walpole and conversed with him for two hours, deploring the general situation and appearing to be homesick for his days as Whig leader. He was discouraged at the attitude of Frederick of Prussia. No progress was being made on the Northern Alliance, for Frederick was wary of the frequent change of ministries in England, and was occupied with a scheme for the division of Poland. On domestic matters Pitt made complimentary remarks regarding Conway, commending him particularly for his Whiggism.

"And am not I, Lord Camden, and Lord Shelburne, Whigs?" Chatham added.

He then came to the subject of the King, saying that his Majesty was very gracious to him, that he believed the King was in earnest—and then while still on the subject of his Majesty, Chatham added the surprising comment, "If I was in possession of the citadel of Lisle, and was told there was a mine under my feet, I would say, 'I do not believe it.'" On which Walpole observed, in his *Memoirs*: "His opinion of his Majesty's sincerity was therefore exactly the same as mine."

In the first three months of his Ministry, Chatham had not been well enough to appear in the House of Lords, but on November 11 he made his maiden speech there in defense of his embargo, asserting, with some justice, that this action was in a different category from the personal exercise of authority by the King.

" 'If there comes to be a question between the executive power and the people about a thing claimed as prerogative,' " he said, quoting from Locke, " 'the exercise of such a prerogative to the good or hurt of the people will easily decide that question.' "

His position was at least plausible, but he did not speak with the old-time fire, and the new audience was less susceptible to oratory. Mansfield took delight in being able to speak this time on the side of the Constitution and to remind Lord Chatham of his supposed devotion to it, and William Pitt, Earl of Chatham, for once was ineffective before his old-time rival.

Before long, new difficulties occurred in the Administration. Chatham demanded the resignation of Lord Edgecumbe as Treasurer of the Household. Edgecumbe had been unsympathetic to the Pitt regime in the past, and the Minister did not wish to have an enemy so close to the Throne. The action stirred up much protest, however, and eight men in leading Government offices resigned, including Chatham's old friends, Saunders and Keppel. There was trouble, also, in the House of Commons, for when Beckford moved to investigate the East India Company, Townshend, who was speculating in the stocks, voted on the other side. The most painful rebuff of all, however, occurred in the House of Lords on December 10, 1766, when Chatham appeared to speak in favor of a bill indemnifying those who had suffered financially from the embargo on grain. In the course of these remarks Chatham said that when the people should condemn him he would tremble, but that he "would set his face against the proudest connection in this country."

Richmond jumped to the conclusion that this was aimed at the Rockingham Whigs, and replied that "he hoped the nobility would not be browbeaten by an insolent Minister."

When the Chair called Richmond to order he apologized by saying that he was aware that "the truth should not be spoken at all times and in all places."

Chatham challenged the Duke to give an instance in which he had treated any man with insolence. If the instance was not produced, he said, the charge of insolence would lie on his Grace.

Richmond replied that he could not give the instance without betraying private conversations, but he wished to congratulate Lord Chatham on his new connections, whereupon he looked directly at Lord Bute.

Chatham, embarrassed for the second time, was overwhelmed at this attack from Richmond, who had always been one of his most loyal and devoted friends. If his scheme of a coalition Cabinet placed him in the position of being a friend of Bute and of alienating him from his most beloved associates, his career had indeed come to a heart-rending conclusion. He returned home from the Lords, sick at heart, measurably worse both in mind and body.

Though Parliament was again in session, Chatham was unable to take any further part either in Cabinet meetings or in the Lords. He went down to Bath at Christmas time and remained ill there for many weeks, trying to give some direction to Government by occasional letters to his colleagues which revealed the vagaries of a sick mind,—and were largely disregarded.

In this state of affairs, Charles Townshend thought that he saw the opportunity to put on the toga. On January 14, 1767, he spoke in the Commons against the inquiry into the East India Company, saying that he knew that the Company would soon make an advantageous proposal, and hence there was no need for an investigation. He attacked Chatham's American views, approved of the Stamp Act, and pledged himself "to find a revenue in America."

On March 2, 1767, Chatham was able to drag himself up to London, where his first task was to try to settle affairs with Mr. Townshend. He offered Townshend's job at the Exchequer to Lord North, but the latter refused. The only other man in the Ministry who was competent to fill the office was Sir Gilbert Elliot, Treasurer of the Chambers; but Elliot had wrecked his personal finances by his lavish expenditures for the procurement of young girls, and his consequent ill-reputation did not commend him to Chatham, to the other Ministers, or to the nation. Since Elliot had ruined himself and North refused promotion, Chatham was helpless, as he could not re-align the Ministry without a competent man in the Exchequer.

Again beaten down by disappointment and illness, Chatham took to his bed, and Townshend had a field day. Elated by the fact that Chatham had been unable to oust him, Townshend now advanced a series of measures affecting America, vigorously abetted by Elliot, and by Rigby representing the Bedford faction. One proposal was a colonial tax on tea. Townshend's presentation of the subject was most adroit, alleging that it was an external and not an internal tax, saying that it would gratify the colonists because it was laid on British manufactures, and pointing out that it was trivial. He also carried his bill to establish an American Customs Board to be established at Boston for the further restriction of smuggling; and, on June 15, 1767, in spite of earlier opposition by the Cabinet, he obtained the suspension of the legislative power of the New York Assembly, pending compliance with the Mutiny Act.

Meanwhile, Chatham had become so ill that he was unable to understand what was taking place. On May 31, 1767, the Duke of Grafton had driven out to North End desperately trying to get some hint of instruction, some guidance as to a line of action. Grafton, as First Lord of the Treasury, was nominally in superior authority to Townshend and was sincerely anxious to carry on the Ministry along Chatham principles, if he could find out what they were. His report revealed conditions at North End to be far worse than the Ministry or the public imagined:

> Though I expected to find Lord Chatham very ill indeed, his situation was different from what I had imagined; his nerves and spirits were affected to a dreadful degree, and the sight of his great mind bowed down, and thus weakened by disorder, would have filled me with grief and concern, even if I had not

long borne a sincere attachment to his person and character. . . .
The interview was truly painful.

At this news the King, who was still skeptical regarding
Chatham's illness, made six different attempts to stir some
reply from his chief Minister, repeatedly urging Chatham
to return "to break up faction," but all of his Majesty's
efforts were in vain. The King had been so pleased, however, at his vacation from dictation by ministers that he
would not think of making a change in Government. If
Chatham would not help him to end the party system, it was
at least an advantage to have an inactive chief Minister;
and, furthermore, in spite of all that had taken place, the
name of William Pitt, Lord Chatham, still had a luster
with the public which the King could employ to advantage.

The achievements of the Chatham Ministry had been
pitiful compared with the great expectations. Little had
been accomplished in foreign affairs, new irritations had
been added to American relationships, and the only constructive move was a bill, finally passed by Parliament,
limiting the profit of the East India Company to ten
percent.

At North End House, Chatham continued in his state
of depression. He lived by himself in a little room on the
top floor, refusing to speak to anyone, frantic if anyone
came near him. A hole was cut in the doorway of the room
and a shelf made so that food could be passed in and out
without the intrusion of a servant. He would go without
eating for hours, and then suddenly become ravenously
hungry, rapping on the floor with his crutch as a signal of
demanding food. To meet this situation, chickens were
kept roasting at all hours of the day and night, and attendants were constantly within call, even though not permitted in his presence. On rare occasions he expressed a
desire to take a drive and was allowed to go out in the
company of a servant.

In August, 1767, Hester obtained full power of attorney
to conduct Chatham's affairs. This was fortunate, because
his mania now took a new turn. He got the impression

that the whole trouble with him was his living quarters. Though he confined himself to one room at North End, he conceived the idea that the place would be comfortable only if it had an addition of thirty-four rooms, and he persuaded the landlord to consent to the scheme. Before this was carried out, he became obsessed with the thought that he would be healthy again if he could but live at Hayes, and he urged Hester to repurchase the place. Thomas Walpole was at first unwilling to sell, but Hester pleaded with him that Chatham's life might depend on it; and Walpole finally obliged her graciously, while making a profit of more than £5,000 in the transaction.

In September, 1767, fortunately for the Ministry, Charles Townshend unexpectedly died. The Duke of Grafton at the Treasury was recognized as the head of the Ministry in the absence of Chatham. Lord North finally agreed to take Townshend's place at the Exchequer, as his refusal to fill that vacancy would have probably caused the appointment of a new Ministry and the loss of his job at the Pay Office. A new office, a Third Secretary of State, was established to deal with the affairs of the American colonies. Here again the arrangements were satisfying to the King. Grafton was not a forceful leader, North was pliable, and by placing the colonies in a separate department they were removed from Shelburne's jurisdiction where they had formerly belonged. Shelburne had strong views on colonial affairs, corresponding to those of Mr. Pitt in his prime; but Hillsborough, who was now transferred to the Third Secretaryship, was a man lacking in ideas and knowing how to take orders.

Toward the end of 1767 Dr. Addington, Chatham's physician, began to be more optimistic about his condition. The poisoned condition of the patient's blood over a period of years had been relieved by fits of gout which seemed to bring about concentration of the poison, thereby relieving his system. Dr. Addington also believed in the therapeutic value of fever.

"I flatter myself his Lordship will have a salutary fit of gout in the middle of January or sooner," he wrote to

Hester. "It is not expected that these posthumous editions of gout will be violent, or of long continuance; but I believe my Lord will have the benefit of them at proper intervals while he has fever; and that he will and ought to have fever, till the whole poison of his disease is expelled from his constitution."

The doctor's predictions came true toward the end of December, by which time Chatham had moved to Hayes, but the patient then had a bad relapse though his mental condition was improved. Hester, however, insisted that he should not be bothered with affairs of state. The Ministry were eager to respect her wishes in this regard, but there was one incident which proved to be unavoidable.

Norborne Berkeley, Lord Botetourt, a promoter of corporations, a Tory, and an active member of the Court set, desired a charter to establish a brass foundry under the authority of the Privy Seal. During Chatham's illness the affairs of his office of Lord Privy Seal had become badly scrambled, and there were scores of public documents awaiting the technical approval of the Seal. Botetourt needed the prestige of the Seal for the success of his company and was unwilling to suffer a delay. Various caveats had been entered against his petition and he demanded to have his case heard. The Ministry were inclined to brush him aside, but he threatened to enter a complaint against Chatham in the House of Lords.

The only solution to avoid such a crisis was to put the Great Seal into commission, though the Ministry feared that Chatham would take this proposal as a hint to resign. To the relief of his colleagues, however, he understood the situation, and agreed with Botetourt's right to be heard. The incident brought joy to Hester, Chatham's friends, and the Ministry, because it showed that his mind was clearing, that he could comprehend a situation and deal with it rationally and without excitement.

In April, 1768, a new Parliament was elected; and the Crown spent money in excess of all ordinary times to secure a majority. Various East India nabobs, lush with money and socially ambitious, came into the market, bidding for

Parliamentary seats. Moreover, the public was favorable to change, and John Wilkes, returned from abroad, was elected to Parliament from Middlesex,—and was thrown into jail again on the old libel charge. If Chatham had been active, he could have prevented the Throne from again making Wilkes a hero by silly and unwarranted persecution, which only served to bring authority into contempt. Lady Sarah Lennox (now Lady Sarah Bunbury) observed in a letter to her cousin Susan:

> Are you still politician enough to be eager about the fuss they make with Mr. Wilkes? If you are, I wish you would write an anonymous letter to His M. to advise him not to sculk in his den like—I don't know what, for I must not say what a *pauvre animal* I think him; but it really provokes me to see him so bullied; but you know *we* always prophesied he would never make a figure when once he ceased being in our good graces, & *we* never were mistaken certainly. Do you know that he has made his brat (the future George IV) the proudest little imp you ever saw, just like himself.

Another affront to Chatham loyalties was the treatment which the Throne accorded to General Amherst. Amherst had been given certain military appointments in reward for his services in the New World and had also been made absentee Governor of Virginia, on his express stipulation that he would not be called upon to reside there. Compared to the rewards of Marlborough and many other military heroes this compensation was negligible. Amherst had made no complaint regarding this modest treatment, and Chatham, who was out of office when the General returned from the New World in 1763, was not in a position to provide a more ample recognition.

Now, however, it appeared that all persons with American sympathies were to be proscribed. Amherst was known to have numerous friends in the colonies and to be carrying on correspondence with them. On his return, he had refused an offer of a seat in Parliament and had said that he was not interested in politics. Such a man was of no political use to the Crown. Accordingly, the General was notified one day, without prior warning, that he was relieved of the Governorship of Virginia and that Norborne Berkeley, Lord Botetourt, had been named in his place.

The third evidence of the scuttling of Mr. Pitt's ideas was the treatment which had been accorded Shelburne. The American business had been taken out of his hands, and, further, France had been allowed to annex Corsica without protest by England. Shelburne had urged the Cabinet to resist this action, had been voted down, and had forthwith resigned.

The Wilkes, Amherst, and Shelburne incidents were but symptoms of the deplorable state into which Government had fallen. The King had the opportunity at this time, as never before or after, to be a great popular monarch leading his people in the paths of their natural destiny while their chief Minister was critically ill. Instead, George III, who had little gift for kingship, kept encroaching on the Constitution by petty acts and reprisals with which the helpless Grafton seemed unable to cope. Criticism and apprehension were widespread. The famous letters of *Junius* were appearing in periodical form and were boldly exposing the errors of Government. They harped on the ingratitude to General Amherst, until Lord Albemarle (whose brother, Admiral Keppel, had resigned from the Chatham Ministry) wrote to Chatham urging a meeting of Whigs—forget the coalition!—on the Amherst issue. *Junius* also blistered the hide of Grafton on his sex life. Grafton, who was trying to conduct the Ministry somehow in his blundering, inept way, became desperate at these personal attacks, and pleaded to Hester that he must see her at least "for one quarter of an hour."

Grafton hoped, in talking with Lady Chatham, to soften the impression that the errors of his Ministry might have made in that household, but his visit had the opposite result. The recital of events by the First Lord of the Treasury served to emphasize the lamentable errors of the Throne and the Cabinet. Chatham was now well enough to be given some account of public affairs through Hester, and he realized that the Ministry was being conducted in a way which could not have his approval.

The Grafton interview was on October 9, 1768. On the 12th, Chatham addressed Grafton in Hester's handwriting:

> Though unable to enter into business, give me leave, my Lord, not to conclude without expressing to your Grace that I cannot enough lament the removal of Sir Jeffrey Amherst and that of Lord Shelburne. I will add no more to your Grace's present trouble, than to desire your Grace will accept my sincerest acknowledgments of all your goodness to me.

The letter also requested the royal permission to resign the Privy Seal.

The King replied, "I think I have a right *to insist* on your remaining in my service; for I with pleasure look forward to the time of your recovery, when I may have your assistance in resisting the torrent of Factions this country so much labours under."

To insist! No wonder Lord Chatham had had his fill of a coalition Ministry. This was his reward for attempting to oblige the King. To insist! Shades of Charles I and James II! Shades of Hardwicke instructing the rebellious George II in English Constitutionality! To insist that William Pitt, the Great Commoner, Earl of Chatham, remain in his Majesty's service. On October 14, Chatham wrote his formal resignation to the Throne, and when he appeared again in the public arena it was under the Whig banner.

CHAPTER XXXVIII

THE SCARECROW OF VIOLENCE

With Chatham out of the Government, the Grafton Ministry succumbed entirely to the King's wishes and used their majority in Parliament for the most flagrant abuses of the Constitution. His Majesty and the Court party, freed from the fear of Chatham, pressed every opportunity to exalt the power of the Throne, and punish any resistance.

Throughout the spring of 1769 the Wilkes case came to the forefront again. This troublesome gentleman was again elected to Parliament from Middlesex and was promptly expelled. At each new election the same procedure was followed, until, on the fourth election of Wilkes by Middlesex, Parliament declared that his opponent, Colonel Luttrell, was the duly chosen member. This arbitrary action by the Commons aroused great public resentment, particularly against the King, who was known to have dictated the policy.

The public believed, and rightly, that the unjust treatment of Wilkes by the authorities was due largely to his stand for free speech. In the colonies there were now numerous "45" clubs, so-called in honor of the No. 45 issue of *The North Briton*. In Pennsylvania a town was named Wilkes-Barré, in tribute to Wilkes and Col. Isaac Barré. The latter had remained loyal to Pitt and had become a steadfast supporter of the American cause.

The Ministry, while fostering the policy against Wilkes, was also causing more friction in America. Massachusetts had instituted a boycott of British goods and had circularized the other colonies to join with them. Lord Hillsborough, in reprisal, dissolved the Assembly of the province and promised the same action against any other colony which joined with Massachusetts. That the colonists were

479

hot-headed and unjust in their conduct was generally conceded, even by their advocates, but the harsh repressive
measures of the Court kept making conciliation more difficult. Pressure was brought upon the Cabinet by the British
merchants and manufacturers who were continuing to suffer
from this situation; and in May, 1769, Hillsborough finally
made the gesture of repealing all the Townshend taxes
except the one on tea. Actually this helped but little, as
the tea tax was the chief point at issue.

While the Ministry was moving along in its fool's paradise, unconcerned with trouble ahead, the Earl of Chatham
was gradually recovering his health. On July 6, to the
astonishment of everyone, he appeared at the King's levee,
looking better than in some years with more meat on his
tall frame than ever before. Always of commanding height,
his added weight gave an imposing appearance. Everyone
stared at him as if seeing a man risen from the dead. Chatham bowed coldly to Bedford and Grafton, but warmly
embraced the Marquis of Granby. Granby, at the head
of the Army, had voted with the rest of the Cabinet for
measures which Chatham disapproved, but the former Minister always had a soft spot in his heart for the military,
and, besides, he had plans for that gentleman which would
have made him tremble.

No one was more concerned over this appearance of
Chatham than his royal Majesty. The ex-minister indulged in his usual deep obeisances of Oriental respect, but
George III had learned not to take these too seriously.
The King was, moreover, devoured with curiosity to know
the cause of this unexpected appearance, and invited Chatham to remain after the levee for a private audience.

When the two were alone, Chatham, in words of suave
but insistent courtesy, proceeded to tell George III that
everything he was doing was wrong. Chatham held the
King responsible for the Wilkes case, for American affairs,
and for the failure to clean up the situation in India. He
said that unless the Throne changed its policies he might
have to discuss these matters in Parliament, not from any
ambition for office—which his health would not permit him

to take—but because the Throne had violated and was violating the Constitution. He did not cite, nor was it necessary for him to mention, the name of Charles I to under-
score the implications of his remarks.

The King listened to these observations in baleful silence,
reflecting on all that he had suffered from this obnoxious
subject, who could have been so useful in establishing kingship as his Majesty conceived it. When Chatham had finished and perceived by the silence that he had made no
favorable impression, he withdrew, never again to be afforded an interview.

Chatham had been a friend of the King in the latter's
younger days. It will be recalled that Mr. Pitt had been
on the official staff of George III's father and had lived in
the Prince's household even before the days of Lord Bute.
He was credited with assisting George in the affair of
Hannah Lightfoot, he knew the handicaps of the King's
early training, and he was inclined to blame the Bute influence for the mistakes of the Throne. He had come at
last thoroughly to mistrust George III in the early days of
the Chatham Ministry; but he had made his final attempt
to induce the King to see the errors of his ways. He had
hoped to convince the morose young monarch that a king
could not possibly expect to achieve his ambition of ruling
over a loving and united people except on terms consistent
with English history. Now that this effort had failed,
Chatham determined to concentrate his efforts on reorganization of the Whig party, which he had all too successfully
broken up in his recent ill-fated Ministry, and to direct it to
check the King and restore Constitutional procedure.

The first opportunity to rally the Whig forces came on
January 9, 1770, at the opening of Parliament. The state
of public affairs was such as might have frightened a less
obdurate monarch. Thousands of unemployed weavers who
were jobless because of the American embargo thronged
the streets outside of the Houses of Parliament, as the
session convened. The King was greeted with hisses and
jeers, and Lord Mansfield's carriage was stoned. When
the doors of the Lords were thrown open the mob pressed

forward, and commoners jostled with Peers in the rush to witness the proceedings.

One of the onlookers, a Mr. Cradock, was shoved along into the main chamber and in bewilderment seated himself on one of the earl's benches next to Lord Chatham. Chatham made no move to disturb the visitor, for from now on, William Pitt, Earl of Chatham, was going to appeal to the public, over the heads of the Parliament, and it was a stroke of good fortune to have this sample of public opinion right at hand.

The King's address on the state of the nation, in general avoided the issues of the day. It dismissed American matters, by referring to the colonies' "unwarrantable" conduct, and it dealt at length with the innocuous topic of the spread of distemper among the cattle.

After the address had been moved and seconded, Chatham arose, amid a stir of interest. It was his first address since the day when he had endured the rebuff from Richmond. All felt that his first appearance in the Lords had been a failure, that his last Ministry had been pitiful; but rumor said that his renewed health had made him a new man; and not a few had heard of his defiance of the King.

He began by saying that at his time of life he might have been excused, perhaps, to continue in retirement; but the alarming state of the nation had forced him to come forward once more and execute the duty which he owed to God, to his Sovereign, and to his country. He felt it the duty of the Lords to lay before the Sovereign the discontent which universally prevailed among the subjects and the true causes of the unhappy state of affairs.

He observed sarcastically that he had heard with great concern of the distemper among the cattle and he was glad to give his approval to the prudent measures for putting a stop to so dreadful a calamity, but there were other matters on which he wished to speak. With respect to America he said:

"Let us be cautious how we invade the liberties of our fellow-subjects, however mean, however remote; for be assured, my Lords, that in whatever part of the Empire you suffer slavery to be established, whether it be in America or in Ireland, or here at home, you will find it a disease which spreads by contact, and soon reaches from the extremities to the heart. The man who has lost his own freedom, becomes from that moment an instrument in the hands of an ambitious prince, to destroy the freedom of others.

"These reflections, my Lords, are but too applicable to our present situation. The liberty of the subject is invaded, not only in provinces, but here at home. The English people are loud in their complaints: they proclaim with one voice the injuries they have received; they demand redress, and depend upon it, my Lords, that one way or other they will have redress. They will never return to a state of tranquillity until they are redressed; nor ought they; for in my judgment, my Lords, and I speak it boldly, it were better for them to perish in a glorious contention for their rights than to purchase a slavish tranquillity at the expense of a single iota of the Constitution."

Regarding Wilkes he said: "I have considered the matter with most serious attention; and as I have not in my own breast the smallest doubt that the present universal discontent of the nation arises from the proceedings of the House of Commons upon the expulsion of Mr. Wilkes, I think that we ought, in our address, to state that matter to the King."

He said considerably more, exhorting the Peers to action, but his voice was not in good condition, and his manner hesitating. He realized that he had not stirred his audience.

Turning to the commoner Cradock, as he sat down, he said, "Have you ever heard me before?"

"Not in this House, my Lord."

"And in no House, I hope, have I ever before so disgraced myself," Chatham replied. "I feel quite ill and have been alarmed and annoyed this morning before I arrived; I scarce know what I have been talking about."

Lord Camden, however, for one at least, had been impressed and stirred by the appearance of his former chief.

He arose and gave the astonishing performance of recant-
ing his actions in the recent Ministry. He said that he had
not meant "to be trammeled by his Majesty's Ministers";
that he had often "hung down his head in Council"; that
he was of the same opinion with Lord Chatham; and that in
the future he would "openly and boldly speak his sentiments."

Lord Mansfield aroused at this new note of rebellion
entered into a long harangue, defending the House of
Commons in the Wilkes case, basing his argument chiefly
on the contention that it was none of the business of the
House of Lords and that there was no precedent to warrant
their interference.

The unblushing Toryism of Mansfield stirred Chatham
out of his lethargy. He leaped to his feet.

"I confess, my Lords," he said, "that I am apt to distrust
the refinements of learning, because I have seen the ablest
and the most learned men equally liable to deceive themselves, and to mislead others.

"But Providence has taken better care of our happiness,
and given us, in the simplicity of common sense, a rule for
our direction, by which we shall never be misled. The
evidence which truth carries with it, is superior to all argument; it neither wants the support, nor dreads the opposition, of the greatest abilities.

"I did not say that the House of Commons had done
either right or wrong; but, when his Majesty was pleased
to recommend it to us to cultivate unanimity amongst ourselves, I thought it the duty of this house, as the great
hereditary council of the Crown, to state to his Majesty the
distracted condition of his dominions, together with the
events which had destroyed unanimity among his subjects.

"Is it not indisputably true, my Lords, that Mr. Wilkes
had a common right, and that he lost it no other way but
by a resolution of the House of Commons?

"Will any man presume to affirm that Colonel Luttrell
is the free choice of the electors of Middlesex? We all
know the contrary. We all know that Mr. Wilkes (whom
I mention without either praise or censure) was the fa-

vourite of the county, and chosen by a very great and acknowledged majority, to represent them in Parliament. If the noble Lord dislikes the manner in which these facts are stated, I shall think myself happy in being advised by him how to alter it.

"The Constitution of this country has been openly invaded in fact; and I have heard, with horror and astonishment, that very invasion defended on principle. What is this mysterious power, undefined by law, unknown to the subject, which we must not approach without awe, nor speak of without reverence, which no man may question, and to which all men must submit?

"My Lords, I thought the slavish doctrine of passive obedience had long since been exploded: and, when our kings were obliged to confess that their title to the Crown, and the rule of their Government, had no other foundation than the known laws of the land, I never expected to hear a divine right, or a divine infallibility, attributed to any other branch of the legislature.

"My Lords, I beg to be understood; no man respects the House of Commons more than I do, or would contend more strenuously than I would to preserve them their just and legal authority. Within the bounds prescribed by the Constitution, that authority is necessary to the well-being of the people: beyond that line, every exertion of power is arbitrary, is illegal; it threatens tyranny to the people, and destruction to the State. Power without right is the most odious and detestable object that can be offered to the human imagination: it is not only pernicious to those who are subject to it, but tends to its own destruction.

"My Lords, I am a plain man, and have been brought up in a religious reverence for the original simplicity of the laws of England. By what sophistry they have been perverted, by what artifices they have been involved in obscurity is not for me to explain; the principles, however, of the English laws are still sufficiently clear: they are founded in reason, and are the masterpiece of the human understanding; but it is in the text that I would look for a direction to my judgment, not in the commentaries of modern professors.

"What then, my Lords, are all the generous efforts of our ancestors, are all those glorious contentions, by which they meant to secure themselves, and to transmit to their posterity a known law, a certain rule of living, reduced to this conclusion, that instead of the arbitrary power of a King, we must submit to the arbitrary power of a House of Commons? If this be true, what benefit do we derive from the exchange? Tyranny, my Lords, is detestable in every shape; but in none so formidable as when it is assumed and exercised by a number of tyrants.

"It is *your* ancestors, my Lords,—it is to the English barons that we are indebted for the laws and Constitution we possess.

"Let us not, then, degenerate from the glorious example of our ancestors. Those iron barons (for so I may call them when compared with the silken barons of modern days), were the guardians of the people; yet *their* virtues, my Lords, were never engaged in a question of such importance as the present. A breach has been made in the Constitution—the battlements are dismantled—the citadel is open to the first invader—the walls totter—the Constitution is not tenable. What remains then, but for *us* to stand foremost in the breach, to repair it or perish in it? . . . Unlimited power is apt to corrupt the minds of those who possess it; and this I know, my Lords, that where law ends, tyranny begins!"

After this dynamic plea for liberty, delivered with all his old-time glow and fire, Chatham sank down, exhausted but satisfied. He turned to Cradock and shook his hand.

"I hope now your Lordship is satisfied?" Cradock inquired.

"Yes Sir," Chatham replied with a smile, "I think I have now redeemed my credit."

Camden's act of recantation, following the opening of Chatham's address, was a favorable omen for the rebirth of the Whig party. The Throne promptly dismissed Camden from the Lord Chancellorship; and four other members of the Ministry handed in their resignations. Chatham was particularly eager for Granby to resign, but the Marquis at first was reluctant to take the step. It was not easy to forego the chief command of the Army, and though he necessarily had voted with the Ministry while serving with it, his post did not call for political activity as such. Nevertheless, he yielded to Chatham's importunities within a few days, and the latter then felt that the course was clear for reorganization, as all the chief Whigs, with the exception of Grafton, were now back in the fold.

The idea which Chatham proposed for the union of the Whigs was noble, but not too appealing to many of the party. The purpose, as Chatham stated it, was: "Not to possess the emoluments of Government, but, if possible, to save the State." The Whigs, over a long period, with all due credit to their Constitutional principles, had always dearly loved the emoluments, and they were somewhat tardy in responding to Chatham's summons to self-sacrifice. Newcastle, who had died in the preceding year, had been the Whigs' most competent organizer, and as a dispenser of the best feed had been a champion hog-caller.

The work, on the new sacrificial plan, went forward slowly. Chatham had written to Rockingham some time before, asking him to come down to Hayes, and Rockingham had replied coldly that he lived at Grosvenor Square. Edmund Burke, who was the secretary and brains of Rockingham, was suspicious and jealous of Chatham, referring to his "significant, pompous, creeping, explanatory, and ambiguous" language, and his policy to "keep hovering in the air over all parties." Chatham, however, did not let his own pride stand in the way, and made a visit to Grosvenor Square in which he obtained Rockingham's lukewarm support.

It was essential to unite all the Whig factions if any progress were to be made, and Chatham, who had never been conspicuous for his tact or his humility with his peers, became a changed man. Perhaps in the seriousness of his recent illness he had realized the folly of arrogance. At any rate, immediately on his recovery the preceding autumn he had effected a reconciliation with Temple and George Grenville, and had allowed it to be publicly announced that he was the one who had sought the reconciliation. He was also ready to forget the harsh words of Richmond, but this reunion proved to be more difficult because the Grenvilles and the Richmonds were jealous of each other, and each side was suspicious of reunion. Here again, however, Chatham was successful.

Realizing that he needed someone with the gifts of party management, Chatham made the fortunate choice of a John Calcraft, the one-time clerk in Henry Fox's pay office, a solicitor who had served as an Army agent. In the latter capacity Calcraft had acted as trustee for Amherst and for many others in the Army and Navy who were unable to attend to their affairs while in active service. He had made quantities of money in this career, but had made it honestly and had retained the friendship of a wide range of clients. He had also loaned considerable sums of money to various clients, including Granby, and conducted this phase of his business profitably to himself and to the satisfaction of the borrowers. Obviously, he was a man of exceptional abilities, integrity, and tact.

The chief disappointment of Chatham in the situation was the lack of zeal on the part of the Whigs who had made the pact of friendship. At a Guildhall banquet Chatham gave the toast: "May the wicked be taken away from before the King, that his Throne may be established in righteousness." This was all very well, but less stirring to the Whigs without the promise of emoluments; yet Chatham realized that if the party should be susceptible to the favors distributed by the Throne, there could be no curtailment of the King's influence.

The Marquis of Granby, who was a popular soldier, was particularly disappointing. Granby was only forty-eight, and Chatham had hoped to groom him for leadership, presumably as his successor at the head of the Whig party. Granby, however, was reluctant; and Chatham saw that he himself must exert superhuman efforts to stir the party into action.

Chatham found, moreover, that Granby was not more anxious than Rockingham to take a vigorous part, and wrote to Calcraft on July 28, 1770:

> I was in town on Wednesday last, saw Lord Rockingham, and learnt nothing more than what I knew before; namely, that the Marquis is an honest and honourable man, but that "moderation, moderation!" is the burden of the song among the body. For myself, I am resolved to be in earnest for the public, and shall be a *scarecrow of violence* to the gentle warblers of the grove, the moderate Whigs and temperate statesmen.

"In earnest for the public,"—that had not been such a difficult task in the days of the Cobham Cubs; but the Whigs had become a party of tired liberals, unable to see much hope for their ideas and, for the most part, caring little.

Chatham hitherto had directed his fire against specific abuses by the Throne and by Ministers; but the subservience of Parliament to the King, notably in the Wilkes case, made him realize that the heart of the difficulty was in the distorted structure of the Government. Theoretically, the King was responsible to his Ministers, the Ministers to Parliament, and the Commons to the public. Actually, the Commons had become removed from public opinion by the existence of the numerous boroughs which were controlled by the Court and by families whose influence had been purchased through offices dispensed by the Crown. In only a few sections such as London and Middlesex were the members of Parliament elected by wide popular representation. Now the Wilkes case had demonstrated that a majority of the borough members, representing at best a small sector of the public, could exclude a man elected by popular vote. Chatham might appeal to the public to redress the violations of the Constitution and the invasion of the liberty of the subject; but the people, under the current election laws, had no means of making their voice effective.

The Commons had ceased to live up to its name and had become, for the most part, a group of place-holders.

On January 22, 1770, William Pitt, the Earl of Chatham, poured forth a torrent of eloquence which ultimately, some years later, brought reform.   It was, in fact, an elaboration of his views on "rotten boroughs" on which he had spoken in the Commons on January 14, 1766.   He hardly expected that his proposal would win support from the majority of place-holders who benefited from the old system, but the force and logic of the presentation made an immediate impression on many, and further weakened the Grafton Ministry.

"The boroughs of this country have properly enough been called the rotten parts of the Constitution," said Chatham.   "I have lived in Cornwall, and without entering into any invidious particularity have seen enough to justify the appellation.   But in my judgment, my Lords, these boroughs, corrupt as they are, must be considered as the natural infirmity of the Constitution.   Like the infirmities of the body, we must bear them with patience, and submit to carry them about with us.   The limb is mortified, but the amputation might be death.

"Let us try, my Lords, whether some gentler remedies may not be discovered.   Since we cannot cure the disorder, let us endeavour to infuse such a portion of new health into the Constitution as may enable it to support its most inveterate diseases.

"The representation of the counties is, I think, still preserved pure and uncorrupted.   That of the greatest cities is upon a footing equally respectable; and there are many of the larger trading towns which still preserve their independence.   The infusion of health which I now allude to would be to permit every county to elect one member more in addition to their present representation.

"The knights of the shires approach nearest to the Constitutional representation of the country, because they represent the soil.

"It is not in the little dependent boroughs, it is in the

great cities and counties that the strength and vigor of the Constitution resides, and by them alone, if an unhappy question should ever rise, will the Constitution be honestly and firmly defended. It would increase that strength, because I think it is the only security we have against the profligacy of the times, the corruption of the people, and the ambition of the Crown."

After giving this epoch-making statement, Chatham then referred to a motion which had been made by the Marquis of Rockingham and used it as the means to declare to the country the reunion of the Whig party:

"The friends of this country will, I doubt not, hear with pleasure, that the noble Lord and his friends are now united with me and mine, upon a principle which, I trust, will make our union indissoluble. It is not to possess, or divide, the emoluments of government; but, if possible, to save the State. Upon this ground we met—upon this ground we stand, firm and inseparable. No ministerial artifices, no private offers, no secret seduction can divide us."

The Great Commoner's strategy, at the least, resulted in a clear definition between Whig and Tory party and principles. The Throne was no longer able to form a group which included some men from each faction as a means of controlling the whole. Chatham had succeeded in undoing to that extent the unsound principle on which the Chatham Ministry had been formed. The Duke of Grafton realized that for him to continue as First Lord of the Treasury would alienate him permanently from the whole Whig connection, and on January 28 he resigned.

The King promptly appointed Lord North in Grafton's place, and the issue between Tory and Whig principles was clearly posed for the first time. The King now had a Minister thoroughly willing to carry out his views. Lord North was the ideal man for such a position. He was a streamlined model of Newcastle. He possessed all of the older statesman's gifts for election management, bribery, giving orders, and punishing the disobedient, but he was free from

Newcastle's absurdities. He was urbane, good-natured, and had his moments of courage. He had the misfortune in history to be the head man, and hence the villain, of George III's ill-fated attempt to increase the powers of the Throne, but North was non-moral rather than wicked. He was a stout, near-sighted, amiable fellow who had the best job that the Crown could give him, and he did his best to please the boss.

All through the session of Parliament in the winter of 1770 Chatham was in attendance, ringing the changes on the issue of rotten boroughs and attacking the control of the Court over the members of the Commons, who, he said on February 2, "so far forget what their privileges are that they have added to the long list of venality from Esau to the present day." He returned to the Wilkes case, to the American scene, and to the usurpation of power by the Throne,—taking part, in all, in ten debates.

His campaign, however, was carried on amid discouragement and sorrow, for during the year Beckford, Granby, and George Grenville died, leaving large gaps in the ranks. Especially severe was the loss of Beckford, who for years had been Chatham's adviser, supporter, and chief contact with the opinion of the general public.

When Parliament opened again in the fall, Chatham again fought for the freedom of the press, as the Crown had now filed a libel against Woodfall, the printer of the *Junius* papers. While Chatham's efforts remained unabated, his followers were growing tired. They felt that he was going too far. On November 24, 1770, he inveighed against the corruption of the Court, attacked Mansfield for his excessive "zeal to the reigning family" and concluded by saying "there are some distinctions which are inherent in the nature of things. There is a distinction between right and wrong—between Whig and Tory." He followed this on November 28, 1770, with a blistering attack on the King:

"Is it that the King," he exclaimed, "like a stranger in England, knows nothing of its feelings? Or that, encompassed with the complaints of his people, they neither reach

his heart nor his attention? Strange unconstitutional in-
sensibility, productive of despair, not loyalty! . . . And
when the people are obliged to despair, my Lords, the
consequences must be terrible. In this conjuncture, so critical and so alarming, I hope something may happen astonishing, stupendous like a peal of thunder, or that some figure
like that which

> Drew Priam's curtain in the dead of night,
> And would have told him half his Troy was burn'd:—
> But Priam found the fire, ere he his tongue—

may open his eyes if they are closed and let in upon his
mind the distracted and degraded state of his Empire."

The presiding officer called him to order, whereupon
Chatham replied:

"I am misunderstood. I said, *if* they are closed—but
I now withdraw the condition and say they are closed and
must be opened to the state of his Empire, to which he
is a stranger."

This sort of talk was a challenge to reprisals. Chatham
was not afraid of any action which might be taken against
him, and seemed even to be inviting commitment to the
Tower, but his colleagues continued to be inclined to moderation. The majority, on the other hand, were so alarmed at
the effect which his oratory might have on the public mind
that they revived the order against the presence of strangers
in the House of Lords and thereby made the reporting of
his speeches more difficult.

This action was a shrewd move on the part of the Court
faction. Chatham's oratory had become famous and the
word that he was going to appear always brought a throng
to the chamber. Men of wealth and influence, as well as
plain commoners, were frequent attendants on these occasions. And even the Court group, reasonably secure in its
majority, was not wholly immune to public opinion.

Chatham was one of only a few men in either House of
Parliament to realize, and to proclaim, that the oppression
of subjects in the American colonies, if successful, would be
only a prelude to oppression at home. In the debate on the

Stamp Act he had already declared that the colonials were entitled to "all natural rights" and to share equally with all other Englishmen in their privileges, their laws and the protection of the Constitution "of this free country." Significantly, while affirming America's birthright of freedom, he emphasized it as the freedom to which all subjects of the Crown were equally entitled. The Court and Tory party knew just as well as Chatham what principles were at stake, and each side was settling down more grimly to the struggle.

There was an uproar in the Lords when the first attempt was made to enforce the order on December 10. Even visiting members of the Commons, waiting below the Bar, were ejected amid violence and tumult. Chatham vainly tried to calm the storm, and finally left the chamber in protest.

Chatham continued his vigorous leadership without pulling any of his punches, but the clearing of strangers from the Lords had to some extent clipped his wings, and in his final speech of the session, after taking part in twenty-two debates, he sounded a note of discouragement.

"Were I but ten years younger," he said, "I should spend the remainder of my days in America, which has already given the most brilliant proofs of its independent spirit."

CHAPTER XXXIX

"I May Last as Long as Great Britain"

The loss of Alderman Beckford had proved to be a greater blow to the Whigs than even Chatham had expected. Wilkes saw the opportunity to run for Beckford's former office of Lord Mayor of London and, thanks chiefly to his persecution by the Court, he was elected. Wilkes had no love for Chatham, who had always taken pains to disavow him personally though defending his legal rights. Wilkes also was such a disreputable and irresponsible character that any support from him would be a liability. Yet the potential rebirth of the Whigs depended on gaining strength in the commercial and industrial classes, who had their chief political strength in London. The division of ranks caused by the Wilkes faction was well-nigh fatal.

Early in 1772, therefore, Chatham went into virtual retirement at Burton Pynsent, discouraged over the situation and marking time until events might form a new guide to action. On January 10 he wrote to Shelburne:

> A headlong, self-willed spirit has sunk the City into nothing; attempting powers it has no colour of right to, it has lost the weight to which it is entitled. In another quarter, the narrow genius of old-corps' connection has weakened Whiggism, and rendered national union on revolution principles impossible; and what but such an union can have any chance to withstand the present corruption?
>
> In this deplorable conjuncture, it is a species of happiness to be resolved what *not* to do. Negative plans are, I confess, not very brilliant, and in their nature slow; but time, the great discoverer of truth, seldom fails to vindicate the real lovers of their country.

Meanwhile he enjoyed the pleasures of country life to the full, since formerly most of his periods of vacation had been marred by illness. He renewed his friendship with Garrick and invited him in verse to visit:

> Leave, Garrick, the rich landscape, proudly gay,
> Docks, forts, and navies, bright'ning all the bay:
> To my plain roof repair, primeval seat! . . .
> Come, then, immortal spirit of the stage
> Great nature's proxy, glass of ev'ry age!
> Come, taste the simple life of patriarchs old,
> Who, rich in rural peace, ne'er thought of pomp or gold.

These unpretentious rhymes delighted Garrick as a mark of personal attention from one of the chief men in England, and he accepted with alacrity.

Hester, now that the children had passed the babyhood stage, did considerable traveling, visiting London and also stopping with the Temples and Grenvilles. She usually left one or more of the children at home with Chatham, who liked nothing better than playing daddy. He wrote numerous letters about the children to Hester, cheerfully unperturbed even when the family were quarantined with measles. He wrote to Hester on April 11, 1772:

> My dearest life will read with joy that the boys go on well. I believe William's *sequestration,* as he learnedly terms it, agrees better with his contemplative constitution than more talk and more romps. Airing, literature, the arts, tea-table, sober whist. and lecturing papa for staying out too' late, together with the small amusement of devouring a joint of mutton, or so, before I can look about, make up our daily occupations.

The chief cloud in the family sky was the matter of finances, to which Chatham himself seemed to be personally indifferent. Hester was the one who did the money-raising, and from now on her task was increasingly difficult. The Chatham income during the 1770's was in the neighborhood of £7,000 a year from all sources, but the expenses were huge. Chatham was maintaining three country estates, at Burton Pynsent, Hayes, and Bath. On one of his journeys to Stowe there were listed twenty-six servants as accompanying the family, and this was presumably only part of the total staff.

The pinch was first felt acutely in the spring of '72, when the Chathams tried to offer Hayes for sale and approached Thomas Walpole on the proposition, but he declined, saying that "a disappointed passion does not quickly return." The Chathams were finally able to rent Hayes Place for the summer to Admiral Hood. Hood had long been a protégé of the Temple connection and had married Molly West, one of Chatham's early admirers and a cousin to Hester. Chatham had visited with the Hoods frequently in Harley Street, London, and they were soon to be his chief source of financial aid.

Politics during the year was largely forgotten, except for one address which Chatham made on the Dissenters Bill, speaking in the Lords on May 19, 1772. This address was in support of a bill to relieve dissenters who had conscientious objections to serving in certain public offices. Chatham, on this measure, was his usual colorful self, and it gave him a new opportunity to affirm his views on religious toleration. In the conclusion of the debate he said:

> The dissenting Ministers are represented as men of close ambition: they are so, my Lords, and their ambition is to keep close to the college of fishermen—not of cardinals—and to the doctrine of inspired apostles—not to the degrees of interested and aspiring bishops. But, my Lords, perhaps I may affront your rank or learning by applying to such humble antiquated authorities, for I must confess there is a wide difference between the bishops of those times and these. . . . You talk of our English Church system; but we have no system: we have a Calvinistic creed, a Popish liturgy, and an Arminian clergy. The dissenters you revile contend for a spiritual creed and spiritual worship. . . . I am for this bill, my Lords, because I am for toleration, that sacred right of nature and bulwark of truth and most interesting of all objects to fallible man.

His appeal to the Lords, however, was unavailing, and the bill was rejected by a vote of 102 to 29. Chatham, partly because of ill health, and more particularly because of discouragement, did not speak in the Lords again until the spring of 1774.

Meanwhile the money pressure continued. In June, 1772, the Chathams were able to persuade Temple to sell £15,000 of the Trust Funds to meet financial emergencies. As the market was down, these yielded only £9500. Lord Clive bought Chatham's house at Bath, and Hood unsuccessfully acted as a real estate agent for Hayes, trying to find customers. In March, the following year, Hood lent Chatham £1,000, secured by an equity in Hayes, although it was already heavily mortgaged, and later in the year Hood lent £6,000 on Burton Pynsent at five percent interest. This source of relief was reaching its limit, however, as Hood wrote that he had just been obliged to buy a house for himself—and "I must put my credit to the utmost stretch in raising further sums."

At the same time, with an understanding of Chatham's financial vagueness, the Admiral put in writing various transactions which had taken place, and expressed a doubt to Lady Chatham "upon the object of money transactions. I am fearful that they oftener occasion a separation of friends than promote closer ties of friendship. I am certain this cannot happen between Lord Chatham and me, but, unless Lord Pitt [the oldest son] and your Ladyship's children are fully acquainted with the sum borrowed on the Burton Pynsent estate, they may be alarmed at it hereafter."

Another rescuer in this situation was Thomas Coutts, the banker, who handled various financial affairs for the family with the greatest discretion and friendliness. His freedom from partisan leanings in business was indicated by the fact that one daughter married a son of Lord Bute and another a son of Lord North, yet Coutts was able, and apparently eager, to help the leader of the Whigs. His dealings, after February, 1773, were entirely with Hester rather than with Chatham; and he had a great admiration for her, calling her "the cleverest *man* of her time."

Lady Chatham, in fact, was clearly one of the great unsung women of history who made possible her husband's career. She worshiped her husband, was an intellectual companion to him, protected him from annoyances, and exercised tact in all her relationships.

A neighboring farmer named Petty said of her to a Mr. Bowring, "She is a woman of business."

"What a fine creature to breed out of," Mr. Bowring responded enthusiastically. "Such a family is not elsewhere to be seen!"

The months rolled on peacefully at Burton Pynsent, while Chatham remained away from the political scene. In June he joined his two sons at the beach at Lyme Regis, where he found that the younger generation were growing up, as his letter to Hester indicated:

> I found, on my arrival, all at church, Mr. Wilson preaching. Beef of Old England ready—not at an Old England hour—at four o'clock, on account of evening service. Papa better pleased to find so exemplary a family. The sea continues kind to our race; Pitt [the oldest son] and William striving who shall, by good looks, carry the vogue among the ladies of our Vauxhall. Engagements for tea this evening too far advanced to be retracted, in any way becoming a *cavalier*: so papa insists on playing a solo.

By the end of the year 1773, troubles began brewing again on the political front. The Irish Parliament had voted a tax on absentee landlords, and the Ministry were inclined to reject it arbitrarily. So many Whig families, including the Pitt-Chathams, had a large stake in this matter that Shelburne, who was also financially affected, wrote to Chatham for advice on the course to take. Chatham agreed that the measure was unjust, that it would be costly to him and his friends, but he replied that the Commons of Ireland were exercising "their inherent exclusive right by raising supplies in the manner they judge best. This great principle of Constitution is so fundamental, and with me, so sacred and indispensable, that it outweighs all other considerations."

American matters were again reaching the boiling point.

In April, 1773, Lord North had tried to make the tax on tea more palatable by permitting tea exportation directly from India to the colonies, so that the price was reduced even though the tax was added.

This move was typical of the King's appraisal of human nature; he assumed that the appeal to the pocketbook exceeds all other interests. The colonists, far from being gratified, were incensed at the suggestion that they would abandon their principles for a petty bribe; and in December, when a shipment of tea arrived in Boston Harbor, a group of men disguised as Indians boarded the vessels and threw the cargo overboard.

The colonists, though the Court still failed to realize it, were solid in their convictions of their rights as English freemen. Chatham's speeches were not the idle rhetoric of a malcontent, but the philosophy of what the English freemen at home and in the provinces felt and believed.

In the New World Benjamin Franklin was continuing his work as the chief philosopher of the colonies, and Shelburne gave Chatham data by Franklin discussing the situation in Boston. When Franklin had been in England earlier, as agent for Pennsylvania, he had not met the Great Commoner, and Chatham in turn had not anticipated that the American troubles would be of such long duration.

In fact, no one could have predicted that his Majesty would have been so blind, even to self-interest, to refuse reasonable conciliation. Every month, however, the obstinacy of the Throne on this subject was more evident. In March, 1774, the Cabinet retaliated on Boston by closing the port, quartering troops in the town, taking away the charter of Massachusetts, and passing a bill to remove offenders for trial to Nova Scotia or England.

These were patently acts of war, and Chatham was horrified at their probable result. During April he was prostrated with illness, but on May 27 he came up to the Lords to make protest against the Crown policies and to plead for peace.

"Had the British colonies been planted by any other

kingdom than our own," he said, "the inhabitants would have carried with them the chains of slavery, and spirit of despotism; but as they are they ought to be remembered as great instances to instruct the world what great exertions mankind will naturally make, when they are left to the free exercise of their own powers.

"And, my Lords, notwithstanding my intention to give my hearty negative to the question now before you, I cannot help condemning, in the severest manner, the late turbulent and unwarrantable conduct of the Americans in some instances, particularly in the late riots at Boston.

"But, my Lords, the mode which has been pursued to bring them back to a sense of their duty to their parent state has been so diametrically opposite to the fundamental principles of sound policy, that individuals, possessed of common understanding must be astonished at such proceedings.

"By blocking up the harbour of Boston, you have involved the innocent trader in the same punishment with the guilty profligates who destroyed your merchandise; and instead of making a well-concerted effort to secure the real offenders, you clap a naval and military extinguisher over their harbour, and punish the crime of a few lawless depredators and their abettors upon the wholy body of the inhabitants.

"My Lords, this country is little obliged to the framers and promoters of this tea tax. The Americans had almost forgot, in their excess of gratitude for the repeal of the Stamp Act, any interest but that of the mother country; there seemed an emulation among the different provinces who should be most dutiful and forward in their expressions of loyalty to their real benefactor; as you will readily perceive by the following letter from Governor Bernard [of Massachusetts] to a noble Lord then in office:—

" 'The House of Representatives,' says he, 'from the time of opening the session to this day, has shown a disposition to avoid all dispute with me; everything having passed with as much good humour as I could desire. They have acted, in all things, with temper and moderation; they have avoided some subjects of dispute, and have laid a foundation for removing some causes of former altercation.'

"This, my Lords, was the temper of the Americans; and would have continued so, had it not been interrupted by your fruitless endeavors to tax them without their consent: but the moment they perceived your intention was renewed to tax them, under a pretense of serving the East India Company, their resentment got the ascendant of their moderation, and hurried them into actions contrary to law, which, in their cooler hours, they would have thought on with horror; for I sincerely believe the destroying of the tea was the effect of despair.

"But, my Lords, from the complexion of the whole of the proceeding, I think that administration has purposely irritated them into those late violent acts for which they now so severely smart; purposely to be revenged on them for the victory they gained by the repeal of the Stamp Act; a measure in which they seemingly acquiesced, but to which at the bottom they were real enemies. For what other motive could induce them to dress taxation, that father of American sedition, in the robes of an East India Director, but to break in upon that mutual peace and harmony which then so happily subsisted between them and the mother country? . . .

"It has always been my received and unalterable opinion . . . *that this country had no right under Heaven to tax America.* It is contrary to all the principles of justice and civil policy, which neither the exigencies of the State, nor even an acquiescence in the taxes, could justify upon any occasion whatever.

"Such proceedings will never meet their wished-for success; and, instead of adding to their miseries, as the bill now before you most undoubtedly does, adopt some lenient measures, which may lure them to their duty; proceed like a kind and affectionate parent over a child whom he tenderly loves; * and, instead of those harsh and severe proceed-

* Again he was using the affectionate-parent simile which he had used years before in the Jew bill.

ings, pass an amnesty on all their youthful errors; clasp them once more in your fond and affectionate arms; and, I will venture to affirm, you will find them children worthy of their sire.

"But should their turbulence exist after your proffered terms of forgiveness, which I hope and expect this House will immediately adopt, I will be among the foremost of your Lordships to move for such measures as will effectually prevent a future relapse, and make them feel what it is to provoke a fond and forgiving parent!, a parent, my Lords, whose welfare has ever been my greatest and most pleasing consolation.

"This declaration may seem unnecessary; but I will venture to declare, the period is not far distant, when she will want the assistance of her most distant friends: but should the all-disposing hand of Providence prevent me from affording her my poor assistance, my prayer shall be ever for her welfare—length of days be in her right hand, and in her left riches and honour; may her ways be ways of pleasantness, and all her paths be peace!"

Chatham was now thoroughly aroused as an advocate for the colonial cause. When the North American provinces objected to the Quebec Act he rather inconsistently lent his support to the protest. The terms of the Quebec Act were similar to those granted by General Amherst in the terms of surrender at the time when Mr. Pitt was Secretary of State. The French legal system was continued, instead of trial by jury, as that was the custom and preference of the French Canadians; the populace were permitted to continue in their services of worship according to the Roman Catholic religion, without prejudice, though this was more latitude than was then permitted in most parts of the British Empire.

The colonists felt, however, that the Quebec Act would be used as a precedent for abolishing jury trials throughout America. The Act also went beyond the terms of capitulation in the religious matter, in that it permitted the priests of the Roman Catholic Church to exact tithes. Chatham attacked the measure furiously on this point, alleging that the right of tithes would officially establish a State church, giving aid to a church which at that time was in politics and was the official church of the Bourbon enemies of England.

Chatham's zeal for the colonial cause was strengthened in the summer of 1774, when he entertained Dr. Franklin and other Americans who had crossed the Atlantic to promote sympathy in England. Among the visitors was a sculptress, a Mrs. Patience Wright of Bordentown, New Jersey. She was the widow of a poor farmer who had lived across the road from the American painter, Francis Hopkinson. Under his encouragement she had become a modeler in wax and had opened a studio in New York which had met with considerable success. General Amherst had his army headquarters in New York at the time and Mrs. Wright had made numerous acquaintances among the General's staff and their families.

Now she had come to England with excellent introductions and shrewdly was associating with all parties. She was accepted on terms of friendship by the King and Queen, even though she accepted commissions wherever she could find them. There was no reason, of course, why an artist should have regard for the politics of her sitters, but Mrs. Wright was a patriot as well as an artist. She was a close friend of Silas Deane, the American agent, and later on she was a volunteer informer (though rather an inefficient one) for Dr. Franklin. Mrs. Wright, who was a Quaker, was a vigorous, dynamic woman, prone to swearing and colorful speech. She struck Chatham's fancy and prevailed on him to sit for her. Her talents were considerable, and her bust of Chatham has found a permanent place in Westminster Abbey.

In the fall of 1774 there was a new election in Parliament, and the King's friends again exerted the utmost efforts, successfully, to elect a Commons which would obey the dictates of the Administration. The outlook for America was gloomier than ever.

There were also new shadows on Chatham's financial

affairs. His older daughter, Hester, was engaged to Lord Mahon whom she was to marry on December 19, 1774. This meant that a dowry must be provided. The sum fixed upon was £6,000. The price of settling a daughter had evidently declined in the past dozen years, along with the general fall of stocks, as it will be recalled that Lady Hardwicke in 1762 had quoted the figure for an earl's daughter at £20,000, compared with £10,000 for the daughter of a baron.* Even so, £6,000 was sufficient to cripple the Chatham bank deposits, causing difficulties which were apparent the following year.

The money was raised, however, and the marriage took place according to plan. In the following month, January, 1775, Lady Chatham went up to London to present the bride and groom at Court. This was a great occasion for her, as neither the Temples nor the Chathams had been particularly active in formal society, and she enjoyed the excitement.

"Duchesses, grandees, and others have dropped their cards of visits to me in every street I think," she wrote to her husband, specifying the street addresses of the Grenvilles and other families she had visited, where cards had been presented. "The seeking so much about to be civil is flattering at least." Chatham, however, was suspicious of the wiles of the social lobby, and replied: "Your Duchesses and archbishops *littering* all the streets with cards, to catch you in your passage, is indeed flattering enough . . . as for gracious verbiage, I make but small account of such moonshine."

He was interested, nevertheless, in the presentation of their daughter at Court, and said, "I am anxious to hear how our dear couple came off." The presentation was on January 19, 1775, and Lady Chatham wrote to him at eight the next morning:

His Majesty was very gracious, for *him*. Three or four sentences of a general sort. Her Majesty, a conversation wishing of

* The quotation on Hester Grenville, sister of an Earl, in 1754, had been £12,000.

joy, glad of what made me so happy. Impossible now, but that having such agreeable calls, must come to town. . . . The deficiency in graciousness was in not asking about my Love, but I think that might be occasioned by the disappointment of not seeing him there. You was in general expected. The Drawing Room extremely thin. It had been put in the papers, that there was not to be any; on purpose I believe. . . . Our girl acquitted herself well and both Majesties were very civil.

Chatham, at this time, had made up his mind to appear in the Lords and make a further effort on the correction of American policy. He had been studying a petition which had been sent to the King from the General Congress of the American Colonies sitting at Philadelphia, and he hoped that this might open the way to ending the American troubles.

Feeling was so high in Court circles on this subject that Hester was frightened for Chatham's safety. She had written him the day before their daughter's presentation that reports were being circulated from authoritative sources that Chatham was no longer troubling himself about American affairs and certainly would not come to town. "It proves how much there is to be afraid of, of jockeyship, and whatever is bad." She urged him to see that the windows were down and the doors shut in his lodgings "that you may not be *made* to catch cold."

He had written to Hester on the day of the Court presentation: "America is deeply entered upon her defense, and seems to put more of solidity and prudence into *her* plan, than the wiseacres who surround his Majesty have known how to give to *their* schemes of destruction."

He had also advised Shelburne that he meant "to look the *Tapestry* and Bishops in the face tomorrow," and had said: "I mean to-morrow to touch only the threshold of American business and knock at the Minister's door to wake him, as well as show I attend to America. I shall move for an address, to send orders immediately for removing the forces from the town of Boston as soon as practicable."

Chatham assured his wife that he would be careful, and

of course adhered to his program of appearing in the House of Lords. There, on January 20, 1775, he made one of his most eloquent pleas for the settlement of the American issue.

His themes were, to a large extent, the points which he had made previously at numerous times,—the assertion that England had no right to tax America, the injustice of taxation without representation, and the need for conciliation if America were to be brought back within the family of the Empire. As was Mr. Pitt's habit, his eloquence was an ascending spiral. He could come back to the same theme repeatedly and usually give it a fresh and sharper treatment in the light of current events; so, in this instance, he returned to the American subject treating with familiar themes but with new eloquence and new considerations, and offering a specific proposal:

"As I have not the honour of access to his Majesty, I will endeavor to transmit to him, through the Constitutional channel of this House, my ideas of America, to rescue him from the misadvice of his present Ministers. I congratulate your Lordships, that the business is *at last* entered upon, by the noble Lord's laying the papers before you. As I suppose your Lordships too well apprized of their contents, I hope I am not premature in submitting to you my present motion:

" 'That an humble address be presented to his Majesty, humbly to desire and beseech his Majesty, that in order to open the way towards a happy settlement of the dangerous troubles in America, by beginning to allay ferments and soften animosities there; and, above all, for preventing, in the meantime, any sudden and fatal catastrophe at Boston, now suffering under the daily irritation of an army before their eyes, posted in their town, it may graciously please his Majesty, that immediate orders be dispatched to General Gage, for removing his Majesty's forces from the town of Boston, as soon as the rigour of the season, and other circumstances indispensable to the safety and accommodation of the said troops may render the same practicable.'

"I wish, my Lords, not to lose a day in this urgent, pressing crisis; an hour now lost in allaying ferments in America may produce years of calamity. . . .

"When I urge this measure of recalling the troops from Boston, I urge it on this pressing principle, that it is necessarily preparatory to the restoration of your peace, and the establishment of your prosperity. It will then appear that you are disposed to treat amicably and equitably; and to consider, revise, and repeal, if it should be found necessary, as I affirm it will, those violent acts and declarations which have disseminated confusion throughout your Empire.

"Resistance to your acts was necessary as it was just; and your vain declarations of the omnipotence of Parliament, and your imperious doctrines of the necessity of submission, will be found equally impotent to convince, or to enslave your fellow-subjects in America, who feel that tyranny, whether *ambitioned* by an individual part of the legislature or the bodies who compose it, is equally intolerable to British subjects. . . .

"I therefore urge and conjure your Lordships immediately to adopt this conciliating measure. I will pledge myself for its immediately producing conciliatory effects by its being thus well timed: but if you delay till your vain hope shall be accomplished, of triumphantly dictating reconciliation, you delay for ever. . . .

"Is the spirit of persecution never to be appeased? Are the brave sons of those brave forefathers to inherit their sufferings, as they have inherited their virtues? Are they to sustain the infliction of the most oppressive and unexampled severity, beyond the accounts of history, or description of poetry: *'Rhadamanthus habet durissima regna, castigatque, AUDITQUE!'* So says the wisest poet, and perhaps the wisest statesman and politician. But our Ministers say, *the Americans must not be heard.* They have been condemned *unheard.*—The indiscriminate hand of vengeance has lumped together innocent and guilty; with all the formalities of hostility, has blocked up the town [Boston] and reduced to beggary and famine thirty thousand inhabitants.

"But his Majesty is advised, that the union in America cannot last! Ministers have more eyes than I, and should have more ears; but with all the information I have been able to procure, I can pronounce it an union, solid, permanent, and effectual. Ministers may satisfy themselves, and delude the public, with the report of what they call commercial bodies in America. They are *not* commercial; they are your packers and factors: they live upon nothing—for I call commission nothing. I mean the ministerial *authority* for this American intelligence; the runners for government, who are paid for their intelligence. But these are not the men, nor this the influence, to be considered in America, when we estimate the firmness of their union. Even to extend the question, and to take in the really mercantile circle, will be totally inadequate to the consideration.

"Trade indeed increases the wealth and glory of a country; but its real strength and stamina are to be looked for among the cultivators of the land: in their simplicity of life is found the simpleness of virtue—the integrity and courage of freedom. These true genuine sons of the earth are invincible: and they surround and hem in the mercantile bodies; even if these bodies, which supposition I totally disclaim, could be supposed disaffected to the cause of liberty. Of this general spirit existing in the British nation (for so I wish to distinguish the real and genuine Americans from the pseudo-traders I have described)—of this spirit of independence, animating the *nation* of America, I have the most authentic information. It is not new among them; it is, and has ever been, their established principle, their confirmed persuasion: it is their nature, and their doctrine.

"I remember, some years ago, when the repeal of the Stamp Act was in agitation, conversing in a friendly confidence with a person of undoubted respect and authenticity on that subject; and he assured me with a certainty which his judgment and opportunity gave him, that these were the prevalent and steady principles of America—that you might destroy their towns, and cut them off from the super-fluities, perhaps the conveniences, of life; but that they were prepared to despise your power, and would not lament their loss, whilst they have—what, my Lords?—their *woods* and their *liberty*. The name of my authority, if I am called upon, will authenticate the opinion irrefragably.*

"If illegal violences have been, as it is said, committed in America, prepare the way, open the door of possibility, for acknowledgment and satisfaction: but proceed not to such coercion, such proscription; cease your indiscriminate in-flictions; amerce not thirty thousand; oppress not three millions, for the fault of forty or fifty individuals. Such severity of injustice must forever render incurable the wounds you have already given your colonies; you irritate them to unappeasable rancour. What though you march from town to town, and from province to province; though you should be able to enforce a temporary and local submis-sion, which I only suppose, not admit—how shall you be able to secure the obedience of the country you leave behind you in your progress, to grasp the dominion of eighteen hundred miles of continent, populous in numbers, possessing valour, liberty, and resistance?

"This resistance to your arbitrary system of taxation might have been foreseen: it was obvious from the nature of things, and of mankind; above all, from the Whiggish spirit flourishing in that country. The spirit which now resists your taxation in America is the same which formerly opposed loans, benevolences, and ship-money, in England; the same spirit which called all England *on its legs,* and by the Bill of Rights vindicated the English Constitution; the same spirit which established the great fundamental, essential maxim of your liberties, *that no subject of Eng-land shall be taxed but by his own consent.*

"This glorious spirit of Whiggism animates three mil-

* The editors of the *Chatham Correspondence,* published in 1838, made the footnote that Chatham referred to Dr. Franklin. Chatham here, how-ever, was talking of the Stamp Act period before he had become intimate with Franklin, and from the context he probably meant General Amherst. These were Amherst's views and would presumably, from his experience, be generally accepted as authoritative.

lions in America; who prefer poverty with liberty, to gilded chains and sordid affluence; and who will die in defense of their rights as men, as freemen. What shall oppose this spirit, aided by the congenial flame glowing in the breasts of every Whig in England, to the amount, I hope, of double the American numbers? Ireland they have to a man. In that country, joined as it is with the cause of the colonies, and placed at their head, the distinction I contend for is and must be observed. This country superintends and controls their trade and navigation; but they *tax themselves*. And this distinction between external and internal control is sacred and insurmountable; it is involved in the abstract nature of things. Property is private, individual, absolute. Trade is an extended and complicated consideration: it reaches as far as ships can sail or winds can blow: it is a great and various machine. To regulate the numberless movements of its several parts, and combine them into effect, for the good of the whole, requires the superintending wisdom and energy of the supreme power in the Empire. But this supreme power has no effect towards internal taxation; for it does not exist in that relation; there is no such thing, *no such idea in this Constitution, as a supreme power operating upon property*. Let this distinction then remain forever ascertained; taxation is theirs, commercial regulation is ours. As an American, I would recognise to England her supreme right of regulating commerce and navigation: as an Englishman by birth and principle, I recognise to the Americans their supreme unalienable right in their property; a right which they are justified in the defense of to the last extremity. To maintain this principle is the common cause of the Whigs on the other side of the Atlantic, and on this ' 'Tis liberty to liberty engaged' that they will defend themselves, their families, and their country. In this great cause they are immovably allied: it is the alliance of God and nature—immutable, eternal,—fixed as the firmament of Heaven. . . .

"I hear General Gage censured for inactivity, I must retort with indignation on those whose intemperate measures and improvident councils have betrayed him into his present situation. His situation reminds me, my Lords, of the answer of a French General in the civil wars of France— Monsieur Condé opposed to Monsieur Turenne: he was asked, how it happened that he did not take his adversary prisoner, as he was often very near him: '*J'ai peur,*' replied Condé, very honestly, '*j'ai peur qu'il ne me prenne,*'—'I'm afraid lest he take me.'

"When your Lordships look at the papers transmitted us from America; when you consider their decency, firmness, and wisdom, you cannot but respect their cause, and wish to make it your own. For myself, I must declare and avow, that in all my reading and observation—and it has been my favorite study—I have read Thucydides, and have studied and admired the master-states of the world—that for solidity of reasoning, force of sagacity, and wisdom of conclusion, under such a complication of difficult circumstances, no nation or body of men can stand in preference to the General Congress at Philadelphia.

"I trust it is obvious to your Lordships, that all attempts to impose servitude upon such men, to establish despotism over such a mighty continental nation, must be vain, must be fatal. We shall be *forced ultimately to retract;* let us retract while we can, not when we must. I say we must necessarily undo these violent oppressive acts: *they must be repealed—you will repeal them; I pledge myself for it, that you will in the end repeal them; I stake my reputation on it; I will consent to be taken for an idiot, if they are not finally repealed.*—Avoid, then, this humiliating, disgraceful necessity. With a dignity becoming your exalted situation, make the first advances to concord, to peace and happiness: for *that* is your true dignity, to act with prudence and justice. That *you* should first concede is obvious, from sound and rational policy. Concession comes with better grace and more salutary effect from superior power; it reconciles superiority of power with the feelings of men; and establishes solid confidence on the foundations of affection and gratitude. . . .

"Every danger and every hazard impend, to deter you from perseverance in your present ruinous measures. Foreign war hanging over your heads by a slight and brittle thread: France and Spain watching your conduct, and waiting for the maturity of your errors:—with a vigilant eye to America, and the temper of your colonies, more than to their own concerns, be they what they may.

"To conclude, my Lords: If the ministers thus persevere in misadvising and misleading the King, I will not say, that they *can* alienate the affections of his subjects from his crown; but I will affirm, *that they will make the crown not worth his wearing*—I will not say that the King is betrayed; but I will pronounce, *that the kingdom is undone.*"

Chatham, however, was talking to a group of men who, in the main, were unable to see where the American issue was of any particular concern to them. The House of Lords was made up in general of large landed proprietors who were not directly touched by what transpired in America. Their interests were remote from the merchants, the manufacturers, and the industrial populace. They had an inherited contempt for persons who were in trade and little regard for any individual who gained his livelihood as a result of his own diligence. Hence those interests in England which supported the American cause had little influence in the Lords. Even the doctrine of the rights of the English freemen had only a moderate appeal for them, as they were the class which was on top and did not feel their own liberty to be threatened. Lord Chatham, it is true, had pointed out, and emphasized later, that the interests of the entire kingdom were involved in the long run, but the fox-hunting, idle peers had little mental capacity to look that far ahead. The reports of the debates in the House of Lords did not indicate any special enthusiasm for the war against America, but the Peers were little disposed to interfere with the ministerial policy and inclined to follow what seemed to be the line of least resistance by endorsing its conduct. Therefore, when Lord Chatham's motion came to a vote, the motion for which he had pleaded with his utmost energy, only eighteen votes were recorded in favor and sixty-eight against.

This remarkable address by Chatham worried the Administration, even if it did not shake their fundamental policy. The American sympathizers naturally were overjoyed, and Franklin wrote to Lord Stanhope: "Dr. Franklin is filled with admiration of that truly great man! He has seen, in the course of life, sometimes eloquence without wisdom, and often wisdom without eloquence: in the present instance, he sees both united, and both, as he thinks, in the highest degree possible."

Franklin now became Chatham's chief adviser on American matters. Chatham was proposing to bring in a bill to make effective the principles of his speech and invited Franklin to visit him at Hayes on January 27, where the American arrived at eleven A.M. and stayed to dinner. On the 29th, Chatham came to town and visited Franklin at his lodgings in Craven Street. He stayed for two hours, while his equipage waited outside and people coming home from church noticed it and talked about it. This was another gratifying solace to Franklin's feelings, in contrast to the rough treatment which he had received previously at the hands of the Court. There was another conference between the two men on the 31st at Hayes, lasting for four hours; and on February 1, Chatham brought in his bill.

The bill was particularly notable for the fact that it recognized the Continental Congress within the framework of the sovereignty of the British Empire. Chatham, some months before, had said to Franklin that he thought the colonists would be insistent on independence, and Franklin had disagreed. The proposal to recognize the Congress was expected to satisfy the desire for independence without sacrificing the authority of the kingdom. The Congress would function essentially as a dominion parliament.

The idea was naturally anathema to the Ministry, and was regarded as daring by other conservative elements. Though Camden, Richmond, and Shelburne approved, Temple and Grafton were opposed. From the Ministerial bench Lord Gower dismissed it contemptuously as the work of an old man; and Lord Sandwich, turning to Franklin, who was standing at the Bar, said, "It is evidently the work of some American, and I fancy that I have in my eye the person who drew it up, one of the bitterest and most mischievous enemies this country has ever known!"

"The bill is entirely my own," Chatham replied. ". . . But I do not scruple to affirm that if I were first minister * . . . I should not be ashamed of calling to my assistance a person so perfectly acquainted with the whole of American affairs as the gentleman alluded to and so injuriously reflected upon; one, I am pleased to say, whom all Europe holds in high estimation for his knowledge and wisdom, and ranks with our Boyles and Newtons; one who is an honour not to the English nation only, but to human nature!"

He concluded with this savage thrust: "On reconsideration I must allow you one merit, a strict attention to your own interests: in that view you appear sound statesmen and politicians. You well know, if the present measure should prevail, that you must instantly relinquish your places. . . . Such then being your precarious situations, who should wonder that you can put a negative on any measure which must annihilate your power, deprive you of your emoluments, and at once reduce you to that state of insignificance for which God and nature designed you."

Chatham's advocacy of the American cause, though brilliant, had not had the support of good political management. The unexpected death of Calcroft had again left Chatham without adequate aid in Parliamentary tactics. Under proper organization neither Temple nor Grafton should have been allowed to enter a demurrer, and would hardly have done so if they had been adequately prepared. Even so, of course, a majority could hardly have been obtained. The effort did at least convince the Government that some steps needed to be taken, and Lord North introduced a measure on February 27 which offered to remit taxation imposed by Parliament to any colony that would contribute for the common defense a sum approved by the King and both Houses of Parliament. This, however, did

---

* Note that even at this date the term "prime minister" had not come into official use.

not meet many of the main issues and was substantially taxation in another form.

On March 22, Burke made his famous speech on the conciliation of the American colonies, though Burke was not willing to go as far as Chatham in recognizing the Continental Congress.

Chatham returned to Hayes in March, 1775, sick with disappointment; and his illness kept him out of active participation in public affairs until the end of May, 1777. The family financial affairs continued to be in worse shape than ever. Hood ultimately increased his loans to a total of £10,000, reducing the interest rate from five to four and one-half percent. Coutts and Temple each made loans of £1,000 each and Jouvencel, a clerk in the Treasury, loaned £500. Lord North, having heard something of Chatham's difficulties, proposed to the King that Chatham was entitled to the full £3,000 pension granted him years before, and that some way should be found to make up the difference of the deductions which had been made through Treasury fees and taxes. Furthermore, the pension was many months in arrears, because the King's family had prior claim on the Plantation duties. The King, however, was not sympathetic to the suggestion, and replied:

> The making Lord Chatham's family suffer for the conduct of the father is not in the least agreeable to my sentiments; but I should choose to know him totally unable to appear on the public stage before I agree to any offer of that kind, lest it should be wrongly construed a fear of him; and, indeed, his political conduct the last winter was so abandoned, that he must, in the eyes of the dispassionate, have totally undone the merit of his former conduct. As to any gratitude to be expected from him or his family, that would be absurd, when the whole tenour of their lives have shewn them void of that most honourable sentiment; but when decrepitude or death puts an end to him as a trumpet of sedition, I shall make no difficulty of placing the second son's name instead of the father, and making up the pension £3,000.

Since the Ministry ignored the petition from the Continental Congress, the dispute between the Throne and the colonies had reached an impasse. On April 19, 1775, the Minutemen at Lexington "fired the shot heard 'round the world." The next move by the Government was to replace Lord Hillsborough with the most incompetent possible choice in the person of Lord George Sackville, who had now become Lord George Germain. He had changed his name in order to inherit the fortune of Lady Betty Germain.*

Sackville-Germain had long been a friend and toady to the King. It will be recalled that he had been court-martialed at Minden and had bitterly resented the failure of Mr. Pitt to save his hide. For many years he had hung around the Court, looking for favors, and had succeeded in being made Vice-Treasurer of Ireland in 1765 under the Rockingham Ministry. When the Grafton Ministry had fallen, Sackville had taken to cover and had joined the reorganization of the Whig party, thinking that it would become successful. He was, however, suspect by his colleagues and soon tired of his associations. As a man of some experience in the Army, and as a boyhood friend of General Amherst, he was thought to have some knowledge of American affairs, an illusion which was very soon dispelled.

The action at Lexington was shortly followed by the Battle of Bunker Hill, in which many British officers of leading families lost their lives. The country at last woke up to the fact that it had a serious war on its hands. The feeling in some quarters on the situation was illustrated in paragraphs which Lady Sarah Lennox Bunbury wrote in July, 1775, in letters to her cousin Susan:

> I suppose you are violent for your American friends. I hope they are good sort of people, but I don't love Presbetiryans & I love the English soldiers, so that I at present have a horror of those who use them ill beyond the laws of war, which *scalping* certainly is, & I don't believe a word of the soldiers doing more than they ought; you know one is always unreasonable when one's prejudiced. . . .
>
> Since I began this I've heard the news of the action near

* Also spelled Germaine.

Boston. Oh Lord! how it makes one's blood run cold to think of *any action,* much more such a bloody one as that, & among one's own people almost. Thank God our friends are safe. . . .

Mrs. Howe is vastly better since the General was made Commander-in-Chief, for he is at least safe for a *time,* & safe from *bush fighting,* which seemed the most to be dreaded as being more frequent than a regular action; besides she flatters herself his advice will be a little attended to, & she knows he wishes to have a peace that is creditable to both. . . .

And yet I hate the King should conquer too, because he sits there at his ease at Windsor, and fancies he has nothing to do but to *order* to conquer such a place as America; he will grow so insolent about it that it will provoke me beyond all patience, and were it not for the blood, every drop of which I think of full as much consequence as the King's (of some, of a great deal more) I should wish him to have a compleat mortification in having Ireland whisk'd away from him whilst his troops are sailing, and so have him obliged to give up America, and look like a fool without Ireland. . . .

Meanwhile Chatham, feeling that he might not live to see the outcome, wrote a statement to Dr. Addington which he wished preserved as evidence of his "unshaken" opinions:

. . . that he continued in the same sentiments, with regard to America, which he had always professed, and which stand so fully explained in the Provisional Act offered by him to the House of Lords. To this he added, that unless effectual measures were speedily taken for reconciliation with the colonies, he was fully persuaded, that, in a very few years, France will set her foot on English ground. That, in the present moment, her policy may probably be to wait some time, in order to see England more deeply engaged in this ruinous war, *against herself,* in America; as well as to prove how far the Americans, abetted by France *indirectly* only, may be able to make a stand, before she takes an *open* part, by declaring war upon England.

The affairs of the Ministry in carrying on the American war became steadily worse. On July 4, 1776, as no present-day American needs to be told, the colonies published their Declaration of Independence.

The Throne was desperate in its attempt to get efficient officers to put down the rebellion. Usually the monarch is the mere figurehead of a State at war, representing the policies of his people, but this conflict was specifically the war of George III. The trading classes, the manufacturers, the timid Whigs, and the Army were all against it. True enough, the man in the street "jostled the Throne," as Franklin expressed it, in his attempts to assert what should be done to the colonies, but the leadership was that of the King supported by a docile Ministry and an apathetic House of Lords.

The question of a commander-in-chief presented great difficulties. General Gates had been recalled because he had married an American girl, was openly sympathetic to the colonies, and was an avowed supporter of Chatham. General Howe was conducting the war as evasively as possible, in the hope that peace would soon be obtained. He was a friend of the Richmonds and their Whig connections, and a believer in conciliation.

A new move on the part of the King, who thought he had discovered a bright idea, was to rescue General Amherst from obscurity, restore him to his regiments, and give him the

A contemporary cartoon

LORD AMHERST

He said the colonies could not be conquered.

title of Baron Amherst. When this had been done, the Throne informed Amherst that he was nominated to take the field as the commander of the forces in North America. No one was better qualified; but, to the astonishment and anger of his Majesty, Amherst flatly refused to go, and offered to resign his regiments. Amherst, furthermore, told the Cabinet that to conquer the colonies was an impossibility. He suggested that the only feasible means of attack would be to attempt a naval blockade and harass the ship-ping. The colonies might then yield to economic pressure.

Lord George Germain, however, flattered the King with the idea that the rebellion could be put down; and the staff operations were left in his bungling hands, while Amherst was made commander-in-chief of the home forces and a member of the Cabinet, and Howe was left in command in the field. Even in his Cabinet post Amherst was of little help on American affairs, as he refused to discuss policies and merely voted yes or no on motions presented.

The public, meanwhile, waited for news of some out-standing victory, but the chief news was the list of killed and wounded. Lady Sarah again expressed a human re-action, though a strongly biased one, in her letter to her cousin Susan (who had lived for a time in America) on November 5, 1776:

> I was vastly struck with the accounts you give of your feels about the war being in the very spot of ground you lived in; I understand your horror perfectly well, & feel all *goose skin* with the very idea of it, it makes me creep all over. Only think of the horrible attempt of burning the town, think of the poor sick in it! My God! what a horrible thing it is alltogether! You talk of the time when we used to *fancy great things;* I am sure I can thank God very sincerely I am not Queen, for in the first place, I should have quarrell'd with His Majesty long before this, & my head would have been off probably. But if I had loved & liked him, & not had interest enough to prevent this war, I should certainly go mad, to think a person I loved was the cause of such a shameful war.

The following year brought no improvement in the situ-ation. On May 30, 1777, Chatham returned to the scene and made a motion for the cessation of hostilities. The House divided for the motion, 28 for; against 199.

In the fall session Chatham was again active, speaking against the use of Indians in the war. On December 2, he attacked the state of the national defense and ridiculed the claims of the Ministry that they were adequately pre-pared to win an ultimate victory.

The charge was even more true than he realized, for the bungling Germain had made a fatal mistake, though his culpability was not discovered until sometime afterwards. He had ordered General Burgoyne to march south from Canada into the province of New York, while the English forces at New York City were to advance northward. This plan was intended to cut off New England and break the colonies in two. The dispatches were sent to Burgoyne; but Germain decided to go down to the country as the dispatches to the New York City forces were being completed, and he did not take the time to sign them. Instead, he placed the papers in his overcoat pocket; and when he came up to London again he was wearing another coat and forgot that the dispatches had not been sent.

The New York City forces thus knew nothing of Burgoyne's plan. Burgoyne advanced southward under orders and, as history knows, was bagged by the colonials at Saratoga. Word of this disaster reached Chatham on December 3, independently of Government dispatches, and on December 5, 1777, in the House of Lords he again pleaded with the Ministry to abandon their hopeless and disastrous enterprise:

America . . . has been the great support of this country; she has produced millions; she afforded soldiers and sailors; she has given our manufacturers employment and enriched our merchants. The gentlemen of landed property would probably feel this; for when commerce fails—when new burdens are incurred—when the means by which those burdens were lightened are no more—the land-owner will feel the double pressure of heavy taxes; he will find them doubled in the first instance, and his rents proportionably decreased. But, for what have we sacrificed all those advantages? The pursuit of a *pepper-corn!* * And how have we treated America?—Petitions rejected—complaints unanswered—dutiful representations treated with contempt—an attempt to establish despotism on the ruins of constitutional liberty—measures to enforce taxation by the point of the sword. Ministers have insidiously betrayed us into a war; and what are its fruits? Let the sad catastrophe which has fallen Mr. Burgoyne speak the success.

* Again Pitt referred to Hans Stanley's famous observation.

But the majority of the Lords refused to be stirred. The Christmas holidays were drawing near, and at the session on December 11, 1777, the Earl of Oxford moved that the House adjourn until January 20, 1778. Chatham was staggered at this indifference to the national safety. The proposal of a six weeks' adjournment at this time seemed to him incredible, and he concluded:

> I tremble for this country; I am almost led to despair, that we shall ever be able to extricate ourselves. Whether or not the day of retribution is at hand, when the vengeance of a much injured and afflicted people will fall heavily on the authors of their ruin, I am strongly inclined to believe, that before the day to which the proposed adjournment shall arrive, the noble Earl who moved it will have just cause to repent of his motion.

The motion for the adjournment was carried by 47 against 17.

Things had reached a state which had confirmed only too fully Chatham's dire predictions.

"Where is this ruin to end?" he wrote to Dr. Addington on January 14, 1778. "Heaven only knows. I hold out without gout hitherto; perhaps I may last as long as Great Britain."

CHAPTER XL

"In the Cause of My Country"

The defeat of General Burgoyne revealed to the British public the depths to which the conduct of the King and the Lord North Ministry had plunged the country. George III had succeeded in his plan of being a "patriot king" whose ministers would do his bidding. In matters of State policy he had become an absolute monarch and was well-nigh an absolute failure.

His achievement of this degree of power had been effected slowly and shrewdly, first under the tutoring of Bute and Grenville and later under the guidance of his own dour judgment. He had developed into a tough-minded, ill-tempered and diligent monarch, impatient of all correction and satisfied only by yes-men.

Lord Sandwich, at the head of the Admiralty, knew virtually nothing of the state of the Navy, even though his ignorance was exposed at various times in Parliament. Lord Amherst, who remained as one of the few reputable persons in the Government, was overruled in his military policies by Lord George Germain, as Secretary for the American Colonies. Lord North, an amiable and kindly man, lacked the backbone to correct the King, knowing that such an act might cost him his place. Nowhere on the public scene was there a man, other than Chatham, who had sufficient strength and following to challenge the present state of affairs. Chatham continued to find that his scheme of a coalition cabinet, breaking up the structure of party government, had proved to be a fatal error. The Whigs remained dis-united while the Court group were tied together solidly by the self-interest of office-holding.

The despair of the nation was reaching such a point, however, that some change in ministry seemed inevitable, and many minds naturally turned to the distinguished invalid who, fifteen years earlier, when he was Mr. Pitt, had raised a fallen England to new heights of glory. Richmond, Rockingham, Thomas Coutts (the banker), Temple, and Shelburne, were among those who wrote to Chatham, urging him to form a ministry. Even Lord Bute sent a messenger to Dr. Addington, asking that he propose to Chatham to rescue the country from its mismanagement.

Such a proposal, however, was impractical unless the King and the Lord North Ministry were ready to make a change, for Chatham's strength was not adequate to plan and direct the sustained strategy which would be necessary to win a majority in Parliament; and only by a clear-cut defeat in Parliament could the North Ministry be expected to retire.

Hester, in particular, was opposed to having her husband at the head of an administration, even if it were feasible. The fiasco of the Chatham Ministry had demonstrated that his health could not stand the strain, and ten years had passed since that time. Another obstacle was a basic difference of opinion between himself and his closest political friends. He still cherished the notion that the Americans could be induced to return to the mother country. He could not bear the thought of the colonies becoming independent and thereby putting an end to his lifelong dream of a vast empire of freemen under the British flag. Richmond and Rockingham, even Camden, pleaded with him to favor negotiations with the colonies on the basis of independence, and then to work out some terms of friendly alliance which might still leave America within the imperial system. Richmond pointed out urgently that Chatham himself had favored independence in respect to taxation, colonial assemblies, and on virtually every other basic point except the Acts of Navigation. Why insist on the word "sovereignty" if that were to be the stumbling block. Chatham received these appeals graciously and calmly, but he was set in his opinion.

He was, nevertheless, somewhat hopeful that the Parliament and the Ministry might be persuaded to make changes in policy which would save the situation. He refused to

Lord North, the good-humored and ill-fated Minister of George III.

Bedford House in 1772, home of the truculent Duke of Bedford, who had his own political gang and thereby offended the other Whigs, including Mr. Pitt.

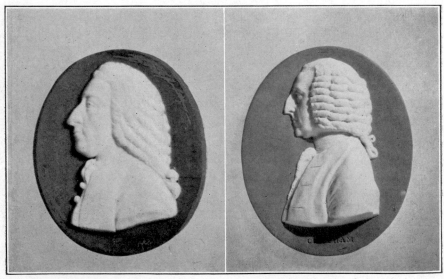

Two Wedgwood medallions of Pitt, both marked Wedgwood and Bentley. The one on the left was modeled by Flaxman in 1778.

consider allying himself with any group which would compromise his opinion and, before all, of course, he had no thought of returning to power at the solicitation of Lord Bute.

"What can this officious emissary mean by the nonsense he has at times thrown out to you?" Chatham wrote to Dr. Addington regarding an approach which had been made by Bute's agent. "Let him remember, the next attempt he makes to surprise your integrity by courtly insinuation, that his great patron and your village friend differ in this: one has ruined the King and Kingdom; the other still endeavours to save it."

Neither the Whigs nor Bute nor any man could save the country, in Chatham's opinion, until the Throne and the Court had a complete change of heart. He directed Hester to express this view definitely in a letter to Coutts on January 22, 1778:

> To rescue a falling country from the last consequences of their own fatal errors, until those errors are fully perceived, and, from conviction, sincerely renounced, is a work too dangerous (not to say impossible) for presumption itself to undertake, unbidden, and uncommanded. To obtrude ideas, now, perhaps, in any case, too late, would be folly, as well as presumption; courting extreme danger to no good end, and being but too likely to sink under the load of the faults of others. Nothing short of commands can be a motive to act in desperate cases: zeal, duty, and obedience may outlive hope.

Within a month Lord North had such a change of heart, for he learned that France had entered into alliance with America, which meant that the chances of British victory were highly improbable. To the astonishment of the country, on February 17, 1778, North asked the Commons to pass a bill which would appoint five Commissioners to deal with the colonies, granting the Commission the widest powers to make peace on virtually any terms that they could obtain. This was a complete reversal of the Government's former stand.

Lord North realized, more fully than ever before, that his Ministry was incapable of dealing with this acute crisis. He was convinced that William Pitt, the Earl of Chatham, was the one man who might extricate the country from its desperate plight, and he summoned the courage to lay this proposal before the King.

The rage of the oft-thwarted George knew no bounds. Again and again different sets of ministers had failed to carry out his orders successfully, and always finished by suggesting that he must call in Mr. Pitt, now Lord Chatham. This step invariably had meant humiliation for the King. While other men yearned for office and would yield obedience, even for minor favors, the Great Commoner had the impudence, at all times, to state the terms on which he would serve, and frequently had refused to serve at all. True enough, Chatham was always courteous, always reverential to the kingly office. His letters were couched in the most obsequious terms, but George III knew better than anyone else that Chatham's reverence was for the office of kingship, as an office which must express the policies of the Ministry, the Parliament, and the people. His Majesty replied to North in a frenzy. Chatham, of all persons. The one man who in an otherwise timid and somnolent era had blocked the King's purposes. Said his Majesty:

> No advantage to this country, nor personal danger to myself, can ever make me address myself to Lord Chatham, or to any other branch of the Opposition. Honestly, I would rather lose the Crown I now wear than bear the ignominy of possessing it under their shackles. . . . Should Lord Chatham wish to see me before he gives an answer, I shall most certainly refuse it. I have had enough of personal negotiation; and neither my dignity nor my feelings will ever let me again submit to it.
>
> You have now full power to act, but I do not expect Lord Chatham and his crew will come to your assistance.

"Lord Chatham must be head of any Administration in which he acts," Lord North replied, with a courageous candor which might have saved George III's reputation even at that late date, "and it would be vain and useless to expect him on any other footing."

The King, however, would not yield to such an idea. Even so, North, without hopes of success, delegated William Eden, one of the Commissioners for America, to feel out Chatham's views with respect to taking office. As North had expected, Chatham said that he would need to have the confidence of the Throne, that he must be known publicly as the head of the Ministry, not as a subordinate to anyone; and must be allowed to appoint "efficient men" in the key positions.

North advised his Majesty to accept whatever terms the Chatham group might ask, as the longer the move was delayed the more obdurate they would be, but the royal eyes merely bulged with obstinacy and anger. North, while weak and easy-going, was an astute judge of men and events, and he persisted in his recommendations that Chatham's services were absolutely essential. Finally the King inquired of North if he were going to play the traitor to him as Grafton had done, and on that appeal North abandoned the last effort to bring Chatham into office.

If George III had at this point called back to office the man who, as Mr. Pitt, had conceived the idea of a liberal British empire embracing both continents, the history of the next century and a half might have been quite different. The colonists were set on independence, and Mr. Pitt was determined to retain the principle of sovereignty, but he had proved himself in the past to be a resourceful negotiator on world affairs, and it is reasonable to think that he might have found some diplomatic formula, possibly the recognizing of the Continental Congress, which would have preserved the essential of his dream.

Richmond and the other younger men in Parliament, now that the King had refused to accept the Great Commoner, determined to force the issue on the North Ministry. Richmond's strategy was to move the withdrawal of troops from the thirteen colonies, and to follow this with a vote of censure on the North Administration. He introduced the motion to withdraw the troops, in the House of Lords on March 22, 1778, and this was lost by a vote of 56 against 28. Undiscouraged, he determined that on April 7 he would move an address to the King, recapitulating the misconduct of the war, entreating his Majesty to dismiss his ministers, and to withdraw his forces from the revolted provinces. Two days before this event Richmond paid Chatham the courtesy of advising him of these intentions, and urged him, if possible, to support the program.

"I am willing to hope," he wrote, "that differences of opinion were more apparent than real, and arose only from want of opportunities to communicate and to explain; for as I believe your Lordship and those I have the honor to act with were agreed as to the impracticability of compelling America to subjection by war, I think the difference could only be as to the more or less sanguine expectations we might form of what could be obtained by their consent. The circumstances are much changed of late, and may possibly now make our degrees of hope more similar."

Richmond's efforts were unavailing except that he received in reply a note written in friendly terms by Lord Chatham's son at the father's direction and hinting that Chatham would introduce some proposal of his own:

> Lord Chatham presents his respects to the Duke of Richmond, and desires to express his best thanks for the great honour of the communication of the motion intended by his Grace on Tuesday.
>
> It is an unspeakable concern to him, to find himself under so very wide a difference with the Duke of Richmond, as between the *sovereignty* and *allegiance* of America, that he despairs of bringing about successfully any honourable issue. He is inclined to try it, before *this bad* grows worse. Some weakness still continues in his hands; but he hopes to be in town to-morrow.

Richmond could not surmise what Chatham might have meant in his note by the phrase "he is inclined to try it." It had been characteristic of Mr. Pitt in his later days as Chatham to cherish within himself any idea of great moment until he was ready to proclaim it publicly. Though he consulted his colleagues and even the humblest subject on the techniques of subjects on which they were skilled, though his war strategy was the composite of ideas submitted by dozens of citizens familiar with the scene, in matters of major state policy he was inclined to consult his own judgment primarily. Certainly in the final stages of the formulation of an idea he seemed to feel that it would lose something of its shine and velocity by being exposed to a dress rehearsal, that he might yield in some fashion, through consultation, against his better sense, and that above all his voice was most persuasive, not in the drawing-room but in the theater of the Parliament.

Richmond, however, had reached his conclusions after earnest consultation with the chief men of the Opposition and he felt that already too much time had been lost. On the fateful day of April 7, 1778, Richmond and most of the other peers were on hand promptly for the opening of the session. Most of them were already seated when there was a stir in the corridor and Chatham entered the chamber supported by his son, William, and his son-in-law, Lord Mahon. He appeared like Mr. Pitt come alive again and risen from his death-bed, pale, emaciated, but with his great Roman nose and his piercing eyes the dominating features under his large gray wig.

He was dressed not in the crimson robe of a peer, but in the black velvet suit which had been familiar for so many years in the House of Commons. His legs were swathed about with flannel so that he could barely walk; and as he with difficulty made his way to his seat, the Lords rose to receive him while he bowed from side to side in acknowledgment of their courtesy. Taking his crutches in hand he then seated himself at the side of Temple and waited for the proceedings to begin.

Richmond moved his address to the Throne for the dismissal of Ministers, the withdrawal of troops, etc., according to plan. Lord Weymouth then made the reply on behalf of the Government. When Weymouth had concluded, Chatham rose to his feet, leaning on his crutches, and speaking in the midst of absolute silence. The Peers hung eagerly on his words, not only in tribute to their most distinguished member, but also to learn what solution the greatest living mind in England might have for this national crisis.

At first the speaker's voice was barely audible, so that his opening remarks have been lost to history, but as he warmed to his subject, his voice became more distinct and his manner animated. Taking one hand from his crutches, and raising the hand with his eyes lifted toward Heaven, he thanked God that he had been enabled to come that day to do his duty.

"I am old," he said, "and infirm; have one foot, more than one foot, in the grave. I am risen from my bed to stand up in the cause of my country, perhaps never again to speak in this House. I have made an effort, almost beyond my strength, to come here this day, to express my indignation at an idea which has gone forth of yielding up America."

He recited the history of the American war, of the measures to which he had objected and of all the evils which he had prophesied would result. As he summarized each one and stated his prophecy, he concluded in each case, "and so it proved!"

"My Lords," he continued, "I rejoice that the grave has not closed upon me; that I am still alive to lift up my voice against the dismemberment of this ancient and most noble monarchy! Pressed down as I am by the hand of infirmity, I am little able to assist my country in this most perilous conjuncture; but, my Lords, while I have sense and memory, I will never consent to deprive the royal offspring of the House of Brunswick, the heirs of the Princess Sophia, of their fairest inheritance.

"Where is the man that will dare to advise such a measure?

"My Lords, his Majesty succeeded to an empire as great in extent as its reputation was unsullied. Shall we tarnish the lustre of this nation by an ignominious surrender of its rights and fairest possessions?

"Shall this great kingdom, that has survived whole and

entire the Danish depredations, *the Scottish inroads*,"—
here he looked keenly at Lord Mansfield—"and the Norman conquest; that has stood the threatened invasion of the
Spanish armada, now fall prostrate before the House of
Bourbon? Surely, my Lords, this nation is no longer what
it was!

"Shall a people that fifteen years ago was the terror of
the world now stoop so low as to tell its ancient inveterate
enemy, 'Take all we have, only give us peace.'

"It is impossible! I wage war with no man, or set of men.
I wish for none of their employments; nor would I co-
operate with men who still persist in unretracted error; or
who, instead of acting on a firm decisive line of conduct,
halt between two opinions, where there is no middle path.

"In God's name, if it is absolutely necessary to declare
either for peace or war, and the former cannot be preserved
with honour, why is not the latter commenced without hesitation.

"I am not, I confess, well informed of the resources of
this kingdom; but I trust it has still sufficient to maintain
its just rights, though I know them not. But, my Lords,
any state is better than despair.

"Let us at least make one effort; and if we must fall, let
us fall like men!"

Richmond, Shelburne, and Camden listened in stunned
silence. Surely, this was not the whole of what Chatham
had to say. It was undoubtedly a severe blow that America should be allied with the House of Bourbon above all
others, that the colonies whose interests had been fostered
steadfastly by the Great Commoner should now be linked
with a totalitarian state which he regarded as a menace to
civilization. If England should declare war on France, in
a last desperate effort, that might be wise international
strategy, but it still would not solve the issues existing between England and the provinces. Where was the solution
about which Chatham had hinted? Perhaps he meant to
advise, as he had before, to recognize their Congress, within
the English system.

There was evidently something more to come, for as Chatham was seated Lord Temple turned to him and said, "You forgot to mention what we talked of; shall I get up?" "No, no," Chatham replied, "I will do it by and by."

Richmond, under the necessity of defending his plan, replied in terms of kindness and courtesy, acknowledging Chatham's great abilities, but reciting the feeble state of the country in the present situation.

When he had finished Chatham again rose to his feet in evident excitement, but suddenly pressed his hand to his heart, staggered, and fell into the arms of Temple and the Duke of Cumberland. He was, to all appearances, in the agony of death, and the whole room was thrown into confusion. One member opened the windows, another produced smelling salts, and the room was cleared of strangers. The Peers crowded about their chief member. In the forefront of the anxious circle was Lord Amherst, whom he had raised from obscurity to be one of the greatest generals in the nation's history; also Pitt's schoolmate, Charles Pratt, Lord Camden, whom he had advanced to one of the first positions in the kingdom; also Richmond, Shelburne, Temple, and others whose careers had been lighted by his genius. Even the Government Peers who had endured his biting criticism realized that they were present at a stirring moment in history, and paid their respects to the man who had accomplished so much for their country.

Only one person in the entire gathering sat apart. This was William Murray, Lord Mansfield. Murray, who had won the Latin competition at Oxford; Murray, whose precise and methodical nature loathed the theatricalities and vitality of Mr. Pitt. Murray was certain that his own monumental mind had always been greater than that of the dying mountebank, and yet he had been compelled to endure criticisms and sarcasms without having the facility to reply in quick debate. Murray was one of the three men under George II who, twenty-three years before, had been given the job of annihilating Mr. Pitt.

He had failed then, but could triumph now, for Death would soon do what he had failed to accomplish. Murray,

The collapse of William Pitt, Earl of Chatham, from the stroke which interrupted his final address in the House of Lords. Note that Murray, Lord Mansfield, remains seated.

The statue of Pitt by Joseph Wilton, R.A., in the City Hall Park, Charleston, S. C. Voted by the Colony in 1766, it originally stood at the intersection of Broad and Meeting Streets.

Lord Mansfield, alone among the body of Peers, sat quiet, and did not move a muscle.

Chatham, still alive, was removed to an adjacent room where he showed some faint signs of recovery. Later the same day he was taken to a house on Downing Street and two days later he was carried in a coach to Hayes. Life continued to flicker within him for a number of days, though at all times he was just on the borderland. While he was lingering at Hayes, his oldest son was called to join his regiment at Gibraltar, but hesitated whether he should respond at once, in view of his father's condition.

"Go, my son," Chatham advised him, "go whither your country calls you . . . spare not a moment which is due her service in weeping over an old man who soon will be no more."

On May 11, Lord Chatham became even weaker, and he called to his son William, asking him to read the description of the death of Hector from the *Iliad*. William read, in the original Greek, the following passage:

> *The shadow of death came down upon him, and his soul flew forth of his limbs and was gone to the house of Hades, wailing her fate, leaving her vigour and youth.*
>
> *Then to the dead man spake noble Achilles:*
> *"Die: for my death, I will accept it whensoever Zeus and the immortal gods are minded to accomplish it."*

On the same day he died. Immediately, with his passing, even his political enemies realized that the nation had lost a towering figure, a man of great conceptions and great purpose, the chief defender of the liberty of the subject. The House of Lords desired to attend his funeral in a body, and the King's approval was requested. His Majesty disapproved, and even so the motion was lost by only one vote.

Other proposals for honoring the Great Commoner were also viewed coldly by the King. He wrote to Lord North:

> I am rather surprised at the vote of a public funeral and monument for Lord Chatham. But I trust it is worded as a testimony of gratitude for his rousing the nation at the be-

ginning of the late war, and his conduct as Secretary of State, or this compliment, if paid to his general conduct, is rather an offensive measure to me personally. As to adding a trifle to the pension, I have no objection.

Parliament, in spite of the King's reluctance, voted a public funeral in Westminster Abbey, a monument, £20,000 to pay Chatham's debts, and a permanent annuity of £4,000 attached to the Earldom of Chatham. Lord North, regardless of the sentiments of his royal master, was an eager supporter of the various measures. He was absent when the bill for a public monument was proposed, but on hearing of it returned and entered the House in great haste. As reported in the *Chatham Correspondence:* "He declared his happiness in arriving in time enough to give his vote for the motion, which he hoped would pass unanimously; and lamented, that he had not breath enough, from the hurry in which he came down, to express himself with that degree of respect which he wished to show on so great an occasion."

Pending the lengthy discussions of where and how William Pitt, Lord Chatham, should be buried, his body remained at Hayes. The Mayor, Aldermen, and Common Council of London desired the funeral to be held at St. Paul's, but arrangements had already been made for Westminster. The City, however, erected a monument to the statesman in the Guildhall.

The body at last, on June 7, was brought to London where it lay in state in the Painted Chamber, between the House of Lords and the House of Commons. The funeral procession began at two o'clock on June 9th, leading through Westminster Hall where Lord Talbot's horse had made his Whiggish gesture, through the New Palace Yard, along Parliament Street, left on Bridge Street, left again on King Street to the Broad Sanctuary to the west door of the Abbey.

It was a curious, lonely procession, for the passing of one of England's greatest men. The Court was conspicuously absent and the noted figures among those present were almost wholly from the Opposition.

The procession was led by the High Constable of Westminster followed by several officials. Then came the commoners represented by seventy poor men in cloaks, accompanied by a standard, bearing the badges of the crest of the Pitt family.

There followed personal servants, physicians, clergy, and officials from the College of Heraldry. Next in line came Col. Isaac Barré who had served with Wolfe at Quebec, with Amherst at Montreal, and with Mr. Pitt in the House of Commons.

Attending Barré, in deep mourning, were the Dukes of Richmond, Northumberland, and Manchester, and the Marquis of Rockingham.

After more heralds and heraldic devices came the coffin, over which was a pall borne by Edmund Burke, Sir George Savile, John Dunning, and Thomas Townshend, an eloquent and appropriate quartet to officiate in the last rites of the Great Commoner. Then came members of the immediate family, other peers of the Opposition including Camden and Fortescue, followed by additional relations of the deceased, and concluding with the banner of the arms of Pitt.

More keenly even than in England, the passing of William Pitt, Earl of Chatham, was felt beyond the seas. He, more than anyone else in England, had been the friend of the American colonies, and it was he pre-eminently who had given them both courage and a philosophy.

He had fought consistently for the safeguards of the Constitution, in the New World as well as at home. Long before the Revolution he had popularized the sentiment that taxation without representation is tyranny. He had said, "I rejoice that America has resisted." He had described the American colonies as "an union solid, permanent and effectual."

It was his philosophy which was being echoed in the words of James Otis, Patrick Henry, and Tom Paine. He had defended the cause of Anglo-Saxon freedom, of "liberty and independency," as America's birthright; and his words continued to burn in the hearts of the Americans after he had passed on.

The events which immediately followed in British affairs are so familiar that they may be briefly recited. King George now reveled in the opportunity to have his own way. "May not the political exit of Lord Chatham incline you to continue at the head of my affairs?" he had asked Lord North the day after Chatham's final speech in the Lords. North had agreed, and the war was continued hopelessly and ineptly.

Two years later, in 1780,—a year before Cornwallis' surrender at Yorktown—a battery of George III's artillery was erected on James Island in the harbor of Charleston, South Carolina. It opened fire on the city, where William Lyttleton, cousin of Mr. Pitt, had once been a colonial governor. A shell, by an incredible irony of history, screamed across the Ashley River, up Meeting Street, past St. Michael's Church, into the intersection of Broad Street, and crashed into the statue of Mr. Pitt which the colony had commissioned fourteen years previously. The missile broke off the right arm, and shattered the right hand which held a copy of the Magna Carta.

Today, more than a hundred and fifty years later, in the City Hall Park of Charleston, South Carolina, U.S.A., the statue is still standing.

THE END

INTRODUCTION TO NOTES

Ralph Thompson, in the *New York Times,* Sept. 19, 1938 issue, wrote of the need for biography to find some happy medium between absence of annotation and the use of references so frequent as to impede the narrative.

He pointed out then and on other occasions that the reader who cares is entitled to have some assurances of the ground which the writer has covered, and that, conversely, display of diligence may be carried to excess.

I have tried to have regard for Mr. Thompson's wise warnings in the handling of this biography. The reader is certainly entitled to be assured that any new life of William Pitt, Earl of Chatham, has been written with the knowledge of the works on the subject by Basil Williams, Von Ruville, Lord Rosebery, Francis Thackeray, Lord Macaulay, and Tunstall. The lives by Harrison and by Green are also worth consulting.

In the handling of notes to the individual chapters, I have given citations only where the points seem to me to be controversial or could not readily be verified by consulting the indices of the various works in the bibliography of this book. If, however, any biographer or historian wishes to question any point about which he is in doubt or disagreement, I shall be glad to enter into correspondence, giving the citations of sources.

This is not the place to appraise the merits of the various published biographies of Chatham, but any student of the period would be ungrateful not to emphasize the magnificent notes and bibliography of Professor Williams' book, which can be of exceptional assistance to anyone working on the eighteenth century.

A writer on this period should also be able to affirm that he has covered the work of Horace Walpole the younger, both the *Memoirs* and the various *Letters* which are applicable to the subject in hand. Walpole himself, however, confesses to a lack of precise accuracy and needs to be checked where possible against the work of more careful scholars. On Walpole's behalf it should be said that usually his accounts of debates in Parliament agree closely with the reports of other contemporary writers.

537

One reason for the emergence of a new biography of William Pitt, Earl of Chatham, at this time, is the significance of his life in current world affairs and the fact that prior biographies, even when relating the bulk of Pitt's activities and speeches on behalf of liberty, have seemingly underestimated their significance. This is not surprising, for most of them were written in periods when the democratic idea was unchallenged, and Mr. Pitt was therefore, to the reader, apparently only stating what was generally accepted. Today, when the issues are comparable, in part, to those of Pitt's lifetime, the clarity and forcefulness of his thoughts and action shine with a new light.

The availability of much new material in recent years and new syntheses of old material also call for a new biography on this character. The publication of the correspondence of George III, the discovery of the General Amherst Papers, the thoroughly documented analysis of eighteenth-century politics by L. B. Namier, and the book, *Poor Fred,* on Frederick, Prince of Wales, by Sir George Young, all give new information on the period.

While Sir George Young's work is conspicuously partisan, it gives convincing proofs that the pivotal figure of Prince Frederick was much maligned for political reasons. The loyalty of Pitt and others to the Prince's party is now seen to be not wholly a matter of expediency.

The work of L. P. Gipson on the twenty-five years preceding the American Revolution is important for economic background; and numerous specialty works have appeared in the last year or two, such as *The North Briton* by George Nobbe, making more understandable certain aspects of the period.

One of the most fortunate events for American students of William Pitt, the elder, is the acquisition of the Stowe Collection by the Henry E. Huntington Library and Art Gallery, San Marino, California. These are the papers of the Grenville family, to whom Mr. Pitt became connected by marriage and with whom he was distantly connected through the Villiers blood on the maternal side. Many parts of the Stowe Collection have already been published, but many have not. Notable among the documents apparently unconsulted hitherto is the copy of the marriage settlement of William Pitt and Hester Grenville, which disposes at last of the controversy as to by what extent Pitt became financially benefited through his marriage.

Most commentators on Pitt have expressed the uncertainty of anyone knowing whether or not many of Pitt's speeches were accurately reported, because reporters were officially barred from Parliament. There is not space here to discuss the comparative conditions of present-day and eighteenth-century reporting; but I wish to express the confidence in the probable reliability of the accounts which have been handed down. The rules of Parliament were circumvented in various ways, and where several versions of a speech are available their similarity is remarkable. Williams' translations of French reports of Pitt's addresses tend to confirm substantial accuracy of the English records.

ACKNOWLEDGMENTS

In making any list of acknowledgments, it is perhaps obvious, yet true, to say that any biographer is in debt to hundreds of persons living and dead who have already worked in the field he is covering. I may also add that perhaps I may unwittingly omit the name of someone who has been of material assistance and, if so, I shall hope to be forgiven.

I wish to make acknowledgment to Dixon Ryan Fox, President of Union College, to whom this book is dedicated, for guidance and suggestion on research in the period.

To Dr. Max Farrand, Director of the Huntington Library, San Marino, California; and to Capt. Reginald Berti Haselden and Miss Haydée Noya of the Manuscript Division of that Library.

To Prof. L. P. Gipson, of Lehigh University, for comment and recommendations in research.

To Miss Louise Ernst, for research assistance and comment.

To Miss Elizabeth Schuyler Dunlop, of Pasadena, California, and Miss Muriel Gooden, for research in the Huntington Library.

To Miss Isabel Stewart, of San Francisco, for comment and suggestion.

To Howard S. Leach, Librarian, and Miss Myrtle Helms, of the Lehigh University Library.

To Miss Harriet Root, Librarian, and Miss Elizabeth Burrows of the Bethlehem, Pa., Public Library.

To the staff of the Enoch Pratt Memorial Library, Baltimore, Md., the University of Pennsylvania Library, the New York Society Library, and the New York Public Library, the Haverford College

Library, Princeton University Library, the Philadelphia Library, and above all, to the Henry E. Huntington Library and Art Gallery for permission to use and reprint documents.

To R. Malcolm Sills, in charge of the Mason-Franklin Collection, Yale University Library, for permission to consult its extraordinary resources of pamphlet material.

To Stanley G. Remington, of Baltimore, Md., for assistance in getting old and rare books.

To the American Philosophical Society, for research, especially with respect to the letters of Patience Wright.

To His Excellency, the Marquis of Lothian.

To Charles W. and Hope Williams, who prodded me into undertaking a new book, and to Horace W. Stokes who was present at, and persisted in, the prodding.

To the Earl Amherst who has made available to me the use of the Amherst Papers.

To the British Museum and the British Public Record Office.

To Thomas Furlong, for consultation on art sources and illustrations.

To Arthur Pound, for help on the Temple genealogy.

To Miss Elsie Shipman and Miss Alice Smith, for assistance in research.

To Miss Mary Gregorie Trott for checking on Charleston, S. C., sources.

To R. T. H. Halsey, not only for permission to reproduce items from his collections, but also for wise counsel.

To Homer M. Smith for aid in locating rare Americana.

NOTES

CHAPTER I

The numerous sources on which this chapter draws indicate the necessity of choosing between the precise annotation of every statement, or the alternative of general observations as to evidence. I have chosen the latter course, standing ready to answer any specific inquiries from a biographer or historian relative to the authority for any specific facts. The list of the various Pitts in Parliament and the places for which they sat is taken from various contemporary records. The statements that certain characters were school and university mates of Mr. Pitt are based on books dealing with Eton or taken from biographies of the persons concerned.

The summation of character of Fox is not from any one historical citation but is based on the accumulation of evidence in his acts, the comments of his contemporaries, and the evidence of his own letters. The character of Fox, in the letters of Horace Walpole, for example, differs considerably from the estimation of himself as it appears in his introduction to the *Life and Letters of Sarah Lennox*.

These observations may seem obvious, if not naïve, to the professional historian, but they are given to indicate the great amount of space which would be required if it were decided to give a full annotation of all the sources consulted for a particular chapter.

It may be worth noting that the final scene of the chapter has been evolved from various sources: one source provides a detailed description of St. Stephen's Chapel, another where Mr. Pitt sat, another what he wore and still others the details of the debate and the political background.

CHAPTER II

The term *Whig,* originally referring to a horse-thief, came, by the association of ideas in the English mind, to mean a Scotch Presbyterian. Subsequently, it also meant a rebel, and finally it referred to the political clique which supported the Protestant succession in deposing the Stuart line of kings.

Tory was also a slang term (comparable to the modern slang word "harp"), meaning Irish Catholic. The designations *Whig* and

Tory came into political use during the struggle which resulted in "the Glorious Revolution of 1688" when the Stuart king, James II, was obliged to abdicate in favor of a Protestant monarch. For many years after this event the word *Whig* had only a rather general meaning of designating the group which had brought in the new dynasty, while *Tory* applied to Stuart sympathizers or to those who were merely anti-Whigs. In the course of years the Whig doctrine became associated with the idea of constitutional democratic government, while Tories were held to be royalists believing, more or less, in the personal rule of a monarch supported by a subservient ministry. See *Encyclopædia Britannica* and Murray's *New English Dictionary* (Oxford Dictionary).

CHAPTERS III AND IV

Letters are quoted from Lord Rosebery's *Lord Chatham.*

CHAPTERS V, VI, AND VII

Von Ruville displays the unreliability of his powers of deduction in commenting on this period of Pitt's life. In Chapter IV of his *William Pitt, Earl of Chatham,* for example, the author deduces that Luneville would not have been a suitable place for William to choose, doubts that he went there, and assumes that "his brother Thomas had nothing to spare for him." All three guesses are proved erroneous by letters quoted by other scholars.

Von Ruville also accepts without question the theory that William Pitt wrote the "Letter on Superstition" appearing in the London *Journal* in 1733. Basil Williams, in his life of Pitt, Volume I, p. 216 n., presents strong evidence that the paper was written by a James Pitt who was one of a group of professed unbelievers.

Most of the letters in these chapters are quoted from Lord Rosebery's *Lord Chatham.* The translations from French into English are my own.

The discovery of these letters by Lord Rosebery is an interesting evidence of the fact that even the most authoritative scholars can at times be in error.

According to: Historical Mss. Commission, 13th Report, Appendix, Part III, Vol. I (the Dropmore Collection), published in 1892, there were no letters extant between Ann Pitt and her brother.

Page XIV of the Introduction says:

It is noteworthy that, although the correspondence preserved by Miss Pitt ranges over a period of more than thirty years, from 1734 to 1768, during which her brother William fills so great a place in English history, it does not contain a single letter from him, or indeed, any definite allusion to him.

Lord Rosebery was evidently undeterred by this categorical statement, for he independently examined the Dropmore manuscripts and found there this rich store of letters, given in his book, which was printed in 1910. I am not aware of what may be the explanation of the failure of the Historical Manuscripts Commission to find the letters, but I cite the instance to show the need for skepticism and persistence in the face of affirmations that such and such historical data is unavailable.

CHAPTER VIII

It seems probable that Mr. Pitt's uncle, Col. John Pitt, had as his first wife, Diana Howard, half-sister of the ninth Earl of Suffolk who was the husband of Lady Suffolk. *Burke's Peerage* records the marriage of Lady Diana Howard to Col. John Pitt; and Lady Suffolk's early interest in Ann indicates some special reason for their acquaintanceship, though this may have been accounted for by their more distant Villiers connection. I have, however, been unable to establish positive evidence that Diana Howard's husband was the same Col. John Pitt as Mr. Pitt's uncle.

The quotation from the Duchess of Argyle to Lady Suffolk is contained in the *Suffolk Correspondence*. It was written when each was a favorite of King George and before either had succeeded to her respective title.

CHAPTER IX

The partial list of the art collection at Stowe is from Britton and Brayley's *The Beauties of England and Wales*.

A check by Thomas Furlong in the Frick Library, New York City, and the library of the Metropolitan Museum of Art, New York City, did not discover any reference to the Stowe collection. In certain instances the painters listed at Stowe had made many pictures under the heading given, such as the numerous portraits of his father by Rembrandt. In other cases it was not recorded that the painter had ever painted the subject mentioned, as for instance, Van Dyck's *Sir Richard Leveson*.

The account given in the authority cited is, however, so precise in many of the details regarding Stowe, and so many of the details check accurately with other sources, where available, that the presumption is in favor of the list of paintings being correctly given. It is suggested, therefore, that students of art and the history of art may find *The Beauties of England and Wales* a useful reference with respect to unknown paintings or the duplicates of paintings.

CHAPTER X

Downing Street was laid out in 1633-71 and was named for Sir George Downing, who was a graduate of Harvard University. He was a member of the class of 1642, the first class to be graduated from Harvard. Downing was a secretary of state in 1668. During the days when the Earl of Lichfield owned No. 10, the houses on the street were used by persons of eminence, but in Pitt's time many of the homes had become lodging houses occupied chiefly by Scottish and Irish members of Parliament. Boswell had lodgings in Downing Street in 1763, and Tobias Smollett tried to establish himself as a surgeon in Downing Street offices in 1744.

CHAPTER XI

Pitt was living in Burlington Buildings, Cork Street. Rosebery, apparently through a typographical error, gives the address as York Street.

CHAPTER XII

The status of the Holy Roman Empire from 1556 is almost as confusing as the War of the Austrian Succession. Eighteenth-century writers and correspondents often refer to The Empire in a way which would suggest an organized nation. Basil Williams, in *The Whig Supremacy,* gives a map which shows The Empire as including Austria. Technically this is correct, as the presiding heads of the Empire (Francis I in 1745 and Joseph II in 1765) were appointees of the Hapsburg family. In actuality, the central German states constituting The Empire were a loose confederation which I have shown on a map as "dependent states." The *Encyclopædia Britannica* refers to the Emperor at this period as being less than "an interstate arbitrator." This is a just designation, since the various states nominally within The Empire from time to time independently allied themselves with powers which were hostile to Austria. Austria's ambition was to dominate an area extending from northern Italy throughout most of the territory occupied by twentieth-century Germany, but this alliance was an historical fiction and never an actuality.

The existence of the idea of The Empire, allied with France and Spain, however, ultimately became a serious threat to British interests, as Pitt realized when he came to power.

CHAPTER XIII

It is interesting to observe in this chapter the early developments of Mr. Pitt's stand for a big navy policy. Since the history of England had so clearly indicated that the days of her greatness had been accompanied by a big navy policy, it is curious that Mr. Pitt should have been one of the few advocates of this idea in his era. The lack of such vision on the part of the other statesmen of the times may be regarded as a consequence of the prejudice against learning in high places. A coronet was a far better passport to political eminence than a knowledge of history or statecraft.

CHAPTER XIV

Readers are referred to *Poor Fred* by Sir George Young, for a more temperate presentation of Lord Bute than is available in the commentaries of his time.

CHAPTER XV

Basil Williams, in his biography of Pitt, Volume I, pp. 187, 188, discussing the death of Prince Frederick and Mr. Pitt's tribute to the Prince, takes the view that the tribute was given in order to curry favor with the Princess Dowager.

This interpretation does not seem plausible. Pitt could and did seek the favor of the Princess in various ways and it was unnecessary from this motive to praise her late husband and to make a sarcastic reference to the attitude of the King. In fact, it seems clear that Pitt had everything to lose and nothing to gain by his generous tribute to the late Prince, and that he spoke out of affection for, and loyalty to, a departed friend.

See also *Poor Fred,* by Sir George Young.

CHAPTER XVI

Students interested in a thorough study of the Jewish question in England in 1753 may find it elaborately presented in the issues of the *Gentleman's Magazine* for that period, and exceptionally full accounts of Parliamentary debates on the subject are to be found in *Parliamentary History* covering that year.

CHAPTER XVII

Most of the letters in this chapter have been quoted by Rosebery, though others which he did not use, but which appear here, are from the *Chatham Correspondence.*

CHAPTER XVIII

There is a question as to whether the portrait by Reynolds at Knole is "Mrs. Axford" or "Miss Axford." John Heneage Jesse states it to be Mrs. Axford, but most present-day listings do not so give it. The portrait is sometimes said to be that of a daughter of Hannah Lightfoot.

William J. Thoms, F.S.A., wrote *Hannah Lightfoot,* published in 1867, in which he assailed the entire legend, and even asserted that letters to the magazines from the supposed relatives of Miss Lightfoot were forgeries perpetrated with the connivance of one of the magazine editors.

The Fair Quaker by Mary Pendered, published in 1910, is more inclined to believe there was something in the story and attacks certain grounds of Mr. Thoms' skepticism. The Pendered book, however, does not add to the store of positive proof. In spite of the persistence of the tale, with its circumstantial mention of names, it is entirely possible that the incident may be only a myth.

On the other hand, it is difficult to believe that anyone would start such a rumor about the royal family without some basis. At the very least it is probable that certain circumstantial facts did originate from the younger Beckford. The acquaintanceship of Pitt with Miss Chudleigh and Miss Taylor was not a matter of general mention and not remarked upon by the biographies of him extant at the time.

The husbands of Lady Elizabeth Montagu and Lady Mary Wortley Montague were first cousins, but spelled their names differently, the latter family using the final "e."

CHAPTER XIX

In the *Love-letters of William Pitt,* edited by Ethel Ashton Edwards, there is a curious error in Pitt's letter of October 21, 1754, which is quoted as saying: "I have writ this night to my poor sister Ann, she is well enough to return to England this winter."

The line should read: "She is not well enough to return to England this winter."

The point is mentioned here, even though seemingly trivial, for if Ann had been well enough to come to England Hester's succeeding correspondence with her, emphasizing the fact of Ann's not returning to England, would have been extraordinarily uncordial.

CHAPTER XX

Most of the Pitt biographies quote a passage from an address which Mr. Pitt made on November 13, 1755, in which he inferentially compared Granville to the river Rhône and Newcastle to the Saône. As most of his fellow-members had made the grand tour and were familiar with these rivers, the passage made a great impression, but to a modern generation the metaphor requires too much explanation to be of much interest. The climax of the comparison was in these words:

I remember at Lyons to have been carried to see the conflux of the Rhône and the Saône: this is a gentle feeble languid stream, and though languid of no depth—the other a boisterous and overbearing torrent—but they meet at last; and long may they continue united, to the comfort of each other, and to the glory, honour and happiness of this nation.

CHAPTER XXI

Further data on the investiture and customs of the House of Lords may be found in A. S. Turberville's excellent work on that subject. Complete details of the ceremonies attendant upon the opening of a new Parliament are given in the *Parliamentary History* of the period.

CHAPTER XXII

The lengthy debates fully detailed in *Parliamentary History* for the year 1757, as well as the proceedings of the court-martial, give a dramatic picture of the extraordinary efforts made to obtain the conviction of Byng and throw further light on the courage of Mr. Pitt in opposing a popular, powerful, and well-organized movement.

CHAPTER XXIII

The estimates of population for various countries in the mid-eighteenth century are necessarily vague, as accurate population statistics for most countries were not available until some years later.

The estimate given for England is by Basil Williams in *The Whig Supremacy*. According to the Encyclopædia Britannica, France had 27,340,000 in 1801, Spain had 10,268,000 in 1787, Austria had 29-770,000 in 1818. It is doubtful if Frederick of Prussia ruled over more than 2,500,000, and his ally, Ferdinand of Brunswick may not have had that many. Frederick's Prussia was actually about the size and location of East Prussia in August, 1939. As Frederick intermittently conquered and lost Silesia, Saxony, and other German provinces it would be difficult to draw a fixed boundary for his kingdom. As late as 1880 all the German states in the Prussian confederation totaled only 27,000,000 in population, a smaller figure than for France or Austria at the beginning of the century. It will be seen, therefore, that the value of Frederick's aid was in his energy and genius. England and the German states combined were much inferior in population to the Bourbon allies.

CHAPTER XXIV

Readers who may be in doubt with respect to certain particulars of military strategy as recited in this and succeeding chapters are requested to make special study of the Bibliography, as there reference will be found to very special works on different phases of the campaigns. *Louisbourg*, by J. S. McLennan, for example, is a thoroughly documented work which gives a considerably different account of the siege from that found in Corbett. While Corbett's *Seven Years War* is still the outstanding work on that subject, research and manuscript discoveries of recent years modify Corbett's account in various details, especially in respect to the American scene.

CHAPTER XXV

Various biographies of William Pitt, Earl of Chatham, refer to an incident in September, 1759, in which Earl Temple resigned the office of Privy Seal, because the King had refused to appoint Temple to the Order of the Garter. Mr. Pitt felt affronted at the King's refusal since this was the only request that had been made of the Crown by Pitt's political connection, and under this pressure his Majesty soon afterwards yielded to Temple's importunities. A full description of the incident has been omitted from this chapter because the affair was of no special significance in a year which was crowded with matters of overwhelming moment both to Pitt and the kingdom. Readers who wish to be further informed on the incident are referred to *Chatham Correspondence,* Vol. I, pp. 438, 439, 474.

CHAPTER XXVI

Excellent and full accounts of the European phases of the war are given in J. S. Corbett's *Seven Years War.*

CHAPTER XXVII

Bolingbroke's *The Idea of a Patriot King,* from which only excerpts could be given here for reasons of space, is well worth study by anyone dealing with the technique of absolutism and dictatorship.

CHAPTER XXVIII

The incidents and conversations in this chapter are based on: *The Life and Letters of Lady Sarah Lennox;* with an introductory memoir by Henry Fox; *Memoirs of the Reign of George III* by Horace Walpole; *Letters of Horace Walpole; Historical Memoirs* by Nathaniel Wraxall, and the *Grenville Papers.* The *Memoirs of George III* by J. H. Jesse was also consulted, but this material is not by a contemporary and is drawn almost wholly from the other sources cited.

It is unusual to find such detailed description of conversations and scenes of a love affair between historical characters because of the very nature of the occasion. In this case, however, the contemporary accounts are in substantial agreement. It is interesting to observe that the *Grenville Papers,* usually concerned with dry affairs of state, contain copious records on this subject, indicating its importance to the Pitt and Temple-Grenville connections.

The accounts differ in one particular. According to Henry Fox, Lord Holland, Lady Sarah did not at any time accept the King's proposal, and probability tends to support this version. Once Sarah had accepted the King, presumably the affair would have moved to a more sharply defined crisis. On the other hand, the commentary by Captain Henry Napier, R.N., a son of Sarah Lennox, given in *The Life and Letters of Sarah Lennox* affirms that Lady Sarah told him that she had accepted the King in one interview with him, indicating that had she chosen to do so she might have been Queen of England. This perhaps was a wishful reminiscence on the lady's part. Her version, however, is supported by a letter of Thomas Pitt (William Pitt's nephew), written to George Grenville at the time. Tom Pitt was of the same generation as Sarah and a cordial friend both then and in later years. He may have been more in her confidence than was her uncle. He tells that she was receptive to the King's proposal.

Lord Holland apparently errs in at least one particular, in thinking that Lady Sarah entirely lost interest in Lord Newbottle. In a letter to Lady Susan several years after this incident, she referred to meeting Lord Newbottle in London, and on that occasion at least there was a renewal of the old attraction. He was already married to someone else, and Sarah suggested that they had better see no more of each other because of the talk that might be occasioned by it.

CHAPTER XXIX

Several of the letters quoted in this chapter are from the Dropmore Collection, and the originals are undated, as to the year. Rosebery and others have assumed that they belong to this general period, as their internal evidence would indicate. I feel that it is justifiable to assume that the correspondence took place immediately prior to November 4, 1760. The letter from Pitt to Ann on that date refers to the pension subject; and all prior correspondence in this chapter by Hester, Ann and William led up to Ann's plea that she had come to London to look into the pension possibility—"a safe and honourable retreat," as she called it. Though question has been raised at placing this group of letters in October, since Ann in one of them says, "I writ you word from the Bath that I had thoughts of coming to Town" etc., I do not feel that this limited her to arriving just before the Christmas holidays, especially as the correspondence shows that she visited a number of friends in different localities around London.

CHAPTER XXX

Pitt's youngest child, James Charles, was born April 24, 1761 at St. James Square during the critical period of his struggles with the Cabinet on the Peace issue. The birth dates and places of his other children were: Hester, born November, 1755, at the Pay Office; John, born October 10, 1756, at Hayes; Harriot, born April, 1758, in London; William, born May 28, 1759, at Hayes.

CHAPTER XXXI

The events of this chapter have been assembled from a multitude of sources, especially as related to the struggle within the Cabinet.

I do not know of any other place where they have been arranged specifically in relationship to the calendar, though I feel that the timing of the various events is particularly important. Brian Tunstall's biography of Pitt is particularly full and illuminating on this period.

The quotations from the marriage ceremony are from the *Prayer Book* printed at that time.

Additional details on the Coronation may be found in the *Gentleman's Magazine* and in Horace Walpole's *Memoirs of George III.*

PARTICULARS OF HESTER'S CORONATION ROBE

To Countess Temple
    Bill for Coronation Robe

The R^t Hon^{le} Countess Temple

B^{ot} of (Crest)   Barrett (Late Basnett's) Laceman at the
                Goat, the corner of Craven Street in
                the Strand

London

1761
Aug. 21 9 yds Fine silver Clinean Point d'Esprit at 3/6   1.11.6
     28 A very rich gold Point d'Espagne Shape for
         Shoes and narrow for the Heels and
         Quarters   0.19.6
Sep. 9 A very rich silver open spangled Girdle &
         Tassels at   0.13.6
         A Fine very rich gold Point d'Espagne Trim-
         ming for the Coronation Petticoat Trimmed
         with very rich Gold Plate Roses and board-
         ered with rich Gold spangled Fringe with
         a rich Gold Embroidered spangled Head   47.10
         2 yds 1/2 very deep Exceeding rich gold
         spangled Fringe with a very rich gold Point
         d'Espagne & Embroidered Head for the Bot-
         tom of the Petticoat

                                                   ————————
                                                   50.14.6
Rec'd 29th Sepr 1761 the full contents and demands
                        for Mr Bry^t Barrett
                        Jacob Gibson
(Courtesy of Huntington Library)

CHAPTER XXXII

The *Annual Register,* 1761 issue, has numerous interesting comments on the events of this chapter.

CHAPTER XXXIII

The publication of the official notice of the Government regarding the resignation of Mr. Pitt, given as an illustration to this book, is not available in any other work of reference, as far as I have been able to find. The original from which this was photographed is in the Rare Book Room of the Library of Congress.

CHAPTER XXXIV

Basil Williams and Horace Walpole differ in their accounts of these debates with respect to what remarks were made on what day. Walpole places some of Pitt's remarks as of February 14, and cites the record late adjournment on that date. A footnote in *Chatham Correspondence,* Vol. II, p. 287, also gives February 14 as the record session of the House. Williams gives the date as the 17th. *Parliamentary History,* Vol. XV, gives the 17th as the day when Mr. Pitt spoke to the motion, while the footnote in *Chatham Correspondence,* Vol. II, p. 288, places these remarks on the 19th. The discrepancies are understandable, since the debates lasted over a several-day period and were not reported immediately. It is probable that the participants themselves did not recall accurately the exact time of the various speeches. Basil Williams' work is exceptionally careful in appraisal of source material, but I beg leave to differ with Williams in certain instances on the hour and date probabilities in this particular event, as may be seen by comparison of the text of this chapter with Vol. II, Chapter XX of the Williams biography.

All authorities are in substantial agreement, however, as to what was said, the difference being only in respect to time.

CHAPTER XXXV

See notes to Chapter XXX which will indicate the ages of the Pitt children at this period.

Chapter XXXVI

Horace Walpole's *Memoirs of George III* give a detailed, informative view of the surrounding politics of this period, in fuller scope than is necessary here, but very rewarding for anyone with a special interest in the eighteenth century.

Chapter XXXVII

The *Chatham Correspondence* of this period gives additional evidence of the worn and twisted condition of Chatham's mind.

Chapter XXXVIII

The quotation referring to "a scarecrow of violence" is from *Chatham Correspondence,* Vol. III, p. 469. In Williams, Vol II, p. 266, there was apparently a misprint, as the quotation is given "a scarecrow of violence to . . . timid statesmen" instead of "temperate statesmen."

Chapter XXXIX

For refusal of General Amherst to take the American command see *Correspondence of King George the Third,* Vol. IV, Nos. 2161, 2162.

For General Amherst's opinion on the necessary strategy in America see above reference Nos. 2161, 2170. The latter instance quotes Amherst's opinion as given in the Cabinet, Jan. 17, 1778. See also letter No. 2229.

Chapter XL

The ineptness and subservience of the King's Cabinet in 1778 is borne out by the comments of contemporaries as well as by events.

The Government consisted of a Cabinet of only seven men, as follows:

First Lord of the Treasury and Chancellor of the Exchequer—
  Lord North
First Lord of the Admiralty—Lord Sandwich
Secretaries of State—Lord Hillsborough and Lord Stormont
  (a nephew of Mansfield!)
Secretary of State for the Colonies—Lord George Germain
Lord Chancellor—Lord Thurlow
Commander in Chief of the Forces in Great Britain—General,
  Lord Amherst

According to the notes of the Cabinet meetings made at the time by General Amherst (and now in the Private Letters collection of the present Earl Amherst at 1 Wilton Crescent, Knightsbridge, London), these seven men made the major decisions and carried out the King's wishes.

They did not meet at the Government offices or at the palace, but, according to the evidence of the Amherst notes, convened about once a week in rotation at the homes of the various members. Lord North, Lord George Germain, and Lord Sandwich did most of the talking. This is borne out by the *Historical Memoirs* of Sir N. W. Wraxall, who has elaborated on the theme. He tells that after dinner it was customary for the table to be cleared for business. Lord Chancellor Thurlow would then line up several chairs in a row, stretch out on them, and go to sleep until the meeting was over. Amherst made little, if any, comment. Wraxall reports that "at the Cabinet dinners . . . though he [Amherst] usually gave his decided affirmative or negative to the specific measure proposed, yet he always did it in a few words, often by a monosyllable."

There were occasions of Mansfield and Attorney General Wedderburn being called in for an opinion; and Lord Gower, the Lord President of the Council, was occasionally consulted, but the seven men listed above were the chief figures in the ill-fated Ministry.

Earl Bathurst was Lord Chancellor from January 23, 1771, until June 3, 1778, when Edward Thurlow, Baron Thurlow, succeeded to the office. Thurlow had been a member of the inner Cabinet in his prior post of Attorney General, which he had held from 1771, while Bathurst seems to have been less frequently included in the Cabinet councils.

The ineptitude of this small Cabinet, or its lack of independence, may be indicated by the fact that at the meeting where General Amherst gave his opinion on the American war only three other members were present, North, Suffolk, and Sandwich. (See *Correspondence of King George the Third,* Vol. IV, No. 2170.) The Earl of Suffolk, though for a brief time and on that occasion one of the principal Secretaries of State, was not an influential factor in the Ministry.

The extent to which this was the King's war is indicated in his *Correspondence* wherein Lord North urgently advises a conciliatory attitude toward the colonies and the King rejects the proposal. Vol. IV, Nos. 2179, 2182.

The attitude of the King on bringing Chatham into the Ministry is to be seen in *Corres. Geo. III,* Vol. IV, Nos. 2235, 2237, 2240, and in the complete letter quoted in part in this biography, i.e. No. 2232.

The King's complete letter on the "political exit" of Chatham is No. 2284, and on the proposal for a public funeral, No. 2236.

Basil Williams, in his biography of William Pitt, refers to the cannon-ball which struck the Pitt statue as being fired from a ship. This apparently is an error. Prof. Williams cites the *Magazine of American History,* Vol. VIII, pp. 214 et seq. That account, however, states that the ball was fired from a battery on James Island and is consistent with other accounts. The *Magazine of American History* gives as its source the *Southern Literary Journal,* Vol. I, No. 5, January, 1836.

The Pitt statue at Charleston, S. C., originally stood in the intersection of Broad and Meeting Streets.

BIBLIOGRAPHY

Acts and Resolves of the Province of Massachusetts Bay.
Acts of the Privy Council of England, Colonial Series.
Additional Mss. (Brit. Mus.).
Adolphus, John, Esq.: *The History of England from the Accession of King George the Third to the Conclusion of Peace in the Year 1783.*
Almon, John: *Parliamentary Register.*
Alvord, C. W.: *Genesis of the Proclamation of 1763.*
Amherst Papers (Private).
Amherst Papers (W. O. 34).
Amherst, Jeffery: *Journal.*
Amherst, William: *Journal.*
Andrews, Alexander: *Eighteenth Century.*
Anglo-Saxon Review, The.
Anson, W. T.: *Law and Custom of the Constitution.*
Arkell, R. L.: *Caroline of Ansbach, George the Second's Queen.*
Ashbourne, Lord: *Pitt.*
Aspinwall Papers, Collections of the Massachusetts Historical Society.
Authentic Records of the Court of England for the Last Seventy Years, The.

Bancroft, George: *History of the United States.*
Barrington, Shute: *Political Life of William Wildman, Viscount Barrington.*
Bayne-Parnell, Rosamond: *The English Child in the 18th Century.*
Beatson, Robert: *A Political Index to the Histories of Great Britain and Ireland.*
Beer, George Louis: *British Colonial Policy, 1754-1765.*
Bisset, Robert: *A History of the Reign of George III.*
Bolingbroke, Lord: *Works—Idea of a Patriot King.*
Book of the Court.
Boston Record Commissioners Reports.
Botsford, J. B.: *English Society in the 18th Century.*
Bowdoin and Temple Papers (Preface to *Collections of the Massachusetts Historical Society*).

557

Britton, John, and Brayley, Edward Wedlake: *The Beauties of England and Wales.*
Broadley, A. M., and Melville, Lewis: *The Beautiful Lady Craven.*
Bryce, John: *The Holy Roman Empire.*
Buckle, Henry Thomas: *History of Civilization in England.*
Burke, Edmund: *Annual Register.*
Burke, Sir John Bernard: *Peerage.*
Burke's Extinct and Dormant English Peerage.

Campbell, John: *Lives of the Chancellors.*
Campbell, John: *Lives of the Chief Justices of England.*
Campbell, Thomas: *Frederick the Great, His Court and Times.*
Cannon, Richard: *Historical Record of the Life Guards.*
Carlson, C. Lennart: *The First Magazine, A History of the Gentleman's Magazine.*
Century Dictionary and Cyclopedia, The.
Channing, Edward: *A History of the United States.*
Chart, D. A.: *The Story of Dublin.*
Clarke, *The Georgian Era* (Pub. London, 1847; initials of author not given).
Cobbett, Wm.: *Parliamentary History.*
Collins, A.: *Peerage.*
Colonial Office Papers (Brit.); *A. and W. I.*
Commager, H. S., and Nevins, Allan: *The Heritage of America.*
Corbett, J. S.: *England in the Seven Years War.*
Court and City Register (London).
Cross, Wilbur L.: *The History of Henry Fielding.*
Cunningham, G. G.: *Lives of Eminent and Illustrious Englishmen.*
Cunningham, George H.: *London.*
Curtis, Edward E.: *Organization of the British Army in the American Revolution.*

Dasent, Arthur Irwin: *The History of St. James's Square.*
Davies, A. Mervyn: *Clive of Plassey.*
Day, R. E.: *Calendar of the Sir Wm. Johnson Manuscripts in the N. Y. State Library.*
Debrett, John: *The Peerage of the United Kingdom of Great Britain and Ireland.*
Derrick, Charles: *Memoirs of the Rise and Progress of the Royal Navy.*
Dictionary of American Biography.
Dictionary of English History.
Dictionary of National Biography.

Dietz, Frederick C.: *A Political and Social History of England.*
Dobson, Austin: *Fielding.*
Dodington: *Diary of the Late George Bubb Dodington, Baron Melcombe.*
Donne, W. Bodham: *The Correspondence of King George the Third with Lord North.*
Doubleday's Encyclopædia.
Drinkwater, John: *Charles James Fox.*
Durand, R. A.: *Oxford: Its Buildings and Gardens.*

Encyclopædia Americana.
Encyclopædia Britannica (American Edition).
Encyclopædia Britannica (British Edition).
English Historical Review.
English Illustrated Magazine.

Fitzmaurice, Lord: *Life of Shelburne.*
Fortescue, Sir J. W.: *History of the British Army.*
Franklin, Benjamin: *Life of Franklin* (Ed. by John Bigelow).
French, John H.: *Gazetteer of the State of New York.*

Galt, John: *George the Third, His Court and Family.*
Gentleman's Magazine.
George III: *Correspondence, 1760-1783* (Ed. by Sir J. W. Fortescue).
Godden, G. M.: *Henry Fielding.*
Granville, Mary: *Autobiography and Correspondence.*
Grattan, Henry: *Memoirs of the Life.*

Haldimand, Sir Frederick: *Diary.*
Halsey, R. T. H.: *Franklin and His Circle.*
Hamilton, F. W.: *Origin and History of the First Grenadier Guards.*
Hare, A. J. C.: *Walks in Paris.*
Harris, George: *Life of Lord Chancellor Hardwicke.*
Harrison, Frederic: *Chatham.*
Hawkes, Major John: *Orderly Book and Journal.*
Hayes, I. Minis: *The Franklin Bicentennial Celebration—Calendar of the Franklin Papers.*
Hearnshaw, F. J. C.: *British Prime Ministers of the 18th Century.*
Hemstreet, Charles: *Nooks and Corners of Old New York.*
Hervey, John: *Memoirs of the Reign of George II.*
History of Crawford County (Pa.).

Holt, Edward: *The Public and Domestic Life of His Late Most Gracious Majesty, George the Third.*
Hotblack, K.: *The Peace of Paris, 1763.*
Hudleston, F. J.: *Gentleman Johnny Burgoyne.*
Huish, Robert: *The Public and Private Life of His Late Excellent and Most Gracious Majesty George the Third.*
Hunt, Rev. Wm.: *Political History of England.*
Hutchinson, Thomas: *Diary and Letters.*
Hutchinson, Thomas: *History of Massachusetts Bay.*
Hutton, Lawrence: *Literary Landmarks of London.*

Jesse, John Heneage: *George Selwyn and His Contemporaries.*
Jesse, John Heneage: *London: Its Celebrated Characters and Remarkable Places.*
Jesse, John Heneage: *Memoirs of the Court of England from the Revolution to the Death of George the Second.*
Jesse, John Heneage: *Memoirs of the Life and Reign of George the Third.*
Journals of the House of Commons.
Journals of the House of Lords.

Kingsford, William: *History of Canada.*
Knight's Cyclopædia of London.
Knox, John: *Historical Journal of the Campaigns in North America.*

Lambert, B.: *History and Survey of London and its Environs.*
Lawrence, Frederick: *Life of Henry Fielding.*
Lecky, W. E. H.: *History of England in the 18th Century.*
Lee Papers—New York Historical Society Collection.
Lee: *Concise Dictionary of National Biography.*
Lefranc, Jean: *Bougainville et ses Compagnons.*
Leigh, R. A. Austen: *Guide to the Buildings of Eton College.*
Lewis, Samuel: *A Topographical Dictionary of England.*
Lodge, Edmund: *Portraits of Illustrious Personages of Great Britain.*
London and Its Environs Described.
Long, J. C.: *Lord Jeffery Amherst.*
Lovat, J. A.: *John Stuart, Earl of Bute.*
Lyte, Sir H. C. Maxwell: *History of Eton College, 1440-1910.*

MacDonagh, Michael: *The English King.*
Mackenzie, Compton: *Windsor Tapestry.*
Magazine of American History, Vol. VIII.
Mahon, Lord: *History of England.*

Malleson, G. B.: *Rulers of India, Lord Clive.*
Mallet, Charles Edward: *A History of the University of Oxford.*
Mayo, Lawrence Shaw: *Jeffery Amherst.*
McLennan, J. S.: *Louisburg from Its Foundation to Its Fall, 1713-1758.*
Melville, L.: *Life and Letters of William Beckford.*
Melville, Lewis: *The Life and Letters of Tobias Smollett.*
Memoirs of Barbara, Duchess of Cleveland (Ed. by G. S. Steinman).
Miller, Sanderson: *Correspondence.*
Monroe, Paul: *Cyclopædia of Education.*
Montague, Lady Mary Wortley: *Letters.*
Monthly Magazine.
Montresor, John: *Journals.*
Morison, S. E.: *Maritime History of Massachusetts.*
Morley, John: *Walpole.*
Munro, Wm. Bennett: *Seignoral System in Canada.*
Murray, Sir James Augustus Henry: *The New English Dictionary* (Oxford).
Myers Collection of Mss. (N. Y. Public Library).

Namier, L. B.: *England in the Age of the American Revolution.*
Namier, L. B.: *Structure of Politics at the Accession of George the Third.*
Napier, Lady Sarah: *The Life and Letters of Lady Sarah Lennox.*
National Gazetteer of Great Britain and Ireland, The.
Nelson, S. B.: *Nelson's Biographical Dictionary and Historical Reference Book of Erie Co., Pa.*
Nevins, Allan, and Commager, H. S.: *The Heritage of America.*
New International Encyclopædia, The.
New Monthly Magazine.
N. Y. Gazette and Weekly Post Boy.
N. Y. Mercury.
Nobbe, George: *The North Briton.*

O'Callaghan, E. B.: *Documentary History of the State of New York.*
O'Mahony, Charles: *The Viceroys of Ireland.*

Pargellis, Stanley McCrory: *Lord Loudoun in North America.*
Parish Register of Kensington (Harlein Society).
Parkman, Francis: *Montcalm and Wolfe.*
Parkman, Francis: *The Conspiracy of Pontiac.*
Parsons, Henry: *Parsons Family.*

Paston, George: *Little Memoirs of the Eighteenth Century.*
Pemberton, W. Baring: *Lord North.*
Pendered, Mary: *The Fair Quaker.*
Penny Magazine, The.
Petrie, Sir Charles: *The Four Georges.*
Pitt, William: *Correspondence with Colonial Governors, Etc.* (Ed. by G. S. Kimball).
Pitt, William: *Correspondence* (Ed. by W. S. Taylor and Capt. J. H. Pringle).
Pitt, William: *The Love-Letters of William Pitt, First Lord Chatham* (Ed. by Ethel Ashton Edwards).
Pittsburgh and the Pittsburgh Spirit (Addresses in the Chamber of Commerce of Pittsburgh, 1927-1298).
Pound, Arthur: *Johnson of the Mohawks.*
Prime, Temple: *Some Account of the Temple Family.*

Quarterly Review.

Redding, Cyrus: *Memorials of W. Beckford.*
Renton and Phillimore: *Colonial Laws and Courts.*
Report of the Record Commissioner of the City of Boston.
Report on Canadian Archives (Private Diary of General Haldimand).
Retrospective Review.
Rockingham, Charles, Marquis of: *Memoirs.*
Rogers, Robert: *Journals.*
Roscoe, E. S.: *The English Scene in the 18th Century.*
Rose, Rev. Hugh James: *A New General Biographical Dictionary.*
Rosebery, Lord: *Lord Chatham.*
Rosebery, Lord: *Miscellanies, Literary and Historical.*

Sackville-West, V.: *Knole and the Sackvilles.*
Secret History of the Court of England.
Seward, William: *Anecdotes of Distinguished Persons.*
Shortt, Adam, and Doughty, Arthur G.: *Documents Relating to the Constitutional History of Canada.*
Sibley, J. L.: *Biographical Sketches of Graduates of Harvard University.*
Sitwell, Edith: *Bath.*
Skrine, Francis Henry: *Fontenoy.*
Smalley, G. W.: *London Letters.*
Smith, John Thomas: *An Antiquarian Ramble in the Streets of London.*

Smith, V. A.: *The Oxford History of India.*
Smith, W. J.: *Grenville Papers.*
Smollett, Tobias George: *History of England.*
Smollett, Tobias: *The Expedition of Humphry Clinker.*
Smollett, Tobias: *Letters of Tobias Smollett.*
Smollett, Tobias: *Works of Tobias Smollett with Memoirs of His Life.*
Smyth, Albert Henry: *The Writings of Benjamin Franklin.*
Sparks, Jared: *Writings of George Washington.*
Stanhope, Philip Henry, Earl of: *History of England.*
Stark, James H.: *The Loyalists of Massachusetts.*
Statutes of United Kingdom.
Stevens, B. F.: *Clinton-Cornwallis Controversy.*
Stopford-Sackville Manuscripts.
Stowe Collection (at Huntington Library, San Marino, Calif.).
Suffolk: *Letters to and from Henrietta, Countess of Suffolk, and her Second Husband, the Hon. George Berkeley.*

Taswell-Langmead, Thomas Pitt: *English Constitutional History.*
Taylor, G. R. Stirling: *Modern English Statesmen.*
Temple, Levi Daniel: *Some Temple Pedigrees.*
Thackeray, Francis: *A History of the Life of Chatham.*
Thackeray, W. M.: *The Four Georges.*
Thoms, W. J.: *Hannah Lightfoot.*
Thomson, Mark A.: *The Secretaries of State, 1681-1782.*
Thornbury, Walter (Edited by Edward Walford): *Haunted London.*
Timbs, John: *School Days of Eminent Men.*
Torrens, William, and Torrens, McCullagh: *History of Cabinets.*
Townshend, C. V. F.: *Life of Field Marshal George Townshend.*
Trevelyan, Sir George Otto: *American Revolution.*
Trotter, L. J. (Revised by W. H. Hutton): *History of India.*
Tunstall, Brian: *Wm. Pitt, the Earl of Chatham.*
Turberville, A. S.: *Johnson's England.*
Turberville, A. S.: *The House of Lords in the 18th Century.*

Universal Magazine, The.

Von Ruville, Albert: *William Pitt, Earl of Chatham.*

Waddington, Richard: *La Guerre de Sept Ans.*
Wade, John: *British History Chronologically Arranged.*
Waldegrave, James: *Memoirs from 1754 to 1758.*

Walford, Edward: *Old and New London.*
Walpole, Horace: *Last Journals.*
Walpole, Horace: *Letters.*
Walpole, Horace: *Memoirs of the Reign of George III.*
Warburton, Eliot: *Walpole.*
Watson, Elkanah: *Memoirs of the Times of the Revolution or Memoirs of Elkanah Watson.*
Watson, Elkanah: *Holy Roman Empire.*
Watts, John: *Letter Book.*
Webster, J. Clarence: *The Journal of Jeffery Amherst* (edited).
Webster, J. Clarence: *The Journal of William Amherst* (edited).
Westminster Review.
Wharton, Grace and Philip: *The Wits and Beaux of Society.*
Whitaker's *Peerage.*
Whitton, Lt. Col. F. E.: *Wolfe and North America.*
Williams, Basil: *Life of William Pitt.*
Williams, Basil: *Stanhope.*
Williams, Basil: *The Whig Supremacy.*
Willson, Beckles: *Life and Letters of James Wolfe.*
Wilson, George: *Life of Cavendish.*
Wilson, P. W.: *William Pitt, the Younger.*
Windham, Rt. Hon. William: *Life and Correspondence.*
Winsor, Justin: *Reader's Handbook of the American Revolution.*
Woodfall, H. S.: *Miscellaneous Letters Ascribed to Junius.*
Woodfall, H. S.: *Parliamentary History.*
Wraxall, Sir N. W.: *Historical Memoirs.*
Wraxall, Sir N. W.: *Posthumous Memoirs.*
Wright, Robert: *The Life of Major-General James Wolfe.*
Wright, Thomas: *England Under the House of Hanover.*
Wright, Thomas: *Caricature History of the Georges.*

Yorks, Philip C.: *Life and Correspondence of Philip Yorke.*

INDEX

565